THE MATERIAL QUEER

Queer Critique

Series Editor
Gary Thomas, University of Minnesota

Opera in the Flesh: Sexuality in Operatic Performance, Sam Abel

The Material Queer: A LesBiGay Cultural Studies Reader,
Donald Morton

FORTHCOMING
Queer Consumption, Danae Clark

THE MATERIAL QUEER

A LesBiGay Cultural Studies Reader

edited by
Donald Morton

Syracuse University

WestviewPress

A Division of HarperCollins*Publishers*

Queer Critique

Frontispiece photograph: Candlelight AIDS rally at the Mall, Washington, D.C., October 1992. Time-lapse photograph courtesy of Scott Severance.

Published in 1996 in the United States of America by Westview Press, Inc., 5500 Central Avenue, Boulder, Colorado, 80301-2877, and in the United Kingdom by Westview Press, 12 Hid's Copse Road, Cumnor Hill, Oxford OX2 9JJ

Library of Congress Cataloging-in-Publication Data
The material queer : a LesBiGay cultural studies reader / edited by
Donald Morton.
   p. cm.—(Queer critique)
  Includes bibliographical references.
  ISBN 0-8133-1926-9—ISBN 0-8133-1927-7 (pbk.)
  1. Gay and lesbian studies.   2. Homosexuality—Philosophy.
3. Lesbianism—Philosophy.   I. Morton, Donald E.   II. Series.
HQ75.15.M37   1996
306.76'6'01—dc20   96-7423
                                                            CIP

CONTENTS

DOSSIER 3: IDENTITY MATTERS

DOSSIER 4: QUEER DESIRE

Contents   ix

PREFACE

At the outset I want to address the readers of *The Material Queer: A LesBiGay Cultural Studies Reader* by offering some comments on and critiques of the cultural space in which the book has been produced. This anthology is being published at a time when not only academic and intellectual circles but also the culture industry itself is dominated by post-al (what I refer to throughout the editorial materials as "ludic") theories of sexuality—theories deriving largely from deconstruction, (post)-structuralism, and Foucauldian genealogy—that have problematized the discipline of Gay and Lesbian Studies as it had been established earlier. These post-al theories are all founded—either directly or indirectly—upon what Jean-François Lyotard, among others, identifies and promotes as a libidinal (as opposed to a conceptual) economy model of culture, and these theories are absorbed mainly with questions of ethics, pleasure, and "playfulness." In such a cultural environment as the one prevailing at this historical moment, a book like *The Material Queer* is bound to raise a number of questions in the minds of its readers, who are influenced mainly by the contemporary post-al environment I have just described. (For a further elaboration and critique of various aspects of today's dominant post-al understandings of culture, see Zavarzadeh, Ebert, and Morton 1995.)

Of all the questions that such an encounter may raise for readers, the question above all questions would be something like this: If *The Material Queer* is finally (as it seems to be) critical of all that now exists in the fields of queer theory and gay and lesbian studies, does that not automatically place *The Material Queer* and its editor in the cultural site commonsensically designated as the space of the malcontent? Are

the book and the editor then not merely sites of cultural/intellectual disgruntlement? From my point of view, what needs to happen next is not the easy endorsement of such a commonsensical reaction on the readers' part but instead an investigation of the assumptions on which such a reaction is based. The assumption behind the construction of the book/editor as sites of disgruntlement and malcontent are the following: If an anthology is to have any purchase on contemporary reality and is therefore to be influential, it has to be at least partially affirmative of what has been achieved over the past several decades. In other words, for a writer/a book to have any critical credibility, he/it has to earn that credibility by accepting—at least in part—what is already available. However, in the last analysis, this argument for affirming the already available is in fact a strategy of crisis management—for managing the very crisis produced by the call to go quite beyond the available knowledges. To ask the book/the writer to be, at least in part, affirmative is nothing less than to ask that the book/the writer locate its/his practices WITHIN the prevailing system of understanding.

Now, on the surface, such a call for affirmation and support of what exists in order to go beyond the existing sounds reasonable and unexceptionable. Part of the reasonableness of this line of thinking derives from the fact that it implies a certain theory of knowledge: It implies the idea that all progress is made on the basis of acceptance (to some extent) of what has already been done (on the shoulders of the proverbial giants). Yet this line of thought is not just a theory of knowledge, it is also a politics of knowledge. It is ultimately a strategy for limiting legitimate knowledges to already available, immanent knowledge (knowledge within). By situating all beginnings or departure points within the existing system of knowledge, the trajectory of innovative knowledges is—to a very large extent—predetermined. Once a project is located within the system, I believe, it becomes—as I have argued at some length in my introduction to this volume—an insider's knowledge, and the knowledge-worker is thereby reduced to being a bureaucrat/expert/technician of existing knowledges. This protocol of intellectual inquiry, which proceeds on the basis of "immanent critique," ultimately ensures that there will be no effective interruptions of business as usual in the understandings being investigated and that all changes will take place within the domain of what the established knowledges regard as the "possible." In other words, the historicity of the possible (and the interests served by limiting the idea of the possible to that foreseen only within the existing system) is obscured by such an approach.

Not following the dominant protocol, *The Material Queer* is located in a transgressive space that begins with this premise: A new anthology is in fact urgently needed today because the existing anthologies can in no way be affirmed. Of course, this does not mean that none of the essays in some of the existing anthologies is helpful, but rather that an anthology is not simply an ensemble of essays. An anthology either implicitly or explicitly situates the reader in a particular position from which to understand the issues it addresses. Basically *The Material Queer* claims to rearticulate a field of understanding; and when I say that there is nothing existing that can be affirmed, I mean that there is nothing that can be affirmed in terms of the different articulation offered in this anthology.

Of course, one has to be prepared for the fact that the intellectual and academic caretakers of the dominant view are always alert to any deviations from immanent critique that might break with business as usual and imperil their lock on knowledge-production. They are quick to notice and police such deviations. Such policing is carried out through a set of concepts and vocabularies, at the core of which is the question that I have already mentioned: Is this not just the work of a disappointed person, a malcontent? On the contrary, the application of such labels is but one more strategy deployed to divert attention from the insufficiencies of available knowledges of the "queer" and thus to block efforts at radically transformative social change.

*   *   *

The following persons have given their sustained intellectual support to this project: Teresa Ebert; David Jenemann; Gordon Massman; Benjamin, Karen, and Samantha Morton; Connie Oehring; Scott Severance; Meredith Sund; Gary Thomas; and Mas'ud Zavarzadeh.

This book is for Scott.

Donald Morton
Syracuse, New York

References

Zavarzadeh, Mas'ud, Teresa Ebert, and Donald Morton, eds. (1995) *Post-ality: Marxism and Postmodernism.* (Transformation: Marxist Boundary Work in Theory, Economics, Politics, and Culture 1.) Washington, D.C.: Maisonneuve Press.

A NOTE ON (THE POLITICS OF) TEXT SELECTION

In selecting the texts for this volume, I have not aimed at coverage of the lesbian/gay/queer thematics of everyday life but have tried to construct an anthology that is intellectually effective as an inventory of concepts. The aim here has been to provide a wider horizon of concepts than is available, on my view, in the already published anthologies. In other words, the goal here is to resituate discussions of the queer in a broader historical and theoretical context.

Following this plan and keeping in mind the pedagogical uses (both in the classroom sense and the broader cultural sense of pedagogy) of such a volume, it seemed to me important to include texts not only by new and less known writers but also by some familiar writers on the subject, even if their texts are available elsewhere and even if their perspectives (like the perspectives of many other writers included here) are not necessarily ones I share. I therefore made space for many of them and following the usual arrangements, the publisher was quite willing to pay them the going rate in permissions fees for reprinting their texts. The fact that some of them—Teresa de Lauretis, Lee Edelman, Diana Fuss, and Eve Sedgwick—rejected, either directly or indirectly, my request to reprint their previously published texts is a part of the history of the formation of this volume. These aspects of the book's publication history, on my view, should not be privatized and passed over in silence, as is usually done, but should rather provide an occasion for inquiring into the politics of publishing—specifically, the politics of publishing today in the "booming" area of queer theory and queer studies.

These writers' self-exclusion of their texts from this anthology I read finally neither as "incidental" (just one of those things that happens in the course of so complicated a project) nor "personal" (directed to me) but rather as ideological resistance to the theories developed in this book, which provides a context that resituates their writings. At a general level, it is inevitable that the works of writers well known within certain established and familiar arenas of ideas will look different (perhaps quite different) when they are resituated in a larger and "other" context and relocated within a different set of intellectual and political relations and parameters. But there is more to these self-exclusions than this. In the terms developed in the general introduction, "Changing the Terms: (Virtual) Desire and (Actual) Reality" (to which I refer the reader), these writers are basically proponents of the "autonomy of desire" theory of sexuality (which I have critiqued in previously published writings and critique more extensively in this volume), who regard the perspective of this book as "extreme" (illiberal) because it situates queer desire along the axis of class and the social division of labor.

To me, what is remarkable about the politics of these particular acts of self-exclusion is that these writers are, without exception, persons who officially—one gathers from their writings—oppose all forms of oppression, repression, and the exclusion of ideas and represent themselves as interested in nothing less than a totally democratic and open dialogue about sexual (and other) politics. In other words, they officially promote the free expression of all persons' ideas without any restraint at all—as a part of the ongoing intellectual debate over sexuality in the public sphere. It is notable, then, that these advocates of free expression have actually resisted opening up a political and theoretical space in this anthology to enable the development of a society free from repression. Regarding the unrestrained circulation of ideas, the instance of Professor de Lauretis is symptomatic. At first she rejected my request to reprint her text on technical grounds (she found the letter I originally sent her unclear in its description of the book project—although apparently not a single other respondent to what was essentially a form letter had any trouble deciphering its meaning), but then later when the publisher approached her, she was willing to have her text reprinted, but only on the payment of a permissions fee that she knew could not be met. Either what is "unrestrained" in this case is the commodification of knowledges (one markets one's intellectual work at the highest possible fee) or the fee was knowingly set so high as to restrain the text's reprinting.

Again my interest here is neither personal nor incidental: The contradiction between the supposed endorsement of the free exchange of ideas, on the one hand, and actual repression of such exchange, on the other, is ultimately part of the larger dilemmas of liberalism that this book in part addresses. From my perspective, all liberalism does is allow some subjects to find a small space of "relative freedom" in a larger, globally exploitative society where they and those close to them can pursue their own personal desires without ever asking the question of how their pursuit of desire relates to the problems of class, the division of labor, and the exploitation produced by surplus value.

Although they could not be published here because permission was denied, the texts by de Lauretis, Edelman, Fuss, and Sedgwick, along with a text by Larissa MacFarquhar about Judith Butler (for which permission to reprint was also denied by the editors of *Lingua franca*—it was "offensive" to Professor Butler), are nevertheless cited by author and title in the table of contents, inserted at the point where they would otherwise have appeared. Such insertion will allow readers, who can find these texts elsewhere, to see how they would be situated on the conceptual horizon of this anthology.

A NOTE ON CULTURAL STUDIES

At the present historical juncture, an urgent contestation is now under way in America over how culture itself is to be theorized: this struggle is being fought out between proponents of textual studies, on the one hand, and cultural studies, on the other.[1] Although these two forms of cultural understanding have both been shaped by the impact of (post)modern thought, they nevertheless have distinct presuppositions and point in significantly different political directions.[2] Textual studies, which relies on (post)-structuralist theory and its privileging of the concept of "textuality," is concerned with the mechanics of signification, the "playful" relation of signifier to signified (hence the term *ludic*), and therefore stresses the supposedly decisive rupture produced by Saussurean linguistics. It basically defines "politics" as those reading activities that "delay" the connection of the signifier to the signified and disrupt the easy trafficking of meaning in culture.[3] This disruption is understood as the continual subversion of the denotative or literal meanings of the texts of culture by their ever-shifting and unstable connotative or figural undersides. Furthermore, this interminable sliding along the chain of signifiers is driven by unsatisfiable "desire." This slide cannot stop, in Derrida's terms, because the signifier can no longer acquire representational authority by anchoring itself in the "transcendental signified."[4] From such a perspective the term *culture* in cultural studies is itself the effect of logocentric metaphysics: a transcendental signified which aims at a coercive stopping of the "free play" of the signifier. For textual studies, culture is merely another signifier. On the textualist view, the "material" is the material part of the sign, that is, the signifier. And inasmuch as the sign is conceived of as being deployed specif-

ically in textualist thought by the *speaking subject,* the material is also associated by ludic textualism with the domain of the body; for, as Barthes—a queer theorist before the letter—has proposed, the body contributes to moments of signification through the phatic dimension of speech which folds an opacity (a meaninglessness) into the process of meaning-production.[5] This move of delaying the easy trafficking of meaning in culture, far from being a trivial philosophical game (as some seem to think), is actually aimed ultimately at rendering knowledge itself unreliable. Thus, for textual studies, there really can be no "knowable" "public sphere" understood as the site of a collective political project; in fact, as post-Marxist textualists like Ernesto Laclau avow, society—being itself a text operating as the "infinite play of differences"—is "impossible."[6] Thus, textual studies puts in question the very validity of cultural studies in general; for since it regards culture itself to be textual (and thus subject to the effects of *différance*), culture is not really available for investigation in any reliable manner.

As developed in Britain, particularly through the Birmingham School, cultural studies by contrast depends on the continuing possibilities of speaking "knowledgeably" and "effectively" about entities called "culture" and "society." Although it takes signification into account (seeing language as a form of social praxis), cultural studies is suspicious of textual studies' overtextualization of all cultural phenomena and is primarily concerned with the reproduction and maintenance of subjectivities. More specifically, it is concerned with the reproduction and maintenance of subjectivities *in ideology and in the accompanying social/economic/cultural/political . . . structures that produce social inequalities.* Thus, for cultural studies, the "material" means (not as in textual studies, the signifier or the body, but) these structures as well as the supposedly "abstract" ideas that support and legitimate them. Thus, although cultural studies is concerned with "subjects," its analytics moves away from the narrowly "personal" and toward the "transpersonal" and "collective."

The story of recent developments does not end here, however, for under the impact of current cultural politics, cultural studies has itself split into two opposing modes, a "critical" and "experiential" mode. The dominant form of cultural studies today, which is exemplified in the theoretically updated work of writers such as John Fiske, Constance Penley, and Andrew Ross,[7] must be called "experiential cultural studies." It "describes" various emerging, suppressed cultural groups and its goal is to give voice to their previously un- or little-known "experience," to let them "speak for themselves." Over against this dominant form stands "critical cultural studies" (a reaffirmation of the concerns of classic cultural studies) which, even in the wake of (post)modern thought, still privileges conceptuality (while accounting for textuality), takes as its radical political project the transformation of the very social/political/economic . . . structures which have suppressed those groups in the first place and prevented them from speaking. Unlike experiential cultural studies, whose mode is "descriptive" and whose effect is to give the (native) bourgeois student of culture the pleasure of encounter with the exotic "other," the mode of critical cultural studies is "explanatory" and its effect is to alter the settled and exploitative relations between the bourgeois reader and her/his "other." The point of critical cultural studies is not simply to "witness" cultural events but to intervene in them, that is, to produce socially transformative cultural understandings. It does so by refusing to take "experience" (either the sensations of empirical traditionalism or the signs of a supposedly anti-empirical textualism)[8] as a given, for to do so is to accept a highly restricted and restricting understanding of the "materiality" of culture, that is, as what a given subject

"experiences": her thoughts, feelings, opinions, physical and bodily states. . . . Of course, under the impact of "textualism" (which has presumably torn the philosophical ground out from under what traditionalists understand as "experience"), there is today a greatly increased sophistication about the notion of "experience": "experience" itself has been reunderstood, not in traditional terms as the direct contact of an "essentialized" subject with her own self-expressive and self-defining thoughts and sensations but rather in ludic (post)modern terms as the recognition of one's textual and linguistic construction. In other words, "experience" today is also understood by many theorists as the experience of the "slide along the chain of signifiers" that produces one as a subject. In this way, something called "experience" has today become the space in which, for the sake of a politically "safe" eclectic approach to the study of culture, the very distinctions between the theories underlying textual studies and cultural studies are being blurred: Many of the dominant academy's most "sophisticated" critics swing uncertainly today between the two. This new elision of textual and cultural studies allows one to begin to understand why the essentialism/constructionism debate has dwindling force today, since each approach still enables the privileging of "experience."[9] Rather than focusing on experience and the "everyday," critical cultural studies "moves beyond" experience (as given) and understands the "materiality" of culture as the historical conditions and the social and economic—the material—structures which in fact produce that "experience." While for its part experiential cultural studies tends to restrict the understanding of the "material" to the level of micro-practices, critical cultural studies understands the "material" at the level of macro-practices in relation to the level of micro-practices.

It is important to add that no matter how theoretically sophisticated it may be, experiential cultural studies (whether it thinks of "experience" in traditionalist or ludic "textualist" terms) is, in the last analysis, hostile to "theory" (that is, to "conceptuality"), seeing it ultimately as a potentially "oppressive" (Enlightenment) structure of abstract and "totalizing" (even "totalitarian") ideas, threatening to disrupt the individual subject's "security" by breaking his grip on "his experience." For its part, critical cultural studies sees theory not as something to be resisted in general but as itself—as Mas'ud Zavarzadeh has strongly argued—a form of resistance.[10]

In its focus on the production and maintenance of subjectivities in ideology, critical cultural studies—of which this book is an example—understands "politics" ultimately as a struggle over access to the material base of power/knowledge/resources. Rather than being any form of opacity (of the signifier, the body . . .), the material is understood in this perspective as the overdetermination and effectivity of all cultural phenomena as they are grasped "socially," which is to say, rendered intelligible through the mediation of the concept. On this view, theory itself, as Marx has argued, is a "material force."[11] Desire here is not the localized and privatized entity it is in textual studies (not "my" desire attached to "my" body driving me along "my" chain of signifiers) but is reunderstood in relation to the collective requirements of social justice. Marx is again relevant here: "Men make their own history, but they do not make it just as they please; they do not make it under circumstances chosen by themselves, but under circumstances directly found, given and transmitted from the past."[12] Among these circumstances, as critical cultural studies proposes, is the construction of those desires, under presently prevailing relations of power, which we call "our" desires.

Notes

1. For recent discussions of cultural studies, see Patrick Brantlinger, *Crusoe's Footprints: Cultural Studies in Britain and America* (New York, London, 1990); Graeme Turner, *British Cultural Studies: An Introduction* (Boston, 1990); L. Grossberg et al., *Cultural Studies* (New York, 1991); Donald Morton and Mas'ud Zavarzadeh, *Theory/Pedagogy/Politics: Texts for Change* (Chicago and London, 1991), 22 ff.

2. For a theorization of the differences between ludic (post)modernism and resistance (post)modernism, see Teresa Ebert, "Rewriting the (Post)Modern: Resistance (Post)Modernism," *Legal Studies Forum* 15, no. 4 (1991): 291–303; Teresa Ebert, "Political Semiosis in/of American Cultural Studies," *American Journal of Semiotics* 8, no. 1/2 (1991): 113–136; and Teresa Ebert, "Ludic Feminism, the Body, Performance, and Labor: Bringing *Materialism* Back into Feminist Cultural Studies," *Cultural Critique* 23 (Winter 1992–93): 5–50.

3. For an extended theorization of these points, see Mas'ud Zavarzadeh, "Theory as Resistance," *Rethinking Marxism* 2, no. 1 (1989): 50–70.

4. Jacques Derrida, *Of Grammatology*, trans. Gayatri Spivak (Baltimore, 1976), 20.

5. For an articulation of these questions, see Donald Morton, "The Body and/in the Text: The Politics of Clitoral Theoretics," *American Journal of Semiotics* 6, no. 2/3 (1989): 299–305.

6. Ernesto Laclau, "The Impossibility of Society," *Canadian Journal of Political and Social Theory* 15, no. 1–3 (1991): 25.

7. See, for example, John Fiske, *Reading the Popular* (Boston, 1989); John Fiske, *Understanding Popular Culture* (Boston, 1989); Constance Penley, Elizabeth Lyon, Lynn Spiegel, and Janet Bergstrom, eds., *Close Encounters: Film, Feminism, and Science Fiction* (Minneapolis, 1991); Andrew Ross, *Strange Weather* (New York, 1991); and Andrew Ross, *No Respect* (New York, 1989).

8. On the question of ludic theory's supposed "break" with empiricism, see Mas'ud Zavarzadeh and Donald Morton, *Theory/(Post)Modernity/Opposition: An "Other" Introduction to Literary and Cultural Studies*, chap. 5.

9. Compare Michael Warner, "Fear of a Queer Planet," *Social Text* 22 (1991): "The major theoretical debate over constructionism seems exhausted" (5). Recent discussions of aspects of constructionism are available in such texts as David F. Greenberg, *The Construction of Homosexuality* (Chicago, 1988); Diana Fuss, *Essentially Speaking: Feminism, Nature, and Difference* (New York, London, 1989); Judith Butler, *Gender Trouble: Feminism and the Subversion of Identity* (New York, London, 1990); Edward Stein, *Forms of Desire: Sexual Orientation and the Social Constructionist Controversy* (New York and London, 1992); and Anja van Kooten Niekerek and Theo van der Meer, eds., *Homosexuality? Which Homosexuality? Essays from the International Scientific Conference on Lesbian and Gay Studies* (London, 1989).

A recent interview with John Boswell (see Lawrence Mass, "Sexual Categories, Sexual Universals: An Interview with John Boswell," *Christopher Street* 151 [1990]: 23ff.) makes it clear that what is far more important than the constructionist/essentialist debate today is the question of the "empirical" or "experience" as the ground of knowledge, a premise which unites both arch-conservatives like Boswell and ludic (post)modernists. Indeed the desire of the Reagan/Bush era culture industry to "secure" and "stabilize" thinking about sexuality is indicated by the fact that Boswell's attack on constructionism, in the guise of a review of Greenberg's book, was published not in a journal for historians but in the popular *Atlantic*. Although Boswell represents himself as the "objective" historian whose "authority" rests on the "accuracy" (ideology-free-ness) of his handling of "facts," his review is nothing more than a tissue of reassertions of empiricist and historicist clichés of traditional humanist ideology. See John Boswell, "Gay History," rev. of David F. Greenberg, *The Construction of Homosexuality*, *Atlantic* 163, no. 2 (February 1989): 74–78.

10. Again, see Zavarzadeh, "Theory as Resistance."

11. Karl Marx, *Early Writings*, trans. R. Livingston and G. Benton (New York, 1975), 251.

12. Karl Marx and Friedrich Engels, *Collected Works* (New York, 1978), 11: 103.

Changing the Terms: (Virtual) Desire and (Actual) Reality

1

The Material Queer is a different anthology, and the difference lies in its emphasis on reopening the question of the status of desire in (post)-modern discourses.[1] Most currently available anthologies on queer theory (see the sustained discussion that follows in section 6) begin with the premise that their approach to queer studies—as a development taking place in the (post)-modern moment and enabled by (post)modern theory—represents a decisive and radical advance over modernism (and its precursors), which has always assigned questions of desire and sexuality to a merely secondary status in social and intellectual inquiry. Even while giving sexuality and desire a place of central importance in his theory, Freud himself, as a modernist thinker still committed to such Enlightenment assumptions as the need for reason in social organization, nevertheless stressed the necessity of regulating sexuality and desire in order to sustain civilized life. Such regulation (institutionalized in social taboos and emblematized by the name Oedipus) is necessary, in Freud's view, even though it produces the inevitable "discontents" that accompany civilization.

Against such supposedly outmoded modernist assumptions, (post)modern theory has produced an atmosphere of sexual "deregulation." As a—if not *the*—leading element in this development, queer theory (as understood in the other available anthologies) is seen as making an advance by opening up a new space for the subject of desire, a space in which *sexuality becomes primary.* These anthologies, in other words, are premised on the notion that, as a prominent queer-studies spokesperson has put it, "an understanding of virtually any aspect of modern Western culture must be, not merely incomplete, but damaged in its central substance to the degree that it does not incorporate a critical analysis of modern homo/heterosexual definition" (Sedgwick 1990, 1). In this new space of inquiry, however, desire is not merely promoted as primary but is in fact regarded as *autonomous—unregulated and unencumbered.* This shift is evident in the contrast between the model of *necessary sexual regulation* promoted by Freud in, for example, *Civilization and Its Discontents,* with the notion of *sexual deregulation* proposed and enacted by Gilles Deleuze and Felix Guattari in *Anti-Oedipus: Capitalism and Schizophrenia* and *A Thousand Plateaus: Capitalism and Schizophrenia.* Their deregulating process is represented as a breakthrough into a space beyond the Oedipus complex (for Deleuze and Guattari, that "grotesque triangle" [1977, 171]), which colonizes the subject and restricts desire. For Deleuze and Guattari, such restriction is unnecessary, and moving beyond such restriction amounts to the liberation of humankind from oppression. Since the Oedipal model of sexual regulation is explicitly heterosexual, its supersession has a special appeal to many queer theorists, who have likewise taken up the call for sexual deregulation.

Associated with the deregulation of desire is a new (post)modern model of reading on which most queer anthologies are also premised: In them reading the texts of culture is reunderstood as the search for *jouissance* (or "the pleasure of

1

the text"). Roland Barthes, a queer theorist before the letter and the leading pedagogue of this mode of reading, calls it listening for "the *grain of the voice* . . . the pulsional incidents, the language lined with flesh, . . . the grain of the throat, the patina of consonants, the voluptuousness of vowels, a whole carnal stereophony: the articulation of the body, of the tongue, not that of meaning, of language" (Barthes 1975, 66–67). It is, Barthes continues, listening for what is captured in the cinematic close-up:

> It suffices that the cinema capture the sound of speech *close up* (this is, in fact, the generalized definition of the "grain" of writing) and make us hear in their materiality, their sensuality, the breath, the gutturals, the fleshiness of the lips, a whole presence of the human muzzle (that the voice, that writing, be as fresh, supple, lubricated, delicately granular and vibrant as an animal's muzzle), to succeed in shifting the signified a great distance and in throwing, so to speak, the anonymous body of the actor into my ear: it granulates, it crackles, it caresses, it grates, it cuts, it comes: that is bliss (1975, 67).

In the Barthesian spirit, the currently available queer studies anthologies attempt to treat the status of desire as if it were a fairly settled and closed matter. They do so by following the general (post)modern program of establishing a tradition of thinking—emblematized in Barthes's image of the anonymous body thrown into the ear—that asserts the *primariness of sexuality/libidinality, the autonomy of desire, and the freedom of the sexual subject from all constraints.*

This idealist notion of freedom from constraint, of course, is hardly new and can be found in a very wide range of discourses. One ancient though still culturally influential example is Plato's argument for sexuality as essence: Viewed from the perspective of his Allegory of the Cave, this implies that we should understand sexuality, like other questions, in relation to a "free" transcendental horizon (the realm of true essences) rather than in relation to the "constrained" realm of worldly sexuality (the

space of mere appearances). Again, a contemporary example is Deleuze and Guattari's notion of unregulated desire as a form of what they call "pure intensities" (1987, 4), a kind of desire for which the very idea of Oedipal or any other constraint is irrelevant. In this space of pure intensities, other changes also take place: The normative territorialization of the body, for example, in which different organs are assigned different "proper" functions is overturned. Instead of having a body, in this space one has an unregulated, desirous "body-without-organs," which according to Deleuze and Guattari "is continually dismantling the organism, causing asignifying particles or pure intensities to pass or circulate, and attributing to itself subjects that it leaves with nothing more than a name as a trace of an intensity" (1987, 4).

Contesting this tradition of the autonomy of desire is a countertradition, which finds representatives ranging also from the ancients to the (post)moderns. This tradition has, on the one hand, acknowledged the significance of desire but, on the other, has also insisted on relating desire to the historical world (not some ideal world) and tying it to the materiality of that worldliness. One can find versions of the materialist tradition among the ancients, for example, in Heraclitus; but the tradition becomes especially critical with the rise of early capitalism and class society and thus finds expression in the writings of eighteenth-century European Enlightenment philosophers and its strongest theorization in Marx's historical materialism. Marx, of course, sees history as a series of events representing changing social organization generated by changes in the mode of production. The encompassing commitments of historical materialism are expressed through its goal "of comprehending theoretically the historical movement as a whole" (Marx 1988, 64). Here Marx defines materialism as an understanding that is theoretical, historical, and global in scope. In this perspective, desire too must be theorized, historicized, and situated in global social relations. Those working within this countertradition agree in denying desire's au tonomy. Here too, however, there are diverse discourses providing different accounts of how desire is conditioned, how it is material rather than ideal, what—in its materiality—it relates to or depends upon. One of the main goals of this anthology in queer theory is to place these two traditions against one another, in order to reveal that the social injustices that persist today are not due to the moral failures resulting from "bad attitudes" or "prejudicial opinions" but are related to the operations of ideology in U.S. society that occlude questions of need by promoting an obsession with desire. Since, however, idealism reigns in the already available anthologies, what bringing the two traditions together means in effect is that, while amply representing the idealist position, *The Material Queer* aims to bring back to contemporary discussions of sexuality (queer, straight, bisexual, . . .) the issue of materiality and to stage the contestation over the autonomy of desire as one of the most urgent issues for contemporary cultural and social theory. This anthology argues that what is needed at this historical moment of the (post)modern is intellectual inquiry into sexualities that develops a critique-al position in relation to both (a pro-Enlightenment) modernism and (an anti-Enlightenment) (post)-modernism and that shows the theoretical and political limitations of both of these frames of understanding.[2]

It will no doubt be pointed out by some readers that materialism is in fact everywhere in mainstream academic and intellectual writing, including queer theory. They will say that the axis along which the distinction between idealism and materialism is being formulated here is overdrawn: After all, a very broad range of cultural and social critics and theorists—among them, those working within the frames of (post)structuralism, psychoanalysis, feminism, Foucauldianism, and the New Historicism—espouse something called materialism today. Even in the quotation presented earlier, does not Barthes himself invoke the notion of the materiality of the body? However, these claims must be critiqued; what (post)modernists mean by the "material" must be carefully investigated. With respect to the groups just mentioned, all influenced by ludic (post)modernism (by which I mean mainly deconstruction and [post]structuralism), what their materialism finally comes down to is their general agreement that—against humanism's essentializing of the individual—the subject is *constructed.* Yet in (post)modernism the subject's construction is accounted for ultimately in terms of mode of signification and not mode of production. In the frame of mode of signification, the material is what Ferdinand de Saussure calls the material part of the sign, that is, the signifier (1966, 66). And inasmuch as the subject is understood as the *speaking subject,* the material is also associated with the domain of the body, as in the Barthesian notion of *jouissance* discussed previously. Since (post)modernism conceives of both the signifier and the body as meaningless opacities that by definition subvert the possibility of a conceptual grasp of the social totality, historical materialism sees this "discursive and/or bodily materiality" as a form of ahistorical idealism. The (post)modern body and the signifier become, on this view, the contemporary equivalents of what older forms of empiricism thought they could grasp as "raw nature"—a kind of "matter"; and so (post)-modern materialism, like the modernists' "raw nature," is a kind of "matter-ism." (This matter is not literally physical, but physical-like: As Saussure emphasizes, the signifier is not "a purely physical thing," not a sound but a "sound-image" [1966, 66].)

In the texts provided in this book, the reader can begin to trace the long genealogy of negotiations over the question of the autonomy of desire between the idealist position, which postulates an autonomous queer subject, and the materialist position, which holds that the queer subject is a "material" (nonautonomous) entity. The reader can also begin to clarify some of the competing claims to what is variously understood as "materialism" (the general observations offered here are expanded in the more specific headnotes to the anthology's various sections). However, because the principal focus of the book is on queer theory, a very recent development accompanying the emphatic return of the word *queer* in the last decade of the twentieth century, it is necessary to foreground here the more recent phases of this contestation. What is ultimately at stake in (post)modern theories that promote the autonomy of desire can be grasped in the exemplary work of Jean Baudrillard. However, it may be useful first to clarify at a general level the (post)modern account of desire, that is to say, the understanding of desire developed in the wake of *the linguistic turn.*

2

Whereas the modernist Freud used more biological- and physiological-sounding terms (he refers to sexuality, for instance, as "the most unruly of the instincts," [1962, 27]), (post)modern discourses articulate desire (and its unruliness) in linguistic and significatory terms. "Desire," it is said, "is the perpetual effect of symbolic articulation" (Lacan 1977, viii). Although the (post)-modern notion that desire is always "desire in language" (to use Julia Kristeva's phrase) seems to suggest that desire, being related to language, is not autonomous, such is not the case. Since in the (post)modern paradigm everything is ultimately language-based, this is not the distinguishing mark of desire. The distinctiveness of desire arises because it is finally that unruly and uncontainable excess that accompanies the production of meaning. Generated in the unbridgeable gap between organic *need* and linguistic or symbolic *demand* (the subject's call for satisfaction of its need via language), desire "is not an appetite: it is essentially excentric and insatiable" (Lacan 1977, 311). Desire, then, is that excess produced at the moment of the human subject's entry into the codes and conventions of culture. As such, desire is an autonomous entity outside history; it is that uncapturable, inexpressible, and actually meaningless *remainder* left over when the human person becomes a socialized subject, a civilized participant in what Jacques Lacan calls the "Symbolic." (Post)structuralist theorists articulate the disruption of conscious,

convention-bound, and voluntary meaning-making by unconscious desire as the process of the disruption of the signified (s^d, that is, the conceptual, meaning-full part of the sign) by the signifier (s^r, the sensory-like, meaning-less, sound-image part of the sign). In short, (post)-structuralism represents desire as an autonomous, if language-embedded entity, which inexorably disrupts sociality, the domain of collective codes and conventions.

The texts of Jean Baudrillard provide an exemplary theoretical staging—in the name of the "breakthrough" that (post)modernism is supposed to represent—of the displacement of the economic account of need by the linguistic account of desire. He proposes a theoretical shift from (Marxist) political economy (or mode of production—what Baudrillard refers to as "utility," "needs," "use value," "economic rationality" [1981, 191]) to "the political economy of the sign" (or mode of signification). Marxism, Baudrillard proposes, has made a false distinction between use value (in which "lard is valued as lard and cotton as cotton" and they "cannot be substituted for each other, nor thus 'exchanged'") and the more "abstract and general" level of exchange value (1981, 130). Capitalism, which needs exchangeability or equivalence between commodities, is founded on exchange value and is driven by the need to produce from exchange value a surplus value that is itself responsible for the difference of class. Overcoming capitalism would involve a return to the more fundamental level of addressing human *need,* represented by use value, and a consequent cancellation of all those *(needless) desires* produced by capitalist commodity fetishism at the level of exchange-become-surplus-value. But, against Marx, Baudrillard argues that "use value is [also] an abstraction. It is an abstraction of the *system of needs* cloaked in the false evidence of a concrete destination and purpose, an intrinsic finality of goods and products" and thus that both "use value and exchange value" are "regulated by an identical abstract logic of equivalence" (1981, 131). There is thus no way that an overturning of capitalism would return man to a "simple relation to his work and his products" (1981, 130). What this means is that the level of use value is not distinct from but rather is dependent on the level of exchange value, and both are equally subject to the operations of commodification and fetishization and must be accounted for ultimately in terms of desire. Need itself is therefore caught up in the same systematic, language-based relations as is desire. Baudrillard expresses this relation in a modification of the Saussurean formula (Sign = Signified/Signifier):

$$\frac{\text{Exchange Value}}{\text{Use Value}} = \frac{\text{Signifier}}{\text{Signified}}$$

Commenting on this ratio following the standard (post)structuralist understandings, Baudrillard remarks that

> absolute preeminence redounds to exchange value and the signifier. Use value and needs are only an effect of exchange value. Signified and [referent] are only an effect of the signifier. . . . Neither [signified nor referent] is an autonomous reality that either exchange value or the signifier would express or translate in their code. At bottom, they are only simulation models, produced by the play of exchange value and of signifiers. . . . Use value and the signified do not constitute an *elsewhere* with respect to the systems of the other two; they are only their alibis (1981, 137).

This means not simply that, as a theoretical procedure, mode of production (as the basis for accounting for need) is subsumed by mode of signification (as the basis for accounting for desire) but that, in broad terms, those human needs to which materialism, in its various forms, might want to respond are themselves merely simulacra of desire. Thus, in particular, historical materialism's social goals (based on a rational concept-based understanding of the social totality)—and any of its possible allied political aims and agendas, such as emancipation from injustice and exploitation—are rendered merely chimerical. At the level of the contestation between materialism and idealism, Baudrillard's idealist notion of simulacra can be

seen as a more recent version, albeit in a different historical context and in quite different language, of what in Plato's system are referred to as appearances.

It is important to note that Baudrillard's modification of the Saussurean formula for the sign *reverses* the relation of concept (signified) to sound-image (signifier): In other words, it subordinates concept to sound-image (the idea to the sensory), or—to follow Baudrillard's thinking here—it renders the concept (signified) as merely a mirage of the operations of sound-images (signifiers). Writing on the "subversion" of the subject, Lacan articulated this at the level of the individual when he suggested—reversing the more familiar understanding of the relation of the subject to language—the subject's dependency on the signifier: "My definition of the signifier (there is no other) is as follows: A signifier is that which represents the subject for another signifier" (Lacan 1977, 316). On the collective, social level, what this means is that the conventional meanings (concepts) by which collective social life is conducted and that form the basis of its commonality are merely evanescent mirages thrown up by the processes of signification (driven by an autonomous and ultimately socially meaningless desire). The principal philosophical point here is that in the end, whether we are talking about Platonic essences or (post)modern signifiers, both are finally postulated as autonomous, as outside history and its materiality. A further epistemological (and political) conclusion is also drawn from these premises: These illusory, concept-based social understandings, then, do not constitute reliable knowledges that can be the basis of an effective political position. This conclusion is perhaps most evident in the work of deconstructionists who propose that pedagogy should not be regarded as the production of concepts but as the unleashing of desire: Exemplary here are such (post)structuralist theorists as Barbara Johnson, who speaks of "teaching ignorance" (1987, 68) and Jane Gallop, who speaks even more pointedly of "thinking through the body" (1988) and writes about pedagogy in relation to "The Teacher's

Breasts" (1995). In queer studies, the same position is articulated still more emphatically by Ed Cohen in his slogan about what is to be done with ideas: "We fuck with categories" (1990, 174–175). The (post)structuralist notion of pedagogy as the pedagogy of desire has been recently institutionalized as the very mode of lesbian/gay/queer pedagogy in the book *Professions of Desire,* edited by George E. Haggerty and Bonnie Zimmerman and published by the Modern Language Association. According to the editors, the field of lesbian/gay/queer studies is "a field that one does not so much enter as come out in" (1995, 2). In other words, one does not so much enter the field by beginning to work with concepts but rather by revealing one's own "desire" (the implications of this mode of pedagogy as self-revelation and of lesbian/gay/queer criticism as "intimate critique" are investigated more fully in section 6 of this introduction).

In order to reemphasize the conclusions about the possibilities for social change that (post)modernism finally draws and the trajectory that the pedagogy of desire takes, I quote Baudrillard again, who lumps together capitalists and Marxists in the same category as taking all concepts—and especially the concept of *need*—too seriously: "Positivized under the sign of progress by the bourgeoisie, or dialecticized under the sign of revolution by Marxism, [the call for social change] is always the case of an imposition of a meaning, the rational projection of an objective finality opposing itself to the radicality of desire which, in its non-meaning, cuts through all finality" (1975, 155).

Just how difficult it is, in today's intellectual and political climate, to resist such ahistorical notions of the "material" is illustrated in the discussion of theory found in the concluding chapter of *Postmodernism, or, the Cultural Logic of Late Capitalism* by one of the foremost defenders of materialism, Fredric Jameson. Here Jameson addresses the critical issue of whether and, if so, how the differences between competing and incommensurate theoretical systems can be overcome. His example centers on exactly what we have been investigating here, the

problematic issue of the autonomy of desire or the incommensurability between idealism and materialism. The "difficulties of yoking two thought systems together," he observes, can be seen in "the older attempt at a Freudo-Marxism" (1991, 394), referring to efforts like those of such modernist theorists as Wilhelm Reich and Herbert Marcuse, who try to merge psychoanalytic idealism (the Freudian libido-oriented theory concerned with desire) and Marxist materialism (the concept-oriented theory concerned with need). Jameson, the materialist, identifies the theorization of Baudrillard discussed previously as "virtually the paradigm gesture" (1991, 395) for overcoming such theoretical gaps. Jameson's account of Baudrillard's theoretical "success" depends on Jameson's own (ludic-sounding) retheorization of the manner in which theoretical change takes place. In his view, the older (rather mechanical-sounding) approach of "synthesis" has to be superseded by the (post)modern (rather desirous-sounding) "sparking": Theoretical change, Jameson says, is a result of "the sparks struck by the 'theoretical' setting of two codes in equivalence with each other" (1991, 396). Jameson's reverential treatment of Baudrillard in the face of his displacement of need with desire, his recurrent use of such nostalgic rhetoric as "something like our old friends base and superstructure" (1991, 396), and his treatment of the concept of *hegemony* as a kind of semiotic formalism (although Antonio Gramsci, who developed the term, firmly tied it to the class struggle) are all features that reveal the strains materialism is under today. To bring the discussion more directly to the question of sexuality, it is a contradiction of some interest that whereas a few years ago Jameson appeared to speak, on the level of the everyday, in an unproblematized manner of "gay promiscuity" (1988, 2), at the theoretical level he seems ready in the text just discussed to accept the Baudrillardian semiotic "promiscuity" of "insatiable signifiers."

In any case, historical materialism does not rely ultimately on either synthesis or sparking to explain how theoretical change takes place: Change takes place *dialectically* through class conflict. Theoretical change, like social change, is driven by the material collision of two classes (the bourgeoisie and the proletariat) in a historical struggle over the mode of production and over the exploitation that results from capitalist extraction of surplus value from the labor of workers—a recognition that seems rather remote in the Jameson text. Today's dominant idealist, (post)modern theories operate in the mode of *dialogics, not dialectics*. The space of dialogics is the space that assumes the autonomy of desire as it is manifested in all its variety: The dialogical space is the pluralist space of the convening of and conversation between different available and self-evident utterances, self-evident because they are based on autonomous desires. (This is the space of the kind of "carnivalesque" dialogue theorized by Mikhail Bakhtin [1965] and further elaborated by Julia Kristeva [1980].) This type of conversation occurs within an already agreed-upon framework; it therefore begins and continues *indefinitely* by following the established rules of the game, which can never be changed. The only change that can be registered is the increasing virtuosity of the players; and even this virtuosity—a heightened intensity of play—and its recognition are themselves finally nothing more than the expression of the autonomy of desire. The more innovative the players, the more intense the conversation becomes. In spite of the endlessly repeated claims that the game is characterized by openness, everybody knows the rules and no one will ever be even startled, much less frightened, by the radical appearance of the unexpected. In other words, dialogics is not open to the unexpectedness of history (in its ultimate form, called revolution), which can and does change the very rules of the established social/economic/political . . . game.

In contrast to the dialogical, which is marked by sophistication, urbanity, virtuosity, and originality ("sparking" as the expression of the autonomy of desire), the dialectical is not interested in what kind of games are allowed but in the historical clash of frames that represent different class interests. In this sense, the dialectical refuses to allow desire to reify the kinds of boundaries generated in and by the dialogical. The dialectical is not interested in originality but in effectivity, in pushing the frames in order to open them up and show what lies behind them. It reveals the clash between the ideal (the frame of desire) and the material (the frame of need) by disclosing the fact that what lies behind (and is occluded by) the promotion of cultural understandings articulated in relation to mode of signification are ultimately questions about the mode of production. In the context of the present discussion, it raises, for example, that very "unliterary" question of the relation of sexuality (language-embedded desire) to wages (material need). To clarify further: Defending dialogics against dialectics, Jean-François Lyotard declares it "oppressive" . . . "to import into a language game a question that comes from another one and to impose it" (Lyotard and Thébaud 1985, 53). Whereas Lyotard argues that it is oppressive to import to the language game called desire (mode of signification) a question from the language game called need (mode of production), the materialist argues that it would be oppressive *not* to ask the question of need, since the historical effect of not asking under contemporary conditions would be to support existing inequalities.

In their critique of nineteenth-century idealist thinkers who, defending middle-class interests, directed their readers' attention away from "property" (mode of production) as such and toward "the language of property" (mode of signification), Marx and Engels provide a paradigm for reading today's bourgeois fascination with signs, language, and etymology (ludic [post]modernism's exclusive emphasis on signification and textualism) as ultimately a cover for the defense of private property:

Having thus made private property and personality identical, Destutt de Tracy with a play on the words *propriété* and *propre* (One's own—Ed.), like Stirner with his play on the words *Mein* (Mine—Ed.) and *Meinung* (Opinion, view.—Ed.), *Eigentum* (Property—Ed.) and *Eigenheit* (Peculiarity—Ed.), arrives at the following conclusion: "It is therefore, quite futile to argue about whether it would be better for none of us to have anything of our own . . . " (Marx and Engels 1970, 100–101).

Marx and Engels go on to observe: "All this theoretical nonsense [that is to say, this idealism], which seeks refuge in etymology, would be impossible if the actual private propery that the communists want to abolish had not been transformed into the abstract notion of 'property'" (1970, 101).

Marx and Engels's critique here of the diversion of attention from mode of production to mode of signification, the latter being an idealism that poses as materialism, applies as well to today's deconstructive meditations on language. A relevant example is Derrida's commentary on the classical motif of cleaning the Augean stables: "The word *proper* plays, expropriating itself and reappropriating itself to itself, right in the manure. It works right into the matter. In the linen (of the body), its tissue, its text, *proper* envelops both propriety and property" (Derrida 1984, 46). Here, as in the examples Marx and Engels critique, the metaphoricity of language, its messy adhesiveness, is taken to be the very mark of materiality itself. This rhetorical "materialism" is, however, only a familiar form of "matter-ism." For Derrida, it is the operations of metaphor (the slippage of the signifier, the swamping of a word's denotative meaning by its connotative undersides) that account for the agitation of meaning in society. Derrida, however, treats metaphors as transhistorical: Once a metaphor, always a metaphor. Yet the boundary separating the metaphorical from the literal is historically defined and redefined. In other words, that boundary *shifts*: What was literal truth in the Middle Ages (alchemy) is only a metaphor today. Metaphor itself must be historicized. For historical materialism the shiftingness, the agitation in the meanings of words, is produced not by the inherent slipperiness of language but by the ongoing contestations between different groups and social classes over, say, the meaning of *woman, family, queer,* . . .

Ludic (post)modernism does indeed challenge the humanist notion that representation functions mimetically, that there is a one-to-one, mirror-like, reflective relationship between any given representation and what it is supposed to represent in the world. But historical materialism has another account of the distortions of representation. For Marx and Engels, language is tied not so much to desire as to need:

> Language is as old as consciousness, language *is* practical consciousness that exists also for other men, and for that reason alone really exists for me personally as well; language, like consciousness, only arises from the need, the necessity of intercourse with other men. . . . Consciousness is, therefore, from the very beginning a social product, and remains so as long as men exist at all (Marx and Engels 1970, 51).

Yet for historical materialism language is not a merely transparent reflection of reality. Language also distorts reality; but these distortions come about not by the slippage of the signifier, but by the mystifications produced by ideology:

> Existence reflected in sign is not merely reflected but *refracted*. How is this refraction of existence in the ideological sign determined? By an intersecting of differently oriented social interests within one and the same sign community, i.e., *by the class struggle*.
> Class does not coincide with the sign community . . . various different classes will use one and the same language. . . . Sign becomes the arena of class struggle (Vološinov 1986, 23).

Elaborating on this notion in more recent times—particularly with the work of Louis Althusser (but also the work of such ludic theorists as Barthes, Lacan, Kristeva, Derrida, Phillipe Sollers, . . . and such Marxist theorists as Joseph Stalin, Georg Lukács, Bertolt Brecht, Mao Tse-tung, . . .) in mind—Rosalind Coward and John Ellis articulate the materiality of language in the following terms:

Ideology produces the subject as the place where a specific meaning is realised in signification. It is thus an active part of social relations since it creates their intelligibility, an intelligibility which in a capitalist society tends to serve the interest of one class. This process of production of representations and subjects for those representations is reinforced by certain material apparatuses, which ensure and support the physical reproduction of ideology and social contradictions. However, its real effectivity is established in a more complex movement of the production of a subject as [the] place where an ideological signified is realized (Coward and Ellis 1977, 68).

Their stress on the ideological nature of signs thus strives to incorporate contemporary notions of subject construction into historical materialist theory.

Undoubtedly all people in all times and places have needs and desires; nevertheless, the forms they take are different depending on changing historical conditions. A century ago no one either needed or desired a computer, for instance. Whether or not one has a computer does not depend on what (post)modernism refers to as "desire-in-language" (one can dream or fantasize about computers, of course) but on the availability of resources and existing power relations that determine whether that need will be fulfilled. (It is unfortunately true that in the past decade the lesbian/gay community—like the larger community—worldwide has had to come to terms, whatever its desires, with need as redefined by the imperatives of the AIDS epidemic.) The different forms need and desire take have to do ultimately with economic conditions (mode of production). It is not that materialism equates desire with need; the two concepts cannot simply be collapsed into one another. But materialism does envision both need and desire in relation to what is *socially productive*. Thus needs and desires have to be theorized in terms of their global social value, which would be determined—at a minimum— by the equitable distribution of resources of all kinds on a global scale. On its own terms and by

definition, capitalism (committed to the principle of extraction of surplus value from the labor of the workers) is exploitative and produces inequality in the distribution of resources and, therefore, results in social injustice. In the classless society envisioned by historical materialism, a different principle would govern resource distribution: "From each according to his ability, to each according to his needs!" (Tucker 1978, 531).

As we have seen in Deleuze and Guattari, Baudrillard, Lyotard, and others, (post)modernism devotes itself energetically to the dissociation of desire from need, to the deregulation of desire, to letting the signifier play, to the search for *jouissance*, to the pleasure of the text. This movement is premised on the notion drawn from Freudian theory and promoted also by some left thinkers such as Marcuse and Reich, that desire is repressed and in need of liberation. Yet it is also a commonplace of (post)modern thought—familiarly articulated by Michel Foucault in *The History of Sexuality* (1980, 3ff.), but more forcefully theorized by Marx in the concept of commodity fetishism (1977, 163ff.)— that desire is not so much repressed and in need of liberation as it is produced and regulated, and thus its production and regulation are in urgent need of investigation.

Since Foucault's work has had such a significant impact on contemporary discussions of sexuality in general and on queer theory in particular, the attention given here to such theorists as Deleuze and Guattari, Barthes, and Baudrillard may seem disproportionate. Yet an investigation of the outcome *on the political plane* of these presumably different theories will show that Foucault's work converges finally with that of Baudrillard and the others and diverges from that of Marx. It is undoubtedly the seeming agreement between Marx and Foucault (that desire is produced rather than repressed) that results in the use of such misleading phrases as *Foucauldian Marxism* (Kernan 1990, 207), an expression that not only blurs the differences between Foucault's and Marx's respective forms of materialism but also serves the ideological function of creating the impression that Foucauldian "materialism" is, in the end, a better (because more up-to-date) Marxism. It is certainly true that Foucault rejected the idea that his work was a part of the development of (post)structuralism (he rejected Derrida's pantextualism, the notion that "there is no outside the text" [1976, 158]). In a vigorous public dispute with Derrida, Foucault defended the notion that there is an "outside to the text" and named that outside "history." Nevertheless, in spite of his differences with (post)structuralists, the outcome of Foucault's work coincides in crucial ways with the results of (post)modern theory, which I have already described. The produced desire/sexuality he writes about in *The History of Sexuality* is, after all, discursive: Sex is "produced" in those interminable discourses generated, first in earlier centuries of Western European history, in church confessionals and, then in more recent times, on the psychiatrist's couch. What Foucault does, of course, is to extend the notion of materiality (beyond textualism) by tying the generation of discourses to specific historically developed institutions such as the church, the prison, the asylum, and so on. Those theorists and critics called the "New Historicists" have followed the Foucauldian model of materialist inquiry by examining how a large range of institutions in a wide variety of social and cultural sites operate. But while introducing this kind of extended materialism, Foucault, at the very same time, theorizes these institutions as purely local sites that "emerge" island-like on the surface of a culture and finally are—like Lyotard's language games—incommensurate with each other, that is, no common measure can encompass them all (Foucault 1977, 148ff). The effect of Foucault's localization of the material is to block the possiblity of theorizing, as Marx does, systematic global connections in relation to the mode of production.

Other aspects of Foucault's work reveal its convergence with the ludic (post)modernist position, which can be characterized, in Jean-François Lyotard's broad formula, as the displacement of the *conceptual economy* model of

culture by the *libidinal economy* model (Lyotard 1993). In his well-known essay, "Nietzsche, Genealogy, History," Foucault reiterates this shift away from the conceptual and toward the libidinal (the bodily) by arguing that "effective history" (the kind he wishes to write) "has more in common with medicine than philosophy . . . since among the philosopher's idiosyncrasies is a complete denial of the body" (1977, 156). In other words, effective history will shun the kind of abstraction philosophy deals with for the concreteness (of the body) medicine attends to. Foucault's later work, particularly the final published volume of his history of sexuality, *The Care of the Self,* anchors the new split, post-individual subject in the body (Foucault 1990). Just as Barthes promotes a mode of "reading with the body" by attending to what is "close up," Foucault likewise declares that "effective history studies what is closest" (1977, 156). His notion of materialist politics is captured finally in this declaration: "The essence of being radical is *physical*" (Miller 1993, 182). In the end, although Foucault's work does not, in an outright manner, reject theoretics for erotics—as today's queer theory does—it nevertheless moves strongly in that direction. Foucault himself indicated quite clearly the distance between his materialism and that of Marx by observing, specifically in the *History of Sexuality,* that his aim is "to move less toward a 'theory' of power than toward an 'analytics' of power" (1980, 82). This *analytics* is finally the name for a middle ground between a historical materialist, concept-based theoretics and (the destination toward which Foucault finally pointed) today's queer erotics.

3

In the (post)modern moment, desire has displaced need, the signifier has displaced the signified, exchange value has displaced use value, mode of signification has displaced mode of production, textuality has displaced conceptuality, the meaningless has displaced the meaningful, indeterminacy has displaced determination, undecidability has displaced causality, feeling has displaced knowing, difference has displaced commonality, and so on. So also, in relation to these complex shifts, *the "queer" has "returned" to displace the "gay."*

What is widely referred to as the "advance" in cultural and social understanding brought about by (post)modernism is actually the contemporary shift toward a theoretically updated version of idealism and away from historical materialism: In the domain of sexuality, queer theory—as a supersession of the older, and presumably outmoded, gay and lesbian theory—must also be grasped—theoretically, historically, globally, as Marx proposed—as a product of these transformations. In other words, the return of the "queer" cannot be explained commonsensically simply as the oppressed minority's revalencing as positive what was once a negative word, or as the outcome of a search for an umbrella term for representing the concerns of both female and male homosexuals and bisexuals of both sexes, or as the younger and hipper homosexual generation's embrace of the latest fashion and its rejection of the older generation's "square" style. Much more is at stake than this: That is why the appearance of the queer has a strongly contestatory, even violent, edge.

Popular accounts of the birth of the queer have emphasized its negative relation to the gay: "The one thing on which everybody was agreed was that whatever else it may or may not be, queer definitely is not gay" (Mitchell and Olafimihan 1992, 38). More pointedly still, the authors of a queer Canadian "zine" declare:

> BIMBOX is at war against lesbians and gays. A war in which modern queer boys and queer girls are united against the prehistoric thinking and demented self-serving politics of the above-mentioned scum. BIMBOX renounces *its* past use of the term lesbian and/or gay in a positive manner. This is a civil war against the ultimate evil, and consequently we must identify us and them in no uncertain terms. . . . So, dear lesbian woman or gay man to whom perhaps BIMBOX has been inappropriately sent . . . prepare to pay dearly for the way you and

your kind have fucked things up (Cooper 1992, 31).

Declaring the queer to be the "quintessentially pomo homo," another writer asserts that "queerness refuses to fit within any conventional category, thereby calling into question the very notion of categories," and reinforces queerity's anticonceptuality by observing that "same-sex relations long preceded the concept of a homosexual identity" (Solomon 1992, 29). The same writer nevertheless points to the very issues being investigated in this anthology by asking finally whether "a queer politics can be forged *without* a gay or lesbian identity? And what would that be like?" (29). Alisa Solomon's recent comments recall not only the long tradition of lesbian and gay efforts to theorize a different (non-gendered, non-patriarchal) identity for women and men (a classic instance is the Radicalesbian manifesto, "The Woman-Identified Woman" [*Liberation Now!* 1971, 287–293]) but also the women's movement's special appreciation of lesbian/gay theoretical efforts to account for "the nature and underlying causes of [women's] oppression" (1971, [vii]). If the impulse behind the BIMBOX outburst is the conclusion that gay liberation failed to meet its goals, this is certainly true. In a more thoughtful account, one historian of the movement has come to the same conclusion: "The paradox of the 1970's was that gay and lesbian liberation did not produce the gender-free communitarian world it envisioned, but faced an unprecedented growth of gay capitalism and a new masculinity" (Adam 1987, 97). The question that needs to be asked, however, is this: Did the failure of lesbian/gay liberation result from the limitations of particular persons (as the discourses of BIMBOX implies), or is it the result of the limitations of the earlier movement's theoretical grasp of its project? Does the very project of emancipation itself need to be abandoned (along with notions of reliable knowledge, conceptuality, theory, and, most importantly, the notion of need), as the queer perspective suggests, or does the project of emancipation need to be retheorized to overcome previous weaknesses, notably a weakness that only helped produce "an unprecedented growth of gay capitalism"? This anthology supports the latter conclusion and questions whether the idealist direction taken by post-gay theories of sexuality is a politically productive one.

Queer theory has to be reunderstood as the result, in the domain of sexuality, of the (post)modern encounter with—and rejection of—Enlightenment views concerning the role of the conceptual, the rational, the systematic, the structural, the normative, the progressive, the liberatory, the revolutionary, and so on, in social change. The queer commitment to desire, captured in the emblematic title of the recent book *The Culture of Desire* (1993), is a commitment to a queerness that, as the author Frank Browning forthrightly remarks, is on "a journey separate from the path to equity, democracy, and justice" (1993, 104). Gay liberation did *not* promote such separation: To repeat, gay liberation "envisioned" a "gender-free, communitarian world" (Adam 1987, 97). Hence, it must be asked *how and why* queer theory has taken so different a route, since this is not self-evident.

Following the paradigm of Baudrillard, which disrupts the entire conceptual series of Enlightenment thought by elevating desire and displacing need, queer theory produces a similar disruption by rewriting the sexual ratio as follows:

$$\frac{\text{Queer}}{\text{Gay}} = \frac{\text{Signifier}}{\text{Signified}} = \frac{\text{Desire}}{\text{Need}}$$

The reading of this ratio starts from the observation that gay liberation grew historically out of the lessons of the civil rights and feminist movements of the 1960s and depended for its self-understanding and its political agenda on *conceptualization,* the formation of a reliable knowledge on which a politics could be grounded. This is to say that gay liberation depended on the development of concepts such as exploitation and oppression, on the one hand, and social justice, on the other, that could form the basis of the *collective* goal of overcoming the former in order to achieve the latter (it thus depended also, and not incidentally, on the con-

cept of causality). But, as (post)modernism proposes, the conceptual part of the sign (the signified) is merely a mirage, a simulacrum, the mere illusion of a stabilized meaning produced by the slippage of the signifier. It is thus only a meaning-effect. Need also is just an illusion generated by desire, a need-effect. Likewise, from the queer theory perspective, gayness is nothing more than a mirage of signification—a gay-effect. Sensing the ghostly status of the gay in the current cultural environment, Barbara Smith, a lesbian political worker, recently observed that "today's 'queer' politicos seem to operate in a historical and ideological vacuum" so that "revolution seems like a largely irrelevant concept to the gay movement of the nineties" (1993, 13). Smith is correct, but if we are to understand the shift she points to, the deeper theoretical changes have to be investigated. It is not simply the concepts of history, ideology, and revolution that have been displaced in (queer) politics but *conceptuality itself:* "Rational politics, in the sense of the concept, is over," declares Lyotard, "that is the swerve of this *fin-de-siècle*" (Lyotard and Thébaud 1985, 75). Thus queer theory, embracing the libidinal economy paradigm and rejecting the conceptual economy paradigm, brackets the Enlightenment project for social progress envisioned by gay studies. In the end, through its allegiance to "ex-centric and insatiable" signifiers and its rejection of signifieds as concepts that are agreed-upon social conventions, queer theory renounces all commonality in the name of "uncapturable" difference: "Erotic desire always introduces the phenomenon of difference," Karl Toepfer remarks, "which subverts the great unifying ambition of revolution" (1991, 136). Thus Lyotard insists that the possibility of commonality has passed in our time: The "social universe is formed by a plurality of games" for which there is "no common measure" (Lyotard and Thébaud 1985, 58, 50).

The rejection of the signified, of course, has consequences at the level of subjectivities. Difference politics forbids anyone to "speak for the other"; in queer theory this injunction is carried further. As nothing more than insatiable signifiers of insatiable signifiers, the authors of the queer zines are said to "speak for no one— not for an emerging generation *and not even for themselves*. If anything, they position themselves as savage cheerleaders feeding off and fueling their contemporaries' violent mood swings" (Cooper 1992, 31, emphasis added). In other words, queer subjects, who exist in a dimensionless dimension and in an immaterial materiality, devote themselves to the further intensification of "pure intensities." Composed of "quirky outcasts," the queer community (if it can be called that) is "intense" but "scattered," which is to say that it is unorganized and in fact unorganizable (31). As "pure intensity," the queer represents an almost instinctive (as "instinctive"-effect) sensitivity to exclusion, but can have no principles (concepts) of inclusion/exclusion (and therefore cannot be organized): "They don't expect anything close to a consensus, and so are able to fight among themselves with a degree of affection" (31). Again, if occasions call for judgment, then following the lead of Lyotard, the queer subject "judges without criteria" (Lyotard and Thébaud 1985, 16).

If—in intersubjective terms—the space of the queer is the space of "quirky outcasts" who "fight among themselves with a degree of affection," this is because it is a libidinal space for exchanges of self-evident utterances needing no conceptual argument or explanation. It is therefore what was described previously as a dialogical, rather than dialectical, space. In other words, it is the space where subjects can only engage in what is now known as (post)modern *performance*, which stands in contrast to the historical materialist understanding of *practice*. Whereas performance art (in, for example, the work of Karen Finley or Laurie Anderson or the Pomo Afro Homos) is widely recognized as an exemplary element in (post)modern culture, the *theory* of performance is less well known. The concept of practice (as something to which the subject could be committed) is tied to a number of assumptions, among them, that action should be guided by principles or priorities (not envisioned in modernist or Enlightenment

fashion as either transcendental or ahistorical, but historically grounded, principles), that these principles come from a conceptual grasp of the social totality, that effective action for social change is indeed possible, and that this effectivity can be rationally assessed and evaluated through critique, and that after modifications in principles, further actions can consequently be undertaken.

Equally important, practice also assumes a distance (sometimes called "critical distance") from the object of knowledge, a distance needed in order to grasp what it is. This distance does not have to be literally spatial: It is a distance from the sensoriness of the object (the object-as-experienced) needed to form a concept of the object (the object-as-conceived rather than perceived). (Post)modernism not only reverses the priority between the experiential (the sensory) and the theoretical (the conceptual) but also shrinks the distance between them to infinitesimal proportions (to whatever distance, if any, exists between signifier and signified). Conceptuality can no longer, through critical distance, "take a perspective on" the object. Thus (post)modernism announces the end of practice, which is based on concepts, requires critique-al distance (the distinction between inside and outside), and guides itself by principles. As should be evident by now, today's dialogical and performative (post)modernism completely displaces these assumptions.

(Post)modernism argues, as we have already seen, that principles are never anything more than principle-effects, mirages on which it would be foolish to think of grounding action. The (post)modern subject (like the queer subject) is deprived not only of the possibility of "speaking for" (others or even itself) but of the possibility of "speaking in the name of": That is, it cannot speak in the name of any principle (concept) such as social justice. The ludic academy's thoroughgoing rejection of any commitment to principled actions is nowhere more strongly signaled than in Stanley Fish's proud declaration: "I don't have any principles" (1993, 360). As a social construct that can only act self-reflexively by deconstructing itself, the (post)modern subject can only "perform" not "practice." In the terms made familiar by Judith Butler, whose work deconstructs the notion of (gender) identity, the subject's actions are "not expressive but performative" (Butler 1990, 141). In other words, a subject's actions are not expressive of either its inner essence (soul, spirit, psyche), as the modernist tradition proposes, or even of some constructed and prior existing identity, as the (post)modernist position might imply. Just as Baudrillard understands the simulacrum to be a copy for which there is no original, which renders all representations as copy-effects (see Baudrillard, 1983), Butler understands gender as a gender-effect, a simulation or mimicry of nothing that is prior to it, a non-referential repetition. "There is," Butler argues, "no gender identity behind expressions of gender; that identity is performatively constituted by the very 'expressions' that are said to be its results" (1990, 25). The subject's identity (or identities) is then only a mirage produced by the play of signifiers. It does not act, it "acts out" or "performs." The subject becomes, again in the language of Deleuze and Guattari, an "asignifying particle." From the materialist perspective identities are not textual mirages but intersections of historically produced subject positions in which various marginalized subjects are exploitatively and oppressively situated. The textualist position (which is only interested in deconstructing—rendering "mirage"-like—those identities) leads Butler to declare that although she will use "the sign of lesbian," she will do so only on the condition that it is "permanently unclear what precisely that sign signifies" (1991, 14). In the end, the textualist position renders identity-effect as a form—in Butler's words—of "trappings"; and "the Being of Gayness" becomes a "Necessary Drag" (18). From this follows the sudden explosion of the culture industry's interest in, and unthoughtful celebration of, transvestism, suggested by the reception of books such as Marjorie Garber's *Vested Interests* (1991).

Ultimately the shift from gay studies to queer studies has been accompanied by another displacement: The foregrounding of sexuality has meant the displacement of gender as too conceptual a notion. In fact, Eve Sedgwick insists that the dissociation of gender from sexuality is "axiomatic" for today's "antihomophobic inquiry" (1990, 27). In contrast to today's queer studies, gay studies—which was an "intense critique of gender" (Adam 1987, 97)—was grounded on the premise that in order to fight effectively against sexual oppression and exploitation, it is necessary to develop reliable knowledges that *explain* the causes of sexual oppression and exploitation in the first place. Like pre-deconstructive feminism then, gay/lesbian studies conceptualized gender as a part of a larger determinative system: Gay/lesbian studies theorized gender as a *structural and systematic* regulation of sexual practices resulting from the binary power arrangements generated by patriarchy. On this logic, gay liberation could only comprehend the struggle against sexual oppression as a struggle to overthrow the gender system and the patriarchy as the causal structures. In other words, it had explanatory, causal, determinative, and globalizing impulses, all of which are unacceptable to queer theory. If BIMBOX writer Johnny Noxema is able to say that "sex is the last thing" on the minds of himself and his friends (Cooper 1992, 32), that does not mean that queer interest has been rekindled in questions such as gender, rather that sexuality has simply been absorbed into the broader operations of desire in today's libidinal economy.

4

Gay theory was forward-looking: It had a historical vision of a differently ordered and more just future. Caught in the interminable processes of deconstruction (the playful self-dismantling operations of textuality), queer theory points ultimately not toward a differently ordered *utopia* but toward a nonconditioned and non-ordered *atopia* (a no place outside history). When queer theory does envision a future, it formulates that future in terms of an ever-expanding region of sensuous pleasure (articulated as an expanding domain of "sexual expression"). Such a "vision" is a-topic because it ignores the historical constraints that need itself places on pleasure. Despite its a-topic claims, queer theory—like ludic (post)modernism in general—can in fact be critically situated and understood historically and materially as a part of the confluence of elements that constitutes the moment of late capitalism: Queer theory shares fundamental features with the hyperspace, cyberspace, and cyberpunk of contemporary technoculture. In fact, in today's "return of the queer," what we are witnessing is actually the (techno)birth of the cyberqueer.

Hints at these shared features between queer theory and cyberspace appear, for instance, when cyberspace is described in the same nostalgic, ahistorical, and atavistic formulas used to describe the "queer." Just as the queer is said to be older than "gay identity," so too it is said that "cyberspace tap[s] into desires far older than digital computers" (Davis 1993, 11). The ahistoricity of the "queer" is indicated by its violent separation from the historically minded "gay." In his definitional essay, Dennis Cooper, in a first move, describes the queer as "the punky, anti-assimilationist, transgressive movement on the fringe of lesbian and gay culture" (Cooper 1992, 31). Then, in a further development, he yokes the punk (also called "phreak") and the queer to a common anti-Left position: "In fact both punk and Queercore spring from an idealism that radicals have abandoned for the pleasures of a compromised but stable Left" (Cooper 1992, 31). Here the perception that the difference between the gay and the queer is in part generational can be seen as a mask for what is basically a political difference. The gay movement had a social idealism too, but it tied its idealism to conceptual understandings of material and historical conditions and to an optimism about a theoretically grounded politics (the kind recognized by the Left as at least related to the political tradition promoted by Marx). Gay theory envisioned a differently ordered society with different norms. "Cybercized" queer theory envisions a norm-less society (if that is not a contradiction in terms). In contrast with gay idealism, queer idealism—fol-

lowing the path laid down by ludic (post)modernism—sees its roots not in the historical materialism of Marx but in the anarchic skepticism of Nietzsche. Indeed one cyberpunk locates his project as a post-Nietzschean one: " 'Nihilism,' he says, 'doesn't go far enough for me' " (Caniglia 1993, 95). As we have already learned, in the "new" queer space, the word *compromised* cannot mean merely *complicit* in the "old" political sense; after all, any position whatsoever that is "stable" is already "compromised" in the queer perspective since it can only be an illusion. Thus what Cooper calls queer and punk "idealism" cannot be the kind of social idealism supported by materialist Left theory (the commitment to social progress) that shaped gay liberation. In its association with cyberspace (entry to which is literally not open to all), queer idealism is rendered more clearly as allied with the self-interested individualistic idealism of the bourgeois subject: As one cyberpunk reportedly puts it, his goal in life is "to move up" (Caniglia 1993, 92).

Cyberspace is that universe of virtual reality produced by the cybernetic electronic systems (computers, televisions, videos, faxes, and the various electronically spawned "nets") of our contemporary "plugged-in" and/or "air-wave" technoculture. Mainstream accounts of cyberspace as a cultural phenomenon frame it partly in practical or managerial terms and partly in aesthetic terms. On the one hand, we are told that contemporary technoculture has become so vast, sophisticated, and complex that the efficient electronic management of the information-overload is an urgent, practical necessity. On the other hand, cyberspace is said to be a development of the human imagination, an enhancement of the natural excitement generated when abstraction is rendered concrete, for example, when mathematical formulas are turned into three-dimensional representations such as charts and graphs (Davis 1993, 10). In other words, today the old "3-D" has now become the new "VR." The technology producing virtual reality is light years ahead of mere charts and graphs. "VR may ultimately project the user into the midst of a digital space as concrete, chimerical, and manipulable as a lucid dream" (Davis 1993, 10).

This last assessment—which, considered in global terms, associates cyberspace with the dreams of its Euro-American inventors—points beyond the merely practical and aesthetic dimensions to the *politics* of cyberspace. Cyberspace is a bourgeois "designer" space in which the privileged Western (or Westernized) subject entertains the fantasy of being able, so to speak, to choose (and write) his own history rather than be chosen by history. Virtual reality machines are a way, as one commentator has put it, of supposedly "grasping reality through illusion" (Rheingold 1991, 13). What actually happens, however, is that by manipulating the machines, the user-subject writes a "preferred" history (creates a virtual reality) according to his or her own desires rather than dealing with the actuality of present historical conditions. In other words, the mainstream understanding and use of cyberspace is symptomatic of the (post)modern displacement of need by desire (the material by the ideal). Cyberspace's connection to (post)structuralist notions of textuality is emphasized by Julian Dibbell, who says that "cyberspace is a place all right, but it is an insistently textual one," and its purpose is the same as that of all writing, which, according to Derrida, is "to fake presence" (Dibbell 1993, 13–14). This is true especially of the kind of cyberspace known to cyberfans as "tactile telepresence" (Rheingold 1991, 346). Cyberspace is not only part of Derrida's textualist world, it is a part of what Lyotard calls the "libidinal economy." Cyberspace was produced, Davis remarks, by "connecting the libidinal pleasures of video-game joysticks with dry data banks" (1993, 10).

For the present discussion, one of the most important new zones in this technocultural expansion of the bourgeois subject's desire is called "cybersex." As Howard Rheingold reports, "the most lurid implications of VR have already been trumpeted in the mass media, via reports of what it just might make possible—such as 'teledildonics' (simulated sex at a distance) or 'electronic LSD' (simulations so powerfully addictive that they replace reality)" (1991, 19). Again, like cyberspace, cybersex is often accounted for in pragmatic terms. In the age of AIDS, cybersex, which produces what sex evangelist Susie Bright refers to as "the virtual orgasm" (1992, 60), is the newest form of "safe sex," made possible by the development of fiber-optic communications cables ("tactile telepresence" requires "fiberoptic networks" with what is called "high bandwidth" for transmitting a high density of information [Rheingold 1991, 346–347]). Through various technical means, from telephone sex lines, which still rely on the user's imagination, to erotic messages with pictures transmitted by e-mail on computer bulletin boards, to the full-fledged graphic "virtual sexual experiences" enabled by VR goggles and gloves, cybersex provides that Derridean "fake presence" that simulates the conditions and sensations required to produce sexual stimulation and release. According to one prediction, "thirty years from now, when portable telediddlers become ubiquitous, most people will use them to have sexual experiences with other *people,* at a distance, in combinations and configurations undreamed of by precybernetic voluptuaries. Through a marriage of virtual reality technology and telecommunication networks, you will be able to reach out and touch someone—or an entire population—in ways humans have never before experienced" (Rheingold 1991, 345).

Susie Bright's more modest, "lower tech" account of a telephone sex operation run by two friends reveals not so much the pragmatics as the political economy of cybersex. Bright situates the experience in tellingly contradictory discourses: On the one hand, she describes telephone sex as "out of the body travel" (into body-less-ness); on the other hand, such travel is clearly undertaken in search of sensuous experience that requires a body in order to appreciate the experience (into body-full-ness). The contradiction is resolvable in material terms: Cybersex enables travel out of the actual, historical body and into a virtual body of Deleuzean "pure intensity." Bright listens as one sexline hostess describes to a heterosexual male client not her real body ("Perry's hips haven't seen thirty-six inches in about ten years") but a virtual body meant to satisfy the customer ("I'm a 36C-25-36") (60). This virtual body, in other words, is not the historical body but the commodified, ahistorical body fetishized by the Imaginary and promoted for profit by Madison Avenue and hundreds of savvy entrepreneurs. "You can be any BODY you want to be," we are told, "on a fiber optic network" (61). Although the features fetishized in different representations will of course vary depending on whether the target audience is heterosexual or homosexual (indeed for Madison Avenue's purposes a wholly bisexual target audience would prove ultimately most efficient—and this may indeed be the direction in which things are headed), the same process is nevertheless at work throughout contemporary U.S. culture (from explicit pornography to the suggestive crotch-grabbing performances of such cultural icons as Madonna, Michael Jackson, and Marky Mark).

Bright's account also reveals not just the micropolitical dimensions of virtual reality (its use to enhance erotic consciousness) but its macro- and geopolitical dimensions (its use by Western powers as an alibi to salve bad consciences). We learn not only that the U.S. Defense Department has "the most advanced telerobotic, long distance computer scanning equipment" available but also that it was used to make the war with Iraq a "'virtual' war" (63). With cyberspace equipment in the Persian Gulf War, what bomber pilots could do was "strap on goggles, see where they are going and where they're going to drop bombs" (63). The advantage is that this method of "technological imaging" "get[s] human beings out of the loop" (63). Virtual reality seems to provide then another kind of (post)modern reversibility. For sexual stimulation it gets bodies into places they really aren't in; for warfare it gets (guilty) bodies out of places where they really are. Although sex-evangelist Bright sees this use of virtual reality to produce a different kind of war as "the dead opposite of the technoeroticism," in which she is interested, ultimately these micro-uses and macro-uses converge on the political plane:

Virtual reality situates both bomber pilots and cybersex users in an ahistorical space supposedly disconnected from actuality, and the subjects inhabiting that space are therefore beyond social responsibility.

Alongside Bright's popular account of virtual reality (and produced by the same dominant assumptions), there lie such sophisticated theoretical accounts of contemporary cyberculture as that, for instance, found in Avital Ronell's *The Telephone Book: Technology, Schizophrenia, Electronic Speech*. Ronell's work is, of course, quite self-consciously informed by all the ludic (post)modern assumptions (articulated previously) that result from giving primacy to mode of signification. The signifiers of the telephone book are taken to constitute the human community (thus understood as a linguistic entity). Therefore, Ronell situates her inquiry into the operation of the telephone not in the space of "reflection" (that is, of philosophy in the traditional sense) but rather in the ludic (post)modern performative space of "response," of "answering a call" (Ronell 1989, 3). As Ronell projects it, the telephone is not so much a technological instrument developed at a particular historical moment but an emblem of an endless panhistorical connectedness: "The telephone splices a party line stretching through history" (295). Ronell theorizes the subject of this panhistorical party line as the schizophrenic. In other words, Deleuze and Guattari's schizo "desiring machine" becomes more specifically for Ronell the subject "who has distributed telephone receivers along her body" (4). Thus Ronell's contemporary subject exists in a state of generalized perversity (queerness), in which it is difficult to decide or conclude any question whatsoever. Human intersubjectivity is a system of shifting relays; hence, in this telephonic cosmos, it is difficult to know the answers to such undecidable questions as: Who calls? Who answers? Therefore, the same political question of social responsibility that haunts Bright's essay (in terms of the Defense Department and the Persian Gulf War) also haunts Ronell's book. Perhaps her primary political question concerns philosopher Martin

Heidegger's complicity with fascism; but another is today's Arab-Israeli conflict, which Ronell references as "The Telephone Wars of the Egyptians and the Hebrews" (296). The question of responsibility and the need to take a position haunts any understanding of culture and society (including queer theory) that sees desire as autonomous.

If today's BIMBOX queers and cyberpunks mix what one writer calls "youthful rage and technological terrorism" (Caniglia 1993, 88), the difference is that cyberpunks derive their technology from differential, digital, and binary computer culture whereas the new queer subjects derive their techno-theory from the differential and binary theories of ludic (post)modernism. Both technologies are, of course, the consequence of contemporary historical conditions under late capitalism. Both post-gay queerity and post-left-political cyberpunk are virtual realities, "post-al" realities that are supposedly "beyond" historical consciousness, spaces where those who can afford it can choose their reality. As such, these modes of thought are the latest forms of contemporary bourgeois idealism. (For a sustained inquiry into today's post-al cultural and social theories, see Zavarzadeh, Ebert, and Morton.)

Although the imposition of virtual reality over historical actuality—which is the matrix-move for the birth of the cyberqueer—is most strikingly visible in some of the examples already mentioned, that same violence is present even in quieter, more "civilized" queer studies writing. That violence can be found, for instance, in Eve Sedgwick's intimate essay, "White Glasses," written as a memorial-in-advance for a friend dying of AIDS (the gay poet, teacher, scholar, and activist, Michael Lynch). The essay, in the form of a journal or memoir, deals also with the author's own sense of mortality brought home to her by the parallel discovery of her own breast cancer. Certainly such issues are commonsensically personal, but what better opportunity to raise transpersonal, collective issues? Rather than opening a space for inquiring into the global historical conditions that determine health care availability and quality, rather than using AIDS and breast cancer as occasions

for a conceptual inquiry into unjust patterns of resource distribution on a global scale, Sedgwick's essay follows the queer mode: It lets desire "play" (in a manner reminiscent of Nabokov's *Lolita,* in which a closely similar object also becomes an obsessive image) by fetishizing a signifier (white glasses) associated metonymically with the dying friend. (Lynch was wearing white glasses on the day Sedgwick met and "fell in love with" him [194].) My critique of Sedgwick's text is not personal in commonsensical terms. The problem is not simply that Sedgwick, in a private moment, gives in to the impulse to organize her writing about a friend with AIDS around what she herself calls "obsessive imagery" (198). The problem is rather that the fetishized white glasses become the very emblem of today's privileged "ludic" mode of understanding (based on the autonomy of desire) not only for questions of health and illness, and not only (since Lynch and Sedgwick have played such prominent roles in its development) for the new mode of queer studies and for "otherness" itself but for any kind of inquiry. My critique concerns the broader effects of "White Glasses" as the text of a committed intellectual and pedagogue working in queer studies by promoting fetishes. This modality is an intellectual problem, because (to put it concisely) as Laura Mulvey has recently done, the function of the fetish is not to produce new understanding, but "to guard against the encroachment of knowledge" (Mulvey 1993, 12). By wearing white glasses, one produces local (fashion) effects: One sets oneself apart by associating with a new "desire" (the signifier, white glasses), by having the "experience" of a "new" difference, and by extension, a feeling of control over "difference" itself. As Mulvey's comment hints, however, the substitution of feeling for knowledge trivializes the understanding of how differences get produced in the first place and the place of particular differences within prevailing knowledge/power relations. The point here is neither to deny or erase fetishes (everyone has them), but to inquire into the consequences of their use. In the course of Sedgwick's essay, what starts out as a personal fetish ("to me the glasses meant [mean] nothing but Michael," 195) is transformed ultimately into a universal fetish, a "prosthetic device that attaches to, extends, and corrects the faulty limb of our vision" (197). Sedgwick's essay provides a particularly striking instance of the merger of the fetish as erotic with the fetish as commodity. Sedgwick reports that her "first thought" on seeing Lynch wearing the glasses was, "Within a year, every fashion-conscious person in the United States is going to be wearing white glasses. . . . I want white glasses first" (193). In the "magical" realm (197) made available by the white glasses (which create, Sedgwick says, a "series of uncanny effects" [197]), what has to be called a *queering* of reality takes place. Not only can a woman who thinks of herself (and believes that others think of her) as "fat" somehow escape that historical condition but that same woman can also slip the moorings of her own social construction and become "along with Michael," her friend, "a gay man" (198). In the end, the white glasses produce the same effect as the VR goggles. The bourgeois subject, whose desire is (relatively) autonomous, is in a position not only to have the latest commodity first but also, in broader terms, to write her own virtual history. In a recent interview with Sedgwick conducted by Jeffrey Williams (Williams 1993), Sedgwick hints that she is moving—on what she refers to as a "hunch"—toward the space of the cyberqueer. As I have argued here, however, such texts as "White Glasses" show her to be already there, that is, already "at home" in the world of virtual reality.

In view of the dominant queer theory's promotion of social space as an ahistorical virtual reality (the space of autonomous desire), *The Material Queer* insists on the urgent importance of bringing back into the discussion of sexuality the question of need in all its historical and material actuality.

5

Although the ahistorical thinking characteristic of queer theory and cyberspace seems most readily visible in avant-garde texts or in the texts of what Richard Kadrey calls "fringe" or "covert culture" (1993), it is constitutive of the understanding of the real—as it is being renovated today—in all texts of the dominant culture, including popular ones. For purposes of further clarification, it may be helpful here to discuss briefly a popular example at the intersections of queerity, perversion, psychopathology, cyberspace, and virtual reality: the much-discussed film released in 1992, Paul Verhoeven's *Basic Instinct*, starring Sharon Stone and Michael Douglas. Queer activists vigorously protested the making and distribution of this film because of its negative images of homosexuals in the characters of Catherine, Roxy, and Beth, all women involved in lesbian sex and either at some point intending to be, suspected of being, or finally proven to be murderers. The queer activists' critique, however, is basically ethical and moral and, therefore, idealistic: The producers of the film, who knew very well that most lesbians and gay men are not murderers, nevertheless recirculated this false negative stereotype. This critique is, however, only a mirror-image of the religious fundamentalists' own account of homosexuality. Whereas the latter privilege negative associations with homosexuality, the former privilege positive ones. A materialist critique will investigate the very terms of this "producing" (positive or negative) and will therefore connect questions of sexuality and sexual orientation not to morality but to the politics of class and other struggles against oppression and to ideology, of which morality is one expression.

One of the most urgent aspects of *Basic Instinct* is its demand that the viewer reunderstand sexuality by separating it from humanist, modernist, and moralist frames of reference. The film's central female character, Catherine Trammell, an exemplary ludic (post)modern subject (with a double major degree in literature and psychology from Berkeley), is also a writer (a producer of texts). She has written a mystery story that anticipates in its details the murder of one of her lovers (this sensational ice-pick murder of a man by a woman at the point of orgasm during sexual intercourse is the opening scene of the film). Now, in the context of this (post)modern filmic narrative, the term *lover* has to be problematized: It is too over-coded by conventional (humanist and modernist) social understandings about sexuality. And Catherine works hard to separate her understanding of sexuality in general and their relationship in particular from normative social views. It was not a "loving" (social) relationship she had with the dead man, Catherine argues, but specifically a "sexual" relationship of "pure" desire. Correcting one detective who is interviewing her about this relationship, Catherine remarks, "I wasn't dating him, I was fucking him." As it unfolds, the film becomes a ludic (post)modern investigation not only of the (post)structuralist principle that history itself is nothing more than a text but also of the related notion that the meaning of all texts is ultimately undecidable. On the one hand, Catherine Trammell becomes the prime suspect because her sex partner's murder follows the plot of her fictional account; on the other hand, she has the perfect alibi (she wouldn't be so stupid as to murder someone following her own fictional plot). As the narrative proceeds and Catherine (Sharon Stone) becomes involved sexually with Nick Curran (Michael Douglas), she is also writing (on computer) a novel about a detective who "falls for" the wrong woman, who in the end kills him. Part of the tension of the film derives from the fear that fiction may repeat itself and that Catherine may kill Nick, who has fallen for her. Eventually the relationship of the rich and "free" woman and the employed and thus "constrained" detective takes on the aspect of an allegory not just of class relations but also of the contrast between modernist and ludic (post)modernist ways of living. The representation of Nick is produced through familiar discourses: He is an ordinary Joe, an ex-alcoholic and ex-cocaine-user, who is trying to resist falling off the wagon. For Nick, who must work for a living ("I don't have any money," he says), desire is still pitted against need. In Catherine's case, however, her wealth not only sustains her pleasure-seeking adventures (drugs, sex, and so on) but appears to produce a different state of consciousness in which

desire seems to have escaped mere need (for her, the regulation of desire—resisting temptation—seems as irrelevant as Oedipal regulation seems to Deleuze and Guattari).

From the materialist perspective, the demonstrations against the film are misdirected. For queers to protest against the queer character as murderess is only to offer a moral criticism. It is much more urgent to inquire into and critique the kind of queered reality explored in *Basic Instinct* and to understand its message in relation to the queer political project at large. Although the nominal star is Douglas playing the completely straight Nick, the film's main interest centers around queerness and perversity and thus around Catherine (the role that suddenly made Sharon Stone, who had already appeared in seventeen films in the previous fifteen years, a star). The central character is not just queer and a murder suspect but, more importantly, the bourgeois subject (in fact, a multi-millionaire heiress) free to write her own virtual reality. In writing the novel, Catherine writes her own *jouissance* (her "pure intensity"—Nick calls her "the fuck of the century") and lives her desire out in history. Having her needs more than taken care of, Catherine can afford to let her desire play. As the film itself acknowledges, not everyone can. Gus, the middle-aged detective who is not only Nick's sidekick and best friend but also a prime voice of normative reality, remarks, "I can get laid by blue-haired women, but I don't want 'em." In the terms developed here, Nick's remark is a reminder that desire is (relatively) autonomous only for some people, not all. His recognition therefore problematizes the claim of some spokespersons that the goal of today's queer agenda is to achieve free sexual expression for all. For the ludic (post)modern subject like Catherine (who is wealthy by any standard and beautiful by conventional white, middle-class U.S. standards) desire is relatively autonomous. Although the film's sex scenes don't immediately recall the technically engineered pleasures of the new cybersex, the sex is nevertheless technically (that is, pharmacologically and otherwise) enhanced. Virtual reality is certainly not unfamiliar to the film's director, Verhoeven, who also directed the technoculture hit, *Robocop*. Catherine is the subject for whom historical reality is only, in the end, a reality-effect (a virtual reality) and thus open to her manipulation. Her game is to use her novel to problematize—for those trying to solve the crime—her identity as murderess; this problematization (representation) thus works also as an alibi. At another level, Catherine's freedom to manipulate representations according to her desire recalls queer theorist Judith Butler's similar free manipulation of gender identity. Both Catherine and Butler situate gender in relation to desire and occlude the connections of gender and sexuality to need (class).

Right-wing criticism of the film would no doubt also focus on the film's language, but again in a moral frame. From their perspective, which assumes the existence of timeless and universal truths (and seeks a "proper," "pure," and thus "moral" language for the expression of those truths), conservatives would no doubt find the frank sexual language of *Basic Instinct* (like that of today's pornotopic culture in general) to be a sign of moral decay in the contemporary United States and an affront to their family values. If one were to take this criticism seriously, one could make a case for saying that the film is not a confirmation of, but actually an affront to, bourgeois morality. This analysis, however, would overlook the way in which bourgeois morality itself must change under changing historical conditions to keep up with changes in the mode of production. The morality needed by the bourgeoisie under earlier stages of capitalism and the morality needed by the same class today under late, multinational capitalism are different moralities. Thus, the film's frank sexual language is not so much a calculated "transgression" of bourgeois values for shock effect (although it may appear this way in some circles) as it is the mark of a transition in bourgeois consciousness; the frank language is the inevitable result of the (post)modern erasure of the distinction between the public and the private, the outside and the inside. It is often remarked that modernist

"depth" has disappeared and we are left with nothing but (post)modern "surfaces" (Jameson 1991, 6). On this view, nothing is any longer hidden; the outside is the inside and vice versa. In this perspective, the human subject no longer has an "interiority": Consciousness and unconsciousness are written on the surface of the body, which is itself a text. Hence, in the new world of the cyberqueer, any form of modesty or reticence in speech or behavior is also irrelevant. The frank language of *Basic Instinct* is, therefore, a result of the collapse of the public (the space of "civil" behavior) into the private (the informal space of "instinctual" reaction).

In the last analysis, one of the most telling aspects of the queer response to *Basic Instinct* is that while rejecting the negative image of homosexuals, the queer perspective would nevertheless support the new frank language—and would follow both lines of thinking on moral grounds (or grounds of accuracy of representation). The recognition of the skewedness of this response allows one, in the end, to pose another urgent question that I have yet to see posed in queer studies: Is it not finally the case that the new cyberqueerity (which, drawing on contemporary technoculture, promotes the supposed autonomy of desire and suppresses the question of need), while seeming to oppose it, is in fact playing a pivotal role in the transition to a new bourgeois morality and state of consciousness that is desperately needed by late multinational capitalism to maintain its exploitative and oppressive regime of class relations?

The more general point is that, on the view promoted by ludic (post)modernism, today's culture of "libidinal economy" (which has arrived, from the materialist perspective, because of underlying transformations in the capitalist mode of production) is an inevitably more intimate culture: not one that is just more intensely subjective but subjective in new ways. Such a new culture, which necessarily results in new attitudes toward all social and cultural phenomena (what kind of language is socially acceptable, for instance), will inevitably spawn new genres of artistic and intellectual expression. We have already seen how the libidinal theory has resulted in the development of the innovative genres of the performance piece and the texts of virtual reality. Beyond this, however, the new language of intimacy in the texts of popular culture (where even such euphemisms as "the F-word" are no longer necessary to cover up the nakedness of the act itself) is being matched today with a new intimacy at the level of academic and intellectual writing. One developing new genre—an example of which we have already examined in Sedgwick's "White Glasses"—is called "intimate critique" by some (Freedman et al. 1993) and "personal criticism" by others (Dubrow 1993). Since ludic (post)-modernism has problematized and rejected the possibility of any form of "objective" (transpersonal) writing, insisting that all texts come from a specific and personal locale (from a subject situated in particular discourses), it follows that all writing is, in this sense, autobiographical. Unlike the older form of autobiographical essay, in which both author and reader voluntarily crossed over from the (more objective, formal) public sphere to the (personal and intimate) private sphere for the (again voluntary) moment of a personal writing/reading, intimate critique belongs to the ludic space in which the public has imploded into the private. One result of this implosion—which is basically the result of the continual subversion of the signified (conceptuality) by the signifier (textuality)—is the odd (queer) juxtaposition of diverse discourses and rhetorics or—in Lyotard's terms—the confluence of incommensurate "language games."

Perhaps because the discourse of sexuality is already regarded as the most intimate of discourses, many mainstream academics and intellectuals inquiring into the question of sexuality (including those in queer studies) appear to find the new intimate writing especially appealing. A striking example of the odd juxtaposition of formal and informal discourses (the queering of language) that results from the implosion of the public into the private is available in the "acknowledgments" section of Alexander Doty's *Making Things Perfectly Queer* (1993). I

cite this text not simply because it rather clearly illustrates the point I wish to make but also because it is being promoted today as exemplary: Doty, the jacket cover quotes Constance Penley as saying, "is on the verge of being recognized as the single most important figure in gay media studies." Doty's discourses are therefore currently being understood within the academy and academic publishing as symptomatic not of already existing but of *emerging queer discourses.* Like dedications and indexes, the acknowledgments section is usually one of the most heavily coded and conventional elements of a book. In tune with these codes, Doty begins his words of thanks with a more conventional and formal rhetoric ("There are many people to thank in connection with this book"); but he then immediately shifts to a very different and decidedly intimate register ("First, I'd like to say, Corey Creekmur, you're a great pal and an insightful reader. When this thing finally comes out, we're going to put our feet up, have some champagne, and watch *Leave Her to Heaven* again" [1993, ix]). At the commonsense level, there could be no objection to an author celebrating the publication of a book with his friends, just as there could be no objection to a woman writing an essay mourning a dying friend, or no objection to queer activists protesting Hollywood's promotion of a negative image of lesbians. Again, however, something more is at stake than common sense recognizes: For the very project of intellectual work itself, important consequences follow from adopting the new mode of personal criticism. Historically, intellectual discourses have been most productive socially when they are a form of intervention against received ideas. In other words, intellectual discourses produce innovative and oppositional knowledges (alternative conceptual understandings) by critiquing a society's common sense and the hierarchies of power that common sense serves to support. Thus from the materialist perspective, the ideological function of the new intimate critique is to disrupt this process of conceptual innovation not only by constantly displacing—as in Doty's example—the conceptual with the social but also by denying that there is finally any significant difference between the desire and the concept anyway.

One must note, however, that the discourses of Doty's "acknowledgments" are also a form of dis-acknowledgment. Doty's relaxed social discourse appears to assume unproblematically the availability to all the world of a space like that of the bourgeois living room (TV room, den, or bedroom, for that matter), whose comforts he and his friends are able to enjoy. Thus the importance of class analysis of such discourses; for this is not simply a naive assumption but in fact a violent ideological erasure of the historical actuality of spaces available to other kinds of subjects in the world. Beyond this broad class dimension of the represented space (the living room) in Doty's discourses is the question of labor itself. The author speaks in the sentence previously quoted of the need for rest ("we'll put our feet up") as if after prodigious intellectual production. Actually he has produced a "thin" volume in more than one sense: In physical terms, Doty has published a text whose body comprises little more than a hundred pages; in theoretical terms, he apologizes for never achieving conceptual clarity and coherence about the meaning of the term *queer* ("I try to be as clear and coherent as possible" [xiii]) but never explains why he holds on to such criteria while writing a basically ludic book, when ludic theory itself has abandoned these very criteria. Doty's confused commitment to ludic premises in cultural inquiry is manifested in the continual formula by which "making things queer" is equated basically with multiplying pleasure (straight, gay, lesbian, queer). In the end, as the reference to champagne suggests, this is in no way a case of rest after hard labor but rather a case of upper-middle-class self-coddling. In the last analysis, the same process we saw at work in the film *Basic Instinct* and in the essay "White Glasses" is also at work in Doty's discourses: Just as in the film, unleashed desire (in the form of frank sexual language and visual images) is "at play" to

swamp a conceptual grasp of issues of need, just as in the essay, unleashed desire (in the form of white glasses that turn into VR goggles) is "at play" to keep us from asking about the historical and material conditions that produce the injustices of the health care system, so in Doty's acknowledgments (as elsewhere in his text), unleashed desire (in the form of casual sociality and the search for pleasure) is "at play" for similar occlusive ideological purposes. In the final analysis, intimate critique is another new (post)modern genre that works to obliterate the distinction between the inside and the outside as the difference between the private (domain of experience and the personal) and the public (domain of the conceptual and the collective). With Corey Creekmur, Doty has also edited an anthology, *Out in Culture: Gay, Lesbian, and Queer Essays on Popular Culture,* which continues to "queer" the texts of popular culture by extending the (post)modern obliteration of the distinction "inside/outside" and by (post)modernizing the concept of "camp" as a mode of cultural pedagogy that "has the ability to 'queer' straight culture by asserting that there is queerness at the core of mainstream culture even though that culture tirelessly insists that its images, ideologies, and readings were always only about heterosexuality" (1995, 3). While Creekmur and Doty acknowledge that some essays in their collection "are more informative than analytical, more polemical than theoretical," they maintain that this signals merely the "range of modes as well as topics in queer cultural commentary" (7). Such an effort to situate (post)-modernist modes unproblematically alongside modernist ones obscures the conflictual theoretical relations and completely mystifies the politics of (post)modern theory's impact on gay/lesbian/queer studies. (The same taming and naturalizing moves are made for readers of *PMLA* by Lauren Berlant and Michael Warner in their essay, "What Does Queer Theory Teach Us About X?" written by invitation of the editors of *PMLA* to contest preemptively the kind of historical materialist analysis of queer theory I am offering here and that also appeared in my essay, "Birth of the Cyber-queer," which was published in the same volume of *PMLA*.)

Another highly instructive example of the political consequences of the anti-cognitivism of intimate critique is found in Henry Abelove's essay, "From Thoreau to Queer Politics." The significance of this essay lies not so much in what it says: Abelove does not undertake to articulate concepts theoretically but merely names them and thereby "evokes" a sense of the contemporary theoretical ambience. What the essay strikingly reveals is the tremendous depth of political anxiety today in academic and intellectual circles and the maneuvers currently being deployed to evade rigorous materialist inquiry by promoting the return of "repressed sensations" (through intimate critique) in order to block ideology critique. Not only has Abelove's text acquired the institutional prestige of being published in *The Yale Journal of Criticism* (as Doty's is heralded as the work of that writer "on the verge of being recognized as the single most important figure in gay media studies"), but furthermore Abelove's notes to the text indicate that he was invited to give "versions" of this paper "during the academic year 1992–1993" at no less than six universities (26), five in the United States (Brown, New York University, Stanford, Berkeley, and Davis) and one in Australia (Australian National University), a point I shall return to in a moment.

Abelove's essay weaves together two "impressionistic" narratives: One articulates Abelove's impressions of the impressions produced by homophobic readers of Thoreau's impressions recorded in *Walden* at the time of the book's first publication (its literal textual impression); the other articulates Abelove's own impressions of his participation in a "local chapter of Queer Nation" (17) (which like other chapters appears to specialize in making "queer impressions") while he was in Salt Lake City, Utah, during the 1991/1992 academic year. Like any other impressionistic essay, this one cannot really arrive at an intellectually grounded conclusion: Such concluding would require a knowledge-based conviction. Abelove pointedly calls attention to

this lack of conviction. Even though Abelove remarks that "we should try to believe" (26), his essay "ends" with a necessarily inconclusive ("unbelieving") conclusion: "We who are queer do not yet fully believe our own claims to centrality. *That is my impression*" (26, emphasis added). Without being able to conclude, Abelove nevertheless ends his essay with an idea that queers should believe in, if they can: "What Queer Nation really means is America" (26). This confident formulation is finally just rhetoric, only a kind of "whistling in the dark" to buck up one's flagging spirits and not an argument. The essay in fact gives no argument for this equation (it cannot do so). All Abelove does is render overt ludic theory's antitheoreticism by dismissing those who have in fact tried to theorize (render conceptual) the meaning of Queer Nation: "I do not think that the signification of this name is as mysterious and difficult as most commentators on the subject have assumed" (26). What is finally missing, of course, from Abelove's impressions of theory is any theory of impressions. Ultimately, the very ideological function of this impressionistic criticism or intimate critique is to evade argument: instead of providing an argument, the essay performs an invocation (and a rhetorical queering) of the texts of a canonical white male U.S. writer—Thoreau.

The final paragraphs of Abelove's essay are situated within a politically very telling contradiction. Along one line of thought, the ending, like the rest of the essay, is enabled (although not very consciously informed) theoretically by the very principle of ludic undecidability (a principle that underpins the genre of which it is an example); yet along another line of thought that lies athwart the first, the ending expresses a deep nostalgia for certainty (which ludic principles render impossible). As Abelove himself suggests, his entire essay is haunted by a lack of belief in the "centrality" of the "queer." This is what makes wide acceptance of texts like Abelove's (and Doty's as well) in intellectual and academic circles so politically instructive. Those texts that are accepted as representing the strongest political interests of the queer (and whose creators are therefore invited to speak for those interests in many institutional sites or are promoted by the culture industry as the leading spokesperson in subfield "x") are just those texts expressing uncertainty and confusion about that very project. In the terms being developed in this anthology, the problem is that the very kind of knowledge of the social totality that would bring—by means of conceptual explanations—a certainty about the "materiality" of the oppression of the queer is the dangerous knowledge associated with taking ideology seriously. If Abelove could grasp the oppression of queers in the United States or anywhere else as a result of the operations of ideology (and the material contradictions of class relations and other differences) and gain certain knowledge from this cognition, he would be unable just to stop there but would instead then have to explain the global implications of his new cognitive understanding and his own situatedness in relation to that knowledge. In other words, this knowledge would entail certain further obligations. Abelove's hesitation—which, as the academy's eagerness to hear and publish his views indicates, he doubtless articulates for many others—comes from his deep fear that he is too "queer" to be "American." In this he repeats, in parallel, the same fear articulated by Frank Lentricchia, once known as a leading Marxist critic, who reportedly said not long ago that he is "too American to be a Marxist" (Atlas 1988, 27). In tone, the conclusion of Abelove's "uncertain" essay (itself an instance of "queer" reading) shares the kind of ludic melancholy that characterizes Lentricchia's essay, also in the genre of intimate critique, "En Route to Retreat: Making It to Mepkin Abbey" (1992), whose very title signals a withdrawal from worldly contestations and that aims finally at queering the concept by invoking the specter of the ineffable. Abelove—uncertain about the centrality of queers—and Lentricchia—in retreat from the world—join together in the ahistorical space of the queer sublime. On the political level, the underlying connection between Lentricchia's and Abelove's statements is that both of them know very well

that America *as it is* is incompatible with both homosexuality and Marxism. However, neither seems willing to make the effort to overcome this situation, except through local gestures that have, at best, only very short-term effects, effects that come, for instance, from the license plate Lentricchia sports on his car ("Go Left") and from "the buttons, signs and illustrated t-shirts" worn by Queer Nation members (while in Mormon Salt Lake City, Abelove favored wearing the T-shirt marked "Elder Queer" [26]).

6

I have dwelled at some length on the new genre of "intimate critique" because examining it helps to clarify still further (beyond the points presented earlier in this introduction) the difference between this anthology on (homo)sexuality and the other available anthologies. Broadly speaking, it helps to clarify the consequences for sexual politics of following the idealist project of the dominant anthologies, which, under the hegemonic sway of ludic theory, take the autonomy of desire for granted. It also helps to clarify the consequences of following a materialist understanding of sexualities by reopening—as *The Material Queer* does—the question of the autonomy of desire through rearticulating the contestation between idealism and materialism. The very point of undertaking the production of another anthology on (homo)sexuality—which is inevitably not merely an editorial but also a pedagogical task (for sustained theorizations of pedagogy in the broad sense, see Morton and Zavarzadeh 1991)—is not to repeat what a number of anthologies are already doing, but to provide a *different* understanding of the issues. The aim of *The Material Queer* is certainly not to erase—as the Right wants to do—all discussion of "other" sexualities from the discourses of culture, but to inquire into whether today's prevailing understandings of "other" sexualities (especially those on the Left) are indeed socially productive. Neither is the point to pretend that desire and

pleasure do not exist: However, desire and pleasure are not simply to be acknowledged and celebrated (naturalized) but must instead be in-
terrogated and critiqued (denaturalized and
historicized), and their production in the global
series of social phenomena thereby understood.

The prevailing theory of desire (as autonomous) is articulated not only thematically in
dominant anthologies but is in fact the principle of selection and organization of these anthologies. In other words, the notion of desire
in (post)modern theory is an understanding of
desire as "immanent"—as a self-intelligible
given without any relations of "dependency"
with an outside of desire. In fact, the very binary of the inside/outside (following Derrida's
classic deconstruction of it in *Of Grammatology*) is obscured in the dominant cultural
studies today precisely in order to further enhance the prevailing logic of immanence.

As a principle of editing, the idea of desire as
immanent and self-supporting leads to editorial practices that assume that the topic being
addressed, whatever it happens to be, can indeed be understood "on its own terms." Following this pattern, existing anthologies on
queerity usually bring together texts that either
thematize the topic (are "about" queerity) or
perform queerity itself (are written in the queer
mode). In either case, it is assumed that all of
the relevant questions about the focal phenomenon are situated and contained within the field
of queerity itself. In other words, there is a
queer knowledge *as such* and scholarship on the
topic will inevitably be a further elaboration
and annotation of that knowledge *from within.*
The production, reproduction, and extension
of this "inside knowledge" is one of the marks
of the academic institutionalization and bourgeois professionalization of a "new" area of
knowledge: its "settling down" within the status
quo.

Those scholars and intellectuals who work as
if "on the inside," as one might say, show their
credentials by learning to speak the various
queer idioms and vernaculars. The result is that
in the process of acquiring this inside knowledge and learning to speak and write queerly

about the queer, these critics and scholars become what might be called the technocrats of
queer studies. They take on the task of refining
queer knowledge-in-itself and rendering it—in
the dialogical process theorized previously—
ever more sophisticated and subtle. They do
this for the most part, however, without ever
asking how this new queer knowledge came to
be what it is. This working assumption, which
protects inside knowledge by pretending that
there is no outside, holds today (not only in
queer studies but also in African-American
studies, in feminism, and in other marginal inquiries anxious to establish their "autonomy"
and secure a place in presently existing institutional arrangements), in spite of the fact that
(post)modernism has supposedly shifted all
productive intellectual and critical work away
from the plane of traditional disciplinarity and
toward the plane of the transdisciplinary. Those
who are fascinated with *queerity as such* somehow manage to overlook the open secret that
this "as suchness" (its self-evident "thereness")
changes under changing historical conditions.
The queer of twenty years ago is something
quite different from the queer of today. In other
words, as I have argued at length here, the "return of the queer" marks a return with a difference. This means that queerity is not an entity
in itself, but, on the contrary, is open to its outside, which—in an ongoing historical process—
conditions what the queer is.

Based on different assumptions and moving
along a different trajectory, *The Material Queer*
rejects the ghettoization of queer knowledge by
raising questions *from without* the localized domain of the queer-as-such. In other words, this
volume interprets the title of the series in which
it appears, "Queer Critique," to mean not only—
as common sense might suggest—critique of
the non-queer world from the inside of the
queer (although many of the texts published
here undertake this project) but also a critique-al resituating of the queer itself in relation to the larger social and historical series of
which it is a part. (This resituating, of course,
proceeds by critiquing the prevailing dominant
"queer" discourses.) Thus this text goes against

the dominant logic today, which tends to regard any effort to bring into the discussion understandings from outside the field of the phenomenon under study as a violation of that phenomenon's supposed integrity. This anthology assumes that you cannot interpret queerity (or anything else for that matter) without a theoretical understanding of *prior questions*. For example, the work of the historian of science, Donna Haraway (see, for instance, Haraway 1991) has recently introduced the notion of the (post)modern subject as the *cyborg*, a term that seems to have taken on a life of its own and now circulates widely in cultural studies texts. However, the term is not self-intelligible: To make sense of it, one has to have at least a minimal understanding of the principles of cybernetics, a science that may at first seem remote from the analysis of subjectivity. The same may be said of Gilles Deleuze and Felix Guattari's notion (elaborated previously) of the "body without organs." Such a notion depends on a prior knowledge of the "body *with* organs." With these considerations in view, the present anthology argues that the queer cannot be understood "on its own terms" because it is a historical phenomenon—that is, one conditioned by social, cultural, economic . . . forces.

The aim here, therefore, is to open queer studies up to its outside, which is to say to place it within the context of the historical. There is, one must add, nothing sacrosanct about the category of history. The value of the historicizing logic emphasized here lies in its inclusive character—inclusive, not in the empirical or quantitative sense, but in terms of its capacity to connect disparate seemingly unconnected and unconnectable phenomena on many different levels. It may appear, for instance, that there is no connection between the way Plato, in the *Symposium,* situates questions of love and sexuality in relation to the ladder to Truth, on the one hand, and the theory of queerity Michael Warner articulates in "Fear of a Queer Planet," on the other (see these texts reprinted in this volume). I would argue, however, that the enabling socioeconomic conditions of these idealistic positions on (homo)sexuality are very

much the same: Whereas Plato's position was enabled by the existence of a class of slaves in ancient Greek society, Warner's is enabled by the existence of a class of workers in the U.S. society of today.

The evidence of (idealist) ludic influence on most available lesbian/gay/queer anthologies (that is, their commitment to the ludic [post]-modern premises that support the notion of the autonomy of desire and the autonomy of the new queer studies) is not hard to adduce, as these instances suggest: the very titles of Joseph Bristow's *Sexual Sameness: Textual Differences in Lesbian and Gay Writing* (Routledge, 1992) and Susan J. Wolfe and Julia Penelope's *Sexual Practice, Textual Theory: Lesbian Cultural Criticism* (Blackwell, 1993); and the titular binarism and the presiding performative spirit set by Judith Butler's lead essay in Diana Fuss's *Inside/Out: Lesbian Theories, Gay Theories* (Routledge, 1991). A very direct and overt example is furnished by Sally Munt's candid acknowledgment that her *New Lesbian Criticism: Literary and Cultural Readings* (Columbia University Press, 1992) had as its working, programmatic title "Dykonstruction," which she says signaled its "indebtedness to poststructuralism" (Munt 1992, xiii). However, the most prominent instance is the anthology (which names itself, in the singular as) *The Lesbian and Gay Studies Reader,* published in 1993 by Routledge. The book was produced under the coeditorship of Henry Abelove (a practitioner, as we have just seen, of "intimate critique"), Michèle Aina Barale (whose work focuses on producing self-described "queer readings"—reversible textual representations [Abelove et al. 1993, 604]), and David Halperin (whose Foucauldian commitments are already well known), and it is, furthermore, punctuated with texts by ludic-oriented/-influenced writers (Eve Sedgwick, Monique Wittig, Simon Watney, D. A. Miller, Biddy Martin, Sue-Ellen Case, Judith Butler, Marjorie Garber, Joan Scott, Lee Edelman, and others). Like all editors of anthologies these days, Abelove, Barale, and Halperin confront a stark contradiction: At one level, market considerations, among other pressures (such as community-building and participants's career considerations), urge decisions that will produce both the broadest possible sales and thus the broadest sense of "inclusiveness" (Routledge advertises *The Lesbian and Gay Studies Reader* as "the biggest and most comprehensive multidisciplinary anthology of critical work in lesbian/gay studies" [Routledge, 1993]); on another level, editors must draw certain boundaries and in the light of the demystification of institutional practices in recent years, it is very difficult today for editors to pretend that their boundary-drawing editorial work is objective or "un-positioned."

Rather than theorizing their editorial position(s), however, these editors hedge the hard issues. On the one hand, they offer rather vague and impressionistic criteria for what they have *included* ("what we take to be some of the best and most significant recent English-language work" [xv]; "comprehensiveness" [xvii]; "essays that reflect contemporary trends and tendencies" [xvii]; "essays that convey the intellectual intricacy and cohesiveness of current work" [xvii]; and what they "admired" [xvii]); on the other hand, they offer a substantial list of "Suggestions for Further Reading" (653–666) to compensate for what they have *excluded*. These maneuvers help to avoid an inquiry into how their inclusions/exclusions produce ideologically coded boundaries. Furthermore, their avoidance of developing the emergent notion of the "queer" suggests that, in spite of the announced wish to "reflect contemporary trends and tendencies," the underlying agenda of the volume is aimed more at institutionalizing writings that are already safely established and dependably commodifiable, in other words, at creating a professional and academic "inside."

What they do forthrightly acknowledge is that their anthology is completely in tune with the contemporary commitment of the dominant lesbian/gay/queer theory (which they represent) to displace the category of gender with the category of sexuality (in other words, to move toward underwriting the autonomy of desire). Given their ludic learning, the editors cannot pretend that their process of selection

merely "reflects" (in a referential gesture toward the world) already existing trends, but must realize that they are themselves, by their very selections, producing and perpetuating (in an act of cultural pedagogy) certain understandings of sexuality and of the world at large. Their anthology's ideological agenda (what we might call, borrowing a term from Abelove, its commitment to *desire-evangelism*—see Abelove 1990) is strikingly evident in the editors' choice of the keynote text for the entire collection: Gayle Rubin's essay, "Thinking Sex: Notes for a Radical Theory of the Politics of Sexuality." Rubin's widely cited essay becomes the fulcrum for a key theoretical—or rather, antitheoretical—shift. This essay supersedes an earlier and also well-known text of hers, "The Traffic in Women: Notes on the 'Political Economy' of Sex" (Reiter 1975). Exemplifying the trajectory of ludic theory in the United States, Rubin's more recent essay promotes sexuality (the space for the investigation of "impressions" and "sensations") as a category that displaces the category of gender, which earlier was a *conceptually theorized* category—producing not an "impression" but a "cognition"—that had taken its place alongside such already established categories as "class." The shift in Rubin's essay recapitulates the dominant academy's move (a move whose theoretical genealogy and political consequences this anthology is devoted to investigating): the erasure of questions of need and the promotion of the autonomy of desire.

The dominant anthologies, for example, take such new developments as "intimate critique" for granted. *The Material Queer,* by contrast, insists that the new genre of "intimate critique" must be reunderstood—like the "return of the queer" itself—in historical terms as a "return-with-a-difference." "Intimate critique"—which is quietly being "naturalized" in dominant gay/lesbian/queer discourses today—actually represents the return—under the auspices of the antitheory theory of ludic (post)modernism—of that "impressionistic criticism" rejected some decades ago by the New Criticism, whose theorists promoted instead rigorous textual-structural readings that could produce clear, if also ambiguous, meanings of texts. We can better grasp this "return" if we keep in mind that the new impressionism, which takes the form of reading/writing for Barthesian "pleasure of the text," is basically an effort to subvert the very possibility of ideology critique. This point was hinted at recently by Graeme Turner, who remarks in discussing cultural studies that "The notion of pleasure has increasingly been placed in opposition to that of ideology" (Turner 1990, 119). This opposition pits "meanings," which (as Turner recognizes) are "socially produced," against "physical pleasures," which are supposedly not social but personal ("our own," 119). As I have already argued, ludic theory pits sensations (impressions) against concepts. Reading for pleasure becomes a strategy for producing interruptions of continuous ideological knowledge through the return of repressed sensations that produces an intermittency of cognition. "Intimate critique," then, is not merely a new aesthetic form but rather a contemporary strategy for resisting intelligibility and the very possibility of ideology critique. The mode of reading inscribed in "intimate critique" produces a reading/writing subject who ends up being impressed by the knowledge she or he encounters, but who does not turn this impression into a cognitive knowing on which a political practice could be based. Against the dominant practice, it is this latter politically alert and directed kind of knowing that *The Material Queer* supports.

Finally, *The Material Queer* insists on the need to make *global connections* between understandings of sexuality and other cultural/social/economic/political . . . struggles. At first glance, it appears that the dominant queer theory wants to make large connections also, as suggested, for instance, in the generality of Doty's title, *Making Things Perfectly Queer*. Whereas Dennis Altman in the early 1980s spoke more modestly of "the homosexualization of America" (Altman 1982), queer theorists of the 1990s speak of "queering the planet" (Warner 1991). With such broad formulations, queer theory seems to situate itself in relation to a network of all-encompassing transforma-

tions. However, after a visit to the United States again a few years ago, where he attended a conference in which the new queer theory was being developed, Altman himself remarked that today "politics, in the large sense of the word, is not sufficiently central in the creation of lesbian and gay studies" (1990, 65). Altman then issued a new call for gay studies to "get global": "Gay liberation," he remarked (recalling the importance of pre-queer assumptions), "cannot exist in a vacuum and only ask 'Is it good for the gays?'" (65). As Altman's text clearly indicates, for him getting global does not mean "queering the planet" but going in the other direction we are also investigating here—"getting historical, material, and collective." If we think in these terms, we must finally ask very different kinds of questions from those today's dominant queer theory poses from within its idealist frame of understanding.

One of the most important questions would be this: Why does the appearance of queer theory coincide historically with the fall of the Berlin Wall? The Berlin Wall symbolized, of course, not simply a particular post–World War II partitioning by Allied powers of a country on the "losing" side. As Ronald Reagan and George Bush's obsession with it indicated, the Berlin Wall symbolized, most importantly, the dividing line between the spheres of influence of two competing visions of the social and their allied modes of production: one, capitalism, devoted to the expansion, reproduction, and commodification of desires (for profit); and another, socialism, concerned with fulfilling needs. Ultimately, today's queer theory—which belongs, as I have shown, with the former and not with the latter—is the kind of Eurocentric theory (it takes its de-historicized notion of desire to be desire as such) that sees the fall of the Berlin Wall as what the bourgeois apologist Francis Fukuyama calls "the end of history" itself (1989). The queer theory that dominates academic and intellectual circles at the present time is, in the last analysis, just one strand of today's dominant Eurocentric theories, which desperately want to see the burden of history (along with the West's collective social responsibilities) disappear. Dominant queer theory's program for this disappearance is what it calls "queering the planet" (that is, establishing the autonomy of desire and erasing need). These theories, which hail the present post–Cold War moment to be the moment of the arrival of "freedom for all" (that is, of the desire of "all"), only serve to occlude the worldwide needs that remain to be fulfilled (in Bosnia, Somalia, the Middle East, Africa, Central and South America, and elsewhere, not to mention U.S. inner cities). In other words, today's queer theory is finally only part of that idealist, bourgeois history currently being written through VR goggles and "white glasses." Ultimately the most productive and responsible contribution will be made by a materialist queer studies that theorizes sexuality in relation to the largest possible understanding of social need.[3] Rather than working indefatigably—as ludic (post)modernism and its bourgeois proponents do—to mystify the very category of "the other" (as an interminable and basically unknowable—and unexplainable, but only describable—series of emerging differences), a materialist queer theory will account—within a rigorous (but not eternally fixed) conceptual frame of understanding—for existing, historically produced "othernesses" of all kinds and work against the oppression and exploitation to which those othernesses—while today's queer desire is celebrating its autonomy—remain subject.

Notes

1. As I understand the term, *(post)modernism* is not a positive entity "out there," but rather a political construct—the collectivity of reading strategies that are deployed to make sense of a particular historical series. Following Teresa L. Ebert's theorization of (post)modernism (Ebert, 1992–1993), I designate as "ludic (post)modernism" the understanding of (post)modernity that makes sense of it as a problematics of representation and, furthermore, conceives *representation* as a rhetorical issue, a matter of signification, in which the very process of signification itself articulates the signified. Representation is always incommensurate with the represented, since it is subject to the law of *différance*. Ludic

(post)modernism, therefore, posits the real as an instance of simulation and in no sense the origin of the truth that can provide a ground for a political project. *Différance* is regarded as the effect of the unending playfulness (thus the term *ludic*) of the signifier in signifying processes that can no longer acquire representational authority by anchoring themselves in what Jacques Derrida has called the "transcendental signified" (*Of Grammatology,* 20). For a further discussion of the different understandings of (post)-modernity in relation to today's competing forms of cultural studies, see my "A Note on Cultural Studies" in this volume and Zavarzadeh and Morton (1991). For a sustained critique of queer theory, see my "The Politics of Queer Theory in the (Post)modern Moment."

2. For sustained critiques of liberal pluralism in both its modernist and its (post)modernist forms, see Zavarzadeh and Morton (1993). For a discussion of the current crisis of liberalism in literary/cultural studies, see Morton, "The Crisis of Liberalism."

3. For a more sustained discussion of contemporary sexualities in materialist terms, see Morton, "Queerity and Ludic Sado-Masochism."

References

Abelove, Henry. (1990) *The Evangelist of Desire: John Wesley and the Methodists.* Stanford: Stanford University Press.

———. (1993) "From Thoreau to Queer Politics." *The Yale Journal of Criticism* 6.2 (Fall): 17–27.

Abelove, Henry, Michèle Aina Barale, and David M. Halperin, eds. (1993) *The Lesbian and Gay Studies Reader.* New York and London: Routledge.

Adam, Barry D. (1987) *The Rise of a Gay and Lesbian Movement.* Boston: Twayne Publishers.

Altman, Dennis. (1982) *The Homosexualization of America.* Boston: Beacon Press.

———. (1990) "My America and Yours: A Letter to US Activists." *Outlook: National Lesbian & Gay Quarterly* 8 (Spring 1990):62–65.

Atlas, James. (1988) "The Battle of the Books." *New York Times Magazine,* June 5:24ff.

Bakhtin, Mikhail. (1965) *Rabelais and His World.* Cambridge, Mass.: MIT Press.

Barthes, Roland. (1975) *The Pleasure of the Text.* Trans. Richard Miller. New York: Hill & Wang.

Baudrillard, Jean. (1981) *For a Critique of the Political Economy of the Sign.* Trans. Charles Levin. St. Louis: Telos Press.

————. (1975) *The Mirror of Production.* Trans. Mark Poster. St. Louis: Telos Press.

————. (1983) *Simulations.* Trans. Paul Foss and Paul Patton. New York: Semiotext(e).

Berlant, Lauren, and Michael Warner. (1995) "What Does Queer Theory Teach Us About X?" *PMLA* 110:343–349.

Boone, Joseph A., and Michael Cadden, eds. (1990) *Engendering Men: The Question of Male Feminist Criticism.* New York and London: Routledge.

Bright, Susie. (1992) *Sexual Reality: A Virtual Sex World Reader.* Pittsburgh and San Francisco: Cleis Press.

Bristow, Joseph, ed. (1992) *Sexual Sameness: Textual Differences in Lesbian and Gay Writing.* London and New York: Routledge.

Browning, Frank. (1993) *The Culture of Desire: Paradox and Perversity in Gay Lives Today.* New York: Crown Publishers, Inc.

Butler, Judith. (1990) *Gender Trouble: Feminism and the Subversion of Identity.* New York and London: Routledge.

————. (1991) "Imitation and Gender Insubordination." In Diana Fuss, ed. *Inside/Out: Lesbian Theories, Gay Theories.* New York and London: Routledge, pp. 13–31.

Caniglia, Julie. (1993) "Cyberpunks Hate You." *Utne Reader* (July/August):88–96.

Cohen, Ed. (1990) "Are We (Not) What We Are Becoming? Gay 'Identity,' 'Gay Studies,' and the Disciplining of Knowledge." In Boone and Cadden, eds., pp. 161–175.

Cooper, Dennis. (1992) "Johnny Noxzema to the Gay Community: 'You Are the Enemy.'" *The Village Voice,* (June 30):31–32.

Coward, Rosalind, and John Ellis. (1977) *Language and Materialism: Developments in Semiology and the Theory of the Subject.* Boston, London, and Henley: Routledge & Kegan Paul.

Creekmur, Corey K., and Alexander Doty, eds. (1995) *Out in Culture: Gay, Lesbian, and Queer Essays on Popular Culture.* Durham, N.C.: Duke University Press.

Davis, Erik. (1993) "A Computer, A Universe: Mapping an Online Cosmology." *The Voice Literary Supplement,* (March):10–11.

Deleuze, Gilles, and Felix Guattari. (1977) *Anti-Oedipus: Capitalism and Schizophrenia.* Trans. Robert Hurley, Mark Seem, and Helen R. Lane. New York: Viking Press.

————. (1987) *A Thousand Plateaus: Capitalism and Schizophrenia.* Trans. Brian Massumi. Minneapolis: University of Minnesota Press.

Derrida, Jacques. (1976) *Of Grammatology.* Trans. Gayatri C. Spivak. Baltimore and London: The Johns Hopkins University Press.

————. (1984) *Signsponge.* Trans. Richard Rand. New York: Columbia University Press.

Dibbell, Julian. (1993) "Let's Get Digital: The Writer à la Modem." *Voice Literary Supplement,* (March): 13–14.

Doty, Alexander. (1993) *Making Things Perfectly Queer: Interpreting Mass Culture.* Minneapolis and London: University of Minnesota Press.

Dubrow, Heather. (1993) Announcement of special topic for future issue of *PMLA. PMLA* 108.3 (May):399.

Ebert, Teresa L. (1992–1993) "Ludic Feminism, the Body, Performance, and Labor: Bringing *Materialism* Back into Feminist Cultural Studies." *Cultural Critique* 23 (Winter): 5–50.

Fish, Stanley. (1993) *There Is No Such Thing as Free Speech . . . And It's a Good Thing, Too.* New York: Oxford University Press.

Foucault, Michel. (1990) *The Care of the Self.* Vol. 3 of *The History of Sexuality.* Trans. Robert Hurley. New York: Vintage Books.

————. (1980) *The History of Sexuality. Volume 1: An Introduction.* Trans. R. Hurley. New York: Vintage Books.

————. (1977) *Language, Counter-Memory, Practice: Selected Essays and Interviews.* Trans. D. F. Bouchard and S. Simon. Ithaca: Cornell University Press.

Freedman, Diane P., O. Frey, and F. M. Zauhar, eds. (1993) *The Intimate Critique: Autobiographical Literary Criticism.* Durham, N.C. and London: Duke University Press.

Freud, Sigmund. (1961) *Civilization and Its Discontents.* New York: Norton.

————. (1962) *Three Essays on the Theory of Sexuality.* Trans. James Strachey. New York: Basic Books.

Fukuyama, Francis. (1989) "The End of History." *National Interest* (Summer):3–18.

Fuss, Diana. (1991) *Inside/Out: Lesbian Theories, Gay Theories.* New York and London: Routledge.

Gallop, Jane. (1988) *Thinking Through the Body.* New York: Columbia University Press.

————. (1995) "The Teacher's Breasts." In Jane Gallop, ed. *Pedagogy: The Question of Impersonation.* Bloomington and Indianapolis: Indiana University Press.

Garber, Marjorie. (1991) *Vested Interests: Cross Dressing & Cultural Anxiety.* New York: Routledge.

Haggerty, George E., and Bonnie Zimmerman, eds. (1995) *Professions of Desire: Lesbian and Gay Studies in Literature.* New York: Modern Language Association.

Haraway, Donna. (1991) *Simians, Cyborgs, and Women: The Reinvention of Nature.* New York: Routledge.

Jameson, Fredric. (1988) *The Ideologies of Theory: Essays, 1971–1986.* 2 vols. Minneapolis: University of Minnesota Press.

———. (1991) *Postmodernism, or, the Cultural Logic of Late Capitalism.* Durham, N.C.: Duke University Press.

Johnson, Barbara. (1987) *A World of Difference.* Baltimore and London: Johns Hopkins University Press.

Kadrey, Richard. (1993) *Covert Culture Sourcebook.* New York: St. Martin's Press.

Kernan, Alvin. (1990) *The Death of Literature.* New Haven, Conn.: Yale University Press.

Kristeva, Julia. (1980) *Desire in Language: A Semiotic Approach to Literature and Art.* Trans. T. Gora, A. Jardine, and L. S. Roudiez. New York: Columbia University Press.

Lacan, Jacques. (1977) *Écrits: A Selection.* Trans. Alan Sheridan. New York and London: W. W. Norton & Company.

Lentricchia, Frank. (1992) "En Route to Retreat: Making It to Mepkin Abbey." *Harper's* Jan.:68ff.

Liberation Now! Writings from the Women's Liberation Movement. (1971) New York: Dell.

Lyotard, Jean-François. (1993) *Libidinal Economy.* Trans. Iaian H. Grant. Bloomington: Indiana University Press.

Lyotard, Jean-François, and Jean-Loup Thébaud. (1985) *Just Gaming.* Trans. Wlad Godzich. Minneapolis: University of Minneapolis Press.

Marx, Karl. (1977) *Capital: A Critique of Political Economy. Volume One.* Trans. Ben Fowkes. New York: Vintage.

———. (1988) *The Communist Manifesto.* Ed. Frederic L. Bender. New York and London: W. W. Norton.

Marx, Karl, and Friedrich Engels. (1970) *The German Ideology: Part One.* New York: International Publishers.

Miller, D. A. (1992) *Bringing out Barthes.* Berkeley: University of California Press.

Miller, James. (1993) *The Passion of Michel Foucault.* New York: Simon & Schuster.

Mitchell, Hugh, and Kayode Olafimihan. (1992) "A Queer View." *Living Marxism* (November):39.

Morton, Donald. (1995) "Birth of the Cyberqueer." *PMLA* 110:369–381.

———. "The Crisis of Liberalism in Literary/Cultural Studies." *Red Orange* 1 (forthcoming, Spring 1996).

———. (1993) "The Politics of Queer Theory in the (Post)modern Moment." *Genders* 17:180–230.

———. "Queerity and Ludic Sado-Masochism: Compulsory Consumption and the Emerging Post-al Queer." In Zavarzadeh, Ebert, and Morton, eds. *Post-ality: Marxism and Postmodernism.* 189–215.

Morton, Donald, and Mas'ud Zavarzadeh. (1991) *Theory/Pedagogy/Politics: Texts for Change.* Urbana and Chicago: University of Illinois Press.

Mulvey, Laura. (1993) "Some Thoughts on Theories of Fetishism in the Context of Contemporary Culture." *October* 65 (Summer):3–20.

Munt, Sally, ed. (1992) *New Lesbian Criticism: Literary and Cultural Readings.* ("Between Women—Between Men: Lesbian and Gay Studies") New York: Columbia University Press.

Rheingold, Howard. (1991) *Virtual Reality.* New York: Summit Books.

Ronell, Avital. (1989) *The Telephone Book: Technology, Schizophrenia, Electronic Speech.* Lincoln: University of Nebraska Press.

Routledge, Chapman, and Hall, Inc. (1993) Announcement and Order Form for *The Lesbian and Gay Studies Reader.*

Rubin, Gayle. (1993, originally 1984) "Thinking Sex: Notes for a Radical Theory of the Politics of Sexuality." In Abelove, Barale, and Halperin eds., pp. 1–44.

———. (1975) "The Traffic in Women: Notes on the 'Political Economy' of Sex." In R. Reiter, ed. *Toward an Anthropology of Women.* New York: Monthly Review Press, pp. 157–210.

Saussure, Ferdinand de. (1966) *Course in General Linguistics.* Trans. Wade Baskin. New York: McGraw-Hill.

Sedgwick, Eve Kosofsky. (1990) *Epistemology of the Closet.* Berkeley: University of California Press.

———. (1992) "White Glasses." *Yale Journal of Criticism* 5.3 (Fall):193–208.

Smith, Barbara. (1993) "Where's the Revolution?" *The Nation* (July 5):12–16.

Solomon, Alisa. (1992) "Breaking Out." *The Village Voice,* (June 30) 27, 29.

Toepfer, Karl. (1991) *Theatre, Aristocracy, and Pornocracy: The Orgy Calculus.* New York: PAJ Publications.

Tucker, Robert C., ed. (1978) *The Marx-Engels Reader.* 2d ed. New York: W. W. Norton.

Turner, Graeme. (1990) *British Cultural Studies: An Introduction.* Boston: Unwin Hyman.

Vološinov, V. N. (1986) *Marxism and the Philosophy of Language.* Trans. L. Matejka and I. R. Titunik. Cambridge and London: Harvard University Press.

Warner, Michael. (1991) "Introduction: Fear of a Queer Planet." *Social Text* 29:3–17.

Williams, Jeffrey. (1993) "Sedgwick Unplugged (An Interview with Eve Kosofsky Sedgwick)." *The Minnesota Review* n.s., 40 (Spring/Summer):53–64.

Wolfe, Susan J., and Julia Penelope. (1993) *Sexual Practice, Textual Theory: Lesbian Cultural Criticism.* New York: Blackwell.

Zavarzadeh, Mas'ud, and Donald Morton. (1993) *The Resistance to Theory: Politics and Culture After (Post)Structuralism.* New York: Guilford Publications, Inc.

———. (1991) *Theory, (Post)Modernity, Opposition: An "Other" Introduction to Literary and Cultural Theory.* Washington, D.C.: Maisonneuve Press.

Zavarzadeh, Mas'ud, Teresa Ebert, and Donald Morton, eds. (1995) *Post-ality: Marxism and Postmodernism.* (Transformation: Marxist Boundary Work in Theory, Economics, Politics, and Culture 1) Washington, D.C.: Maisonneuve Press.

Queer Consensus/ Socialist Conflict

I open *The Material Queer* with a(n unorthodoxly) "queer" move: I take the book's reader on a detour into the "thick" of the contestation before the fuller dimensions of the contemporary struggle—articulated in the bulk of the texts reprinted in the anthology—are made available. The essays included here at the outset stage the (post)modern contestation over the queer in rather sharp terms. In Michael Warner's essay, "Tongues Untied: Memoirs of a Pentecostal Boyhood," the axis of inquiry is the shift from a "Pentecostal Boyhood" to "queer atheist intellectual" adulthood. Along one line of thought, the text represents this shift as a marker of a radical difference, of a "rupture" within the self, and reads this personal rupture in public terms—as a key element in the larger narrative of America ("a certain carelessness about starting over is very much in the national taste,"); along another line, there is an intimate connection between these diverse selves: the later one (queer literary critic) is but a paler version of the earlier one (charismatic, receiver of "the gift of the Holy Ghost"). The point to be emphasized here is that—as Warner's "undecidable" narrative makes quite clear—the "giving up" of the most patent idealism of religions does not necessarily lead to the "giving up" of the secular idealism (he is now inscribed in the new idealism of the dominant queer theory).

As I have just suggested, Warner acknowledges some similarities between the two frames: Both Pentecostalism and queer theory are of course (like all frames of intelligibility) "hermeneutic," as Warner claims them to be; but they are idealist and not materialist hermeneutics. More important for my purposes is the fact that in the end, the "speaking in tongues" that characterizes the Pentecostal frame is not all that different from the "speaking in bodies" that characterizes today's dominant queer theory. Barthesian *jouissance* and Pentecostal *rapture* produce politically similar effects. In Warner's text about "coming out" as queer (which is for him analogous to religious "witnessing"), the space of the queer is promoted as the space of subversive and interventionist practices into heteronormativity. But its subversiveness is wholly ludic, that is, it works toward its aim by opening a post-historical space: a space *after* and *beyond* the history that has been written, rewritten, and overwritten by the regime of heterosexualities, the patriarchal and bourgeois family, the laws of inheritance, and by all the other elements of that order, which is so necessary to the continuation of today's regimented world. In Warner's discourses, the concerns of socialism with, for instance, the production of subjects as consumers is a very minor side issue because compared to religious rapture, the "satisfaction provided in consumer culture, is by contrast, low-budget monochrome." One might add that to this kind of subjectivity, the satisfactions of concept-formation (for addressing questions of need) can hardly compete with the thrills of (queer, straight, or bisexual) *jouissance* (desire). "If you lick my nipple," Warner remarks, "the world suddenly seems comparatively insignificant." For Warner, as for Butler and many other dominant queer theorists, identity (whether religious or secular) is the "performance" of desire. And the measure of "authenticity" of identity is sensuous excitement.

The second text, by Lance Selfa, "What's Wrong with Identity Politics," opens a different site for understanding identity: Identity is not performative but ideological. Identity is not a mode of being by which one achieves membership in a consensual community of desire, but rather a site of ideological and material contestation over need. In Warner's terms, coming out is joining (and trying to gain legitimacy for) such a consensual community of desire. By contrast, Selfa argues that a politics of desire will lead not to a radical transformation of the very structuring of desire but only to the addition to the existing structure of new quarters for homosexual inhabitants. In other words, the change that is needed cannot come about merely by legitimizing "new desires" for the very reason that heterosexuality is *not* the regime of desire. Against Warner's desire-bound notions, Selfa theorizes heterosexuality not as a regime for maximizing the pleasure-yield of desire, but for maximizing the social division of labor for profit. In this regime of profit, the difference of the homosexual, like the differences of persons of color, of women, and so on, is used ultimately to justify social differences that are generated in the social division of labor. Selfa further argues that solidarity is not grounded in gender, race, or sexuality, but in class. On his view, patriarchal capitalism, in other words, will not be transformed by the transferral of power from the straight to the gay, from man to woman, from white to those of color, and so on. It will change if—and only if—the prevailing mode of private ownership of the means of production is transformed to public ownership. To be sure, this materialist position is—as the cultural and theoretical cliché proposes—"reductive." However, this is the same "reductiveness" with which critics reproached Marx, who answered:

> You reproach us, therefore, with intending to do away with a form of property, the necessary condition for whose existence is the non-

existence of any property for the immense majority of society.

> In one word, you reproach us with intending to do away with your property. Precisely so; that is just what we intend (Marx 1988, 69–70).

The whole point of opening with these texts is to clearly indicate that this anthology is situated in the space of contestation between Warner's proposal that the world will change if we desire it into becoming a "queer planet" and Selfa's argument that Warner's notion is simply the latest form of a long tradition of "idealist radicalism" in the West: a radicalism that has always seen the world as the effect of the consciousness of the subject and that, at different historical moments, has found different names for that particular element of consciousness. In Warner's text—as in all those texts produced under the aegis of ludic (post)modernism—that name is *desire*. From Selfa's point of view, although Warner's text posits itself as an "odd" text (which claims to intervene effectively in the regime of the heterosexual), it is finally radical only in that it "redeems" consciousness—it offers a tale that redeems the queer from the straight by "oddly" resituating the queer in the straight world as it presently exists. This form of idealist radicalism reaches a high degree of populist effectivity precisely because it argues for a personal and voluntaristic (nonstructural) change that finally does not transform anything. All it does is alter the subject's "feeling" about his/her relations to the world. Warner's text ends by supporting the voluntarist and ahistorical notion of identity: that one can just "be somebody else." Hence, rather than changing the world, Warner instead—to repeat—applies mind-altering strategies in order to—in the words of today's most influential idealist philosopher, Richard Rorty—"redescribe" the world. It turns out that in the Warnerian/Rortian world "redescribed" by that "new somebody" that you have mysteriously (performatively) become, the queer will now "oddly" fit. Of course, the world itself has not changed. All that has happened is that the world has been redescribed for the consciousness of the subject in such a way that its new topography will "accommodate" the queer.

By contrast Selfa argues that all such re-descriptions are basically extensions (accommodations to the structure) of the regime of wage labor and capital; rather than bringing about material change, they only bring about changes of perception. In the end, this is all that Warner, Rorty, Derrida, Kristeva, and others have done and all that they claim is in fact doable. As far as Rorty is concerned, the competing narratives of Warner and Selfa are not translatable to each other; all that can be done is to re-perceive the world so that it can accommodate both narratives. What this produces then is only a quantitative not a qualitative change: a change of dimension, not of the logic that structures the world. In other words, the only legitimate change is a pluralistic one. In Warner's story, the change of consciousness allows the Pentecostal child to grow up *according to his desire*. It is precisely this kind of disembodied (immaterial) desire that is contested throughout this anthology by a line of materialist thinkers, who pose the question of *need*.

It is the aim of this book, therefore, to intervene in the very terms of the contemporary debate over the queer. This volume resituates the contestation over sexualities as not so much a struggle between the straight (desire) and the queer (desire) as one between desire and need, socialism and capitalism, the individual and the collective, and so on. Such an intervention is absolutely necessary because today's reigning ludic queer theory has managed to formulate the issues in such a way that it lets capitalism off the hook. In ludic theory's formulations of the radical/non-radical axis, the queer is promoted as the radical and the straight, as the conserva-

tive. Under this understanding, all ludic queer theory aims at, finally, is a radical reappropriation of desire, not a radical transformation of society (through a reappropriation of property). Ludic queerity is the kind of radicalism critiqued in the opening moves of *The German Ideology* as left Hegelianism. To quote Marx in this more recent context, in spite of their "'world-shattering statements,'" today's ludic queer radicals turn out to be "the staunchest conservatives" (Marx and Engels 1970, 41). The agenda of this anthology is to demystify today's queer conservatism, which promotes itself as a form of radicalism. The argument of *The Material Queer* is that the only effective radicalism is historical and materialist, the kind that provides revolutionary praxis rather than the kind "popular" today in the dominant academy, which only aims at appropriating and recuperating the rights of the heterosexual—as they exist in an oppressive and exploitative class society—for the homosexual.

The third text in this opening section, a manifesto prepared by the Chicago Gay Liberation group for the Revolutionary People's Constitutional Convention plenary session, held in Philadelphia in September 1970, insists—as does this anthology—that what is required for sexual liberation is "changing objective conditions" of society and that sexual liberation is "inextricably bound to the liberation of all oppressed people."

References

Marx, Karl. (1988) *The Communist Manifesto*. Ed. Frederick L. Bender. New York: Norton.

Marx, Karl, and Friedrich Engels. (1970) *The German Ideology*. New York: International Publishers.

Tongues Untied: Memoirs of a Pentecostal Boyhood

Michael Warner

I was a teenage Pentecostalist. Because that is so very far from what I am now—roughly, a queer atheist intellectual—people often think I should have an explanation, a story. Was I sick? Had I been drinking? How did I get here from there? For years I've had a simple answer: "It was another life." If you had spent adolescence passing out tracts in a shopping mall, you might have the same attitude. My memory gives me pictures of someone speaking in tongues and being "slain in the spirit" (a Pentecostalist style of trance: you fall backward while other people catch you). But recognizing myself in these pictures takes effort, as though the memories themselves are in a language I don't understand, or as though I had briefly passed out.

Once, when I said, "It was another life," someone told me, "That's a very American thing to say." And it's true; a certain carelessness about starting over is very much in the national taste. On average, we afford ourselves a great deal of incoherence. Americans care about the freedom not only to have a self, but to discard one or two. We tend to distrust any job—peasant, messiah, or queen, for example—that requires people grown specially for the purpose. We like some variety on the résumé (though not necessarily a degree from Oral Roberts University, as in my case). We like people who take you aside, very privately, and whisper, "I'm Batman." In fact there's an impressive consistency on this point in the national mythology, from Rip Van Winkle to Clark Kent and Samantha on *Bewitched*.

Still, even allowing for the traditional naiveté and bad faith that is my birthright as a citizen of this, the last of history's empires, I have never been able to understand people with consistent lives—people who, for example, grow up in a liberal Catholic household and *stay* that way; or who in junior high school are already laying down a record on which to run for president one day. Imagine having no discarded personalities, no vestigial selves, no visible ruptures with yourself, no gulf of self-forgetfulness, nothing that requires explanation, no alien version of yourself that requires humor and accommodation. What kind of life is that?

For us who once were found and now are lost—and we are legion—our other lives pose some curious problems. Is there no relation at all between our once and present selves, or only a negative one? Is there some buried continuity, or some powerful vestige? In my case it would be hard to imagine a more complete revolution of personality. From the religious vantage of my childhood and adolescence, I am one of Satan's agents. From my current vantage, that former self was exotically superstitious. But I distrust both of these views of myself as the other. What if I were to stop saying "It was another life"? What if that life and this one are not so clearly opposed?

Of course, my life in the bosom of Jesus influenced me; but what interests me more is the way religion supplied me with experiences and ideas that I'm still trying to match. Watching

Katherine Kuhlman do faith healing, for example, didn't just influence my aesthetic sense for performance and eloquence; it was a kind of performance that no one in theater could duplicate. Religion does things that secular culture can only approximate.

Curiously enough, considering that fundamentalism is almost universally regarded as the stronghold and dungeon-keep of American anti-intellectualism, religious culture gave me a passionate intellectual life of which universities are only a pale ivory shadow. My grandfather had been a Southern Baptist preacher in North Carolina mountain towns like Hickory and Flat Rock, but my family migrated through various Protestant sects, including Seventh-Day Adventists, winding up in the independent Pentecostalist congregations known as "charismatic." We lived, in other words, in the heart of splinter-mad American sectarianism. In that world, the subdenomination you belong to is bound for heaven; the one down the road is bound for hell. You need arguments to show why. And in that profoundly hermeneutic culture, your arguments have to be *readings:* ways of showing how the church down the road misreads a key text. Where I come from, people lose sleep over the meaning of certain Greek and Hebrew words.

The whole doctrine of Pentecostalism rests on the interpretation of one brief and difficult passage in the book of Acts. The apostles have been sitting around with nothing to do: "And there appeared unto them cloven tongues like as of fire, and it sat upon each of them. And they were all filled with the Holy Ghost, and began to speak with other tongues, as the Spirit gave them utterance." In the late 19th century, certain Americans decided you not only could but should do the same thing. In 1901, for example, Agnes Ozman of Topeka, Kansas, asserted that after being filled with the Holy Ghost she spoke and wrote Chinese for three days. (The Paraclete's literary tastes seem to have changed; nowadays people who speak in tongues favor a cross between Hebrew and baby talk.)

Pentecostalism interprets this verse as a model to be followed mainly because of an-

other verse that comes a little later, in which Peter tells passersby to be baptized and "receive the gift of the Holy Ghost." My mother, my brother, and I, like other Pentecostalists, accepted an interpretation in which "the gift" means not the Holy Ghost himself (i.e., "receive the Holy Ghost as a gift"), but the glossolalia given by him/it (i.e., "receive incomprehensible speech from the Holy Ghost as a gift"). We were known as "charismatics" because of this interpretation of the word *gift* (charisma); on the basis of this one interpretation my family was essentially forced out of our Baptist church. But only after a lot of talk about the texts and their interpretation. Throughout my childhood and adolescence, I remember being surrounded by textual arguments in which the stakes were not just life and death, but eternal life and death.

When I was 15 or so, my family moved to Tidewater, Virginia, in part to be closer to the great new revival led by the then obscure Pat Robertson. There, we went to special Bible study sessions for charismatics, held in the basement of a Lutheran church on nights when the room wasn't needed by Alcoholics Anonymous. (The Lutherans were the only Protestants in town who cared so little about theology that their scorn for us was only social rather than cosmic. For just this reason, of course, we regarded the Lutherans with limitless contempt, while in their basement we studied the grounds of their damnation.) The leader of these Bible study groups was a brilliant and somewhat unsettled man who by day worked as an engineer for International Harvester and by night set up as the Moses Maimonides of the greater Tidewater area. He had flip charts that would have impressed Ross Perot. He also had a radical argument: God could not possibly be omniscient. The Old Testament, he said, clearly showed God acting in stories, stories that, like the concept of free will itself, made no sense unless God doesn't know the future. If God does know the future, including your own decisions, then narrative time is illusory and only in farce can you be held responsible for your decisions. (Like most modern fundamentalists, he was deeply committed to a contract ideal of justice.)

Every Wednesday night without fail, as this man wound himself through an internal deconstruction of the entire Calvinist tradition, in a fastidiously Protestant return to a more anthropomorphic God, foam dried and flecked on his lips. For our petit-bourgeois family it was unbearable to watch, but we kept coming back. I remember feeling the tension in my mother's body next to me, all her perception concentrated on the desire to hand him the Kleenex which, as usual, she had thoughtfully brought along.

Being a literary critic is nice, I have to say, but for lip-whitening, vein-popping thrills it doesn't compete. Not even in the headier regions of Theory can we approximate that saturation of life by argument. In the car on the way home, we would talk it over. Was he right? If so, what were the consequences? Mother, I recall, distrusted an argument that seemed to demote God to the level of the angels; she thought Christianity without an omniscient God was too Manichaean, just God and Satan going at it. She also complained that if God were not omniscient, prophecy would make no sense. She scored big with this objection, I remember; at the time, we kept ourselves up to date on Pat Robertson's calculations about the imminent Rapture. I, however, cottoned onto the heretical engineer's arguments with all the vengeful pleasure of an adolescent. God's own limits were in sight; this was satisfaction in its own right, as was the thought of holding all mankind responsible in some way.

Later, when I read Nietzsche on the ressentiment at the heart of Christianity—the smell of cruelty and aggression in Christian benevolence—I recognized what that pleasure had been about. In my experience, ressentiment wasn't just directed against Power. It was directed against everything: the dominant cadres of society, of course, parents, school, authority in general; but also God, the material world, and one's own self. Just as the intellectual culture of religion has an intensity that secular versions lack, so also Protestant culture has an intricate and expressive language of power and abjection that in secular life has to be supplied in relatively impoverished ways. The world has

not the least phenomenon that cannot, in Christian culture, be invested both with world-historical power and with total abjection. You are a soldier of the Lord, born among angels, contemplated from the beginning of time and destined to live forever. But you are also the unregenerate shit of the world. Your dinner-table conversation is the medium of grace for yourself and everyone around you; it also discloses continually your fallen worthlessness. Elevation and abasement surround you, in every flicker of your half-conscious thoughts. And the two always go together.

People often say, as though it's a big discovery, that Christians have a finely honed sadomasochistic sensibility. But this doesn't come close to appreciating religion's expressive language for power and abjection. The secular equivalents, such as Foucauldian analysis, have nothing like the same condensation. I realize this every time I read Jonathan Edwards:

> The sun does not willingly shine upon you to give you light to serve sin and Satan; the earth does not willingly yield her increase to satisfy your lusts; nor is it willingly a stage for your wickedness to be acted upon; the air does not willingly serve you for breath to maintain the flame of life in your vitals.... And the world would spew you out, were it not for the sovereign hand of Him who hath subjected it in hope.... The sovereign pleasure of God, for the present, stays His rough wind; otherwise it would come with fury, and your destruction would come like a whirlwind, and you would be like the chaff of the summer threshing floor.

You almost expect the next paragraph to be a manifesto for ecofundamentalism. Not even the final paragraphs of *The Order of Things* contain a more thorough distrust of everything in the human order. American religion has lost much of that antihumanism, even in the fundamentalist sects that rail against the "religion" of secular humanism, but they retain the imagination of abjection. And the abjection can be exquisite:

> The bow of God's wrath is bent, and the arrow made ready on the string, and justice bends the

arrow at your heart, and strains the bow, and it is nothing but the mere pleasure of God, and that of an angry God, without any promise or obligation at all, that keeps the arrow one moment from being made drunk with your blood.

In the film version the role of *you* will be played by a trembling and shirtless Keanu Reeves. Stuff like this can displace almost any amount of affect because of the strobe light alternation of pleasure and obliteration: "it is nothing but His mere pleasure that keeps you from being this moment swallowed up in everlasting destruction." *Nothing but pleasure,* indeed. When I read this my blood heats up. I can hardly keep from reading it aloud. (Maybe that comes from hanging out with Oral Roberts.) The displacement and vicarious satisfaction provided in consumer culture is, by contrast, low-budget monochrome.

About the same time that we were going to hear the holy prophet of International Harvester, my mother made a new church friend, Frankie. Frankie was very butch. She was sweet to me, but visibly seething toward most of the world. Her sidekick Peggy, however, was the devoted servant of everybody, making endless presents of macramé before finally opening her own macramé store in a strip mall. Frankie, Peggy, and my mother belonged to a circle of women who held Bible studies in one another's living rooms (furnished in Ethan Allen early American, most of them), swapped recipes, came to each other in trouble, and prostrated themselves in the power of the Holy Spirit together.

I remember watching the way they wept together, their implicit deference to Frankie, their constant solicitation of one another's sufferings. Most of them worked. All were unhappy in the family dramas to which they nevertheless held absolute commitments. None of them liked her lot in life. They would pray in tongues while vacuuming the shag carpet. When the bills could be paid, it was because Jesus provided the money. In church, weeping in the intense but unfathomable love of Jesus, they repeated certain gestures: head slowly shaking no, eyes closed above damp cheeks, arms stretched out on invisible crosses, the temporarily forgotten Kleenex clenched in the hand. (Because Pentecostalists exalt weeping and catarrh so much, I still associate the smell of tissue with church.)

At the time I remember thinking that this social-devotional style, in which I was often a half-noticed participant, had a special meaning for these women. Not that it was a mere displacement or substitute for an articulate feminism; my mother and her friends felt, I'm sure, that Jesus spoke to them on more levels, and deeper ones, than did the feminism they had encountered. But certainly the redemption of Jesus compensated sufferings that were already framed by women's narrative. Think about the consequences of having fundamental parts of your life—gender, especially—filtered through fundamentalism's expressive language of power and abjection. In their descriptions of the love of Jesus—undeserved, devastating benignity—one heard always the articulation of a thorough resentment of the world and themselves, but also of hitherto unimaginable pleasures, and of an ideal which was also an implicit reproach against their social world. It was not lost on me that we migrated to more extreme versions of Protestant fundamentalism as my mother saw more and more clearly her dissatisfaction with the normal life to which she was nevertheless devoted. Even now, her sons have left home, three husbands have been reluctantly divorced, her friends have parted ways, and she's had to go back to teaching school—but Jesus still pays the bills.

C. S. Lewis once complained that English pictures of Jesus always made him look like an adolescent girl; I think this was and is part of the appeal, for me, for my mother's friends, *and* for Lewis, whose desire for a butch deity said more about his own queeny tastes than about the Jesus we continue to reinvent. As Harold Bloom has pointed out in his recent book *The American Religion,* many American Protestants, particularly Southern Baptists, have essentially reduced the trinity to Jesus. "He walks with me, and he talks with me, and he tells me I am His own," as we always sang. During this hymn, I would look around to make sure no one noticed that these words were coming, rather too pleasurably, from my mouth.

Jesus was my first boyfriend. He loved me, personally, and he told me I was his own. This was very thrilling, especially when he was portrayed by Jeffrey Hunter. Anglo-American Christian culture has developed a rich and kinky iconography of Jesus, the perma-boy who loves us, the demiurge in a dress. Here, for example, is Emerson's Divinity School Address of 1838: "Jesus Christ belonged to the true race of prophets. He saw with open eye the mystery of the soul. Drawn by its severe harmony, ravished with its beauty, he lived in it, and had his being there. . . . He said, in this jubilee of sublime emotion, 'I am divine.'" Well, it's fun to exclaim, "I am divine," and Emerson's point is that we all should. But he does some extra fantasy work in this picture of Jesus the happily ravished, Jesus the perpetual jubilee of sublime affect. Jesus, it seems, is coming all the time. This wouldn't make him good for much *except* being a fantasy boyfriend. With spikes in him.

Since the early days of Methodism, of course, it has been commonplace to see enthusiastic religion as sexual excess. In a characteristically modern way, writers such as Lacan and Bataille have regarded all religion as an unrecognized form of sexuality. Bloom, in *The American Religion,* writes that "there is no way to disentangle the sexual drive from Pentecostalism." He calls it "sadomasochistic sexuality," "a kind of orgiastic individualism," a "pattern of addiction," "an ecstasy scarcely distinguishable from sexual transport."

There's something to this, but I worry about putting it like that. You can reduce religion to sex only if you don't especially believe in either one. When I learned what orgasm felt like, I can't say that the difference between it and speaking in tongues was "scarcely distinguishable." It seemed like a clear call to me. And the two kinds of ecstasy quickly became, for me at least, an excruciating alternative. God, I felt sure, didn't want me to come. And he always wanted to watch.

The agony involved in choosing between orgasm and religion, as I was forced to do on a nightly basis, is the sort of thing ignored by any account that treats religion as sublimated, displaced, or misrecognized sexuality. At the beginning of *Two Serious Ladies,* the great Jane Bowles novel, one little girl asks another to play a new game. "It's called 'I forgive you for all your sins,'" she says. "Is it fun?" asks the other. "It's not for fun that we play it, but because it's necessary to play it." This, undoubtedly, is just why religion is so queer; it's not for fun that we play it.

What I think critics like Bloom are trying to say, against their own anerotic reductivism, is that religion makes available a language of ecstasy, a horizon of significance within which transgressions against the normal order of the world and the boundaries of self *can be seen as good things.* Pentecostalists don't get slain in the spirit just by rubbing themselves, or by redirecting some libido; they require a whole set of beliefs about the limitations of everyday calculations of self-interest, about the impoverishment of the world that does not willingly yield its increase to satisfy your lusts. In this way ecstatic religions can legitimate self-transgression, providing a meaningful framework for the sublime play of self-realization and self-dissolution. And once again, the secular versions often look like weak imitations. Only the most radical theories of sexual liberation (Marcuse's *Eros and Civilization,* for example) attribute as much moral importance to self-dissolution as fundamentalist religion does. (And nobody believes them any more.) Simple affirmations of desire, by contrast, don't supply a horizon of significance at all.

The bliss of Pentecostalism is, among other things, a radical downward revaluing of the world that despises Pentecostalists. Like all religions, Pentecostalism has a world-canceling moment; but its world-canceling gestures can also be a kind of social affirmation, in this case of a frequently despised minority. I suspect that the world-canceling rhetorics of queer sexuality work in a similar way. If you lick my nipple, the world suddenly seems comparatively insignificant. Ressentiment doubles your pleasure.

Both my moral, Christian self and my queer, atheist one have had to be performed as minority identities. What queers often forget, jeopardized as we are by resurgent fundamentalisms in the United States, is that fundamentalists themselves are not persuaded by "moral majority" or "mainstream values" rhetoric; they too consider themselves an oppressed minority. In their view the dominant culture is one of a worldliness they have rejected, and bucking that trend comes, in some very real ways, with social stigmatization. For instance, as far as I can make out, Jehovah's Witnesses believe in almost nothing *but* their own minority status and the inevitable destruction of the mainstream.

The radical Protestant and quasi-Protestant (i.e., Mormon) sects in this country have helped, willingly or not, to elaborate minoritarian culture. Left political thought has been remarkably blind to this fact. Most of us believe, I think, that we are in favor of all oppressed minorities, and that you can tell an oppressed minority because the people concerned say that's what they are. Who gets to say, and by what standards, that Pentecostalists, or Mormons, are not the oppressed minority they claim to be? This is not a rhetorical question.

One way that fundamentalists have contributed to the culture of minority identities is by developing the performative genres of identity-talk. Sentences like "I'm Batman" or "We're here, we're queer, get used to it" take for granted a context in which people are accorded the power of declaring what they are. In the world of Southern Baptists and charismatics, people practice a genre known as witnessing, in some ways the Ur-form of all modern autobiographical declarations. Witnessing might mean telling a conversion narrative or a miracle narrative in church, but it also might mean declaring yourself in suburban shopping malls. It is the fundamentalist version of coming out, and explained to the budding Pentecostalist in much the same language of necessity, shame and pride, stigma and cultural change.

In writing all of this, of course, I am stuck between witnessing and coming out. One of the most interesting things about the gap between religious and secular culture is that no matter which side you stand on, conversion or deconversion, the direction seems inevitable. Religious people always suppose that people start out secular and have to get religion. People like me don't secularize: we *backslide.* Of course, I have slid back to places I never was or thought of being, and it may be to halt this endless ebb that my mother has recently begun trying out a new paradigm: she's willing to consider me as having a lifestyle. I might prefer backsliding, but the concept of an alternative path marks progress in our relations. Meanwhile, those of us who have gotten over religion find ourselves heir to a potent Enlightenment mythology that regards religion as a primitive remnant, a traditional superstition. This has been the opinion not only of thinkers with very little religious imagination, like Marx and Freud, but even those who have given us our most profound analyses: Nietzsche, Weber, Durkheim, Bataille. (William James is a rare exception.) It's almost impossible to broach the subject of religion without taking the movement of this narrative for granted. To be secular is to be modern. To be more secular is to be more modern. But religion clearly isn't withering away with the spread of modern rationalism and home entertainment centers. In a recent Gallup study 94 per cent of Americans say they believe in God. Better still: 88 per cent believe that God loves them personally. Yet this is the country that has always boasted of *not* having a feudal past, of being the world's most modern nation. It's enough to make you ask: Are we sick? How did we get here from there?

I'm as secular and modern as the next person, but I doubt that these statistics indicate a residue of pre-Enlightenment superstition. And I don't think that my own personal incoherence is entirely of the linear and progressive type. Even to raise the subject of personal incoherence, identity, and rupture is to see that, in a way, the secular imagination and the religious one have already settled out of court. For both the notion of having a rupture with your self *and* the notion of narrated personal coherence are Protestant conventions, heightened in all the American variants of Protestantism. No other culture goes as far as ours in making everything an issue of identity. We've invented an impressive array of religions: Mormons, Southern Baptists, Jehovah's Witnesses, Pentecostalists, the Nation of Islam, Christian Sci-entists, Seventh-Day Adventists—every last one of them a conversion religion. They offer you a new and perpetual personality, and they tell you your current one was a mistake you made. They tell you to be somebody else. I say: believe them.

What's Wrong with "Identity Politics"

Lance Selfa

Earlier this year, the San Francisco chapter of the gay and lesbian rights group Queer Nation suspended operations because its members could not agree on proposed internal guidelines prohibiting racist, sexist, anti-Semitic and homophobic comments.

In Chicago, the movement against AIDS is fragmented among several different organizations whose politics hardly differ.

Instead of one chapter of the AIDS Coalition to Unleash Power (ACTUP), there are two: one which involves only gay men with HIV, and one which involves everyone else who wants to fight AIDS.

How could these organizations, which many consider to represent a new kind of activist politics, fall prey to such internal squabbling?

The answer lies within the assumptions of the "politics of identity," which form the basis of these groups' activities and form of organization.

The proponents of "identity politics" argue that political activity is not simply a means to a political end, but is above all, an affirmation of one's identity as a member of an oppressed group.

Perhaps these politics are most clearly expressed today by the two main political organizations in the forefront of struggles for gay liberation, ACTUP and Queer Nation.

ACTUP, founded in New York in 1987, has experienced substantial growth, with new chapters forming around the country.

Initially focused on advocacy for people with AIDS, it has widened its political appeal to include demands for national health care, for free needle distribution and for lower prices for AIDS drugs.

Queer Nation, born from struggles against gay-bashing in New York in 1989, has also produced chapters throughout the country.

Need for Visibility

Concerned that ACTUP's focus on AIDS would undercut its identity as a gay organization, Queer Nation activists have asserted the need for "visibility" for gays and the development of a separate "queer" identity.

Both organizations have fought for and have won essential battles in the fight against AIDS and homophobia.

Many of their activists have also joined the movements for abortion rights and against the Gulf War. Their efforts must be supported.

However, many of the ideas that form the politics of ACTUP and Queer Nation act as obstacles to broadening and deepening a movement against all oppression—let alone one against gay oppression.

Many Queer Nation and ACTUP activists accept the notion that only those oppressed have the right to struggle against their oppression.

This idea is an outgrowth of a "personal politics," for which personal, subjective experience is considered more important than political or strategic discussions about the best way to build a movement.

This kind of politics, developed initially in the 1960s civil rights movement, was carried over to the women's liberation, and later, the gay and lesbian liberation movements.

It is often true that personal experience can spur people to political activity.

But accepting the notion that one's personal experience should dictate one's politics depoliticizes and, ultimately, weakens a movement.

If one's experience as a person with AIDS is all that is needed to give a lead in the struggle against AIDS, then there is no need for discussions and arguments about strategy and tactics.

It means that the soundness of strategies and tactics are not judged on their merits in contributing to building a movement, but on *who* is making the argument.

By this logic, arguments put forward by HIV-positive Republicans should be granted a greater hearing than those of non-HIV positive socialists.

Moreover, the idea that only specific oppressed groups have a right to combat their specific oppression presents two problems.

On the one hand, it can lead to fragmentation which can divide, and thus weaken the movement.

Splits

It has led to splits within groups between men and women, gays and bisexuals, Jews and gentiles, Blacks, whites and Latinos.

On the other hand, oppressed minorities do not have the political clout to win their demands without appealing for support to other sections of the population who do not suffer that particular form of oppression.

If only gays have the right to combat gay oppression, then the struggle for gay liberation is confined to only 10 to 20 percent of the population.

What is more, a politics which defines all except members of the particular oppressed group as "the enemy," reinforces that ghettoization.

It is one thing to recognize the minority and ghettoized status of gays in society, but quite another to celebrate the ghetto.

The choice of the identification "queer" among some gay activists accepts the ghetto's confines.

The word "queer" connotes something out of the ordinary—beyond the pale.

For that very reason, it has been a slur that anti-gay bigots have used *against* gays.

That is why the gay liberation movement that developed after the 1969 Stonewall Rebellion rejected "queer" in favor of "gay."

Even the notion of a specific "queer" identity raises problems.

Gay people are represented in every social category—in every race, in both sexes and in all classes in society.

Sexual Orientation

Though they share sexual orientation, gays differ from each other in nearly every other way.

Thus, the attempt to establish a separate "queer" identity can amount to little more than ascribing a political content to a particular lifestyle which is predominantly available only to a minority of gays, generally to middle-class men.

Patronizing gay-owned businesses or dressing a certain way are personal, not political, choices. They contribute nothing to the struggle for gay and lesbian liberation.

Most gay men and lesbians—who are working-class—are locked in the closet, afraid for their jobs or relationships if they reveal their sexuality.

For them, the challenge is not to express a "queer identity," as defined by a particular lifestyle, but is in being able to be open about their sexuality with friends, co-workers and family.

What kind of movement is needed to push the struggle against gay oppression forward?

The most effective type of gay liberation movement is one which wins greater numbers of people—both gay and straight—to a politics of gay liberation.

Activities, like demonstrations and rallies, which unite gays and straights in struggle, need to be built.

Too often, the tactics and media-influenced "zaps" of Queer Nation and ACTUP reject this aim.

For example, Queer Nation contingents at political demonstrations often chant vulgar slogans whose intent seems to be to shock passersby rather than to persuade them to endorse the demonstration's aims.

At the same time, ACTUP and Queer Nation members often are the most vocal in opposing slogans like "*Gay, straight, Black, white—same-struggle, same fight.*"

This is a far cry from the Gay Liberation Front, formed in 1969, which identified openly with other oppressed groups, like Blacks and the Vietnamese fighting the U.S. military.

A movement whose politics or whose tactics do not afford it opportunities to grow can quickly be thrown back on itself. Internal discord and further isolation from the "outside world" can result.

A more serious mistake is the tactic of "outing"—exposing publicly the concealed homosexuality of some celebrity or politician.

Hollywood Stars

At the April Academy Awards show, Queer Nation activists threatened to "out" Hollywood stars in protest of Hollywood's portrayal of gays in films.

A gay man's or lesbian's decision to "come out" to friends, family or co-workers is an expression of confidence and pride. Outing does exactly the opposite.

It mirrors the efforts of right-wingers to force gays out of "the closet."

It can contribute to a situation in which "outed" people are fired, denied promotions, refused health insurance, kicked out of their apartments or ostracized by friends and family.

The fact that the targets of outing are rich and famous does not matter. A tactic which can unleash such manifestations of gay oppression must be condemned, no matter who suffers them.

Outing is sometimes defended as a misguided, but understandable, expression of outrage at the hypocrisy of famous gays.

This is a defense which no serious person who wants to build a broad, fighting movement can accept.

Moral outrage may motivate some people to get involved in a struggle around a political issue.

But a movement cannot sustain itself, grow or thrive on moral outrage.

The real questions that any movement faces—what strategies to adopt, what tactics to use, who its allies and enemies are, and how to extend its influence—are not moral questions, but political ones.

They are questions for which "identity politics" gives the wrong answers.

Working Paper for the Revolutionary People's Constitutional Convention

Chicago Gay Liberation

A. Introduction

Although we recognize that homosexuals have been oppressed in all societies, it is the struggle against that oppression in the context of Amerikan imperialism that faces us. In addition to the usual forms of oppression, we, as homosexuals, are forced to hide our identities in order to keep our jobs and avoid being social outcasts—in order to "make it" in straight Amerika. As gay liberation, we now take the position that, because of the rampant oppression we see—of black, Third World people, women, workers—in addition to our own; because of the corrupt values, because of the injustices, we no longer want to "make it" in Amerika. For to make it is to accept the oppression of others (in addition to our own). We are joining the Revolutionary People's Constitutional Convention and reject what Amerikan imperialism has to offer us. Rather we will fight for our liberation, and we will get it by any means necessary.

Our particular struggle is for sexual self-determination, the abolition of sex-role stereotypes and the human right to the use of one's own body without interference from the legal and social institutions of the state. Many of us have understood that our struggle cannot succeed without a fundamental change in society which will put the source of power (means of production) in the hands of the people who at present have nothing. Those now in power will oppose this change by violent repression, which in fact is already in motion. Not all of our sisters and brothers in gay liberation share this view, or may feel that personal solutions might work. But as our struggle grows, it will be made clear by the changing objective conditions that our liberation is inextricably bound to the liberation of all oppressed people.

This position paper does not intend to speak for the Black Caucus or Women's Caucus of Chicago Gay Liberation; we recognize that black homosexuals and female homosexuals live with doubly or triply oppressed conditions. But since anti-homosexual prejudice is rampant throughout society, homosexuals can be treated as outcasts even within an already oppressed group. Therefore this paper should speak in a general way for homosexuals as homosexuals.

B. Grievances Common to All Homosexuals

1. Employment and Other Economic Factors

a. Hiring: In addition to the particular discrimination against black, female and poor homosexuals, we are at a disadvantage because of discriminatory hiring practices—unless, of course, we "pass." There is a tracking system which determines the positions open to homosexuals where we are able to work in the company of other homosexuals. We often take these jobs even though we may not like them and the pay may be low, just so we won't have to worry about being found out. Our women may become physical education teachers and nurses; our men may become beauticians or ribbon clerks for those reasons. There is nothing wrong with those jobs, but the choice should be based on interest and ability. There are no "gay jobs"; there are no "women's jobs." For *known* homosexuals, *there is no employment* at all except in a few fields, e.g., theater, music, etc., which require special talents.

b. Firing: Since firing of known homosexuals is notorious, most of us hold jobs which would be closed to us if we didn't "pass." We do so at a tremendous and cruel personal cost, for we must hide what, in our hearts, we know to be important and beautiful—our sexuality. Forced to wear a heterosexual mask, we are brainwashed (without even knowing it) into believing that our sex is shameful and unnatural— this belief is usually expressed as a tendency toward compulsive promiscuity, sexual objectification of each other, and loneliness.

c. Income: The jobs into which we are tracked are often low-paying and certainly alienating. And the higher federal income taxation of "single" people—that is, those whose relationships are not recognized as legal—discriminates against us economically.

2. Political

a. Electoral Politics: As homosexuals we have *no* representation in the government, and never have had. Third World and female homosexuals are especially unrepresented, but even the white male as a homosexual has no voice. Presently there are politicians in New York and California who are trying to attract the "gay vote." But they are not homosexual and cannot represent our needs and interests. Furthermore, their political parties are corrupted by racism, sexism (male chauvinism) and anti-homosexual prejudice and are tied economically to those who are responsible, ultimately, for our continued oppression. How can these politicians be on our side, in practice? We have never had an admitted homosexual in public office, and our heterosexual "representatives" have never done anything for us although we have worked in their campaigns and given them our votes. But even if we could find spokesmen and women, they would be ineffective as part of a social system that is based on oppression, anyway.

b. The "Movement": As we in gay liberation look around us to find out who are our friends and potential allies, we see that the Black Panther Party, personified by its Supreme Commander Huey P. Newton, is the first national organization to give us such warm, public support, as well as official recognition. For years, many of us have worked in radical organizations always hiding our identities, always working in the struggles of others. Some so-called "Marxist" organizations do not allow homosexual membership. This has been very oppressive to us and has kept many of us, who were potential radicals, from radicalization. These groups and individuals treat us as badly as their supposed enemy, the "ruling class" that they are always talking about. In abusing homosexuals they show they cannot tell the difference between their friends and their enemies and are probably unable to make principled political alliances. Failing to recognize our grievances as legitimate, these "revolutionaries" and "radicals" are not only inhumane but also counter-revolutionary. We will no longer work within such groups.

3. Social Institutions

a. The Law and the State: Our most immediate oppressors are the pigs. We are beaten, entrapped, enticed, raided, taunted, arrested and jailed. In jail we are jeered at, gang-raped, beaten and killed, with full encouragement and participation by the pigs. Every homosexual lives in fear of the pigs, except that we are beginning to fight back! The reasons are not that the pigs are just prejudiced (which they are) or that they "over-react," but that they are given silent approval by the power structure for their violence against us. Since our *lives* are defined as illegal, immoral, and unnatural, there is no reason why the pigs shouldn't harass us—and they are never punished for it. The law is against us, but changing laws makes no difference. That must be crystal clear; any homosexual from Chicago, where homosexuality is legal, will tell you that changing the law makes no difference. The pigs must be fought, but we must see beyond them to ultimate sources of power—an elite of super-rich, white males who control production and therefore the prevailing ideology. Their representatives may try to tempt us with reforms, "progress," divide us by class and skin privileges, buy us off with a piece of the pie or male supremacy because we have just begun to join the revolutionary and progressive people. But common sense tells us that as long as the power rests in the hands of a few and not with the people—both straight and gay—that power can be used to oppress homosexuals.

b. Housing—The Homosexual Ghetto: Homosexuals are frequently denied housing, much more so if they are also female or black. We avoid the anti-homosexual discrimination by "passing." But life for homosexuals is so psychologically oppressive in a heterosexual neighborhood that we tend to live in homosexual neighborhoods which take on ghetto-like characteristics. These conditions should not be confused with the immiseration and oppression in the black, brown and poor white ghettos, but there are some similarities. No sooner is it established that a neighborhood is "gay" than rents and real estate prices rise. Those that exploit us as consumers know that we will pay through the nose, even when we aren't well off, for the psychological comfort of living among "our own kind." Most of us probably live outside of these communities, but ghetto institutions are still part of our lives. We neither control nor own the institutions which we use. These bars, shops, movie-houses, etc., are owned by businessmen who serve their own interests or the Mafia's but do not serve us at all. The prices are notoriously high, and the practices are often racist, sexist and anti-working class. This materially oppresses female, black and poor homosexuals and also reinforces the false consciousness (racism, sexism, class-chauvinism) which divides us as a group and, in the end, oppresses us all.

c. Education: We have no stake in education which is racist, male-chauvinist, anti-working class and anti-homosexual. The schools are not people's schools and therefore do not serve the people. They certainly do not serve us as homosexuals, but teach ideology that is destructive to us and helps to keep us social outcasts. What child would have disdain for homosexuals? They have to be taught that. There are no positive educational programs on homosexuality which would alleviate anti-homosexual prejudice and our own self-hate, which comes when we discover what we are. The subject is avoided in the schools, and is usually assumed to be taboo and dirty by the students. It is wrong to mislead the people this way and perpetuate attitudes which harm us. The only models for love and sexuality according to our "educators" are heterosexual ones in the context of state-sanctioned monogamous white relationships which oppress women. Homosexual authors are usually ignored, especially if they write about their homosexuality, like James Baldwin. Others, like Walt Whitman or Gertrude Stein, are taught but never as homosexual writers. Like blacks and women, we are taught, by omission, that we have no heroes and heroines and certainly no role-models.

d. Medical Care: The branch of medicine we are most concerned with is psychiatry. The American medical profession is oblivious to the needs of oppressed people, and psychiatrists are clearly hostile to homosexuality. They (not Freud) have created and spread the ideology that we are sick, neurotic, paranoid and other bullshit. Yet they never hesitate in taking money from brothers and sisters who are fed up with having to live in such a sick society, and who could use some *honest* advice. Because psychiatrists emphasize "adjustment" and conformity rather than liberation, because they tell us to become good citizens rather than good revolutionaries, because they favor individual solutions rather than social change, we recognize that they are not the helpers of homosexuals or any oppressed people, but serve our oppressors.

4. Culture

Although we have certainly contributed to this country's cultural life as a group we have been robbed of our culture. The culture of any period is defined by a ruling elite; and the rulers of Amerika have defined homosexuals as outcasts. The culture available to us is clearly heterosexual and alienating to us. Athletics are based upon men competing with each other, one winning at the other's expense; while homosexual men relate by loving each other, not by competition. In movies or on TV, women are always shown as objects of the love (?) of men, but homosexual women love each other; and the standards of female beauty, defined by society as what *men* want, is irrelevant to lesbians. Art,

books, plays don't relate to homosexuality except in trying to say how bad it is. As individuals we are prevented from cultural expression, for sexuality cannot be suppressed without suppression of personality at the same time. And our sexuality must be suppressed because of the legal, economic and social penalties for it. We see culture not as the output of a few great men and women, but as a possession of all people and as activities (whether sports, hobbies or arts) which all people can participate in. In spite of the restrictions homosexuals have, in fact, become artists, athletes, writers, but the masses of homosexuals have had no benefit from this fact. We have had to depend on the ruling elites who have taken over our talents and used them for their own profit, like the Kennedys who decorated their court with Gore Vidal. This is an expropriation of our cultural resources. We refuse to entertain them any longer with "camp" for their profit.

5. Class Status and Homosexuality

Homosexuals from the proletariat (whether working-class or lumpen) lead a particularly prison-like, straight-jacketed existence. Because of their particular relationship (actual or potential) to production, the custom is to marry at a young age. It is not surprising that white working-class communities are among the most up-tight about homosexuals due to the role of the family structure in the capitalist mode of production. Homosexuals from these communities often marry and have children before discovering their homosexuality. All the doors that can be opened by middle-class privilege are closed. The women cannot afford to follow their homosexual preferences; they are tied economically to men due to the low salaries and restricted job opportunities open to women in general. The men cannot afford divorce, support of their family and the expense of setting up a new life as a homosexual. Nor can they afford the notoriously high legal fees used to pay off the pigs, which keep middle-class and wealthy homosexuals out of jail.

6. *Sexual Capitalism*

a. Social Attitudes: The most frequently described grievance is the prejudice most homosexuals find in heterosexuals. Anti-homosexual feeling among the masses of Americans cannot be our ultimate problem; in fact straight people too are harmed by rigid, stereotyped ideas about sex and sex-roles. These ideas can only persist because of the institutions which support them: news media, entertainment media, schools, medical establishment, etc. These institutions are not owned by the people, and only a small minority profit from them. Certainly the masses of American people receive no long-range benefits from their contempt for homosexuals.

b. Psychological Attitudes: Possibly the most devastating aspect of these attitudes is that we learn them ourselves during our "formative years" and are therefore filled with self-contempt when we become homosexual. In American society, we are taught that people are supposed to get what they *deserve* rather than what they *need*. It is a "meritocracy," not a democracy. Translated into sexual life, we see how this defeats us. Through advertising and the entertainment media, artificial standards of beauty are learned and internalized. Youth, white Aryan aggressive "masculinity" and submissive "femininity" are constantly stressed. We begin to act as though only certain "types" who approach these phony standards *deserve* our love and sexual attention, and we become more and more unresponsive to people's *needs* for love and sex. We respond to what "turns us on," and we have learned to be "turned on" by merit and not by other's needs. Taking on, as individuals, the ethic of the capitalist system which despises the needs of the people, especially the poor and oppressed, we act against our own long-run interests. Those who do not approach the stereotypes because they may be older, homely, physically deformed, etc., may be among the most miserable and lonely people in society. And we do not even have the family structure which helps most people to help these lonely persons forget how unhappy they are.

Dossier 1: Outing the Concepts

These readings "out" some basic concepts required to render questions of sexualities intelligible. This outing involves a double move: On the one hand, the reader will encounter here some texts on sexual theory (such as those by Plato, Freud, and Marcuse) that predate the (post)modernist views on sexuality that dominate discussions today (and thus rely on a different conceptual series); on the other hand, the reader will encounter texts that aim to resituate questions about sexuality in the context of the larger contestation between idealism (represented in ancient philosophy by Plato) and materialism (by Heraclitus) and that thus help to develop the conceptual frames on which these opposing understandings depend. Whereas materialism—in the broad philosophical sense—regards reality to be constituted by matter in motion and holds that all phenomena—including mind, consciousness, and spirit—are due to material agency, idealism maintains the reverse, that reality is constituted by thought and that the objects of external perception consist of ideas. Materialism therefore gives priority to the material world (the objective) over consciousness (the subjective), whereas idealism gives priority to human consciousness over materiality (that is, argues for the autonomy of consciousness).

In his dialogues, *The Republic* and *The Phaedo,* Plato put forward the notion that the only true reality is that composed of immutable Ideas or Forms, of which the phenomena of the physical world are only secondary reflections or shadows. Behind the mere appearances of the world, then, Plato sees the permanent and au-

tonomous order of a harmonious and unchanging reality of ideal forms. Heraclitus, by contrast, holds to the materialist understanding of reality as matter in motion, an endless and ongoing process emblematized for him in the element of fire. Furthermore, Heraclitus is said to be "the most radical dialectician of ancient times," the philosopher who not only "employed dialectic [the mode in which the process of change takes place] in the most far-reaching way" but also "set a model for both Hegel and Marx" (Williams 1989, 1). The fragments of Heraclitus (and the remarks on them by later commentators—Hegel and Engels—also published here) point to his theory of materiality, flux, and the unity of opposites in the dialectic.

The selection printed from the "Symposium" not only presents understandings of homosexual relations in Greek society of the time but also situates these relations emphatically within Plato's idealistic view of human existence. Sexual/erotic relations are evaluated not in terms of their historical and material effects, but in terms of whether or not they live up to the Platonic idea of the unchanging and eternal Good. The political conservatism of the Platonic view, which is reasserted today in the right wing's insistence on upholding its set of ahistorical, idealistic, supposedly permanent, and universal "family values" (the reader may want to consult these best-selling contemporary instances of idealism: William Bennett's *The Book of Virtues* and his *Children's Book of Virtues*) is revealed in the notion that such inequalities as existed in ancient Greek society, such as that between master and slave, are in fact ordained by the ideal forms themselves. Although these selections from Plato hint at the process of acquiring knowledge through dialectical reasoning, this form of dialectic is idealistic in the sense that it always leads back to a permanent and unchanging set of given truths. In other words, any "change" the dialectical process might hint at here is itself only an appearance.

The investigation of dialectics is continued here in the dialogue between Enlightenment thinkers Jean d'Alembert and Denis Diderot, which, among other questions, briefly addresses sexuality in terms of the material process of human reproduction and insists on the materiality of not only our sensations but our thoughts. The radicality of the materialism being promoted is suggested by Diderot's insistence that inferences themselves (usually thought of as voluntary cognitive processes taking place in consciousness) are actually "drawn by nature" (the material). Unlike the merely apparent change envisioned in Platonic dialectics, actual change can take place in this Enlightenment form of dialectics since it sees matter as evolving dialectically, taking on different forms of organization that produce very different results (matter is not only constitutive of the mineral and the animal, for instance, but also the human). Inert matter can become thinking, sensing matter (consciousness). In other words, Diderot gives a materialist account of the construction of subject, which has, first, feelings and sensations, which when organized give rise to memory, by means of which one can connect impressions and produce a narrative of one's life and through that narrative finally acquire a sense of one's "identity." The possibility of differently organized matter can be extended, in political terms, to the possibility of different forms of social organization (which itself is but the organization of the material on a different plane).

In his discussion of the sexual aberrations, Freud seems to open the space for a kind of materialist account of sexuality. He begins by assuming that sexual needs are driven by something called "libido," which he theorizes as the

sexual analog to hunger, the motor of the human need for food. Unlike genital sexuality, libido is not simply manifested in adulthood but has a preadult history. One of the changes Freud's argument in *Three Essays on the Theory of Sexuality* brought about was a recognition that since libido is with human beings from the beginning, some form of libidinality or sexuality is present also in infants and children. Freud argues that libido goes through several stages of cultural/social training: the oral, anal, and genital stages and that the trajectory of this training regarding questions of gender depends on the successful resolution of the Oedipus complex. One of the markers of infantile libidinality, however, is that, in its association with orality and nutritive nurturance, it combines into one moment both the survival instinct and the pleasure principle. These principles get separated in later stages where survival is not simply a matter of animal needs but of a large field of other "needs" developed through cultural mediation and negotiation, many of which are "unconscious" (do not fit with the pattern of need-fulfillment practiced in the given subject's "reality") and thus fall under the operations of the Imaginary. Under the increasing complexities of later stages of social development, indeed pleasure (desire) and survival (need) come increasingly into conflict with each other. One of the tests of any social theory is whether or not its account of this conflict is in fact socially progressive. Freudian theory seems to tie libido to questions of the common good in two ways: (1) positively, in that survival of the species depends (or has depended until the recent invention of new reproductive technologies) on heterosexual intercourse; and (2) negatively, in that individuals must delay the gratification of their immediate libidinal impulses—that is, libido must be repressed and sublimated—for the common good.

A critique of the heterosexism of the Freudian view of what he calls the "sexual aberrations" begins from the observation that the exaggerated emphasis on the survival of the species dictates that for him sexuality is by definition heterosexuality. His privileging of heterosexual genital intercourse as the norm (and his universalization of this norm as transhistorical), along with his formula that marks the neuroses as the inverse of the perversions, results in a situation in which homosexuals (those who live outside or against the norm) must be classified either as neurotics (if their homosexual desires remain repressed) or perverts (if they act on those desires and make them a part of "reality"). An effective critique of the Freudian view from the homosexual perspective would not simply become a defense of homosexual practices but an inquiry into the historical construction of sexualities at large (including homosexuality).

The materialist critique of the Freudian take on sexual theory begins from the observation that the mere survival of the species hardly provides much ground for evaluating anything like social progress. In a historical perspective, this worry about the survival of the human race appears as a symptom of the anxieties produced by wars and conflicts in his part of the world in the early part of this century and thus is an index of Freud's Eurocentrism. Furthermore, to the degree that libido is an instinct that is thought of primarily as biological, analysis of the laws of biological life would displace social and historical analysis. The Lacanian (post)-modernizing of Freudian theory, which transforms libido into desire-in-language, seems, at first glance, to be one effective way—on the theoretical level—to block this collapse of the social into the merely biological. However, in the general introduction to this text, I have already critiqued the notion of desire-in-language to show that this (post)modernization of Freud also leads to a treatment of desire as autonomous and ahistorical. Lacan's notion of desire-in-language refers to the same kind of

space as does Freud's notion of biologism—a space outside history. Among subsequent thinkers who tried to overcome the ahistoricity of Freudian theory by synthesizing Freud with Marx (connecting class oppression to sexual repression) are Wilhelm Reich and Herbert Marcuse; a text from Marcuse's *Eros and Civilization* is presented in this volume. It is important to notice that in the passage on surplus repression and the performance principle, Marcuse finds it necessary to create a set of terms that in some way parallels but does not equal or displace similar Freudian terms (pleasure principle, reality principle, and the like). The works of Reich, Marcuse, Fromm, and Juliet Mitchell are critiqued here by Ann Foreman, who concludes that "from the very beginning the Freudian theory of the libido and the sexual instincts was irreconcilable with the marxist analysis of revolutionary change" precisely because "Marx's basic approach was an historical one," whereas for Freud "the instincts . . . were essentially ahistorical." The final text republished here, written by Dennis Altman, occupies the conceptual space of the pre-"queer" era of gay liberation.

References

Bennett, William J., ed. (1993) *The Book of Virtues: A Treasury of Great Moral Stories.* New York: Simon and Schuster.

———. (1995) *Children's Book of Virtues.* New York: Simon and Schuster.

Freud, Sigmund. (1962) *Three Essays on the Theory of Sexuality.* Trans. James Strachey. New York: Basic Books.

Williams, Howard. (1989) *Hegel, Heraclitus, and Marx's Dialectic.* New York: St. Martin's Press.

From the Fragments, with Commentaries of Hegel and Engels

Heraclitus

From the Fragments

XLIX

Cold warms up, warm cools off, moist parches, dry dampens.

L

As they step into the same rivers, other and still other waters flow upon them.

LI

[[One cannot step twice into the same river, nor can one grasp any mortal substance in a stable condition, but it scatters and again gathers; it forms and dissolves, and approaches and departs.]]

LII

[[It rests by changing.]]

XCI

[[Men asleep are laborers and co-workers in what takes place in the world.]]

XCII

Immortals are mortal, mortals immortal, living the others' death, dead in the others' life.

XCIII

The same . . . : living and dead, and the waking and the sleeping, and young and old. For these transposed are those, and those transposed again are these.

XCIX

[[The beginning and the end are shared in the circumference of a circle.]]

CII

For souls it is death to become water, for water it is death to become earth; out of earth water arises, out of water soul.

CIII

The way up and down is one and the same.

CXXIV

Graspings: wholes and not wholes, convergent divergent, consonant dissonant, from all things one and from one thing all.

CXXV

[[The fairest order in the world is a heap of random sweepings.]]

Commentary: G.W.F. Hegel, from *Lectures on the History of Philosophy*

If we put aside the Ionics, who did not understand the Absolute as Thought, and the Pythagoreans likewise we have the pure Being of the Eleatics, and the dialectic which denies all finite relationships. Thought to the latter is the process of such manifestations; the world in itself is the apparent, and pure Being alone the true. The dialectic of Zeno thus lays hold of the determinations which rest in the content itself, but it may, in so far, also be called subjective dialectic, inasmuch as it rests in the contemplative subject, and the one, without this movement of the dialectic, is abstract identity. The next step from the existence of the dialectic as movement in the subject, is that it must necessarily itself become objective. If Aristotle blames Thales for doing away with motion, because change cannot be understood from Being, and likewise misses the actual in the Pythagorean numbers and Platonic Ideas, taken as the substances of the things which participate in them, Heraclitus at least understands the absolute as just this process of the dialectic. The dialectic is thus three-fold: (α) the external dialectic, a reasoning which goes over and over again without ever reaching the soul of the thing; (β) immanent dialectic of the object, but falling within the contemplation of the subject; (γ) the objectivity of Heraclitus which takes the dialectic itself as principle. The advance requisite and made by Heraclitus is the progression from Being as the first immediate thought, to the category of Becoming as the second. This is the first concrete, the Absolute, as in it the unity of opposites. Thus with Heraclitus the philosophic Idea is to be met with in its speculative form; the reasoning of Parmenides and Zeno is abstract understanding. Heraclitus was thus universally esteemed a deep philosopher and even was decried as such. Here we see land; there is no proposition of Heraclitus which I have not adopted in my Logic.

. . .

In his system Heraclitus did not rest content with thus expressing himself in Notions, or with what is purely logical. But in addition to this universal form in which he advanced his principle, he gave his idea a real and more natural form, and hence he is still reckoned as belonging to the Ionic school of natural philosophers. However, as regards this form of reality, historians are at variance; most of them, and amongst others, Aristotle (Met. I. 3, 8), say that he maintained fire to be the existent principle; others, according to Sextus (adv. Math. IX. 360; X. 233), say it was air, and others again assert that he made vapour to be the principle rather than air, even time is, in Sextus (adv. Math. X. 216), given as the primary existence. The question arises as to how this diversity is to be comprehended. It must not be believed that all these accounts are to be ascribed to the inaccuracy of historians, for the witnesses are of the best, like Aristotle and Sextus Empiricus, who do not speak casually of these forms, but definitely, without, however, remarking upon any such differences and contradictions. We seem to have a better reason in the obscurity of the writing of Heraclitus, which might, by the confusion of its expression, give occasion to misunderstanding. But when regarded closer, this difficulty, which is evident when merely looked at superficially, disappears; it is in the profoundly significant conceptions of Heraclitus that the true way out of this difficulty manifests itself. Heraclitus could no longer, like Thales, express water, air or anything similar as an absolute principle— he could no longer do so in the form of a primeval element from which the rest proceeds—because he thought of Being as identical with non-being, or the infinite Notion; thus the existent, absolute principle cannot with him come forth as a definite and actual thing such as water, but must be water in alteration, or as process only.

. . .

There is still something else to consider, and that is what position in this principle Heraclitus gives to consciousness; his philosophy has, on the whole, a bent towards a philosophy of nature, for the principle, although logical, is apprehended as the universal nature-process. How does this λόγος come to consciousness? How is it related to the individual soul? I shall explain this here in greater detail: it is a beautiful, natural, child-like manner of speaking truth of the truth. The universal and the unity of the principle of consciousness and of the object, and the necessity of objectivity, make their first appearance here. Several passages from Heraclitus are preserved respecting his views of knowledge. From his principle that everything that is, at the same time is not, it immediately follows that he holds that sensuous certainty has no truth; for it is the certainty for which something exists as actual, which is not so in fact. Not this immediate Being, but absolute mediation, Being as thought of, Thought itself, is the true Being. Heraclitus in this relation says of sensuous perception—according to Clement of Alexandria—(Strom. III. 3, p. 520): "What we see waking is dead, but what we see sleeping, a dream," and in Sextus (adv. Math. VII. 126, 127), "Men's eyes and ears are bad witnesses, for they have barbarous souls. Reason (λόγος) is the judge of truth, not the arbitrary, but the only divine and universal judge"—this is the measure, the rhythm, that runs through the Being of everything. Absolute necessity is just the having the truth in consciousness; but every thought, or what proceeds from the individual, every relation in which there is only form and which has the content of the ordinary idea, is not such; what is so is the universal understanding, the developed consciousness of necessity, the identity of subjective and objective. Heraclitus says in this connection, according to Diogenes (IX. 1): "Much learning (πολυμαθίη) does not instruct the mind, else it had instructed Hesiod, Pythagoras, Xenophanes and Hecatæus. The only wisdom is to know the reason that reigns over all."

. . .

Reason is this process with the objective: when we are not in connection with the whole, we only dream. "Separated, the understanding loses the power of consciousness (μνημονικὴν δύναμιν) that it formerly had." The mind as individual unity only, loses objectivity, is not in individuality universal, is not the Thought which has itself as object. "In a waking condition, however, the understanding—gazing through the channels of sense as though it were through a window, and forming a relationship with the surroundings—maintains the logical power." We here have the ideal in its native simplicity. "In the same way as coals which come near fire, themselves take fire, but apart from it, go out, the part which is cut off from the surroundings in our bodies becomes, through the separation, almost irrational." This confutes those who think that God gives wisdom in sleep or in somnambulism. "But in connection with the many channels it becomes similar to the whole." This whole, the universal and divine understanding, in unity with which we are logical, is, according to Heraclitus, the essence of truth.

Commentary: Friedrich Engels, from *Socialism, Utopian and Scientific*

In the meantime, along with and after the French philosophy of the eighteenth century had arisen the new German philosophy, culminating in Hegel. Its greatest merit was the taking up again of dialectics as the highest form of reasoning. The old Greek philosophers were all born natural dialecticians, and Aristotle, the most encyclopædic intellect of them, had already analysed the most essential forms of dialectic thought. The newer philosophy, on the other hand, although in it also dialectics had brilliant exponents (*e.g.* Descartes and Spinoza), had, especially through English influence, become more and more rigidly fixed in the so-called metaphysical mode of reasoning, by which also the French of the eighteenth century were almost wholly dominated, at all events in their special philosophical work. Outside philosophy in the restricted sense, the French nevertheless produced masterpieces of dialectic. We need only call to mind Diderot's *Le Neveu de Rameau*, and Rousseau's *Discours sur l'origine et les fondements de l'inégalité parmi les hommes*. We give here, in brief, the essential character of these two modes of thought.

When we consider and reflect upon nature at large, or the history of mankind, or our own intellectual activity, at first we see the picture of an endless entanglement of relations and reactions, permutations and combinations, in which nothing remains what, where, and as it was, but everything moves, changes, comes into being and passes away. We see, therefore, at first the picture as a whole, with its individual parts still more or less kept in the background; we observe the movements, transitions, connections, rather than the things that move, combine, and are connected. This primitive, naïve, but intrinsically correct conception of the world is that of ancient Greek philosophy, and was first clearly formulated by Heraclitus: everything is and is not, for everything is fluid, is constantly changing, constantly coming into being and passing away.

But this conception, correctly as it expresses the general character of the picture of appearances as a whole, does not suffice to explain the details of which this picture is made up, and so long as we do not understand these, we have not a clear idea of the whole picture. In order to understand these details we must detach them from their natural or historical connection and examine each one separately, its nature, special causes, effects, etc. This is, primarily, the task of natural science and historical research; branches of science which the Greeks of classical times, on very good grounds, relegated to a subordinate position, because they had first of all to collect materials for these sciences to work upon.

. . .

The analysis of nature into its individual parts, the grouping of the different natural processes and objects in definite classes, the study of the internal anatomy of organised bodies in their manifold forms—these were the fundamental conditions of the gigantic strides in our knowledge of nature that have been made during the last four hundred years. But this method of work has also left us as legacy the habit of observing natural objects and processes in isolation, apart from their connection with the vast whole; of observing them in repose, not in motion; as constants, not as essentially variables; in their death, not in their life. And when this way of looking at things was transferred by Bacon and Locke from natural science to philosophy, it begot the narrow, metaphysical mode of thought peculiar to the last century.

To the metaphysician, things and their mental reflexes, ideas, are isolated, are to be considered one after the other and apart from each other, are objects of investigation fixed, rigid, given once for all. He thinks in absolutely irreconcilable antitheses. "His communication is 'yea, yea; nay, nay'; for whatsoever is more than these cometh of evil." For him a thing either exists or does not exist; a thing cannot at the same time be itself and something else. Positive and negative absolutely exclude one another; cause and effect stand in a rigid antithesis one to the other.

. . .

Dialectics, on the other hands, comprehends things and their representations, ideas, in their essential connection, concatenation, motion, origin and ending. Such processes as those mentioned above are, therefore, so many corroborations of its own method of procedure.

Nature is the proof of dialectics, and it must be said for modern science that it has furnished this proof with very rich materials increasing daily, and thus has shown that, in the last resort, nature works dialectically and not metaphysically; that she does not move in the eternal oneness of a perpetually recurring circle, but goes through a real historical evolution.

. . .

This new German philosophy culminated in the Hegelian system. In this system—and herein is its great merit—for the first time the whole world, natural, historical, intellectual, is represented as a process, *i.e.,* as in constant motion, change, transformation, development; and the attempt is made to trace out the internal connection that makes a continuous whole of all this movement and development. From this point of view the history of mankind no longer appeared as a wild whirl of senseless deeds of violence, all equally condemnable at the judgment seat of mature philosophic reason, and which are best forgotten as quickly as possible, but as the process of evolution of man himself. It was now the task of the intellect to follow the gradual march of this process through all its devious ways, and to trace out the inner law running through all its apparently accidental phenomena.

That the Hegelian system did not solve the problem it propounded is here immaterial. Its epoch-making merit was that it propounded the problem.

. . .

From the *Symposium*

Plato

[Socrates speaking:] I want to talk about some lessons I was given, once upon a time, by a Mantinean woman called Diotima—a woman who was deeply versed in this and many other fields of knowledge. It was she who brought about a ten years' postponement of the great plague of Athens on the occasion of a certain sacrifice, and it was she who taught me the philosophy of Love. And now I am going to try to connect her teaching—as well as I can without her help—with the conclusions that Agathon and I have just arrived at. Like him, I shall begin by stating who and what Love is, and go on to describe his functions, and I think the easiest way will be to adopt Diotima's own method of inquiry by question and answer. I'd been telling her pretty much what Agathon has just been telling me—how Love was a great god, and how he was the love of what is beautiful, and she used the same arguments on me that I've just brought to bear on Agathon to prove that, on my own showing, Love was neither beautiful nor good.

Whereupon, My dear Diotima, I asked, are you trying to make me believe that Love is bad and ugly?

Heaven forbid, she said. But do you really think that if a thing isn't beautiful it's therefore bound to be ugly?

Why, naturally.

And that what isn't learned must be ignorant? Have you never heard of something which comes between the two?

And what's that?

Don't you know, she asked, that holding an opinion which is in fact correct, without being able to give a reason for it, is neither true

knowledge—how can it be knowledge without a reason?—nor ignorance—for how can we call it ignorance when it happens to be true? So may we not say that a correct opinion comes midway between knowledge and ignorance?

Yes, I admitted, that's perfectly true.

Very well, then, she went on, why must you insist that what isn't beautiful is ugly, and that what isn't good is bad? Now, coming back to Love, you've been forced to agree that he is neither good nor beautiful, but that's no reason for thinking that he must be bad and ugly. The fact is that he's between the two.

And yet, I said, it's generally agreed that he's a great god.

It all depends, she said, on what you mean by 'generally.' Do you mean simply people that don't know anything about it, or do you include the people that do?

I meant everybody.

At which she laughed, and said, Then can you tell me, my dear Socrates, how people can agree that he's a great god when they deny that he's a god at all?

What people do you mean? I asked her.

You for one, and I for another.

What on earth do you mean by that?

Oh, it's simple enough, she answered. Tell me, wouldn't you say that all the gods were happy and beautiful? Or would you suggest that any of them were neither?

Good heavens, no! said I.

And don't you call people happy when they possess the beautiful and the good?

Why, of course.

And yet you agreed just now that Love lacks, and consequently longs for, those very qualities?

Yes, so I did.

Then, if he has no part in either goodness or beauty, how can he be a god?

I suppose he can't be, I admitted.

And now, she said, haven't I proved that you're one of the people who don't believe in the divinity of Love?

Yes, but what can he be, then? I asked her. A mortal?

Not by any means.

Well, what then?

What I told you before—halfway between mortal and immortal.

And what do you mean by that, Diotima?

A very powerful spirit, Socrates, and spirits, you know, are halfway between god and man.

What powers have they, then? I asked.

They are the envoys and interpreters that ply between heaven and earth, flying upward with our worship and our prayers, and descending with the heavenly answers and commandments, and since they are between the two estates they weld both sides together and merge them into one great whole. They form the medium of the prophetic arts, of the priestly rites of sacrifice, initiation, and incantation, of divination and of sorcery, for the divine will not mingle directly with the human, and it is only through the mediation of the spirit world that man can have any intercourse, whether waking or sleeping, with the gods. And the man who is versed in such matters is said to have spiritual powers, as opposed to the mechanical powers of the man who is expert in the more mundane arts. There are many spirits, and many kinds of spirits, too, and Love is one of them.

Then who were his parents? I asked.

I'll tell you, she said, though it's rather a long story. On the day of Aphrodite's birth the gods were making merry, and among them was Resource, the son of Craft. And when they had supped, Need came begging at the door because there was good cheer inside. Now, it happened that Resource, having drunk deeply of the heavenly nectar—for this was before the days of wine—wandered out into the garden of Zeus

and sank into a heavy sleep, and Need, thinking that to get a child by Resource would mitigate her penury, lay down beside him and in time was brought to bed of Love. So Love became the follower and servant of Aphrodite because he was begotten on the same day that she was born, and further, he was born to love the beautiful since Aphrodite is beautiful herself.

Then again, as the son of Resource and Need, it has been his fate to be always needy; nor is he delicate and lovely as most of us believe, but harsh and arid, barefoot and homeless, sleeping on the naked earth, in doorways, or in the very streets beneath the stars of heaven, and always partaking of his mother's poverty. But, secondly, he brings his father's resourcefulness to his designs upon the beautiful and the good, for he is gallant, impetuous, and energetic, a mighty hunter, and a master of device and artifice—at once desirous and full of wisdom, a lifelong seeker after truth, an adept in sorcery, enchantment, and seduction.

He is neither mortal nor immortal, for in the space of a day he will be now, when all goes well with him, alive and blooming, and now dying, to be born again by virtue of his father's nature, while what he gains will always ebb away as fast. So Love is never altogether in or out of need, and stands, moreover, midway between ignorance and wisdom. You must understand that none of the gods are seekers after truth. They do not long for wisdom, because they are wise—and why should the wise be seeking the wisdom that is already theirs? Nor, for that matter, do the ignorant seek the truth or crave to be made wise. And indeed, what makes their case so hopeless is that, having neither beauty, nor goodness, nor intelligence, they are satisfied with what they are, and do not long for the virtues they have never missed.

Then tell me, Diotima, I said, who are these seekers after truth, if they are neither the wise nor the ignorant?

Why, a schoolboy, she replied, could have told you that, after what I've just been saying. They are those that come between the two, and one of them is Love. For wisdom is concerned with the loveliest of things, and Love is the love of what is lovely. And so it follows that Love is a lover of wisdom, and, being such, he is placed between wisdom and ignorance—for which his parentage also is responsible, in that his father is full of wisdom and resource, while his mother is devoid of either.

Such, my dear Socrates, is the spirit of Love, and yet I'm not altogether surprised at your idea of him, which was, judging by what you said, that Love was the beloved rather than the lover. So naturally you thought of Love as utterly beautiful, for the beloved is, in fact beautiful, perfect, delicate, and prosperous—very different from the lover, as I have described him.

Very well, dear lady, I replied, no doubt you're right. But in that case, what good can Love be to humanity?

That's just what I'm coming to, Socrates, she said. So much, then, for the nature and the origin of Love. You were right in thinking that he was the love of what is beautiful. But suppose someone were to say, Yes, my dear Socrates. Quite so, my dear Diotima. But what do you mean by the love of what is beautiful? Or, to put the question more precisely, what is it that the lover of the beautiful is longing for?

He is longing to make the beautiful his own, I said.

Very well, she replied, but your answer leads to another question. What will he gain by making the beautiful his own?

This, as I had to admit, was more than I could answer on the spur of the moment.

Well then, she went on, suppose that, instead of the beautiful, you were being asked about the good. I put it to you, Socrates. What is it that the lover of the good is longing for?

To make the good his own.

Then what will he gain by making it his own?

I can make a better shot at answering that, I said. He'll gain happiness.

Right, said she, for the happy are happy inasmuch as they possess the good, and since there's no need for us to ask why men should want to be happy, I think your answer is conclusive.

Absolutely, I agreed.

This longing, then, she went on, this love—is it common to all mankind? What do you think, do we all long to make the good our own?

Yes, I said, as far as that goes we're all alike.

Well then, Socrates, if we say that everybody always loves the same thing, does that mean that everybody is in love? Or do we mean that some of us are in love, while some of us are not?

I was a little worried about that myself, I confessed.

Oh, it's nothing to worry about, she assured me. You see, what we've been doing is to give the name of Love to what is only one single aspect of it; we make just the same mistake, you know, with a lot of other names.

For instance . . . ?

For instance, poetry. You'll agree that there is more than one kind of poetry in the true sense of the word—that is to say, calling something into existence that was not there before, so that every kind of artistic creation is poetry, and every artist is a poet.

True.

But all the same, she said, we don't call them all poets, do we? We give various names to the various arts, and only call the one particular art that deals with music and meter by the name that should be given to them all. And that's the only art that we call poetry, while those who practice it are known as poets.

Quite.

And that's how it is with Love. For 'Love, that renowned and all-beguiling power,' includes every kind of longing for happiness and for the good. Yet those of us who are subject to this longing in the various fields of business, athletics, philosophy, and so on, are never said to be in love, and are never known as lovers, while the man who devotes himself to what is only one of Love's many activities is given the name that should apply to all the rest as well.

Yes, I said, I suppose you must be right.

I know it has been suggested, she continued, that lovers are people who are looking for their other halves, but as I see it, Socrates, Love never longs for either the half or the whole of anything except the good. For men will even have their hands and feet cut off if they are once convinced that those members are bad for them. Indeed I think we only prize our own belongings in so far as we say that the good belongs to us, and the bad to someone else, for what we love is the good and nothing but the good. Or do you disagree?

Good heavens, no! I said.

Then may we state categorically that men are lovers of the good?

Yes, I said, we may.

And shouldn't we add that they long for the good to be their own?

We should.

And not merely to be their own but to be their own forever?

Yes, that must follow.

In short, that Love longs for the good to be his own forever?

Yes, I said, that's absolutely true.

Very well, then. And that being so, what course will Love's followers pursue, and in what particular field will eagerness and exertion be known as Love? In fact, what *is* this activity? Can you tell me that, Socrates?

If I could, my dear Diotima, I retorted, I shouldn't be so much amazed at *your* grasp of the subject, and I shouldn't be coming to you to learn the answer to that very question.

Well, I'll tell you, then, she said. To love is to bring forth upon the beautiful, both in body and in soul.

I'm afraid that's too deep, I said, for my poor wits to fathom.

I'll try to speak more plainly, then. We are all of us prolific, Socrates, in body and in soul, and when we reach a certain age our nature urges us to procreation. Nor can we be quickened by ugliness, but only by the beautiful. Conception, we know, takes place when man and woman come together, but there's a divinity in human propagation, an immortal something in the midst of man's mortality which is incompatible with any kind of discord. And ugliness is at odds with the divine, while beauty is in perfect harmony. In propagation, then, Beauty is the goddess of both fate and travail, and so when procreancy draws near the beautiful it grows genial and blithe, and birth follows swiftly on conception.

But when it meets with ugliness it is overcome with heaviness and gloom, and turning away it shrinks into itself and is not brought to bed, but still labors under its painful burden. And so, when the procreant is big with child, he is strangely stirred by the beautiful, because he knows that beauty's tenant will bring his travail to an end. So you see, Socrates, that Love is not exactly a longing for the beautiful, as you suggested.

Well, what is it, then?

A longing not for the beautiful itself, but for the conception and generation that the beautiful effects.

Yes. No doubt you're right.

Of course I'm right, she said. And why all this longing for propagation? Because this is the one deathless and eternal element in our mortality. And since we have agreed that the lover longs for the good to be his own forever, it follows that we are bound to long for immortality as well as for the good—which is to say that Love is a longing for immortality.

So much I gathered, gentlemen, at one time and another from Diotima's dissertations upon Love.

And then one day she asked me, Well, Socrates, and what do you suppose is the cause of all this longing and all this love? Haven't you noticed what an extraordinary effect the breeding instinct has upon both animals and birds, and how obsessed they are with the desire, first to mate, and then to rear their litters and their broods, and how the weakest of them are ready to stand up to the strongest in defense of their young, and even die for them, and how they are content to bear the pinch of hunger and every kind of hardship, so long as they can rear their offspring?

With men, she went on, you might put it down to the power of reason, but how can you account for Love's having such remarkable effects upon the brutes? What do you say to that, Socrates?

Again I had to confess my ignorance.

Well, she said, I don't know how you can hope to master the philosophy of Love, if *that's* too much for you to understand.

But, my dear Diotima, I protested, as I said before, that's just why I'm asking you to teach me—because I realize how ignorant I am. And I'd be more than grateful if you'd enlighten me as to the cause not only of this, but of all the various effects of Love.

Well, she said, it's simple enough, so long as you bear in mind what we agreed was the object of Love. For here, too, the principle holds good that the mortal does all it can to put on immortality. And how can it do that except by breeding, and thus ensuring that there will always be a younger generation to take the place of the old?

Now, although we speak of an individual as being the same so long as he continues to exist in the same form, and therefore assume that a man is the same person in his dotage as in his infancy, yet, for all we call him the same, every bit of him is different, and every day he is becoming a new man, while the old man is ceasing to exist, as you can see from his hair, his flesh, his bones, his blood, and all the rest of his body. And not only his body, for the same thing happens to his soul. And neither his manners, nor his disposition, nor his thoughts, nor his desires, nor his pleasures, nor his sufferings, nor his fears are the same throughout his life, for some of them grow, while others disappear.

And the application of this principle to human knowledge is even more remarkable, for not only do some of the things we know increase, while some of them are lost, so that even in our knowledge we are not always the same, but the principle applies as well to every single branch of knowledge. When we say we are studying, we really mean that our knowledge is ebbing away. We forget, because our knowledge disappears, and we have to study so as to replace what we are losing, so that the state of our knowledge may seem, at any rate, to be the same as it was before.

This is how every mortal creature perpetuates itself. It cannot, like the divine, be still the same throughout eternity; it can only leave behind new life to fill the vacancy that is left in its species by obsolescence. This, my dear Socrates, is how the body and all else that is temporal partakes of the eternal; there is no other way. And so it is no wonder that every creature prizes its own issue, since the whole creation is inspired by this love, this passion for immortality.

Well, Diotima, I said, when she had done, that's a most impressive argument. I wonder if you're right.

Of course I am, she said with an air of authority that was almost professorial. Think of the ambitions of your fellow men, and though at first they may strike you as upsetting my argument, you'll see how right I am if you only bear in mind that men's great incentive is the love of glory, and that their one idea is 'To win eternal mention in the deathless roll of fame.'

For the sake of fame they will dare greater dangers, even, than for their children; they are ready to spend their money like water and to wear their fingers to the bone, and, if it comes to that, to die.

Do you think, she went on, that Alcestis would have laid down her life to save Admetus, or that Achilles would have died for the love he bore Patroclus, or that Codrus, the Athenian king, would have sacrificed himself for the seed of his royal consort, if they had not hoped to win 'the deathless name for valor,' which, in fact, posterity has granted them? No, Socrates, no. Every one of us, no matter what he does, is longing for the endless fame, the incomparable glory that is theirs, and the nobler he is, the greater his ambition, because he is in love with the eternal.

Well then, she went on, those whose procreancy is of the body turn to woman as the object of their love, and raise a family, in the blessed hope that by doing so they will keep their memory green, 'through time and through eternity.' But those whose procreancy is of the spirit rather than of the flesh—and they are not unknown, Socrates—conceive and bear the things of the spirit. And what are they? you ask. Wisdom and all her sister virtues; it is the office of every poet to beget them, and of every artist whom we may call creative.

Now, by far the most important kind of wisdom, she went on, is that which governs the ordering of society, and which goes by the names of justice and moderation. And if any man is so closely allied to the divine as to be teeming with these virtues even in his youth, and if, when he comes to manhood, his first ambition is to be begetting, he too, you may be sure, will go about in search of the loveliness—and never of the ugliness—on which he may beget. And hence his procreant nature is attracted by a comely body rather than an ill-favored one, and if, besides, he happens on a soul which is at once beautiful, distinguished, and agreeable, he is charmed to find so welcome an alliance. It will be easy for him to talk of virtue to such a listener, and to discuss what human goodness is and how the virtuous should live—in short, to undertake the other's education.

And, as I believe, by constant association with so much beauty, and by thinking of his friend when he is present and when he is away, he will be delivered of the burden he has labored under all these years. And what is more, he and his friend will help each other rear the issue of their friendship—and so the bond between them will be more binding, and their communion even more complete, than that which comes of bringing children up, because they have created something lovelier and less mortal than human seed.

And I ask you, who would not prefer such fatherhood to merely human propagation, if he stopped to think of Homer, and Hesiod, and all the greatest of our poets? Who would not envy them their immortal progeny, their claim upon the admiration of posterity?

Or think of Lycurgus, she went on, and what offspring he left behind him in his laws, which proved to be the saviors of Sparta and, perhaps, the whole of Hellas. Or think of the fame of Solon, the father of Athenian law, and think of all the other names that are remembered in Grecian cities and in lands beyond the sea for the noble deeds they did before the eyes of all the world, and for all the diverse virtues that they fathered. And think of all the shrines that have been dedicated to them in memory of their immortal issue, and tell me if you can of *anyone* whose mortal children have brought him so much fame.

Well now, my dear Socrates, I have no doubt that even you might be initiated into these, the more elementary mysteries of Love. But I don't know whether you could apprehend the final revelation, for so far, you know, we are only at the bottom of the true scale of perfection.

Never mind, she went on, I will do all I can to help you understand, and you must strain every nerve to follow what I'm saying.

Well then, she began, the candidate for this initiation cannot, if his efforts are to be rewarded, begin too early to devote himself to the beauties of the body. First of all, if his preceptor instructs him as he should, he will fall in love with the beauty of one individual body, so that his passion may give life to noble discourse. Next he must consider how nearly related the beauty of any one body is to the beauty of any other, when he will see that if he is to devote himself to loveliness of form it will be absurd to deny that the beauty of each and every body is the same. Having reached this point, he must set himself to be the lover of every lovely body, and bring his passion for the one into due proportion by deeming it of little or of no importance.

Next he must grasp that the beauties of the body are as nothing to the beauties of the soul, so that wherever he meets with spiritual loveliness, even in the husk of an unlovely body, he will find it beautiful enough to fall in love with and to cherish—and beautiful enough to quicken in his heart a longing for such discourse as tends toward the building of a noble nature. And from this he will be led to contemplate the beauty of laws and institutions. And when he discovers how nearly every kind of beauty is akin to every other he will conclude that the beauty of the body is not, after all, of so great moment.

And next, his attention should be diverted from institutions to the sciences, so that he may know the beauty of every kind of knowledge. And thus, by scanning beauty's wide horizon, he will be saved from a slavish and illiberal devotion to the individual loveliness of a single boy, a single man, or a single institution. And, turning his eyes toward the open sea of beauty, he will find in such contemplation the seed of the most fruitful discourse and the loftiest thought, and reap a golden harvest of philosophy, until, confirmed and strengthened, he will come upon one single form of knowledge, the knowledge of the beauty I am about to speak of.

And here, she said, you must follow me as closely as you can.

Whoever has been initiated so far in the mysteries of Love and has viewed all these aspects of the beautiful in due succession, is at last drawing near the final revelation. And now, Socrates, there bursts upon him that wondrous vision which is the very soul of the beauty he has toiled so long for. It is an everlasting loveliness which neither comes nor goes, which neither flowers nor fades, for such beauty is the same on every hand, the same then as now, here as there, this way as that way, the same to every worshiper as it is to every other.

Nor will his vision of the beautiful take the form of a face, or of hands, or of anything that is of the flesh. It will be neither words, nor knowledge, nor a something that exists in something else, such as a living creature, or the earth, or the heavens, or anything that is—but subsisting of itself and by itself in an eternal oneness, while every lovely thing partakes of it in such sort that, however much the parts may wax and wane, it will be neither more nor less, but still the same inviolable whole.

And so, when his prescribed devotion to boyish beauties has carried our candidate so far that the universal beauty dawns upon his inward sight, he is almost within reach of the final revelation. And this is the way, the only way, he must approach, or be led toward, the sanctuary of Love. Starting from individual beauties, the quest for the universal beauty must find him ever mounting the heavenly ladder, stepping from rung to rung—that is, from one to two,

and from two to *every* lovely body, from bodily beauty to the beauty of institutions, from institutions to learning, and from learning in general to the special lore that pertains to nothing but the beautiful itself—until at last he comes to know what beauty is.

And if, my dear Socrates, Diotima went on, man's life is ever worth the living, it is when he has attained this vision of the very soul of beauty. And once you have seen it, you will never be seduced again by the charm of gold, of dress, of comely boys, or lads just ripening to manhood; you will care nothing for the beauties that used to take your breath away and kindle such a longing in you, and many others like you, Socrates, to be always at the side of the beloved and feasting your eyes upon him, so that you would be content, if it were possible, to deny yourself the grosser necessities of meat and drink, so long as you were with him.

But if it were given to man to gaze on beauty's very self—unsullied, unalloyed, and freed from the mortal taint that haunts the frailer loveliness of flesh and blood—if, I say, it were given to man to see the heavenly beauty face to face, would you call *his,* she asked me, an unenviable life, whose eyes had been opened to the vision, and who had gazed upon it in true contemplation until it had become his own forever?

And remember, she said, that it is only when he discerns beauty itself through what makes it visible that a man will be quickened with the true, and not the seeming, virtue—for it is virtue's self that quickens him, not virtue's semblance. And when he has brought forth and reared this perfect virtue, he shall be called the friend of god, and if ever it is given to man to put on immortality, it shall be given to him.

A Conversation

Jean d'Alembert and Denis Diderot

d'Alembert: I confess that a Being who exists somewhere and yet corresponds to no point in space, a Being who, lacking extension, yet occupies space; who is present in his entirety in every part of that space, who is essentially different from matter and yet is one with matter, who follows its motion, and moves it, without himself being in motion, who acts on matter and yet is subject to all its vicissitudes, a Being about whom I can form no idea; a Being of so contradictory a nature, is an hypothesis difficult to accept. But other problems arise if we reject it; for if this faculty of sensation, which you propose as substitute, is a general and essential quality of matter, then stone must be sensitive.

Diderot: Why not?

d'Alembert: It's hard to believe.

Diderot: Yes, for him who cuts, chisels, and crushes it, and does not hear it cry out.

d'Alembert: I'd like you to tell me what difference there is, according to you, between a man and a statue, between marble and flesh.

Diderot: Not much. Flesh can be made from marble, and marble from flesh.

d'Alembert: But one is not the other.

Diderot: In the same way that what you call animate force is not the same as inanimate force.

d'Alembert: I don't follow you.

Diderot: I'll explain. The transference of a body from one place to another is not itself motion, it is the consequence of motion. Motion exists equally in the body displaced and in the body that remains stationary.

d'Alembert: That's a new way of looking at things.

Diderot: True none the less. Take away the obstacle that prevents the displacement of a stationary body, and it will be transferred. Suddenly rarefy the air that surrounds the trunk of this huge oak, and the water contained in it, suddenly expanding, will burst it into a hundred thousand fragments. I say the same of your own body.

d'Alembert: That may be so. But what relation is there between motion and the faculty of sensation? Do you, by any chance, distinguish between an active and an inactive sensitiveness, as between animate and inanimate force? An animate force which is revealed by displacement, an inanimate force which manifests itself by pressure; an active sensitiveness which would be characterized by certain recognizable behaviour in the animal and perhaps in the plant, while your inactive sensitiveness only makes itself known when it changes over to the active state?

Diderot: Precisely; just as you say.

d'Alembert: So, then, the statue merely has inactive sensitiveness; and man, animals, perhaps even plants, are endowed with active sensitiveness.

Diderot: There is undoubtedly that difference between the marble block and living tissue; but you can well imagine that's not the only one.

d'Alembert: Of course. Whatever likeness there may be in outward form between a man and a statue, there is no similarity in their internal organization. The chisel of the cleverest sculptor cannot make even an epidermis. But there is a very simple way of transforming an inanimate force into an animate one—the experiment is repeated a hundred times a day before our eyes; whereas I don't quite see how a body can be made to pass from the state of inactive to that of active sensitiveness.

Diderot: Because you don't want to see it. It is just as common a phenomenon.

d'Alembert: And what is this common phenomenon, if you please?

Diderot: I'll tell you, since you want to be put to shame; it occurs every time you eat.

d'Alembert: Every time I eat!

Diderot: Yes, for what do you do when you eat? You remove obstacles that prevented the food from possessing active sensitiveness. You assimilate it, you turn it into flesh, you make it animal, you give it the faculty of sensation, and, what you do to this foodstuff, I can do, when I please, to marble.

d'Alembert: And how?

Diderot: How? I shall make it edible.

d'Alembert: Make marble edible? That doesn't seem easy to me.

Diderot: It's my business to show you the process. I take the statue you see there, I put it in a mortar, then with great blows from a pestle . . .

d'Alembert: Careful, please; that's Falconet's masterpiece! If it were only by Huez or some one like that—.

Diderot: Falconet won't mind; the statue is paid for, and Falconet cares little for present respect and not at all for that of posterity.

d'Alembert: Go on then, crush it to powder.

Diderot: When the block of marble is reduced to impalpable powder, I mix it with humus or leaf-mould; I knead them well together; I water the mixture, I let it decompose for a year or two or a hundred, time doesn't matter to me. When the whole has turned into a more or less homogeneous substance, into humus, do you know what I do?

d'Alembert: I'm sure you don't eat humus.

Diderot: No; but there is a means of connection, of assimilation, a link, between the humus and myself, a *latus* as the chemist would say.

d'Alembert: And that is plant life?

Diderot: Quite right, I sow peas, beans, cabbages, and other vegetables; these plants feed on the soil and I feed on the plants.

d'Alembert: Whether it's true or false, I like this passage from marble into humus, from humus to the vegetable kingdom, from the vegetable to the animal kingdom, to flesh.

Diderot: So, then, I make flesh, or soul as my daughter said, an actively sensitive substance; and if I do not thus solve the problem you set me, at any rate I get pretty near solving it; for you will admit that a piece of marble is much further removed from a being that can feel, than a being that can feel is from a being that can think.

d'Alembert: I agree. But nevertheless the feeling being is not yet the thinking being.

Diderot: Before going one step further let me tell you the history of one of the greatest geometricians[1] in Europe. What was this wonderful creature to begin with? Nothing.

d'Alembert: What, nothing? Nothing comes from nothing.

Diderot: You take my words too literally. I mean to say that, before his mother, the beautiful and wicked Madame de Tencin, had reached the age of puberty, and before the adolescence of the soldier La Touche, the molecules which were to form the first rudiments of our geometrician were scattered throughout the frail young bodies of these two, filtering through with the lymph, circulating with the blood, till at last they reached the vessels whence they were destined to unite, the germ cells of his father and mother. The precious germ, then, is formed; now according to the common belief, it is brought through the Fallopian tubes to the womb, it is attached to the womb by a long cord; it grows gradually and develops into a foetus; now comes the moment for it to leave the dark prison; it is born, abandoned on the steps of Saint-Jean-le-Rond, whence it receives its name; now, taken from the foundlings' home it is put to the breast of good Madame Rousseau, the glazier's wife; it is given suck, it grows in body and mind, becomes a man of letters, an engineer, a geometrician. How was all this done? Just through eating and other purely mechanical operations. Here, in four words you have the general formula. Eat, digest, distil *in vasi licito, et fiat homo secundum artem.*[2] And to expound before the Academy the process of the formation of a man or an animal, one need employ only material agents, the successive results of which would be an inert being, a feeling being, a thinking being, a being solving the problem of the precession of the equinoxes, a sublime being, a marvelous being, a being growing old, fading away, dying, dissolved and given back to the soil.

*   *   *

Diderot: Can you tell me what constitutes the existence of a perceiving being, for that being itself?

d'Alembert: The consciousness of continued identity from the first moment of reflection to the present.

Diderot: And on what is this consciousness based?

d'Alembert: On the memory of its actions.

Diderot: And without this memory?

d'Alembert: Without this memory it would have no identity, since, realizing its existence only at the instant of receiving an impression, it would have no life-story. Its life would be an interrupted series of sensations with nothing to connect them.

Diderot: Very good. And what is this memory? Whence does it spring?

d'Alembert: From a certain organization, which develops, grows weaker, and is sometimes lost entirely.

Diderot: Then, if a being that can feel, and that possesses this organization that gives rise to memory, connects up the impressions it receives, forms through this connection a story which is that of its life, and so acquires consciousness of its identity, it can then deny, affirm, conclude and think.

d'Alembert: So it appears to me; there is only one more difficulty.

Diderot: You are wrong; there are many more.

d'Alembert: But one chief one; that is, it seems to me that we can only think of one thing at a time, and that to form even a simple proposition, let alone those vast chains of reasoning that embrace in their course thousands of ideas, one would need to have at least two things present—the object, which seems to remain in the mind's eye while that mind considers the quality which it is to attribute or to deny to that object.

Diderot: I think that is so; that has made me sometimes compare the fibres of our organs to sensitive vibrating strings which vibrate and resound long after they have been plucked. It is this vibration, this kind of inevitable resonance, which holds the object present, while the mind is busied about the quality that belongs to that object. But vibrating strings have yet another property, that of making other strings vibrate; and that is how the first idea recalls a second, the two of them a third, these three a fourth and so on, so that there is no limit to the ideas awakened and interconnected in the mind of the philosopher, as he meditates and hearkens to himself amid silence and darkness. This instrument makes surprising leaps, and an idea once aroused may sometimes set vibrating an harmonic at an inconceivable distance. If this phenomenon may be observed between resonant strings that are lifeless and separate, why should it not occur between points that are alive and connected, between fibres that are continuous and sensitive?

d'Alembert: Even if it's not true, that is at least very ingenious. But I am inclined to think that you are, without realizing it, slipping into a difficulty that you wished to avoid.

Diderot: What is that?

d'Alembert: You are opposed to making a distinction between the two substances.

Diderot: I don't deny it.

d'Alembert: And if you look closer, you'll see that you are making of the philosopher's mind a being distinct from the instrument, a musician, as it were, who listens to the vibrating strings and decides as to their harmony or dissonance.[3]

Diderot: I may have laid myself open to this objection, but you might not have made it if you had considered the difference between the instrument philosopher and the instrument harpsichord. The philosopher is an instrument that has the faculty of sensation; he is, at the same time, both the musician and the instrument. As he can feel, he is immediately conscious of the sound he gives forth; as he is an animal, he retains the memory of it. This faculty of the organism, connecting up the sounds within him, produces and preserves the melody there. Just suppose that your harpsichord has the power to feel and to remember, and tell me if it will not know and repeat of its own accord the airs that you have played on its keys. We are instruments endowed with feeling and memory; our senses are so many keys that are struck by surrounding nature, and that often strike themselves. This is all, in my opinion, that happens in a harpsichord which is organized like you or me. An impression is created by some cause either within or outside the instrument, a sensation is aroused by this impression, a sensation that persists, since you cannot imagine it arising and dying instantaneously; another impression follows, which equally has its cause either within or outside the animal, a second sensation, and voices to indicate them by natural or conventional sounds.

d'Alembert: I understand. So then, if this harpsichord were not only sensitive and animate but were further endowed with the faculty of feeding and reproducing itself, it would live and breed of itself, or with its female, little harpsichords, also living and vibrating.

Diderot: Undoubtedly. In your opinion, what, other than this, is a chaffinch, a nightingale, a musician or a man? And what other difference do you find between a bird and a bird-organ?[4] Do you see this egg? With this you can overthrow all the schools of theology, all the churches of the earth. What is this egg?

An unperceiving mass, before the germ is introduced into it; and after the germ is introduced, what is it then? still only an unperceiving mass, for this germ itself is only a crude inert fluid. How will this mass develop into a different organization, to sensitiveness, to life? By means of heat. And what will produce the heat? Motion. What will be the successive effects of this motion? Instead of answering me, sit down and let's watch them from moment to moment. First there's a dot that quivers, a little thread that grows longer and takes on colour; tissue is formed; a beak, tiny wings, eyes, feet appear; a yellowish material unwinds and produces intestines; it is an animal. This animal moves, struggles, cries out; I hear its cries through the shell; it becomes covered with down; it sees. The weight of its head, shaking about, brings its beak constantly up against the inner wall of its prison; now the wall is broken; it comes out, it walks about, flies, grows angry, runs away, comes near again, complains, suffers, loves, desires, enjoys; it has the same affections as yourself, it performs the same actions. Are you going to assert with Descartes that it is a purely imitative machine? Little children will laugh at you, and philosophers will retort that if this be a machine then you, too, are a machine. If you admit that between the animal and yourself the difference is merely one of organization, you will be showing good sense and reason, you will be honest; but from this there will be drawn the conclusion that refutes you; namely that, from inert matter, organized in a certain way, and impregnated with other inert matter, and given heat and motion, there results the faculty of sensation, life, memory, consciousness, passion and thought. You have only two courses left to take: either to imagine within the inert mass of the egg a hidden element that awaited the egg's development before revealing its presence, or to assume that this invisible element crept in through the shell at a definite moment in the development. But what is this element? Did it occupy space or did it not? How did it come, or did it escape without moving? What was it doing there or elsewhere? Was it created at the instant it was needed? Was it already in existence? Was it waiting for a home? If it was homogeneous it was material; if heterogeneous, one cannot account for its previous inertia nor its activity in the developed animal. Just listen to yourself, and you will be sorry for yourself; you will perceive that, in order to avoid making a simple supposition that explains everything, namely the faculty of sensation as a general property of matter or a product of its organization, you are giving up common sense and plunging headlong into an abyss of mysteries, contradictions and absurdities.[5]

d'Alembert: A supposition! It pleases you to say so. But suppose this quality is in its essence incompatible with matter?

Diderot: And how do you know that the faculty of sensation is essentially incompatible with matter, you who do not know the essence of anything, either of matter or of sensation? Do you understand the nature of motion any better, how it comes to exist in a body, and its transmission from one to another?

d'Alembert: Without understanding the nature of sensation or that of matter, I can see that the faculty of sensation is a simple quality, entire, indivisible, and incompatible with a subject or substratum which is divisible.

Diderot: Metaphysico-theological nonsense! What! don't you see that all the qualities, all the forms by which nature becomes perceptible to our senses, are essentially indivisible? You cannot have more or less impenetrability. There is half a round body, but there is not a half of roundness; you can have motion to a greater or less degree, but either there is motion or there is not. You cannot have half, or a third, or a quarter of a head, an ear, a finger, any more than half, a third, or a quarter of a thought. If in the universe no one particle is like another, in a particle no one point like another, acknowledge that the atom itself possesses an indivisible quality or form; acknowledge that division is incompatible with the essence of forms, since it destroys them. Be a physicist, and acknowl-

edge the produced character of an effect when you see it produced, even if you cannot explain all the steps that led from the cause to the effect. Be logical, and do not substitute for a cause which exists and which explains everything, another cause which cannot be comprehended, whose connection with the effect is even more difficult to grasp, which engenders an infinite number of difficulties and solves not one of them.

d'Alembert: But what if I give up this cause?

Diderot: There is only one substance in the universe, in man and in the animal. The bird-organ is made of wood, man of flesh. The bird is of flesh, the musician of flesh differently organized; but both of them have the same origin, the same formation, the same functions and the same end.

d'Alembert: And how is the convention of sounds established between your two harpsichords?

Diderot: Since an animal is a perceiving instrument, resembling any other in all respects, having the same structure, being strung with the same chords, stimulated in the same way by joy, pain, hunger, thirst, colic, wonder, terror, it is impossible that at the Pole and at the Equator it should utter different sounds. And so you will find that interjections are about the same in all languages, living and dead. The origin of conventional sounds must be ascribed to need and to proximity. The instrument endowed with the faculty of sensation, or the animal, has discovered by experience that when it uttered a certain sound a certain result followed outside it, feeling instruments like itself or other animals drew nearer, went away, asked or offered things, hurt or caressed it. All these consequences became connected in its memory and in that of others with the utterance of these sounds; and note that human intercourse consists only of sounds and actions. And, to appreciate the power of my system, notice further that it is subject to the same insurmountable difficulty that Berkeley brought against the existence of bodies. There came a moment of madness when the feeling harpsichord thought that it was the only harpsichord in the world, and that the whole harmony of the universe resided in it.

d'Alembert: There's a lot to be said on all that.

Diderot: True.

d'Alembert: For instance, your system doesn't make it clear how we form syllogisms or draw inferences.

Diderot: We don't draw them; they are all drawn by nature. We only state the existence of connected phenomena, which are known to us practically, by experience, whose existence may be either necessary or contingent; necessary in the case of mathematics, physics, and other exact sciences; contingent in ethics, politics and other conjectural sciences.

d'Alembert: Is the connection between phenomena less necessary in one case than in another?

Diderot: No, but the cause undergoes too many particular vicissitudes which escape our observation, for us to be able to count with certainty upon the result that will ensue. Our certainty that a violent-tempered man will grow angry at an insult is not the same as our certainty that one body striking a smaller body will set it in motion.

d'Alembert: What about analogy?

Diderot: Analogy, in the most complex cases, is only a rule of three working out in the feeling instrument. If a familiar natural phenomenon is followed by another familiar natural phenomenon, what will be the fourth phenomenon that will follow a third, either provided by nature or imagined in imitation of nature? If the lance of an ordinary warrior is ten feet long, how long will the lance of Ajax be? If I can throw a stone weighing four pounds, Diomedes must be able to shift a large block of rock. The strides of gods and the leaps of their horses will correspond to the imagined proportion between gods and men. You have here a fourth chord in harmony with and proportional to three others; and the animal awaits its resonance, which always occurs within itself, though not always in nature. The poet doesn't mind about that, it doesn't affect his kind of truth. But it is otherwise with the philosopher; he must proceed to examine nature which often shows him a phenomenon quite different from what he had supposed, and then he perceives that he had been seduced by an analogy.

d'Alembert: Farewell, my friend, good evening and good night to you.

Notes

1. Namely, d'Alembert himself.

2. In a suitable vessel, let a man be made by art.

3. An allusion to Simmias' theory of the relation of mind to body in Plato's *Phaedo*. (Simmias uses the metaphor of the lyre.)

4. Mechanical musical-box to teach a canary tunes.

5. Diderot's point here is that sensation as a faculty of matter, as conjectured by Locke, is more plausible than Cartesian dualism, which d'Alembert favors.

The Sexual Aberrations[1]

Sigmund Freud

The fact of the existence of sexual needs in human beings and animals is expressed in biology by the assumption of a 'sexual instinct', on the analogy of the instinct of nutrition, that is of hunger. Everyday language possesses no counterpart to the word 'hunger', but science makes use of the word 'libido' for that purpose.[2]

Popular opinion has quite definite ideas about the nature and characteristics of this sexual instinct. It is generally understood to be absent in childhood, to set in at the time of puberty in connection with the process of coming to maturity and to be revealed in the manifestations of an irresistible attraction exercised by one sex upon the other; while its aim is presumed to be sexual union, or at all events actions leading in that direction. We have every reason to believe, however, that these views give a very false picture of the true situation. If we look into them more closely we shall find that they contain a number of errors, inaccuracies and hasty conclusions.

I shall at this point introduce two technical terms. Let us call the person from whom sexual attraction proceeds the *sexual object* and the act towards which the instinct tends the *sexual aim*. Scientifically sifted observation, then, shows that numerous deviations occur in respect of both of these—the sexual object and the sexual aim. The relation between these deviations and what is assumed to be normal requires thorough investigation.

(1) Deviations in Respect of the Sexual Object

The popular view of the sexual instinct is beautifully reflected in the poetic fable which tells how the original human beings were cut up into two halves—man and woman—and how these are always striving to unite again in love.[3] It comes as a great surprise therefore to learn that there are men whose sexual object is a man and not a woman, and women whose sexual object is a woman and not a man. People of this kind are described as having 'contrary sexual feelings', or better, as being 'inverts', and the fact is described as 'inversion'. The number of such people is very considerable, though there are difficulties in establishing it precisely.[4]

(A) Inversion

Behaviour of Inverts: Such people vary greatly in their behaviour in several respects.

(*a*) They may be *absolute* inverts. In that case their sexual objects are exclusively of their own sex. Persons of the opposite sex are never the object of their sexual desire, but leave them cold, or even arouse sexual aversion in them. As a consequence of this aversion, they are incapable, if they are men, of carrying out the sexual act, or else they derive no enjoyment from it.

(*b*) They may be *amphigenic* inverts, that is, psychosexual hermaphrodites. In that case their sexual objects may equally well be of their own or of the opposite sex. This kind of inversion thus lacks the characteristic of exclusiveness.

(*c*) They may be *contingent* inverts. In that case, under certain external conditions—of which inaccessibility of any normal sexual object and imitation are the chief—they are capable of taking as their sexual object someone of their own sex and of deriving satisfaction from sexual intercourse with him.

Again, inverts vary in their views as to the peculiarity of their sexual instinct. Some of them accept their inversion as something in the natural course of things, just as a normal person accepts the direction of *his* libido, and insist energetically that inversion is as legitimate as the normal attitude; others rebel against their inversion and feel it as a pathological compulsion.[5]

Other variations occur which relate to questions of time. The trait of inversion may either date back to the very beginning, as far back as the subject's memory reaches, or it may not have become noticeable till some particular time before or after puberty.[6] It may either persist throughout life, or it may go into temporary abeyance, or again it may constitute an episode on the way to a normal development. It may even make its first appearance late in life after a long period of normal sexual activity. A periodic oscillation between a normal and an inverted sexual object has also sometimes been observed. Those cases are of particular interest in which the libido changes over to an inverted sexual object after a distressing experience with a normal one.

As a rule these different kinds of variations are found side by side independently of one another. It is, however, safe to assume that the most extreme form of inversion will have been present from a very early age and that the person concerned will feel at one with his peculiarity.

Many authorities would be unwilling to class together all the various cases which I have enumerated and would prefer to lay stress upon their differences rather than their resemblances, in accordance with their own preferred view of inversion. Nevertheless, though the distinctions cannot be disputed, it is impossible to overlook the existence of numerous intermediate examples of every type, so that we are driven to conclude that we are dealing with a connected series.

Nature of Inversion: The earliest assessments regarded inversion as an innate indication of nervous degeneracy. This corresponded to the fact that medical observers first came across it in persons suffering, or appearing to suffer, from nervous diseases. This characterization of inversion involves two suppositions, which must be considered separately: that it is innate and that it is degenerate.

Degeneracy: The attribution of degeneracy in this connection is open to the objections which can be raised against the indiscriminate use of the word in general. It has become the fashion to regard any symptom which is not obviously due to trauma or infection as a sign of degeneracy. Magnan's classification of degenerates is indeed of such a kind as not to exclude the possibility of the concept of degeneracy being applied to a nervous system whose general functioning is excellent. This being so, it may well be asked whether an attribution of 'degeneracy' is of any value or adds anything to our knowledge. It seems wiser only to speak of it where

1.   several serious deviations from the normal are found together, and
2.   the capacity for efficient functioning and survival seem to be severely impaired.[7]

Several facts go to show that in this legitimate sense of the word inverts cannot be regarded as degenerate:

1.   Inversion is found in people who exhibit no other serious deviations from the normal.
2.   It is similarly found in people whose efficiency is unimpaired, and who are indeed distinguished by specially high intellectual development and ethical culture.[8]
3.   If we disregard the patients we come across in our medical practice, and cast our eyes round a wider horizon, we shall come in two directions upon facts which make it impossible to regard inversion as a sign of degeneracy:

a. Account must be taken of the fact that inversion was a frequent phenomenon—one might almost say an institution charged with important functions—among the peoples of antiquity at the height of their civilization.

b. It is remarkably widespread among many savage and primitive races, whereas the concept of degeneracy is usually restricted to states of high civilization (cf. Bloch); and, even amongst the civilized peoples of Europe, climate and race exercise the most powerful influence on the prevalence of inversion and upon the attitude adopted towards it.[9]

Innate Character: As may be supposed, innateness is only attributed to the first, most extreme, class of inverts, and the evidence for its rests upon assurances given by them that at no time in their lives has their sexual instinct shown any sign of taking another course. The very existence of the two other classes, and especially the third [the 'contingent' inverts], is difficult to reconcile with the hypothesis of the innateness of inversion. This explains why those who support this view tend to separate out the group of absolute inverts from all the rest, thus abandoning any attempt at giving an account of inversion which shall have universal application. In the view of these authorities inversion is innate in one group of cases, while in others it may have come about in other ways.

The reverse of this view is represented by the alternative one that inversion is an acquired character of the sexual instinct. This second view is based on the following considerations:

1. In the case of many inverts, even absolute ones, it is possible to show that very early in their lives a sexual impression occurred which left a permanent after-effect in the shape of a tendency to homosexuality.

2. In the case of many others, it is possible to point to external influences in their lives, whether of a favourable or inhibiting character, which have led sooner or later to a fixation of their inversion. (Such influences are exclusive relations with persons of their own sex, comradeship in war, detention in prison, the dangers of heterosexual intercourse, celibacy, sexual weakness, etc.)

3. Inversion can be removed by hypnotic suggestion, which would be astonishing in an innate characteristic.

In view of these considerations it is even possible to doubt the very existence of such a thing as innate inversion. It can be argued (cf. Havelock Ellis [1915]) that, if the cases of allegedly innate inversion were more closely examined, some experience of their early childhood would probably come to light which had a determining effect upon the direction taken by their libido. This experience would simply have passed out of the subject's conscious recollection, but could be recalled to his memory under appropriate influence. In the opinion of these writers inversion can only be described as a frequent variation of the sexual instinct, which can be determined by a number of external circumstances in the subject's life.

The apparent certainty of this conclusion is, however, completely countered by the reflection that many people are subjected to the same sexual influences (e.g. to seduction or mutual masturbation, which may occur in early youth) without becoming inverted or without remaining so permanently. We are therefore forced to a suspicion that the choice between 'innate' and 'acquired' is not an exclusive one or that it does not cover all the issues involved in inversion.

Explanation of Inversion: The nature of inversion is explained neither by the hypothesis that it is innate nor by the alternative hypothesis that it is acquired. In the former case we must ask in what respect it is innate, unless we are to accept the crude explanation that everyone is born with his sexual instinct attached to a particular sexual object. In the latter case it may be questioned whether the various accidental influences would be sufficient to explain the acquisition of inversion without the co-operation of something in the subject himself. As we have already shown, the existence of this last factor is not to be denied.

Bisexuality: A fresh contradiction of popular views is involved in the considerations put forward by Lydston [1889], Kiernan [1888] and Chevalier [1893] in an endeavour to account for the possibility of sexual inversion. It is popularly believed that a human being is either a man or a woman. Science, however, knows of cases in which the sexual characters are obscured, and in which it is consequently difficult to determine the sex. This arises in the first instance in the field of anatomy. The genitals of the individuals concerned combine male and female characteristics. (This condition is known as hermaphroditism.) In rare cases both kinds of sexual apparatus are found side by side fully developed (true hermaphroditism); but far more frequently both sets of organs are found in an atrophied condition.[10]

The importance of these abnormalities lies in the unexpected fact that they facilitate our understanding of normal development. For it appears that a certain degree of anatomical hermaphroditism occurs normally. In every normal male or female individual, traces are found of the apparatus of the opposite sex. These either persist without function as rudimentary organs or become modified and take on other functions.

These long-familiar facts of anatomy lead us to suppose that an originally bisexual physical disposition has, in the course of evolution, become modified into a unisexual one, leaving behind only a few traces of the sex that has become atrophied.

It was tempting to extend this hypothesis to the mental sphere and to explain inversion in all its varieties as the expression of a psychical hermaphroditism. All that was required further in order to settle the question was that inversion should be regularly accompanied by the mental and somatic signs of hermaphroditism.

But this expectation was disappointed. It is impossible to demonstrate so close a connection between the hypothetical psychical hermaphroditism and the established anatomical one. A general lowering of the sexual instinct and a slight anatomical atrophy of the organs is found frequently in inverts (cf. Havelock Ellis, 1915). Frequently, but by no means regularly or even usually. The truth must therefore be recognized that inversion and somatic hermaphroditism are on the whole independent of each other.

A great deal of importance, too, has been attached to what are called the secondary and tertiary sexual characters and to the great frequency of the occurrence of those of the opposite sex in inverts (cf. Havelock Ellis, 1915). Much of this, again, is correct; but it should never be forgotten that in general the secondary and tertiary sexual characters of one sex occur very frequently in the opposite one. They are indications of hermaphroditism, but are not attended by any change of sexual object in the direction of inversion.

Psychical hermaphroditism would gain substance if the inversion of the sexual object were at least accompanied by a parallel change-over of the subject's other mental qualities, instincts and character traits into those marking the opposite sex. But it is only in inverted women that character-inversion of this kind can be looked for with any regularity. In men the most complete mental masculinity can be combined with inversion. If the belief in psychical hermaphroditism is to be persisted in, it will be necessary to add that its manifestations in various spheres show only slight signs of being mutually determined. Moreover the same is true of somatic hermaphroditism: according to Halban (1903),[11] occurrences of individual atrophied organs and of secondary sexual characters are to a considerable extent independent of one another.

The theory of bisexuality has been expressed in its crudest form by a spokesman of the male inverts: 'a feminine brain in a masculine body'. But we are ignorant of what characterizes a feminine brain. There is neither need nor justification for replacing the psychological problem by the anatomical one. Krafft-Ebing's attempted explanation seems to be more exactly framed than that of Ulrichs but does not differ from it in essentials. According to Krafft-Ebing (1895, 5), every individual's bisexual disposition endows him with masculine and feminine brain centres as well as with somatic organs of sex; these centres develop only at puberty, for the most part under the influence of the sex-gland, which is independent of them in the original disposition. But what has just been said of masculine and feminine brains applies equally to masculine and feminine 'centres'; and incidentally we have not even any grounds for assuming that certain areas of the brain ('centres') are set aside for the functions of sex, as is the case, for instance, with those of speech.[12]

Nevertheless, two things emerge from these discussions. In the first place, a bisexual disposition is somehow concerned in inversion, though we do not know in what that disposition consists, beyond anatomical structure. And secondly, we have to deal with disturbances that affect the sexual instinct in the course of its development.

Sexual Object of Inverts: The theory of psychical hermaphroditism presupposes that the sexual object of an invert is the opposite of that of a normal person. An inverted man, it holds, is like a woman in being subject to the charm that proceeds from masculine attributes both physical and mental: he feels he is a woman in search of a man.

But however well this applies to quite a number of inverts, it is, nevertheless, far from revealing a universal characteristic of inversion. There can be no doubt that a large proportion of male inverts retain the mental quality of masculinity, that they possess relatively few of the secondary characters of the opposite sex and that what they look for in their sexual object are in fact feminine mental traits. If this were not so, how would it be possible to explain the fact that male prostitutes who offer themselves to inverts—today just as they did in ancient times—imitate

women in all the externals of their clothing and behaviour? Such imitation would otherwise inevitably clash with the ideal of the inverts. It is clear that in Greece, where the most masculine men were numbered among the inverts, what excited a man's love was not the *masculine* character of a boy, but his physical resemblance to a woman as well as his feminine mental qualities—his shyness, his modesty and his need for instruction and assistance. As soon as the boy became a man he ceased to be a sexual object for men and himself, perhaps, became a lover of boys. In this instance, therefore, as in many others, the sexual object is not someone of the same sex but someone who combines the characters of both sexes; there is, as it were, a compromise between an impulse that seeks for a man and one that seeks for a woman, while it remains a paramount condition that the object's body (i.e. genitals) shall be masculine. Thus the sexual object is a kind of reflection of the subject's own bisexual nature.[13]

The position in the case of women is less ambiguous; for among them the active inverts exhibit masculine characteristics, both physical and mental, with peculiar frequency and look for femininity in their sexual objects—though here again a closer knowledge of the facts might reveal greater variety.

Sexual Aim of Inverts: The important fact to bear in mind is that no one single aim can be laid down as applying in cases of inversion. Among men, intercourse *per anum* by no means coincides with inversion; masturbation is quite as frequently their exclusive aim, and it is even true that restrictions of sexual aim—to the point of its being limited to simple outpourings of emotion—are commoner among them than among heterosexual lovers. Among women, too, the sexual aims of inverts are various: there seems to be a special preference for contact with the mucous membrane of the mouth.

Conclusion: It will be seen that we are not in a position to base a satisfactory explanation of the origin of inversion upon the material at present before us. Nevertheless our investigation has put us in possession of a piece of knowledge which may turn out to be of greater importance to us than the solution of that problem. It has been brought to our notice that we have been in the habit of regarding the connection between the sexual instinct and the sexual object as more intimate than it in fact is. Experience of the cases that are considered abnormal has shown us that in them the sexual instinct and the sexual object are merely soldered together—a fact which we have been in danger of overlooking in consequence of the uniformity of the normal picture, where the object appears to form part and parcel of the instinct. We are thus warned to loosen the bond that exists in our thoughts between instinct and object. It seems probable that the sexual instinct is in the first instance independent of its object; nor is its origin likely to be due to its object's attractions.

(B) Sexually Immature Persons and Animals as Sexual Objects

People whose sexual objects belong to the normally inappropriate sex—that is, inverts—strike the observer as a collection of individuals who may be quite sound in other respects. On the other hand, cases in which sexually immature persons (children) are chosen as sexual objects are instantly judged as sporadic aberrations. It is only exceptionally that children are the exclusive sexual objects in such a case. They usually come to play that part when someone who is cowardly or has become impotent adopts them as a substitute, or when an urgent instinct (one which will not allow of postponement) cannot at the moment get possession of any more appropriate object. Nevertheless, a light is thrown on the nature of the sexual instinct by the fact that it permits of so much variation in its objects and such a cheapening of them—which hunger, with its far more energetic retention of its objects, would only permit in the most extreme instances. A similar consideration applies to sexual intercourse with animals, which is by no means rare, especially among country people,

and in which sexual attraction seems to override the barriers of species.

One would be glad on aesthetic grounds to be able to ascribe these and other severe aberrations of the sexual instinct to insanity; but that cannot be done. Experience shows that disturbances of the sexual instinct among the insane do not differ from those that occur among the healthy and in whole races or occupations. Thus the sexual abuse of children is found with uncanny frequency among school teachers and child attendants, simply because they have the best opportunity for it. The insane merely exhibit any such aberration to an intensified degree; or, what is particularly significant, it may become exclusive and replace normal sexual satisfaction entirely.

The very remarkable relation which thus holds between sexual variations and the descending scale from health to insanity gives us plenty of material for thought. I am inclined to believe that it may be explained by the fact that the impulses of sexual life are among those which, even normally, are the least controlled by the higher activities of the mind. In my experience anyone who is in any way, whether socially or ethically, abnormal mentally is invariably abnormal also in his sexual life. But many people are abnormal in their sexual life who in every other respect approximate to the average, and have, along with the rest, passed through the process of human cultural development, in which sexuality remains the weak spot.

*   *   *

The most general conclusion that follows from all these discussions seems, however, to be this. Under a great number of conditions and in surprisingly numerous individuals, the nature and importance of the sexual object recedes into the background. What is essential and constant in the sexual instinct is something else.[14]

(2) Deviations in Respect of the Sexual Aim

The normal sexual aim is regarded as being the union of the genitals in the act known as copulation, which leads to a release of the sexual tension and a temporary extinction of the sexual instinct—a satisfaction analogous to the sating of hunger. But even in the most normal sexual process we may detect rudiments which, if they had developed, would have led to the deviations described as 'perversions'. For there are certain intermediate relations to the sexual object, such as touching and looking at it, which lie on the road towards copulation and are recognized as being preliminary sexual aims. On the one hand these activities are themselves accompanied by pleasure, and on the other hand they intensify the excitation, which should persist until the final sexual aim is attained. Moreover, the kiss, one particular contact of this kind, between the mucous membrane of the lips of the two people concerned, is held in high sexual esteem among many nations (including the most highly civilized ones), in spite of the fact that the parts of the body involved do not form part of the sexual apparatus but constitute the entrance to the digestive tract. Here, then, are factors which provide a point of contact between the perversions and normal sexual life and which can also serve as a basis for their classification. Perversions are sexual activities which either (a) extend, in an anatomical sense, beyond the regions of the body that are designed for sexual union, or (b) linger over the intermediate relations to the sexual object which should normally be traversed rapidly on the path towards the final sexual aim.

(A) Anatomical Extensions

Overvaluation of the Sexual Object: It is only in the rarest instances that the psychical valuation that is set on the sexual object, as being the goal of the sexual instinct, stops short at its genitals. The appreciation extends to the whole body of the sexual object and tends to involve every sensation derived from it. The same overvaluation spreads over into the psychological sphere: the subject becomes, as it were, intellectually infatuated (that is, his powers of judgement are weakened) by the mental achievements and perfections of the sexual object and he submits to the latter's judgements with credulity. Thus the credulity of love becomes an important, if not the most fundamental, source of *authority*.[15]

This sexual overvaluation is something that cannot be easily reconciled with a restriction of the sexual aim to union of the actual genitals and it helps to turn activities connected with other parts of the body into sexual aims.[16]

The significance of the factor of sexual overvaluation can be best studied in men, for their erotic life alone has become accessible to research. That of women—partly owing to the stunting effect of civilized conditions and partly owing to their conventional secretiveness and insincerity—is still veiled in an impenetrable obscurity.[17]

Sexual Use of the Mucous Membrane of the Lips and Mouth: The use of the mouth as a sexual organ is regarded as a perversion if the lips (or tongue) of one person are brought into contact with the genitals of another, but not if the mucous membranes of the lips of both of them come together. This exception is the point of contact with what is normal. Those who condemn the other practices (which have no doubt been common among mankind from primaeval times) as being perversions, are giving way to an unmistakable feeling of *disgust,* which protects them from accepting sexual aims of the kind. The limits of such disgust are, however, often purely conventional: a man who will kiss a pretty girl's lips passionately, may perhaps be disgusted at the idea of using her tooth-brush, though there are no grounds for supposing that his own oral cavity, for which he feels no disgust, is any cleaner than the girl's. Here, then, our attention is drawn to the factor of disgust, which interferes with the libidinal overvaluation of the sexual object but can in turn be overridden by libido. Disgust seems to be one of the forces which have led to a restriction of the sexual aim. These forces do not as a rule extend to the genitals themselves. But there is no doubt that the genitals of the opposite sex can in themselves be an object of disgust and that such an attitude is one of the characteristics of all hysterics, and especially of hysterical women. The sexual instinct in its strength enjoys overriding this disgust.

Sexual Use of the Anal Orifice: Where the anus is concerned it becomes still clearer that it is disgust which stamps that sexual aim as a perversion. I hope, however, I shall not be accused of partisanship when I assert that people who try to account for this disgust by saying that the organ in question serves the function of excretion and comes in contact with excrement—a thing which is disgusting in itself—are not much more to the point than hysterical girls who account for their disgust at the male genital by saying that it serves to void urine.

The playing of a sexual part by the mucous membrane of the anus is by no means limited to intercourse between men: preference for it is in no way characteristic of inverted feeling. On the contrary, it seems that *paedicatio* with a male owes its origin to an analogy with a similar act performed with a woman; while mutual masturbation is the sexual aim most often found in intercourse between inverts.

Significance of Other Regions of the Body: The extension of sexual interest to other regions of the body, with all its variations, offers us nothing that is new in principle; it adds nothing to our knowledge of the sexual instinct, which merely proclaims its intention in this way of getting possession of the sexual object in every possible direction. But these anatomical extensions inform us that, besides sexual overvaluation, there is a second factor at work which is strange to popular knowledge. Certain regions of the body, such as the mucous membrane of the mouth and anus, which are constantly appearing in these practices, seem, as it were, to be claiming that they should themselves be regarded and treated as genitals. We shall learn later that this claim is justified by the history of the development of the sexual in-

stinct and that it is fulfilled in the symptomatology of certain pathological states.

Unsuitable Substitutes for the Sexual Object— Fetishism: There are some cases which are quite specially remarkable—those in which the normal sexual object is replaced by another which bears some relation to it, but is entirely unsuited to serve the normal sexual aim. From the point of view of classification, we should no doubt have done better to have mentioned this highly interesting group of aberrations of the sexual instinct among the deviations in respect of the sexual *object*. But we have postponed their mention till we could become acquainted with the factor of sexual overvaluation, on which these phenomena, being connected with an abandonment of the sexual aim, are dependent.

What is substituted for the sexual object is some part of the body (such as the foot or hair) which is in general very inappropriate for sexual purposes, or some inanimate object which bears an assignable relation to the person whom it replaces and preferably to that person's sexuality (e.g. a piece of clothing or underlinen). Such substitutes are with some justice likened to the fetishes in which savages believe that their gods are embodied.

A transition to those cases of fetishism in which the sexual aim, whether normal or perverse, is entirely abandoned is afforded by other cases in which the sexual object is required to fulfil a fetishistic condition—such as the possession of some particular hair-colouring or clothing, or even some bodily defect—if the sexual aim is to be attained. No other variation of the sexual instinct that borders on the pathological can lay so much claim to our interest as this one, such is the peculiarity of the phenomena to which it gives rise. Some degree of diminution in the urge towards the normal sexual aim (an executive weakness of the sexual apparatus) seems to be a necessary precondition in every case.[18] The point of contact with the normal is provided by the psychologically essential overvaluation of the sexual object, which inevitably extends to everything that is associated with it. A certain degree of fetishism is thus habitually present in normal love, especially in those stages of it in which the normal sexual aim seems unattainable or its fulfilment prevented:

> *Schaff' mir ein Halstuch von ihrer Brust,*
> *Ein Strumpfband meiner Liebeslust!*[19]

The situation only becomes pathological when the longing for the fetish passes beyond the point of being merely a necessary condition attached to the sexual object and actually *takes the place* of the normal aim, and, further, when the fetish becomes detached from a particular individual and becomes the *sole* sexual object. These are, indeed, the general conditions under which mere variations of the sexual instinct pass over into pathological aberrations.

Binet (1888) was the first to maintain (what has since been confirmed by a quantity of evidence) that the choice of a fetish is an after-effect of some sexual impression, received as a rule in early childhood. (This may be brought into line with the proverbial durability of first loves: *on revient toujours á ses premiers amours.*) This derivation is particularly obvious in cases where there is merely a fetishistic condition attached to the sexual object. We shall come across the importance of early sexual impressions again in another connection.[20]

In other cases the replacement of the object by a fetish is determined by a symbolic connection of thought, of which the person concerned is usually not conscious. It is not always possible to trace the course of these connections with certainty. (The foot, for instance, is an age-old sexual symbol which occurs even in mythology;[21] no doubt the part played by fur as a fetish owes its origin to an association with the hair of the *mons Veneris.*) None the less even symbolism such as this is not always unrelated to sexual experiences in childhood.[22]

(B) Fixations of Preliminary Sexual Aims

Appearance of New Aims: Every external or internal factor that hinders or postpones the attainment of the normal sexual aim (such as impotence, the high price of the sexual object or the danger of the sexual act) will evidently lend support to the tendency to linger over the preparatory activities and to turn them into new sexual aims that can take the place of the normal one. Attentive examination always shows that even what seem to be the strangest of these new aims are already hinted at in the normal sexual process.

Touching and Looking: A certain amount of touching is indispensable (at all events among human beings) before the normal sexual aim can be attained. And everyone knows what a source of pleasure on the one hand and what an influx of fresh excitation on the other is afforded by tactile sensations of the skin of the sexual object. So that lingering over the stage of touching can scarcely be counted a perversion, provided that in the long run the sexual act is carried further.

The same holds true of seeing—an activity that is ultimately derived from touching. Visual impressions remain the most frequent pathway along which libidinal excitation is aroused; indeed, natural selection counts upon the accessibility of this pathway—if such a teleological form of statement is permissible[23]—when it encourages the development of beauty in the sexual object. The progressive concealment of the body which goes along with civilization keeps sexual curiosity awake. This curiosity seeks to complete the sexual object by revealing its hidden parts. It can, however, be diverted ('sublimated') in the direction of art, if its interest can be shifted away from the genitals on to the shape of the body as a whole.[24] It is usual for most normal people to linger to some extent over the intermediate sexual aim of a looking that has a sexual tinge to it; indeed, this offers them a possibility of directing some proportion of their libido on to higher artistic aims. On the other hand, this pleasure in looking [scopophilia] becomes a perversion (a) if it is restricted exclusively to the genitals, or (b) if it is connected with the overriding of disgust (as in the case of *voyeurs* or people who look on at ex-cretory functions), or (*c*) if, instead of being *preparatory* to the normal sexual aim, it supplants it. This last is markedly true of exhibitionists, who, if I may trust the findings of several analyses,[25] exhibit their own genitals in order to obtain a reciprocal view of the genitals of the other person.[26]

In the perversions which are directed towards looking and being looked at, we come across a very remarkable characteristic with which we shall be still more intensely concerned in the aberration that we shall consider next: in these perversions the sexual aim occurs in two forms, an *active* and a *passive* one.

The force which opposes scopophilia, but which may be overridden by it (in a manner parallel to what we have previously seen in the case of disgust), is *shame*.

Sadism and Masochism: The most common and the most significant of all the perversions—the desire to inflict pain upon the sexual object, and its reverse—received from Krafft-Ebing the names of 'sadism' and 'masochism' for its active and passive forms respectively. Other writers [e.g. Schrenck-Notzing (1899)] have preferred the narrower term 'algolagnia'. This emphasizes the pleasure in *pain,* the cruelty; whereas the names chosen by Krafft-Ebing bring into prominence the pleasure in any form of humiliation or subjection.

As regards active algolagnia, sadism, the roots are easy to detect in the normal. The sexuality of most male human beings contains an element of *aggressiveness*—a desire to subjugate; the biological significance of it seems to lie in the need for overcoming the resistance of the sexual object by means other than the process of wooing. Thus sadism would correspond to an aggressive component of the sexual instinct which has become independent and exaggerated and, by displacement, has usurped the leading position.[27]

In ordinary speech the connotation of sadism oscillates between, on the one hand, cases merely characterized by an active or vio-lent attitude to the sexual object, and, on the other hand, cases in which satisfaction is entirely conditional on the humiliation and maltreatment of the object. Strictly speaking, it is only this last extreme instance which deserves to be described as a perversion.

Similarly, the term masochism comprises any passive attitude towards sexual life and the sexual object, the extreme instance of which appears to be that in which satisfaction is conditional upon suffering physical or mental pain at the hands of the sexual object. Masochism, in the form of a perversion, seems to be further removed from the normal sexual aim than its counterpart; it may be doubted at first whether it can ever occur as a primary phenomenon or whether, on the contrary, it may not invariably arise from a transformation of sadism.[28] It can often be shown that masochism is nothing more than an extension of sadism turned round upon the subject's own self, which thus, to begin with, takes the place of the sexual object. Clinical analysis of extreme cases of masochistic perversion show that a great number of factors (such as the castration complex and the sense of guilt) have combined to exaggerate and fixate the original passive sexual attitude.

Pain, which is overridden in such cases, thus falls into line with disgust and shame as a force that stands in opposition and resistance to the libido.[29]

Sadism and masochism occupy a special position among the perversions, since the contrast between activity and passivity which lies behind them is among the universal characteristics of sexual life.

The history of human civilization shows beyond any doubt that there is an intimate connection between cruelty and the sexual instinct; but nothing has been done towards explaining the connection, apart from laying emphasis on the aggressive factor in the libido. According to some authorities this aggressive element of the sexual instinct is in reality a relic of cannibalistic desires—that is, it is a contribution derived from the apparatus for obtaining mastery, which is concerned with the satisfaction of the other and, ontogenetically, the older of the great instinctual needs.[30] It has also been maintained that every pain contains in itself the possibility of a feeling of pleasure. All that need be said is that no satisfactory explanation of this perversion has been put forward and that it seems possible that a number of mental impulses are combined in it to produce a single resultant.[31]

But the most remarkable feature of this perversion is that its active and passive forms are habitually found to occur together in the same individual. A person who feels pleasure in producing pain in someone else in a sexual relationship is also capable of enjoying as pleasure any pain which he may himself derive from sexual relations. A sadist is always at the same time a masochist, although the active or the passive aspect of the perversion may be the more strongly developed in him and may represent his predominant sexual activity.[32]

We find, then, that certain among the impulses to perversion occur regularly as pairs of opposites; and this, taken in conjunction with material which will be brought forward later, has a high theoretical significance.[33] It is, moreover, a suggestive fact that the existence of the pair of opposites formed by sadism and masochism cannot be attributed merely to the element of aggressiveness. We should rather be inclined to connect the simultaneous presence of these opposites with the opposing masculinity and femininity which are combined in bisexuality—a contrast which often has to be replaced in psycho-analysis by that between activity and passivity.[34]

(3) The Perversions in General

Variation and Disease: It is natural that medical men, who first studied perversions in outstanding examples and under special conditions, should have been inclined to regard them, like inversion, as indications of degeneracy or disease. Nevertheless, it is even easier to dispose of that view in this case than in that of inversion. Everyday experience has shown that most of these extensions, or at any rate the less

severe of them, are constituents which are rarely absent from the sexual life of healthy people, and are judged by them no differently from other intimate events. If circumstances favour such an occurrence, normal people too can substitute a perversion of this kind for the normal sexual aim for quite a time, or can find place for the one alongside the other. No healthy person, it appears, can fail to make some addition that might be called perverse to the normal sexual aim; and the universality of this finding is in itself enough to show how inappropriate it is to use the word perversion as a term of reproach. In the sphere of sexual life we are brought up against peculiar and, indeed, insoluble difficulties as soon as we try to draw a sharp line to distinguish mere variations within the range of what is physiological from pathological symptoms.

Nevertheless, in some of these perversions the quality of the new sexual aim is of a kind to demand special examination. Certain of them are so far removed from the normal in their content that we cannot avoid pronouncing them 'pathological'. This is especially so where (as, for instance, in cases of licking excrement or of intercourse with dead bodies) the sexual instinct goes to astonishing lengths in successfully overriding the resistances of shame, disgust, horror or pain. But even in such cases we should not be too ready to assume that people who act in this way will necessarily turn out to be insane or subject to grave abnormalities of other kinds. Here again we cannot escape from the fact that people whose behaviour is in other respects normal can, under the domination of the most unruly of all the instincts, put themselves in the category of sick persons in the single sphere of sexual life. On the other hand, manifest abnormality in the other relations of life can invariably be shown to have a background of abnormal sexual conduct.

In the majority of instances the pathological character in a perversion is found to lie not in the *content* of the new sexual aim but in its relation to the normal. If a perversion, instead of appearing merely *alongside* the normal sexual aim and object, and only when circumstances are unfavourable to *them* and favourable to *it*—if, instead of this, it ousts them completely and takes their place in *all* circumstances—if, in short, a perversion has the characteristics of exclusiveness and fixation—then we shall usually be justified in regarding it as a pathological symptom.

The Mental Factor in the Perversions: It is perhaps in connection precisely with the most repulsive perversions that the mental factor must be regarded as playing its largest part in the transformation of the sexual instinct. It is impossible to deny that in their case a piece of mental work has been performed which, in spite of its horrifying result, is the equivalent of an idealization of the instinct. The omnipotence of love is perhaps never more strongly proved than in such of its aberrations as these. The highest and the lowest are always closest to each other in the sphere of sexuality: 'vom Himmel durch die Welt zur Hölle.'[35]

Two Conclusions: Our study of the perversions has shown us that the sexual instinct has to struggle against certain mental forces which act as resistances, and of which shame and disgust are the most prominent. It is permissible to suppose that these forces play a part in restraining that instinct within the limits that are regarded as normal; and if they develop in the individual before the sexual instinct has reached its full strength, it is no doubt they that will determine the course of its development.[36]

In the second place we have found that some of the perversions which we have examined are only made intelligible if we assume the convergence of several motive forces. If such perversions admit of analysis, that is, if they can be taken to pieces, then they must be of a composite nature. This gives us a hint that perhaps the sexual instinct itself may be no simple thing, but put together from components which have come apart again in the perversions. If this is so, the clinical observation of these abnormalities will have drawn our attention to amalgama-

tions which have been lost to view in the uniform behaviour of normal people.[37]

List of Abbreviations

S.E. Standard Ed. = Freud, *Standard Edition* (24 vols.), London, from 1953

Notes

Editor's Note: The notes to Freud's text are preserved from the edition published by Basic Books, 1975, from which the text itself is reprinted.

1. The information contained in this first essay is derived from the well-known writings of Krafft-Ebing, Moll, Moebius, Havelock Ellis, Schrenck-Notzing, Löwenfeld, Eulenburg, Bloch and Hirschfeld, and from the *Jahrbuch für sexuelle Zwischenstufen*, published under the direction of the last-named author. Since full bibliographies of the remaining literature of the subject will be found in the works of these writers, I have been able to spare myself the necessity for giving detailed references. [*Added* 1910:] The data obtained from the psycho-analytic investigation of inverts are based upon material supplied to me by I. Sadger and upon my own findings.

2. [*Footnote added* 1910:] The only appropriate word in the German language, '*Lust*', is unfortunately ambiguous, and is used to denote the experience both of a need and of a gratification. [Unlike the English 'lust' it can mean either 'desire' or 'pleasure'.]

3. [This is no doubt an allusion to the theory expounded by Aristophanes in Plato's *Symposium*. Freud recurred to this much later, at the end of Chapter VI of *Beyond the Pleasure Principle* (1920).]

4. On these difficulties and on the attempts which have been made to arrive at the proportional number of inverts, see Hirschfeld (1904).

5. The fact of a person struggling in this way against a compulsion towards inversion may perhaps determine the possibility of his being influenced by suggestion [*added* 1910:] or psycho-analysis.

6. Many writers have insisted with justice that the dates assigned by inverts themselves for the appearance of their tendency to inversion are untrustworthy, since they may have repressed the evidence of their heterosexual feelings from their memory. [*Added* 1910:] These suspicions have been confirmed by psycho-analysis in those cases of inversion

to which it has had access; it has produced decisive alterations in their anamnesis by filling in their infantile amnesia. [In the first edition (1905) the place of this last sentence was taken by the following one: 'A decision on this point could be arrived at only by a psycho-analytic investigation of inverts.']

7. Moebius (1900) confirms the view that we should be chary in making a diagnosis of degeneracy and that it has very little practical value: 'If we survey the wide field of degeneracy upon which some glimpses of revealing light have been thrown in these pages, it will at once be clear that there is small value in ever making a diagnosis of degeneracy.'

8. It must be allowed that the spokesmen of 'Uranism' are justified in asserting that some of the most prominent men in all recorded history were inverts and perhaps even absolute inverts.

9. The pathological approach to the study of inversion has been displaced by the anthropological. The merit for bringing about this change is due to Bloch (1902–3), who has also laid stress on the occurrence of inversion among the civilizations of antiquity.

10. For the most recent descriptions of somatic hermaphroditism, see Taruffi (1903), and numerous papers by Neugebauer in various volumes of the *Jahrbuch für sexuelle Zwischenstufen.*

11. His paper includes a bibliography of the subject.

12. It appears (from a bibliography given in the sixth volume of the *Jahrbuch für sexuelle Zwischenstufen*) that E. Gley was the first writer to suggest bisexuality as an explanation of inversion. As long ago as in January, 1884, he published a paper, 'Les aberrations de l'instinct sexuel', in the *Revue Philosophique*. It is, moreover, noteworthy that the majority of authors who derive inversion from bisexuality bring forward that factor not only in the case of inverts, but also for all those who have grown up to be normal, and that, as a logical consequence, they regard inversion as the result of a disturbance in development. Chevalier (1893) already writes in this sense. Krafft-Ebing (1895, 10) remarks that there are a great number of observations 'which prove at least the virtual persistence of this second centre (that of the subordinated sex)'. A Dr. Arduin (1900) asserts that 'there are masculine and feminine elements in every human being (cf. Hirschfeld, 1899); but one set of these—according to the sex of the person in question—is incomparably more strongly developed than the other, so far as heterosexual individuals are concerned. . . .' Herman (1903) is convinced that

'masculine elements and characteristics are present in every woman and feminine ones in every man', etc. [*Added* 1910:] Fliess (1906) subsequently claimed the idea of bisexuality (in the sense of *duality of sex*) as his own. [*Added* 1924:] In lay circles the hypothesis of human bisexuality is regarded as being due to O. Weininger, the philosopher, who died at an early age, and who made the idea the basis of a somewhat unbalanced book (1903). The particulars which I have enumerated above will be sufficient to show how little justification there is for the claim.

[Freud's own realization of the importance of bisexuality owed much to Fliess (cf. p. 86 *n.*), and his forgetfulness of this fact on one occasion provided him with an example in his *Psychopathology of Everyday Life,* 1901, Chapter VII (11). He did not, however, accept Fliess's view that bisexuality provided the explanation of repression. See Freud's discussion of this in 'A Child is Being Beaten' (1919, half-way through Section VI). The whole question is gone into in detail by Kris in Section IV of his introduction to the Fliess correspondence (Freud, 1950).]

13. [This last sentence was added in 1915.—*Footnote added* 1910:] It is true that psycho-analysis has not yet produced a complete explanation of the origin of inversion; nevertheless, it has discovered the psychical mechanism of its development, and has made essential contributions to the statement of the problems involved. In all the cases we have examined we have established the fact that the future inverts, in the earliest years of their childhood, pass through a phase of very intense but short-lived fixation to a woman (usually their mother), and that, after leaving this behind, they identify themselves with a woman and take *themselves* as their sexual object. That is to say, they proceed from a narcissistic basis, and look for a young man who resembles themselves and whom *they* may love as their mother loved *them*. Moreover, we have frequently found that alleged inverts have been by no means insusceptible to the charms of women, but have continually transposed the excitation aroused by women on to a male object. They have thus repeated all through their lives the mechanism by which their inversion arose. Their compulsive longing for men has turned out to be determined by their ceaseless flight from women.

[At this point the footnote proceeded as follows in the 1910 edition only: 'It must, however, be borne in mind that hitherto only a single type of invert has been submitted to psycho-analysis—persons whose sexual activity is in general stunted and the residue of which is manifested as inversion. The problem of inversion is a highly complex one and includes very various types of sexual activity and development. A strict conceptual distinction should be drawn between different cases of inversion according to whether the sexual character of the *object* or that of the *subject* has been inverted.']

[*Added* 1915:] Psycho-analytic research is most decidedly opposed to any attempt at separating off homosexuals from the rest of mankind as a group of a special character. By studying sexual excitations other than those that are manifestly displayed, it has found that all human beings are capable of making a homosexual object-choice and have in fact made one in their unconscious. Indeed, libidinal attachments to persons of the same sex play no less a part as factors in normal mental life, and a greater part as a motive force for illness, than do similar attachments to the opposite sex. On the contrary, psycho-analysis considers that a choice of an object independently of its sex—freedom to range equally over male and female objects—as it is found in childhood, in primitive states of society and early periods of history, is the original basis from which, as a result of restriction in one direction or the other, both the normal and the inverted types develop. Thus from the point of view of psycho-analysis the exclusive sexual interest felt by men for women is also a problem that needs elucidating and is not a self-evident fact based upon an attraction that is ultimately of a chemical nature. A person's final sexual attitude is not decided until after puberty and is the result of a number of factors, not all of which are yet known; some are of a constitutional nature but others are accidental. No doubt a few of these factors may happen to carry so much weight that they influence the result in their sense. But in general the multiplicity of determining factors is reflected in the variety of manifest sexual attitudes in which they find their issue in mankind. In inverted types, a predominance of archaic constitutions and primitive psychical mechanisms is regularly to be found. Their most essential characteristics seem to be a coming into operation of narcissistic object-choice and a retention of the erotic significance of the anal zone. There is nothing to be gained, however, by separating the most extreme types of inversion from the rest on the basis of constitutional peculiarities of that kind. What we find as an apparently sufficient explanation of these types can be equally shown to be present, though less strongly, in the constitution of transitional types and of those whose manifest attitude is normal. The differences

in the end-products may be of a qualitative nature, but analysis shows that the differences between their determinants are only quantitative. Among the accidental factors that influence object-choice we have found that frustration (in the form of an early deterrence, by fear, from sexual activity) deserves attention, and we have observed that the presence of both parents plays an important part. The absence of a strong father in childhood not infrequently favours the occurrence of inversion. Finally, it may be insisted that the concept of inversion in respect of the sexual object should be sharply distinguished from that of the occurrence in the subject of a mixture of sexual characters. In the relation between these two factors, too, a certain degree of reciprocal independence is unmistakably present.

[*Added* 1920:] Ferenczi (1914) has brought forward a number of interesting points on the subject of inversion. He rightly protests that, because they have in common the symptom of inversion, a large number of conditions, which are very different from one another and which are of unequal importance both in organic and psychical respects, have been thrown together under the name of 'homosexuality' (or, to follow him in giving it a better name, 'homo-erotism'). He insists that a sharp distinction should at least be made between two types: 'subject homo-erotics', who feel and behave like women, and 'object homo-erotics', who are completely masculine and who have merely exchanged a female for a male object. The first of these two types he recognizes as true 'sexual intermediates' in Hirschfeld's sense of the word; the second he describes, less happily, as obsessional neurotics. According to him, it is only in the case of object homo-erotics that there is any question of their struggling against their inclination to inversion or of the possibility of their being influenced psychologically. While granting the existence of these two types, we may add that there are many people in whom a certain quantity of subject homo-erotism is found in combination with a proportion of object homo-erotism.

During the last few years work carried out by biologists, notably by Steinach, has thrown a strong light on the organic determinants of homo-erotism and of sexual characters in general. By carrying out experimental castration and subsequently grafting the sex-glands of the opposite sex, it was possible in the case of various species of mammals to transform a male into a female and vice versa. The transformation affected more or less completely both the somatic sexual characters and the psychosexual attitude (that is, both subject and object erotism). It appeared that the vehicle of the force which thus acted as a sex-determinant was not the part of the sex-gland which forms the sex-cells but what is known as its interstitial tissue (the 'puberty-gland'). In one case this transformation of sex was actually effected in a man who had lost his testes owing to tuberculosis. In his sexual life he behaved in a feminine manner, as a passive homosexual, and exhibited very clearly-marked feminine sexual characters of a secondary kind (e.g. in regard to growth of hair and beard and deposits of fat on the breasts and hips). After an undescended testis from another male patient had been grafted into him, he began to behave in a masculine manner and to direct his libido towards women in a normal way. Simultaneously his somatic feminine characters disappeared. (Lipschütz, 1919, 356–7.)

It would be unjustifiable to assert that these interesting experiments put the theory of inversion on a new basis, and it would be hasty to expect them to offer a universal means of 'curing' homosexuality. Fliess has rightly insisted that these experimental findings do not invalidate the theory of the general bisexual disposition of the higher animals. On the contrary, it seems to me probable that further research of a similar kind will produce a direct confirmation of this presumption of bisexuality.

14. [*Footnote added* 1910:] The most striking distinction between the erotic life of antiquity and our own no doubt lies in the fact that the ancients laid the stress upon the instinct itself, whereas we emphasize its object. The ancients glorified the instinct and were prepared on its account to honour even an inferior object; while we despise the instinctual activity in itself, and find excuses for it only in the merits of the object.

15. In this connection I cannot help recalling the credulous submissiveness shown by a hypnotized subject towards his hypnotist. This leads me to suspect that the essence of hypnosis lies in an unconscious fixation of the subject's libido to the figure of the hypnotist, through the medium of the masochistic components of the sexual instinct. [*Added* 1910:] Ferenczi (1909) has brought this characteristic of suggestibility into relation with the 'parental complex'.—[The relation of the subject to the hypnotist was discussed by Freud much later, in Chapter VIII of his *Group Psychology* (1921). See also 1905, *S.E.*, 7, 294 ff.]

16. [In the editions earlier than 1920 this paragraph ended with the further sentence: 'The emergence of these extremely various anatomical extensions clearly implies a need for variation, and this has been described by Hoche as "craving for stimulation".' The first two sentences of the footnote which follows were added in 1915, before which date it had begun with the sentence: 'Further consideration leads me to conclude that I. Bloch has overestimated the theoretical importance of the factor of craving for stimulation.' The whole footnote and the paragraph in the text above were recast in their present form in 1920:] It must be pointed out, however, that sexual overvaluation is not developed in the case of *every* mechanism of object-choice. We shall become acquainted later on with another and more direct explanation of the sexual role assumed by the other parts of the body. The factor of 'craving for stimulation' has been put forward by Hoche and Bloch as an explanation of the extension of sexual interest to parts of the body other than the genitals; but it does not seem to me to deserve such an important place. The various channels along which the libido passes are related to each other from the very first like inter-communicating pipes, and we must take the phenomenon of collateral flow into account.

17. [*Footnote added* 1920:] In typical cases women fail to exhibit any sexual overvaluation towards men; but they scarcely ever fail to do so towards their own children.

18. [*Footnote added* 1915:] This weakness would represent the *constitutional* precondition. Psycho-analysis has found that the phenomenon can also be *accidentally* determined, by the occurrence of an early deterrence from sexual activity owing to fear, which may divert the subject from the normal sexual aim and encourage him to seek a substitute for it.

19. [*Get me a kerchief from her breast*
  A garter that her knee has pressed.
Goethe, *Faust*, Part I, Scene 7. (*Trans.* Bayard Taylor.)]

20. [*Footnote added* 1920:] Deeper-going psycho-analytic research has raised a just criticism of Binet's assertion. All the observations dealing with this point have recorded a first meeting with the fetish at which it already aroused sexual interest without there being anything in the accompanying circumstances to explain the fact. Moreover, all of these 'early' sexual impressions relate to a time after the age of five or six, whereas psycho-analysis makes it doubtful whether fresh pathological fixations can occur so late as this. The true explanation is that behind the first recollection of the fetish's appearance there lies a submerged and forgotten phase of sexual

development. The fetish, like a 'screen-memory', represents this phase and is thus a remnant and precipitate of it. The fact that this early infantile phase turns in the direction of fetishism, as well as the choice of the fetish itself, are constitutionally determined.

21. [*Footnote added* 1910:] The shoe or slipper is a corresponding symbol of the *female* genitals.

22. [*Footnote added* 1910:] Psycho-analysis has cleared up one of the remaining gaps in our understanding of fetishism. It has shown the importance, as regards the choice of a fetish, of a coprophilic pleasure in smelling which has disappeared owing to repression. Both the feet and the hair are objects with a strong smell which have been exalted into fetishes after the olfactory sensation has become unpleasurable and been abandoned. Accordingly, in the perversion that corresponds to foot-fetishism, it is only dirty and evil-smelling feet that become sexual objects. Another factor that helps towards explaining the fetishistic preference for the foot is to be found among the sexual theories of children (see below p. 61): the foot represents a woman's penis, the absence of which is deeply felt. [*Added* 1915:] In a number of cases of foot-fetishism it has been possible to show that the scopophilic instinct, seeking to reach its object (originally the genitals) from underneath, was brought to a halt in its pathway by prohibition and repression. For that reason it became attached to a fetish in the form of a foot or shoe, the female genitals (in accordance with the expectations of childhood) being imagined as male ones.—[The importance of the repression of pleasure in smell had been indicated by Freud in two letters to Fliess of January 11 and November 14, 1897 (Freud, 1950, Letters 55 and 75). He returned to the subject at the end of his analysis of the 'Rat Man' (Freud, 1909), and discussed it at considerable length in two long footnotes to Chapter IV of *Civilization and its Discontents* (1930*a*). The topic of fetishism was further considered in Freud's paper on that subject (1927) and again still later in a posthumously published fragment on the splitting of the ego (1940*b* [1938]) and at the end of Chapter VIII of his *Outline of Psycho-Analysis* (1940*a* [1938]).]

23. [The words in this parenthesis were added in 1915.]

24. [This seems to be Freud's first published use of the term 'sublimate', though it occurs as early as May 2, 1897, in the Fliess correspondence (Freud, 1950*a*, Letter 61). It also appears in the 'Dora' case history, 1905*e*, actually published later than the present work (*S.E.*, 7, pp. 50 and 116) though drafted in 1901. The concept is further discussed below on p. 44.—*Footnote added* 1915:] There is to my mind no doubt that the concept of 'beautiful' has its roots in sexual excitation and that its original meaning was 'sexually stimulating'. [There is an allusion in the original to the fact that the German word '*Reiz*' is commonly used both as the technical term for 'stimulus' and, in ordinary language, as an equivalent to the English 'charm' or 'attraction'.] This is related to the fact that we never regard the genitals themselves, which produce the strongest sexual excitation, as really 'beautiful'.

25. [In the editions before 1924 this read 'of a single analysis'.]

26. [*Footnote added* 1920:] Under analysis, these perversions—and indeed most others—reveal a surprising variety of motives and determinants. The compulsion to exhibit, for instance, is also closely dependent on the castration complex: it is a means of constantly insisting upon the integrity of the subject's own (male) genitals and it reiterates his infantile satisfaction at the absence of a penis in those of women.

27. [In the editions of 1905 and 1910 the following two sentences appeared in the text at this point: 'One at least of the roots of masochism can be inferred with equal certainty. It arises from sexual overvaluation as a necessary psychical consequence of the choice of a sexual object.' From 1915 onwards these sentences were omitted and the next two paragraphs were inserted in their place.]

28. [*Footnote added* 1924:] My opinion of masochism has been to a large extent altered by later reflection, based upon certain hypotheses as to the structure of the apparatus of the mind and the classes of instincts operating in it. I have been led to distinguish a primary or *erotogenic* masochism, out of which two later forms, *feminine* and *moral* masochism, have developed. Sadism which cannot find employment in actual life is turned round upon the subject's own self and so produces a *secondary* masochism, which is superadded to the primary kind. (Cf. Freud, 1924*c*.)

29. [This short paragraph was in the first edition (1905), but the last two, as well as the next one, were only added in 1915.]

30. [*Footnote added* 1915:] Cf. my remarks below [p. 64] on the pregenital phases of sexual development, which confirm this view.

31. [*Footnote added* 1924:] The enquiry mentioned above [in footnote 2 on p. 24] has led me to assign a peculiar position, based upon the origin of the instincts, to the pair of opposites constituted by sadism and masochism, and to place them outside the class of the remaining 'perversions'.

32. Instead of multiplying the evidence for this statement, I will quote a passage from Havelock Ellis (1913, 119): 'The investigation of histories of sadism and masochism, even those given by Krafft-Ebing (as indeed Colin Scott and Féré have already pointed out), constantly reveals traces of both groups of phenomena in the same individual.'

33. [*Footnote added* 1915:] Cf. my discussion of 'ambivalence' below.

34. [The last clause did not occur in the 1905 or 1910 editions. In 1915 the following clause was added: 'a contrast whose significance is reduced in psycho-analysis to that between activity and passivity.' This was replaced in 1924 by the words now appearing in the text.]

35. ['From Heaven, across the world, to Hell.'

Goethe, *Faust*, Prelude in the Theatre. (*Trans.* Bayard Taylor.) In a letter to Fliess of January 3, 1897 (Freud 1950a, Letter 54), Freud suggests the use of this same quotation as the motto for a chapter on 'Sexuality' in a projected volume. This letter was written at a time when he was beginning to turn his attention to the perversions. His first reference to them in the Fliess correspondence dates from January 1, 1896 (Draft K).]

36. [*Footnote added* 1915:] On the other hand, these forces which act like dams upon sexual development—disgust, shame and morality—must also be regarded as historical precipitates of the external inhibitions to which the sexual instinct has been subjected during the psychogenesis of the human race. We can observe the way in which, in the development of individuals, they arise at the appropriate moment, as though spontaneously, when upbringing and external influence give the signal.

37. [*Footnote added* 1920:] As regards the origin of the perversions, I will add a word in anticipation of what is to come. There is reason to suppose that, just as in the case of fetishism, abortive beginnings of normal sexual development occur before the perversions become fixated. Analytic investigation has already been able to show in a few cases that perversions are a residue of development towards the Oedipus complex and that after the repression of that complex the components of the sexual instinct

which are strongest in the disposition of the individual concerned emerge once more.

Bibliography

Arduin (1900) 'Die Frauenfrage und die sexuellen Zwischenstufen', *Jb. sex. Zwischenst.*, **2**. (9)

Binet, A. (1888) *Études de psychologie expérimentale: le fétichisme dans l'amour*, Paris. (20, 37)

Bloch, I. (1902–3) *Beiträge zur Ätiologie der Psychopathia sexualis* (2 vols.), Dresden. (5)

Ellis, Havelock (1910) *Studies in the Psychology of Sex*, Vol. I: *The Evolution of Modesty; the Phenomena of Sexual Periodicity; and Auto-erotism*, 3rd ed., Philadelphia. (1st ed., 'Leipzig' [London], 1899.) (47)

———. (1913) *Studies in the Psychology of Sex*, Vol. III: *Analysis of the Sexual Impulse; Love and Pain; the Sexual Impulse in Women*, 2nd ed., Philadelphia. (1st ed., Philadelphia. 1903.) (25, 39–40, 56, 89)

———. (1915) *Studies in the Psychology of Sex*, Vol. II: *Sexual Inversion*, 3rd ed., Philadelphia. (1st Engl. ed., London, 1897.) (6, 8)

Ferenczi, S. (1909) 'Introjektion und Übertragung', *Jb. psychoanal. psychopath. Forsch.*, **1**, 422. (16) [*Trans.:* 'Introjection and Transference', *First Contributions to Psycho-Analysis*, London, 1952, Chap. II.]

———. (1914) 'Zur Nosologie der männlichen Homosexualität (Homoërotik)', *Int. Z. Psychoanal.*, **2**, 131 (12) [*Trans.:* 'The Nosology of Male Homosexuality (Homoerotism)', *First Contributions to Psycho-Analysis*, London, 1952, Chap. XII.]

Fliess, W. (1906) *Der Ablauf des Lebens*, Vienna. (9)

Freud, S. (1901) *Zur Psychopathologie des Alltagslebens*, Berlin. (*G.S.*, **4**; *G.W.*, 4.) (xiii, 9, 41, 112) [*Trans.: The Psychopathology of Everyday Life, Standard, Ed.*, **6**.]

———. (1905) 'Psychische Behandlung (Seelenbehandlung)', *G.W.*, 5, 289 (16)

———. (1905) 'Bruchstück einer Hysterie-Analyse', *G.S.*, 8, 3; *G.W.*, 5, 163. (xiii, 22, 29, 31, 33) [*Trans.:* 'Fragment of an Analysis of a Case of Hysteria', *C.P.*, 3, 13; *Standard Ed.*, 7, 3.]

———. (1909) 'Bemerkungen über einen Fall von Zwangsneurose, *G.S.*, **8**, 269; *G.W.*, 7, 381. (21, 92) [*Trans.:* 'Notes on a Case of Obsessional Neurosis', *C.P.*, 3, 293; *Standard Ed.*, 10, 155.]

———. (1919) '"Ein Kind wird geschlagen"', *G.S.*, 5, 344; *G.W.*, 12, 197. (9) [*Trans.:* '"A Child is being Beaten'", *C.P.*, **2**, 172; *Standard Ed.*, **17**, 177.]

————. (1920) *Jenseits des Lustprinzips*, Vienna. (*G.S.*, **6**, 191; *G.W.*, **13**, 3.) (2, 34) [*Trans.: Beyond the Pleasure Principle, Standard Ed.*, **18**, 3; *I.P.L.*, **4**.]

————. (1921) *Massenpsychologie und Ich-Analyse*, Vienna. (*G.S.*, 6, 261; [*G.W.*, **13**, 73.) (16) [*Trans.: Group Psychology and the Analysis of the Ego, Standard Ed.*, **18**, 67; *I.P.L.*, **6**.]

————. (1924) 'Das ökonomische Problem des Masochismus', *G.S.*, **5**, 374; *G.W.*, **13**, 371. (24, 71, 75) [*Trans.:* 'The Economic Problem of Masochism', *C.P.*, **2**, 255; *Standard Ed.*, **19**, 157.]

————. (1927) 'Fetischismus', *G.S.*, **11**, 395; *G.W.*, **14**, 311. (21) [*Trans.:* 'Fetishism', *C.P.*, **5**, 198; *Standard Ed.*, **21**, 149.]

————. (1930) *Das Unbehagen in der Kultur*, Vienna. (*G.S.*, **12**, 29; *G.W.*, **14**, 421.) (21, 86, 112) [*Trans.: Civilization and its Discontents*, London, 1930; New York, 1961; *Standard Ed.*, **21**, 59.]

————. (1940 [1938]) *Abriss der Psychoanalyse*, *G.W.*, **17**, 67. (21) [*Trans.: An Outline of Psycho-Analysis*, London and New York, 1949; *Standard Ed.*, **23**.]

————. (1940 [1938]) 'Die Ichspaltung im Abwehrvorgang', *G.W.*, **17**, 59. (21) [*Trans.:* 'Splitting of the Ego in the Process of Defence', *C.P.* **5**, 372; *Standard Ed.*, **23**.]

————. (1950 [1887–1902]) *Aus den Anfängen der Psychoanalyse*, London. Includes 'Entwurf einer Psychologie' (1895). (x–xiii, 9, 22, 28, 31, 33, 50–1, 82, 91, 101, 102) [*Trans.: The Origins of Psycho-Analysis*, London and New York, 1954. (Partly, including 'A Project for a Scientific Psychology', in *Standard Ed.*, **1**.)]

Gley, E. (1884) 'Les aberrations de l'instinct sexuel', *Revue philosophique*, **17**, 66. (9)

Halban, J. (1903) 'Die Entstehung der Geschlechtscharaktere', *Arch. Gynaek.*, **70**, 205. (8)

Herman, G. (1903) *'Genesis', das Gesetz der Zeugung*, Bd. 5, *Libido und Mania*, Leipzig. (9)

Hirschfeld, M. (1899) 'Die objecktive Diagnose der Homosexualität', *Jb. sex. Zwischenst.*, **1**, 8. (9)

————. (1904) 'Statistiche Untersuchungen über den Prozentsatz der Homosexuellen', *Jb. sex. Zwischenst.*, **6**. (2)

Lipschütz, A. (1919) *Die Pubertätsdrüse und ihre Wirkungen*, Bern. (13, 43, 81)

Lydston, G. F. (1889) *Philadelphia Med. Surg. Rep.*, Sept. 7. (7)

Moebius, P. J. (1900) 'Über Entartung', *Grenzfr. Nerv.-u. Seelenleb.*, **3**. (4)

Moll, A. (1898) *Untersuchungen über die Libido sexualis*, Bd. I, Berlin. (35, 46)

————. (1909) *Das Sexualleben des Kindes*. Berlin. (39–40, 46)

Schrenck-Notzing, A. von (1899) 'Literaturzusammenstellung über die Psychologie und Psychopathologie der Vita sexualis', *Z. Hypnot.*, **9**, Heft 2, 98. (23)

Taruffi, C. (1903) *Hermaphroditismus und Zeugungsunfähigkeit* (German trans. by R. Teuscher), Berlin. (7)

The Content of Consciousness as Ideology

V. N. Vološinov

We know that Freudianism began from a position of distrust of the conscious and fundamental criticism of motives such as those a person is likely, in all honesty and sincerity, to use as explanations for and commentary on his behavior (let us recall Bernheim's experiment). Consciousness is in fact *that commentary* which every adult human being brings to bear on every instance of his behavior. According to Freud, this commentary is invalid; any psychology that takes such commentary as its basis is likewise invalid.

Wherever Freud criticizes the psychology of consciousness, we can join in full accord with him. A person's conscious motivation of his actions is certainly in no instance to be taken as a scientific explanation of his behavior. But we go further than that. Neither do the motives of the unconscious explain his behavior in the least, for, as we have seen, the Freudian unconscious does not fundamentally differ from consciousness; it is only another form of consciousness, only an ideologically different expression of it.

The motives of the unconscious that are disclosed at psychoanalytical sessions with the aid of "free association" are just such *verbal reactions* on the patient's part as are all other, ordinary motives of consciousness. They differ from the latter not in kind of "being," that is, not ontologically, but only in terms of content, that is, *ideologically*. In this sense Freud's unconscious can be called the "unofficial conscious" in distinction from the ordinary "official conscious."

From the objective point of view, both sets of motives, those of the unofficial as well as of the official conscious, are given completely alike in inner and in outward speech and both alike are not a cause of behavior but a component, an integral part of it. For objective psychology, every human motive belongs to human behavior as a part of it and not a cause of it. Human behavior may be said to break down into motor reactions ("acts" in the narrow sense of the word) and reactions of *inner and outward speech* (verbal reactions) that accompany motor reactions. Both these components of the whole of human behavior are objective and material in nature and require for their explanation factors that are likewise objective and material with respect both to the human organism itself and to the surrounding natural and social environment.

The verbal component of behavior is determined in all the fundamentals and essentials of its content by objective-social factors.

The social environment is what has given a person words and what has joined words with specific meanings and value judgements; the same environment continues ceaselessly to determine and control a person's verbal reactions throughout his entire life.

Therefore, nothing verbal in human behavior (inner and outward speech equally) can under any circumstances be reckoned to the account of the individual subject in isolation; the verbal is not his property but the property of his *social group* (his social milieu).

In the preceding chapter we pointed out that every concrete utterance always reflects the *immediate* small social event—the event of communication, of exchange of words between persons—out of which it directly arose. We saw that Freud's "dynamics" reflected the psychoanalytical session with its struggle and peripeteia—that social event out of which the patient's verbal utterances were engendered. In the present chapter what interests us is not the immediate context of utterance but the broader, more enduring and steadfast social connections out of whose dynamics are generated all elements of the form and content of our inner and outward speech, the whole repertoire of value judgements, points of view, approaches, and so on with the help of which we illuminate for ourselves and for others our actions, desires, feelings, and sensations.

This content of our consciousness and of our psyche in its entirety and, likewise, the separate and individual utterances with the help of which that content and that psyche manifest themselves outwardly are in every respect determined by socioeconomic factors.

We shall never reach the real, substantive roots of any given single utterance if we look for them within the confines of the single, individual organism, even when that utterance concerns what appears to be the most private and most intimate side of a person's life. Any motivation of one's behavior, any instance of self-awareness (for self-awareness is always verbal, always a matter of finding some specifically suitable verbal complex) is an act of gauging oneself against some social norm, social evaluation—is, so to speak, the socialization of oneself and one's behavior. In becoming aware of myself, I attempt to look at myself, as it were, through the eyes of another person, another representative of my social group, my class. Thus, *self-consciousness,* in the final analysis, always leads us to *class consciousness,* the reflection and specification of which it is in all its fundamental and essential respects. Here we

have the *objective roots* of even the most personal and intimate reactions.

How do we reach those roots?

With the help of those objective-sociological methods that Marxism has worked out for the analysis of various ideological systems—law, morality, science, world outlook, art, religion.

In bourgeois philosophy the contention has long held sway, and is even now quite widespread, that a work of cultural creativity can be considered fully explained if the analyst succeeds in reducing it to the specific individual states of mind and psychical experiences of the person who created it. This contention, as we have seen, is upheld by the Freudians, as well. But in actual fact there is no fundamental dividing line between the content of the individual psyche and formulated ideology. In any case, the content of the individual psyche is not the least bit easier to understand or clearer than the content of cultural creativity and, therefore, cannot serve as explication for it. An experience of which an individual is conscious is already ideological and, therefore, from a scientific point of view, can in no way be a primary and irreducible datum; rather, it is an entity that has already undergone ideological processing of some specific kind. The haziest content of consciousness of the primitive savage and the most sophisticated cultural monument are only extreme links in the single chain of ideological creativity. Between them exists a whole unbroken series of degrees and transitions.

The more clarified a thought of mine becomes, the closer it will approach the formulated products of scientific creativity. What is more, my thought will be able to achieve final clarity only when I find exact verbal formulation for it and bring it into contact with scientific postulations that have a bearing on the same topic—in other words, my thought will not achieve final clarity until I transform it into an authoritative scientific product. Similarly, a feeling cannot achieve culmination and definitiveness without finding its external expression, without nurturing itself on words, rhythm, color, that is, without being forged into a work of art.

The route leading from the content of the individual psyche to the content of culture is a long and hard one, but it is a single route, and throughout its entire extent at every stage it is determined by one and the same socioeconomic governance.

At all stages of this route the human consciousness operates through words—that medium which is the most sensitive and at the same time the most complicated refraction of the socioeconomic governance. For the study of verbal reactions in their most primitive, pragmatic form, the same methods must be used as Marxism has worked out for the study of complex ideological constructs, since the laws of the refraction of objective necessity in verbal discourse are one and the same in both instances.

Any human verbal utterance is an ideological construct in the small. The motivation of one's behavior is juridical and moral creativity on a small scale; an exclamation of joy or grief is a primitive lyric composition; pragmatic considerations of the causes and consequences of happenings are germinal forms of scientific and philosophical cognition, and so on and so forth. The stable, formulated ideological systems of the sciences, the arts, jurisprudence, and the like have sprung and crystallized from that seething ideological element whose broad waves of inner and outward speech engulf our every act and our every perception. Of course, an ideology, once it has achieved formulation, exerts, in turn, a reverse influence on our verbal reactions.

Let us call that inner and outward speech that permeates our behavior in all its aspects "behavioral ideology." This behavioral ideology is in certain respects more sensitive, more responsive, more excitable and livelier than an ideology that has undergone formulation and become "official." In the depths of behavioral ideology accumulate those contradictions which, once having reached a certain threshold, ultimately burst asunder the system of the official ideology. But, on the whole, we may say that behavioral ideology relates just as much to the socioeconomic basis and is subject to the same laws of development as ideological superstruc-

tures in the proper sense of the term. Therefore, the methods for its study should be, as already stated, basically the same methods, only somewhat differentiated and modified in accordance with the special nature of the material.

Let us now return to those "psychical" conflicts upon which psychoanalysis is based and which psychoanalysis attempts to explain in terms of a struggle between the conscious and the unconscious. From an objective point of view, all these conflicts are played out in the element of inner and outward speech (in addition, of course, to their purely physiological aspect), that is to say, they are played out in the element of behavioral ideology. They are not "psychical" but ideological conflicts and, therefore, they cannot be understood within the narrow confines of the individual organism and the individual psyche. They not only go beyond the conscious, as Freud believes, they also go beyond the individual as a whole.

Dream, myth, joke, witticism, and all the verbal components of the pathological formations reflect the struggle of various ideological tendencies and trends that take shape within *behavioral ideology.*

Those areas of behavioral ideology that correspond to Freud's official, "censored" conscious express the most steadfast and the governing factors of class consciousness. They lie close to the formulated, fully fledged ideology of the class in question, its law, its morality, its world outlook. On these levels of behavioral ideology, inner speech comes easily to order and freely turns into outward speech or, in any case, has no fear of becoming outward speech.

Other levels, corresponding to Freud's unconscious, lie at a great distance from the stable system of the ruling ideology. They bespeak the disintegration of the unity and integrity of the system, the vulnerability of the usual ideological motivations. Of course, instances of the accumulation of such inner motives—ones that erode the unity of behavioral ideology—can bear an incidental character and testify merely to the *assumption of a social déclassé status* on the part of separate individuals, but more often they testify to the emergent disintegration if not of the class as a whole then of certain of its groups. *In a healthy community and in a socially healthy personality, behavioral ideology, founded on the socioeconomic basis, is strong and sound—* here, there is no discrepancy between the official and the unofficial conscious.

The content and composition of the unofficial levels of behavioral ideology (in Freudian terms, the content and composition of the unconscious) are conditioned by historical time and class to the same degree as are its levels "under censorship" and its systems of formulated ideology (morality, law, world outlook). For example, the homosexual inclinations of an ancient Hellene of the ruling class produced absolutely no conflicts in his behavioral ideology; they freely emerged into outward speech and even found formulated ideological expression (e.g., Plato's *Symposium*).

All those conflicts with which psychoanalysis deals are characteristic in the highest degree for the European petite bourgeoisie of modern times. Freud's "censorship" very distinctly reflects the behavioral-ideological point of view of a petit bourgeois, and for that reason a somewhat comical effect is produced when Freudians transfer that point of view to the psyche of an ancient Greek or a medieval peasant. The monstrous overestimation on Freudianism's part of the sexual factor is also exceedingly revealing against the background of the present disintegration of the bourgeois family.

The wider and deeper the breach between the official and the unofficial conscious, the more difficult it becomes for motives of inner speech to turn into outward speech (oral or written or printed, in a circumscribed or broad social milieu) wherein they might acquire formulation, clarity, and rigor. Motives under these conditions begin to fail, to lose their verbal countenance, and little by little really do turn into a "foreign body" in the psyche. Whole sets of organic manifestations come, in this way, to be excluded from the zone of verbalized behavior and may become *asocial.* Thereby the sphere of the "animalian" in man enlarges.

Of course, not every area of human behavior is subject to so complete a divorce from verbal

ideological formulation. After all, neither is it true that every motive in contradiction with the official ideology must degenerate into indistinct inner speech and then die out—it might well engage in a struggle with that official ideology. If such a motive *is founded on the economic being of the whole group,* if it is not merely the motive of a déclassé loner, then it has a chance for a future and perhaps even a victorious future. There is no reason why such a motive should become asocial and lose contact with communication. Only, at first a motive of this sort will develop within a small social milieu and will depart into the underground—not the psychological underground of repressed complexes, but the salutary political underground. That is exactly how a *revolutionary ideology* in all spheres of culture comes about.

There is one other extremely important area of human behavior in which verbal connections are put in order with great difficulty and which, therefore, is especially liable to fall out of social context, lose its ideological formulatedness, and degenerate into an aboriginal, animalian state. This is the area of *the sexual.* The disintegration of an official ideology is reflected first and foremost in this area of human behavior. It becomes the center for the accumulation of asocial and antisocial forces.

This area of human private life is preeminently the one most easily made the base for social deviations. The sexual "pair," as a sort of *social minimum,* is most easily isolated and transformed into a microcosm without the need for anything or anybody else.

All periods of social decline and disintegration are characterized by *overestimation of the sexual* in life and in ideology, and what is more, of the sexual in an extreme unidimensional conception; its *asocial* aspect, taken in isolation, is advanced to the forefront. The sexual aims at becoming a surrogate for the social. All human beings are divided above all into males and females. All the remaining subdivisions are held to be inessential. Only those social relations that can be sexualized are meaningful and valuable. Everything else becomes null and void.

The present day success of Freudianism throughout Europe bespeaks the complete disintegration of the *official ideological system*. A "behavioral ideology" has supervened that is turned in upon itself, disjointed, unformulated. Each aspect of life, each happening and object, goes out of kilter with a smoothly operating and universally respected context of *class and social values*. Each thing, as it were, turns its sexual, not its social, side to the human gaze. Behind every word in a poetic or philosophical text glares some stark sexual symbol. All other aspects of words, and especially the social-historical values inherent in them, cease to be heard by a modern European bourgeois—they have become merely overtones to the basic note of sexuality.

An extremely indicative and immensely interesting feature of Freudianism is its *wholesale sexualization of the family* and all family relationships in toto (the Oedipus complex). The family, that castle and keep of capitalism, evidently has become a thing economically and socially little understood and little taken to heart; and that is what has brought on its wholesale sexualization, as if thereby it were made newly meaningful or "made strange" as our formalists would say.[1] The Oedipus complex is indeed a magnificent way of making the family unit "strange." The father is not the entrepreneur, and the son is not his heir—the father is only the mother's lover, and his son is his rival!

Precisely this novel and piquant "meaningfulness," imparted to all those aspects of life that have lost their meaning, is what has attracted so broad a public to Freudianism. The obviousness and certitude of sexual drives contrast here with the ambiguity and uncertainty of all other social ideological values. Sexuality is declared the supreme criterion of *reality*, of *essentiality*. And the more déclassé a person is, the more keenly he senses his "naked naturalness," his "elementalness."

Freudianism—the psychology of the déclassés—is becoming the acknowledged ideological persuasion of the widest strata of the European bourgeoisie. Here is a fact profoundly symptomatic and indicative for anybody who wishes to grasp the spirit of Europe today.

The basic aspiration of the philosophy of our time is *to create a world beyond the social and the historical*. The "cosmism" of Steiner's anthroposophy, the "biologism" of Bergson, and, finally, the "psychobiologism" and "sexualism" of Freud that we have examined here—all these three trends, sharing the entire bourgeois world among them, have, each in its own way, served the aspiration of the latest philosophy. They have endowed with their own features the physiognomy of the modern *Kulturmensch*—the Steinerian, the Bergsonian, the Freudian—and they have raised the *three altars* of his belief and veneration—*Magic, Instinct* and *Sex*. Where the creative paths of history are closed, there remain only the blind alleys of the individual "livings out" of a life bereft of meaning.

Notes

1. "Making strange" (*ostranenie*) is a verbal device whereby an ordinary and familiar thing is made to appear new and strange. [On the Russian formalist notion of *ostranenie*, see V. Erlich, *Russian Formalism (History-Doctrine)* (The Hague, 1955) pp. 150–151; on the formalists and Vološinov's position in their regard, see pp. 96–97 of V. N. Vološinov, *Marxism and the Philosophy of Language*. Trans. L. Matejka and I. R. Titunik (Cambridge, Mass: Harvard University Press 1986) and Appendix 2 in V. N. Vološinov, *Marxism and the Philosophy of Language* (New York and London; Seminar Press 1973), especially pp. 175–180. *Translator*]

Surplus Repression

Herbert Marcuse

. . . The reality principle sustains the organism in the external world. In the case of the human organism, this is an *historical* world. The external world faced by the growing ego is at any stage a specific socio-historical organization of reality, affecting the mental structure through specific societal agencies or agents. It has been argued that Freud's concept *reality principle* obliterates this fact by making historical contingencies into biological necessities: his analysis of the repressive transformation of the instincts under the impact of the reality principle generalizes from a specific historical form of reality to reality pure and simple. This criticism is valid, but its validity does not vitiate the truth in Freud's generalization, namely, that a repressive organization of the instincts underlies *all* historical forms of the reality principle in civilization. If he justifies the repressive organization of the instincts by the irreconcilability between the primary pleasure principle and the reality principle, he expresses the historical fact that civilization has progressed as organized *domination*. This awareness guides his entire phylogenetic construction, which derives civilization from the replacement of the patriarchal despotism of the primal horde by the internalized despotism of the brother clan. Precisely because all civilization has been organized domination, the historical development assumes the dignity and necessity of a universal biological development. The "unhistorical" character of the Freudian concepts thus contains the elements of its opposite: their historical substance must be recaptured, not by adding some sociological factors (as do the "cultural" Neo-Freudian schools), but by unfolding their own content. In this sense, our subsequent discussion is an "extrapolation," which derives from Freud's theory notions and propositions implied in it only in a reified form, in which historical processes appear as natural (biological) processes.

Terminologically, this extrapolation calls for a duplication of concepts: the Freudian terms, which do not adequately differentiate between the biological *and* the socio-historical vicissitudes of the instincts, must be paired with corresponding terms denoting the specific socio-historical component. Presently we shall introduce two such terms:

a. *Surplus-repression:* the restrictions necessitated by social domination. This is distinguished from (basic) *repression:* the "modifications" of the instincts necessary for the perpetuation of the human race in civilization.

b. *Performance principle:* the prevailing historical form of the *reality principle.*

Behind the reality principle lies the fundamental fact of Ananke or scarcity (*Lebensnot*), which means that the struggle for existence takes place in a world too poor for the satisfaction of human needs without constant restraint, renunciation, delay. In other words, whatever satisfaction is possible necessitates *work,* more or less painful arrangements and undertakings for the procurement of the means for satisfying needs. For the duration of work, which occupies practically the entire existence of the mature individual, pleasure is "suspended" and pain prevails. And since the basic instincts strive for the prevalence of pleasure and for the absence of pain, the pleasure principle is incompatible with reality, and the instincts have to undergo a repressive regimentation.

However, this argument, which looms large in Freud's metapsychology, is fallacious in so far as it applies to the brute *fact* of scarcity what actually is the consequence of a specific *organization* of scarcity, and of a specific existential attitude enforced by this organization. The prevalent scarcity has, throughout civilization (although in very different modes), been organized in such a way that it has not been distributed collectively in accordance with individual needs, nor has the procurement of goods for the satisfaction of needs been organized with the objective of best satisfying the developing needs of the individuals. Instead, the *distribution* of scarcity as well as the effort of overcoming it, the mode of work, have been *imposed* upon individuals—first by mere violence, subsequently by a more rational utilization of power. However, no matter how useful this rationality was for the progress of the whole, it remained the rationality of *domination,* and the gradual conquest of scarcity was inextricably bound up with and shaped by the interest of domination. Domination differs from rational exercise of authority. The latter, which is inherent in any societal division of labor, is derived from knowledge and confined to the administration of functions and arrangements necessary for the advancement of the whole. In contrast, domination is exercised by a particular group or individual in order to sustain and enhance itself in a privileged position. Such domination does not exclude technical, material, and intellectual progress, but only as an unavoidable by-product while preserving irrational scarcity, want, and constraint.

The various modes of domination (of man and nature) result in various historical forms of the reality principle. For example, a society in which all members normally work for a living requires other modes of repression than a society in which labor is the exclusive province of one specific group. Similarly, repression will be different in scope and degree according to whether social production is oriented on individual consumption or on profit; whether a market economy prevails or a planned economy; whether private or collective property. These differences affect the very content of the reality principle, for every form of the reality principle must be embodied in a system of societal institutions and relations, laws and values which transmit and enforce the required "modification" of the instincts. This "body" of the reality principle is different at the different stages of civilization. Moreover, while any form of the reality principle demands a considerable degree and scope of repressive control over the instincts, the specific historical institutions of the reality principle and the specific interests of domination introduce *additional* controls over and above those indispensable for civilized human association. These additional controls arising from the specific institutions of domination are what we denote as *surplus-repression.*

For example, the modifications and deflections of instinctual energy necessitated by the perpetuation of the monogamic-patriarchal family, or by a hierarchical division of labor, or by public control over the individual's private existence are instances of surplus-repression pertaining to the institutions of a *particular* reality principle. They are added to the basic (phylogenetic) restrictions of the instincts which mark the development of man from the human animal to the *animal sapiens.* The power to restrain and guide instinctual drives, to make biological necessities into individual needs and desires, increases rather than reduces gratification: the "mediatization" of nature, the breaking of its compulsion, is the human form of the pleasure principle. Such restrictions of the instincts may first have been enforced by scarcity and by the protracted dependence of the human animal, but they have become the privilege and distinction of man which enabled him to transform the blind necessity of the fulfillment of want into desired gratification.

The "containment" of the partial sexual impulses, the progress to genitality belong to this basic layer of repression which makes possible intensified pleasure: the maturation of the organism involves normal and natural maturation of pleasure. However, the mastery of instinctual drives may also be used *against* gratification; in the history of civilization, basic repression and surplus-repression have been inextricably intertwined, and the normal progress to genitality has been organized in such a way that the partial impulses and their "zones" were all but desexualized in order to conform to the requirements of a specific social organization of the human existence. The vicissitudes of the "proximity senses" (smell and taste) provide a good example for the interrelation between basic repression and surplus-repression. Freud thought that "the coprophilic elements in the instinct have proved incompatible with our aesthetic ideas, probably since the time when man developed an upright posture and so removed his organ of smell from the ground."[1] There is, however, another aspect to the subduing of the proximity senses in civilization: they succumb to the rigidly enforced taboos on too intense bodily pleasure. The pleasure of smell and taste is "much more of a bodily, physical one, hence also more akin to sexual pleasure, than is the more sublime pleasure aroused by sound and the least bodily of all pleasures, the sight of something beautiful."[2] Smell and taste give, as it were, unsublimated pleasure *per se* (and unrepressed disgust). They relate (and separate) individuals immediately, without the generalized and conventionalized forms of consciousness, morality, aesthetics. Such immediacy is incompatible with the effectiveness of organized *domination,* with a society which "tends to isolate people, to put distance between them, and to prevent spontaneous relationships and the 'natural' animal-like expressions of such relations."[3] The pleasure of the proximity senses plays on the erotogenic zones of the body—and does so only for the sake of pleasure. Their unrepressed development would eroticize the organism to such an extent that it would counteract the desexualization of the organism required by its social utilization as an instrument of labor.

Throughout the recorded history of civilization, the instinctual constraint enforced by scarcity has been intensified by constraints enforced by the hierarchical distribution of scarcity and labor; the interest of domination added surplus-repression to the organization of the instincts under the reality principle. The pleasure principle was dethroned not only because it militated against progress in civilization but also because it militated against a civilization whose progress perpetuates domination and toil. Freud seems to acknowledge this fact when he compares the attitude of civilization toward sexuality with that of a tribe or a section of the population "which has gained the upper hand and is exploiting the rest to its own advantage. Fear of a revolt among the oppressed then becomes a motive for even stricter regulations."[4]

The modification of the instincts under the reality principle affects the life instinct as well as the death instinct; but the development of the latter becomes fully understandable only in the light of the development of the life instinct, i.e., of the repressive *organization of sexuality.* The sex instincts bear the brunt of the reality principle. Their organization culminates in the subjection of the partial sex instincts to the primacy of genitality, and in their subjugation under the function of procreation. The process involves the diversion of libido from one's own body toward an alien object of the opposite sex (the mastery of primary and secondary narcissism). The gratification of the partial instincts and of non-procreative genitality are, according to the degree of their independence, tabooed as perversions, sublimated, or transformed into subsidiaries of procreative sexuality. Moreover, the latter is in most civilizations channeled into monogamic institutions. This organization results in a quantitative and qualitative restriction of sexuality: the unification of the partial instincts and their subjugation under the procreative function alter the very nature of sexuality: from an autonomous "principle" governing the entire organism it is turned into a specialized temporary function, into a means for an end. In terms of the pleasure principle governing the "unorganized" sex instincts, reproduction is merely a "by-product."

The primary content of sexuality is the "function of obtaining pleasure from zones of the body"; this function is only "subsequently brought into the service of that of reproduction."[5] Freud emphasizes time and again that without its organization for such "service" sexuality would preclude all non-sexual and therefore all civilized societal relations—even at the stage of mature heterosexual genitality:

> . . . The conflict between civilization and sexuality is caused by the circumstance that sexual love is a relationship between two people, in which a third can only be superfluous or disturbing, whereas civilization is founded on relations between larger groups of persons. When a love relationship is at its height no room is left for any interest in the surrounding world; the pair of lovers are sufficient unto themselves, do not even need the child they have in common to make them happy.[6]

And earlier, in arguing the distinction between sexual and self-preservation instincts, he points up the fatal implications of sexuality:

> It is undeniable that the exercise of this function does not always bring advantage to the individual, as do his other activities, but that for the sake of an exceptionally high degree of pleasure he is involved by this function in dangers which jeopardize his life and often enough exact it.[7]

But how does this interpretation of sexuality as an essentially explosive force in "conflict" with civilization justify the definition of Eros as the effort "to combine organic substances into ever larger unities,"[8] to "establish ever greater unities and to preserve them thus—in short, to bind together"?[9] How can sexuality become the probable "substitute" for the "instinct towards perfection,"[10] the power that "holds together everything in the world"?[11] How does the notion of the asocial character of sexuality jibe with the "supposition that love relationships (or, to use a more neutral expression, emotional ties) also constitute the essence of the group mind?"[12] The apparent contradiction is not

solved by attributing the explosive connotations to the earlier concept of sexuality and the constructive ones to Eros—for the latter includes both. In *Civilization and Its Discontents,* immediately following the passage quoted above, Freud joins the two aspects: "In no other case does Eros so plainly betray the core of his being, his aim of making one out of many; but when he has achieved it in the proverbial way through the love of two human beings, he is not willing to go further." Nor can the contradiction be eliminated by locating the constructive cultural force of Eros only in the sublimated modes of sexuality: according to Freud, the drive toward ever larger unities belongs to the biological-organic nature of Eros itself.

At this stage of our interpretation, rather than trying to reconcile the two contradictory aspects of sexuality, we suggest that they reflect the inner unreconciled tension in Freud's theory: against his notion of the inevitable "biological" conflict between pleasure principle and reality principle, between sexuality and civilization, militates the idea of the unifying and gratifying power of Eros, chained and worn out in a sick civilization. This idea would imply that the *free* Eros does not preclude lasting civilized societal relationships—that it repels only the supra-repressive organization of societal relationships under a principle which is the negation of the pleasure principle. Freud allows himself the image of a civilization consisting of pairs of individuals "libidinally satisfied in each other, and linked to all the others by work and common interest."[13] But he adds that such a "desirable" state does not exist and never has existed, that culture "exacts a heavy toll of aim-inhibited libido, and heavy restrictions upon sexual life are unavoidable." He finds the reason for culture's "antagonism to sexuality" in the aggressive instincts deeply fused with sexuality: they threaten time and again to destroy civilization, and they force culture "to call up every possi-ble reinforcement" against them. "Hence its system of methods by which mankind is to be driven to identifications and aim-inhibited love-relationships; hence the restrictions on sexual life."[14] But, again, Freud shows that this repressive system does not really solve the conflict. Civilization plunges into a destructive dialectic: the perpetual restrictions on Eros ultimately weaken the life instincts and thus strengthen and release the very forces against which they were "called up"—those of destruction. This dialectic, which constitutes the still unexplored and even tabooed core of Freud's metapsychology, will be explored later on; here, we shall use Freud's antagonistic conception of Eros for elucidating the specific historical mode of repressiveness imposed by the established reality principle.

In introducing the term *surplus-repression* we have focused the discussion on the institutions and relations that constitute the social "body" of the reality principle. These do not just represent the changing external manifestations of one and the same reality principle but actually change the reality principle itself. Consequently, in our attempt to elucidate the scope and the limits of the prevalent repressiveness in contemporary civilization, we shall have to describe it in terms of the specific reality principle that has governed the origins and the growth of this civilization. We designate it as *performance principle* in order to emphasize that under its rule society is stratified according to the competitive economic performances of its members. It is clearly not the only historical reality principle: other modes of societal organization not merely prevailed in primitive cultures but also survived into the modern period.

The performance principle, which is that of an acquisitive and antagonistic society in the process of constant expansion, presupposes a long development during which domination has been increasingly rationalized: control over social labor now reproduces society on an enlarged scale and under improving conditions. For a long way, the interests of domination and the interests of the whole coincide: the profitable utilization of the productive apparatus fulfills the needs and faculties of the individuals. For the vast majority of the population, the scope and mode of satisfaction are determined by their own labor; but their labor is work for an apparatus which they do not control, which operates as an independent power to which individuals must submit if they want to live. And it becomes the more alien the more specialized the division of labor becomes. Men do not live their own lives but perform pre-established functions. While they work, they do not fulfill their own needs and faculties but work in *alienation*. Work has now become *general*, and so have the restrictions placed upon the libido: labor time, which is the largest part of the individual's life time, is painful time, for alienated labor is absence of gratification, negation of the pleasure principle. Libido is diverted for socially useful performances in which the individual works for himself only in so far as he works for the apparatus, engaged in activities that mostly do not coincide with his own faculties and desires.

Notes

1. "The Most Prevalent Form of Degradation in Erotic Life," in *Collected Papers* (London: Hogarth Press, 1950), IV, 215.

2. Ernest Schachtel, "On Memory and Childhood Amnesia," in *A Study of Interpersonal Relations,* ed. Patrick Mullahy (New York: Hermitage Press, 1950), p. 24.

3. *Ibid.,* p. 26.

4. *Civilization and Its Discontents,* p. 74.

5. *An Outline of Psychoanalysis,* p. 26.

6. *Civilization and Its Discontents,* pp. 79–80.

7. *A General Introduction to Psychoanalysis* (New York: Garden City Publishing Co., 1943), p. 358.

8. *Beyond the Pleasure Principle,* p. 57.

9. *An Outline of Psychoanalysis,* p. 20.

10. *Beyond the Pleasure Principle,* p. 57.

11. *Group Psychology and the Analysis of the Ego* (New York: Liveright Publishing Corp., 1949), p. 40.

12. *Ibid.*

13. *Civilization and Its Discontents,* p. 80. See also *The Future of Illusion* (New York: Liveright Publishing Corp., 1949), pp. 10–11.

14. *Civilization and Its Discontents,* pp. 86–87.

Marxism and Psychoanalysis

Ann Foreman

. . . There was an obvious parallel between marxism and psychoanalysis in Marx's concept of ideology and Freud's concept of the unconscious and it was here that the first attempts at a fusion between the two systems of thought started. Any development in the understanding of ideology would, of course, be invaluable in providing the groundwork for integrating an analysis of the relations between the sexes into socialist theory. But those radical writers who have attempted to fuse together marxism and psychoanalysis have been faced with huge problems. Both were well developed and drastically different systems. To attempt a synthesis was similar to a rider setting off at a gallop balanced on two horses which tended to pull in opposite directions. Nevertheless a number of writers have tackled the course.

The work of Wilhelm Reich represented the first serious attempt and in many ways he was the harbinger of all the hazards that awaited such a project. Herbert Marcuse and Erich Fromm returned to the problem a generation later and from the differing directions of political theory and psychoanalysis. And more recently, Juliet Mitchell has used psychoanalysis specifically to reappraise the marxist analysis of women's oppression.

But while all four writers applied themselves to the problems that had originated from an economic determinist approach to the analysis of society they nonetheless accepted its dualist heritage. All of them in their own way reproduced the separation of ideology from economics. Wilhelm Reich, Erich Fromm and Juliet Mitchell openly adopted it, and even Herbert Marcuse's conclusions were conditioned by it.

For example, Wilhelm Reich explained the relation of marxism to psychoanalysis in these terms: 'Marxism overthrows the old values by economic revolution and materialist philosophy; psychoanalysis does the same, or could do the same, in the sphere of the psyche.'[1] The same method is echoed by Juliet Mitchell: 'in analysing contemporary Western society we are (as elsewhere) dealing with two autonomous areas; the economic mode of capitalism and the ideological mode of patriarchy.'[2] She applied marxism to the first and psychoanalysis to the second. In both the original division between ideology and economics was retained. Similarly Erich Fromm in his turn attempted to use the psychoanalytic theory of the sexual instincts to place them alongside economic relations as the base forces in the social process.

But there is an important difference among the four writers which reflects on the seriousness of each attempt to synthesise the ideas of Marx and Freud. We have already made the point that Freudian psychoanalysis constitutes a coherent system of thought. Now it is necessary to introduce to the discussion the additional factor that psychoanalysis is not only a system of thought, but one which also had a certain dynamic. The development of Freud's theories and their continuing coherence depended on his notion of opposing forces acting within the human mind—that is, on his theory of the libido. A measure of the seriousness with which each writer approached Freudian psychoanalysis is the extent to which they treated it as a dynamic system of thought—the extent to which they confronted the problems posed by the libido theory.

Freud developed the notion of libido in the course of his clinical work as an explanation of the relation between his two major areas of concern, the understanding of sexuality and the unconscious. From his observation of parapraxes (slips of the tongue), the revelations of events by patients under hypnosis and also from his study of dreams, Freud concluded that there were elements within each individual's mind that were repressed from consciousness. He considered that in this idea of repression lay the key to understanding the incidence of neuroses. A neurosis, he suggested, was the eruption in the present life of the patient of an instinct which in the past had been unsuccessfully blocked and which up to that point had been hidden in an unconscious area of his or her mind. This idea of repression and eruption in turn led Freud to put forward the notion that there was a dynamic principle at work, to which he gave the term libido. The libido, Freud explained, represented the force of the sexual instincts.

Once Freud had established the notion of the libido he developed his own version of a theory of the instincts. To begin with, he considered that the child is born with two sets of instincts, the sexual and the self-preservative instincts. In the early phase of the child's life these two sets of instincts are at one with each other. Through suckling the mother's breast the child obtains the necessary nourishment to keep it alive. However, the self-preservative and the sexual instincts soon become opposed, and it is out of the growing antagonism between them that the structuring of the psyche takes place.

The sexual instincts aim for pleasurable gratification, a process which Freud referred to as the pleasure principle. At first the ego instincts (self-preservative instincts), have the same aim, but under the influence of reality they learn that pleasurable gratification is not always possible. Since the failure to satisfy a sexual urge causes unpleasant irritation the ego instincts discover that it is necessary to renounce immediate satisfaction in order to guarantee satisfaction in the long term. Freud termed this factor the reality principle. Thus we have the separa-

tion of the psyche into two major seats, the conscious and the unconscious, each maintained by different instincts and under the sway of a different principle, and each governed by a different agency, the ego and the id.

As Freud's work developed he continually modified his analysis of the structure of the psyche, and at each move made it less rigid and more complex. He emphasised that the conscious and unconscious regions of the mind do not have fixed boundaries. More and more he considered the force of the id, of the sexual, libidinal instincts, as the primary power within the psyche. Indeed he was to drop the division between the ego and the sexual instincts and explain the ego as a development out of the id.

Accordingly, Freud suggested that the ego was the result of past identifications of the id. In order for the ego to gain any control over the id it had to acquiesce to a large extent in its demands. One way it could do this was by presenting itself as a love object to the id. Thus, for example, the child in thumb-sucking was able to detach itself from total dependency on the mother and therefore to develop its sense of being a separate entity. But in carrying this through the ego was only able to change the direction of sexual energy and not to contain it.

In his later writings[3] Freud introduced his final version of the instinct theory, that is of the opposition between Eros and the death instinct. His abandonment of the original division that he made between the self-preservative instincts of the ego and the sexual instincts of the id paved the way for his understanding of Eros. Eros was the force of life, the instinctual aim of the human organism, as well as all other organisms, to preserve living substance and to join it into ever larger units. But acting against Eros was the death instinct, a force aiming to dissolve those units and return them to their original state of dispersion. Freud's postulate of the existence of these two instincts enabled him to account for the previously inexplicable phenomena of sadism and masochism. In both the sexual instinct took the form of a destructive impulse—in the first directed against the other, in the second directed against the self. Freud believed that these phenomena could now be explained by the combination of the death instinct with Eros, which resulted in a fusion of eroticism and destructiveness.

But while Freud's theory of the instincts underwent these changes and sophistications, the underlying concept that remained constant and gave coherence to those developments was that of the libido. The concept of the libido gave meaning to the opposition between the self-preservative and sexual instincts and later between Eros and the death instinct. It was in terms of the libido that he accounted for the structuring of the psyche into the conscious and unconscious, governed by the agencies of the ego and the id. Freud considered that all these were ultimately reducible to the 'economics' of the libido. What then in more detail was his understanding of this force?

Freud's view of the libido was based on the idea that each human being formed a closed system with a static quantity of energy which could be redirected but not increased or diminished. Similarly, Freud believed that the libido was a form of energy that could not be contained; its force had to express itself in some way, whether it was in sexual pleasure, neuroses, or in its other sublimated and repressed forms. This is clear from Freud's discussion of the libido in *The Introductory Lectures on Psychoanalysis*:

> The quantitative factor is no less decisive as regards capacity to resist neurotic illness. It is a matter of *what quota* of unemployed libido a person is able to hold in suspension and of *how large a fraction* of his libido he is able to divert from sexual to sublimated aims. The ultimate aim of mental activity, which may be described qualitatively as an endeavour to obtain pleasure and avoid unpleasure, emerges, looked at from the economic point of view, as the task of mastering the amounts of excitation (mass of stimuli) operating in the mental apparatus and of keeping down their accumulation which creates unpleasure.[4]

So elementary was libido to human life that Freud considered that the whole development of civilisation, including men's basic capacity for thought, rested on its sublimation and repression. 'If thought-processes in the wider sense are to be included among these displacements [of libido] then the activity of thinking is also supplied from the sublimation of these erotic motive forces.'[5]

The relation of the repression of libido and the growth of civilisation is best expressed through Freud's concept of the super-ego. This was the last category of physical agency that Freud developed after those of the ego and the id and it is crucial in completing his theory of the unconscious. The concept of the super-ego adds the finishing touches to the relation between sexuality, its repression, the structuring of the unconscious and the development of civilisation. For the super-ego is the inheritance within the psyche of the individual's childhood sexual urges. The repression that took place through the Oedipus complex prepared the child to enter adult civilised life. The strength of the super-ego, which acts as the continual force of individual conscience, is in proportion to the force of the repressed libido. Freud spoke of the super-ego as 'the expression of the most powerful impulses and most important libidinal vicissitudes of the id.'[6] And in turn Freud considered that the strength of each individual's super-ego in society was an index of the development of civilisation.

Drop the Freudian notion of the libido, then, and the relation between the theory of sexuality and the structuring of the psyche into the conscious and unconscious systems dissolves. This was the dilemma that faced the four writers who tried to combine marxism and psychoanalysis. Wilhelm Reich and Herbert Marcuse retained it, with its problems, in their work, while Erich Fromm and Juliet Mitchell abandoned it.

Fromm's approach boiled down to taking a little of what he fancied from both marxism and psychoanalysis. He dropped the marxist theory of revolutionary change but retained the importance of environment in conditioning the form of human life. Then later, in *The Art of Loving*, he dropped the term sexual instincts in favour of the all-embracing one of love. Indeed by this stage Fromm had even dropped the claim to be concerned in an analysis of the individual and society, preferring rather to give a little sermon on the importance of love. Since at best Fromm's work represented an eclectic rather than a synthetic approach to Marx and Freud his writings contain little, from our point of view, of lasting interest.

*   *   *

Juliet Mitchell's attempt to side-step the problems posed by Freud's theory of the libido and the instincts is more sophisticated than Fromm's. In translating the German term *trieb* as drive rather than instinct she hoped to avoid the biological determinism that lurks within psychoanalysis. Unfortunately, despite the fact that Mitchell insisted that a psychoanalytic theory of the instincts was a humanised one and that as such no comparison was intended between men and animals, in doing so she contradicted what Freud actually wrote. For in introducing his most refined version of the instinct theory in *Beyond the Pleasure Principle* (1920) Freud spent considerable time discussing the instinctual life of the simplest living organisms. And it was from this discussion that he put forward the hypothesis of a life and a death instinct to explain the many characteristics that he considered these organisms had in common with human beings. 'The present development of human beings requires, as it seems to me,' he concluded, 'no different explanation for that of animals.'[7]

Indeed it was a feature of Freud's later writings that he minimised the ability of men to 'humanise' their instincts. He considered that the power of the individual's ego, that is, of human consciousness, was feeble compared to the instinctual urges of the id. So, for example, in *Civilization and Its Discontents* we find Freud talking of the ego as a mere 'façade' of the id.

But in down-playing Freud's concept of the libido Mitchell incurred problems in establishing a clear interpretation of the psychoanalytic theory of the unconscious. For, as we have seen, in explaining the force of the sexual instincts,

the libido also made sense of the structuring of the psyche. Consequently, when Mitchell uses the term 'the unconscious' in *Psychoanalysis and Feminism* we are never sure what she actually means by it. Is the unconscious an unchanging feature of the individual's mind, or is it a feature of the mind within patriarchal capitalism that will disappear with its abolition? In the last chapter of *Psychoanalysis and Feminism* Mitchell talked about new structures gradually coming to be represented in the unconscious after a revolution in social relations.[8] But does this mean therefore that she considered that the repression of the libidinal force of the sexual instinct was inevitable in all forms of society? For the Freudian theory of the unconscious is meaningless without the notion of a repression and redirection of sexual energy.

This in turn means that Mitchell's claim to explain the hold of ideology within patriarchal society is severely damaged. For at one point she had argued that the concept of the unconscious was the key to understanding ideology: 'the unconscious that Freud analysed,' she wrote, 'could thus be analysed as the domain of the reproduction of culture or ideology.'[9] But if the unconscious remains a constant within both a patriarchal capitalistic society and a non-patriarchal socialist one then in what way is it a useful concept to explain the hold of ideology? And if the unconscious and ideology are mutually dependent concepts, as Mitchell appears to assume, then presumably ideology will also exist in a non-patriarchal society. But if this is the case, what is the basic difference between the two types of society? Mitchell leaves these crucial questions unanswered.

Similarly, it is unclear where Mitchell stands in relation to the Oedipus complex. As we have seen, the original Oedipal situation marked the beginning of human society for Freud. But with Mitchell we are never quite sure whether she meant it to represent the beginning of human society or of civilisation—something quite different. However, since on balance she equates patriarchy with human society more frequently than with civilisation, we will have to assume this meaning.[10] But if this is the case then the same argument that can be made against Freud applies equally to Mitchell. That is, Mitchell is also open to the criticism that the Freudian Oedipus complex assumes without explanation the original domination of men over women. On top of this, however, in dismissing a social and historical explanation of that relation the Oedipus complex rests on a biological one. In other words, Mitchell's adherence to the Oedipus complex leads her to the conclusion that the social and cultural distinctions between men and women are ultimately reducible to biological differences. Set against her specific aim to explain by means of psychoanalytic theory the origins and basis of femininity, such a conclusion, and the criticism of it, have even more serious implications than they did for Freud. Perhaps, it might be suggested in her defence, Mitchell had intended to use a weaker version of the Oedipus complex? Perhaps, for example, she meant that while it was a universal feature of all societies up to this point, it would become redundant within a non-patriarchal one? But if this were so, then she would have had to make the appropriate alteration to Freud's theory of the unconscious. For, as we have seen, the Oedipus complex was a central and not an accidental feature of that theory. But again Mitchell remains silent.

Ironically, it is Mitchell's critique of other feminist interpretations of Freud which reveals the basic error in her approach to psychoanalysis. She accused such writers of reading Freud as a prescriptive account of society. That is, she felt they took Freud to be saying that women *should* behave in a certain way when in fact he was analysing how they actually *do* behave. While there is an element of truth in this, Mitchell deduced from it a mistaken conclusion. For she took from it justification for a far stronger claim, namely that psychoanalysis was, by that fact, a science. In other words she accepted without further question that Freud's basic concepts were unbiased, that they were not conditioned by the ideology of a specific culture at a specific historical point in time. However, not only the Oedipus complex but also Freud's theory of the unconscious, of the libido and its re-

pression, were affected by his experience of capitalism, as I shall show later. But even without this, the error of Mitchell's attempt to pluck such theories from Freud's particular conceptual framework and to place them unaltered within a revolutionary feminist one, is clear. They mix just about as well as oil and water.

What then are the implications of this for Mitchell's synthesis of marxism and psychoanalysis? In accepting the scientific status of psychoanalysis to be the same as that of marxism, Mitchell assumed that there was no problem in the relation between them. Consequently she made no provision for reconciling the fundamental differences that exist between them on the nature of human society. Thus she, like Fromm before her, failed in her project. Instead of synthesising marxism and psychoanalysis she treated them as two autonomous bodies of thought, each with a separate function in the analysis of society. And in doing so she reproduced, perhaps in a stronger form than it had ever occurred before, the dualism within radical thought.

*   *   *

In contrast to Juliet Mitchell and Erich Fromm, Wilhelm Reich's work maintains a notion of the libido throughout. His starting-point was to apply a class analysis to the Freudian theory of repression and sublimation of sexual energy. Through his therapeutic work with working class patients he had come to the conclusion that their neuroses were directly connected to their appalling living conditions. Sexual repression was the result of poverty and bad housing. From this premise Reich simplified Freud's concept of repression from a process which was necessary in all societies to one which occurred only in specific ones. In *The Invasion of Compulsory Sex-Morality* he argued that the repression of sexuality did not exist within primitive cultures and only emerged with the development of class interests. One of the cardinal ways in which a ruling class was able to maintain its domination in society was through the suppression of sexuality. In this way Reich was able to tie together the

'Freudian' concept of the unconscious and the 'marxist' concept of ideology. Repressed sexuality, he argued, expressed itself in the hold of bourgeois ideology and moral sentiments over the minds of the working class. While Reich's move to submit Freud's theories to an historical analysis was a step forward, the conclusions that he himself drew from it in many ways were a step backwards. The way that he theorised the connection between historically specific conditions and a healthy sex life involved a regressive revaluation of Freud's distinction between 'normal' and 'perverse' sexuality.

As we saw earlier, Freud made a distinction between 'normal' and 'perverse' sexuality on the basis of whether it corresponded to adult or infantile forms. Sexuality in the childhood stages was 'polymorphously perverse' and adult sexuality was only established after a long and hazardous journey through the different infantile forms. The sexual urges could return to an early or 'perverse' phase of development. This explained the occurrence of homosexuality, which was a regression or fixation of sexuality at an infantile stage of its development. Reich, however, used his own new understanding of the relation between material conditions and sexuality to draw a much more rigid line than Freud's between its 'normal' and 'perverse' forms. 'Perverse' sexuality, he argued, which included masturbation as well as homosexuality, was an expression of the repression by *class society* of 'normal' genital satisfaction.

> The perverse and neurotic modes of gratification against which society should be protected are in themselves only substitutes for genital gratification and arise only if genital gratification is disturbed or made impossible.[11]

Thus, within Reich's system the primacy of genital sexuality acquired an entirely new dimension. Genital sexuality in itself was a liberating force. Its repression or sublimation had the particular effect of strengthening reactionary forces in society rather than being a necessary precondition for social interchange of

any kind. Thus at the same time as making Freud's approach to sexuality more rigid he drastically simplified the process of the redirection of libido. But while the ruling class in capitalist society actively repressed the sex lives of the working class, the latter still retained their revolutionary potential. According to Reich, 'anal urges seem to be much more strongly marked in the middle classes than in the working class, whereas, conversely genital urges are more intense in the working class'.[12] Hence the working class was the revolutionary force in both the sexual and the economic 'spheres'. So, at the expense of knocking off a few corners Reich had managed to combine the marxist theory of class struggle with the importance that Freud gave to sexuality.

Reich used his conclusions on the repression of genital sexuality within capitalism to emphasise the importance of the family as the major arena where this process took place. This emphasis on the family is the most positive and lasting influence that Reich has had on the development of a theory of sexual liberation. He looked at the family primarily through his work on character analysis. A person's character, he argued, was an armour formed as a defence against the hard knocks of reality. But in the sense that it limited the individual's ability to experience life, both within and without in its full intensity, it was a negative development. The family, as a product of definite economic conditions and the structure in which the individual was primarily moulded, forged the type of character which would cling to the status quo. For it was the function of the family to suppress all manifestations of genital sexuality in children and adolescents.

But with his theories on character analysis Reich moved further away from the Freudian concept of the unconscious which was the original starting point for the link up with marxism, via an analysis of ideology. The dynamic for the structuring of the psyche into the conscious, pre-conscious and unconscious systems had, according to Freud, come from the force of the opposition between the reality principle and the sexual instincts. But Reich had denied that this opposition was a necessary one. Consequently he was faced with the task of redefining the psychic make-up. He replaced Freud's model of dynamic interconnecting systems with the three tier construction of the human personality. This construction was analogous to a chocolate fruit cake where all the goodness has sunk to the bottom in the process of cooking. The bottom layer was made up with the individual's natural energies, the enjoyment of work and sociality, or what was essentially the same thing to Reich, the spontaneous sexual urges. These were silted up by the perversions of the second layer which were the result of the sex-negating nature of class society. This layer, he maintained, was equivalent to the Freudian unconscious. And finally on the top, the icing covering everything over, was the individual's character, full of artificial sweetness and politeness.

Given Reich's new definition of the psychic make-up the 'unconscious' no longer explained the hold of ideology but was, rather, a result of it. The 'unconscious' was not a necessary element of the psyche but the historical residue from the damming up of genital satisfaction. If men were instead to express their genital sexuality they could sweep away that residue and realise their natural personality. As Reich himself put it: 'The man who attains genital satisfaction is honourable, responsible, brave and controlled, without making much of a fuss about it.'[13] But if the individual was able to accomplish this, then, through the free expression of genital sexuality repeated at the level of society as a whole, the repressive ideology of capitalism could be brought tumbling down like the walls of Jericho.

With this final step, Reich's logic takes an ironic twist. He had begun with the belief that material conditions caused sexual neuroses and that these had to be changed before a cure could be made. It was because of this premise that he turned to marxism. However, by developing his theory of the revolutionary force of genital sexuality he eventually arrived at the conclusion

that there was no need to fight for the political transformation of society.

'It is not necessary to create anything new,' he wrote towards the end of his life,

we must merely remove the obstacles that limit the natural social functions, no matter in what form these obstacles turn up. . . . In short, work-democracy is a newly discovered bio-socio-logic, natural and basic function of society. It is not a political programme.[14]

His theories of 'work-democracy' and 'biophysical orgone therapy' aimed simply at releasing men's positive life force. By this time Wilhelm Reich had left far behind his early intentions to weld together psychoanalysis and marxism, and yet there was an undeniable logic which linked together his original serious premises and his final bizarre conclusions. That logic was the logic of the theory of the libido as a quantitative sexual force.

While he was prepared to modify or abandon all of Freud's other concepts, Wilhelm Reich maintained a terrier-like hold on the libido theory. And by redefining repression and sublimation in historical terms he elevated that theory to a position of preeminence. It was a small step from that to his final obsessive concentration on attempting to measure and analyse the material components of the libido.

The ultimate assessment of Reich's work has to be that it contributed little to countering the weaknesses in radical thought. His 'synthesis' of marxism and psychoanalysis had been a string-and-sticky-paper job, which fell apart once his own enthusiasm for the task dwindled. Although he set himself the important task of analysing the links between economic relations, sexuality and ideology his conclusions dissolved the problems rather than resolving them. Genital sexuality would solve everything. Theory became unimportant and therapy all important. In the same way Reich considered it unnecessary to develop an analysis of female sexuality. Since genital heterosexuality was eminently natural, its free expression would resolve any historical problems in the relations between men and women. Indeed in the course of his life Reich became more and more hostile to the conscious analysis of sexuality. Even consciousness of one's own sexuality was bad and finally he concluded that self-consciousness was at the root of all human malaise.

*   *   *

Like Wilhelm Reich, Herbert Marcuse eagerly grasped the nettle of the libido theory. In his book *Eros and Civilization* he considered that it was possible to integrate the major theses of psychoanalysis with a marxist approach precisely because its essence, the libido theory, was revolutionary. What was required was the reworking of the central psychoanalytic concepts to reveal their revolutionary kernel which had been hidden even from Freud himself. Unlike Reich, Marcuse agreed with Freud that the repression of libido was a necessary condition for cultural advance. However, he drew a distinction between basic repression that is 'the "modification" of the instincts necessary for the perpetuation of the human race in civilisation' and surplus repression, 'the restrictions necessitated by social domination'.[15] Similarly he introduced a sophistication into the reality principle, the restrictive force of reality on the sexual desire, by suggesting that in different historical periods it took different forms. Marcuse argued that these distinctions were an historical extrapolation of Freud's basic ideas rather than external additions to them.

Under the strictures of the performance principle, he suggested, the libido was both spatially and temporally reduced. Firstly, the use of the body primarily as an instrument of labour required the repression of libido and limited its release to a particular and short period of the worker's life—during recreation. Secondly, the libido was concentrated in one area of the body—the genitals—leaving the rest of the body free for work.

By making explicit the form of the reality principle in capitalist society Marcuse believed that he had made possible the theorisation of a non-repressive civilisation that was derivable from Freud's original theory of the instincts. If the working day and the necessary energy required for labour could be reduced to a minimum, then the reason for the restrictions placed upon the libido by the performance principle would be removed. Since the body would no longer be primarily an instrument of labour then as a whole it could become 'resexualised'. This development in turn would allow the decline of genital sexuality in favour of 'polymorphous sexuality'. Freud had argued against the possibility of such a release of the libido from the reality principle as it was this which kept its anti-social force in check. Marcuse, however, considered that its release need not be disruptive because it would take place in the form of a 'spread rather than an explosion of libido'.[16] The equation of the resexualisation of the body with the diminishing strength of the reality principle balanced, given Freud's concept of a quantitative amount of libido.

So far so good, but Marcuse still had to deal with Freud's concept of the death instinct. Freud had developed this concept in his later writings, as we have seen, to help account amongst other things for the aggressive elements present in interpersonal relations. Since the existence of a death instinct posed a threat to the mere continuation of civilisation, repressive or non-repressive, Marcuse had to be able to theorise a situation where the development of society involved a weakening of its hold. But first let us recapitulate on Freud's understanding of the death instinct.

The death instinct took its meaning from its relation and contrast to the force of the sexual instinct, or Eros as Freud sometimes termed it. While the tendency of Eros was to bind bodies together in ever larger units, that of the death instinct was conservative, to return bodies to their original state of dispersion. Therefore in contrast to Eros the death instinct was a destructive force.

Again, Marcuse applied the premise of a static and quantitative amount of instinctual energy to an apparently irreconcilable contradiction within Freud's original theory. He argued that if the body was resexualised then the accompanying release of libido, which had previously been turned back on itself through repression, would weaken the force of the death instinct. For destructive energy, he concluded, could only manifest itself in the space made available by the repression of libido.

But while his application of the economics of the libido was consistent, the form of Marcuse's application involved a corruption and simplification of what Freud had actually understood to be the relation between Eros and the death instinct. Although Freud made a conceptual distinction between Eros and the death instinct he believed that the two forces were inextricably bound together in practice. He wrote in *Beyond the Pleasure Principle* when he first put forward this version of the instinct theory, 'if . . . we are not to abandon the hypothesis of death instincts, we must suppose them to be associated from the very first with life instincts.'[17] Indeed Freud pointed to their coexistence to explain why unimpeded sexual relations within a collective tended to fragment it and to break social ties. The maintenance of such ties involved rather the sublimation of the sexual instincts and their re-emergence in the form of love. It was, therefore, the sublimation not the release of libido that held the destructive force of the death instinct in check. And so Marcuse's simple separation of the death instinct and Eros into one force acting against and one acting for the good of society was quite out of keeping with Freud's analysis.

However, Marcuse was not only faced with the problem of remaining consistent with Freud's basic concepts. If he was actually to synthesise psychoanalysis with marxism he had to do more than theorise the possibility of a non-repressive society. If his theory was to withstand the charge of being utopian, and therefore unmarxist, he had to be able to indicate how such a society could be realised in practice. Specifically, he had to be able to explain why the force of reality should cease, at some historical

point in time, its repression of the sexual instinct and allow the resexualisation of the body.

Marcuse's response was to point to two developments. The first was that of technological advance. Here Marcuse argued that the performance principle, the historical form of the reality principle in capitalist society, was based primarily on the need to overcome material scarcity. The strength and efficiency of the performance principle had been illustrated by the extensive improvements in industry and technology that had taken place in the capitalist epoch. But at the same time this advance removed the problem of scarcity and therefore weakened the basis of the performance principle. When this process becomes complete then the dynamic for repression itself would be removed. As Marcuse himself put it,

> the quantum of instinctual energy still to be diverted into necessary labour (in turn completely mechanised and rationalised) would be so small that a large area of repressive constraints and modifications, no longer sustained by external forces, would collapse.[18]

This all has a pleasing logic, but there is one important snag that I will mention here and return to in greater detail later. Marcuse postulated that these radical changes in the form of social relations all took place without a development in the consciousness of the individuals in society. It all would happen as it were behind their backs, or to be more precise, within the unconscious and instinctual realm of their psyches. Indeed, if anything, as the process developed their consciousness coagulated, for we find Marcuse talking about the reduction of the individual in advanced capitalism to an automaton unable to distinguish 'between war and peace, between civilian and military populations, between truth and propaganda.'[19]

The second development that Marcuse pointed to was the decline of the family. The existence of such a development was vital to his analysis that the super-ego and the accompanying sense of guilt, which were central features of the human condition in civilised society, were on the wane. For Freud had seen both as measures of the increasing level of repression in society. Indeed in *Civilization and Its Discontents* he talked about his intention,

> to represent the sense of guilt as the most important problem in the development of civilisation and to show that the price we pay for our advance in civilisation is a loss of happiness through the heightening of the sense of guilt.[20]

This sense of guilt originated from the killing of the father at the beginning of human history, but had been reintegrated into the super-ego of every generation since then through the Oedipal situation in the family. The family then was vital to conditioning the strength of the super-ego and thereby, the sense of guilt. Thus if Marcuse could point to a decline in family relations he would reasonably be able to deduce from it that the super-ego, the sense of guilt, and the level of sexual repression were also in decline. But was his crucial premise, that the importance of the family was declining, true?

Marcuse analysed development of the state organisation of society, the provision of state education as signs of the cumulative erosion of the family's social function which lead to what he termed the 'technological abolition of the individual'.[21] But was he justified in taking the undeniable changes in the family as indications of its progressive abolition? Rather, its survival after decades of state education and the creation of a range of state services in conjunction with and not replacing it suggest otherwise. Moreover, Marcuse's announcement of the technological abolition of the individual seems off the mark. Instead, the family appears within an automated society more important than ever as a haven of human and individual values. His conclusion that 'the formation of the mature super-ego seems to skip the stage of individualisation; the generic atom becomes directly a social atom . . .'[22] fits in with his theoretical needs but not, unfortunately, with reality.

Marcuse, then, failed both to theorise a non-repressive civilisation and to analyse how it could be brought about in practice. Freudian psychoanalysis could not be revolutionised. But from the point of view of marxism, his theories are even less satisfactory.

Like Reich, Marcuse's theoretical contortions could be traced to the theory of the sexual instincts and the libido. Despite his protestations it was profoundly un-marxist, and could not be squeezed into a revolutionary framework. By making the libido the dynamic of change Marcuse was faced with the problem that any development took place primarily outside the individual's awareness. For the realm of the libido was the realm of the unconscious. But for Marx a qualitative social change was impossible without the development of a revolutionary consciousness within the proletariat. And so from the very beginning the Freudian theory of the libido and the sexual instincts was irreconcilable with the marxist analysis of revolutionary change. In attempting to reconcile the irreconcilable Marcuse found himself in an ironic situation. He had turned to psychoanalysis as a reaction against the reduction of marxism to economic determinism. But in basing himself on a force, the libido, that acted outside of the individual's conscious activity and replaced it as the force for social change, he put forward a form of psychological determinism. In short, Herbert Marcuse had failed to renounce the dualist heritage.

But is it surprising that the attempts to overcome economic determinism through psychoanalysis should be so unsuccessful? Freud and Marx had a radically different outlook on both the nature of interpersonal relations and the relation of the individual to reality. And, moreover, these differences centred on Freud's sexual instinct theory and Marx's emphasis on conscious activity.

Marx's basic approach was an historical one. But Freud considered that while the instincts might manifest themselves differently in specific historical and cultural conditions they themselves were essentially ahistorical. The instincts were ahistorical because they were not determined by their relation to their object. As Freud explained,

The object of an instinct is that in or through which it can achieve its aim. *It is the most variable thing about an instinct* and it is not originally connected with it, but becomes attached to it only in the consequence of being peculiarly fitted to provide satisfaction.[23]

So while the object might be subject to historical change the sexual instinct was not. The relation was similar to that of an electrical current to a fitting. The fitting might change, it might be a lamp or an iron, but the electricity that powered it remained unaltered.

Marx's analysis of the relation of the individual to objective reality was totally different. Unlike Freud he considered that it was impossible to separate the object of a relation from the relation itself—human beings from their objective reality. Both were subject to historical change as men acted on reality and by changing it, changed themselves. Consequently human beings were always in the process of transforming the very form of their being. All their relations, including their sexual ones, were subject to historical development. But there was one more crucial element in the process. By acting on reality and changing it human beings developed their consciousness. This development of knowledge, which again stood them in a new relation to reality, was what Marx considered as defining the difference between the human species and animals. In the *1844 Manuscripts* he wrote:

The animal is immediately one with its life activity. It does not distinguish itself from it. It is *its life activity.* Man makes his life activity itself the object of his will and of his consciousness. He has conscious life activity. It is not a determination with which he directly emerges. Conscious life activity distinguishes man immediately from animal life activity.[24]

With Freudian psychoanalysis this distinction between animal and human life was blurred. Men's ability to regulate their sexual instincts was at best an uncertain affair. Ultimately, Freud's theory of the unconscious

put severe limits on the ability of the individual to take conscious control over his or her life. But if conscious control was a limited factor in the life of the individual, Freud considered it to be almost non-existent in a group situation. In *Group Psychology and the Analysis of the Ego* (1921) he wrote,

. . . when individuals come together in a group all their individual inhibitions fall away and all the cruel, brutal and destructive instincts, which lie dormant in individuals as relics of a primitive epoch, are stirred up to find free gratification.[25]

Thus to accept Freud's theory of the unconscious and the instincts would in effect require abandoning the marxist theory of revolutionary change. For marxism's central premise was that a development in consciousness not simply at an individual level, but at the level of a whole class, the working class, was possible; and the concept of socialism took its meaning from the idea of collective and conscious control. In short, to synthesise marxism and psychoanalysis was an impossible task.

Notes

1. W. Reich, *Dialectical Materialism and Psychoanalysis,* Socialist Reproduction 1972, p.53.

2. J. Mitchell, *Psychoanalysis and Feminism,* Pelican Books 1975, p.412.

3. From 'Beyond the Pleasure Principle' (1921) onwards.

4. S. Freud, 'The Paths to the Formation of Symptoms' (1917), *Introductory Lectures on Psychoanalysis,* Pelican Books 1974, p.422, emphasis in the original.

5. S. Freud, *The Ego and the Id* (1923), Hogarth Press 1962, p.35.

6. *ibid.* p.26.

7. S. Freud, 'Beyond the Pleasure Principle' (1921), in J. Strachey (ed), *The Standard Edition of the Complete Psychological Works of Sigmund Freud,* vol. XVIII, Hogarth Press 1957, p.42.

8. J. Mitchell, *op. cit.* p.415.

9. *ibid.* p.413.

10. *ibid.* p.369.

11. W. Reich, *The Sexual Revolution*, Vision Press 1972, p.16.

12. W. Reich, *Dialectical Materialism and Psychoanalysis*, Socialist Reproduction 1972, p.25.

13. W. Reich, *The Mass Psychology of Fascism*, Pelican Books 1975, p.39.

14. *ibid.* p.138.

15. H. Marcuse, *Eros and Civilization*, Abacus 1972, p.42.

16. *ibid.* p.145.

17. S. Freud, *op. cit.* p.57.

18. H. Marcuse, *op. cit.* p.115.

19. *ibid.* p.81.

20. S. Freud, 'Civilization and Its Discontents' (1929), in J. Strachey (ed), *The Standard Edition of the Complete Psychological Works of Sigmund Freud*, Hogarth Press 1961, vol. XXI, p.134.

21. H. Marcuse, *op. cit.* p.78.

22. *ibid.*

23. S. Freud, 'Instincts and Their Vicissitudes' (1915), in J. Strachey (ed), *Collected Papers of Sigmund Freud*, vol. IV, Hogarth Press 1925, p.65, emphasis added.

24. K. Marx, *Economic and Philosophical Manuscripts of 1844*, Lawrence and Wishart 1968, p.113.

25. S. Freud, 'Group Psychology and the Analysis of the Ego' (1921), in J. Strachey (ed), *The Standard Edition of the Complete Psychological Works of Sigmund Freud*, vol. XVIII, Hogarth Press 1957, p.79.

Coming Out:
The Search for Identity

Dennis Altman

To be a homosexual in our society is to be constantly aware that one bears a stigma. Despite the recent upsurge in open discussion—"the love that dare not speak its name," said one observer, "has become the neurosis that doesn't know when to shut up"—there is still little genuine acceptance of homosexuality as a valid sexual and social life-style. As a homosexual I am constantly made aware of this, in the jokes and caricatures of stage and films, in the pain of my parents, in my own uncertainties as to how I may be affected by a book like this, written under my own name.

Over the past few years I have come to realize that my homosexuality is an integral part of my self-identity, and that to hide it can only make my life, if less precarious, more difficult and unsatisfying. Yet I have not totally escaped the necessity to live a double life, at least in certain situations, nor rid myself of the tenseness that results from being constantly with people who assume everyone is straight and are incapable of the imagination or empathy necessary to transcend this attitude. Like most gay people, I know myself to be part of a minority feared, disliked, and persecuted by the majority and this gives my life a complexity and an extra dimension unknown to straights.

Our society, of course, stigmatizes other groups: nonwhites most obviously, and women, at least in some circumstances. Even worse perhaps are the stigmas borne by the old, the invalid, the crippled, the ugly. Yet the stigma of

the homosexual is unique in one central sense. Our gayness is not something, like skin color, or sex, or infirmity, immediately apparent to both us and others. We have to discover our homosexuality, and having discovered it, we have a wide range of options, hardly available to others who are stigmatized, as to how far we should reveal our stigma.

I shall in later chapters seek to develop some theories that explain just why homosexuals are so stigmatized, and what changes would be necessary to remove that stigma. For the moment I am concerned with the experience of being-a-homosexual in contemporary Western society. For, let there be no confusion: the very concept of homosexuality is a social one, and one cannot understand the homosexual experience without recognizing the extent to which we have developed a certain identity and behavior derived from social norms.

The conventional definition of homosexuality has always been a behavioral one: a homosexual is anyone who engages in sexual acts with another of his or her sex (homosexual is a generic term, including both men and women). If he or she has sex with both men and women, then he or she is bisexual. What could be simpler?

Yet a moment's thought will show the inadequacy of the purely behavioral approach. Human beings are distinguished by a capacity for experience as well as by their behavior, and homosexuality is as much a matter of emotion as of genital manipulation. Celibacy, for example, is not an unknown state (we are all celibate for a time, and some manage life-long celibacy, either through determination or bad luck), yet are we to deny a celibate any sexual definition at all? Homosexuals often discover their homosexuality before any overt sexual experience, yet they are no less homosexual for that. Equally, many men or women have engaged in homosexual acts without being in any experiential sense homosexuals, for example in prison, at school, as prostitutes. As we each examine our own sense of identity we realize how much more complex is the question of homosexuality than a mere Kinsey-like computation of orgasms.

Three cases:

I am sitting on some steps in the East Village in New York City with a very attractive kid called Robbie. We rap about being gay. He is not, he claims, but he has many gay friends. Moreover he is going to a gay dance that night; perhaps he will see me there? I hope so, I say. I want to ask him home with me, but am a little scared.

After a ten-year-old marriage a well-known journalist announces he is divorced. The children stay with him, in their suburban home, and his male secretary moves in to help keep house. It appears they have been sleeping together for six years.

In the Tombs, Manhattan's House of Detention for Men, a friend of mine spent three weeks. While there he was raped, frequently, brutally, and with much resulting physical and mental pain. The rapists included wardens and fellow prisoners. All considered themselves straight, bragged of their adventures with women, and vehemently denounced "faggots."

Gore Vidal has claimed that "homosexual" should be used only as an adjective to describe a sexual activity, not as a noun to describe a recognized type, for we are all basically bisexual (more of that later). In an ideal society this would undoubtedly be true, and one might expect that if, as most writers in the field suggest, there is a continuum between homo- and heterosexuality, sexual behaviour would reflect this. Yet most people seem to regard the two as mutually exclusive categories and there is con-

siderable emphasis on the need to identify as either straight or gay. Thus the expression "coming out," common among homosexuals, implies much more than a first sexual act with another man or woman. Rather it is bound up with the whole process whereby persons come to identify themselves as homosexual, and recognize thereby their position as part of a stigmatized and half-hidden minority. For the moment I shall consider bisexuals as part of this minority, although their case is somewhat different. Nonetheless, author Kate Millett has had reason to note that it is her homo- rather than her heterosexuality with which she is branded.

The development of a homosexual identity is a long process that usually begins during adolescence, though sometimes considerably later. Because of the fears and ignorance that surround our views of sex, children discover sexual feelings and behavior incompletely, and often with great pangs of guilt. This is true even for the heterosexual, as a whole literary tradition, whose recent variations include Philip Roth's *Portnoy's Complaint* and Dan Wakefield's *Going All the Way,* makes clear. How much greater, then, is the guilt of the teenager who discovers himself attracted to others of his or her own sex? Dave McReynolds, the pacifist and political activist who first wrote openly of his homosexuality in 1969, has described how he waited for each birthday hoping he would become "normal" and his guilt on realizing he was irredeemably "queer." Others, like myself, manage to enter into our twenties without a full realization that we are not like others—that we are, in fact, one of *them.*

The actual origins of homosexuality remain a mystery, despite a profusion of psychoanalytic theories. We know that much of what is considered natural sexual behavior is, in fact, learned, and that somewhere along the way homosexuals diverge from the more common path and develop a different pattern of sexual response. To many this is proof of a pathology, and men like Dr. Irving Bieber and Dr. Charles Socraides, both well-known exponents of "curing" homosexuals, have made their name by so branding homosexuals. "We consider," writes Bieber in his book *Homosexuality: A Psychoanalytic Study of Male Homosexuals* "homosexuality to be a pathologic biosocial, psychosexual adaptation consequent to pervasive fears surrounding the expression of heterosexual impulses." Of course his study is based exclusively on men sufficiently disturbed to be undergoing treatment.

Most psychiatrists tend to locate the origin of homosexuality in "maladjusted" family life, yet such an explanation is not altogether convincing. Too many homosexuals have strong and loving fathers, too many heterosexuals have dominant mothers for any very obvious connection to be seen. It is probably true that in modern Western societies *most* mothers overdominate their sons, and this fact is often disregarded by those concerned to discover the etiology of homosexuality. What Americans call "momism" is a general feature of our culture, reflected both in homosexual sons (e.g., Sebastian in Tennessee Williams' *Suddenly Last Summer*) or heterosexual (e.g., Portnoy). Which is not to deny that there may be some relationship, only to point out that it is more complex than popularized versions of Freudian psychiatry would suggest. Those particularly influenced by Freud see homosexuality as determined in very early childhood, and there is a strong emphasis on childhood experiences in novels such as Radclyffe Hall's *Well of Loneliness* or Sanford Friedman's *Totempole*. Others have sought to demonstrate some genetic origin, on the whole not very convincingly, although recent research does suggest there may be some correlation between homosexual behavior and chemical balance in certain hormones. A correlation however is far from being a cause.

Too often speculation on homosexuality tends to confuse it with effeminacy in boys or butchness in girls. Thus one comes across statements such as that by Robert Stoller, a Los Angeles professor of psychiatry, in his book *Sex and Gender* that "masculine homosexual men are an exception I cannot discuss since I do not yet understand them." Most studies of homosexuality, however, and certainly my own experience, tend to suggest that the majority are in fact masculine or feminine as we measure these

things in our society. Most homosexuals do not have doubts about their own masculinity or femininity, nor do they wish to be taken for or in fact become the opposite sex: many transvestites and transsexuals consider themselves determinedly heterosexual. As Simone de Beauvoir wrote in *The Second Sex,* "homosexuality can be for a woman a mode of flight from her situation or a way of accepting it."

This confusion of sex roles with sexual preference continues to influence the public imagination and even the psychiatric. There is a connection, but it is far more complicated than the assumption that homosexuality involves wanting-to-be-the-other-sex. Norman Mailer, whom I shall have frequent reason to quote, refers for example to "queers" as "humans-with-phalluses who choose to be female." Which is nonsense: most homosexuals choose no such thing, they choose rather to love/sleep with others of their own sex which is a completely different phenomenon.

Mailer uses the word "choose" which would be rejected by both biological and psychiatric determinists, and indeed probably by most homosexuals. "I can't help what I am" is a frequent comment in homosexual conversation. I suspect this is less true than the orthodox wisdom suggests, and that there is at least sometimes an element of deliberate choice in the adoption of homosexuality. Robert Lindner in his book *Must You Conform?* refers to homosexuality as "a form of rebellion" and the homosexual as a "non-conformist" and there is some truth in this. To become a homosexual, particularly for women, is to reject the program for marriage, family, and home that our society holds up as normal.

I must admit to considerable confusion in my own mind as to the way in which we develop our various patterns of sexual response. The interaction of biological urges and social pressures is a process that is little understood. Homosexuality, as we now know, exists in some form in virtually all human societies, and is associated with very different personality types and adjustment to sex roles. Thus some people can simultaneously assert that *most* fashion models and *most* masculine women are lesbians. Perhaps the most sensible conclusion is that there are many reasons which may account for an individual's homosexuality, that this becomes part of her or his total concept of identity, and that it is almost impossible to eradicate it without doing damage to the whole personality. (It may, of course, be possible to frighten a "patient" out of overt sexual acts, an approach which underlies so-called aversion therapy.)

The "problem" of the genesis of homosexuality ceases to be of great concern once one is prepared to accept homosexuality as neither a sin nor a pathology but rather as one way of ordering one's sexual drive, intrinsically no better nor worse than the heterosexual and with the same potential for love and hate, fulfillment or disappointment. In Iris Murdoch's novel *A Fairly Honourable Defeat,* remarkable among books that touch on the gay experience because the homosexuals end more happily than the heterosexuals, one of the protagonists, Axel, sees his homosexuality as "a fundamental and completely ordinary way of being a human being." Such is my own perspective.

Dossier 2: Signsex

The readings presented here constitute a sustained and rigorous articulation of that "textual/sexual" reading practice promoted by (post)structuralism and discussed in the general introduction (see especially section 2). The investigative focus of these readings is on the process of the (post)modernization of questions of sexuality and desire, which is to say the transmutation of the quasi-biological framework provided by Freud into the discursive framework theorized by ludic (post)modernists. What is fundamentally at stake in this allegiance to a theory of culture and the social posited in terms of mode of signification is the question of how "difference" is itself produced. Any address to the issue of social inequality necessarily involves assumptions about what constitutes politically meaningful differences. In textual/sexual materialism, signs do not refer to the objects they are taken to represent in the world (that is, meaning is not referential) but instead refer back to the ongoing processes of signification itself (meaning is differential). Difference is significatory difference, which Derrida theorizes as *différance:* the signifier always exceeds the limits of meaning set by the signified and enters a chain of *différance* in signification that is unstoppable and unmasterable. In a series of readings of various texts, Derrida demonstrates that, rather than being self-present and determinable, meaning is a constant drift of *différance,* a semantic chase, an unresting referral of one sign to other signs in endless deferment. As Baudrillard argues, following this line of theorization, economic need is itself absorbed into the operations of differ-

ential slipping signifiers. Like everything else, the sexual is also textualized and understood as a site of the play of *différance.*

Ludic (post)modern theorists argue that the naturalistic/biologistic or mechanistic/hydraulic vocabularies that mark Freud's texts ("instinct," "drive," "repression") are mere rhetorical residues, mere symptoms of the impact of those sciences that happened to have tremendous influence in Freud's time (a prestige on which Freud drew in order to promote his new science of psychoanalysis). Hence these vocabularies (especially the biologistic terminology), (post)modernists argue, do not constitute the core terms of the psychoanalytic frame itself. They thus sharply separate Freud's work from the natural sciences and situate it as a part of the social—particularly the hermeneutical or interpretive—sciences, stressing Freudian analytics as a form of reading the texts of culture, particularly reading the unconscious (sexually repressed) dimensions of the human psyche as text (as Freud himself does, for example, in *The Interpretation of Dreams*).

(Post)modernist theorists thus absorb Freudian organicism into mode of signification, as for example in the textualization of the psyche promoted in Lacan's "The Agency of the Letter in the Unconscious," the second part of which is reprinted in this volume. Lacan makes it clear (at the opening of the first part) that it is not the instincts (the organic) that constitute the unconscious but rather that "what the psychoanalytic experience discovers in the unconscious is the whole structure of language" (1977, 147). Drawing on Saussurean analytic principles in order to investigate the unconscious-as-discourse, Lacan insists that by the "letter in the unconscious" he means "literally" "the material support that concrete discourse borrows from language" (147) (or the signifier, the sound-image part of the sign). In order to bring Saussurean linguistics into relation with Freud's decentering of consciousness by the discovery of the unconscious, Lacan rewrites the Saussurean algorithm (as S/s or S^r/s^d) to emphasize the free play of the signifier in the unconscious. It is only an "illusion," he argues, "that the signifier answers to the function of representing the signified, or better, that the signifier has to answer for its existence in the name of any signification whatsoever" (150). In other words, once again we encounter in Lacan what we find in Baudrillard (see the general introduction to this text, section 2): not only a notion of materiality that refers above all to the kind of "materiality" the signifier has but also the insistence on the subordination of conventional and collective meaning (the signified) to the metaphorical and metonymical "play" of the signifer (meaningless in itself). The problem that results is that the interminable deconstructive process, which is the hallmark of Lacan's mode of writing/speaking, continually subverts (through the play of the signifier) all forms of knowing and renders it impossible to set (however provisionally) a knowledge that could serve as the basis for political praxis. In other words, the operations of desire always undermine and subvert any grasp or understanding of need.

Aware of what is at stake in the political arena, Lacan remarks that existing socialist societies (in his time) had not been able to develop "an esperanto in which the relations of language to socialist realities would have rendered any literary formalisms radically impossible" (149). What this means (in part) is that there could never be any form of society in which signifiers do not "slip." However, as I indicated in the general introduction, Marxism has produced a historical materialist account of the agitation of social meaning that understands the slippage of meaning politically, not just semiotically.

Lacan insists on the "letter" in the unconscious (the unconscious as intelligible in terms of the operations of such figures as metaphor and metonymy), but in "The Molecular Unconscious" Deleuze and Guattari take a more "radical" micro-level approach to subjectivity. In order to deregulate desire, they reject the very distinction between the literal (the body as "organism") and the figurative (the body as "mechanism"). From their viewpoint the Lacanian model of the unconscious is a "molar" model still concerned with larger units such as subjectivity itself and its components (id, ego, superego, or Imaginary, Symbolic, Real). They argue that the "molecular" level is the level at which the literal/figural distinction disappears, along with these larger units, and the subject is seen merely as the trace of the operations of the desiring machines (see again the general introduction).

Still willing to name the (larger) molar unit called "the lover," in *A Lover's Discourse,* Barthes offers an index to the textual/sexual field of signifiers in which the amorous subject is constructed. The lover's Imaginary articulates itself through a complex string of interwoven connotations organized by the arbitrariness of the alphabet. Although named as an identifiable unit, the amorous subject remains "anonymous" in *A Lover's Discourse,* where the concreteness and specificity of the historical is suspended in the textualized field of playing signifiers. Barthes's own history, however, makes its (re)appearance in a set of texts posthumously published in 1992 under the title *Incidents,* which comprise an intimate journal of some of Barthes's sexual contacts in Paris and Morocco, a slim book that was published by the University of California Press as half of a banded set, the other half of which was D. A. Miller's essay on *Bringing Out Barthes.*

The short selection on "writing aloud" from Barthes's *The Pleasure of the Text* reveals in concentrated form a number of features of ludic (post)modern thought. It not only sums up Barthes's orgasmic theory of reading/writing as an act of *jouissance* but also shows his own tendency to collapse, like Deleuze and Guattari, the figurative into the literal (with "writing aloud" the body of the actor is thrown, Barthes says, into his ear). This passage also marks ludic (post)modern theory's effort to subvert the signified (conceptuality) with the signifier (textuality) using the idea of "shifting the signified a great distance [away]."

In the pantextual universe of ludic (post)-modernism, in which everything seems "always already" to have happened (that is, everything exists in a "post" state), the historical record (itself a text) is undecidable and indeterminate. As one commentator puts it, "Postmodern awareness is born of the recognition that the past that was never present eternally returns as the future that never arrives to displace all contemporaneity and defer forever the presence of the modern" (Taylor 1986, 34). In Derrida's *The Post Card,* history as objective causal relations is bracketed and instead becomes a set of reversible representations. Derrida's reading of the depiction of Plato *behind* Socrates makes of the engraving an emblematic instance of the undecidability of history through the unleashing of desire (in this case marked specifically as homosexual) in signification. While the *historical* record says that Plato followed *after* and wrote down in the dialogues the lessons of his tutor, Socrates, the engraving situates Plato graphically *after* (in the sense of behind) his mentor who in this version of their relationship is the one who writes. Derrida speculates, furthermore, that a reversal of roles has taken place: It appears as if Plato is directing Socrates's writing. Since for (post)structuralism, the enabling condition of the production of meaning is the unleashing of irrepressible desire, we therefore find incorporated into the "excitement" of this reversal of history and (phallic) authority a homoerotic excitement: It looks as if Plato has an erection pressed against Socrates's backside. The postcard becomes then not only an emblem of the "slippage of the signifier" but that "slippage" becomes the kind of "queering of meaning" promoted by today's norm-busting queer theory (the picture disrupts all norms—of history, of writing, of sexuality, and so on). In the same desirous spirit, in *The Post Card: From Socrates to*

Freud and Beyond Derrida continually addresses his principal "object of desire" and thus thematizes his text as a "lover's discourse," something which, in a broader sense, all texts—operating by the unleashing of desire—"already are," according to (post)structuralism.

In "That Dangerous Supplement," Derrida offers a reading of Jean-Jacques Rousseau's *Confessions* focusing on Rousseau's anxiety about masturbation. In his discussion, Derrida uses his "differential" and "supplementary" logic to deconstruct the familiar hierarchy by which sexual intercourse (here specifically heterosexual) is privileged as a genuine and authentic form of sexuality whereas autoeroticism is merely regarded as a poor substitute. The effect of Derrida's reading is to show that there is no sexual practice of any kind that is free of imaginary and autoerotic components and thus that sexuality is not in any simple sense "social" (an unmediated and "pure" connecting of the one person with another). Like other moves of ludic (post)modern theory, such a deconstruction tends to divert attention away from the social character of sexual practices. (For a more sustained discussion of these issues, see Zavarzadeh and Morton, *Theory, (Post)Modernity, Opposition,* pp. 181–184.)

Although she accepts the desire-orientation of her male (post)structuralist tutors, Luce Irigaray inaugurates a line of feminist inquiry that critiques Freud and Lacan and the psychoanalytic institution at large for promoting phallocentric desire as desire itself. One of the focal points of her critique is the phallocratic psychoanalytic tradition's treatment particularly of female homosexuality: Because male psychoanalytic theorists are so unconsciously and narcissistically convinced of the desirability of the masculine subject, they understand male homosexuality, while generally observing the taboo against it. What they refer to as homosexuality Irigaray rewrites as "hom(m)osexuality" to indicate (through the masculine prefix, "hommo-") the patriarchal and masculinist ideology in which it is entangled. However, because of the merely "secondary" status of the feminine subject in the phallic economy (in which woman is just another object of exchange), woman's desire for woman remains mysterious. In Irigaray's understanding, this means that woman's desire remains uncharted territory, which her work proposes to begin mapping. However, because her theorizing is premised on ludic (post)modern assumptions (with a clear indebtedness to the supposedly feminocentric writings of Derrida), Irigaray's work hovers between deconstructing phallocentric texts (negating "masculinist" desire) and re-essentializing woman's desire by centering it on the supposedly centerless body of woman (for instance, by substituting an analytics of the labial for an analytics of the phallic).

In her essay titled "Sexual Indifference and Lesbian Representation" (behind which lies not only the work of Irigaray but Adrienne Rich's well-known essay, "Compulsory Heterosexuality and Lesbian Existence"), Teresa de Lauretis further elaborates on "hom(m)osexuality"—which Irigaray attributes to *the sexual indifference that underlies the truth of any science [understood as masculinist "knowing"], the logic of every discourse*" (Irigaray 1985, 69). (Permission to reprint this essay in this anthology was denied; see my "A Note on [the Politics of] Text Selection.") De Lauretis's theorizations confirm the proposition that the lesbian is outside sociality itself (that is, by definition, "unknowable" within phallocratic discourses). A result, however, of the introduction of difference as textual/sexual *différance* (the play of the signifier) is to render the process of differentiation as interminable (undecidable). In other words, rigorous deconstruction does not allow the "play of the signifer" ever to stop long enough to permit a particular representation of "woman," "lesbian," "homosexual," to persist or insist in the discourses of culture. Maintaining this deconstructive rigor in "Imitation and Gender Insubordination," Judith Butler follows the Barthesian principle of embrace of the "letter" and rejection of the "name": In other words, she will accept the term *lesbian* so long as it is "permanently unclear" what *lesbian* means. This outcome is peculiar in the sense that for woman-as-mystery (produced through phallocratic discourses) is substituted woman-as-mystery (produced through deconstructive discourses). As Sue-Ellen Case has put it, these theorizations produce the subject as in a constant state of "mobility," as always in a state of process or transit (1990). Elizabeth Meese's essay reprinted here clearly situates the "lesbian" as a "mobile" material entity in the (post)structuralist sense of a "textual" (the signifier) and/or "bodily" materiality. The short extract by Kaja Silverman also reprinted in the dossier suggests that this transitivity allows even the female subject to pass through the defile of signifiers marking the gay male Imaginary. Just as male theorists such as Deleuze and Guattari speak of "becoming woman," Silverman—like Sedgwick in "White Glasses" (see the general introduction, section 4)—discursively enacts the woman "becoming a (gay) man." The interminably transitive subject of ludic (post)modernism, however, never arrives at any destination, nor can it come to any—even provisional—conclusion. It is, in other words, a thoroughgoingly ahistorical subject, a subject always "in process" (to borrow Kristeva's phrase), unconnected to any origin or telos or to any "cause."

The AIDS epidemic is, sadly, one moment when such "textual"/"sexual" "transitivity" (based on the autonomy of desire) does not seem finally to be very productive, a moment when history cannot be bracketed. It represents an instance in which "need" (for material resources, of money, treatments, medical personnel, and so on) overwhelms the desire-bound Imaginary. This outcome is clearly articulated in the self-described "somber" conclusion of an essay by Lee Edelman on AIDS ("The Plague of Discourse"), which indicates that playful deconstructive readings that can unleash *desire* and produce a politics of "representations" cannot finally address those *needs*. (Permission to reprint this essay in this anthology was denied; see my "A Note on [the Politics of] Text Selection.")

References

Barthes, Roland. (1992) *Incidents*. Trans. Richard Howard. Berkeley: University of California Press.

Case, Sue-Ellen, ed. (1990) *Performing Feminisms: Feminist Critical Theory and Theatre.* Baltimore and London: The Johns Hopkins University Press.

de Lauretis, Teresa. (1990) "Sexual Indifference and Lesbian Representation." In Sue-Ellen Case, ed., *Performing Feminisms: Feminist Critical Theory and Theatre.* Baltimore: Johns Hopkins University Press: 17–39.

Derrida, Jacques. (1987) *The Post Card: From Socrates to Freud and Beyond.* Trans. Alan Bass. Chicago: University of Chicago Press.

Edelman, Lee. (1989) "The Plague of Discourse: Politics, Literary Theory, and AIDS." In Ronald R. Butters, John M. Clum, and Michael Moon, eds., *Displacing Homophobia.* Special issue of *South Atlantic Quarterly* 88.1 (Winter): 301–317.

Irigaray, Luce. (1985) *This Sex Which Is Not One.* Trans. Catherine Porter. Ithaca: Cornell University Press.

Lacan, Jacques. (1977) *Écrits.* New York and London: W. W. Norton.

Miller, D. A. (1992) *Bringing Out Barthes.* Berkeley: University of California Press.

Taylor, Mark. (1986) *Deconstruction in Context: Literature and Philosophy.* Chicago and London: University of Chicago Press.

Zavarzadeh, Mas'ud, and Donald Morton. (1991) *Theory, (Post)Modernity, Opposition: An "Other" Introduction to Literary and Cultural Theory.* Washington, D.C.: Maisonneuve Press.

The Letter in the Unconscious

Jacques Lacan

. . . In the complete works of Freud, one out of every three pages is devoted to philological references, one out of every two pages to logical inferences, everywhere a dialectical apprehension of experience, the proportion of analysis of language increasing to the extent that the unconscious is directly concerned.

Thus in 'The Interpretation of Dreams' every page deals with what I call the letter of the discourse, in its texture, its usage, its immanence in the matter in question. For it is with this work that the work of Freud begins to open the royal road to the unconscious. And Freud gave us notice of this; his confidence at the time of launching this book in the early days of this century[1] only confirms what he continued to proclaim to the end: that he had staked the whole of his discovery on this essential expression of his message.

The first sentence of the opening chapter announces what for the sake of the exposition could not be postponed: that the dream is a rebus. And Freud goes on to stipulate what I have said from the start, that it must be understood quite literally. This derives from the agency in the dream of that same literal (or phonematic) structure in which the signifier is articulated and analysed in discourse. So the unnatural images of the boat on the roof, or the man with a comma for a head, which are specifically mentioned by Freud, are examples of dream-images that are to be taken only for their value as signifiers, that is to say, in so far as they allow us to spell out the 'proverb' presented by the rebus of the dream. The linguistic structure that enables us to read dreams is the very principle of the 'significance of the dream', the *Traumdeutung*.

Freud shows us in every possible way that the value of the image as signifier has nothing whatever to do with its signification, giving as an example Egyptian hieroglyphics in which it would be sheer buffoonery to pretend that in a given text the frequency of a vulture, which is an *aleph*, or of a chick, which is a *vau*, indicating a form of the verb 'to be' or a plural, prove that the text has anything at all to do with these ornithological specimens. Freud finds in this writing certain uses of the signifier that are lost in ours, such as the use of determinatives, where a categorical figure is added to the literal figuration of a verbal term; but this is only to show us that even in this writing, the so-called 'ideogram' is a letter.

But it does not require the current confusion on this last term for there to prevail in the minds of psychoanalysts lacking linguistic training the prejudice in favour of a symbolism deriving from natural analogy, or even of the image as appropriate to the instinct. And to such an extent that, outside the French school, which has been alerted, a distinction must be drawn between reading coffee grounds and reading hieroglyphics, by recalling to its own principles a technique that could not be justified were it not directed towards the unconscious.

It must be said that this is admitted only with difficulty and that the mental vice denounced above enjoys such favour that today's psychoanalyst can be expected to say that he decodes before he will come around to taking the necessary tour with Freud (turn at the statute of Champollion,[2] says the guide) that will make him understand that what he does is decipher; the distinction is that a cryptogram takes on its full dimension only when it is in a lost language.

Taking the tour is simply continuing in the *Traumdeutung*.

Entstellung, translated as 'distortion' or 'transposition', is what Freud shows to be the general precondition for the functioning of the dream, and it is what I designated above, following Saussure, as the sliding of the signified under the signifier, which is always active in discourse (its action, let us note, is unconscious).

But what we call the two 'sides' of the effect of the signifier on the signified are also found here.

Verdichtung, or 'condensation', is the structure of the superimposition of the signifiers, which metaphor takes as its field, and whose name, condensing in itself the word *Dichtung*, shows how the mechanism is connatural with poetry to the point that it envelops the traditional function proper to poetry.

In the case of *Verschiebung*, 'displacement', the German term is closer to the idea of that veering off of signification that we see in metonymy, and which from its first appearance in Freud is represented as the most appropriate means used by the unconscious to foil censorship.

What distinguishes these two mechanisms, which play such a privileged role in the dream-work (*Traumarbeit*), from their homologous function in discourse? Nothing, except a condition imposed upon the signifying material, called *Rücksicht auf Darstellbarkeit*, which must be translated by 'consideration of the means of representation'. (The translation by 'role of the possibility of figurative expression' being too approximative here.) But this condition constitutes a limitation operating *within* the system of writing; this is a long way from dissolving the system into a figurative semiology on a level with phenomena of natural expression. This fact could perhaps shed light on the problems involved in certain modes of pictography which, simply because they have been abandoned in writing as imperfect, are not therefore to be regarded as mere evolutionary stages. Let us say,

then, that the dream is like the parlour-game in which one is supposed to get the spectators to guess some well known saying or variant of it solely by dumb-show. That the dream uses speech makes no difference since for the unconscious it is only one among several elements of the representation. It is precisely the fact that both the game and the dream run up against a lack of taxematic material for the representation of such logical articulations as causality, contradiction, hypothesis, etc., that proves they are a form of writing rather than of mime. The subtle processes that the dream is seen to use to represent these logical articulations, in a much less artificial way than games usually employ, are the object of a special study in Freud in which we see once more confirmed that the dream-work follows the laws of the signifier.

The rest of the dream-elaboration is designated as secondary by Freud, the nature of which indicates its value: they are phantasies or daydreams (*Tagtraum*) to use the term Freud prefers in order to emphasize their function of wish-fulfillment (*Wunscherfüllung*). Given the fact that these phantasies may remain unconscious, their distinctive feature is in this case their signification. Now, concerning these phantasies, Freud tells us that their place in the dream is either to be taken up and used as signifying elements for the statement of the unconscious thoughts (*Traumgedanke*), or to be used in the secondary elaboration just mentioned, that is to say, in a function not to be distinguished from our waking thought (*von unserem wachen Denken nicht zu unterschieden*). No better idea of the effects of this function can be given than by comparing it to areas of colour which, when applied here and there to a stencil-plate, can make the stencilled figures, rather forbidding in themselves, more reminiscent of hieroglyphics or of a rebus, look like a figurative painting.

Forgive me if I seem to have to spell out Freud's text; I do so not only to show how much is to be gained by not cutting it about, but also in order to situate the development of psychoanalysis according to its first guide-lines, which were fundamental and never revoked.

Yet from the beginning there was a general *méconnaissance* of the constitutive role of the signifier in the status that Freud from the first assigned to the unconscious and in the most precise formal manner.

There are two reasons for this, of which the least obvious, of course, is that this formalization was not sufficient in itself to bring about a recognition of the agency of the signifier because the *Traumdeutung* appeared long before the formalizations of linguistics for which one could no doubt show that it paved the way by the sheer weight of its truth.

The second reason, which is after all only the reverse side of the first, is that if psychoanalysts were fascinated exclusively by the significations revealed in the unconscious, it is because these significations derived their secret attraction from the dialectic that seemed to be immanent in them.

I have shown in my seminars that it is the need to counteract the continuously accelerating effects of this bias that alone explains the apparent changes of direction or rather changes of tack, which Freud, through his primary concern to preserve for posterity both his discovery and the fundamental revisions it effected in our knowledge, felt it necessary to apply to his doctrine.

For, I repeat, in the situation in which he found himself, having nothing that corresponded to the object of his discovery that was at the same level of scientific development—in this situation, at least he never failed to maintain this object on the level of its ontological dignity.

The rest was the work of the gods and took such a course that analysis today takes its bearings in those imaginary forms that I have just shown to be drawn 'resist-style' (*en reserve*) on the text they mutilate—and the analyst tries to accommodate his direction to them, confusing them, in the interpretation of the dream, with the visionary liberation of the hieroglyphic aviary, and seeking generally the control of the exhaustion of the analysis in a sort of 'scanning'[3] of these forms whenever they appear, in the idea that they are witnesses of the exhaustion of the regressions and of the remodelling of the object relation from which the subject is supposed to derive his 'character-type'.[4]

The technique that is based on such positions can be fertile in its various effects, and under the aegis of therapy, difficult to criticize. But an internal criticism must none the less arise from the flagrant disparity between the mode of operation by which the technique is justified—namely the analytic rule, all the instruments of which, beginning with 'free association', depend on the conception of the unconscious of its inventor—and, on the other hand, the general *méconnaissance* that reigns regarding this conception of the unconscious. The most ardent adherents of this technique believe themselves to be freed of any need to reconcile the two by the merest pirouette: the analytic rule (they say) must be all the more religiously observed since it is only the result of a lucky accident. In other words, Freud never knew what he was doing.

A return to Freud's text shows on the contrary the absolute coherence between his technique and his discovery, and at the same time this coherence allows us to put all his procedures in their proper place.

That is why any rectification of psychoanalysis must inevitably involve a return to the truth of that discovery, which, taken in its original moment, is impossible to obscure.

For in the analysis of dreams, Freud intends only to give us the laws of the unconscious in their most general extension. One of the reasons why dreams were most propitious for this demonstration is exactly, Freud tells us, that they reveal the same laws whether in the normal person or in the neurotic.

But in either case, the efficacy of the unconscious does not cease in the waking state. The psychoanalytic experience does nothing other than establish that the unconscious leaves none of our actions outside its field. The presence of the unconscious in the psychological order, in other words in the relation-functions of the individual, should, however, be more precisely defined: it is not coextensive with that order, for we know that if unconscious motivation is manifest in conscious psychical effects, as well as in unconscious ones, conversely it is only elementary to recall to mind that a large number of psychical effects that are quite legitimately designated as unconscious, in the sense of excluding the characteristic of consciousness, are nonetheless without any relation whatever to the unconscious in the Freudian sense. So it is only by an abuse of the term that unconscious in that sense is confused with psychical, and that one may thus designate as psychical what is in fact an effect of the unconscious, as on the somatic for instance.

It is a matter, therefore, of defining the topography of this unconscious. I say that it is the very topography defined by the algorithm:

$$\frac{S}{s}$$

What we have been able to develop concerning the effects of the signifier on the signified suggests its transformation into:

$$f(S)\frac{I}{s}$$

We have shown the effects not only of the elements of the horizontal signifying chain, but also of its vertical dependencies in the signified, divided into two fundamental structures called metonymy and metaphor. We can symbolize them by, first:

$$f(S\ldots S')S \cong S(-)s$$

that is to say, the metonymic structure, indicating that it is the connexion between signifier and signifier that permits the elision in which the signifier installs the lack-of-being in the object relation, using the value of 'reference back' possessed by signification in order to invest it with the desire aimed at the very lack it supports. The sign — placed between () represents here the maintenance of the bar—which, in the original algorithm, marked the irreducibility in which, in the relations between signifier and signified, the resistance of signification is constituted.[5]

Secondly,

$$f\left(\frac{S'}{S}\right)S \cong S(+)s$$

the metaphoric structure indicating that it is in the substitution of signifier for signifier that an effect of signification is produced that is creative or poetic, in other words, which is the advent of the signification in question.[6] The sign + between () represents here the crossing of the bar—and the constitutive value of this crossing for the emergence of signification.

This crossing expresses the condition of passage of the signifier into the signified that I pointed out above, although provisionally confusing it with the place of the subject.

It is the function of the subject, thus introduced, that we must now turn to since it lies at the crucial point of our problem.

'I think, therefore I am' (*cogito ergo sum*) is not merely the formula in which is constituted, with the historical high point of reflection on the conditions of science, the link between the transparency of the transcendental subject and his existential affirmation.

Perhaps I am only object and mechanism (and so nothing more than phenomenon), but assuredly in so far as I think so, I am—absolutely. No doubt philosophers have brought important corrections to this formulation, notably that in that which thinks (*cogitans*), I can never constitute myself as anything but object (*cogitatum*). Nonetheless it remains true that by way of this extreme purification of the transcendental subject, my existential link to its project seems irrefutable, at least in its present form, and that: '*cogito ergo sum' ubi cogito, ibi sum*, overcomes this objection.

Of course, this limits me to being there in my being only in so far as I think that I am in my thought; just how far I actually think this concerns only myself and if I say it, interests no one.[7]

Yet to elude this problem on the pretext of its philosophical pretensions is simply to admit one's inhibition. For the notion of subject is indispensable even to the operation of a science such as strategy (in the modern sense) whose calculations exclude all 'subjectivism'.

It is also to deny oneself access to what might be called the Freudian universe—in the way that we speak of the Copernican universe. It was in fact the so-called Copernican revolution to which Freud himself compared his discovery, emphasizing that it was once again a question of the place man assigns to himself at the centre of a universe.

Is the place that I occupy as the subject of a signifier concentric or excentric, in relation to the place I occupy as subject of the signified?— that is the question.

It is not a question of knowing whether I speak of myself in a way that conforms to what I am, but rather of knowing whether I am the same as that of which I speak. And it is not at all inappropriate to use the word 'thought' here. For Freud uses the term to designate the elements involved in the unconscious, that is the signifying mechanisms that we now recognize as being there.

It is nonetheless true that the philosophical *cogito* is at the centre of the mirage that renders modern man so sure of being himself even in his uncertainties about himself, and even in the mistrust he has learned to practise against the traps of self-love.

Furthermore, if, turning the weapon of metonymy against the nostalgia that it serves, I refuse to seek any meaning beyond tautology, if in the name of 'war is war' and 'a penny's a penny' I decide to be only what I am, how even here can I elude the obvious fact that I am in that very act?

And it is no less true if I take myself to the other, metaphoric pole of the signifying quest, and if I dedicate myself to becoming what I am, to coming into being, I cannot doubt that even if I lose myself in the process, I am in that process.

Now it is on these very points, where evidence will be subverted by the empirical, that the trick of the Freudian conversion lies.

This signifying game between metonymy and metaphor, up to and including the active edge that splits my desire between a refusal of the signifier and a lack of being, and links my fate to the question of my destiny, this game, in all its inexorable subtlety, is played until the match is called, there where I am not, because I cannot situate myself there.

That is to say, what is needed is more than these words with which, for a brief moment I disconcerted my audience: I think where I am not, therefore I am where I do not think. Words that render sensible to an ear properly attuned with what elusive ambiguity[8] the ring of meaning flees from our grasp along the verbal thread.

What one ought to say is: I am not wherever I am the plaything of my thought; I think of what I am where I do not think to think.

This two-sided mystery is linked to the fact that the truth can be evoked only in that dimension of alibi in which all 'realism' in creative works takes its virtue from metonymy; it is likewise linked to this other fact that we accede to meaning only through the double twist of metaphor when we have the one and only key: the S and the *s* of the Saussurian algorithm are not on the same level, and man only deludes himself when he believes his true place is at their axis, which is nowhere.

Was nowhere, that is, until Freud discovered it; for if what Freud discovered isn't that, it isn't anything.

*   *   *

The contents of the unconscious with all their disappointing ambiguities give us no reality in the subject more consistent than the immediate; their virtue derives from the truth and in the dimension of being: *Kern unseres Wesen*[9] are Freud's own terms.

The double-triggered mechanism of metaphor is the very mechanism by which the symptom, in the analytic sense, is determined. Between the enigmatic signifier of the sexual trauma and the term that is substituted for it in an actual signifying chain there passes the spark that fixes in a symptom the signification inaccessible to the conscious subject in which that symptom may be resolved—a symptom being a metaphor in which flesh or function is taken as a signifying element.

And the enigmas that desire seems to pose for a 'natural philosophy'—its frenzy mocking the abyss of the infinite, the secret collusion with which it envelops the pleasure of knowing and of dominating with *jouissance,* these amount to no other derangement of instinct than that of being caught in the rails—eternally stretching forth towards the *desire for something else*—of metonymy. Hence its 'perverse' fixation at the very suspension-point of the signifying chain where the memory-screen is immobilized and the fascinating image of the fetish is petrified.

There is no other way of conceiving the indestructibility of unconscious desire—in the absence of a need which, when forbidden satisfaction, does not sicken and die, even if it means the destruction of the organism itself. It is in a memory, comparable to what is called by that name in our modern thinking-machines (which are in turn based on an electronic realization of the composition of signification), it is in this sort of memory that is found the chain that *insists* on reproducing itself in the transference, and which is the chain of dead desire.

It is the truth of what this desire has been in his history that the patient cries out through his symptom, as Christ said that the stones themselves would have cried out if the children of Israel had not lent them their voice.

And that is why only psychoanalysis allows us to differentiate within memory the function of recollection. Rooted in the signifier, it resolves the Platonic aporias of reminiscence through the ascendancy of history in man.

One has only to read the 'Three Essays on Sexuality' to observe, in spite of the pseudo-biological glosses with which it is decked out for popular consumption, that Freud there derives all accession to the object from a dialectic of return.

Starting from Hölderlin's νοστος, Freud arrives less than twenty years later at Kierkegaard's repetition; that is, in submitting his thought solely to the humble but inflexible consequences of the 'talking cure',[10] he was unable ever to escape the living servitudes that led him from the sovereign principle of the Logos to rethinking the Empedoclean antinomies of death.

And how else are we to conceive the recourse of a man of science to a *Deus ex machina* than on that 'other scene' he speaks of as the locus of the dream, a *Deus ex machina* only less derisory for the fact that it is revealed to the spectator that the machine directs the director? How else can we imagine that a scientist of the nineteenth century, unless we realize that he had to bow before the force of evidence that went well beyond his prejudices, valued more highly than all his other works his *Totem and Taboo,* with its obscene, ferocious figure of the primordial father, not to be exhausted in the expiation of Oedipus' blindness, and before which the ethnologists of today bow as before the growth of an authentic myth?

So that imperious proliferation of particular symbolic creations, such as what are called the sexual theories of the child, which supply the motivation down to the smallest detail of neurotic compulsions, these reply to the same necessities as do myths.

Thus, to speak of the precise point we are treating in my seminars on Freud, little Hans, left in the lurch at the age of five by his symbolic environment, and suddenly forced to face the enigma of his sex and his existence, developed, under the direction of Freud and of his father, Freud's disciple, in mythic form, around the signifying crystal of his phobia, all the permutations possible on a limited number of signifiers.

The operation shows that even on the individual level the solution of the impossible is brought within man's reach by the exhaustion of all possible forms of the impossibilities encountered in solution by recourse to the signifying equation. It is a striking demonstration that illuminates the labyrinth of a case which so far has only been used as a source of demolished fragments. We should be struck, too, by the fact that it is in the coextensivity of the development of the symptom and of its curative resolution that the nature of the neurosis is revealed: whether phobic, hysterical, or obsessive, the neurosis is a question that being poses for the subject 'from where it was before the subject came into the world' (Freud's phrase, which he used in explaining the Oedipal complex to little Hans).

The 'being' referred to is that which appears in a lightning moment in the void of the verb 'to be' and I said that it poses its question for the subject. What does that mean? It does not pose it *before* the subject, since the subject cannot come to the place where it is posed, but it poses it *in place* of the subject, that is to say, in that place it poses the question *with* the subject, as one poses a problem *with* a pen, or as Aristotle's man thought *with* his soul.

Thus Freud introduced the ego into his doctrine,[11] by defining it according to the resistances that are proper to it. What I have tried to convey is that these resistances are of an imaginary nature much in the same sense as those coaptative lures that the ethology of animal behaviour shows us in display or combat, and that these lures are reduced in man to the narcissistic relation introduced by Freud, which I have elaborated in my essay on the mirror stage. I have tried to show that by situating in this ego the synthesis of the perceptual functions in which the sensorimotor selections are integrated, Freud seems to abound in that delegation that is traditionally supposed to represent reality for the ego, and that this reality is all the more included in the suspension of the ego.

For this ego, which is notable in the first instance for the imaginary inertias that it concentrates against the message of the unconscious, operates solely with a view to covering the displacement constituted by the subject with a resistance that is essential to the discourse as such.

That is why an exhaustion of the mechanisms of defence, which Fenichel the practitioner shows us so well in his studies of analytic technique (while his whole reduction on the theoretical level of neuroses and psychoses to genetic anomalies in libidinal development is pure platitude), manifests itself, without Fenichel's accounting for it or realizing it himself, as simply the reverse side of the mechanisms of the unconscious. Periphrasis, hyperbaton, ellipsis, suspension, anticipation, retraction, negation, digression, irony, these are the figures of style (Quintilian's *figurae sententiarum*); as catachresis, litotes, antonomasia, hypotyposis are the tropes, whose terms suggest themselves as the most proper for the labelling of these mechanisms. Can one really see these as mere figures of speech when it is the figures themselves that are the active principle of the rhetoric of the discourse that the analysand in fact utters?

By persisting in describing the nature of resistance as a permanent emotional state, thus making it alien to the discourse, today's psychoanalysts have simply shown that they have fallen under the blow of one of the fundamental truths that Freud rediscovered through psychoanalysis. One is never happy making way for a new truth, for it always means making our way into it: the truth is always disturbing. We cannot even manage to get used to it. We are used to the real. The truth we repress.

Now it is quite specially necessary to the scientist, to the seer, even to the quack, that he should be the only one to *know*. The idea that deep in the simplest (and even sickest) of souls there is something ready to blossom is bad enough! But if someone seems to know as much as they about what we ought to make of it . . . then the categories of primitive, prelogical, archaic, or even magical thought, so easy to impute to others, rush to our aid! It is not right that these nonentities keep us breathless with enigmas that prove to be only too unreliable.

To interpret the unconscious as Freud did, one would have to be as he was, an encyclopedia of the arts and muses, as well as an assiduous reader of the *Fliegende Blätter*.[12] And the task is made no easier by the fact that we are at the mercy of a thread woven with allusions, quotations, puns, and equivocations. And is that our profession, to be antidotes to trifles?

Yet that is what we must resign ourselves to. The unconscious is neither primordial nor instinctual; what it knows about the elementary is no more than the elements of the signifier.

The three books that one might call canonical with regard to the unconscious—'The Interpretation of Dreams', 'The Psychopathology of Everyday Life', and 'Jokes and their Relation to the Unconscious'—are simply a web of examples whose development is inscribed in the formulas of connexion and substitution (though carried to the tenth degree by their particular complexity—diagrams of them are sometimes provided by Freud by way of illustration); these are the formulas we give to the signifier in its *transference*-function. For in 'The Interpretation of Dreams' it is in the sense of such a function that the term *Übertragung,* or transference, is introduced, which later gave its name to the mainspring of the intersubjective link between analyst and analysand.

Such diagrams are not only constitutive of each of the symptoms in a neurosis, but they alone make possible the understanding of the thematic of its course and resolution. The great case-histories provided by Freud demonstrate this admirably.

To fall back on a more limited incident, but one more likely to provide us with the final seal on our proposition, let me cite the article on fetishism of 1927,[13] and the case Freud reports there of a patient who, to achieve sexual satisfaction, needed a certain shine on the nose (*Glanz auf der Nase*); analysis showed that his early, English-speaking years had seen the displacement of the burning curiosity that he felt for the phallus of his mother, that is to say, for that eminent *manque-á-être,* for that want-to-be, whose privileged signifier Freud revealed to us, into a *glance at the nose* in the forgotten language of his childhood, rather than a *shine on the nose.*[14]

It is the abyss opened up at the thought that a thought should make itself heard in the abyss that provoked resistance to psychoanalysis from the outset. And not, as is commonly said, the emphasis on man's sexuality. This latter has after all been the dominant object in literature throughout the ages. And in fact the more recent evolution of psychoanalysis has succeeded by a bit of comical legerdemain in turning it into a quite moral affair, the cradle and trysting-place of oblativity and attraction. The Platonic setting of the soul, blessed and illuminated, rises straight to paradise.

The intolerable scandal in the time before Freudian sexuality was sanctified was that it was so 'intellectual'. It was precisely in that that it showed itself to be the worthy ally of all those terrorists whose plottings were going to ruin society.

At a time when psychoanalysts are busy re-modelling psychoanalysis into a right-thinking movement whose crowning expression is the socio-logical poem of the *autonomous ego,* I would like to say, to all those who are listening to me, how they can recognize bad psychoanalysts; this is by the word they use to deprecate all technical or theoretical research that carries forward the Freudian experience along its authentic lines. That word is '*intellectualization*'— execrable to all those who, living in fear of being tried and found wanting by the wine of truth, spit on the bread of men, although their slaver can no longer have any effect other than that of leavening.

Notes

1. Cf. the correspondence, namely letters 107 and 109.

2. Jean-François Champollion (1790–1832), the first scholar to decipher the Ancient Egyptian hieroglyphics [Tr.].

3. That is the process by which the results of a piece of research are assured through a mechanical exploration of the entire extent of the field of its object.

4. By referring only to the development of the organism, the typology fails to recognize (*méconnaît*) the structure in which the subject is caught up respectively in phantasy, in drive, in sublimation. I am at present developing the theory of this structure (note 1966).

5. The sign ≅ here designates congruence.

6. S′ designating here the term productive of the signifying effect (or significance); one can see that the term is latent in metonymy, patent in metaphor.

7. It is quite otherwise if by posing a question such as 'Why philosophers?' I become more candid than nature, for then I am asking not only the question that philosophers have been asking themselves for all time, but also the one in which they are perhaps most interested.

8. '*Ambiguité de furet*'—literally, 'ferret-like ambiguity'. This is one of a number of references in Lacan to the game 'hunt-the-slipper' (*jeu du furet*) [Tr.].

9. 'The nucleus of our being' [Tr.].

10. English in the original [Tr.].

11. This and the next paragraph were rewritten solely with a view to greater clarity of expression (note 1968).

12. A German comic newspaper of the late nineteenth and early twentieth centuries [Tr.].

13. *Fetischismus, Gesammelte Werke* **XIV**: 311; 'Fetishism', *Collected Papers*, **V**: 198; *Standard Edition* **XXI**: 149.

14. English in the original [Tr.].

The Molecular Unconscious

Gilles Deleuze and Felix Guattari

What is the meaning of this distinction between two regions: one molecular and the other molar; one micropsychic or micrological, the other statistical and gregarious? Is this anything more than a metaphor lending the unconscious a distinction grounded in physics, when we speak of an opposition between intra-atomic phenomena and the mass phenomena that operate through statistical accumulation, obeying the laws of aggregates? But in reality the unconscious belongs to the realm of physics; the body without organs and its intensities are not metaphors, but matter itself. Nor is it our intention to revive the question of an individual psychology and a collective psychology, and of the priority of the one or the other; this distinction, as it appears in *Group Psychology and the Analysis of the Ego,* remains completely stymied by Oedipus. In the unconscious there are only populations, groups, and machines. When we posit in one case an involuntariness (*un involontaire*) of the social and technical machines, in the other case an unconscious of the desiring-machines, it is a question of a necessary relationship between inextricably linked forces. Some of these are elementary forces by means of which the unconscious is produced; the others, resultants reacting on the first, statistical aggregates through which the unconscious is represented and already suffers psychic and social repression of its elementary productive forces.

But how can we speak of machines in this microphysical or micropsychic region, *there where there is desire*—that is to say, not only its functioning, but formation and autoproduction? A machine works according to the previous intercommunications of its structure and the positioning of its parts, but does not set itself into place any more than it forms or reproduces itself. This is even the point around which the usual polemic between vitalism and mechanism revolves: the machine's ability to account for the workings of the organism, but its fundamental inability to account for its formations. From machines, mechanism abstracts a *structural unity* in terms of which it explains the functioning of the organism. Vitalism invokes an *individual and specific unity* of the living, which every machine presupposes insofar as it is subordinate to organic continuance, and insofar as it extends the latter's autonomous formations on the outside. But it should be noted that, in one way or another, the machine and desire thus remain in an extrinsic relationship, either because desire appears as an effect determined by a system of mechanical causes, or because the machine is itself a system of means in terms of the aims of desire. The link between the two remains secondary and indirect, both in the new means appropriated by desire and in the derived desires produced by the machines.

A profound text by Samuel Butler, "The Book of the Machines," nevertheless allows us to go beyond these points of view.[1] It is true that this text seems at first merely to contrast the two common arguments, the one according to which the organisms are for the moment only more perfect machines ("Whether those things which we deem most purely spiritual are anything but disturbances of equilibrium in an infinite series of levers, beginning with those levers that are too small for microscopic detection"[2]), the other according to which machines are never more than extensions of the organism ("The lower animals keep all their limbs at home in their bodies, but many of man's are loose, and lie about detached, now here and now there, in various parts of the world"[3]). But there is a Butlerian manner for carrying each of the arguments to an extreme point where it can no longer be opposed to the other, a point of nondifference or *dispersion*. For one thing, Butler is not content to say that machines extend the organism, but asserts that they are really limbs and organs lying on the body without organs of a society, which men will appropriate according to their power and their wealth, and whose poverty deprives them as if they were mutilated organisms. For another, he is not content to say that organisms are machines, but asserts that they contain such an abundance of parts that they must be compared to very different parts of distinct machines, each relating to the others, engineered in combination with the others.

What is essential is this double movement whereby Butler drives both arguments beyond their very limits. *He shatters the vitalist argument by calling in question the specific or personal unity of the organism, and the mechanist argument even more decisively, by calling in question the structural unity of the machine.* It is said that machines do not reproduce themselves, or that they only reproduce themselves through the intermediary of man, but "does any one say that the red clover has no reproductive system because the bumble bee (and the bumble bee only) must aid and abet it before it can reproduce? No one. The bumble bee is a part of the reproductive system of the clover. Each one of ourselves has sprung from minute animalcules whose entity was entirely distinct from our own. . . . These creatures are part of our reproductive system; then why not we part of that of the machines? . . . We are misled *by considering any complicated machine as a single thing*; in truth it is a city or a society, each member of which was bred truly after its kind. We see a machine as a whole, we call it by a name and indi-

vidualize it; we look at our own limbs, and know that the combination forms an individual which springs from a single centre of reproductive action; we therefore assume that there can be no reproductive action which does not arise from a single center; but this assumption is unscientific, and the bare fact that no vapour-engine was ever made entirely by another, or two others, of its own kind, is not sufficient to warrant us in saying that vapour-engines have no reproductive system. The truth is that each part of every vapour-engine is bred by its own special breeders, whose function is to breed that part, and that only, while the combination of the parts into a whole forms another department of the mechanical reproductive system."[4] In passing, Butler encounters the phenomenon of surplus value of code, when a part of a machine captures within its own code a code fragment of another machine, and thus owes its reproduction to a part of another machine: the red clover and the bumble bee; or the orchid and the male wasp that it attracts and intercepts by carrying on its flower the image and the odor of the female wasp.

At *this point of dispersion* of the two arguments, it becomes immaterial whether one says that machines are organs, or organs, machines. The two definitions are exact equivalents: man as a "vertebro-machinate mammal," or as an "aphidian parasite of machines." What is essential is not in the passage to infinity itself—the infinity composed of machine parts or the temporal infinity of the animalcules—but rather in what this passage blossoms into. Once the structural unity of the machine has been undone, once the personal and specific unity of the living has been laid to rest, a direct link is perceived between the machine and desire, the machine passes to the heart of desire, the machine is desiring and desire, machined. Desire is not in the subject, but the machine in desire—with the residual subject off to the side, alongside the machine, around the entire periphery, a parasite of machines, an accessory of vertebro-machinate desire. In a word, the real difference is not between the living and the machine, vitalism and mechanism, but between two states of the machine that are two states of the living as well. The machine taken in its structural unity, the living taken in its specific and even personal unity, are mass phenomena or molar aggregates; for this reason each points to the extrinsic existence of the other. And even if they are differentiated and mutually opposed, it is merely as two paths in the same statistical direction. But in the other more profound or intrinsic direction of multiplicities there is interpenetration, direct communication between the molecular phenomena and the singularities of the living, that is to say, between the small machines scattered in every machine, and the small formations dispersed in every organism: a domain of nondifference between the microphysical and the biological, there being as many living beings in the machine as there are machines in the living. Why speak of machines in this domain, when there would seem to be none, strictly speaking—no structural unity nor any preformed mechanical interconnections? "But there is the possibility of formation of such machines—in indefinitely superimposed relays, in working cycles that mesh with each other—which, once assembled, will obey the laws of thermo-dynamics, but which in the process of assembly do not depend on these laws, since the chain of assembly begins in a domain where by definition there are as yet no statistical laws. . . . *At this level, functioning and formation are still confounded as in the molecule;* and, starting from this level, two diverging paths open up, of which one will lead to the more or less regular accumulations of individuals, the other to the perfectings of the individual organization whose simplest schema is the formation of a pipe."[5]

The real difference is therefore between on the one hand the molar machines—whether social, technical, or organic—and on the other the desiring-machines, which are of a molecular order. Desiring-machines are the following: formative machines, whose very misfirings are functional, and whose functioning is indiscernible from their formation; chronogeneous machines engaged in their own assembly (*montage*), operating by nonlocalizable intercommunications and dispersed localizations, bringing into play processes of temporalization, fragmented formations, and detached parts, with a surplus value of code, and where the whole is itself produced alongside the parts, as a part apart or, as Butler would say, "in another department" that fits the whole over the other parts; machines in the strict sense, because they proceed by breaks and flows, associated waves and particles, associative flows and partial objects, inducing—always at a distance—transverse connections, inclusive disjunctions, and polyvocal conjunctions, thereby producing selections, detachments, and remainders, with a transference of individuality, in a generalized schizogenesis whose elements are the schizzes-flows.

Subsequently—rather, we should say on the other hand—when the machines become unified at the structural level of techniques and institutions that give them an existence as visible as a plate of steel; when the living, too, become structured by the statistical unities of their persons and their species, varieties, and locales; when a machine appears as a single object, and a living organism appears as a single subject; when the connections become global and specific, the disjunctions exclusive, and the conjunctions biunivocal; then desire does not need to project itself into these forms that have become opaque. These forms are immediately molar manifestations, statistical determinations of desire and of *its own* machines. They are the same machines (there is no difference in nature): here, as organic, technical, or social machines apprehended in *their* mass phenomenon, to which they become subordinated; there, as desiring-machines apprehended in their submicroscopic singularities that subordinate the mass phenomena. That is why from the start we have rejected the idea that desiring-machines belong to the domain of dreams or the Imaginary, and that they stand in for the other machines. There is only desire and environments, fields, forms of herd instinct. Stated differently, the molecular desiring-machines are in themselves the investment of the large molar machines or of the configurations that the desiring-machines *form according to the laws of large numbers,*[6] in either or both senses of subordination, in one sense and the other of subordination. Desiring-machines in one sense, but organic, technical, or social machines in the other: these are the same machines under determinate conditions. By "determinate conditions" we mean those statistical forms into which the machines enter as so many stable forms, unifying, structuring, and proceeding by means of large heavy aggregates; the selective pressures that group the parts retain some of them and exclude others, organizing the crowds. These are therefore the same machines, but not at all the same régime, the same relationships of magnitude, or the same uses of syntheses. It is only at the submicroscopic level of desiring-machines that there exists a functionalism—machinic arrangements, an engineering of desire; for it is only there that functioning and formation, use and assembly, product and production merge. All molar functionalism is false, since the organic or social machines are not formed in the same way they function, and the technical machines are not assembled in the same way they are used, but imply precisely the specific conditions that separate their own production from their distinct product. Only what is not produced in the same way it functions has a meaning, and also a purpose, an intention. The desiring-machines on the contrary represent nothing, signify nothing, mean nothing, and are exactly what one makes of them, what is made with them, what they make in themselves.

Desiring-machines work according to régimes of syntheses that have no equivalent in the large aggregates. Jacques Monod has defined the originality of these syntheses, from the standpoint of a molecular biology or of a "microscopic cybernetics" without regard to the traditional opposition between mechanism and vitalism. Here the fundamental traits of synthesis are the indifferent nature of the chemical signals, the indifference to the substrate, and the indirect character of the interactions. Such formulas as these are negative only in appearance, and in relation to the laws of aggregates, but must be understood positively in terms of force (*puissance*). "Between the substrate of an allosteric enzyme and the ligands prompting or inhibiting its activity there exists no chemically necessary relationship of structure or of reactivity. . . . An allosteric protein should be seen as a specialized product of molecular "engineering," enabling an interaction, positive or negative, to come about between compounds without chemical affinity, and thereby eventually subordinating any reaction to the intervention of compounds that are chemically foreign and indifferent to this reaction. The way in which allosteric interactions work hence permits a complete freedom in the "choice" of controls. And these controls, having no chemical requirements to answer to, will be the more responsive to physiological requirements, and will accordingly be selected for the extent to which they confer heightened coherence and efficiency upon the cell or organism. In a word, the very gratuitousness of these systems, giving molecular evolution a practically limitless field for exploration and experiment, enabled it to elaborate the huge network of cybernetic interconnections."[7]

How, starting from this domain of chance or of real inorganization, large configurations are organized that necessarily reproduce a structure under the action of DNA and its segments, the genes, performing veritable lottery drawings, creating switching points as *lines of selection or evolution*—this, indeed, is what all the stages of the passage from the molecular to the molar demonstrate, such as this passage appears in the organic machines, but no less so in the social machines with other laws and other figures. In this sense it was possible to insist on a common characteristic of human cultures and of living species, as "Markov chains": aleatory phenomena that are partially dependent. In the genetic code as in the social codes, what is termed a signifying chain is more a jargon than a language (*langage*), composed of nonsignifying elements that have a meaning or an effect of signification only in the large aggregates that they constitute through a linked drawing of elements, a partial dependence, and a superposition of relays.[8] It is not a matter of biologizing human history, nor of anthropo- logizing natural history. It is a matter of show- ing the common participation of the social machines *and* the organic machines in the desiring-machines. At man's most basic stra- tum, the Id: the schizophrenic cell, the schizo molecules, their chains and their jargons. There is a whole biology of schizophrenia; molecular biology is itself schizophrenic—as is micro- physics. But inversely schizophrenia—the the- ory of schizophrenia—is biological, biocul- tural, inasmuch as it examines the machinic connections of a molecular order, their distrib- ution into maps of intensity on the giant mole- cule of the body without organs, and the statis- tical accumulations that form and select the large aggregates.

Szondi set out on this molecular path, dis- covering a genic unconscious that he contrasted with the Freudian individual unconscious as well as with Jung's collective unconscious.[9] He often calls this genic or genealogical uncon- scious familial; and Szondi himself went on to study schizophrenia using familial aggregates as his units of measure. But the genic unconscious is familial only to a very small degree, much less so than Freud's unconscious, since the diagno- sis is carried out by comparing desire to the photographs of hermaphrodites, assassins, etc., instead of reducing it as usual to the images of daddy-mommy. Finally some relation to the outside! A whole alphabet, an entire axiomatic done with photos of mad people; this has to be tried, testing "the need for paternal feeling" against a series of portraits of assassins. It is no use saying this remains within the bounds of Oedipus, the truth is that it throws them open in a remarkable way. The hereditary genes of drives therefore play the role of simple stimuli that enter into variable combinations following vectors that survey an entire social historical field—an analysis of destiny.

In point of fact, the truly molecular uncon- scious cannot confine itself to genes as its units of reproduction; these units are still expressive, and lead to molar formations. Molecular biol- ogy teaches us that it is only the DNA that is re- produced, and not the proteins. Proteins are

both products and units of production; they are what constitutes the unconscious as a cycle or as the autoproduction of the unconscious—the ultimate molecular elements in the arrange- ment of the desiring-machines and the synthe- ses of desire. We have seen that, *through* repro- duction and its objects (defined familially or genetically), it is always the unconscious that produces itself in a cyclical orphan movement, a cycle of destiny where it always remains a sub- ject. It is precisely on this point that the statu- tory independence of sexuality with regard to generation rests. Szondi senses this direction— according to which one must go beyond the molar to the molecular—so acutely that he takes exception to all statistical interpretations of what is wrongly called his "test." What is more, he calls for going beyond contents to- ward the realm of *functions*. But he makes this advance, follows this direction, only by going from aggregates or classes toward "categories," of which he establishes a systematically closed list—categories that are still only expressive forms of existence that a subject is meant to choose and combine freely. For this reason Szondi misses the internal or molecular ele- ments of desire, the nature of their machinic choices, arrangements, and combinations. He also misses the real question of schizoanalysis: What drives your own desiring-machines? What is their functioning? What are the synthe- ses into which they enter and operate? What use do you make of them, in all the transitions that extend from the molecular to the molar and in- versely, and that constitute the cycle whereby the unconscious, remaining a subject, produces and reproduces itself?

We use the term *Libido* to designate the spe- cific energy of desiring-machines; and the transformations of this energy—*Numen* and *Voluptas*—are never desexualizations or subli- mations. This terminology indeed seems ex- tremely arbitrary. Considering the two ways in which the desiring-machines must be viewed, what they have to do with a properly sexual en- ergy is not immediately clear: either they are as- signed to the molecular order that is their own, or they are assigned to the molar order where they form the organic or social machines, and invest organic or social surroundings. It is in fact difficult to present sexual energy as directly cosmic and intra-atomic, and at the same time as directly sociohistorical. It would be futile to say that love has to do with proteins and society. This would amount to reviving yet once more the old attempts at liquidating Freudianism, by substituting for the libido a vague cosmic energy capable of all of the metamorphoses, or a kind of socialized energy capable of all the investments. Or would we do better to review Reich's final attempt, involving a "biogenesis" that not without justification is qualified as a schizoparanoiac mode of reasoning? It will be remembered that Reich concluded in favor of an intra-atomic cosmic energy—the orgone—generative of an electrical flux and carrying submicroscopic particles, the bions. This energy produced differences in potential or intensities distributed on the body considered from a molecular viewpoint, and was associated with a mechanics of fluids in this same body considered from a molar viewpoint. What defined the libido as sexuality was therefore the association of the two modes of operation, mechanical and electrical, in a sequence with two poles, molar and molecular (mechanical tension, electrical charge, electrical discharge, mechanical relaxation). Reich thought he had thus overcome the alternative between mechanism and vitalism, since these functions, mechanical and electrical, existed in matter in general, but were combined in a particular sequence within the living. And above all he upheld the basic psychoanalytic truth, the supreme disavowal of which he was able to denounce in Freud: the independence of sexuality with regard to reproduction, the subordination of progressive or regressive reproduction to sexuality as a cycle.[10]

If the details of Reich's final theory are taken into consideration, we admit that its simultaneously schizophrenic and paranoiac nature is no obstacle where we are concerned—on the contrary. We admit that any comparison of sexuality with cosmic phenomena such as "electrical storms," "the blue color of the sky and the blue-gray of atmospheric haze," the blue of the or-

gone, "St. Elmo's fire, and the bluish formations [of] sunspot activity," fluids and flows, matter and particles, in the end appear to us more adequate than the reduction of sexuality to the pitiful little familialist secret. We think that Lawrence and Miller have a more accurate evaluation of sexuality than Freud, even from the viewpoint of the famous scientificity. It is not the neurotic stretched out on the couch who speaks to us of love, of its force and its despair, but the mute stroll of the schizo, Lenz's outing in the mountains and under the stars, the immobile voyage in intensities on the body without organs. As to the whole of Reichian theory, it possesses the incomparable advantage of showing the double pole of the libido, as a molecular formation on the submicroscopic scale, and as an investment of the molar formations on the scale of social and organic aggregates. All that is missing is the confirmations of common sense: why, in what sense is this sexuality?

Cynicism has said, or claimed to have said, everything there is to say about love: that it is a matter of a copulation of social and organic machines on a large scale (at bottom, love is in the organs; at bottom, love is a matter of economic determinations, money). But what is properly cynical is to claim a scandal where there is none to be found, and to pass for bold while lacking boldness. Better the delirium of common sense than its platitude. For the prime evidence points to the fact that desire does not take as its object persons or things, but the entire surroundings that it traverses, the vibrations and flows of every sort to which it is joined, introducing therein breaks and captures—an always nomadic and migrant desire, characterized first of all by its "gigantism": no one has shown this more clearly than Charles Fourier. In a word, the social as well as biological surroundings are the object of unconscious investments that are necessarily desiring or libidinal, in contrast with the preconscious investments of need or of interest. The libido as sexual energy is the direct investment of masses, of large aggregates, and of social and organic fields. We have difficulty understanding what principles psychoanalysis uses to support its conception of desire, when it maintains that the libido must be desexualized or even sublimated in order to proceed to the social investments, and inversely that the libido only resexualizes these investments during the course of pathological regression.[11] Unless the assumption of such a conception is still familialism—that is, an assumption holding that sexuality operates only in the family, and must be transformed in order to invest larger aggregates.

The truth is that sexuality is everywhere: the way a bureaucrat fondles his records, a judge administers justice, a businessman causes money to circulate; the way the bourgeoisie fucks the proletariat; and so on. And there is no need to resort to metaphors, any more than for the libido to go by way of metamorphoses. Hitler got the fascists sexually aroused. Flags, nations, armies, banks get a lot of people aroused. A revolutionary machine is nothing if it does not acquire at least as much force as these coercive machines have for producing breaks and mobilizing flows. It is not through a desexualizing extension that the libido invests the large aggregates. On the contrary, it is through a restriction, a blockage, and a reduction that the libido is made to repress its flows in order to contain them in the narrow cells of the type "couple," "family," "person," "objects." And doubtless such a blockage is necessarily justified: the libido does not come to consciousness except in relation to a given body, a given person that it takes as object. But our "object choice" itself refers to a conjunction of flows of life and of society that this body and this person intercept, receive, and transmit, always within a biological, social, and historical field where we are equally immersed or with which we communicate. The persons to whom our loves are dedicated, including the parental persons, intervene only as points of connection, of disjunction, of conjunction of flows whose libidinal tenor of a properly unconscious investment they translate. Thus no matter how well grounded the love blockage is, it curiously changes its function, depending on whether it engages desire in the Oedipal impasses of the couple and the family in the service of the repressive machines, or whether on the contrary it condenses a free energy capable of fueling a revolutionary machine. (Here again, everything has already been said by Fourier, when he shows the two contrary directions of the "captivation" or the "mechanization" of the passions.) But we always make love with worlds. And our love addresses itself to this libidinal property of our lover, to either close himself off or open up to more spacious worlds, to masses and large aggregates. There is always something statistical in our loves, and something belonging to the laws of large numbers. And isn't it in this way that we must understand the famous formula of Marx?—the relationship between man and woman is "the direct, natural, and necessary relation of person to person." That is, the relationship between the two sexes (man and woman) is only the measure of the relationship of sexuality in general, insofar as it invests large aggregates (man and man)? Whence what came to be called the species determination of the sexuality of the two sexes. And must it not also be said that the phallus is not one sex, but sexuality in its entirety, which is to say the sign of the large aggregate invested by the libido, whence the two sexes necessarily derive, both in their separation (the two homosexual series of man and man, woman and woman) and in their statistical relations within this aggregate?

But Marx says something even more mysterious: that the true difference is not the difference between the two sexes, but the difference between the human sex and the "nonhuman" sex.[12] It is clearly not a question of animals, nor of animal sexuality. Something quite different is involved. If sexuality is the unconscious investment of the large molar aggregates, it is because on its other side sexuality is identical with the interplay of the molecular elements that constitute these aggregates under determinate conditions. The dwarfism of desire as a correlate to its gigantism. Sexuality and the desiring-machines are one and the same inasmuch as these machines are present and operating in the social machines, in their field, their formation, their functioning. Desiring-machines are the nonhuman sex, the molecular machinic elements, their arrangements and their syntheses, without which there would be neither a human sex specifically determined in the large aggregates, nor a human sexuality capable of investing these aggregates. In a few sentences Marx, who is nonetheless so miserly and reticent where sexuality is concerned, exploded something that will hold Freud and all of psychoanalysis forever captive: *the anthropomorphic representation of sex!*

What we call anthropomorphic representation is just as much the idea that there are two sexes as the idea that there is only one. We know how Freudianism is permeated by this bizarre notion that there is finally only one sex, the masculine, in relation to which the woman, the feminine, is defined as a lack, an absence. It could be thought at first that such a hypothesis founds the omnipotence of a male homosexuality. Yet this is not at all the case; what is founded here is rather the statistical aggregate of intersexual loves. For if the woman is defined as a lack in relation to the man, the man in his turn lacks what is lacking in the woman, simply in another fashion: the idea of a single sex necessarily leads to the erection of a phallus as an object on high, which distributes lack as two nonsuperimposable sides and makes the two sexes communicate in a common absence— *castration.* Women, as psychoanalysts or psychoanalyzed, can then rejoice in showing man the way, and in recuperating equality in difference. Whence the irresistibly comical nature of the formulas according to which one gains access to desire through castration. But the idea that there are two sexes, after all, is no better. This time, like Melanie Klein, one attempts to define the female sex by means of positive characteristics, even if they be terrifying. At least in this way one avoids phallocentrism, if not anthropomorphism. But this time, far from founding the communication between the two sexes, one founds instead their separation into two homosexual series that remain statistical. And one does not by any means escape castra-

tion. It is simply that castration, instead of being the principle of sex conceived as the masculine sex (the great castrated soaring Phallus), becomes the result of sex conceived as the feminine sex (the little hidden absorbed penis). We maintain therefore that *castration is the basis for the anthropomorphic and molar representation of sexuality.* Castration is the universal belief that brings together and disperses both men and women under the yoke of one and the same illusion of consciousness, and makes them adore this yoke. Every attempt to determine the nonhuman nature of sex—for example, "the Great Other" in Lacan—while conserving myth and castration, is defeated from the start. And what does Jean-François Lyotard mean, in his commentary—so profound, nevertheless—on Marx's text, when he sees the opening of the nonhuman as having to be "the entry of the subject into desire through castration"?[13] Long live castration, so that desire may be strong? Only fantasies are truly desired? What a perverse, human, all-too-human idea! An idea originating in bad conscience, and not in the unconscious. Anthropomorphic molar representation culminates in the very thing that founds it, the ideology of lack. The molecular unconscious, on the contrary, knows nothing of castration, because partial objects lack nothing and form free multiplicities as such; because the multiple breaks never cease producing flows, instead of repressing them, cutting them at a single stroke—the only break capable of exhausting them; because the syntheses constitute local and nonspecific connections, inclusive disjunctions, nomadic conjunctions: everywhere a microscopic transsexuality, resulting in the woman containing as many men as the man, and the man as many women, all capable of entering—men with women, women with men—into relations of production of desire that overturn the statistical order of the sexes. Making love is not just becoming as one, or even two, but becoming as a hundred thousand. Desiring-machines or the nonhuman sex: not one or even two sexes, but n sexes. Schizoanalysis is the variable analysis of the n sexes in a subject, beyond the anthropomorphic representation that society imposes on this subject, and with which it represents its own sexuality. The schizo-analytic slogan of the desiring-revolution will be first of all: to each its own sexes.

Notes

1. Samuel Butler, *Erewhon, Everyman's Library* (New York: E.P. Dutton; London: J. M.Dent, 1965), pp. 146–60.

2. Ibid., p. 148.

3. Ibid., p. 156.

4. Ibid., p. 159.

5. Raymond Ruyer, *La genèse des formes vivantes* (Paris: Flammarion, 1958), pp. 80–81. Taking up certain arguments of Bohr, Schrödinger, Jordan, and Lillie, Ruyer shows that the living is directly coupled to the individual phenomena of the atom, beyond the mass effects that appear in the internal mechanical circuits of the organism as well as in the external technical activities: "Classical physics only concerns itself with mass phenomena. In contrast, micro-physics naturally leads to biology. Starting from the individual phenomena of the atom, one can in fact go in two directions. Their statistical accumulation leads to the laws of common physics. But as these individual phenomena become complicated through systematic interactions—all the while keeping their individuality at the core of the molecule, then at the core of the macromolecule, then of the virus, then of the one-celled organism, by subordinating the mass phenomena—one is led all the way to the organism that, no matter how large, remains in this sense microscopic" (p. 54). These themes are developed at length by Ruyer in *Néo-finalisme* (Paris: Presses Universitaires de France, 1952).

6. Allen Wallis and Harry Roberts, in *Statistics, a New Approach* (New York: Free Press of Glencoe, 1956), define the "law of large numbers" as follows: "the larger the samples, the less will be the variability in the sample proportions . . . the basis of the Law of Large Numbers is that for an improbable event to occur n times is improbable to the nth degree" (p. 123); "the larger the groups averaged, the less the variation" (p. 159). And the consecutive sequences will be "swamped" by a large number of subsequent observations (see L. H. C. Tippett, *Statistics* [New York: Oxford University Press, 1943], p. 87). (*Translators' note.*)

7. Jacques Monod, *Chance and Necessity* (see reference note 27), pp. 77–78. And pp. 90–98: "With the globular protein we already have, at the molecular level, a veritable machine—a machine in its functional properties, but not, we now see, in its fundamental structure, where nothing but the play of blind combinations can be discerned. Randomness caught on the wing, preserved, reproduced by the machinery of invariance and thus converted into order, rule, necessity."

8. On the Markov chains and their applications to the living species as well as to cultural formations, see Ruyer, *La genèse des formes vivantes,* Ch. 8. The phenomena of surplus value of code are clearly explained in this perspective of "semifortuitous sequences." Several times Ruyer compares this with the language of schizophrenia.

9. Lipot Szondi, *Experimental Diagnostics of Drives* (New York: Grune & Stratton, 1952). Szondi's work was the first to establish a fundamental relationship between psychoanalysis and genetics. See also the recent attempt by André Green, in terms of the advances made in molecular biology: "Répétition et instinct de mort," *Revue française de psychanalyse,* May 1970.

10. All of Reich's last studies, biocosmic and biogenetic, are summarized at the end of Wilhelm Reich, *The Function of the Orgasm* (reference note 22), Ch. 7. The primacy of sexuality over generation and reproduction comes to be based on the cycle of sexuality (mechanical tension–electrical charge, etc.), which leads to a division of the cell: pp. 282–86. But very early in his work Reich reproached Freud for having abandoned the sexual position. *It was not only the dissidents from Freud who abandoned this position, it was Freud himself, in a certain fashion:* a first time when he introduces the death instinct, and begins to speak of Eros instead of sexuality (Reich, pp. 124–27); next, when he makes anxiety into the cause of sexual repression, and no longer its result (p. 136); and more generally when he comes back to a traditional primacy of procreation over sexuality (p. 283: "Thus, *procreation* is a function of sexuality, and not vice versa, as was hitherto believed. Freud had maintained the same thing with respect to psychosexuality, when he separated the concepts 'sexual' and 'genital.' But for a reason I was not able to understand, he later stated that 'sexuality in puberty' is 'in the service of procreation.'") Here Reich is obviously referring to Freud's Schopenhauerian or Weismannian texts, where sexuality comes under the sway of the species and the germen: for example,

"On Narcissism: An Introduction," in *Collected Papers* (London: Hogarth Press), Vol. 4, pp. 36–38.

11. Freud, *Three Case Histories* (reference note 42), p. 164: "Persons who have not freed themselves completely from the stage of narcissism, who, that is to say, have at that point a fixation which may operate as a disposing factor for a later illness, are exposed to the danger that some unusually intense wave of libido, finding no other outlet, may lead to a sexualization of their social instincts and so undo the work of sublimation which they had achieved in the course of their development. This result may be produced by anything that causes the libido to flow backwards (i.e., that causes a 'regression'): . . . paranoiacs *endeavour to protect themselves against any such sexualization of their social instinctual cathexes.*"

12. Karl Marx, *Critique of Hegel's "Philosophy of Right,"* trans. Annette Jolin and Joseph O'Malley (New York: Cambridge University Press, 1970), pp. 88–90. And on this text of Marx, see the fine commentary by Lyotard (see reference note 12), pp. 138–41.

13. Jean-François Lyotard, *Discours, figure* (Paris: Klincksieck, 1971).

From *The Pleasure of the Text*

Roland Barthes

If it were possible to imagine an aesthetic of textual pleasure, it would have to include: *writing aloud*. This vocal writing (which is nothing like speech) is not practiced, but it is doubtless what Artaud recommended and what Sollers is demanding. Let us talk about it as though it existed.

In antiquity, rhetoric included a section which is forgotten, censored by classical commentators: the *actio,* a group of formulae designed to allow for the corporeal exteriorization of discourse: it dealt with a theater of expression, the actor-orator "expressing" his indignation, his compassion, etc. *Writing aloud* is not expressive; it leaves expression to the pheno-text, to the regular code of communication; it belongs to the geno-text, to significance; it is carried not by dramatic inflections, subtle stresses, sympathetic accents, but by the *grain* of the voice, which is an erotic mixture of timbre and language, and can therefore also be, along with diction, the substance of an art: the art of guiding one's body (whence its importance in Far Eastern theaters). Due allowance being made for the sounds of the language, *writing aloud* is not phonological but phonetic; its aim is not the clarity of messages, the theater of emotions; what it searches for (in a perspective of bliss) are the pulsional incidents, the language lined with flesh, a text where we can hear the grain of the throat, the patina of consonants, the voluptuousness of vowels, a whole carnal stereophony: the articulation of the body, of the tongue, not that of meaning, of language. A certain art of singing can give an idea of this vocal writing; but since melody is dead, we may find it more easily today at the cinema. In fact, it suffices that the cinema capture the sound of speech *close up* (this is, in fact, the generalized definition of the "grain" of writing) and make us hear in their materiality, their sensuality, the breath, the gutturals, the fleshiness of the lips, a whole presence of the human muzzle (that the voice, that writing, be as fresh, supple, lubricated, delicately granular and vibrant as an animal's muzzle), to succeed in shifting the signified a great distance and in throwing, so to speak, the anonymous body of the actor into my ear: it granulates, it crackles, it caresses, it grates, it cuts, it comes: that is bliss.

From *A Lover's Discourse: Fragments*

Roland Barthes

Inexpressible Love

écrire / *to write*
Enticements, arguments, and impasses generated by the desire to "express" amorous feeling in a "creation" (particularly of writing).

1. Two powerful myths have persuaded us that love could, *should* be sublimated in aesthetic creation: the Socratic myth (loving serves to "engender a host of beautiful discourses") and the romantic myth (I shall produce an immortal work by writing my passion).

   Symposium

   Yet Werther, who used to draw abundantly and skillfully, cannot draw Charlotte's portrait (he can scarcely sketch her silhouette, which is precisely the thing about her that first captivated him). "I have lost . . . the sacred, life-giving power with which I created worlds about me."

   Werther

2. *The full moon this fall,*
   All night long
   I have paced around the pond.

   haiku

   No indirect means could be more effective in the expression of sadness than that "all night long." What if I were to try it, myself?

   > *This summer morning, the bay sparkling,*
   > *I went outside*
   > *To pick a wistaria.*

or:

> *This morning, the bay sparkling,*
> *I stayed here, motionless,*
> *Thinking of who is gone.*

On the one hand, this is saying nothing; on the other, it is saying too much: impossible to *adjust*. My expressive needs oscillate between the mild little haiku summarizing a huge situation, and a great flood of banalities. I am both too big and too weak for writing: I am *alongside it,* for writing is always dense, violent, indifferent to the infantile ego which solicits it. Love has of course a complicity with my language (which maintains it), but it cannot be *lodged* in my writing.

3. I cannot *write myself.* What, after all, is this "I" who would write himself? Even as he would enter into the writing, the writing would take the wind out of his sails, would render him null and void—futile; a gradual dilapidation would occur, in which the other's image, too, would be gradually involved (to write *on* something is to outmode it), a disgust whose conclusion could only be: *what's the use?* What obstructs amorous writing is the illusion of expressivity: as a writer, or assuming myself to be one, I continue to fool myself as to the *effects* of language: I do not know that the word "suffering" expresses no suffering and that, consequently, to use it is not only to communicate nothing but even, and

immediately, to annoy, to irritate (not to mention the absurdity). Someone would have to teach me that one cannot write without burying "sincerity" (always the Orpheus myth: not to turn back). What writing demands, and what any lover cannot grant it without laceration, is to sacrifice *a little* of his Image-repertoire, and to assure thereby, through his language, the assumption of a little reality. All I might produce, at best, is a writing of the Image-repertoire; and for that I would have to renounce the Image-repertoire of writing— would have to let myself be subjugated by my language, submit to the injustices (the insults) it will not fail to inflict upon the double Image of the lover and of his other.

François Wahl

The language of the Image-repertoire would be precisely the utopia of language; an entirely original, paradisiac language, the language of Adam—"natural, free of distortion or illusion, limpid mirror of our senses, a sensual language (*die sensualische Sprache*)": "In the sensual language, all minds converse together, they need no other language, for this is the language of nature."

Boehme

4. To try to write love is to confront the *muck* of language: that region of hysteria where language is both *too much* and *too little,* excessive (by the limitless expansion of the *ego,* by emotive submersion) and impoverished (by the codes on which love diminishes and levels it). Faced with the death of his baby son, in order to write (if only scraps of writing), Mallarmé submits himself to parental division:

Boucou-rechliev

François Wahl: "No one rises on 'his' language without sacrificing to it a little of his image-repertoire, and it is because of this that something in language is committed to function within reality" (*"Chute"*).

Jakob Boehme: Quoted by Norman O. Brown.

Boucourechliev: *Thrène,* on a text by Mallarmé (*Tombeau pour Anatole,* edited by J.-P. Richard).

Mère, pleure
Moi, je pense.
Mother, weep
While I think.

But the amorous relation has made me into an atopical subject—undivided: I am my own child: I am both mother and father (of myself, of the other): how would I divide the labor?

5. To know that one does not write for the other, to know that these things I am going to write will never cause me to be loved by the one I love (the other), to know that writing compensates for nothing, sublimates nothing, that it is precisely *there where you are not*—this is the beginning of writing.

"In the Loving Calm of Your Arms"

étreinte / *embrace*
The gesture of the amorous embrace seems to fulfill, for a time, the subject's dream of total union with the loved being.

1. Besides intercourse (when the Image-repertoire goes to the devil), there is that other embrace, which is a motionless cradling: we are enchanted, bewitched: we are in the realm of sleep, without sleeping; we are within the voluptuous infantilism of *sleepiness:* this is the moment for telling stories, the moment of the voice which takes me, siderates me, this is the return to the mother ("In the loving calm of your arms," says a poem set to music by Duparc). In this companionable incest, everything is suspended: time, law, prohibition: nothing is exhausted, nothing is wanted: all desires are abolished, for they seem definitively fulfilled.

Duparc

Duparc: *"Chanson triste,"* poem by Jean Lahor. Second-rate poetry? But "second-rate poetry" takes the amorous subject into the linguistic register which is all his own: *expression.*

2.   Yet, within this infantile embrace, the genital unfailingly appears; it cuts off the diffuse sensuality of the incestuous embrace; the logic of desire begins to function, the will-to-possess returns, the adult is superimposed upon the child. I am then two subjects at once: I want maternity *and* genitality. (The lover might be defined as a child getting an erection: such was the young Eros.)

3.   A moment of affirmation; for a certain time, though a finite one, a *deranged* interval, something has been successful: I have been fulfilled (all my desires abolished by the plenitude of their satisfaction): fulfillment does exist, and I shall keep on making it return: through all the meanderings of my amorous history, I shall persist in wanting to rediscover, to renew the contradiction—the contraction—of the two embraces.

Exiled from the Image-Repertoire

exil / *exile*
Deciding to give up the amorous condition, the subject sadly discovers himself exiled from his Image-repertoire.

1.   Let me take Werther at that fictive moment (in the fiction itself) when he might have renounced suicide. Then the only thing left to him is exile: not to leave Charlotte (he has already done so once, with no result), but to exile himself from her image, or worse still: to cut off that raving energy known as the Image-repertoire. Then begins "a kind of long insomnia." That is the price to be paid: the death of the Image for my own life.

Hugo
Freud

(Amorous passion is a delirium; but such delirium is not alien; everyone speaks of it, it is

henceforth tamed. What is enigmatic is *the loss of delirium:* one returns to . . . what?)

2.   In real mourning, it is the "test of reality" which shows me that the loved object has ceased to exist. In amorous mourning, the object is neither dead nor remote. It is I who decide that its image must die (and I may go so far as to hide this death from it). As long as this strange mourning lasts, I will therefore have to undergo two contrary miseries: to suffer from the fact that the other is present (continuing, in spite of himself, to wound me) and to suffer from the fact that the other is dead (dead at least as I loved him). Thus I am wretched (an old habit) over a telephone call which does not come, but I must remind myself at the same time that this silence, *in any case,* is insignificant, since I have decided to get over any such concern: it was merely an aspect of the amorous image that it was to telephone me; once this image is gone, the telephone, whether it rings or not, resumes its trivial existence.

(Isn't the most sensitive point of this mourning the fact that I must *lose a language*—the amorous language? No more "I love you's.")

3.   Mourning for the image, insofar as I fail to perform it, makes me anxious; but insofar as I succeed in performing it, makes me sad. If exile from the Image-repertoire is the necessary road to "cure," it must be admitted that such progress is a sad one. This sadness is not a melancholy— or, at least, it is an incomplete melancholy (and not at all a clinical one), for I accuse myself of nothing, nor am I prostrated. My sadness belongs to that fringe of melancholy where the loss of the loved being remains abstract. A double lack: I cannot even invest my misery, as I could when I suffered from being in

Freud

Hugo: "Exile is a kind of long insomnia" (*Pierres*).

Freud: "Mourning incites the ego to renounce the object by declaring that this latter is dead and by offering the ego the reward of remaining alive."

Freud: "In certain circumstances, we may observe that the loss is of a less concrete nature. The object, for instance, is not actually dead, but only lost as an object of love . . ."

love. In those days I desired, dreamed, struggled; the benefit lay before me, merely delayed, traversed by contretemps. Now, no more resonance. Everything is calm, and that is worse. Though justified by an economy—the image dies so that I may live—amorous mourning always has something left over: one expression keeps recurring: "What a shame!"

4.   A proof of love: I sacrifice my Image-repertoire to you—the way a head of hair used to be dedicated. Thus, perhaps (at least, so it is said) I shall accede to "true love." If there is some resemblance between the amorous crisis and the analytic cure, I then go into mourning for my beloved, as the patient goes into mourning for his analyst: I liquidate my transference, and apparently this is how both the cure and the crisis end up. However, as has been pointed out, this theory forgets that the analyst, too, must go into mourning for his patient (or else the analysis risks being interminable); in the same way, the loved being—if I sacrifice to that being an Image-repertoire which nonetheless importuned him—the loved being must enter into the melancholy of his own collapse.

Antoine Compagnon

And concurrently with my own mourning, I must anticipate and assume this melancholy on the part of the other, from which I shall suffer, *for I love the other still.*

The true act of mourning is not to suffer from the loss of the loved object; it is to discern one day, on the skin of the relationship, a certain tiny stain, appearing there as the symptom of a certain death: for the first time I am doing harm to the one I love, involuntarily, of course, but *without panic.*

5.   I try to wrest myself away from the amorous Image-repertoire: but the Image-repertoire burns underneath, like an incompletely extinguished peat fire; it catches again; what was renounced reappears; out of the hasty grave suddenly breaks a long cry.

(Jealousies, anxieties, possessions, discourses, appetites, signs, once again amorous desire was burning everywhere. It was as if I were trying to embrace one last time, hysterically, someone about to die—someone for whom I was about to die: I was performing a denial of separation.)

Freud

Winnicott

Freud: "This rebellion is sometimes so intense that the subject may reach the point of rejecting reality and clinging to the lost object by means of a hallucinatory psychosis of desire."

Winnicott: "Just before this loss is experienced, we may discern in the child, in the excessive utilization of the transitional object, the denial of the fear that this object may lose its signification" (*Playing and Reality*).

Antoine Compagnon: *"L'Analyse orpheline."*

Plato Behind Socrates

Jacques Derrida

6 June 1977

out of this atrocious exclusion that we make of all of them—and of every possible reader. The whole world. The worst of "final solutions," without limit, this is what we are declaring, you and I, when we cipher everything, including our clothes, our steps, what we eat, and not only messages as they say, what we say to each other, write, "signify," etc. And yet the opposite is not less true. All those left out have never been so alive, so harassing even, I call them, like the imperious beggar of the other evening with whom I communed intensely through the pane at the very moment when I was turned toward you, following with my hands

Do you think there are listening devices? That our letters are opened? I don't know if this hypothesis terrifies me or if I need it

Jonathan and Cynthia were standing near me next to the glass case, the table rather, where laid out, under glass, in a transparent coffin, among hundreds of displayed reproductions, this card had to jump out at me. I saw nothing else, but that did not prevent me from feeling that right near me Jonathan and Cynthia were observing me obliquely, watching me look. As if they were spying on me in order to finish the effects of a spectacle they had staged (they have just married more or less)

I no longer knew what to do with myself. How to see to the bottom of all those rectangles between *Socrates'* legs, if it is *Socrates?* I still do not know how to see what there is to see. It gives the impression (look at it

from the other side, turn the card over) that Plato, if it is Plato, does not see either, perhaps does not even want to know, looking elsewhere and further off over the shoulder of the other, what S. is in the middle, *en train,* yes *en train,* of writing or scratching on a last little rectangle, a last little one in the middle of all the others (count them, there are at least 23). This last little one is the most "interior" of all of them, it appears virgin. It is *Socrates'* writing surface, and you can imagine the missive or the rectangular chart, Socrates' post card. To whom do you think he is writing? For me it is always more important to know that than to know what is being written; moreover I think it amounts to the same, to the other finally. And *plato,* distinctly smaller, hitches himself up behind *Socrates,* with one foot in the air as if he wanted to come up to the same height or as if he were running in order to catch a moving train (which is what he did anyhow, no?). Unless he is pushing a baby carriage or wheelchair (*Gängelwagen,* for example, as the great inheritor of the scene will say). Turn it very quickly: *Plato* is pushing himself off on a skateboard (if you can't easily see the scene, put a filter over *Socrates,* multiply the filters, mobilize them, spread them out in every direction, isolate the parts of each personage, put in the film), Plato taking tram fares in a poor country, on the dashboard pushing the young people inside as it gets under way. He is pushing them in the back. *Plato* as the tram conductor, his foot on a pedal or a warning buzzer (he is pretty much a warning himself, don't you think, with his outstretched finger?), and he drives, he

drives avoiding derailment. At the top of the staircase, on the last step, he rings for the elevator.

you always accuse me of being "delirious," and you know very well, alas, what that means in our code

never have I been so delirious

I am

losing my voice calling you, speak to me, tell me the truth

6 June 1977

also jealous of this Matthew Paris, whom I do not know. Want to wake him up to talk to him about all the sleepless nights between us. The card immediately seemed to me, how to put it, obscene. Obscene, understand, in each of its traits. The trait in itself is indiscreet; whatever it traces or represents, it is indecent (my love, free me from the trait). And to these obscene traits I immediately wanted to erect a monument, or a house of cards, sumptuous and fragile, as barely durable, as light as what I have had to let come occasionally to make you laugh (the best memories of us, of my life perhaps, among the ecstasies, that of which I am stupidly the proudest, as of a grace, the only one, that I really deserved). The spectacle is too upsetting and still remains inaccessible for me. I can neither look nor not look, only speculate, you will call it raving again. Later, others will attempt a scientific and competent reading. It must already exist, asleep in the archives, reserved for the rare survivors, the last guardians of our memory. For the moment, myself, I tell you that I see *Plato* getting an erection in *Socrates'* back and see the insane hubris of his prick, an interminable, disproportionate erection traversing Paris's head like a single idea and then the copyist's chair, before slowly sliding, still warm, under *Socrates'* right leg, in harmony or symphony with the movement of this phallus sheaf, the points, plumes, pens, fingers, nails and *grattoirs,* the very pencil boxes which address themselves in the same direction. The di-rection, the dierection of this couple, these old nuts, these rascals on horseback, this is us, in any event, *a priori* (they arrive on us) we are lying on our backs in the belly of the mare as if in an enormous library, and it gallops, it gallops, from time to time I turn to your side, I lie on you and guessing, reconstituting it by all kinds of chance calculations and conjectures, I set up [*dresse*] within you the *carte* of their displacements, the ones they will have induced with the slightest movement of the pen, barely pulling on the reins. Then, without disengaging myself I resettle [*redresse*] myself again

What is going on under *Socrates'* leg, do you recognize this object? It plunges under the waves made by the veils around the plump buttocks, you see the rounded double, improbable enough, it plunges straight down, rigid, like the nose of a stingray to electrocute the old man and analyze him under narcosis. You know that they were both very interested in this paralyzing animal. Would it make him write by paralyzing him? All of this, that I do

not know or do not yet want to see, also comes back from the bottom of the waters of my memory, a bit as if I had drawn or engraved the scene, from the first day that, in an Algiers *lycée* no doubt, I first heard of those two. Do people (I am not speaking of "philosophers" or of those who read Plato) realize to what extent this old couple has invaded our most private domesticity, mixing themselves up in everything, taking their part of everything, and making us attend for centuries their colossal and indefatigable anaparalyses? The one in the other, the one in front of the other, the one after the other, the one behind the other?

I have always known that we are lost and that from this very initial disaster an infinite distance has opened up

this catastrophe, right near the beginning, this overturning that I still cannot succeed in thinking was the condition for everything, not so?, ours, our very condition, the condition for everything that was given us or that we destined, promised, gave, loaned, I no longer know what, to each other

we lost each other—one another, understand me? (I imagine the computer at the listening device attempting to translate or to classify this sentence. Can always run, and us too: who has lost the other losing himself?

One day, years ago, you wrote me this that I, the amnesiac, know by heart, or almost: "it is curious to see that generally I do not answer your letters, nor you mine

or are we delirious, each alone, for ourselves? Are we waiting for an answer or something else? No, since at bottom we are asking for nothing, no, we are asking no question. The prayer

." Okay, I'll call you right away. You know everything, before me

you will always precede me.

6 June 1977

So you are out of my sight. And you, where do you "see" me when you speak to me, when you have me, as you say, on the telephone? On your left, your right, beside you, opposite you, in front, in back, standing up, sitting down? Me, I look out for the noises in the room around you, I try to surprise what you are looking at or looks at you, as if someone were hanging around, someone who might be me at times, there where you are, and often I stop paying attention to what you are saying so that the timbre alone resonates, as in a language that is all the closer for being foreign, and that I understand nothing (this situation might indeed be the one that keeps me close to you, on your string), and then I am lying on my back, right on the ground as in the grand moments you remember, and I would accept death without a murmur, I would want it to come

and I imagine him unable to turn back on *Plato*. He is forbidden to. He is in analysis and must sign, silently, since Plato will have kept the floor; signing what? well, a check, if you will, made out to the other, for he must have paid a lot, or his own death sentence. And first of all, by the same token, the "mandate" to bring back that he himself dispatches to himself at the other's command, his son or disciple, the one he has on his back and who will have played the devil's advocate. For Plato finally says it himself, he sent it to himself, this sign of death, he looked for it, he rushed into it without looking back

and in the homosexual phase which would follow Eurydice's death (and that had therefore preceded it, according to me

) Orpheus sings no more, he writes, and he has another one with Plato. Be aware that everything in our bildopedic culture, in our politics of the encyclopedic, in our telecommunications of all genres, in our telematicometaphysical archives, in our library, for example the marvelous Bodleian, everything is constructed on the protocolary charter of an axiom, that could be demonstrated, displayed on a large *carte,* a post card of course, since it is so simple, elementary, a brief, fearful stereotyping (above all say or think nothing that derails, that jams telecom.). The charter is the contract for the following, which quite stupidly one has to believe: Socrates

comes *before* Plato, there is between them—and in general—an order of generations, an irreversible sequence of inheritance. Socrates is before, not in front of, but before Plato, therefore behind him, and the charter binds us to this order: this is how to orient one's thought, this is the left and this is the right, march. Socrates, he who does not write, as Nietzsche said (how many times have I repeated to you that I also found him occasionally or even always somewhat *on the border* of being naive; remember that photograph of him with his "good guy" side, at the beginning in any event, before the "evil," before the disaster?). He understood nothing about the initial catastrophe, or at least about this one, since he knew all about the others. Like everyone else he believed that Socrates did not write, that he came before Plato who more or less wrote at his dictation and therefore let him write by himself, as he says somewhere. From this point of view, N. believed Plato and overturned nothing at all. The entire "overturning" remained included in the program of this credulity. This is true *a fortiori,* and with an *a fortiori* different each time and ready to blow up otherwise, from Freud and from Heidegger.*
Now, my post card, this morning when I am raving about it or delivering it [*quand je la*

---

*I must note it right here, on the morning of 22 August 1979, 10 A.M., while typing this page for the present publication, the telephone rings. The U.S. The American operator asks me if I accept a *"collect call"* from Martin (she says Martine or martini) Heidegger. I heard, as one often does in these situations which are very familiar to me, often having to call "collect" myself, voices that I thought I recognized on the other end of the intercontinental line, listening to me and watching my reaction. What will he do with the ghost or Geist of Martin? I cannot summarize here all the chemistry of the calculation that very quickly made me refuse *("It's a joke, I do not accept")* after having had the name of Martini Heidegger repeated several times, hoping that the author of the farce would finally name himself. Who pays, in sum, the addressee or the sender? who is to pay? This is a very difficult question, but this morning I thought that I should not pay, at least not otherwise than by adding this note of thanks. I know that I will *délire ou la délivre*] in the state of jealousy that has always terrified me, my post card naively overturns everything. In any event, it allegorizes the catastrophic unknown of the order. Finally one begins no longer to understand what to come [*venir*], to come before, to come after, to foresee [*prévenir*], to come back [*revenir*] all mean—along with the difference of the generations, and then to inherit, to write one's will, to dictate, to speak, to take dictation, etc. One is finally going to be able to love oneself [*s'aimer*]

All of this is not without, it is not to all of you that I will have to teach this, political consequences. They are still difficult to calculate

"One day we will go to Minos."

I am adding several cards, as usual. Why prefer to write on cards? First of all because of the support, doubtless, which is more rigid, the cardboard is firmer, it preserves, it resists manipulations; and then it limits and justifies, from the outside, by means of the borders, the indigence of the discourse, the insignificance of the anecdoque [sic]

I have so much to tell you and it all will have to hold on snapshot post cards—and immediately be divided

among them. Letters in small pieces, torn in advance, cut out, recut. So much to tell you, but all and nothing, more than all, less than nothing—to tell you is all, and a post card supports it well, it is to be but this naked support, to tell it to you, you only, naked. What my picture

You are going to think that I venerate this catastrophic scene (my new fetishes, the "hit" of the summer): *Plato*, teacher, in erection behind *Socrates*, student, for example, and in saying "catastrophic," I am thinking, of course, of the overturning and inversion of relations, but also, suddenly, of the apotrope and the apostrophic: p. a father smaller than his son or disciple, it happens, p., unless it is S., whom he resembles, devilishly, shows him (to others) and at the same time shows him the way, sends him, and at the same time apostrophizes him, which always amounts to saying "go" or "come," *fort, da. Fort/da* of S. and p., this is what it is, this entire post card ontology. What it leaves strangely unexplained, is that himself he addresses himself to S. or to others beyond S. But does one ever know

plato/Socrates, a o/o a. Look closely at their mugs [*bobine*], *plato's* hat flat as a plate and the a in *Socrates* which mimes within the name above the head the very form of his hood. All of this seems very prophylactic, very preservative to me, up to the dot on the small p. But who are they? S is p, my equation with two unknowns. I have always been enchanted by the passage in *Beyond the Pleasure Principle* when, after so many laborious hypotheses and useless detours, Freud comes to state in an apparently embarrassed tone, but within which I have always perceived some wicked satisfaction: the result to which we have come finally, is that instead of one unknown, now we have two. As if he were registering a certain profit at this point. Register, now there's a word, Socrates is keeping a register (secretly, of what the other, the gunner, has lifted from him, the funds he has diverted, the counterfeit money he has had printed with his effigy. Unless this is the effigy of the two greatest counterfeiters of history, comperes preparing the emission we are still plugged into while

---

be suspected of making it all up, since it is too good to be true. But what can I do? It is true, rigorously, from start to finish, the date, the time, the content, etc. Heidegger's name was already written, after "Freud," in the letter that I am in the course of transcribing on the typewriter. This is true, and moreover demonstrable, if one wishes to take the trouble of inquiring: there are witnesses and a postal archive of the thing. I call upon these witnesses (these waystations between Heidegger and myself) to make themselves known. All of this must not lead you to believe that no telephonic communication links me to Heidegger's ghost, as to more than one other. Quite the contrary, the network of my hookups, you have the proof of it here, is on the burdensome side, and more than one switchboard is necessary in order to digest the overload. It is simply, let me say for the ears of my correspondents of this morning (to whom I regret a bit, nevertheless, that I did not speak), that my private relation with Martin does not go through the same exchange.

drawing checks and money orders on it infinitely. In advance they impose everything, they tax, they obliterate the *timbres,* with their own effigy, and from you to me

Would like to address myself, in a straight line, directly, without *courrier,* only to you, but I do not arrive, and that is the worst of it. A tragedy, my love, of destination. Everything becomes a post card once more, legible for the other, even if he understands nothing about it. And if he understands nothing, certain for the moment of the contrary, it might always arrive for you, for you too, to understand nothing, and therefore for me, and therefore not to arrive, I mean at its destination. I would like to arrive to you, to arrive right up to you, my unique destiny, and I run I run and I fall all the time, from one stride to the next, for there will have been, so early, well before us

If you had listened to me, you would have burned everything, and nothing would have arrived. I mean on the contrary that something ineffaceable would have arrived, instead of this bottomless misery in which we are dying. But it is unjust to say that you did not listen to me, you listened closely to the other voice (we were already a crowd in that first envelope) which asked you not to burn, to burn in order to save. Nothing has arrived because you wanted to preserve (and therefore to lose), which in effect formed the sense of the order coming from behind my voice, you remember, so many years ago, in my first "true" letter: "burn everything." You had answered me the next day, and this is how your letter ended: "The letter ends on the exigency of this supreme pleasure: the desire to be torn by you" (you are the mistress of the equivocal and I liked it that you left it to me to attribute this desire to the letter, and then you added) "I am burning. I have the stupid impression of being faithful to you. I am nonetheless saving certain simulacra from your sentences [you have shown me them since]. I am waking up. I remember the ashes. What a chance, to burn, yes yes

." Your letter mandated, commanded, made arrive at its destination everything that we feared. And what has betrayed us, is that you

wanted generality: which is what I call a child. If we had been able to die already, the one or the other, we would have kept each other better. I recall having said to someone, right at the beginning of our history, however, "*I'm destroying my own life.*" I still have to specify: when I first wrote "burn everything," it was neither out of prudence and a taste for the clandestine, nor out of a concern for internal guarding but out of what was necessary (the condition, the given) for the affirmation to be reborn at every instant, without memory. To make anamnesis impossible, symbolically of course, whence the trap. It was within the same impetus that (very sincerely?) I told you, liked to tell you that I liked to approve of your desire even if it were not turned toward me. I was completely crazy, out of my mind, but what a chance! Since then we have reneuronecrosed each other, this was good too, but there you are

Through fidelity to the secret demand you wanted to preserve, to preserve, me too, and here we are deprived of everything. I am still dreaming of a second holocaust that would not come too late. Know that I am always ready, this is my fidelity. I am a monster of fidelity, the most perverse infidel.

The first catastrophe is the ignoble archive which rots everything, the descendence into which everything tumbles

I don't know when I'm coming back, Monday or Tuesday, I'll call and if you can't come to wait for me at the station I

8 June 1977

and I grant you that my "wish" ["*envie*"]—you found the best word—to immortalize the card might appear quite suspect. First of all because without a doubt this was on the two impostors' program, the scene that plays itself out between them, the scene of which Paris made himself the voyeur, or the first *dévoyeur* [corrupter], you could also say *fourvoyeur* [one who leads astray], or *pourvoyeur* [purveyor], ("purveyor of truth," they chose this translation for "*Le facteur de la vérité*"), or further the divulger, but he had to take part in it to do so. The two impostors' program is to have a child by me, them too. And let it be made in the dorsum.

The emission of sense or of seed can be rejected (postmark, stamp, and return to sender). Imagine the day, as I have already, that we will be able to send sperm by post card, without going through a check drawn on some sperm bank, and that it remains living enough for the artificial insemination to yield fecundation, and even desire. But, dear friend, prove to me that this is not a normal tragedy, old as Methuselah, older than our most upsetting techniques?

The *impossible* confession (the one we have risked, the one that the other within us has been able to extort from us by means of this atrocious blackmail by true love), I imagine that it can be delivered only to children, for children, the only ones unable to bear it (in us, of course, for "real" children could also scorn it), and therefore the only ones to deserve it. One can confess everything to adults, everything and nothing, therefore.

To the devil with the child, the only thing we ever will have discussed, the child, the child, the child. The impossible message between us. A child is what one should not be able to "send" oneself. It never will be, never *should* be a sign, a letter, even a symbol. Writings: stillborn children one sends oneself in order to stop hearing about them—precisely because children [*enfants, infans*] are first of all what one wishes to hear speak by themselves. Or this is what the two old men say

They love (the) address. I have too many, too many addresses, too much address. The disease that is killing me.

Suppose that we had given to one of our innumerable (possible) children an accursed name, a name of malediction, the first name of someone who would be in us like the forever open wound (for example

), how we would have loved it. The wound can have (should only have) just one proper name. I recognize that I love—you—by this: that you

leave in me a wound that I do not want to replace.

And they believe that we are two, they want at any price, without knowing how to count, to hang onto this stupidity. Two, neither more nor less. I can see you smile along with me, my sweet love.

I am still sending you the same cards. S. is writing on a medieval scribe's desk as if on a phallus or on a fireplace. Difficult to know if these objects belong to him, but he busies himself on the mount, with both hands. The left, in order to scratch out doubtless, irritates the support, the other dips. Two hands, the mystic writing pad (he destines it, like a post card, to the other bearded old man who wanted to start it all over, anamnesis, twenty-five centuries later, and who, without a warning, nevertheless erases Socrates from the scene of the Symposium [*weg! fort!*]). He is erasing with one hand, scratching, and with the other he is still scratching, writing. Where will all this information have been stocked, everything he will have scratched and scratched, that one? The question deserves a letter to the editor in *le Monde*.

I couldn't answer you on the phone just now, it was too painful. The "decision" you asked me for once again is impossible, you know it. It comes back to you, I send it back to you. Whatever you do I will approve, and I will do so from the day that it was clear that between us never will any contract, any debt, any official custody, any memory even, hold us back—any child even.

Of course this was also the day of the most sacred *liance*, because of it even, but at the moment when the motor started, remember, first gear was passed and we looked at each other through the glass, we said to each other (each to himself aside and each to the other in silence, we said it to each other out loud later, so many times and in so many forms) that the absence of memory and unsworn faith would be the chance, the condition. This was also a vow. Naturally I have never *accepted* it, nor have you, it was not possible, but I still want it, that within me which loves, the only one that can love, I am not speaking of the others, still wants it and adjusts to it. It is killing me of course, but it would be worse otherwise.

I accept [*j'accepte*], this will be my signature henceforth, but don't let it worry you, don't worry about anything. I will never seek you any harm, take this word at its most literal, it is my name, that *j'accepte,* and you will be able to count, to count on it as on the capital clarities, from you *I accept* everything.

8 June 1977

this is the name, like a salvo of post cards, always the same one shooting itself off again, burning its strophes, one after the other in order to try its luck all the way up to you. I had barely posted the preceding one, in order never to miss a pickup when the opportunity presents itself, and here I am again standing up to write you, standing right in the street, so often standing, incapable of waiting—and I do it like an animal, and even against a tree sometimes. But it is also that I like to write you standing up and to accept being surprised doing the thing, exactly the situation I totally reject when it is a question of writing something else, to others and in order to publish it to them. And at the same time, you know that I do not like writing you these miserable scraps, these small dots lost over our immense territory, that let it be seen so little, or even imagined, that occupy it as little as the dot on the I, a single dot on a single I, infinitely small in a book infinitely big. But (I can hardly bear, support this thought in words) on the day that I no longer will be able to do it, when you no longer will let me put the dot on my Is, the sky will fall on my head and the fall will be endless, I will stretch myself out in the other sense

of my support. You said it to me one day, I think, I always write *on* the support, right on the support but also on the subject. Expected result, it deforms it, thereby I broach its destruction, all the while showing it, itself, in the course of *being* that which destroys itself, falls into pieces, a bit theatrical, and then incinerates itself beneath your eyes and there is no

longer anything but your eyes. You understand that this is the insupportable partition of the support. It is within reason not to support it, and I understand this readily to the extent that I am reasonable, like you and like everyone, but precisely at stake there is reason. Okay.

For example I write *on* post cards, oh well I write on post cards. "I" begins again with a reprosuction (say, I just wrote reproSuction: have you noticed that I make more and more strange mistakes, is it fatigue or age, occasionally the spelling goes, phonetic writing comes back in force, as in elementary school where it did not happen to me moreover, only to others whom I confusedly looked down on—plus the *lapsus* or "*slips*" obviously). And by means of a reproduction itself reproduced serially, always the same picture on another support, but an identical support, differing only *numéro*. It dates from when, the post card "properly speaking," do you know? Nineteenth century necessarily, with photography and the stamp, unless . . . Want to write and first to reassemble an enormous library on the *courrier,* the postal institutions, the techniques and mores of telecommunication, the networks and epochs of telecommunication throughout history—but the "library" and the "history" themselves are precisely but "posts," sites of passage or of relay among others, stases, moments or effects of *restance,* and also particular representations, narrower and narrower, shorter and shorter sequences, proportionally, of the Great Telematic Network, the *worldwide connection.* What would our correspondence be,

and its secret, the indecipherable, in this terrifying archive?

The wish to vanquish the postal principle: not in order to approach you finally and to vanquish you, to triumph over distancing, but so that by you might be given to me the distancing which regards me.

Do you think that what went on between S and p regards us? To keep to appearances, but it is only a picture, their eyes are turned elsewhere, they have never had a thought for us.

That Dangerous Supplement

Jacques Derrida

From/Of Blindness to the Supplement

In terms of this problematical scheme, we must therefore think Rousseau's experience and his theory of writing together, the accord and the discord that, under the name of writing, relate Jean-Jacques to Rousseau, uniting and dividing his proper name. On the side of experience, a recourse to literature as reappropriation of presence, that is to say, as we shall see, of Nature; on the side of theory, an indictment against the negativity of the letter, in which must be read the degeneracy of culture and the disruption of the community.

If indeed one wishes to surround it with the entire constellation of concepts that shares its system, the word *supplement* seems to account for the strange unity of these two gestures.

In both cases, in fact, Rousseau considers writing as a dangerous means, a menacing aid, the critical response to a situation of distress. When Nature, as self-proximity, comes to be forbidden or interrupted, when speech fails to protect presence, writing becomes necessary. It must *be added* to the word urgently. I have identified in advance one of the forms of this *addition;* speech being natural or at least the natural expression of thought, the most natural form of institution or convention for signifying thought, writing is added to it, is adjoined, as an image or representation. In that sense, it is not natural. It diverts the immediate presence of thought to speech into representation and the imagination. This recourse is not only "bizarre," but dangerous. It is the addition of a technique, a sort of artificial and artful ruse to make speech present when it is actually absent. It is a violence done to the natural destiny of the language:

> Languages are made to be spoken, writing serves only as a supplement to speech. . . . Speech represents thought by conventional signs, and writing represents the same with regard to speech. Thus the art of writing is nothing but a mediated representation of thought.

Writing is dangerous from the moment that representation there claims to be presence and the sign of the thing itself. And there is a fatal necessity, inscribed in the very functioning of the sign, that the substitute make one forget the vicariousness of its own function and make itself pass for the plenitude of a speech whose deficiency and infirmity it nevertheless only *supplements.* For the concept of the supplement—which here determines that of the representative image—harbors within itself two significations whose cohabitation is as strange as it is necessary. The supplement adds itself, it is a surplus, a plenitude enriching another plenitude, the *fullest measure* of presence. It cumulates and accumulates presence. It is thus that art, *technè,* image, representation, convention, etc., come as supplements to nature and are rich with this entire cumulating function. This kind of supplementarity determines in a certain way all the conceptual oppositions within which Rousseau inscribes the notion of Nature to the extent that it *should* be self-sufficient.

But the supplement supplements. It adds only to replace. It intervenes or insinuates itself *in-the-place-of;* if it fills, it is as if one fills a void.

159

If it represents and makes an image, it is by the anterior default of a presence. Compensatory [*suppléant*] and vicarious, the supplement is an adjunct, a subaltern instance which *takes-(the)-place* [*tient-lieu*]. As substitute, it is not simply added to the positivity of a presence, it produces no relief, its place is assigned in the structure by the mark of an emptiness. Somewhere, something can be filled up *of itself,* can accomplish itself, only by allowing itself to be filled through sign and proxy. The sign is always the supplement of the thing itself.

This second signification of the supplement cannot be separated from the first. We shall constantly have to confirm that both operate within Rousseau's texts. But the inflexion varies from moment to moment. Each of the two significations is by turns effaced or becomes discreetly vague in the presence of the other. But their common function is shown in this: whether it adds or substitutes itself, the supplement is *exterior,* outside of the positivity to which it is super-added, alien to that which, in order to be replaced by it, must be other than it. Unlike the *complement,* dictionaries tell us, the supplement is an "*exterior* addition" (Robert's *French Dictionary*).

According to Rousseau, the negativity of evil will always have the form of supplementarity. Evil is exterior to nature, to what is by nature innocent and good. It supervenes upon nature. But always by way of compensation for [*sous l'espèce de la suppléance*] what *ought to* lack nothing at all in itself.

Thus presence, always natural, which for Rousseau more than for others means maternal, *ought to be* self-sufficient. Its *essence,* another name for presence, may be read through the grid of this ought to be [*ce conditionnel*]. Like Nature's love, "there is no substitute for a mother's love," says *Emile*.[1] It is in no way *supplemented,* that is to say it does not have to be supplemented, it suffices and is self-sufficient; but that also means that it is irreplaceable; what one would substitute for it would not equal it, would be only a mediocre makeshift. Finally it means that Nature does not supplement *itself* at all; Nature's supplement does not proceed from

Nature, it is not only inferior to but other than Nature.

Yet all education, the keystone of Rousseauist thought, will be described or presented as a system of substitution [*suppléance*] destined to reconstitute Nature's edifice in the most natural way possible. The first chapter of *Emile* announces the function of this pedagogy. Although there is no substitute for a mother's love, "it is better that the child should suck the breast of a healthy nurse rather than of a petted mother, if he has any further evil to fear from her who has given him birth" (ibid.) [p. 12]. It is indeed culture or cultivation that must supplement a deficient nature, a deficiency that cannot by definition be anything but an accident and a deviation from Nature. Culture or cultivation is here called habit; it is necessary and insufficient from the moment when the substitution of mothers is no longer envisaged only "from the physiological point of view":

> Other women, or even other animals, may give him the milk she denies him, but there is no substitute for a mother's love. The woman who nurses another's child in place of her own is a bad mother; how can she be a good nurse? She may become one in time; use [habit] will overcome nature . . . (ibid.).

Here the problems of natural right, of the relationship between Nature and Society, the concepts of alienation, alterity, and corruption, are adapted most spontaneously to the pedagogic problem of the substitution of mothers and children:

> And this affection when developed has its drawbacks, which should make every sensible woman afraid to put her child out to nurse. Is she prepared to divide her mother's rights, or rather to abdicate them in favor of a stranger; to see her child loving another as much as and more than herself . . . (ibid.).

If, premeditating the theme of writing, I began by speaking of the substitution of mothers, it is because, as Rousseau will himself say, "more depends on this than you realize."

How emphatically would I speak if it were not so hopeless to keep struggling in vain on behalf of a real reform. More depends on this than you realize. Would you restore all men to their primal duties, begin with the mothers; the results will surprise you. Every evil follows in the train of this first sin; the whole moral order is disturbed, nature is quenched in every breast . . . (p. 18) [p. 13].

Childhood is the first manifestation of the deficiency which, in Nature, calls for substitution [suppléance]. Pedagogy illuminates perhaps more crudely the paradoxes of the supplement. How is a natural weakness possible? How can Nature ask for forces that it does not furnish? How is a child possible in general?

First Maxim.—Far from being too strong, children are not strong enough for all the claims of nature. Give them full use of such strength as they have and which they will not abuse. Second Maxim.—Help them and supply what they lack, in intelligence or in strength, whenever the need is of the body (p. 50) [p. 35].

All the organization of, and all the time spent in, education will be regulated by this necessary evil: "supply [suppléer] . . . [what] . . . is lacking" and to replace Nature. It must be done as little and as late as possible. "One of the best rules of good farming [culture] is to keep things back as much as possible" (p. 274) [p. 193]. "Give nature time to work before you take over her business [act in her place—agir à sa place]" (p. 102; italics added) [p. 71].

Without childhood, no supplement would ever appear in Nature. The supplement is here both humanity's good fortune and the origin of its perversion. The health of the human race:

Plants are fashioned by cultivation, and men by education. If man were born big and strong, his size and strength would be useless to him until he had learned to use them; they would create a prejudice against him, by not allowing others to think of assisting him; and, left to himself, he would die miserably before knowing his needs. We complain of the state of infancy; we do not see that, if man had not begun by being a child, the human race would have perished (p. 67).

The threat of perversion:

While the Author of nature has given children the active principle, He takes care that it shall do little harm by giving them small power to use it. But as soon as they can think of people as tools that they are responsible for activating, they use them to carry out their wishes and to supplement their own weakness. This is how they become tiresome, masterful, imperious, naughty, and unmanageable; a development which does not spring from a natural love of power, but one which gives it to them, for it does not need much experience to realize how pleasant it is to act through the hands of others and to move the world by simply moving the tongue (p. 49; italics added) [p. 34].

The supplement will always be the moving of the tongue or acting through the hands of others. In it everything is brought together: progress as the possibility of perversion, regression toward an evil that is not natural and that adheres to the power of substitution that permits us to absent ourselves and act by proxy, through representation, through the hands of others. Through the written [par écrit]. This substitution always has the form of the sign. The scandal is that the sign, the image, or the representer, become forces and make "the world move."

This scandal is such, and its evil effects are sometimes so irreparable, that the world seems to turn the wrong way (and we shall see later what such a catastrophe can signify for Rousseau); then Nature becomes the supplement of art and society. It is the moment when evil seems incurable: "As the child does not know how to be cured, let him know how to be ill. The one art takes the place of [supplée] the other and is often more successful; it is the art of nature" (p. 31) [p. 22]. It is also the moment when maternal nature, ceasing to be loved, as she ought to be, for herself and in an immediate proximity ("O Nature! O my mother! behold me under thy protection alone! Here there is no cunning or knavish mortal to thrust himself between me and thee." [*Confessions,* Book 12] [p. 669]) becomes the substitute for another love and for another attachment:

> The contemplation of Nature always had a very great attraction for his heart; he found there a supplement to the attachments that he needed; but he would have left the supplement for the thing, if he had had the choice, and he was reduced to converse with the plants only after vain efforts to converse with human beings (*Dialogues,* p. 794).

That botany becomes the supplement of society is more than a catastrophe. It is the catastrophe of the catastrophe. For in Nature, the plant is the most *natural* thing. It is natural *life.* The mineral is distinguished from the vegetable in that it is a dead and useful Nature, servile to man's industry. When man has lost the sense and the taste of true natural riches—plants—he rummages in the entrails of his mother and risks his health:

> The Mineral Kingdom has nothing in itself either amiable or attractive; its riches, enclosed in the breast [womb—*sein*] of the earth, seem to have been removed from the gaze of man in order not to tempt his cupidity; they are there like a reserve to serve one day as a *supplement* to the true wealth which is more within his grasp, and for which he loses taste according to the extent of his corruption. Then he is compelled to call in industry, to struggle, and to labor to alleviate his miseries; he searches the entrails of earth; he goes seeking to its center, at the risk of his life and at the expense of his health, for imaginary goods in place of the real good which the earth offers of herself if he knew how to enjoy it. *He flies from the sun and the day, which he is no longer worthy to see.*[2]

Man has thus put out his eyes, he blinds himself by the desire to rummage in these entrails. Here is the horrible spectacle of the punishment that follows the crime, in sum a simple substitution:

> He buries himself alive, and does well, not being worthy of living in the light of day. There quarries, pits, forges, furnaces, a battery of anvils, hammers, smoke and fire, succeed to the fair images of his rustic labors. The wan faces of the unhappy people who languish in the poisonous vapors of mines, of black forgemen, of hideous cyclops, are the spectacle which the working of the mine substitutes, in the heart [womb] of the earth for that of green fields and flowers, the azure sky, amorous shepherds and robust laborers upon its surface.[3]

Such is the scandal, such the catastrophe. The supplement is what neither Nature nor Reason can tolerate. Neither Nature, our "common mother" (*Reveries,* p. 1066) [p. 143], nor the reason which is reasonable, if not reasoning (*De l'état de nature* [*Pléiade,* vol. 3], p. 478). And had they not done everything to avoid this catastrophe, to protect themselves from this violence and to guard and keep us from this fatal crime? "so that," says the second *Discourse* precisely of mines, "it looks as if nature had taken pains to keep the fatal secret from us" (p. 172) [p. 200]. And let us not forget that the violence that takes us toward the entrails of the earth, the moment of mine-blindness, that is, of metallurgy, is the origin of society. For according to Rousseau, as we shall often confirm, agriculture, marking the organization of civil society, assumes the beginning of metallurgy. Blindness thus produces that which is born at the same time as society: the languages, the regulated substitution of signs for things, the order of the supplement. One goes *from blindness to the supplement.* But the blind person cannot see, in its origin, the very thing he produces to supplement his sight. *Blindness to the supplement* is the law. And especially blindness to its concept. Moreover, it does not suffice to locate its functioning in order to *see* its meaning. The supplement has no sense and is given to no intuition. We do not therefore make it emerge out of its strange penumbra. We speak its reserve.

Reason is incapable of thinking this double infringement upon Nature: that there is *lack* in Nature and that *because of that very fact* something *is added* to it. Yet one should not say that Reason is *powerless to think this;* it is constituted by that lack of power. It is the principle of identity. It is the thought of the self-identity of the natural being. It cannot even determine the supplement as its other, as the irrational and the non-natural, for the supplement comes *naturally* to put itself in Nature's place. The supplement is the image and the representation of Nature. The image is neither in nor out of Nature. The supplement is therefore equally dangerous for Reason, the natural health of Reason.

Dangerous supplement. These are the words that Rousseau uses in the *Confessions*. He uses them in a context which is only apparently different, and in order to explain, precisely, a "condition almost unintelligible and inconceivable [to reason]": "In a word, between myself and the most passionate lover there was only one, but that an essential, point of distinction, which makes my condition almost unintelligible and inconceivable" (*Pléiade,* vol. 1 [p. 111]).

If we lend to the text below a paradigmatic value, it is only provisional and does not prejudge what the discipline of a future reading might rigorously determine. No model of reading seems to me at the moment ready to measure up to this text—which I would like to read as a *text* and not as a document. Measure up to it fully and rigorously, that is, beyond what already makes the text most legible, and more legible than has been so far thought. My only ambition will be to draw out of it a signification which that presumed future reading will not be able to dispense with [*faire économie*]; the economy of a written text, circulating through other texts, leading back to it constantly, conforming to the element of a language and to its regulated functioning. For example, what unites the word "supplement" to its concept was not invented by Rousseau and the originality of its functioning is neither fully mastered by Rousseau nor simply imposed by history and the language, by the history of the language. To speak of the writing of Rousseau is to try to recognize what escapes these categories of passivity and activity, blindness and responsibility. And one cannot abstract from the written text to rush to the signified it *would mean*, since the signified is here the text itself. It is so little a matter of looking for a *truth signified* by these writings (metaphysical or psychological truth: Jean-Jacques' life behind his work) that if the texts that interest us *mean* something, it is the engagement and the appurtenance that encompass existence and writing in the same *tissue,* the same *text.* The same is here called supplement, another name for differance.

Here is the irruption of the dangerous supplement in Nature, between nature and nature, between natural innocence as *virginity* and natural innocence as *pucelage**: "In a word, between myself and the most passionate lover there was only one, but that an essential, point of distinction, which makes my condition almost unintelligible and inconceivable." Here, the lineation should not hide the fact that the following paragraph is destined to explain the "only one point of distinction" and the "almost unintelligible and inconceivable" "condition." Rousseau elaborates:

> I had returned from Italy not quite the same as I had entered it, but as, perhaps, no one of my age had ever returned from it. I had brought back, not my virginity but my *pucelage.* I had felt the progress of years; my restless temperament had at last made itself felt, and its first outbreak, quite involuntary, had caused me alarm about my health in a manner which shows better than anything else the innocence in which I had lived up to that time. Soon reassured, I learned that dangerous means of assisting it [*ce dangereux supplément*], which cheats Nature and saves up for young men of my temperament many forms of excess at the expense of their health, strength, and, sometimes, their life (*Pléiade,* I, pp. 108–09) [p. 111].

**"Pucelage"* is the more earthy French word for the actual physical fact of sexual intactness, in the female the membrane itself. Rousseau applies the word to his own case with some derision, contrasting it to the spiritual innocence of true "virginity."

We read in *Emile* (Book IV): "If once he acquires this dangerous habit [*supplément*] he is ruined" [p. 299]. In the same book, it is also a question of "mak[ing] up . . . by trading on . . . inexperience" [*suppléer en gagnant de vitesse sur l'experience;* literally "supplementing by outdistancing experience"] (p. 437) [p. 315], and of the "mind, which reinforces [*supplée*] . . . the bodily strength" (p. 183) [p. 129].

The experience of auto-eroticism is lived in anguish. Masturbation reassures ("soon reassured") only through that culpability traditionally attached to the practice, obliging children to assume the fault and to interiorize the threat of castration that always accompanies it. Pleasure is thus lived as the irremediable loss of the vital substance, as exposure to madness and death. It is produced "at the expense of their health, strength, and, sometimes, their life." In the same way, the *Reveries* will say, the man who "searches the entrails of earth . . . goes seeking to its center, at the risk of his life and at the expense of his health, for imaginary goods in place of the real good which the earth offers of herself if he knew how to enjoy it" (*Pléiade*, vol. 1, 1067 [p. 145]).

And indeed it is a question of the imaginary. The supplement that "cheats" maternal "nature" operates as writing, and as writing it is dangerous to life. This danger is that of the image. Just as writing opens the crisis of the living speech in terms of its "image," its painting or its representation, so onanism announces the ruin of vitality in terms of imaginary seductions:

> This vice, which shame and timidity find so convenient, possesses, besides a great attraction for lively imaginations—that of being able to dispose of the whole sex as they desire, and to make the beauty which tempts them minister to their pleasures, without being obliged to obtain its consent [*Confessions*, p. 111].

The dangerous supplement, which Rousseau also calls a "fatal advantage," is properly *seductive;* it leads desire away from the good path, makes it err far from natural ways, guides it toward its loss or fall and therefore it is a sort of lapse or scandal (*scandalon*). It thus destroys Nature. But the scandal of Reason is that nothing seems more natural than this destruction of Nature. It is myself who exerts myself to separate myself from the force that Nature has entrusted to me: "Seduced by this fatal advantage, I did my best to destroy the good constitution which Nature has restored to me, and [to] which I had allowed time to strengthen itself." We know what importance *Emile* gives to time, to the slow maturation of natural forces. The entire art of pedagogy is a calculated patience, allowing the work of Nature time to come to fruition, respecting its rhythm and the order of its stages. The dangerous supplement destroys very quickly the forces that Nature has slowly constituted and accumulated. In "out-distancing" natural experience, it runs non-stop [*brûle les étapes*—literally "burns the halting-points"] and consumes energy without possibility of recovery. As I shall confirm, like the sign it bypasses the presence of the thing and the duration of being.

The dangerous supplement breaks with Nature. The entire description of this moving away from Nature has a *scene* [*théâtre*]. The *Confessions* stage the evocation of the dangerous supplement at the moment when it is a question of making visible a distancing which is neither the same nor an other; Nature draws away at the same time as the Mother, or rather "Mamma," who already signified the disappearance of the true mother and has substituted herself in the well-known ambiguous manner. It is therefore now a question of the distance between Mamma and the person she called "Little one."[4] As *Emile* says, all evil comes from the fact that "women have ceased to be mothers, they do not and will not return to their duty" (p. 18) [p. 14]. A certain absence, then, of a certain sort of mother. And the experience of which we speak is such as to reduce that absence as much as to maintain it. A *furtive* experience, that of a thief who needs invisibility: that the mother be invisible and not see. These lines are often quoted:

> I should never have done, if I were to enter into the details of all the follies which the

remembrance of this dear mamma caused me to commit when I was no longer in her presence. How often have I kissed my bed, since she had slept in it; my curtains, all the furniture of my room, since they belonged to her, and her beautiful hand had touched them; even the floor, on which I prostrated myself, since she had walked upon it! Sometimes, even in her presence, I was guilty of extravagances, which only the most violent love seemed capable of inspiring. At table one day, just when she had put a piece of food into her mouth, I exclaimed that I saw a hair in it; she put back the morsel on her plate, and I eagerly seized and swallowed it.[5] In a word, between myself and the most passionate lover there was only one, but that an essential, point of distinction, which makes my condition almost unintelligible and inconceivable ... [A little above, we read] I only felt the full strength of my attachment when I no longer saw her (p. 107) [pp. 110–11].

The Chain of Supplements

The discovery of the dangerous supplement will be next cited *among* these "follies," but it will still retain a privilege; Rousseau evokes it after the others and as a sort of explanation of the state inconceivable to reason. For it is not the question of diverting total enjoyment toward a particular substitute, but now of experiencing it or miming it *directly and in its totality.* It is no longer a question of kissing the bed, the floor, the curtains, the furniture, etc., not even of "swallowing" the "piece ... [that] she had put into her mouth," but of "dispos[ing] of the whole sex as ... [one] desire[s]."

I remarked that the stage of this theater was not only a setting in the generally understood sense: an ensemble of accessories. The topographic disposition of the experience is not unimportant. Jean-Jacques is in the house of Madame de Warens; close enough to *Mamma* to see her and to nourish his imagination upon her but with the possibility of a partition. It is at the moment when the mother disappears that substitution becomes possible and necessary. The play of maternal presence or absence, this

alteration of perception and imagination must correspond to an organization of space; the text argues as follows:

Add to this habit the circumstances of my position, living as I was with a beautiful woman, caressing her image in the bottom of my heart, seeing her continually throughout the day, surrounded in the evening by objects which reminded me of her, sleeping in the bed in which I knew she had slept! What causes for excitement! Many a reader, who reflects upon them, no doubt already considers me as half-dead! Quite the contrary; that which ought to have destroyed me was just the thing that saved me, at least for a time. Intoxicated with the charm of living with her, with the ardent desire of spending my life with her, I always saw in her, whether she were absent or present, a tender mother, a beloved sister, a delightful friend, and nothing more.... She was for me the only woman in the world; and the extreme sweetness of the feelings with which she inspired me did not allow my senses time to awake for others, and protected me against her and all her sex.

This experience was not an event marking an archaic or adolescent period. Not only did it construct or sustain a particular hidden foundation, an edifice of significations. It remained an active obsession whose "present" is constantly reactivated and constituted in its turn, until the end of Jean-Jacques Rousseau's "life" and "text." A little later, a little further on in the text of the *Confessions* (Book IV),[6] "a little incident, which I find some difficulty in relating," [p. 150] is related to us. The encounter with a man "addicted to the same vice." Terrified, Jean-Jacques runs away, "trembling as if" he had just "committed a crime." "The recollection of this incident cured me of it for a long time" [p. 151].

For a long time? Rousseau will never stop having recourse to, and accusing himself of, this onanism that permits one to be himself affected by providing himself with presences, by summoning absent beauties. In his eyes it will remain the model of vice and perversion. Affecting oneself by another presence, one *corrupts* oneself [makes oneself other] by oneself [*on s'altère soi-même*]. Rousseau neither wishes to think nor can think that this alteration does not simply happen to the self, that it is the self's very origin. He must consider it a contingent evil coming from without to affect the integrity of the subject. But he cannot give up what immediately restores to him the other desired presence; no more than one can give up language. This is why, in this respect as well, as he says in the *Dialogues* [*Pléiade*, vol. 1] (p. 800), "to the end of his life he will remain an aged child."

The restitution of presence by language, restitution at the same time symbolic and immediate. This contradiction must be thought. Immediate experience of restitution because as experience, as consciousness or conscience, *it dispenses with passage through the world*. What is touching is touched, auto-affection gives itself as pure autarchy. If the presence that it then gives itself is the substitutive symbol of another presence, it has never been possible to desire that presence "in person" before this play of substitution and this symbolic experience of auto-affection. The thing itself does not appear outside of the symbolic system that does not exist without the possibility of auto-affection. Experience of *immediate* restitution, also because it *does not wait*. It is satisfied then and there and in the moment. If it waits, it is not because the other makes it wait. Pleasure seems no longer to be deferred. "Why give oneself so much trouble in a hope remote from so poor and uncertain a success, when one can, from the very instant . . ." (*Dialogues*).

But what is no longer deferred is also absolutely deferred. The presence that is thus delivered to us in the present is a chimera. Auto-affection is a pure speculation. The sign, the image, the representation, which come to supplement the absent presence are the illusions that sidetrack us. To culpability, to the anguish of death and castration, is added or rather is assimilated the experience of frustration. *Donner le change* ["sidetracking" or, "giving money"]: in whatever sense it is understood, this expression describes the recourse to the supplement admirably. In order to explain his "dislike" for

"common prostitutes," Rousseau tells us that in Venice, at thirty-one, the "propensity which had modified all my passions" (*Confessions*, p. 41) [p. 35][7] has not disappeared: "I had not lost the pernicious habit of satisfying my wants [*donner le change*]" (p. 316) [p. 289].

The enjoyment of the *thing itself* is thus undermined, in its act and in its essence, by frustration. One cannot therefore say that it has an essence or an act (*eidos, ousia, energeia,* etc.). Something promises itself as it escapes, gives itself as it moves away, and strictly speaking it cannot even be called presence. Such is the constraint of the supplement, such, exceeding all the language of metaphysics, is this structure "almost inconceivable to reason." *Almost* inconceivable: simple irrationality, the opposite of reason, are less irritating and waylaying for classical logic. The supplement is maddening because it is neither presence nor absence and because it consequently breaches both our pleasure and our virginity. ". . . abstinence and enjoyment, pleasure and wisdom, escaped me in equal measure" (*Confessions*, p. 12).

Are things not complicated enough? The symbolic is the immediate, presence is absence, the nondeferred is deferred, pleasure is the menace of death. But one stroke must still be added to this system, to this strange economy of the supplement. In a certain way, it was already legible. A terrifying menace, the supplement is also the first and surest protection; against that very menace. This is why it cannot be given up. And sexual auto-affection, that is auto-affection in general, neither begins nor ends with what one thinks can be circumscribed by the name of masturbation. The supplement has not only the power of *procuring* an absent presence through its image; procuring it for us through the proxy [*procuration*] of the sign, it holds it at a distance and masters it. For this presence is at the same time desired and feared. The supplement transgresses and at the same time respects the interdict. This is what also permits writing as the supplement of speech; but already also the spoken word as writing in general. Its economy exposes and protects us at the same time according to the play of forces and of the differences of forces. Thus, the supplement is dangerous in that it threatens us with death, but Rousseau thinks that it is not at all as dangerous as "cohabitation with women." Pleasure *itself*, without symbol or suppletory, that which would accord us (to) pure presence itself, if such a thing were possible, would be only another name for death. Rousseau says it:

> Enjoyment! Is such a thing made for man? Ah! If I had ever in my life tasted the delights of love even once in their plenitude, I do not imagine that my frail existence would have been sufficient for them, I would have been dead in the act (*Confessions,* Book VIII).

If one abides by the universal evidence, by the necessary and a priori value of this proposition in the form of a sigh, one must immediately recognize that "cohabitation with women," hetero-eroticism, can be lived (effectively, really, as one believes it can be said) only through the ability to reserve within itself its own supplementary protection. In other words, between auto-eroticism and hetero-eroticism, there is not a frontier but an economic distribution. It is within this general rule that the differences are mapped out. This is Rousseau's general rule. And before trying—what I do not pretend to be doing here—to encompass the pure singularity of Rousseau's economy or his writing, we must carefully raise and articulate between them all the structural or essential necessities on their different levels of generality.

It is from a certain determined representation of "cohabitation with women" that Rousseau had to have recourse throughout his life to that type of dangerous supplement that is called masturbation and that cannot be separated from his activity as a writer. To the end. Thérèse—the Thérèse of whom we can speak, Thérèse in the text, whose name and "life" belong to the writing we read—experienced it at her cost. In Book XII of the *Confessions*, at the moment when "I must speak without reserve," the "two reasons combined" of certain "resolutions" is confided to us:

> I must speak without reserve. I have never concealed either my poor mamma's faults or my own. I must not show greater favor to Thérèse either; and, pleased as I am to render honor to one who is so dear to me, neither do I wish to conceal her faults, if so be that an involuntary change in the heart's affections is really a fault. I had long since observed that her affection for me had cooled. . . . I was conscious again of an unpleasantness, the effects of which I had formerly felt when with mamma; and the effect was the same with Thérèse. Let us not look for perfections which are not to be found in nature; it would be the same with any other woman whatsoever. . . . My situation, however, was at that time the same, and even aggravated by the animosity of my enemies, who only sought to find me at fault. I was afraid of a repetition; and, not desiring to run the risk of it, I preferred to condemn myself to strict continence, than to expose Thérèse to the risk of finding herself in the same condition again. Besides, I had observed that intercourse with women distinctly aggravated my ill-health. . . . These two reasons combined caused me to form resolutions which I had sometimes been very inconsistent in keeping, but in which I had persevered with greater firmness for the last three or four years (p. 595) [pp. 616–17].

In the *Manuscrit de Paris,* after "distinctly aggravated my ill-health!" we read: "the corresponding vice, of which I have never been able to cure myself completely, appeared to me to produce less injurious results. These two reasons combined . . ."[8]

This perversion consists of preferring the sign and protects me from mortal expenditure. To be sure. But this apparently egotistical economy also functions within an entire system of moral representation. Egotism is redeemed by a culpability, which determines auto-eroticism as a fatal waste and a wounding of the self by the self. But as I thus harm only myself, this perversion is not truly condemnable. Rousseau explains it in more than one letter. Thus: "With that exception and [the exception of] vices that have always done harm to me alone, I can expose to all eyes a life irreproachable in all the secrets of my heart" (to M. de Saint-Germain,

2–26–70). "I have great vices, but they have never harmed anyone but me" (to M. Le Noir, 1–15–72).[9]

Jean-Jacques could thus look for a supplement to Thérèse only on one condition: that the system of supplementarity in general be already open in its possibility, that the play of substitutions be already operative for a long time and that *in a certain way Thérèse herself be already a supplement.* As Mamma was already the supplement of an unknown mother, and as the "true mother" herself, at whom the known "psychoanalyses" of the case of Jean-Jacques Rousseau stop, was also in a certain way a supplement, from the first trace, and even if she had not "truly" died in giving birth. Here is the chain of supplements. The name Mamma already designates one:

Ah, my Thérèse! I am only too happy to possess you, modest and healthy, and not to find what I never looked for. [The question is of "maidenhood" [*pucelage*] which Thérèse has just confessed to have lost in innocence and by accident.] At first I had only sought amusement; I now saw that I had found more and gained a companion. A little intimacy with this excellent girl, a little reflection upon my situation, made me feel that, while thinking only of my pleasures, I had done much to promote my happiness. *To supply the place of* my extinguished ambition, I needed a lively sentiment which should *take complete possession of* [literally "fill"—*remplit*] my heart. In a word, I needed a successor to mamma. As I should never live with her again, I wanted someone to live with her pupil, in whom I might find the simplicity and docility of heart which she had found in me. I felt it necessary that the gentle tranquility of private and domestic life *should make up* to me for the loss of the brilliant career which I was renouncing. When I was quite alone, I felt a void in my heart, which it only needed another heart *to fill.* Destiny had deprived me of, or, at least in part, alienated me from, that heart for which Nature had formed me. From that moment I was alone; for *with me it has always been everything or nothing. I found in Thérèse the substitute [supplément] that I needed.*[10]

Through this sequence of supplements a necessity is announced: that of an infinite chain, ineluctably multiplying the supplementary mediations that produce the sense of the very thing they defer: the mirage of the thing itself, of immediate presence, of originary perception. Immediacy is derived. That all begins through the intermediary is what is indeed "inconceivable [to reason]."

Notes

1. Edition Garnier, p. 17. My references are to the *Oeuvres complètes* (Pléiade edition) only in cases where the text has been published in one of the three volumes that have currently appeared. Other works will be cited from the Garnier editions. Of the *Essay on the Origin of Languages,* which we cite from the 1817 Bélin edition, I indicate, for the sake of convenience, only the numbers of the chapters.

2. *Rêveries.* Septième Promenade (*Pléiade* I, pp. 1066–67 [pp. 144–45]. Italics added. It may be objected that the animal represents a natural life even more animated than the plant, but one can only deal with it dead. "The study of animals is nothing without anatomy" (p. 1068) [p. 146].

3. Ibid. Without looking for a principle of reading there, I refer, out of curiosity and from among many other possible examples, to what Karl Abraham says of the Cyclops, of the fear of being blind, of the eye, of the sun, of masturbation etc. in *Oeuvres complètes,* tr. Ilse Barande [and E. Grin (Payot, 1965)] II, pp. 18 f. Let us recall that in a sequence of Egyptian mythology, Seth, helper of Thoth (god of writing here considered as a brother of Osiris), kills Osiris by trickery (cf. Vandier, op. cit., p. 46). Writing, auxiliary and suppletory, kills the father and light in the same gesture (Cf. supra, p. 101, **328–29 n. 31**).

4. "'Little one' was my name; 'Mama' was hers; and we always remained 'Little one' and 'Mama,' even when advancing years had almost obliterated the difference between us. I find that these two names give a wonderfully good idea of the tone of our intercourse, of the simplicity of our manners, and, above all, of the mutual relation of our hearts. For me she was the tenderest of mothers, who never sought her own pleasure, but always what was best for me; and if sensuality entered at all into her attachment for me, it did not alter its character, but only rendered it more enchanting, and intoxicated

me with the delight of having a young and pretty mamma whom it was delightful to me to caress—I say caress in the strictest sense of the word, for it never occurred to her to be sparing of kisses and the tenderest caresses of a mother, and it certainly never entered my mind to abuse them. It will be objected that, in the end, we had relations of a different character; I admit it, but I must wait a little—I cannot say all at once" (p. 106) [p. 109]. Let us add this sentence from Georges Bataille: "I am myself the 'little one,' I have only a hidden place" (*Le petit* [2d edition (Paris, 1963), p. 9]).

5. This passage is often cited, but has it ever been analyzed for itself? The Pléiade editors of the *Confessions,* Gagnebin and Raymond, are no doubt right in being cautious, as they are, systematically and inevitably, of what they call psychiatry (note p. 1281. This same note checks off very usefully all the texts where Rousseau recalls his "follies" or "extravagances."). But this caution is not legitimate, it seems to me, except to the extent that it concerns the abuse—which has hitherto no doubt been confounded with the use—of psychoanalytic reading, and where it does not prescribe the duplication of the usual commentary which has rendered this kind of text most often unreadable. We must distinguish here between, on the one hand, the often hasty and careless, but often also enlightening, analyses by Dr. René Laforgue ("Etude sur J.-J. Rousseau," in *Revue française de psychanalyse,* I, ii [1927], pp. 370 f.; and *Psychopathologie de l'échec* [1944], [Paris], pp. 114 f.), which moreover do not consider the texts I have just cited, and, on the other hand, an interpretation which would take into more rigorous account, at least in principle, the teachings of psychoanalysis. That is one of the directions in which Jean Starobinski's fine and careful analyses are engaged. Thus, in *L'oeil vivant,* the sentence that has given us pause is reinscribed within an entire series of examples of analogous substitution, borrowed mostly from the *Nouvelle Héloïse;* this one for example, among other "erotic fetishes": "All the parts of your scattered dress present to my ardent imagination those of your body that they conceal. This delicate headdress which sets off the large blond curls which it pretends to cover; this happy bodice shawl against which at least once I shall not have to complain; this elegant and simple gown which displays so well the taste of the wearer; these dainty slippers that a supple foot fills so easily; this corset so slender which touches and embraces . . . what an enchanting form . . . in

front two gentle curves . . . oh voluptuous sight . . . the whalebone has yielded to the force of the impression . . . delicious imprints, let me kiss you a thousand times!" (p. 147 [tr. Judith H. McDowell (University Park and London, 1968), pp. 122–23].

But do the singularity of these substitutions and the articulation of these displacements hold the attention of the interpreter? I wonder if, too concerned with reacting against a reductionist, causalist, dissociative psychology, Starobinski does not in general give too much credit to a totalitarian psychoanalysis of the phenomenological or existentialist style. Such a psychoanalysis, diffusing sexuality in the totality of behavior, perhaps risks blurring the cleavages, the differences, the displacements, the fixations of all sorts that structure that totality. Do the place or the places of sexuality not disappear in the analysis of global behavior, as Starobinski recommends: "Erotic behavior is not a fragmentary given; it is the manifestation of a total individual, and it is as such that it ought to be analyzed. Whether it is to neglect it or to make it a privileged subject of study, one cannot limit exhibitionism to the sexual 'sphere': the entire personality is revealed there, with some of its fundamental 'existential choices.'" (*La transparence et l'obstacle,* pp. 210–11. A note refers us to the *Phénoménologie de la perception* of [Maurice] Merleau-Ponty [(Paris, 1945); *Phenomenology of Perception,* tr. Colin Smith (New York, 1965)].) And does one not, in this way, risk determining the pathological in a very classic manner, as "excess" thought within "existential" categories: "In the perspective of a global analysis, it will appear that certain primary givens of consciousness constitute at the same time the source of Rousseau's speculative thought, and the source of his folly. But these givensources are not morbid by themselves. It is only because they are lived in an excessive manner, that the malady declares itself and is developed. . . . The morbid development will realize the caricatural placing in evidence of a fundamental 'existential' question that consciousness was not able to dominate" (p. 253).

6. Page 165 [p. 171].

7. In these celebrated pages of the first Book of the *Confessions,* Rousseau compares the first experiences of reading ("secret and ill-chosen reading") to the first discoveries of auto-eroticism. Not that the "filthy and licentious [books]" encouraged him in it. Quite the contrary. "Chance aided my modest disposition so well, that I was more than thirty years old

before I set eyes upon any of those dangerous books
which a fine lady finds inconvenient because they
can only be read with one hand" (p. 40) [p. 40].
Without these "dangerous books," Jean-Jacques
gives himself to other dangers. The continuation of
the paragraph which closes thus is well known: "It is
sufficient for me to have defined the origin and first
cause of a propensity which has modified all my passions, and which, restraining them by means of
themselves, has always made me slow to act, owing
to my excessive impetuosity in desire" (p. 41) [p.
41]. The intention and the letter of this passage
should be related to another page of the *Confessions*
(p. 444 [p. 459]. Cf. also the editors' note), and to
the page from which I quote these lines: "for I have
always had a fancy for reading while eating, if I am
alone; it supplies the want of society. I devour alter-

nately a page and a morsel. It seems as if my book
were dining with me" (p. 269) [p. 278].

8. See editors' note, p. 1569. [The English translation includes the sentence quoted in the Pléiade note
on p. 617.]

9. [*Correspondance générale de J.-J. Rousseau*
(Paris, 1934), vol. 19, p. 242, vol. 20, p. 122, the latter
actually addressed to M. de Sartine, Lieutenant-
general of police.]. See also the *Confessions* (p. 109,
editors' note).

10. Pages 331–32 [pp. 340–41] (italics added),
Starobinski (*La transparence et l'obstacle*, p. 221) and
the editors of the *Confessions* (p. 332, n. 1) justly relate the use of the word "supplement" to what is
made of it on p. 109 [p. 111] ("dangerous means of
assisting it" [a literal translation would be "dangerous supplement"]).

Questions About the Premises of Psychoanalytic Theory

Luce Irigaray

To put certain questions to psychoanalysis, to challenge it in some way, is always to risk being misunderstood, and thus to encourage a *pre-critical* attitude toward analytic theory. And yet there are many areas in which this theory merits questioning, in which self-examination would be in order. One of these areas is female sexuality. If we reconsider the terms in which the debate has taken place within the field of psychoanalysis itself, we may ask the following questions, for example:

Why has the alternative between clitoral and vaginal pleasure played such a significant role? Why has the woman been expected to choose between the two, being labeled "masculine" if she stays with the former, "feminine" if she renounces the former and limits herself to the latter? Is this problematics really adequate to account for the evolution and the "flowering" of a woman's sexuality? Or is it informed by the *standardization* of this sexuality according to *masculine parameters* and/or by criteria that are valid—perhaps?—for determining whether auto-eroticism or heteroeroticism prevails in man? In fact, a woman's erogenous zones are not the clitoris or the vagina, but the clitoris and the vagina, and the lips, and the vulva, and the mouth of the uterus, and the uterus itself, and the breasts ... What might have been, ought to have been, astonishing is the *multiplicity of genital erogenous zones* (assuming that the qualifier "genital" is still required) in female sexuality.

Why would the libidinal structuring of the woman be decided, for the most part, before puberty—since at that stage, for Freud and many of his disciples, "the truly feminine vagina is still undiscovered"[1]—unless it is because those feminine characteristics that are politically, economically, and culturally valorized are linked to maternity and mothering? Such a claim implies that everything, or almost everything, is settled as to woman's allotted sexual role, and especially as to the representations of that role that are suggested, or attributed, to her, even before the specific, socially sanctioned form of her intervention in the sexual economy is feasible, and before she has access to a unique, "properly feminine" pleasure. It is understandable that she only appears from then on as "lacking in," "deprived of," "covetous of," and so forth. In a word: castrated.

Why must the maternal function take precedence over the more specifically erotic function in woman? Why, once again, is she subjected, why does she subject herself, to a hierarchical choice even though the articulation of those two sexual roles has never been sufficiently elaborated? To be sure, this prescription has to be understood within an *economy and an ideology of (re)production,* but it is also, or still, the mark of a *subjection to man's desire,* for "even a marriage is not made secure until the wife has succeeded in making her husband her child as well and in acting as mother to him."[2] Which leads to the next question:

Why must woman's sexual evolution be "more difficult and more complicated" than man's?[3] And what is the end point of that evolution, except for her to become in some way her husband's mother? The vagina itself, "now valued [only] as a place of shelter for the penis . . . enters into the heritage of the womb."[4] In other words, does it go without saying that the little girl renounces her first object cathexes, the precociously cathected erogenous zones, in order to complete the itinerary that will enable her to satisfy man's lasting desire to make love with his mother, or an appropriate substitute? Why should a woman have to leave—and "hate"[5]—her own mother, leave her own house, abandon her own family, renounce the name of her own mother and father, in order to take man's genealogical desires upon herself?

Why is the interpretation of female homosexuality, now as always, modeled on that of male homosexuality? The female homosexual is thought to act as a man in desiring a woman who is equivalent to the phallic mother and/or who has certain attributes that remind her of another man, for example her brother.[6] Why should the desire for likeness, for a female likeness, be forbidden to, or impossible for, the woman? Then again, *why are mother-daughter relations necessarily conceived in terms of "masculine" desire* and homosexuality? What is the purpose of this misreading, of this condemnation, of woman's relation to her own original desires, this nonelaboration of her relation to her own origins? To assure the *predominance of a single libido,* as the little girl finds herself obliged to repress her drives and her earliest cathexes. Her libido?

Which leads us to wonder why the active/passive opposition remains so persistent in the controversies surrounding woman's sexu-

ality. Even though this opposition may be defined as characteristic of a pregenital stage, the anal stage, *it continues to leave its mark on the masculine/feminine difference*—which would draw from it its psychological tenor[7]—*just as it determines the respective roles of man and woman in procreation.*[8] What relation continues to maintain that passivity toward the anal-sadistic drives which are permitted to man and forbidden to—inhibited in—woman? What relation guarantees man sole and simultaneous ownership of the child (the product), the woman (the reproductive machine), and sex (the reproductive agent)? *Rape,* if possible resulting in *conception*—rape is depicted moreover by certain male and female psychoanalysts as the height of feminine pleasure[9]—has become the model for the sexual relation.

Why is woman so little suited for sublimation? Does she also remain *dependent upon a relationship with the paternal superego?* Why is woman's social role still largely "transcendent with respect to the order of the contract that work propagates? And, in particular, is it through its effect that the status of marriage is maintained in the decline of paternalism?"[10] These two questions converge perhaps in the fact that women are tied down to domestic tasks without being explicitly bound by any work contract: the marriage contract takes its place.

*   *   *

We have not exhausted the list of questions that psychoanalysis could raise as to the "destiny," in particular the sexual destiny, assigned to woman, a destiny too often ascribed to anatomy and biology—which are supposed to explain, among other things, the very high frequency of female frigidity.

But *the historical determinants of this destiny need to be investigated.* This implies that psychoanalysis needs to reconsider the very limits of its theoretical and practical field, needs to detour through an "interpretation" of the cultural background and the economy, especially the political economy, that have marked it, without its knowledge. And psychoanalysis ought to wonder whether it is even possible to pursue a limited discussion of female sexuality so long as the status of woman in the general economy of the West has never been established. What role has been marked off for her in the *organization of property, the philosophical systems, the religious mythologies* that have dominated the West for centuries?

*   *   *

In this perspective, we might suspect the *phallus* (Phallus) of being the *contemporary figure of a god jealous of his prerogatives;* we might suspect it of claiming, on this basis, to be the ultimate meaning of all discourse, the standard of truth and propriety, in particular as regards sex, the signifier and/or the ultimate signified of all desire, in addition to continuing, as emblem and agent of the patriarchal system, to shore up the name of the father (Father).

Notes

1. Sigmund Freud, "Femininity," in *New Introductory Lectures on Psycho-analysis, The Standard Edition of the Complete Psychological Works of Sigmund Freud*. Ed. James Strachey, 24 vols. (London, 1953–1974), 22:118.

2. Ibid., pp. 133–134.

3. Ibid., p. 117.

4. Freud, "The Infantile Genital Organization: An Interpolation into the Theory of Sexuality," in *The Standard Edition*, 19:145.

5. "Femininity," pp. 121ff.

6. Freud, "The Psychogenesis of a Case of Homosexuality in a Woman," in *The Standard Edition*, 18:156.

7. Freud, "Instincts and Their Vicissitudes," *The Standard Edition*, 14:111–140.

8. See Freud, "Femininity."

9. See Freud, "Femininity"; Helene Deutsch, *The Psychology of Women: A Psychoanalytic Interpretation*, 2 vols. (New York, 1945; rpt. 1967); and Marie Bonaparte, *Female Sexuality*, trans. John Rodker (New York, 1953).

10. See Jacques Lacan, "Propos directifs pour un congrés sur la sexualité féminine," in *Écrits* (Paris, 1966).

Female Hom(m)osexuality

Luce Irigaray

The "Constitutional Factor" Is Decisive

"The extreme achievement of such a masculinity complex would appear to be the influencing of the choice of an object in the sense of manifest homosexuality."[1] The object choice of *a female* homosexual can only be determined by a particularly strong masculinity complex. "Analytic experience teaches us, to be sure, that female homosexuality is seldom or never a direct continuation of infantile masculinity." It should rather be interpreted as a regression "into her early masculinity complex" as a result of the "inevitable disappointments from her father,"[2] whom she has taken as an 'object' once she enters the Oedipus situation. Obviously the significance of these disappointments must not be exaggerated; a girl who is destined to become feminine is not spared them either, though they do not have the same effect. And "the predominance of the constitutional factor seems indisputable."[3] As might have been expected! Be this factor as it may, homosexual woman "play the parts of mother and baby with each other as often and as clearly as those of husband and wife" (!), attitudes which "will mirror" "the two phases in the development of female homosexuality." Would these two phases be, then, "a direct continuation of infantile masculinity" or a regression "into her early masculine complex"? Unless, of course, one of these alternatives, the second, corresponded to the identification with the father that comes after he has been renounced as an "object" of love? Other texts stress the possibility of this.[4] The essential thing, in any case, is to show that the object choice of the homosexual woman is determined by a *masculine* desire and tropism. The female libido is cut off from the active search for its instinctual "object-aims" and its primary "waves." It has in a sense neither aim (telos) nor origin (arche) of its own. The instincts that lead the homosexual woman to choose an object for her satisfaction are, necessarily, "male" instincts.

So we will read, in the argument developed in the text Freud devotes to a case of female homosexuality, that "in her behaviour towards her love-object," the homosexual woman "had throughout assumed the masculine part" and "had thus not only chosen a feminine love-object but had also developed a masculine attitude towards that object" (PCHW, p. 154). Furthermore "she changed into a man and took her mother in place of her father as the object of her love" (PCHW, p. 158). We read that, all the same, her "inversion . . . received its final reinforcement when she found in her 'lady' an object which promised to satisfy not only her homosexual trends, but also that part of her heterosexual libido which was attached still to her brother" (PCHW, p. 160), the same brother whom—after an unremarkable passage through the Oedipus complex—she "had begun to substitute for her father" (PCHW, p. 155). The unusually strong fixation to the lady could thus be explained by the fact that the latter's "slender figure, severe beauty and downright manner reminded her of the brother who was a little older than herself" (PCHW, p. 156).

Homosexual Choice Clearly Expounded

It seems that the phallic instinctual script is never written out so clearly as in the case of

174

female homosexuality: in which a man desires the phallic mother, or another man. Something very obvious but usually unnoticed apparently becomes crystal clear when it shows up in women—that something being the pregnancy, in philosophical terms, of course, of *male homosexuality.* For this whole analysis is about male homosexuality. And Freud could doubtless have reminded us that, as far as the economy of desire goes, *miming*—acting, pretending—is capable of affording *an increase in pleasure* over simple discharges of instincts. He could have pointed out that acting "like" a man, desiring a woman who was "like" a man, just "as" a man does, would be the most satisfying performance of the phallic scenario. But he decides against this, unable to give up so easily the *natural basis* of desire. Therefore he will be on the lookout for the anatomical signs justifying his patient's—masculine—homosexuality. And although he is forced to admit that "there was no obvious deviation from the feminine physical type," that his patient was "beautiful and well-made" and had no "menstrual disturbance," he adds that she had "her father's tall figure, and her facial features were sharp rather than soft and girlish, traits which might be regarded as indicating a physical masculinity." However, "the psycho-analyst customarily forgoes a thorough physical examination of his patients, *in certain cases*[?]" (PCHW, p. 154).

A Cure Fails for Lack of Transferences

Be that as it may, "the analysis went forward almost without any signs of resistance, the patient participating actively with her intellect [thanks to her "intellectual attributes . . . connected with masculinity"], though absolutely tranquil emotionally" (PCHW, p. 163). Once, when Freud "expounded to her a specially important part of the theory, *one touching her nearly,* she replied in an inimitable tone, 'How very interesting', as though she were a grande dame being taken over a museum and glancing through her lorgnon at objects to which she was completely indifferent" (PCHW, p. 163). In-

deed, that homosexual woman must have found Freud's explanations to be very like historical documents that did not touch her at all and left her all her emotional tranquility! As for the use of the lorgnon—the one through which he was looking at her perhaps?—as accessory or prop, responsibility for this has to be laid at Freud's door. It seemed, then, "as though nothing resembling a transference to the physician had been effected" (PCHW, p. 164). At any rate no transference that he recognized as such. None that fitted his theory of "transference," perhaps? Or else none that was practicable within his conception of a cure, and his ways of being, or not being, involved in it? The only hints of transference were supplied by dreams that "he did not *believe*" because they were "*false* or *hypocritical*" and intended to deceive the analyst "just as she habitually deceived her father" (PCHW, p. 164). Why this fear of being misled by the patient's unconscious? Or even by the "preconscious," if not the "waking conscious life" itself, which perhaps whispered their intentions in the dream? Why this fear of being "pleased" by a patient and later, as a result, "disappointed," "misled"? Could it be that all these adventures would be unseemly in the dignified father figure that Freud intends to go on playing and that possibly covers up *his* transference? Therefore he made it clear to the person in question that he was perfectly aware that she wanted to make a fool of him, and he was right to do so since "after I had made this clear, this kind of dream ceased" (PCHW, p. 165). Thus the psychoanalyst can induce or forbid certain dreams. . . . As for the rest, the girl's parents were advised that "if they set store by the psychoanalytic procedure, it should be continued by a woman doctor" (PCHW, p. 164).

So here we have the homosexual woman shown the door by her psychoanalyst, because she refuses to allow herself to be seduced by the father quite as much as he refuses to become the surrogate object of her desire, which in this case would mean his being identified with a *cocotte,* a woman of "bad reputation," who "lived simply by giving her bodily favours" (PCHW, p. 161). Freud's well-brought-up, middle-class super-ego did not permit him such lapses. Or even let him admit that a "beautiful and clever girl, belonging to a family of good standing" might throw over her father (whom Freud knows and likes and is *paid* by) in favor of a whore.

Female Sameness

But isn't there a more unconscious, archaic, and "phylogenetically" remote stratum in Freud's super-ego that forbade him even more strongly to *identify with a woman?* Another good reason for sending the homosexual woman over to a female colleague while remaining skeptical about anything worthwhile coming out of the sessions of female analyst and female patient. For female homosexuality represented for Freud a phenomenon so alien to his imaginary economy that it could only be "neglected by psycho-analytic research" (PCHW, p. 147), and even neglected in the therapy of the homosexual woman patient. This is not to say that what Freud describes does not fit a certain "reality," or that his commentaries or explanations are simply "wrong." Many homosexual women can recognize themselves in this story or could at least try to find their bearings in it. Female homosexuality would nonetheless remain obliterated, travestied—transvestized—and withdrawn from interpretation. For nothing of the special nature of desire *between women* has been unveiled or stated. That a woman might desire a woman "like" herself, someone of the "same" sex, that she might also have auto- and homosexual appetites, is simply incomprehensible to Freud, and indeed inadmissible. Such an idea is rarely encountered in this phallocentric history, in which value is the prerogative of the penis and its equivalents. And in which it is not easy to be outside the system, "off the market." The claims advanced by female homosexuality are obviously not enough to raise doubts about the privilege of the phallus.

This does not mean, however, that woman's desire for herself, for the self-same[5]—a female self, a female same—is not be recognized. Does

not have to discover a possible economy. That this desire is not necessary to balance the desire of the other. That the same-he and same-she do not have to be re-marked for her too if sexual difference is to be expressible without purely and simply incurring death: death of the ego, and therefore of the sexual instincts as well (to refer to a problematic developed by Freud but whose functioning he overlooks somewhat when he is describing the "development of a woman," in which the little girl would have to reject and devalue all representatives, male and female, and representations of her sex in order to turn her desires, her "envies," toward the only sex/organ: the masculine). The prohibition, the depreciation of the desire for the "self-same"—which women would perhaps promote, through their "masculine" phallic super-ego at any rate?—in the development of female sexuality would explain in large measure women's oft-lamented frigidity or lack of sexual appetite. But it could equally serve as an interpretive lever for many other accompanying or derived symptoms: lack of autonomy; narcissistic fragility or hypernarcissim; an incapacity for sublimation that does not exclude an "aethereal" erotism; at best difficult relations with the mother, and indeed with all women; lack of "social interest" and, more generally, of all sustained interest; depressions and chronic somatizations, etc. All these indicate the lack of an auto-erotic, homosexual economy. Or else, or as well as, *death drives.* The "active" enactment of which is forbidden for/in female sexuality. And this ban does not and cannot produce any results, any system of metaphor, any sublimation, simply because a dominant *specular* economy does not tally with female sexuality. The specular organization leaves, in no doubt different ways, both the female sexual function and the female maternal function in an amorphous suspension of their instinctual economy and/or shapes them in ways quite heteronomous to that economy. Their "economy" will be governed by the demands of drives—particularly sadistic or scoptophiliac ones—that only men can actually put into practice. Governed above all by the need to maintain the primacy of the Phallus.

So there will be no female homosexuality, just a hommo-sexuality in which woman will be involved in the process of specularizing the phallus, begged to maintain the desire for the same that man has, and will ensure at the same time, elsewhere and in complementary and contradictory fashion, the perpetuation in the couple of the pole of "matter."[6] Which can be defined as what resists infinite reflection: the mystery (hysteria?) that will always remain modestly *behind every mirror,* and that will spark the desire to see and know more about it. Which relates to the specular only indirectly, through what it offers, or does not offer, to be reflected and echoed by man's desire.

But woman devotes, it is insisted, very little cathexis to auto-erotism, auto-representation, auto-reproduction, even in homosexuality. The possibility that these might give her a specific sexual pleasure is little considered: the pleasure of caresses, words, re-presentations or representations that remind woman of her sex, her sex organs, her sexes[7] would be little in demand, little interested or interesting, within a male heterosexual praxis, because it lacks masculine homologues. It would be a different, complementary or supplementary, sexual pleasure from that sought not only in heterosexuality but also in woman's implication within, or miming of, male homosexuality. There would also be a narcissistic well-being in acting out a regressive relationship with a "good" mother—despite Freud's somewhat incomprehensible insistence that such a relationship is exclusively associated with homosexuality, and, what is more, with the little girl's "virile" desire for (her) mother. Yet what exhilarating pleasure it is to be partnered with someone like oneself. With a sister, in everyday terms. What need, attraction, passion, one feels for someone, for some woman, like oneself. But might not this feeling put an end to the little girl's "penis-envy," or encourage her "penis-desire"? Might it not give her back a phallic urge that was less greedy, frustrated, demanding, or . . . anorexic? But the need, the charm felt for one's like will be repressed, denied, turned into their opposites in what is labeled "normal femininity." In fact, they will only be barely hinted at in the interpretation of masculine homosexuality.

*   *   *

As for his homosexual woman patient, Freud will explain that "the *heterosexual* current" was "*deeper*" and in fact "was deflected into the manifest homosexual one." Woman's desire for her like is thus seen as "secondary," a "reactive formation" in some way to the disappointments her father had caused her, even though, it must be remembered, the little girl's first love object is her mother or else someone of her own sex. Even though Freud makes a point of forgetting this when he affirms about his patient that "from the very early years, therefore, her libido had flowed in two currents, the *one on the surface* being one that we may unhesitatingly designate homosexual. This latter was probably *a direct and unchanged continuation of an infantile fixation* on her mother" (PCHW, p. 168). The libidinal relationship with the mother is therefore more "on the surface" than her "deeper" heterosexual desire and it can "unhesitatingly" and without transformations be called homosexual. Thereby the primary purpose of female desire is *reduced* and *caricatured.* But woman's relationship with her origin must needs be canceled—as well as her original relationship with her mother and her sex, which is deemed to be "on the surface," "secondary," though "manifest"—if the domination of the Phallus is to be established. Emblem of the mastery exercised by and for man within *one* economy of origin. His own.

Notes

1. Sigmund Freud, "Femininity," in *New Introductory Lectures on Psycho-analysis, The Standard Edition of the Complete Psychological Works of Sigmund Freud.* Ed. James Strachey, 24 vols. (London, 1953–1974), 22:130.

2. Ibid., p. 130.

3. Ibid., p. 130.

4. Cf. particularly "The Psychogenesis of a Case of Homosexuality in a Woman," in *The Standard*

Edition, 18:147–172. The "literary" qualities of this "story" and the ideological overdetermination of many of its statements are quite striking. (Page references to this essay—referred to as PCHW—will be made in the text.—Tr.)

5. A self-same that would be "other" than the one that dominates the phallocentric economy of discourse and signifiers. It will be read by half-opening the "volume" elsewhere and otherwise.

6. The assimilation and assignment of woman, the mother, to the pole of "matter" is traditional, as we know. It is found in Freud's work, including this essay on female homosexuality, where it is expressed more or less explicitly in the equally traditional question of whether homosexuality is "congenital" or "later-developed" (Psychogenesis of a Case of Homosexuality in a Woman, pp. 153 and 169), attributable to "physical" or "psychical hermaphroditism" (p. 154), to "body" or "character" (PCHW, p. 170). And even though Freud is somewhat hesi-

tant about positing the problem in this way, many of his statements prove how far his own views coincide with the traditional ones, particularly when it is a question of female sexuality. For example, we shall be told in this text that the independence of one of these factors from the other "is more evident in men than women, where bodily and mental traits belonging to the opposite sex are apt to coincide" (PCHW, p. 154). Woman's psyche, her personality, her "soul," correlate, in fact, better with organic factors than do man's. Perhaps she does not have a soul? People have doubted this in the past. Her homosexuality will thus be put down to her hormones, or her "hermaphroditic ovaries" (PCHW, p. 172).

7. The multiplicity of woman's erogenous zones, the plural nature of her sex, is a differentiating factor that is too rarely considered in the male/female polarity, especially as far as its implications for "signifying" practices are concerned.

Afterword to
Male Subjectivity at the Margins

Kaja Silverman

In the preceding pages, I have attempted to show that our desires and identifications have such important extra-psychic ramifications that it is no exaggeration to speak of a "libidinal politics." I have also tried to complicate the notion of "the feminine"—to show that it designates a number of conditions that are constitutive of all subjectivity, although they are antipathetic to conventional masculinity. Finally, I have struggled to expose the murderous logic of traditional male subjectivity, and to articulate some alternative ways of inhabiting a morphologically masculine body. The marginal male subjectivities that I have most fully valorized are those which absent themselves from the line of paternal succession, and which in one way or another occupy the domain of femininity.

What is my own connection to these "deviant" masculinities? It will perhaps come as no surprise to the reader to learn that while writing this book I often felt myself to be somehow "outside" my corporeal "envelope," and "inside" the subjectivities I was exploring. Since the psychic space into which I thereby stepped was generally one which was familiar to me, I might not seem to have traveled very far away from myself through these exteriorizing identifications. However, for a female subject to re-encounter femininity from within a male body is clearly to experience it under different terms—to live it no longer as disenfranchisement and subordination, but rather as phallic divestiture, as a way of saying "no" to power. It is thus, as I discovered, to alter forever her own relationship to femininity's defining tropes.

Imitation and Gender Insubordination[1]

Judith Butler

So what is this divided being introduced into language through gender? It is an impossible being, it is a being that does not exist, an ontological joke.

—Monique Wittig[2]

Beyond physical repetition and the physical or metaphysical repetition, is there an ontological repetition? . . . This ultimate repetition, this ultimate theatre, gathers everything in a certain way; and in another way, it destroys everything; and in yet another way, it selects from everything.

—Gilles Deleuze[3]

To Theorize as a Lesbian?

At first I considered writing a different sort of essay, one with a philosophical tone: the "being" of being homosexual. The prospect of *being* anything, even for pay, has always produced in me a certain anxiety, for "to be" gay, "to be" lesbian seems to be more than a simple injunction to become who or what I already am. And in no way does it settle the anxiety for me to say that this is "part" of what I am. To write or speak *as a lesbian* appears a paradoxical appearance of this "I," one which feels neither true nor false. For it is a production, usually in response to a request, to come out or write in the name of an identity which, once produced, sometimes functions as a politically efficacious phantasm. I'm not at ease with "lesbian theories, gay theories," for as I've argued elsewhere,[4] identity categories tend to be instruments of regulatory regimes, whether as the normalizing categories of oppressive structures or as the rallying points for a liberatory contestation of that very oppression.

This is not to say that I will not appear at political occasions under the sign of lesbian, but that I would like to have it permanently unclear what precisely that sign signifies. So it is unclear how it is that I can contribute to this book and appear under its title, for it announces a set of terms that I propose to contest. One risk I take is to be recolonized by the sign under which I write, and so it is this risk that I seek to thematize. To propose that the invocation of identity is always a risk does not imply that resistance to it is always or only symptomatic of a self-inflicted homophobia. Indeed, a Foucaultian perspective might argue that the affirmation of "homosexuality" is itself an extension of a homophobic discourse. And yet "discourse," he writes on the same page, "can be both an instrument and an effect of power, but also a hindrance, a stumbling-block, a point of resistance and a starting point for an opposing strategy."[5]

So I am skeptical about how the "I" is determined as it operates under the title of the lesbian sign, and I am no more comfortable with its homophobic determination than with those normative definitions offered by other members of the "gay or lesbian community." I'm permanently troubled by identity categories, consider them to be invariable stumbling-blocks, and understand them, even promote them, as sites of necessary trouble. In fact, if the category were to offer no trouble, it would cease to be interesting to me: it is precisely the *pleasure* produced by the instability of those categories which sustains the various erotic practices that make me a candidate for the category to begin with. To install myself within the terms of an identity category would be to turn against the sexuality that the category purports to describe; and this might be true for any identity category which seeks to control the very eroticism that it claims to describe and authorize, much less "liberate."

And what's worse, I do not understand the notion of "theory," and am hardly interested in being cast as its defender, much less in being signified as part of an elite gay/lesbian theory crowd that seeks to establish the legitimacy and domestication of gay/lesbian studies within the academy. Is there a pregiven distinction between theory, politics, culture, media? How do those divisions operate to quell a certain intertextual writing that might well generate wholly different epistemic maps? But I am writing here now: is it too late? Can this writing, can any writing, refuse the terms by which it is appropriated even as, to some extent, that very colonizing discourse enables or produces this stumbling block, this resistance? How do I relate the paradoxical situation of this dependency and refusal?

If the political task is to show that theory is never merely *theoria,* in the sense of disengaged contemplation, and to insist that it is fully political (*phronesis* or even *praxis*), then why not simply call this operation *politics,* or some necessary permutation of it?

I have begun with confessions of trepidation and a series of disclaimers, but perhaps it will become clear that *disclaiming,* which is no simple activity, will be what I have to offer as a form of affirmative resistance to a certain regulatory

operation of homophobia. The discourse of "coming out" has clearly served its purposes, but what are its risks? And here I am not speaking of unemployment or public attack or violence, which are quite clearly and widely on the increase against those who are perceived as "out" whether or not of their own design. Is the "subject" who is "out" free of its subjection and finally in the clear? Or could it be that the subjection that subjectivates the gay or lesbian subject in some ways continues to oppress, or oppresses most insidiously, once "outness" is claimed? What or who is it that is "out," made manifest and fully disclosed, when and if I reveal myself as lesbian? What is it that is now known, anything? What remains permanently concealed by the very linguistic act that offers up the promise of a transparent revelation of sexuality? Can sexuality even remain sexuality once it submits to a criterion of transparency and disclosure, or does it perhaps cease to be sexuality precisely when the semblance of full explicitness is achieved?[6] Is sexuality of any kind even possible without that opacity designated by the unconscious, which means simply that the conscious "I" who would reveal its sexuality is perhaps the last to know the meaning of what it says?

To claim that this is what I *am* is to suggest a provisional totalization of this "I." But if the I can so determine itself, then that which it excludes in order to make that determination remains constitutive of the determination itself. In other words, such a statement presupposes that the "I" exceeds its determination, and even produces that very excess in and by the act which seeks to exhaust the semantic field of that "I." In the act which would disclose the true and full content of that "I," a certain radical *concealment* is thereby produced. For it is always finally unclear what is meant by invoking the lesbian-signifier, since its signification is always to some degree out of one's control, but also because its *specificity* can only be demarcated by exclusions that return to disrupt its claim to coherence. What, if anything, can lesbians be said to share? And who will decide this question, and in the name of whom? If I claim to be a lesbian, I "come out" only to produce a new and different "closet." The "you" to whom I come out now has access to a different region of opacity. Indeed, the locus of opacity has simply shifted: before, you did not know whether I "am," but now you do not know what that means, which is to say that the copula is empty, that it cannot be substituted for with a set of descriptions.[7] And perhaps that is a situation to be valued. Conventionally, one comes out *of* the closet (and yet, how often is it the case that we are "outted" when we are young and without resources?); so we are out of the closet, but into what? what new unbounded spatiality? the room, the den, the attic, the basement, the house, the bar, the university, some new enclosure whose door, like Kafka's door, produces the expectation of a fresh air and a light of illumination that never arrives? Curiously, it is the figure of the closet that produces this expectation, and which guarantees its dissatisfaction. For being "out" always depends to some extent on being "in"; it gains its meaning only within that polarity. Hence, being "out" must produce the closet again and again in order to maintain itself as "out." In this sense, *outness* can only produce a new opacity; and *the closet* produces the promise of a disclosure that can, by definition, never come. Is this infinite postponement of the disclosure of "gayness," produced by the very act of "coming out," to be lamented? Or is this very deferral of the signified *to be valued,* a site for the production of values, precisely because the term now takes on a life that cannot be, can never be, permanently controlled?

It is possible to argue that whereas no transparent or full revelation is afforded by "lesbian" and "gay," there remains a political imperative to use these necessary errors or category mistakes, as it were (what Gayatri Spivak might call "catachrestic" operations: to use a proper name improperly[8]), to rally and represent an oppressed political constituency. Clearly, I am not legislating against the use of the term. My question is simply: which use will be legislated, and what play will there be between legislation and use such that the instrumental uses of "identity" do not become regulatory imperatives? If

it is already true that "lesbians" and "gay men" have been traditionally designated as impossible identities, errors of classification, unnatural disasters within juridico-medical discourses, or, what perhaps amounts to the same, the very paradigm of what calls to be classified, regulated, and controlled, then perhaps these sites of disruption, error, confusion, and trouble can be the very rallying points for a certain resistance to classification and to identity as such.

The question is not one of *avowing* or *disavowing* the category of lesbian or gay, but, rather, why it is that the category becomes the site of this "ethical" choice? What does it mean to *avow* a category that can only maintain its specificity and coherence by performing a prior set of *disavowals*? Does this make "coming out" into the avowal of disavowal, that is, a return to the closet under the guise of an escape? And it is not something like heterosexuality or bisexuality that is disavowed by the category, but a set of identificatory and practical crossings between these categories that renders the discreteness of each equally suspect. Is it not possible to maintain and pursue heterosexual identifications and aims within homosexual practice, and homosexual identifications and aims within heterosexual practices? If a sexuality is to be disclosed, what will be taken as the true determinant of its meaning: the phantasy structure, the act, the orifice, the gender, the anatomy? And if the practice engages a complex interplay of all of those, which one of these erotic dimensions will come to stand for the sexuality that requires them all? Is it the *specificity* of a lesbian experience or lesbian desire or lesbian sexuality that lesbian theory needs to elucidate? Those efforts have only and always produced a set of contests and refusals which should by now make it clear that there is no necessarily common element among lesbians, except perhaps that we all know something about how homophobia works against women—although, even then, the language and the analysis we use will differ.

To argue that there might be a *specificity* to lesbian sexuality has seemed a necessary counterpoint to the claim that lesbian sexuality is just heterosexuality once removed, or that it is derived, or that it does not exist. But perhaps the claim of specificity, on the one hand, and the claim of derivativeness or non-existence, on the other, are not as contradictory as they seem. Is it not possible that lesbian sexuality is a process that reinscribes the power domains that it resists, that it is constituted in part from the very heterosexual matrix that it seeks to displace, and that its specificity is to be established, not *outside* or *beyond* that reinscription or reiteration, but in the very modality and effects of that reinscription. In other words, the negative constructions of lesbianism as a fake or a bad copy can be occupied and reworked to call into question the claims of heterosexual priority. In a sense I hope to make clear in what follows, lesbian sexuality can be understood to redeploy its 'derivativeness' in the service of displacing hegemonic heterosexual norms. Understood in this way, the political problem is not to establish the specificity of lesbian sexuality over and against its derivativeness, but to turn the homophobic construction of the bad copy against the framework that privileges heterosexuality as origin, and so 'derive' the former from the latter. This description requires a reconsideration of imitation, drag, and other forms of sexual crossing that affirm the internal complexity of a lesbian sexuality constituted in part within the very matrix of power that it is compelled both to reiterate and to oppose.

On the Being of Gayness as Necessary Drag

The professionalization of gayness requires a certain performance and production of a "self" which is the *constituted effect* of a discourse that nevertheless claims to "represent" that self as a prior truth. When I spoke at the conference on homosexuality in 1989,[9] I found myself telling my friends beforehand that I was off to Yale to be a lesbian, which of course didn't mean that I wasn't one before, but that somehow then, as I spoke in that context, I *was* one in some more thorough and totalizing way, at least for the time being. So I *am* one, and my qualifications are even fairly unambiguous. Since I was sixteen, being a lesbian is what I've been. So what's the anxiety, the discomfort? Well, it has something to do with that redoubling, the way I can say, I'm going to Yale to be a lesbian; a lesbian is what I've been being for so long. How is it that I can both "be" one, and yet endeavor to be one at the same time? When and where does my being a lesbian come into play, when and where does this playing a lesbian constitute something like what I am? To say that I "play" at being one is not to say that I am not one "really"; rather, how and where I play at being one is the way in which that "being" gets established, instituted, circulated, and confirmed. This is not a performance from which I can take radical distance, for this is deep-seated play, psychically entrenched play, *and this "I" does not play its lesbianism as a role.* Rather, it is through the repeated play of this sexuality that the "I" is insistently reconstituted as a lesbian "I"; paradoxically, it is precisely the *repetition* of that play that establishes as well the *instability* of the very category that it constitutes. For if the "I" is a site of repetition, that is, if the "I" only achieves the semblance of identity through a certain repetition of itself, then the I is always displaced by the very repetition that sustains it. In other words, does or can the "I" ever repeat itself, cite itself, faithfully, or is there always a displacement from its former moment that establishes the permanently non-self-identical status of that "I" or its "being lesbian"? What "performs" does not exhaust the "I"; it does not lay out in visible terms the comprehensive content of that "I," for if the performance is "repeated," there is always the question of what differentiates from each other the moments of identity that are repeated. And if the "I" is the effect of a certain repetition, one which produces the semblance of a continuity or coherence, then there is no "I" that precedes the gender that it is said to perform; the repetition, and the failure to repeat, produce a string of performances that constitute and contest the coherence of that "I."

But *politically*, we might argue, isn't it quite crucial to insist on lesbian and gay identities precisely because they are being threatened with erasure and obliteration from homophobic quarters? Isn't the above theory *complicitous* with those political forces that would obliterate the possibility of gay and lesbian identity? Isn't it "no accident" that such theoretical contestations of identity emerge within a political climate that is performing a set of similar obliterations of homosexual identities through legal and political means?

The question I want to raise in return is this: ought such threats of obliteration dictate the terms of the political resistance to them, and if they do, do such homophobic efforts to that extent win the battle from the start? There is no question that gays and lesbians are threatened by the violence of public erasure, but the decision to counter that violence must be careful not to reinstall another in its place. Which version of lesbian or gay ought to be rendered visible, and which internal exclusions will that rendering visible institute? Can the visibility of identity *suffice* as a political strategy, or can it only be the starting point for a strategic intervention which calls for a transformation of policy? Is it not a sign of despair over public politics when identity becomes its own policy, bringing with it those who would 'police' it from various sides? And this is not a call to return to silence or invisibility, but, rather, to make use of a category that can be called into question, made to account for what it excludes. That any consolidation of identity requires some set of differentiations and exclusions seems clear. But which ones ought to be valorized? That the identity-sign I use now has its purposes seems right, but there is no way to predict or control the political uses to which that sign will be put in the future. And perhaps this is a kind of openness, regardless of its risks, that ought to be safeguarded for political reasons. If the rendering visible of lesbian/gay identity now presupposes a set of exclusions, then perhaps part of what is necessarily excluded is *the future uses of the sign*. There is a political necessity to use some sign now, and we do, but how to use it in such a way that its futural significations are not *foreclosed*? How to

use the sign and avow its temporal contingency at once?

In avowing the sign's strategic provisionality (rather than its strategic essentialism), that identity can become a site of contest and revision, indeed, take on a future set of significations that those of us who use it now may not be able to foresee. It is in the safeguarding of the future of the political signifiers—preserving the signifier as a site of rearticulation—that Laclau and Mouffe discern its democratic promise.

Within contemporary U.S. politics, there are a vast number of ways in which lesbianism in particular is understood as precisely that which cannot or dare not *be*. In a sense, Jesse Helms's attack on the NEA for sanctioning representations of "homoeroticism" focuses various homophobic fantasies of what gay men are and do on the work of Robert Mapplethorpe.[10] In a sense, for Helms, gay men exist as objects of prohibition; they are, in his twisted fantasy, sadomasochistic exploiters of children, the paradigmatic exemplars of "obscenity"; in a sense, the lesbian is not even produced within this discourse as a prohibited object. Here it becomes important to recognize that oppression works not merely through acts of overt prohibition, but covertly, through the constitution of viable subjects and through the corollary constitution of a domain of unviable (un)subjects—*abjects*, we might call them—who are neither named nor prohibited within the economy of the law. Here oppression works through the production of a domain of unthinkability and unnameability. Lesbianism is not explicitly prohibited in part because it has not even made its way into the thinkable, the imaginable, that grid of cultural intelligibility that regulates the real and the nameable. How, then, to "be" a lesbian in a political context in which the lesbian does not exist? That is, in a political discourse that wages its violence against lesbianism in part by excluding lesbianism from discourse itself? To be prohibited explicitly is to occupy a discursive site from which something like a reverse-discourse can be articulated; to be implicitly proscribed is not even to qualify as an object of prohibition.[11] And though homosexualities of all kinds in this present climate are being erased, reduced, and (then) reconstituted as sites of radical homophobic fantasy, it is important to retrace the different routes by which the unthinkability of homosexuality is being constituted time and again.

It is one thing to be erased from discourse, and yet another to be present within discourse as an abiding falsehood. Hence, there is a political imperative to render lesbianism visible, but how is that to be done outside or through existing regulatory regimes? Can the exclusion from ontology itself become a rallying point for resistance?

*   *   *

Here is something like a confession which is meant merely to thematize the impossibility of confession: As a young person, I suffered for a long time, and I suspect many people have, from being told, explicitly or implicitly, that what I "am" is a copy, an imitation, a derivative example, a shadow of the real. Compulsory heterosexuality sets itself up as the original, the true, the authentic; the norm that determines the real implies that "being" lesbian is always a kind of miming, a vain effort to participate in the phantasmatic plenitude of naturalized heterosexuality which will always and only fail.[12] And yet, I remember quite distinctly when I first read in Esther Newton's *Mother Camp: Female Impersonators in America*[13] that drag is not an imitation or a copy of some prior and true gender; according to Newton, drag enacts the very structure of impersonation by which *any gender* is assumed. Drag is not the putting on of a gender that belongs properly to some other group, i.e., an act of *ex*propriation or *ap*propriation that assumes that gender is the rightful property of sex, that "masculine" belongs to "male" and "feminine" belongs to "female." There is no "proper" gender, a gender proper to one sex rather than another, which is in some sense that sex's cultural property. Where that notion of the "proper" operates, it is always and only *improperly* installed as the effect of a compulsory system. Drag constitutes

the mundane way in which genders are appropriated, theatricalized, worn, and done; it implies that all gendering is a kind of impersonation and approximation. If this is true, it seems, there is no original or primary gender that drag imitates, but *gender is a kind of imitation for which there is no original;* in fact, it is a kind of imitation that produces the very notion of the original as an *effect* and consequence of the imitation itself. In other words, the naturalistic effects of heterosexualized genders are produced through imitative strategies; what they imitate is a phantasmatic ideal of heterosexual identity, one that is produced by the imitation as its effect. In this sense, the "reality" of heterosexual identities is performatively constituted through an imitation that sets itself up as the origin and the ground of all imitations. In other words, heterosexuality is always in the process of imitating and approximating its own phantasmatic idealization of itself—*and failing.* Precisely because it is bound to fail, and yet endeavors to succeed, the project of heterosexual identity is propelled into an endless repetition of itself. Indeed, in its efforts to naturalize itself as the original, heterosexuality must be understood as a compulsive and compulsory repetition that can only produce the *effect* of its own originality; in other words, compulsory heterosexual identities, those ontologically consolidated phantasms of "man" and "woman," are theatrically produced effects that posture as grounds, origins, the normative measure of the real.[14]

*   *   *

Reconsider then the homophobic charge that queens and butches and femmes are imitations of the heterosexual real. Here "imitation" carries the meaning of "derivative" or "secondary," a copy of an origin which is itself the ground of all copies, but which is itself a copy of nothing. Logically, this notion of an "origin" is suspect, for how can something operate as an origin if there are no secondary consequences which retrospectively confirm the originality of that origin? The origin requires its derivations in order to affirm itself as an origin, for origins only make sense to the extent that they are differentiated from that which they produce as derivatives. Hence, if it were not for the notion of the homosexual *as* copy, there would be no construct of heterosexuality *as* origin. Heterosexuality here presupposes homosexuality. And if the homosexual *as* copy *precedes* the heterosexual as *origin,* then it seems only fair to concede that the copy comes before the origin, and that homosexuality is thus the origin, and heterosexuality the copy.

But simple inversions are not really possible. For it is only *as* a copy that homosexuality can be argued to *precede* heterosexuality as the origin. In other words, the entire framework of copy and origin proves radically unstable as each position inverts into the other and confounds the possibility of any stable way to locate the temporal or logical priority of either term.

But let us then consider this problematic inversion from a psychic/political perspective. If the structure of gender imitation is such that the imitat*ed* is to some degree produced—or, rather, *r*eproduced—by imitation (see again Derrida's inversion and displacement of mimesis in "The Double Session"), then to claim that gay and lesbian identities are implicated in heterosexual norms or in hegemonic culture generally is not to *derive* gayness from straightness. On the contrary, *imitation* does not copy that which is prior, but produces and *inverts* the very terms of priority and derivativeness. Hence, if gay identities are implicated in heterosexuality, that is not the same as claiming that they are determined or derived from heterosexuality, and it is not the same as claiming that that heterosexuality is the only cultural network in which they are implicated. These are, quite literally, *inverted* imitations, ones which invert the order of imitated and imitation, and which, in the process, expose the fundamental dependency of "the origin" on that which it claims to produce as its secondary effect.

What follows if we concede from the start that gay identities as derivative inversions are in part defined in terms of the very heterosexual identities from which they are differentiated? If heterosexuality is an impossible imitation of itself, an imitation that performatively constitutes itself as the original, then the imitative parody of "heterosexuality"—when and where it exists in gay cultures—is always and only an imitation of an imitation, a copy of a copy, for which there is no original. Put in yet a different way, the parodic or imitative effect of gay identities works neither to copy nor to emulate heterosexuality, but rather, to expose heterosexuality as an incessant and *panicked* imitation of its own naturalized idealization. That heterosexuality is always in the act of elaborating itself is evidence that it is perpetually at risk, that is, that it "knows" its own possibility of becoming undone: hence, its compulsion to repeat which is at once a foreclosure of that which threatens its coherence. That it can never eradicate that risk attests to its profound dependency upon the homosexuality that it seeks fully to eradicate and never can or that it seeks to make second, but which is always already there as a prior possibility.[15] Although this failure of naturalized heterosexuality might constitute a source of pathos for heterosexuality itself—what its theorists often refer to as its constitutive malaise—it can become an occasion for a subversive and proliferating parody of gender norms in which the very claim to originality and to the real is shown to be the effect of a certain kind of naturalized gender mime.

It is important to recognize the ways in which heterosexual norms reappear within gay identities, to affirm that gay and lesbian identities are not only structured in part by dominant heterosexual frames, but that they are *not* for that reason *determined* by them. They are running commentaries on those naturalized positions as well, parodic replays and resignifications of precisely those heterosexual structures that would consign gay life to discursive domains of unreality and unthinkability. But to be constituted or structured in part by the very heterosexual norms by which gay people are oppressed is not, I repeat, to be claimed or determined by those structures. And it is not necessary to think of such heterosexual constructs as the pernicious intrusion of "the straight mind," one that must be rooted out in its entirety. In a way, the presence of heterosexual constructs and positionalities in whatever form in gay and lesbian identities presupposes that there is a gay and lesbian repetition of straightness, a recapitulation of straightness—which is itself a repetition and recapitulation of its own ideality—within its own terms, a site in which all sorts of resignifying and parodic repetitions become possible. The parodic replication and resignification of heterosexual constructs within non-heterosexual frames brings into relief the utterly constructed status of the so-called original, but it shows that heterosexuality only constitutes itself as the original through a convincing act of repetition. The more that "act" is expropriated, the more the heterosexual claim to originality is exposed as illusory.

Although I have concentrated in the above on the reality-effects of gender practices, performances, repetitions, and mimes, I do not mean to suggest that drag is a "role" that can be taken on or taken off at will. There is no volitional subject behind the mime who decides, as it were, which gender it will be today. On the contrary, the very possibility of becoming a viable subject requires that a certain gender mime be already underway. The "being" of the subject is no more self-identical than the "being" of any gender; in fact, coherent gender, achieved through an apparent repetition of the same, produces as its *effect* the illusion of a prior and volitional subject. In this sense, gender is not a performance that a prior subject elects to do, but gender is *performative* in the sense that it constitutes as an effect the very subject it appears to express. It is a *compulsory* performance in the sense that acting out of line with heterosexual norms brings with it ostracism, punishment, and violence, not to mention the transgressive pleasures produced by those very prohibitions.

To claim that there is no performer prior to the performed, that the performance is performative, that the performance constitutes the appearance of a "subject" as its effect is difficult to accept. This difficulty is the result of a predisposition to think of sexuality and gender as "expressing" in some indirect or direct way a psychic reality that precedes it. The denial of the *priority* of the subject, however, is not the denial of the subject; in fact, the refusal to conflate the subject with the psyche marks the psychic as that which exceeds the domain of the conscious subject. This psychic excess is precisely what is being systematically denied by the notion of a volitional "subject" who elects at will which gender and/or sexuality to be at any given time and place. It is this excess which erupts within the intervals of those repeated gestures and acts that construct the apparent uniformity of heterosexual positionalities, indeed which compels the repetition itself, and which guarantees its perpetual failure. In this sense, it is this excess which, within the heterosexual economy, implicitly includes homosexuality, that perpetual threat of a disruption which is quelled through a reinforced repetition of the same. And yet, if repetition is the way in which power works to construct the illusion of a seamless heterosexual identity, if heterosexuality is compelled to *repeat itself* in order to establish the illusion of its own uniformity and identity, then this is an identity permanently at risk, for what if it fails to repeat, or if the very exercise of repetition is redeployed for a very different performative purpose? If there is, as it were, always a compulsion to repeat, repetition never fully accomplishes identity. That there is a need for a repetition at all is a sign that identity is not self-identical. It requires to be instituted again and again, which is to say that it runs the risk of becoming *de*-instituted at every interval.

So what is this psychic excess, and what will constitute a subversive or *de*-instituting repetition? First, it is necessary to consider that sexuality always exceeds any given performance, presentation, or narrative which is why it is not possible to derive or read off a sexuality from any given gender presentation. And sexuality may be said to exceed any definitive narrativization. Sexuality is never fully "expressed" in a performance or practice; there will be passive and butchy femmes, femmy and aggressive butches, and both of those, and more, will turn out to describe more or less anatomically stable "males" and "females." There are no direct expressive or causal lines between sex, gender, gender presentation, sexual practice, fantasy and sexuality. None of those terms captures or determines the rest. Part of what constitutes sexuality is precisely that which does not appear and that which, to some degree, can never appear. This is perhaps the most fundamental reason why sexuality is to some degree always closeted, especially to the one who would express it through acts of self-disclosure. That which is excluded for a given gender presentation to "succeed" may be precisely what is played out sexually, that is, an "inverted" relation, as it were, between gender and gender presentation, and gender presentation and sexuality. On the other hand, both gender presentation and sexual practices may corollate such that it appears that the former "expresses" the latter, and yet both are jointly constituted by the very sexual possibilities that they exclude.

This logic of inversion gets played out interestingly in versions of lesbian butch and femme gender stylization. For a butch can present herself as capable, forceful, and all-providing, and a stone butch may well seek to constitute her lover as the exclusive site of erotic attention and pleasure. And yet, this "providing" butch who seems *at first* to replicate a certain husband-like role, can find herself caught in a logic of inversion whereby that "providingness" turns to a self-sacrifice, which implicates her in the most ancient trap of feminine self-abnegation. She may well find herself in a situation of radical need, which is precisely what she sought to locate, find, and fulfill in her femme lover. In effect, the butch inverts into the femme or remains caught up in the specter of that inversion, or takes pleasure in it. On the other hand, the femme who, as Amber Hollibaugh has argued, "orchestrates" sexual exchange,[16] may well eroticize a certain dependency only to learn that the very power to orchestrate that dependency exposes her own incontrovertible power, at which point she inverts into a butch or becomes caught up in the specter of that inversion, or perhaps delights in it.

Psychic Mimesis

What stylizes or forms an erotic style and/or a gender presentation—and that which makes such categories inherently unstable—is a set of *psychic identifications* that are not simple to describe. Some psychoanalytic theories tend to construe identification and desire as two mutually exclusive relations to love objects that have been lost through prohibition and/or separation. Any intense emotional attachment thus divides into either wanting to have someone or wanting to be that someone, but never both at once. It is important to consider that identification and desire can coexist, and that their formulation in terms of mutually exclusive oppositions serves a heterosexual matrix. But I would like to focus attention on yet a different construal of that scenario, namely, that "wanting to be" and "wanting to have" can operate to differentiate mutually exclusive positionalities internal to lesbian erotic exchange. Consider that identifications are always made in response to loss of some kind, and that they involve a certain *mimetic practice* that seeks to incorporate the lost love within the very "identity" of the one who remains. This was Freud's thesis in "Mourning and Melancholia" in 1917 and continues to inform contemporary psychoanalytic discussions of identification.[17]

For psychoanalytic theorists Mikkel Borch-Jacobsen and Ruth Leys, however, identification and, in particular, identificatory mimetism, *precedes* "identity" and constitutes identity as that which is fundamentally "other to itself." The notion of this Other *in* the self, as it were, implies that the self/Other distinction is *not* primarily external (a powerful critique of ego psychology follows from this); the self is from the start radically implicated in the "Other." This theory of primary mimetism differs from Freud's account of melancholic incorporation. In Freud's view, which I continue to find useful, incorporation—a kind of psychic miming—is a response to, and refusal of, *loss*. Gender as the site of such psychic mimes is thus constituted by the variously gendered Others who have been loved and lost, where the loss is suspended through a melancholic and imaginary incorpo- ration (and preservation) of those Others into the psyche. Over and against this account of psychic mimesis by way of incorporation and melancholy, the theory of primary mimetism argues an even stronger position in favor of the non-self-identity of the psychic subject. Mime- tism is not motivated by a drama of loss and wishful recovery, but appears to precede and constitute desire (and motivation) itself; in this sense, mimetism would be prior to the possibil- ity of loss and the disappointments of love.

Whether loss or mimetism is primary (per- haps an undecidable problem), the psychic sub- ject is nevertheless constituted internally by dif- ferentially gendered Others and is, therefore, never, as a gender, self-identical.

In my view, the self only becomes a self on the condition that it has suffered a separation (grammar fails us here, for the "it" only be- comes differentiated through that separation), a loss which is suspended and provisionally resolved through a melancholic incorporation of some "Other." That "Other" installed in the self thus establishes the permanent incapac- ity of that "self" to achieve self-identity; it is as it were always already disrupted by that Other; the disruption of the Other at the heart of the self is the very condition of that self's possibility.[18]

Such a consideration of psychic identifica- tion would vitiate the possibility of any stable set of typologies that explain or describe some- thing like gay or lesbian identities. And any effort to supply one—as evidenced in Kaja Silverman's recent inquiries into male homo- sexuality—suffer from simplification, and con- form, with alarming ease, to the regulatory re- quirements of diagnostic epistemic regimes. If incorporation in Freud's sense in 1914 is an ef- fort to *preserve* a lost and loved object and to refuse or postpone the recognition of loss and, hence, of grief, then to become *like* one's mother or father or sibling or other early "lovers" may be an act of love and/or a hateful effort to re- place or displace. How would we "typologize" the ambivalence at the heart of mimetic incor- porations such as these?[19]

How does this consideration of psychic iden- tification return us to the question, what con- stitutes a subversive repetition? How are trou- blesome identifications apparent in cultural practices? Well, consider the way in which het- erosexuality naturalizes itself through setting up certain illusions of continuity between sex, gender, and desire. When Aretha Franklin sings, "you make me feel like a natural woman," she seems at first to suggest that some natural po- tential of her biological sex is actualized by her participation in the cultural position of "wo- man" as object of heterosexual recognition. Something in her "sex" is thus expressed by her "gender" which is then fully known and conse- crated within the heterosexual scene. There is no breakage, no discontinuity between "sex" as biological facticity and essence, or between gen- der and sexuality. Although Aretha appears to be all too glad to have her naturalness con- firmed, she also seems fully and paradoxically mindful that that confirmation is never guar- anteed, that the effect of naturalness is only achieved as a consequence of that moment of heterosexual recognition. After all, Aretha sings, you make me feel *like* a natural woman, sug- gesting that this is a kind of metaphorical sub- stitution, an act of imposture, a kind of sublime and momentary participation in an ontological illusion produced by the mundane operation of heterosexual drag.

But what if Aretha were singing to me? Or what if she were singing to a drag queen whose performance somehow confirmed her own?

How do we take account of these kinds of identifications? It's not that there is some kind of *sex* that exists in hazy biological form that is somehow *expressed* in the gait, the posture, the gesture; and that some sexuality then expresses both that apparent gender or that more or less magical sex. If gender is drag, and if it is an im- itation that regularly produces the ideal it at- tempts to approximate, then gender is a perfor- mance that *produces* the illusion of an inner sex or essence or psychic gender core; it *produces* on the skin, through the gesture, the move, the gait (that array of corporeal theatrics understood as gender presentation), the illusion of an inner

depth. In effect, one way that gender gets naturalized is through being constructed as an inner
psychic or physical *necessity*. And yet, it is always a surface sign, a signification on and with
the public body that produces this illusion of an
inner depth, necessity or essence that is somehow magically, causally expressed.

To dispute the psyche as *inner depth,* however, is not to refuse the psyche altogether. On
the contrary, the psyche calls to be rethought
precisely as a compulsive repetition, as that
which conditions and disables the repetitive
performance of identity. If every performance
repeats itself to institute the effect of identity,
then every repetition requires an interval between the acts, as it were, in which risk and excess threaten to disrupt the identity being constituted. The unconscious is this excess that
enables and contests every performance, and
which never fully appears within the performance itself. The psyche is not "in" the body,
but in the very signifying process through
which that body comes to appear; it is the lapse
in repetition as well as its compulsion, precisely
what the performance seeks to deny, and that
which compels it from the start.

To locate the psyche within this signifying
chain as the instability of all iterability is not the
same as claiming that it is inner core that is
awaiting its full and liberatory expression. On
the contrary, the psyche is the permanent failure of expression, a failure that has its values,
for it impels repetition and so reinstates the
possibility of disruption. What then does it
mean to pursue disruptive repetition within
compulsory heterosexuality?

Although compulsory heterosexuality often
presumes that there is first a sex that is expressed through a gender and then through a
sexuality, it may now be necessary fully to invert
and displace that operation of thought. If a
regime of sexuality mandates a compulsory
performance of sex, then it may be only
through that performance that the binary system of gender and the binary system of sex
come to have intelligibility at all. It may be that
the very categories of sex, of sexual identity, of
gender are produced or maintained in the *ef-*

fects of this compulsory performance, effects
which are disingenuously renamed as causes,
origins, disingenuously lined up within a causal
or expressive sequence that the heterosexual
norm produces to legitimate itself as the origin
of all sex. How then to expose the causal lines as
retrospectively and performatively produced
fabrications, and to engage gender itself as an
inevitable fabrication, to fabricate gender in
terms which reveal every claim to the origin, the
inner, the true, and the real as nothing other
than the effects of *drag,* whose subversive possibilities ought to be played and replayed to make
the "sex" of gender into a site of insistent political play? Perhaps this will be a matter of working sexuality *against* identity, even against gender, and of letting that which cannot fully
appear in any performance persist in its disruptive promise.

Notes

1. Parts of this essay were given as a presentation
at the Conference on Homosexuality at Yale University in October, 1989.

2. "The Mark of Gender," *Feminist Issues* 5 no. 2
(1985): 6.

3. *Différence et répétition* (Paris: PUF, 1968), 374;
my translation.

4. *Gender Trouble: Feminism and the Subversion of
Identity* (New York and London: Routledge, 1990).

5. Michel Foucault, *The History of Sexuality, Vol.
I,* trans. John Hurley (New York: Random House,
1980), 101.

6. Here I would doubtless differ from the very
fine analysis of Hitchcock's *Rope* offered by D. A.
Miller in this volume.

7. For an example of "coming out" that is strictly
unconfessional and which, finally, offers no content
for the category of lesbian, see Barbara Johnson's
deftly constructed "Sula Passing: No Passing" presentation at UCLA, May 1990.

8. Gayatri Chakravorty Spivak, "Displacement
and the Discourse of Woman." In *Displacement: Derrida and After,* ed. Mark Krupnick (Bloomington: Indiana University Press, 1983).

9. Let me take this occasion to apologize to the
social worker at that conference who asked a question about how to deal with those clients with AIDS
who turned to Bernie Segal and others for the pur-

poses of psychic healing. At the time, I understood this questioner to be suggesting that such clients were full of self-hatred because they were trying to find the causes of AIDS in their own selves. The questioner and I appear to agree that any effort to locate the responsibility for AIDS in those who suffer from it is politically and ethically wrong. I thought the questioner, however, was prepared to tell his clients that they were self-hating, and I reacted strongly (too strongly) to the paternalistic prospect that this person was going to pass judgment on someone who was clearly not only suffering, but already passing judgment on him or herself. To call another person self-hating is itself an act of power that calls for some kind of scrutiny, and I think in response to someone who is already dealing with AIDS, that is perhaps the last thing one needs to hear. I also happened to have a friend who sought out advice from Bernie Segal, not with the belief that there is an exclusive or even primary psychic cause or solution for AIDS, but that there might be a psychic contribution to be made to surviving with AIDS. Unfortunately, I reacted quickly to this questioner, and with some anger. And I regret now that I didn't have my wits about me to discuss the distinctions with him that I have just laid out.

Curiously, this incident was invoked at a CLAGS (Center for Lesbian and Gay Studies) meeting at CUNY sometime in December of 1989 and, according to those who told me about it, my angry denunciation of the social worker was taken to be symptomatic of the political insensitivity of a "theorist" in dealing with someone who is actively engaged in AIDS work. That attribution implies that I do not do AIDS work, that I am not politically engaged, and that the social worker in question does not read theory. Needless to say, I was reacting angrily on behalf of an absent friend with AIDS who sought out Bernie Segal and company. So as I offer this apology to the social worker, I wait expectantly that the CLAGS member who misunderstood me will offer me one in turn.

10. See my "The Force of Fantasy: Feminism, Mapplethorpe, and Discursive Excess," *differences* 2, no. 2 (Summer 1990). Since the writing of this essay, lesbian artists and representations have also come under attack.

11. It is this particular ruse of erasure which Foucault for the most part fails to take account of in his analysis of power. He almost always presumes that power takes place through discourse as its instrument, and that oppression is linked with subjection

and subjectivation, that is, that it is installed as the formative principle of the identity of subjects.

12. Although miming suggests that there is a prior model which is being copied, it can have the effect of exposing that prior model as purely phantasmatic. In Jacques Derrida's "The Double Session" in *Dissemination,* trans. Barbara Johnson (Chicago: University of Chicago Press, 1981), he considers the textual effect of the mime in Mallarmé's "Mimique." There Derrida argues that the mime does not imitate or copy some prior phenomenon, idea, or figure, but constitutes—some might say *performatively*—the phantasm of the original in and through the mime:

He represents nothing, imitates nothing, does not have to conform to any prior referent with the aim of achieving adequation or verisimilitude. One can here foresee an objection: since the mime imitates nothing, reproduces nothing, opens up in its origin the very thing he is tracing out, presenting, or producing, he must be the very movement of truth. Not, of course, truth in the form of adequation between the representation and the present of the thing itself, or between the imitator and the imitated, but truth as the present unveiling of the present.... But this is not the case.... We are faced then with mimicry imitating nothing: faced, so to speak, with a double that couples no simple, a double that nothing anticipates, nothing at least that is not itself already double. There is no simple reference.... This speculum reflects no reality: it produces mere "reality-effects."... In this speculum with no reality, in this mirror of a mirror, a difference or dyad does exist, since there are mimes and phantoms. But it is a difference without reference, or rather reference without a referent, without any first or last unit, a ghost that is the phantom of no flesh ... (206)

13. Esther Newton, *Mother Camp: Female Impersonators in America* (Chicago: University of Chicago Press, 1972).

14. In a sense, one might offer a redescription of the above in Lacanian terms. The sexual "positions" of heterosexually differentiated "man" and "woman" are part of the *Symbolic,* that is, an ideal embodiment of the Law of sexual difference which constitutes the object of imaginary pursuits, but which is always thwarted by the "real." These symbolic

positions for Lacan are by definition impossible to occupy even as they are impossible to resist as the structuring telos of desire. I accept the former point, and reject the latter one. The imputation of universal necessity to such positions simply encodes compulsory heterosexuality at the level of the Symbolic, and the "failure" to achieve it is implicitly lamented as a source of heterosexual pathos.

15. Of course, it is Eve Kosofsky Sedgwick's *Epistemology of the Closet* (Berkeley: University of California Press, 1990) which traces the subtleties of this kind of panic in Western heterosexual epistemes.

16. Amber Hollibaugh and Cherríe Moraga, "What We're Rollin Around in Bed With: Sexual Silences in Feminism," in *Powers of Desire: The Politics of Sexuality,* ed. Ann Snitow, Christine Stansell, and Sharon Thompson (New York: Monthly Review Press, 1983), 394–405.

17. Mikkel Borch-Jacobsen, *The Freudian Subject* (Stanford: Stanford University Press, 1988); for citations of Ruth Leys's work, see the following two endnotes.

18. For a very fine analysis of primary mimetism with direct implications for gender formation, see Ruth Leys, "The Real Miss Beauchamp: The History and Sexual Politics of the Multiple Personality Concept," in *Feminists Theorize the Political,* eds. Judith Butler and Joan W. Scott (New York and London: Routledge, forthcoming 1991). For Leys, a primary mimetism or suggestibility requires that the "self" from the start is constituted by its incorporations; the effort to differentiate oneself from that by which one is constituted is, of course, impossible, but it does entail a certain "incorporative violence," to use her term. The violence of identification is in this way in the service of an effort at differentiation, to take the place of the Other who is, as it were, installed at the foundation of the self. That this replacement, which seeks to be a displacement, fails, and must repeat itself endlessly, becomes the trajectory of one's psychic career.

19. Here again, I think it is the work of Ruth Leys which will clarify some of the complex questions of gender constitution that emerge from a close psychoanalytic consideration of imitation and identification. Her forthcoming book manuscript will doubtless galvanize this field: *The Subject of Imitation.*

Body Talk: Lesbian Speculations on "Extra" Textual Letters

Elizabeth A. Meese

No one has imagined us.

> —Adrienne Rich, "Twenty-One Love Poems," in
> *The Dream of a Common Language*

Some say alright all but one way of loving, another says alright all but another way of loving . . . I like loving, I like all the ways any one can have of having loving feeling in them. Slowly it has come to be in me that any way of being a loving one is interesting and not unpleasant to me.

> —Gertrude Stein, *The Making of Americans*

We cannot hide from ourselves the fictional character of the first A.

> —Nicole Brossard, *These Our Mothers*

Dear L,

My title *(Sem)Erotics* opens a space for writing (about) lesbian : letters and lesbian : love. In all honesty, I am writing the book to get to this chapter, or perhaps even beyond it. But this is the chapter that is misunderstood, its relation to the literary, the political, mis-taken, while summation and extension, effects of its placement, are insisted upon.

I refuse to recognize both the lastness and the irrelevance of these "extra" letters. I write my chapter in relation to (because of, in the shadow of the letters—words and texts—that have come before). I am writing with. Surrounded.

I know that there is more to come. There is more (to say about) lesbian : writing, just as we have not yet enumerated the variations on lesbian : eroticism. The uninvented, the unimag-ined remain. The historically uninvited must be invited to speak.

Fore)

(This is about speculation, how I imagine what will interest my lover, turn her on; and then . . . seduction, a seduction in/to the letter.)

The effort of the *fore-* wants to precede the letter, to imagine a feeling be-fore sex, to anticipate what I will say and the positions we will take, what I will do to her, what I want her to do to me. An elaborate(d) invention, a complex fiction. Fore!—-told. Look out ahead.

The *fore-* is the scene of intention, where I reach toward what I don't really have yet, before I imagine or accept the fiction of "A"—the initial form that makes discourse possible, that founds the conceit, so I can write letters to you, my lover. I invent the scene of possibilities, a speculative fiction.

What if the language handed down for generations does not contain you, or what it does say about you, what it sums up in that one word, is rarely spoken or written, and when it is, the inflection is all wrong, suggesting little more than spitefulness and cruelty? Language deceives and language discloses; words speak and words silence. They pose the challenge of what might follow the letter L, how to invent a lesbian and what she means to her lover. How to know one when you see one; how to read and write her story.

The creation of categories requires the production of discourses about them. Hence, the importance of "LESBIAN," "LESBIAN : WRITING," "LESBIAN : READER," "LESBIAN : LOVER." The elaboration of meaning: does it precede or follow the letter? Because "we" are always approaching "us," I speculate in an absence of definition. I make words, writing and more writing, to fill the lack and the imprecision (the unlikeliness of sense) with specification, to create variations on the possible through the shuttle of incalculable losses and gains as we translate each other, me to you, you to me. No one ever told me what my lesbian destiny could be, so I invent us. The terror I find in this results from language's utter dependence on and independence from the world. Flying (almost) blind.

How, beginning in absence, erasure or negation, do we raise this alienated writing to an art? Iterability counts: once, twice, three times. Saying it, over and over, in our own ways helps make it so: L, L, L, L. Dear L, we need to play it again and again and again, patiently recording the variations in our tunes. I want to count my ancestors, to include their texts in mine. I start here by reading one word after another, writing one letter after the next, constructing a long and varied correspondence, (ex)posing myself and you. I am going to speak in tongues, with my tongue, trying to make room for other tongues, different registers, which, when voiced serially, through har-

monics and dissonance, make all sense and non(e). One thing I can say about this book: it will always be (my) LESBIAN : WRITING.

Sex)

Dear L,

When I fucked you at the Big Sur Inn I turned electric—green like the ocean glass ring you wear, the neon blues and pinks of unnatural materials, the metallic tints of space age metals that have never seen the ground. Nothing handmade has ever been this beautiful. It must have been the ever-polite silence of close quarters that transliterated the sounds of pleasure into other forms—geometric, extraterrestrial, spatial landscapes of lesbian : love. This despite (or because of) Big Sur's elemental excesses—rocky shore, sea, limitless sky—observed year after year, but never appearing "natural."

So we went on (coming) on and on and on.

Surely we will keep returning.

Love,
L

This scene invites speculation. A lot can be said and done about it. Painters, they say, go to France for the light, its peculiar brilliance or clarity on the Mediterranean. But what is light to the writer, who, as often as not, composes a letter to her lover after dark, sometime past the day's end, in review, as a labor of memory or longing to have her again. (My lover calls it a "labor for love.") The rhythms of repetition, sex games, excitement: how pleasure makes more pleasure. Happiness writes itself in that.

(Games

she loves me she loves me not she loves me she loves me not she loves me she loves me not she loves me she loves me not she loves loves loves loves loves me

petal after petal after petal

Dropping each petal in the love game, she invents her lesbian : lover. They sit next to each other, counting on the minutes ahead. They tell each other the stories of their lives. They smile and touch, they kiss and tell some more. They shine.

Nicole Brossard says, "A lesbian who does not reinvent the word is a lesbian in the process of disappearing" (*Aerial* 122). Imagine (that is, in one sense, to conjecture, a variant of speculation) or Invent (to come upon). And let's get it right: We are here to stay.

Gotta Get . . . Physi)

I am your lesbian : lover—and who/what is the lesbian behind "lesbian"? The one inscribed in lesbian : writing? There are no hermeneutic victories here, no texts put to rest, their authors discovered and interpreted once and for all. As a lesbian : reader, I am, as you are, the scene of lesbian : writing. I make sense of it, knowing there is more to come. I am one of those I write about, the subject of my own sentence. I live on the page, becoming what my writing tries to materialize, to literalize, to make present at least in the moments of writing and reading. They make me so.

Some days I have little interest in the abstract "Lesbian." I want mine with skin—chocolate or creamy, soft, her eyes brown or green flecked, arms strong. My girl has cunt, clit, lips, tongue—wet and warm. She shares.

I make her skin shine.

(-Cal

Like an astronomer studying the spectra of other galaxies, I try to read your colors, the red of divergence, the blue of convergence, going and coming. I want to know where and how we stand, or lie. I work close up. No telescope.

I see the book of my lesbian: lover's body. As already scripted, that is, understood and felt in someone's words, it writes to me—doing love—one letter to another. It is written in a language I think I can read, and write. We study each other together, perfecting our letters. When I connect them into a lover's alphabet, what meanings can I read there? And my lover—how does she read my hand : writing?

Doing love is a form of speculation—on the body, on the moment, on what is to come. It is an inscription on the lover's body in the name of desire, like characters written on a page, or a love letter I will send or not send.

Ex-)

Ex = X (lover): Ex(it) lover
    Ex-change
    Ex/pressions—pressure to articulate, insisting in the brain, bone or tongue. The ribs of the chest: compression. Ex/tension: circulating the clit.
    Ex-emplar: (L)
    Ex-cavation
    Ex-hilaration
    Ex-cre(a)tion
    Ex-pansion
    Ex-orbitant Ex-stasies of L

The lesbian : body inscribes plot and counterplot; it is text and con/text. In the economy of substitution, transliteration, translation, where women circulate, (some)things are always lost as well as gained. I re-write my interest in equivalence: reduction and expansion. Plot and counterplot. The extra we did not control, the extra that slipped away, the bit that is missing or did not come (lack), and the uninvited guest who did, who takes us by surprise (gift). Higher mathematics.

These are issues of economy, when what was once there is no longer, when what was not there, comes, when that comes but only at this price. Like it or not, this is a form of speculation—the risky bet on a fast and substantial return. A bet on chance. Conjecture shapes capitalism. Like it or not, a lesbian's desire for a house of her own, a red Miata, a leather jacket, issues from the same source. And to write about lesbian : love is a matter of speculation—an investment, betting on a return. When you "invest" affection in your lover, what is it you are hoping for? Some interest or a small dividend. A kiss, a glance, a love letter in return?

Here I am not talking about a "value system" where we make ethical choices about our lives, as though there could be a regulatory system of absolute good (lesbian or other, if this isn't in itself a contradiction) that suggests to us that some things are "good," "better," "best." I am interested in constructing value rather than values, certain engagements, there rather than here. Perhaps the idea of an ethical practice is of interest in writing—an economy of abundance, production of value (shading, hue, tonality, nuance), "more value," regard. As Irigaray says, "We are luminous. Neither one nor two. I've never known how to count. Up to you. In their calculations, we make two. Really, two? Doesn't that make you laugh? An odd sort of two. And yet not one. Especially not one. Let's leave one to them" (*This Sex* 207). The fiction of the number "one" rivals the trace covered over in the letter "A."

A new numeracy, an/other literacy. I'm moving out of here, away from this page, in search of my subject—writing : lesbian energetics. How energy is transformed into tales of lesbian passion. Ex-stasy, the libidinal record of the letter presents itself in the resonances of the words we speak to one another. Language sparks. We can feel it in Derrida's description of how it works: "Language is neither prohibition nor transgression, it compels the two endlessly" (*Grammatology* 267). Prolongations, intensifications, in the f(r)ictional economies of sound and sens(ation).

Like lesbian : writing, I move faster and faster, expanding over time. I fill the bedroom, the hall. I press against the windows. I pull the arcing light of your star toward me, into me. My gravity is inescapable.

I begin to spin, faster and faster, pulling in my luminous spiraling arms toward the radiant center, like a skater rotating on ice, catching you up in the glittery galactic swirl. I spin and spin and spin, throwing off dust made reflective by your light—pinks, greens, yellows, reds, purples—a Milky Way, a southern aurora, across

the dark vaulted sky of the bedroom. Words were never so beautiful.

XXOXX

(Citement

I think that the only "dark continent" is the one that lies beneath the surface of language (the skin that covers it over, masks and smooths "it" out). Language is like a skin, both on the side of the body and out-side of the body, between the body and the world, but also of the body, in the world.

Writing offers rough drafts for loving. It provides blueprints, the steps marked off, itineraries for the thrill of transgression. The perpetual separation of me from you is the *always already* of spacing, the interval pacing our harmonics, the gap that is jumped in the combustion of lesbian : energetics. Sending and receiving depend on the space between. Spacing, as we know, makes-sensemakingpossible. The way we traverse this interval in the chain of separation/substitution marks the human and produces its literatures. It is the originary accident, as well, that separates and conjoins me—the reader—you—the writer; the differences that allow this and every other writing to be read, to be able to (ac)count for (like re-counting or deciding what counts) what happens from the interval constituting the beginning—the letter A or in this (ac)count the letter L—to that other momentous fiction, the ending: how a "then" follows the "if." Somehow we are supposed to find our sentence here, conferred through the "lastness" of this chapter.

Dreaming: A Revision

I had a dream in which I was allowed to try to rewrite my failures with previous lesbian : lovers. The first attempt failed again. I saw my lover, now twenty-five years later, wearing the same brown coat I remember her in. We were at a big street party. I asked her to dance, but she said, "No, thanks. See you again some time." (As though this weren't a capricious dream, and we lived on the same block.) Then the second lover, who was never really my lover except in what compels and preoccupies thought and motivates the letter (we corresponded every day for more than a year, as if every letter were a kiss) appeared to me. She was wearing her old colors, maroon and black, and was still beautiful. She told me to forget my first lover (who had been my second lover in real life). For the first time, in this dream, we kissed each other. I pushed her down on the bed in her room. I was tentative but not too tentative (the cause of our failure years ago). This time she said I could kiss her, before I even mentioned it, asked for it in a way that had never been possible thirty years ago in Ann Arbor.

The release that followed the kiss, the revising of our "affair," woke me up. Now there are other chapters I can begin to rewrite. This must be what is referred to as "setting one's affairs in order."

Wanna)

I say that I want you.

(But I know the less *said* about desire the better, since we always get it wrong. That age-old problem of satisfaction; that is, getting it. So, I say, go for it, right or wrong. Something is better than nothing, isn't it? Economy again.)

We fuck. You are a charged body. I am your electromagnetic field. We spin in our orbit of space-time.

LOVING IT, DOING IT, FLAUNTING IT.

We blaze.

(Do it

Next, the Big Bang, opaque matter, a concentrated glow, then like galaxies in a primordial universe, the energy diffuses, the temperature drops. How many thousands of years will it take for us to materialize? Energy-matter-energy-matter, and vice versa.

Energetics. We shift from level to level. We gleam in the red glow of quanta, exciting one

and then the other. We move, exchanging charges in an avalanche of exhilaration. We hum. My excitement for you throbs in my ears. (My life begins to imitate art. Lesbian: writing provides the lexicon, the pre-texts and texts, of lesbian: eroticism.) I get with the beat.

Rhythm

Pure Sex, or Rendezvous at Nick's: A Riff

They were outrageous. They looked at each other and started to drip. They sat across the table, locked in deep throat looks at each other. They groaned and sighed, rubbed their feet together under the table, inserted their toes into each other's crotch. They picked over their fried chicken and lima beans, choked down the cornbread, and planned their next minutes, orchestrated their next moves, their sexual rhythms:

```
L L L L
L L L L
L L L L
L L L L
L L L L
L L L L
L L L L
L L L L
L L L L
L L L L
L L L L L L L L L L L L
L L L L L L L L L L L L
L L L L L L L L L L L L
```

The question of love is like the question of a story's profluence: how to keep this thing going once it's set in motion. The lover strays from the line and in irregular riffs marks out new chains of sound. The relation of the colon, as in lesbian : writing, marks a connection, a double play. It breaks and joins, a disconnective connective. All rhythm flows from there, two points that are one in space. But what about the tempo? How fast, how slow, do we go from here? Sometimes we speak to each other with our hands through a rare and beautiful grammar. Our fingers fly.

Play)

The letter seeks to connect me with its sense, its sender (whoever that is). It makes me want to take (up) a position, to "strike a pose." But I am thinking of another Madonna. No Pieta her(e). I want to uncover my/your brute instinct.

I could say that these are all wayward or purloined letters, never quite making their way from sender to receiver, stolen or lost, the message never quite what it was thought or meant to be. Sometimes their destinations change; they are sent to obscure places, other readers, without my knowing it. (In some cases, not only is the address unfamiliar, but the addressee—you, dear L—could be said to be unknown, or at least obscure.) The fact that I cannot own these letters leaves more room for doubt as to their meaning. Sometimes their meanings precede the letters, or follow me. These letters concern lesbian anarchists—sexual : textual freewheelers. Rather than Occupant or Resident, they should address the lesbian : reader. Dear Reader,

Dear L,

Tonight I can see my orgasm. A man on a horse wearing a cape and a hat, up in high chaparral country. A mountain meadow in the spring, still full of snow, with the hills banking it, encircling us. This is a vision, not a fantasy. He comes to me, or is it a woman, an uninvited participant in our s(c)ene. With me, but never looking.

Despite the wordless sounds of ecstasy, the scene is always silent, peaceful despite the frenzy of sex, the figure silhouetted, his/her features undiscernible, the vision framed. My orgasm takes me here.

This is my dream, but it is soon supplanted with another in which you star. Ready now? The next scene begins to take shape—the silken blindfold, the fur-lined cuffs with studs, the collar. . . . Now I wonder who you would rather be?

Love,
L

(Play It Again

"How many more than two are there."
—Gertrude Stein, *A Novel of Thank You*

What, for us, might be the future tense of lesbian : love? My cunt is a gateway to the future. Orgasm = intergalactic travel. In the observatory of lesbian : love, our bodies pulsate. We could say that we will burn with the brilliance of the century's supernova, outshining everything else, our luminosity an interstellar reference point for tens of thousands of years to come, visible by night and by day. Lodestars.

MORE.
    HARDER.
        FASTER.
REPEAT.
MORE.
    HARDER.
        FASTER.
AGAIN.
AND AGAIN AND AGAIN AND AND AND AND AND AND.

(I've known from the beginning that this is what my book is all about.)

Dear L,

Through writing I call out the lesbian in me, and in you as you read my letters. Space is opened, between me and the "I" (of) writing, the discursive subject, between the "I" on the page and the reader's "I," or how/who I imagine her to be. Of course, you can decide to read or to put the book down. You agree or disagree, defining a lesbian reader as you go. Together, we create templates, texts, for lesbian : love.

The most amazing thing has happened since the first chapter of this book was published. Queer people have already begun to send me letters. One sent by a gay man in Chicago contained a beautiful photograph of a statue, a boy against an elaborate drape with enormous red and yellow lilies on it. There are red, purple and yellow peppers and some eggplants tucked in and around the s(c)ene. The letter writer said:

> Dear Prof. Meese: I walked into Scenes, a coffee shop in Chicago, carrying you inside like a concealed weapon, inside a book called LESBIAN TEXTS AND CONTEXTS. . . .
>
> I admire your nerve to bring up and in your lover in a letter in the middle of your theorizing thesis about lesbian writing a new law for them/our/selves. . . .
>
> As this letter I am now writing you on mother's day of all days (Gertrude would be proud) shows: I believe in indirect affection. I sent this letter to you and your lover to say I was affected by your writing and have affections for both of you.
>
> > Cheers from Chi Town,
> > Jon-Henri Damski

Also enclosed two auto-graphed photos of/by my friend. . . . He/we believe art should be given away, or it becomes a dead-give-a-way that you are not an artist, but a dealer in commodities.

It's rare to receive gifts, but both this letter and the photos live up to the strictest definition. It makes me understand how my book might be a gift, too. If enough people send me letters, perhaps I can collect them. Writing produces more writing. This story of lesbian : love starts and starts again. No contract compels its profluence, directs its desire, specifies its ending or that it ever end. It breaks open at will. A surprise gift yields other gifts. Why don't you write me when you get a chance. Then you'll understand what a "lesbian" is, the secret involved in writing: lesbian—"(. . . . . .)." I'm hoping for a reply. (A loveletter would be nice.)

> Yours,
> L

Dear Elizabeth,
   Your face looks so remarkable when you're writing

> Love,
> Sandy

Dossier 3: Identity Matters

As the general introduction argues (section 1) the question of constructionism/essentialism is in a somewhat confused state today because there is a widespread tendency to conflate constructionism with materialism itself. Although it is possible to argue that one who theorizes the human person as "constructed" subject is involved in some kind of materialism, what *materialism* means in the specific case is often taken for granted and remains unclarified. The aim of this dossier is to provide texts that reopen the question of what *structure* means in critical and cultural theory today (Does it refer solely to the representational structures deconstruction dismantles?) and that help—once this reopening of the understanding of structure is accomplished—in the task of differentiating between various forms of constructionism/materialism.

Although the inaugural phase of debate over essentialism/constructionism (of the human person as subject, including the homosexual subject) may have played itself out (Warner 1993, x), a case can also be made that the debate today has only shifted to different levels. At one level, a renewed essentialism has recently appeared in the claims of scientists, like Simon LeVay (see for instance, Burr 1993 and Hamer and Copeland 1994), who hope to demonstrate that homosexuality has a genetic cause. Supporters of this view (including some gays and lesbians) who see their primary antagonists as the moralists of the fundamentalist religious right (who brand homosexuality a "sin") seem to believe that the "scientific" discovery of a natural cause of homosexuality will offset, if not cancel, morally grounded opposition. This move repeats the efforts of earlier defenders of homosexuality like Magnus Hirschfield, who in early twentieth-century Germany tried to establish "scientifically" the principle that homosexuality is an essentialized "third sex." Hirschfield's moves clearly did not help homosexuals overcome the persecution associated with the political development of fascism any more than "scientific" evidence of the "naturalness" of queerity will stem the reactionary tide of today's fascist skinheads, whose violence is being encouraged if not overtly supported by right-wing moralists. Gay pro-essentialists—like those who argue that a massive exodus from the closet will be an automatic and significant help in overcoming opposition (see Morton 1993)—are thus neglecting the historical evidence of the oppressions of other groups (women, African-Americans, other people of color, and so on). Race and sex have long been understood as genetically determined, but this understanding has not prevented these markers of difference from being the basis of exploitation and oppression. The ignoring of these social conditions by those in the queer movement suggests that what lies behind their targeting of moralists as the enemy is itself an ideological misrecognition of the "enemy," as if a rapprochement, or standoff, with religious moralists would represent significant progress. This ideological blindness to history produces a contradictory result: At a deeper level, both groups promote an essentialized notion—one "moral," the other "scientific"—of (homosexual) subjectivity. They end up, in other words, supporting a similar ahistorical understanding of social reality and the subject. The gay/lesbian targeting of the religious right as their prime antagonist only flatters the self-righteous, late capitalist, liberal state and its supporters, allowing them to evade their own deep responsibility for gay oppression. Peter Ray's brief text, "It's Not Natural," critiques this resurgent "biologistic" essentialism.

In the arena of avant-garde cultural studies the notion of constructionism does appear to have won out over essentialism. Constructionism's general political logic holds that if social phenomena are constructed, those phenomena are then open to being either perpetually deconstructed (as such critics as Judith Butler propose) and possibly (re)constructed "otherwise," which is to say that for oppressed and exploited groups the current political landscape need not be permanent. Thus the debate now is over which understanding of constructionism is most productive: today's dominant ludic (post)modern notion of the subject's construction through mode of signification with its correlative emphasis on *desire,* or the historical materialist understanding of social construction through mode of production with its correlative emphasis on *need.* Since the ludic view of constructionism/materialism is already quite extensively represented in the texts in Dossier 2 of this volume, the texts included in Dossier 3 accent the Foucauldian and Marxian understandings of constructionism/materialism, the former being represented by the selection from Foucault himself and the one from Bersani and the latter by the selection by Kollontai and— more problematically (for reasons I will discuss)—D'Emilio.

It seems appropriate to open this series of readings by recognizing the effectivity of Monique Wittig's work (represented by "The Straight Mind") in simultaneously putting pressure on the "weak" and merely discursive "materialist" politics of ludic (post)modernism (mode of signification), on the one hand, and on Marxism for the inadequacy of its theorization of the conditions of possibility of sexual practices (in relation to mode of production), on the other. It is also appropriate to recognize

the historical complication of the issue of sexual oppression in relation to identity with the chapters on race (Staples), bisexuality (Udis-Kessler), and AIDS (Watney) included in this dossier.

Although it has already had a long and productive history, the historical materialist account of sexualities has been generally neglected by the U.S. culture industry, which promotes those dominant writers, critics, and theorists who either aestheticize sexualities outright or propose politically limited and philosophically eclectic (non-rigorous) accounts of the material construction of/constraints on sexualities. These questions have been raised, if only briefly and tangentially, by leading queer writers themselves. For example, in the epilogue (titled "Self-Criticism") to his popular and widely familiar account of gay male life in the America of the 1980s, *States of Desire,* Edmund White critiques his book for "its peculiar alternation between snobbism and socialism" (334), seeming himself to write partly within a historical materialist frame (he mockingly compares his text to the practice of auto-critique in "Maoist meetings" [334]). In White's usage, *snobbism* is a code word for class privilege: He describes himself rather apologetically as a "snobbish" self shaped by his experience as a well-educated writer of avant-garde "high-culture" texts with "tastes and values far from those of most Americans" (334). Over against this patent "snobbism," White "discovers" as an afterthought an anti-class countertrend in his book, an inclination "to seek sociological rather than psychological causes" (334), which he calls "socialism." But as White renders it, "socialism" is "more a sympathy than a program" (334); in other words, his socialism is just a (sympathetic) "mental state"—a form of tolerance or good will directed at the exploited by the privileged and not a program for changing fundamental social structures. Although he declares an interest in "witnessing an end to racism, sexism, the exploitation of workers and other social inequities," he supports these goals only "so long as the means for eradicating [the inequities] is consonant with nonviolence and democracy" (335). In his discourses on social struggles, White not only situates himself more as a bystander (a "witness" to inequities) than as a participant but also supports the common-sense definition of *democracy* that holds sway in the liberal state where the word means basically "free speech" (within certain limits) rather than the equitable distribution of economic and other resources. Although the goal of politically serious auto-critique is to find a way of overcoming the contradictions in one's practices, White's epilogue simply renders his contradictions as an "insoluble paradox." Rather than heralding a radical social transformation, White's socialism amounts to little more than a tolerance of local reforms within an overall exploitative system on the part of the (gay) bourgeois male guiltily aware of his privileges. White's fame as an innovative writer of fiction gives his pronouncements a high visibility and others have followed his discourses. In her 1990s book, *Epistemology of the Closet,* Eve Sedgwick, for example, follows the discourses of White in his 1970s book, *States of Desire,* which hold that a rigorous historical materialist account of sexualities based on ideology critique is impossible because, as White says, desire is "anarchic" (336): "Gay life—rich, messy, promiscuous—will never please an ideologue" (336). In this light, the trope in White's title, which articulates the geography of the (gay) United States itself as anarchic desire, suggests—in tune with the notions of ludic (post)-modernism—that all "queer" politics could ever be is the subversion of the social order and not commitment to any particular program of social change. This same contradiction between the disorder of sexuality and the order of the social reappears as the "paradox" investigated in Frank Browning's recent book, *The Culture of Desire* (1993).

Although in agreement with White's view of the limitations of ideological accounts of sexualities, Foucault—whose theories have a privileged place in dominant Euramerican understandings of the queer—argues nevertheless that although not completely "contain-able," desire is still shaped by culture in identifiable ways. Eschewing White's merely descriptive and aesthetic (prehistorical materialist, pre-programmatic) approach, Foucault gives a more "ordered" (but still not theoretical—see section 2 of the general introduction) account of the invention of the homosexual subject as a part of the changes in modes of social regulation and discursive practices Europe has undergone in the past several hundred years. In Foucault's post-historical materialist, post-programmatic account, the homosexual subject was produced as an "object" by the discipline of psychiatry, a development within changing Western institutional formations. Different as they are, White's pre-Marxist materialist and Foucault's post-Marxist forms of knowledge are the ones that—not by accident—dominate contemporary discussions of queer and other sexualities in the (post)modern United States.

John D'Emilio's well-known text, "Capitalism and Gay Identity" (reprinted in this volume) is often taken to be exemplary of the Marxist understanding of constructionism. It is frequently treated as a notable site in academic writing today where historical materialism is given its due. (This text, first published in Snitow's *Powers of Desire,* is reprinted in D'Emilio's own collection of essays called *Making Trouble,* and is included among the texts recently canonized in *The Lesbian and Gay Studies Reader* 1993). His aim, D'Emilio says, is to ground the construction of the homosexual subject in "historically specific . . . concrete social processes." Yet immediately after invoking such Marxist concepts as wage labor and commodity production to explain those processes, D'Emilio cancels the force of his own analysis by insisting not only that capitalism *does not cause* homosexuality, but furthermore, that he is "not trying to claim that capitalism . . . *determines* the form that homosexuality takes." What, however, does *social constructionism* (which D'Emilio claims to be defending) mean except that social factors do indeed "determine the form that homosexuality takes"? Backing away from a materialist explanation, he deploys materialist concepts merely "professionally"—as a methodology to help him produce an inquiry into homosexuality that will look different from that of most other historians. In the end, however, he only thematizes Marxist categories and is not engaged in a sustained Marxist theoretics—indeed, he is "unmaking" trouble. (For a more sustained critique of D'Emilio's text and a fuller discussion of the relation of queer sexuality to capitalist commodification processes, see Morton 1995.)

In the dominant discourses, this axis of contestation between mode of signification and mode of production is continually occluded through various ideological maneuvers. The maneuver favored by the theoretically sophisticated today is to declare that we are living in a universal state of "post-ality," in a post-structural, post-historical, post-ideological, post-production, post-economic, post-need space in which questions of mode of production have all been superseded (on the idea of "post-theory," see Winkler 1993; and for a sustained theorization of "post-ality," see Zavarzadeh 1995). Among the less sophisticated, the favored ideological maneuver is to produce a theoretical and historical "muddlement" of the issues. There are countless instances of both maneuvers: Several examples of the former are readily available to the reader in the selections in Dossier 2 in this volume. However, a signal instance of the latter, the maneuver of theoretical and historical mystification (which is of course not merely cognitive and intellectual but political), is found in Steven Epstein's essay, "Gay Politics, Ethnic Identity: The Limits of Social Constructionism."(Epstein's essay is not included in this volume, but it is widely cited, so I want to discuss it here.) Although it first appeared in a journal *(Socialist Review),* the essay has been reprinted at least twice in book format (in two editions published by different publishers, of *Forms of Desire: Sexual Orientation and the Social Constructionist Controversy*) as one of the canonical texts on these issues. There is room here only to mention the ways in which Epstein's text, which claims to be a clarification of the issues and, which, because it first appeared in a "socialist" journal, is taken to represent a strong Left view, actually mystifies the constructionism/essentialism debate.

The motor of Epstein's analysis, which departs from the recognition of the increasing strength of constructionist theory ("With regard to sexuality, the constructionist critique of essentialism has become the received wisdom in left academic circles," 243), is his observation of a developing/developed "split" in the lesbian/gay community between their practices in the everyday (the increasing sense of a psychological need of a stabilized lesbian/gay identity), on the one hand, and the trajectory of theory toward constructionism (which calls the stability of these identities into question), on the other. In the last instance, the problem as he sees it is that "the strict constructionist perspective" has not "adequately" described "the experiences of gays and lesbians nor" spoken to "their need to understand and legitimate their places in the world" (243–244). His "solution" to this "problem" is to replace the notion of gay "identity" with that of gay "ethnicity," on the argument that the notion of ethnicity implies a looser—less oppressive and strict—form of constructionism than does the notion of identity. The general implication of Epstein's argument is that it is too much to expect lesbians and gays, who have gone through an arduous coming-out process and finally "found" an identity, to want to put that newly acquired identity under the pressure of the theoretical thoughtfulness that rigorous constructionism demands. The point is, of course, that progress against social injustice can only be made if no one is exempt from that kind of necessary ongoing theoretical inquiry. There is an immediate ideological distortion in the way Epstein frames the issues: given the fact that every practice always has a theory (even if unarticulated) inscribed in it, then if there is a divergence between contemporary lesbian/gay practices and lesbian/gay theory, this divergence will *still* have to be thought through *on the theoretical level.* "Experience," in other words, is not some autonomous, free-standing entity set against theory, as Epstein mistakenly suggests it is. There are a number of other problems that make Epstein's a mystifying essay: not the least of these is his treatment of essentialism as if it were only biological essentialism, which sidesteps metaphysical forms of essentialism. Along the same lines, his essay tries to treat the essentialism/constructionism controversy without taking (post)modern thought into account. However, the fundamental problem silently informing Epstein's text, like dozens of other similar texts of the dominant—even Left-liberal and queer—academy today, is the anxiety over the autonomy of experience, which is only a mask for what is basically the "autonomy of desire." In its simplest terms, the question Epstein is posing is this: Can lesbians/gays live as their "experience" tells them they "desire" to live (that is, can they not relax into their new "common sense"), or must they really theorize their practice (that is, must they critique their practices and consider bringing them into relation with their theory)?

In his introduction to *Postmodernist Culture,* Steven Connor articulates the issue of experience in this manner: "It may be that experience is always, if not actually determined, then at least interpreted in advance by the various structures of understanding and interpretation which hold at particular moments in particular societies, and different regions of those societies" (1989, 3). From this perspective, everything we refer to as "experience" is produced by those structures of knowledge that allow us to recognize it as experience in the first place. Writing about lesbian sexuality and theory, Judith Roof has observed the negative impact of trying to separate off "experience" from "theory." In her view, the result of such a move is to both "romanticize the individual (or the category), imagining it as an alienated but pure and innocent space with an originary consciousness" and prevent a "perception of how individuals exist in the complex interplay of representations, material forces, political considerations, and psychic processes" (Roof 1991, 244).

References

Abelove, Henry, Michèle Aina Barale, David M. Halperin, eds. (1993) *The Lesbian and Gay Studies Reader.* New York: Routledge. (D'Emilio's essay is on pp. 467–476.)

Browning, Frank. (1993) *The Culture of Desire: Paradox and Perversity in Gay Lives Today.* New York: Crown.

Burr, Chandler. (1993) "Homosexuality and Biology." *The Atlantic* (March):47–52, 55, 58–62, 64–65.

Connor, Steven. (1989) *Postmodernist Culture: An Introduction to Theories of the Contemporary.* Cambridge and Oxford: Basil Blackwell.

D'Emilio, John. (1992) *Making Trouble: Essays on Gay History, Politics, and the University.* New York and London: Routledge.

Epstein, Steven. (1987) "Gay Politics, Ethnic Identity: The Limits of Social Constructionism." *Socialist Review* 93/94 (May/August):9–54. Reprinted as chapter 10 in Edward Stein, (1992) *Forms of Desire: Sexual Orientation and the Social Constructionist Controversy* (New York and London: Routledge). (First published by Garland Publishing, Inc., in 1990.)

Hamer, Dean, and Peter Copeland. (1994). *The Science of Desire: The Search for the Gay Gene and the Biology of Behavior.* New York: Simon & Schuster.

Morton, Donald. (1995) "Queerity and Ludic Sado-Masochism: Compulsory Consumption and the Emerging Post-al Queer." *Transformation: Marxist Boundary Work in Theory, Economics, Politics and Culture* 1:189–215.

———. (1993) "'Radicalism,' 'Outing,' and the Politics of (Sexual) Knowledges." *The Minnesota Review.* N. S. 40 (Spring/Summer):136–141. (Special issue on "The Politics of AIDS.")

Roof, Judith. (1991) *A Lure of Knowledge: Lesbian Sexuality and Theory.* New York: Columbia University Press.

Sedgwick, Eve Kosofsky. (1990) *Epistemology of the Closet.* Berkeley: University of California Press.

Snitow, Ann, Christine Stansell, and Sharon Thompson, eds. (1983) *Powers of Desire: The Politics of Sexuality.* New York: Monthly Review Press. (D'Emilio's piece is on pp. 100–113.)

Warner, Michael. (1993) "Introduction." In Michael Warner, ed., *Fear of a Queer Planet: Queer Politics and Social Theory.* Minneapolis: University of Minnesota Press, pp. vii–xxxi. (Reprinted in part in Dossier 4 of this volume.)

White, Edmund. (1980) *States of Desire: Travels in Gay America.* New York: Dutton.

Winkler, Karen. (1993) "Scholars Mark the Beginning of the Age of 'Post-Theory.'" *The Chronicle of Higher Education* (October 13):A8–A9, A16–A17.

Zavarzadeh, Mas'ud. (1995) "Post-ality: The (Dis)-Simulations of Cybercapitalism. Book One." *Transformation* 1 (Spring):1–75.

The Straight Mind[1]

Monique Wittig

1980

In recent years in Paris, language as a phenomenon has dominated modern theoretical systems and the social sciences and has entered the political discussions of the lesbian and women's liberation movements. This is because it relates to an important political field where what is at play is power, or more than that, a network of powers, since there is a multiplicity of languages that constantly act upon the social reality. The importance of language as such as a political stake has only recently been perceived.[2] But the gigantic development of linguistics, the multiplication of schools of linguistics, the advent of the sciences of communication, and the technicality of the metalanguages that these sciences utilize, represent the symptoms of the importance of what is politically at stake. The science of language has invaded other sciences, such as anthropology through Lévi-Strauss, psychoanalysis through Lacan, and all the disciplines which have developed from the basis of structuralism.

The early semiology of Roland Barthes nearly escaped from linguistic domination to become a political analysis of the different systems of signs, to establish a relationship between this or that system of signs—for example, the myths of the petit bourgeois class—and the class struggle within capitalism that this system tends to conceal. We were almost saved, for political semiology is a weapon (a method) that we need to analyze what is called ideology. But the miracle did not last. Rather than introducing into semiology concepts which are foreign to it—in this case Marxist concepts—Barthes quickly stated that semiology was only a branch of linguistics and that language was its only object.

Thus, the entire world is only a great register where the most diverse languages come to have themselves recorded, such as the language of the Unconscious,[3] the language of fashion, the language of the exchange of women where human beings are literally the signs which are used to communicate. These languages, or rather these discourses, fit into one another, interpenetrate one another, support one another, reinforce one another, auto-engender, and engender one another. Linguistics engenders semiology and structural linguistics, structural linguistics engenders structuralism, which engenders the Structural Unconscious. The ensemble of these discourses produces a confusing static for the oppressed, which makes them lose sight of the material cause of their oppression and plunges them into a kind of ahistoric vacuum.

For they produce a scientific reading of the social reality in which human beings are given as invariants, untouched by history and unworked by class conflicts, with identical psyches because genetically programmed. This psyche, equally untouched by history and unworked by class conflicts, provides the specialists, from the beginning of the twentieth century, with a whole arsenal of invariants: the symbolic language which very advantageously functions with very few elements, since, like digits (0–9), the symbols "unconsciously" produced by the psyche are not very numerous. Therefore, these

207

symbols are very easy to impose, through therapy and theorization, upon the collective and individual unconscious. We are taught that the Unconscious, with perfectly good taste, structures itself upon metaphors, for example, the name-of-the-father, the Oedipus complex, castration, the murder-or-death-of-the-father, the exchange of women, etc. If the Unconscious, however, is easy to control, it is not just by anybody. Similar to mystical revelations, the apparition of symbols in the psyche demands multiple interpretations. Only specialists can accomplish the deciphering of the Unconscious. Only they, the psychoanalysts, are allowed (authorized?) to organize and interpret psychic manifestations which will show the symbol in its full meaning. And while the symbolic language is extremely poor and essentially lacunary, the languages or metalanguages which interpret it are developing, each one of them, with a richness, a display, that only theological exegeses of the Bible have equalled.

Who gave the psychoanalysts their knowledge? For example, for Lacan, what he calls the "psychoanalytic discourse," or the "analytical experience," both "teach" him what he already knows. And each one teaches him what the other one taught him. But can we deny that Lacan scientifically discovered, through the "analytical experience" (somehow an experiment), the structures of the Unconscious? Will we be irresponsible enough to disregard the discourses of the psychoanalyzed people lying on their couches? In my opinion, there is no doubt that Lacan found in the Unconscious the structures he said he found there, since he had previously put them there. People who did not fall into the power of the psychoanalytical institution may experience an immeasurable feeling of sadness at the degree of oppression (of manipulation) that the psychoanalyzed discourses show. In the analytical experience there is an oppressed person, the psychoanalyzed, whose need for communication is exploited and who (in the same way as the witches could, under torture, only repeat the language that the inquisitors wanted to hear) has no other choice, (if s/he does not want to destroy the implicit

contract which allows her/him to communicate and which s/he needs), than to attempt to say what s/he is supposed to say. They say that this can last for a lifetime—cruel contract which constrains a human being to display her/his misery to an oppressor who is directly responsible for it, who exploits her/him economically, politically, ideologically and whose interpretation reduces this misery to a few figures of speech.

But can the need to communicate that this contract implies only be satisfied in the psychoanalytical situation, in being cured or "experimented" with? If we believe recent testimonies[4] by lesbians, feminists, and gay men, this is not the case. All their testimonies emphasize the political significance of the impossibility that lesbians, feminists, and gay men face in the attempt to communicate in heterosexual society, other than with a psychoanalyst. When the general state of things is understood (one is not sick or to be cured, one has an enemy) the result is that the oppressed person breaks the psychoanalytical contract. This is what appears in the testimonies, along with the teaching that the psychoanalytical contract was not a contract of consent but a forced one.

The discourses which particularly oppress all of us, lesbians, women, and homosexual men, are those which take for granted that what founds society, any society, is heterosexuality.[5] These discourses speak about us and claim to say the truth in an apolitical field, as if anything of that which signifies could escape the political in this moment of history, and as if, in what concerns us, politically insignificant signs could exist. These discourses of heterosexuality oppress us in the sense that they prevent us from speaking unless we speak in their terms. Everything which puts them into question is at once disregarded as elementary. Our refusal of the totalizing interpretation of psychoanalysis makes the theoreticians say that we neglect the symbolic dimension. These discourses deny us every possibility of creating our own categories. But their most ferocious action is the unrelenting tyranny that they exert upon our physical and mental selves.

When we use the overgeneralizing term "ideology" to designate all the discourses of the dominating group, we relegate these discourses to the domain of Irreal Ideas; we forget the material (physical) violence that they directly do to the oppressed people, a violence produced by the abstract and "scientific" discourses as well as by the discourses of the mass media. I would like to insist on the material oppression of individuals by discourses, and I would like to underline its immediate effects through the example of pornography.

Pornographic images, films, magazine photos, publicity posters on the walls of the cities, constitute a discourse, and this discourse covers our world with its signs, and this discourse has a meaning: it signifies that women are dominated. Semioticians can interpret the system of this discourse, describe its disposition. What they read in that discourse are signs whose function is not to signify and which have no *raison d'être* except to be elements of a certain system or disposition. But for us this discourse is not divorced from the real as it is for semioticians. Not only does it maintain very close relations with the social reality which is our oppression (economically and politically), but also it is in itself real since it is one of the aspects of oppression, since it exerts a precise power over us. The pornographic discourse is one of the strategies of violence which are exercised upon us: it humiliates, it degrades, it is a crime against our "humanity." As a harassing tactic it has another function, that of a warning. It orders us to stay in line, and it keeps those who would tend to forget who they are in step; it calls upon fear. These same experts in semiotics, referred to earlier, reproach us for confusing, when we demonstrate against pornography, the discourses with the reality. They do not see that this discourse *is* reality for us, one of the facets of the reality of our oppression. They believe that we are mistaken in our level of analysis.

I have chosen pornography as an example because its discourse is the most symptomatic and the most demonstrative of the violence which is done to us through discourses, as well

as in the society at large. There is nothing abstract about the power that sciences and theories have to act materially and actually upon our bodies and our minds, even if the discourse that produces it is abstract. It is one of the forms of domination, its very expression. I would say, rather, one of its exercises. All of the oppressed know this power and have had to deal with it. It is the one which says: you do not have the right to speech because your discourse is not scientific and not theoretical, you are on the wrong level of analysis, you are confusing discourse and reality, your discourse is naive, you misunderstand this or that science.

If the discourse of modern theoretical systems and social science exerts a power upon us, it is because it works with concepts which closely touch us. In spite of the historic advent of the lesbian, feminist, and gay liberation movements, whose proceedings have already upset the philosophical and political categories of the discourses of the social sciences, their categories (thus brutally put into question) are nevertheless utilized without examination by contemporary science. They function like primitive concepts in a conglomerate of all kinds of disciplines, theories, and current ideas that I will call the straight mind. (See *The Savage Mind* by Claude Lévi-Strauss.) They concern "woman," "man," "sex," "difference," and all of the series of concepts which bear this mark, including such concepts as "history," "culture," and the "real." And although it has been accepted in recent years that there is no such thing as nature, that everything is culture, there remains within that culture a core of nature which resists examination, a relationship excluded from the social in the analysis—a relationship whose characteristic is ineluctability in culture, as well as in nature, and which is the heterosexual relationship. I will call it the obligatory social relationship between "man" and "woman." (Here I refer to Ti-Grace Atkinson and her analysis of sexual intercourse as an institution.[6]) With its ineluctability as knowledge, as an obvious principle, as a given prior to any science, the straight mind develops a totalizing interpretation of history, social reality, culture, language, and all the subjective phenomena at the same time. I can only underline the oppressive character that the straight mind is clothed in in its tendency to immediately universalize its production of concepts into general laws which claim to hold true for all societies, all epochs, all individuals. Thus one speaks of *the* exchange of women, *the* difference between the sexes, *the* symbolic order, *the* Unconscious, Desire, *Jouissance,* Culture, History, giving an absolute meaning to these concepts when they are only categories founded upon heterosexuality, or thought which produces the difference between the sexes as a political and philosophical dogma.

The consequence of this tendency toward universality is that the straight mind cannot conceive of a culture, a society where heterosexuality would not order not only all human relationships but also its very production of concepts and all the processes which escape consciousness, as well. Additionally, these unconscious processes are historically more and more imperative in what they teach us about ourselves through the instrumentality of specialists. The rhetoric which expresses them (and whose seduction I do not underestimate) envelops itself in myths, resorts to enigma, proceeds by accumulating metaphors, and its function is to poeticize the obligatory character of the "you-will-be-straight-or-you-will-not-be."

In this thought, to reject the obligation of coitus and the institutions that this obligation has produced as necessary for the constitution of a society, is simply an impossibility, since to do this would mean to reject the possibility of the constitution of the other and to reject the "symbolic order," to make the constitution of meaning impossible, without which no one can maintain an internal coherence. Thus lesbianism, homosexuality, and the societies that we form cannot be thought of or spoken of, even though they have always existed. Thus, the straight mind continues to affirm that incest, and not homosexuality, represents its major interdiction. Thus, when thought by the straight mind, homosexuality is nothing but heterosexuality.

Yes, straight society is based on the necessity of the different/other at every level. It cannot work economically, symbolically, linguistically, or politically without this concept. This necessity of the different/other is an ontological one for the whole conglomerate of sciences and disciplines that I call the straight mind. But what is the different/other if not the dominated? For heterosexual society is the society which not only oppresses lesbians and gay men, it oppresses many different/others, it oppresses all women and many categories of men, all those who are in the position of the dominated. To constitute a difference and to control it is an "act of power, since it is essentially a normative act. Everybody tries to show the other as different. But not everybody succeeds in doing so. One has to be socially dominant to succeed in it."[7]

For example, the concept of difference between the sexes ontologically constitutes women into different/others. Men are not different, whites are not different, nor are the masters. But the blacks, as well as the slaves, are. This ontological characteristic of the difference between the sexes affects all the concepts which are part of the same conglomerate. But for us there is no such thing as being-woman or being-man. "Man" and "woman" are political concepts of opposition, and the copula which dialectically unites them is, at the same time, the one which abolishes them.[8] It is the class struggle between women and men which will abolish men and women.[9] The concept of difference has nothing ontological about it. It is only the way that the masters interpret a historical situation of domination. The function of difference is to mask at every level the conflicts of interest, including ideological ones.

In other words, for us, this means there cannot any longer be women and men, and that as classes and categories of thought or language they have to disappear, politically, economically, ideologically. If we, as lesbians and gay men, continue to speak of ourselves and to conceive of ourselves as women and as men, we are instrumental in maintaining heterosexuality. I am sure that an economic and political transformation will not dedramatize these categories of language. Can we redeem *slave?* Can we redeem *nigger, negress?* How is *woman* different? Will we continue to write *white, master, man?* The transformation of economic relationships will not suffice. We must produce a political transformation of the key concepts, that is of the concepts which are strategic for us. For there is another order of materiality, that of language, and language is worked upon from within by these strategic concepts. It is at the same time tightly connected to the political field, where everything that concerns language, science and thought refers to the person as subjectivity and to her/his relationship to society. And we cannot leave this within the power of the straight mind or the thought of domination.

If among all the productions of the straight mind I especially challenge the models of the Structural Unconscious, it is because: at the moment in history when the domination of social groups can no longer appear as a logical necessity to the dominated, because they revolt, because they question the differences, Lévi-Strauss, Lacan, and their epigones call upon necessities which escape the control of consciousness and therefore the responsibility of individuals.

They call upon unconscious processes, for example, which require the exchange of women as a necessary condition for every society. According to them, that is what the unconscious tells us with authority, and the symbolic order, without which there is no meaning, no language, no society, depends on it. But what does women being exchanged mean if not that they are dominated? No wonder then that there is only one Unconscious, and that it is heterosexual. It is an Unconscious which looks too consciously after the interests of the masters[10] in whom it lives for them to be dispossessed of their concepts so easily. Besides, domination is denied; there is no slavery of women, there is difference. To which I will answer with this statement made by a Rumanian peasant at a public meeting in 1848: "Why do the gentlemen say it was not slavery, for we know it to have been slavery, this sorrow that we have sor-

rowed." Yes, we know it, and this science of oppression cannot be taken away from us.

It is from this science that we must track down the "what-goes-without-saying" heterosexual, and (I paraphrase the early Roland Barthes) we must not bear "seeing Nature and History confused at every turn."[11] We must make it brutally apparent that psychoanalysis after Freud and particularly Lacan have rigidly turned their concepts into myths—Difference, Desire, the Name-of-the-father, etc. They have even "over-mythified" the myths, an operation that was necessary for them in order to systematically heterosexualize that personal dimension which suddenly emerged through the dominated individuals into the historical field, particularly through women, who started their struggle almost two centuries ago. And it has been done systematically, in a concert of interdisciplinarity, never more harmonious than since the heterosexual myths started to circulate with ease from one formal system to another, like sure values that can be invested in anthropology as well as in psychoanalysis and in all the social sciences.

This ensemble of heterosexual myths is a system of signs which uses figures of speech, and thus it can be politically studied from within the science of our oppression; "for-we-know-it-to-have-been-slavery" is the dynamic which introduces the diachronism of history into the fixed discourse of eternal essences. This undertaking should somehow be a political semiology, although with "this sorrow that we have sorrowed" we work also at the level of language/manifesto, of language/action, that which transforms, that which makes history.

In the meantime, in the systems that seemed so eternal and universal that laws could be extracted from them, laws that could be stuffed into computers, and in any case for the moment stuffed into the unconscious machinery, in these systems, thanks to our action and our language, shifts are happening. Such a model, as for example, the exchange of women, reengulfs history in so violent and brutal a way that the whole system, which was believed to be formal, topples over into another dimension of knowledge. This dimension of history belongs to us, since somehow we have been designated, and since, as Lévi-Strauss said, we talk, let us say that we break off the heterosexual contract.

So, this is what lesbians say everywhere in this country and in some others, if not with theories at least through their social practice, whose repercussions upon straight culture and society are still unenvisionable. An anthropologist might say that we have to wait for fifty years. Yes, if one wants to universalize the functioning of these societies and make their invariants appear. Meanwhile the straight concepts are undermined. What is woman? Panic, general alarm for an active defense. Frankly, it is a problem that the lesbians do not have because of a change of perspective, and it would be incorrect to say that lesbians associate, make love, live with women, for "woman" has meaning only in heterosexual systems of thought and heterosexual economic systems. Lesbians are not women.

Notes

1. This text was first read in New York at the Modern Language Association Convention in 1978 and dedicated to American lesbians.

2. However, the classical Greeks knew that there was no political power without mastery of the art of rhetoric, especially in a democracy.

3. Throughout this paper, when Lacan's use of the term "the Unconscious" is referred to it is capitalized, following his style.

4. For example see Karla Jay and Allen Young, eds., *Out of the Closets* (New York: Links Books, 1972).

5. Heterosexuality: a word which first appears in the French language in 1911.

6. Ti-Grace Atkinson, *Amazon Odyssey* (New York: Links Books, 1974), pp. 13–23.

7. Claude Faugeron and Philippe Robert, *La Justice et son public et les représentations sociales du système pénal* (Paris: Masson, 1978).

8. See, for her definition of "social sex," Nicole-Claude Mathieu, "Notes pour une définition sociologique des catégories de sexe," *Epistémologie Sociologique* 11 (1971). Translated as *Ignored by Some, Denied by Others: The Social Sex Category in Sociology* (pamphlet), Explorations in Feminism 2 (London: Women's Research and Resources Centre Publications, 1977), pp. 16–37.

9. In the same way that in every other class struggle the categories of opposition are "reconciled" by the struggle whose goal is to make them disappear.

10. Are the millions of dollars a year made by the psychoanalysts symbolic?

11. Roland Barthes, *Mythologies* (New York: Hill and Wang, 1972), p. 11.

The Perverse Implantation

Michel Foucault

A possible objection: it would be a mistake to see in this proliferation of discourses merely a quantitative phenomenon, something like a pure increase, as if what was said in them were immaterial, as if the fact of speaking about sex were of itself more important than the forms of imperatives that were imposed on it by speaking about it. For was this transformation of sex into discourse not governed by the endeavor to expel from reality the forms of sexuality that were not amenable to the strict economy of reproduction: to say no to unproductive activities, to banish casual pleasures, to reduce or exclude practices whose object was not procreation? Through the various discourses, legal sanctions against minor perversions were multiplied; sexual irregularity was annexed to mental illness; from childhood to old age, a norm of sexual development was defined and all the possible deviations were carefully described; pedagogical controls and medical treatments were organized; around the least fantasies, moralists, but especially doctors, brandished the whole emphatic vocabulary of abomination. Were these anything more than means employed to absorb, for the benefit of a genitally centered sexuality, all the fruitless pleasures? All this garrulous attention which has us in a stew over sexuality, is it not motivated by one basic concern: to ensure population, to reproduce labor capacity, to perpetuate the form of social relations: in short, to constitute a sexuality that is economically useful and politically conservative?

I still do not know whether this is the ultimate objective. But this much is certain: reduction has not been the means employed for trying to achieve it. The nineteenth century and our own have been rather the age of multiplication: a dispersion of sexualities, a strengthening of their disparate forms, a multiple implantation of "perversions." Our epoch has initiated sexual heterogeneities.

Up to the end of the eighteenth century, three major explicit codes—apart from the customary regularities and constraints of opinion—governed sexual practices: canonical law, the Christian pastoral, and civil law. They determined, each in its own way, the division between licit and illicit. They were all centered on matrimonial relations: the marital obligation, the ability to fulfill it, the manner in which one complied with it, the requirements and violences that accompanied it, the useless or unwarranted caresses for which it was a pretext, its fecundity or the way one went about making it sterile, the moments when one demanded it (dangerous periods of pregnancy or breastfeeding, forbidden times of Lent or abstinence), its frequency or infrequency, and so on. It was this domain that was especially saturated with prescriptions. The sex of husband and wife was beset by rules and recommendations. The marriage relation was the most intense focus of constraints; it was spoken of more than anything else; more than any other relation, it was required to give a detailed accounting of itself. It was under constant surveillance: if it was found to be lacking, it had to come forward and plead its case before a witness. The "rest" remained a good deal more confused: one only has to think of the uncertain status of "sodomy," or the indifference regarding the sexuality of children.

Moreover, these different codes did not make a clear distinction between violations of the rules of marriage and deviations with respect to genitality. Breaking the rules of marriage or seeking strange pleasures brought an equal measure of condemnation. On the list of grave sins, and separated only by their relative importance, there appeared debauchery (extramarital relations), adultery, rape, spiritual or carnal incest, but also sodomy, or the mutual "caress." As to the courts, they could condemn homosexuality as well as infidelity, marriage without parental consent, or bestiality. What was taken into account in the civil and religious jurisdictions alike was a general unlawfulness. Doubtless acts "contrary to nature" were stamped as especially abominable, but they were perceived simply as an extreme form of acts "against the law"; they were infringements of decrees which were just as sacred as those of marriage, and which had been established for governing the order of things and the plan of beings. Prohibitions bearing on sex were essentially of a juridical nature. The "nature" on which they were based was still a kind of law. For a long time hermaphrodites were criminals, or crime's offspring, since their anatomical disposition, their very being, confounded the law that distinguished the sexes and prescribed their union.

The discursive explosion of the eighteenth and nineteenth centuries caused this system centered on legitimate alliance to undergo two modifications. First, a centrifugal movement with respect to heterosexual monogamy. Of course, the array of practices and pleasures continued to be referred to it as their internal standard; but it was spoken of less and less, or in any case with a growing moderation. Efforts to find out its secrets were abandoned; nothing further was demanded of it than to define itself from day to day. The legitimate couple, with its regular sexuality, had a right to more discretion. It tended to function as a norm, one that was stricter, perhaps, but quieter. On the other hand, what came under scrutiny was the sexuality of children, mad men and women, and criminals; the sensuality of those who did not like the opposite sex; reveries, obsessions, petty manias, or great transports of rage. It was time for all these figures, scarcely noticed in the past, to step forward and speak, to make the difficult confession of what they were. No doubt they were condemned all the same; but they were listened to; and if regular sexuality happened to be questioned once again, it was through a reflux movement, originating in these peripheral sexualities.

Whence the setting apart of the "unnatural" as a specific dimension in the field of sexuality. This kind of activity assumed an autonomy with regard to the other condemned forms such as adultery or rape (and the latter were condemned less and less): to marry a close relative or practice sodomy, to seduce a nun or engage in sadism, to deceive one's wife or violate cadavers, became things that were essentially different. The area covered by the Sixth Commandment began to fragment. Similarly, in the civil order, the confused category of "debauchery," which for more than a century had been one of the most frequent reasons for administrative confinement, came apart. From the debris, there appeared on the one hand infractions against the legislation (or morality) pertaining to marriage and the family, and on the other, offenses against the regularity of a natural function (offenses which, it must be added, the law was apt to punish). Here we have a likely reason, among others, for the prestige of Don Juan, which three centuries have not erased. Underneath the great violator of the rules of marriage—stealer of wives, seducer of virgins, the shame of families, and an insult to husbands and fathers—another personage can be glimpsed: the individual driven, in spite of himself, by the somber madness of sex. Underneath the libertine, the pervert. He deliberately breaks the law, but at the same time, something like a nature gone awry transports him far from all nature; his death is the moment when the supernatural return of the crime and its retribution thwarts the flight into counternature. There were two great systems conceived by the West for governing sex: the law of marriage and the order of desires—and the life of Don Juan overturned them both. We shall leave it to psychoanalysts to speculate whether he was homosexual, narcissistic, or impotent.

Although not without delay and equivocation, the natural laws of matrimony and the immanent rules of sexuality began to be recorded on two separate registers. There emerged a world of perversion which partook of that of legal or moral infraction, yet was not simply a variety of the latter. An entire sub-race race was born, different—despite certain kinship ties—from the libertines of the past. From the end of the eighteenth century to our own, they circulated through the pores of society; they were always hounded, but not always by laws; were often locked up, but not always in prisons; were sick perhaps, but scandalous, dangerous victims, prey to a strange evil that also bore the name of vice and sometimes crime. They were children wise beyond their years, precocious little girls, ambiguous schoolboys, dubious servants and educators, cruel or maniacal husbands, solitary collectors, ramblers with bizarre impulses; they haunted the houses of correction, the penal colonies, the tribunals, and the asylums; they carried their infamy to the doctors and their sickness to the judges. This was the numberless family of perverts who were on friendly terms with delinquents and akin to madmen. In the course of the century they successively bore the stamp of "moral folly," "genital neurosis," "aberration of the genetic instinct," "degenerescence," or "physical imbalance."

What does the appearance of all these peripheral sexualities signify? Is the fact that they could appear in broad daylight a sign that the code had become more lax? Or does the fact that they were given so much attention testify to a stricter regime and to its concern to bring them under close supervision? In terms of repression, things are unclear. There was permissiveness, if one bears in mind that the severity of the codes relating to sexual offenses diminished considerably in the nineteenth century and that law itself often deferred to medicine. But an additional ruse of severity, if one thinks of all the agencies of control and all the mechanisms of surveillance that were put into opera-

tion by pedagogy or therapeutics. It may be the case that the intervention of the Church in conjugal sexuality and its rejection of "frauds" against procreation had lost much of their insistence over the previous two hundred years. But medicine made a forceful entry into the pleasures of the couple: it created an entire organic, functional, or mental pathology arising out of "incomplete" sexual practices; it carefully classified all forms of related pleasures; it incorporated them into the notions of "development" and instinctual "disturbances"; and it undertook to manage them.

Perhaps the point to consider is not the level of indulgence or the quantity of repression but the form of power that was exercised. When this whole thicket of disparate sexualities was labeled, as if to disentangle them from one another, was the object to exclude them from reality? It appears, in fact, that the function of the power exerted in this instance was not that of interdiction, and that it involved four operations quite different from simple prohibition.

1. Take the ancient prohibitions of consanguine marriages (as numerous and complex as they were) or the condemnation of adultery, with its inevitable frequency of occurrence; or on the other hand, the recent controls through which, since the nineteenth century, the sexuality of children has been subordinated and their "solitary habits" interfered with. It is clear that we are not dealing with one and the same power mechanism. Not only because in the one case it is a question of law and penality, and in the other, medicine and regimentation; but also because the tactics employed is not the same. On the surface, what appears in both cases is an effort at elimination that was always destined to fail and always constrained to begin again. But the prohibition of "incests" attempted to reach its objective through an asymptotic decrease in the thing it condemned, whereas the control of in-

fantile sexuality hoped to reach it through a simultaneous propagation of its own power and of the object on which it was brought to bear. It proceeded in accordance with a twofold increase extended indefinitely. Educators and doctors combatted children's onanism like an epidemic that needed to be eradicated. What this actually entailed, throughout this whole secular campaign that mobilized the adult world around the sex of children, was using these tenuous pleasures as a prop, constituting them as secrets (that is, forcing them into hiding so as to make possible their discovery), tracing them back to their source, tracking them from their origins to their effects, searching out everything that might cause them or simply enable them to exist. Wherever there was the chance they might appear, devices of surveillance were installed; traps were laid for compelling admissions; inexhaustible and corrective discourses were imposed; parents and teachers were alerted, and left with the suspicion that all children were guilty, and with the fear of being themselves at fault if their suspicions were not sufficiently strong; they were kept in readiness in the face of this recurrent danger; their conduct was prescribed and their pedagogy recodified; an entire medico-sexual regime took hold of the family milieu. The child's "vice" was not so much an enemy as a support; it may have been designated as the evil to be eliminated, but the extraordinary effort that went into the task that was bound to fail leads one to suspect that what was demanded of it was to persevere, to proliferate to the limits of the visible and the invisible, rather than to disappear for good. Always relying on this support, power advanced, multiplied its relays and its effects, while its target expanded, subdivided, and branched out,

penetrating further into reality at the same pace. In appearance, we are dealing with a barrier system; but in fact, all around the child, indefinite *lines of penetration* were disposed.

2. This new persecution of the peripheral sexualities entailed an *incorporation of perversions* and a new *specification of individuals*. As defined by the ancient civil or canonical codes, sodomy was a category of forbidden acts; their perpetrator was nothing more than the juridical subject of them. The nineteenth-century homosexual became a personage, a past, a case history, and a childhood, in addition to being a type of life, a life form, and a morphology, with an indiscreet anatomy and possibly a mysterious physiology. Nothing that went into his total composition was unaffected by his sexuality. It was everywhere present in him: at the root of all his actions because it was their insidious and indefinitely active principle; written immodestly on his face and body because it was a secret that always gave itself away. It was consubstantial with him, less as a habitual sin than as a singular nature. We must not forget that the psychological, psychiatric, medical category of homosexuality was constituted from the moment it was characterized—Westphal's famous article of 1870 on "contrary sexual sensations" can stand as its date of birth[1]—less by a type of sexual relations than by a certain quality of sexual sensibility, a certain way of inverting the masculine and the feminine in oneself. Homosexuality appeared as one of the forms of sexuality when it was transposed from the practice of sodomy onto a kind of interior androgyny, a hermaphrodism of the soul. The sodomite had been a temporary aberration; the homosexual was now a species.

So too were all those minor perverts whom nineteenth-century psychiatrists entomologized by giving them strange baptismal names: there were Krafft-Ebing's zoophiles and zooerasts, Rohleder's auto-monosexualists; and later, mixo-scopophiles, gynecomasts, presbyophiles, sexoesthetic inverts, and dyspareunist women. These fine names for heresies referred to a nature that was overlooked by the law, but not so neglectful of itself that it did not go on producing more species, even where there was no order to fit them into. The machinery of power that focused on this whole alien strain did not aim to suppress it, but rather to give it an analytical, visible, and permanent reality: it was implanted in bodies, slipped in beneath modes of conduct, made into a principle of classification and intelligibility, established as a *raison d'être* and a natural order of disorder. Not the exclusion of these thousand aberrant sexualities, but the specification, the regional solidification of each one of them. The strategy behind this dissemination was to strew reality with them and incorporate them into the individual.

3. More than the old taboos, this form of power demanded constant, attentive, and curious presences for its exercise; it presupposed proximities; it proceeded through examination and insistent observation; it required an exchange of discourses, through questions that extorted admissions, and confidences that went beyond the questions that were asked. It implied a physical proximity and an interplay of intense sensations. The medicalization of the sexually peculiar was both the effect and the instrument of this. Imbedded in bodies, becoming deeply characteristic of individuals, the oddities of sex relied on a technology of health and pathology. And conversely, since sexuality was a medical and medicalizable object, one had to try and detect it—as a lesion, a dysfunction, or a symptom—in the depths of the organism, or on the surface of the skin, or among all the signs of behavior. The power which thus took charge of sexuality set about contacting bodies, caressing them with its eyes, intensifying areas, electrifying surfaces, dramatizing troubled moments. It wrapped the sexual body in its embrace. There was undoubtedly an increase in effectiveness and an extension of the domain controlled; but also a sensualization of power and a gain of pleasure. This produced a twofold effect: an impetus was given to power through its very exercise; an emotion rewarded the overseeing control and carried it further; the intensity of the confession renewed the questioner's curiosity; the pleasure discovered fed back to the power that encircled it. But so many pressing questions singularized the pleasures felt by the one who had to reply. They were fixed by a gaze, isolated and animated by the attention they received. Power operated as a mechanism of attraction; it drew out those peculiarities over which it kept watch. Pleasure spread to the power that harried it; power anchored the pleasure it uncovered.

The medical examination, the psychiatric investigation, the pedagogical report, and family controls may have the over-all and apparent objective of saying no to all wayward or unproductive sexualities, but the fact is that they function as mechanisms with a double impetus: pleasure and power. The pleasure that comes of exercising a power that questions, monitors, watches, spies, searches out, palpates, brings to light; and on the other hand, the pleasure that kindles at having to evade this power, flee from it, fool it, or travesty it. The power that lets itself be invaded by the pleasure it is pursuing; and opposite it, power asserting itself in the pleasure of showing off, scandalizing, or resisting. Capture and seduction, confrontation and mutual reinforcement: parents and children, adults and adolescents, educator and students, doctors and patients, the psychiatrist with his hysteric and his perverts, all have played this game continually since the nineteenth century. These attractions, these evasions, these circular incitements have traced around bodies and sexes, not boundaries not to be crossed, but *perpetual spirals of power and pleasure.*

4. Whence those *devices of sexual saturation* so characteristic of the space and the social rituals of the nineteenth century. People often say that modern society has attempted to reduce sexuality to the couple—the heterosexual and, insofar as possible, legitimate couple. There are equal grounds for saying that it has, if not created, at least outfitted and made to proliferate, groups with multiple elements and a circulating sexuality: a distribution of points of power, hierarchized and placed opposite to one another; "pursued" pleasures, that is, both sought after and searched out; compartmental sexualities that are tolerated or encouraged; proximities that serve as surveillance procedures, and function as mechanisms of intensification; contacts that operate as inductors. This is the way things worked in the case of the family, or rather the household, with parents, children, and in some instances, servants. Was the nineteenth-century family really a monogamic and conjugal cell? Perhaps to a certain extent. But it was also a network of pleasures and powers linked together at multiple points and according to transformable relationships. The separation of grown-

ups and children, the polarity established between the parents' bedroom and that of the children (it became routine in the course of the century when working-class housing construction was undertaken), the relative segregation of boys and girls, the strict instructions as to the care of nursing infants (maternal breast-feeding, hygiene), the attention focused on infantile sexuality, the supposed dangers of masturbation, the importance attached to puberty, the methods of surveillance suggested to parents, the exhortations, secrets, and fears, the presence—both valued and feared—of servants: all this made the family, even when brought down to its smallest dimensions, a complicated network, saturated with multiple, fragmentary, and mobile sexualities. To reduce them to the conjugal relationship, and then to project the latter, in the form of a forbidden desire, onto the children, cannot account for this apparatus which, in relation to these sexualities, was less a principle of inhibition than an inciting and multiplying mechanism. Educational or psychiatric institutions, with their large populations, their hierarchies, their spatial arrangements, their surveillance systems, constituted, alongside the family, another way of distributing the interplay of powers and pleasures; but they too delineated areas of extreme sexual saturation, with privileged spaces or rituals such as the classroom, the dormitory, the visit, and the consultation. The forms of a nonconjugal, nonmonogamous sexuality were drawn there and established.

Nineteenth-century "bourgeois" society—and it is doubtless still with us—was a society of blatant and fragmented perversion. And this was not by way of hypocrisy, for nothing was more manifest and more prolix, or more manifestly taken over by discourses and institutions. Not because, having tried to erect too rigid or too general a barrier against sexuality, society succeeded only in giving rise to a whole perverse outbreak and a long pathology of the sexual instinct. At issue, rather, is the type of power it brought to bear on the body and on sex. In point of fact, this power had neither the form of the law, nor the effects of the taboo. On the contrary, it acted by multiplication of singular sexualities. It did not set boundaries for sexuality; it extended the various forms of sexuality, pursuing them according to lines of indefinite penetration. It did not exclude sexuality, but included it in the body as a mode of specification of individuals. It did not seek to avoid it; it attracted its varieties by means of spirals in which pleasure and power reinforced one another. It did not set up a barrier; it provided places of maximum saturation. It produced and determined the sexual mosaic. Modern society is perverse, not in spite of its puritanism or as if from a backlash provoked by its hypocrisy; it is in actual fact, and directly, perverse.

In actual fact. The manifold sexualities—those which appear with the different ages (sexualities of the infant or the child), those which become fixated on particular tastes or practices (the sexuality of the invert, the gerontophile, the fetishist), those which, in a diffuse manner, invest relationships (the sexuality of doctor and patient, teacher and student, psychiatrist and mental patient), those which haunt spaces (the sexuality of the home, the school, the prison)— all form the correlate of exact procedures of power. We must not imagine that all these things that were formerly tolerated attracted notice and received a pejorative designation when the time came to give a regulative role to the one type of sexuality that was capable of re-

producing labor power and the form of the family. These polymorphous conducts were actually extracted from people's bodies and from their pleasures; or rather, they were solidified in them; they were drawn out, revealed, isolated, intensified, incorporated, by multifarious power devices. The growth of perversions is not a moralizing theme that obsessed the scrupulous minds of the Victorians. It is the real product of the encroachment of a type of power on bodies and their pleasures. It is possible that the West has not been capable of inventing any new pleasures, and it has doubtless not discovered any original vices. But it has defined new rules for the game of powers and pleasures. The frozen countenance of the perversions is a fixture of this game.

Directly. This implantation of multiple perversions is not a mockery of sexuality taking revenge on a power that has thrust on it an excessively repressive law. Neither are we dealing with paradoxical forms of pleasure that turn back on power and invest it in the form of a "pleasure to be endured." The implantation of perversions is an instrument-effect: it is through the isolation, intensification, and consolidation of peripheral sexualities that the relations of power to sex and pleasure branched out and multiplied, measured the body, and penetrated modes of conduct. And accompanying this encroachment of powers, scattered sexualities rigidified, became stuck to an age, a place, a type of practice. A proliferation of sexualities through the extension of power; an optimization of the power to which each of these local sexualities gave a surface of intervention: this concatenation, particularly since the nineteenth century, has been ensured and relayed by the countless economic interests which, with the help of medicine, psychiatry, prostitution, and pornography, have tapped into both this analytical multiplication of pleasure and this optimization of the power that controls it. Pleasure and power do not cancel or turn back against one another; they seek out, overlap, and reinforce one another. They are linked together by complex mechanisms and devices of excitation and incitement.

We must therefore abandon the hypothesis that modern industrial societies ushered in an age of increased sexual repression. We have not only witnessed a visible explosion of unorthodox sexualities; but—and this is the important point—a deployment quite different from the law, even if it is locally dependent on procedures of prohibition, has ensured, through a network of interconnecting mechanisms, the proliferation of specific pleasures and the multiplication of disparate sexualities. It is said that no society has been more prudish; never have the agencies of power taken such care to feign ignorance of the thing they prohibited, as if they were determined to have nothing to do with it. But it is the opposite that has become apparent, at least after a general review of the facts: never have there existed more centers of power; never more attention manifested and verbalized; never more circular contacts and linkages; never more sites where the intensity of pleasures and the persistency of power catch hold, only to spread elsewhere.

Notes

1. Carl Westphal, *Archiv für Neurologie,* 1870.

From *Homos*

Leo Bersani

Homosexual-heterosexual, masculinity-femininity, man-woman: the only proper way of thinking about these categories, many now think, is to investigate their cultural determinants. The dating of homosexuality was a momentous event because it initiated the study of how culture regulates identity. In a recent volume of essays on the controversy between social constructionism and essentialism, Edward Stein defines constructionism as "the view that there are no objective, culture-independent categories of sexual orientation—no one is, independent of a culture, a heterosexual or homosexual."[1] As this suggests, the most radical element in constructionist studies is to question the given or natural status of *heterosexuality*. No longer the stable norm from which same-sex desire deviates (so that the problem is always how the norm was abandoned and how it may be recaptured), heterosexuality, as Lee Edelman puts it, constitutes "a psychic economy that defines itself *against* the historically available category of the 'homosexual.'"[2] The latter would be the invention necessary to keep the always shaky construction of heterosexuality intact. Not only did homosexuals find their existence and identity within the categories from which they had been fashioned by straight society; they were also a distinctively heterosexual fantasy, the internally excluded difference that cements heterosexual identity.

Does this mean that lurking behind heterosexuality is a more "original" homosexuality, a same-sex sex drive that the invention of homosexuality helps to repress? That we may be inclined to answer this question in the negative—or, more effectively, simply to dismiss the question—indicates how far we have come from defending homosexuality on the basis of a presumably natural bisexuality or, even better, polymorphously perverse sexuality. Psychoanalysis has been of great service in the mounting of these defenses. Freud spoke of the repression of a primary bisexuality in all human beings in the normative maturation of desire (and its "satisfactory" climax in genital heterosexuality), and recent critics have emphasized the extent to which, according to Freud himself, the heterosexual denouement of infantile drives is a fragile, defensive, inescapably neurotic resolution to the "series of psychic traumas" that constitute the Oedipus complex.[3] But most of these liberalizing arguments leave intact the fundamental homosexual-heterosexual dichotomy. Since, as Judith Butler has pointed out, bisexuality is conceptualized by Freud in terms of feminine and masculine "dispositions" that have heterosexual aims (it is in desiring like a woman that a boy sees his father as an object of sexual love), bisexuality is simply "the coincidence of two heterosexual desires within a single psyche."[4] As for the polymorphously perverse, while it values free-floating sexuality, its promoters do not attack the idea of a maturational process, where identities are constructed. That process remains as a legitimate description of psychic history; what changes is the most desirable holding position.[5]

We have become far more ambitious: we want to study the effects, and question the necessity, of *all* gendered oppositions. Philosophically, this means deconstructing the assumption that, as

Michael Warner puts it, "gender is the phenomenology of difference itself."[6] That assumption has been shown to operate as the epistemological given even in the purportedly neutral descriptions of the natural sciences. Bonnie Spanier's feminist analysis of the field of molecular biology has uncovered "inaccurate and masculinist superimpositions of Western sex/gender systems onto organisms at the cellular and molecular levels." In tracing "the propensity for and tenacity of genderizing nongendered beings" (for instance, bacteria), Spanier convincingly argues that "the scientific definition of sex—the exchange of genetic material between organisms—is confused with the cultural sense of sex—a sexual act between a male and a female in which the male is the initiator who makes the sex act happen and who donates genetic material while the female is the passive recipient."[7] Such demonstrations lend credibility to Monique Wittig's claim—which we might at first consider to be as ideologically biased as the culture she criticizes—that "heterosexuality is always already there within all mental categories." It is "*the* social contract . . . a political regime." Beginning with Aristotle's *Politics,* in which the first two examples of "those which are ineffective without each other [and therefore] must be unified in a pair" are male and female and ruler and ruled, the heterosexual relationship "has been the parameter of all hierarchical relations."[8]

What Wittig calls the "straight mind" would be more easily recognizable as a political regime if she admitted a difference between heterosexual and heterosexist. But she sees the category of the heterosexual itself as a political arrangement. It is not that we have been ruled by bad heterosexuals; the need to be identified as heterosexual is already a heterosexist position. Wittig gives some plausibility to her claim by defining that need in materialist terms: heterosexuality stabilizes class oppression as a permanent fact of human nature. It creates a ruling class exempt from historical vicissitudes (which frequently redistribute power: from the nobility to the bourgeoisie, from the bourgeoisie to the proletariat). "Men" and "women" in Wittig's

radical argument are political creations designed to give a biological mandate to social arrangements in which one group of human beings oppresses another. Relations among people are always constructed, and the question to be asked is not which ones are the most natural, but rather what interests are served by each construction. Thus, glossing Wittig's gloss of Aristotle, we could say that she sees the first example in the *Politics* as both dictated by and legitimating the second: the case of male and female naturalizes the relation between ruler and ruled as one that must take place. The ruled is as ineffective without the ruler as the implicitly ruled female is without a male ruler; an elementary linguistic axiom (without "ruled" we wouldn't know what "ruler" means, just as "no" gives sense to "yes") is surreptitiously promoted to a political axiom, that the domination of one group by another is a necessary social structure.

The most interesting (and, given our religion of diversity, courageous) aspect of this argument is Wittig's suspicion of difference. She goes further than protesting the equation of gender with the phenomenology of difference itself. The "different-other" is always—would anyone call this a coincidence?—in the inferior position: "Men are not different, whites are not different, nor are the masters. But the blacks, as well as the slaves, are." She concludes: "The concept of difference has nothing ontological about it. It is only the way that the masters interpret a historical situation of domination. The function of difference is to mask at every level the conflicts of interest, including ideological ones."[9]

The straight mind valorizes difference. While you obviously don't have to be straight to think straight, Wittig's association of heterosexuality with a hierarchical view of difference could be defended psychoanalytically. Kenneth Lewes, writing from a Freudian perspective, argues that a primarily heterosexual orientation of desire is, for the little boy, the result of a flight to the father following a horrified retreat from women.[10] Male heterosexuality would be a *traumatic* privileging of difference. Moreover, to the extent that the perception of difference is, for all human subjects, traumatizing, it is perhaps necessarily accompanied by a defensively hierarchical attribution of value. Wittig's remark that the different is always in an inferior position would be justified by this originally self-protective devaluation of a threatening otherness. The cultural consolidation of heterosexuality is grounded in its more fundamental, nonreflective construction as the compulsive repetition of a traumatic response to difference.

The straight mind might be thought of as a sublimation of this privileging of difference. If its achievements in the history of civilization are far more impressive, and civilizing, than Wittig would allow, it has also developed, and made "natural," a system of thinking in which differences are maintained largely through a persistent habit of hierarchical placement. If it is difficult, within this system, to think of differences nonantagonistically, it is because, as I suggested, antagonism is bound up in the very origins of differential perception. Dialectical thinking and dialogue seek to effect reconciliations between opposed terms, but these reconciliations may require the transcendence or even the annihilation of the differential terms. The straight mind thinks alone; as the history of philosophy demonstrates, the thinking of distinctions (that is, philosophical thought) performatively establishes the distinctness, and the distinction, of the thinker. Distinctiveness and distinction: the philosophical performance can't help conferring value on itself, for that value is the very sign of its distinctness and its defense against an "outside" dominated by the assumption that the world, the real, can be an object of thought, can be described, measured, known. So the tonal sign of the straight mind is its seriousness: differences are validated by the thinker's demonstration of how seriously he takes his own statements—and this may be the only validation we can give to the philosophic myth of truth.

It could of course be objected that the straight mind is nothing less than the human mind. Rather than argue for the truth-value of Wittig's argument (which would be to validate it by the very criteria she implicitly attributes to

straight thinking), let's assign it the heuristic value of opening up a new line of inquiry. Is there another way of thinking? Could we authenticate the idea of the straight mind by demonstrating the possibility of thinking outside it? To a certain extent, those designated as homosexuals have acquiesced in the identity thrust upon them. But even that passivity creates a certain divorce from the straight mind that has invented them, clears a space, first of all, for reflection on the heterosexual identity from which they are being excluded. More interestingly, the possibility arises of enacting an alternative to the straight mind. For we are in effect being summoned—unintentionally, to be sure, and the cue provided is still merely etymological—to rethink economies of human relations on the basis of homo-ness, of sameness. Is there a specificity in homo-ness, or, in other terms, how is sameness different?

By this question we do risk repeating the operation I've just criticized with nothing more than a shift in the privileged term of difference. Instead of making the privileging of difference the superior term in the homo-heterosexual opposition we are simply putting it in the inferior position and replacing it with a different structure of relationality. Yet there may be no other way to resist the reduction of homosexuality to the system that would put it down. My argument is that by not accepting and radically reworking the different identity of sameness— by rejecting the whole concept of identity—we risk participating in the homophobic project that wants to annihilate us. Only an emphasis on the specifics of sameness can help us to avoid collaborating in the disciplinary tactics that would make us invisible. In other words, there *is* a "we." But in our anxiety to convince straight society that we are only some malevolent invention and that we can be, like you, good soldiers, good parents, and good citizens, we seem bent on suicide. By erasing our identity we do little more than reconfirm its inferior position within a homophobic system of differences.

Wittig, having laid the basis for precisely the kind of adventure I propose, nonetheless derails that adventure by refusing to grant any sexual specificity to gayness. Her suspicion of difference is so rigorously maintained that she lends herself—unfortunately, for her work is important—to charges of metaphysical quackery. She recasts homosexuality outside the parameters of sexual difference. She is less concerned to collapse the opposition between heterosexual and homosexual than to deconstruct the difference between the sexes that biologically authenticates that opposition. Heterosexuality does not merely privilege different-sex desire over same-sex desire; it promotes the myth that there really is a difference between the sexes. The truly villainous categories are "man" and "woman"; within that opposition heterosexuality grounds itself as natural and stigmatizes homosexuality as a narcissistic rejection of the other. Thus, "the refusal to become (or to remain) heterosexual always meant to refuse to become a man or a woman, consciously or not." Lesbianism has to be redefined in terms far more radical than those provided by the anodyne notion of a "lesbian continuum," which merely allows the category to cover a broad spectrum of relations (sexual and nonsexual) among women. Wittig, in a totally logical and, for many, insane move, asserts: "it would be incorrect to say that lesbians associate, make love, live with women, for 'woman' has meaning only in heterosexual systems of thought and heterosexual economic systems. Lesbians are not women."[11]

What are they, then? In an interesting, largely sympathetic discussion of Wittig, Judith Butler notes that for Wittig only by "effectively lesbianizing the entire world can the compulsory order of heterosexuality be destroyed." Somehow homosexuality is "radically unconditioned by heterosexual norms," and related to its opposite only as an act of protest.[12] Foucault's "reverse discourse" is cut off from that which, for Foucault, made it possible: the production and marginalizing of a homosexual identity by heterosexual power structures. Wittig sees lesbians as socially conditioned only in the sense that heterosexual society compels them to discover their autonomy, and so lesbianism comes per-

ilously close to being a product of nature. We could even say that nature is also hidden at the other extreme. Man *and* woman are heterosexual inventions for Wittig, but who or what, exactly, were the heterosexuals who invented them? The answer has to be "man," since the categories of sex, according to Wittig, were created in order to ensure male domination over women. Then this means that there were men preceding the creation of man. Who were these men, what were they like? If there were "men" before heterosexual "man," what could have motivated them to become that man, except an oppressive intention characterizing that which they had not yet become? At both ends of history, there is something ahistorical: the "afterwards" of the homosexual protest and, more obscurely, the inconceivable "before" necessary to create "man" and "woman" (without that "before," the categories have to be given, natural). Indeed, for Wittig the history of man and woman is fundamentally an ontological fall. Gender seeks to divide originally undivided Being.[13] There are therefore no attributes to be sought in sameness; Wittig is as uninterested in a gay or lesbian identity as she is in femininity or female writing. Homosexuality in her thought is unconditioned because it is a metaphysical category.

So extraordinarily privileged, homosexuality becomes empirically unrecognizable. To say that it designates same-gender desire would be to admit the very categories Wittig tells us to destroy. Finally, she sees very well that the ultimate refuge of those categories is the human body. Particular cultural definitions of man and woman can be challenged without the categories themselves being put into question. Even the repudiation of all notions of masculinity and femininity can leave the distinction between male and female standing. An irreducible bodily binary, it could be said, has been used as the pretext for factitious, ideologically motivated distinctions between feminine and masculine. This would be sensible, but Wittig is, conceptually and politically, far more ambitious. She argues that the body is never merely given; it too is constructed. And the construction is primarily linguistic; the sexual hierarchizing of the body by language is the precondition for the entire system of sexual differences. As Butler puts it: "That penis, vagina, breasts, and so forth, are *named* sexual parts is both a restriction of the erogenous body to those parts and a fragmentation of the body as a whole."[14] Heterosexuality will rise again and again from the ashes of our cultural struggles as long as the heterosexual body remains intact. Thus the violence of Wittig's fiction, in which bodies are (at least textually) torn apart, dismembered, so that they may be configured and eroticized anew. Wittig could be thought of as a Foucauldian warrior, far more guerrilla-like (to borrow the title of one of her books) in taking up Foucault's cause of a new economy of the body's pleasures than Foucault himself ever was. Wittig the martyr, ready to sacrifice her own body to the logic of her lesbian passion: at an incomparably absurd and poignant moment during a lecture at Vassar College, Wittig, asked whether she had a vagina, answered no. That nasty question instantaneously created Wittig as a woman (thus condensing centuries of heterosexual culture's work); her answer, however, just as rapidly reinscribed "lesbian" on her body, effectively erasing the cultural sign and stigma of "woman."

*   *   *

It is doubtful that Wittig herself realizes how politically nonviable such self-erasures are. Judith Butler's *Gender Trouble* is a brilliant attempt to fit some of the radical aspects of Wittig's thought into a workable political program. Echoing Wittig, Butler asks: "To what extent does the category of women achieve stability and coherence only in the context of the heterosexual matrix?" Recognizing the importance of how we think about the body for any successful resistance to the assignment of gendered identities, Butler cites feminist critics of the field of molecular biology whose work suggests that "gendered meanings frame the hypothesis and the reasoning of those biomedical inquiries that seek to establish 'sex' for us as it is

prior to the cultural meanings that it acquires." If even the mundane fact of sex assignment never operates independently of cultural determinants, then we are justified in rethinking the ways in which our bodies are culturally mapped, and in particular how their boundaries are drawn. The description of bodies in terms of binary sex depends on "the cultural discourse that takes external genitalia to be the sure signs of sex," a discourse that itself serves "the social organization of sexual reproduction through the construction of the clear and unequivocal identities and positions of sexed bodies with respect to each other." Citing Mary Douglas' argument in *Purity and Danger* that "the body is a model that can stand for any bounded system" and that "its boundaries can represent any boundaries which are threatened or precarious," Butler emphasizes the dangers for the social system of "permeable bodily boundaries." Homosexual sex—especially anal sex between men—is a threatening "boundary-trespass," a site of danger and pollution for the social system represented synechdochally by the body.[15]

Any activity or condition that exposes the permeability of bodily boundaries will simultaneously expose the factitious nature of sexual differences as they are postulated within the heterosexual matrix. All this is consistent with Wittig's devaluation of difference and her interest in "exploding" the heterosexually sexed body in order to experiment with new ways of being a body and, correlatively, with new cultural orders. Butler separates herself from Wittig in her recognition that the lesbian (and gay male?) body cannot be constructed entirely outside the heterosexuality it would subvert. In insisting on a subversive "resignifying" of heterosexuality rather than its "thoroughgoing displacement," Butler relocates homosexuality itself within the field of cultural politics. So she looks favorably on those gay and lesbian discourses in which terms such as queens, bitches, femmes, girls, dyke queer, and fag are prominent, since they effectively redeploy and destabilize the derogatory categories of homosexual identity.

Within this program of subversive appropria-tion and parodistic redeployment of the domi-nant culture's styles and discourse, drag takes on extraordinary value. In performing a dissocia-tion "not only between sex and performance, but sex and gender, and gender and perfor-mance," drag presumably reveals the original gendered body as itself performative. "*In imitat-ing gender, drag implicitly reveals the imitative structure of gender itself—as well as its contin-gency*" (Butler's emphasis). It invites us to free our subsequent gender experience from what we might have thought of, until the moment of drag's liberating lesson, as an immutable pri-mary gender identification. In *Gender Trouble,* drag appears to satisfy the criteria for a viable politics of resistance, one that Butler opposes to the ideality of Wittig's revolutionary lesbian body: "the normative focus for gay and lesbian practice ought to be on the subversive and paro-dic redeployment of power rather than on the impossible fantasy of its full-scale transcen-dence."[16]

But how subversive is parody? Butler's argu-ment against unequivocal gendered identities is most powerful when it is seen as a strategic re-sponse to the social emphasis on such identities and the terror of trespassing body boundaries. As an assault on *any* coherent identity, it fore-closes the possibility of a gay or lesbian speci-ficity (erasing along the way the very disci-pline—gay and lesbian studies—within which the assault is made): resistance to the heterosex-ual matrix is reduced to more or less naughty imitations of that matrix. At its worst, the em-phasis on parody in *Gender Trouble* has the ef-fect of exaggerating the subversive potential of merely inane behavior. Butler finds that when the gay owners of a neighborhood restaurant, having gone on vacation, put out a sign reading "She's overworked and needs a rest," they are multiplying "possible sites of application" of the feminine, revealing "the arbitrary relation be-tween the signifier and the signified" and desta-bilizing and mobilizing the sign.[17] Heavy stuff for some silly and familiar campiness. Fur-thermore, the politics of parody necessarily un-derplays the elements of longing and venera-

tion in parodistic displays. The leather queen and D. A. Miller's "gay male macho body" are parodistic somewhat at their own expense: if their effect is to parody that which they wor-ship, it is, in the first case, because the tough gay in leather *is* a queen (an involuntary parody of the "real thing," which he worships) and, in the second case, because erotic desire *must* compli-cate the display of muscles with a message of fuckability.

Then, too, the parodistic intentions of the down-and-out drag queens documented in Jennie Livingston's documentary film on Harlem drag balls, *Paris Is Burning,* were all in the minds of the middle-class academic analysts. The drag queens certainly resignified the domi-nant culture, but in ways that could only fortify that culture's dominance. The loving and loyal "families" they constituted could, I suppose, be thought of as an implicit critique of the frequent lack of love and loyalty in the heterosexually in-stitutionalized family, but they remain tributes to the heterosexual ideal of the family itself. And even that critique was nothing more than the in-cidental side effect of what was meant to be a temporary holding position. The point for the drag queens is to get out of the drag family and become a success in the real (straight) fashion and entertainment world (as Willi Ninja did); for those who don't make that move, destitution and even death (as in the case of Venus Xtravaganza) can be counted on to break up the familial inti-macies. The resignifying of heterosexual power in *Paris Is Burning* is really a tribute to that power. It shows how effectively American society can neutralize its margins: in their pathetically minute attention to the styles of a power from which they have been permanently excluded, the oppressed perform nothing more subversive than their own submission to being brain-washed, safely sequestered, and, if necessary, readied for annihilation.

Paris Is Burning reminds us that drag is not al-ways fun and games or the fashion statement of those middle-class gay men who wear skirts out to dinner. The historical and ideological critique of identity surely deserves to inspire more than a taste for crossdressing. In all fairness to Butler, I should say that there has been less emphasis on parody in her recent work than in *Gender Trouble.* She has pulled back from the implication in that book (variously applauded and assailed by her readers) that we can perform ourselves out of gender. "For sexuality," she now argues, "cannot be summarily made or unmade."[18] Rejecting a "voluntarist" account of gender, she writes: "The misapprehension about gender performativity is this: that gender is a choice, or that gender is a role, or that gender is a construction that one puts on, as one puts on clothes in the morning, that there is a 'one' who is prior to this gender, a one who goes to the wardrobe of gender and decides with deliberation which gender it will be today."[19] This misapprehension sounds like a somewhat exasperated parody of *Gender Trouble,* which is understandable given the enthusiastic simplifications of that difficult and frequently abstract work by anti-identitarian activists.

It is nonetheless significant that Butler now emphasizes the constraints on performativity. *Paris Is Burning,* for example, "calls into question whether parodying the dominant norms is enough to displace them; indeed, whether the denaturalization of gender cannot be the very vehicle for a reconsolidation of hegemonic norms." Drag is now, "at best," "a site of a certain ambivalence," although it remains "subversive to the extent that it reflects on the imitative structure by which hegemonic gender is itself produced and disputes heterosexuality's claim on naturalness and originality."[20] The appropriation of hegemonic norms partly subverts them and partly reidealizes them.

These sensible qualifications, however, reveal how dependent on the norms even the utopian subversiveness of *Gender Trouble* was, for the *practice* of reappropriation and attempted resignification is bound to reveal the power of the norms—a power historically fortified by the numerous agencies and networks in which it is embedded—to resist resignification. More exactly, resignification cannot destroy; it merely presents to the dominant culture spectacles of politically impotent disrespect. Is this truly subversive, and, more fundamentally, what does

subversive mean? Subversion, still a central term in Butler's thinking, means first of all, according to the dictionary, overthrowing a system, but in current academic political discourse it seems to mean something much weaker than that, referring to behavior that undermines generally accepted principles. It is, in any case, extremely doubtful that resignification, or redeployment, or hyperbolic miming, will ever overthrow anything. These mimetic activities are too closely imbricated in the norms they continue. As long as the cues for subversion are provided by the objects to be subverted, reappropriation may be delayed but is inevitable: reappropriation, and reidealization. Butler rather touchingly sees in the kinship in the various "houses" to which the drag queens of *Paris Is Burning* belong a lesson for all of us who live outside the heterosexual family. Though she has said that she doesn't think of those relations as simply providing a new and better version of the family, her description of the houses—as mothering, rearing, caring, teaching, sheltering, enabling—is pretty much a catalogue of traditional family values:

> These men "mother" one another, "house" one another, "rear" one another, and the resignification of the family through these terms is not a vain or useless imitation, but the social and discursive building of community, a community that binds, cares, and teaches, that shelters and enables. This is doubtless a cultural reelaboration of kinship that anyone outside of the privilege of heterosexual family (and those within those "privileges" who suffer there) needs to see, to know, and to learn from, a task that makes none of us who are outside of heterosexual "family" into absolute outsiders to this film. Significantly, it is in the elaboration of kinship forged through a resignification of the very terms which effect our exclusion and abjection that such a resignification creates the discursive and social space for community, that we see an appropriation of the terms of domination that turns them toward a more enabling future.[21]

Furthermore, the houses sustain their members "in the face of dislocation, poverty, homelessness." But the structures that sustain those ills are in no way threatened or subverted; here re-signification is little more than a consolatory community of victims.

Notes

1. Edward Stein, "Conclusion: The Essentials of Constructionism and the Construction of Essentialism," *Forms of Desire*, p. 340.

2. Lee Edelman, *Homographesis: Essays in Gay Literary and Cultural Theory* (New York: Routledge, 1994), p. 39. In an analysis of the 1944 film *Laura* in this same volume (and especially of the function of the Clifton Webb character, Waldo), Edelman speaks of the gay man as "both *necessary* to confirm the 'integrity' of the face of male heterosexuality and *intolerable* in so far as his presence is a reminder of the fictionality of that face" (p. 238). Further, in a stunning essay on Alfred Hitchcock's *Rope*, D. A. Miller argues for the "social utility" of castration anxiety in maintaining a heterosexual male identity. Far from being the anxiety-ridden property of the woman and the homosexual, castration may be *needed* in order to generate, in the straight man, the fear and the comfort that keep him securely straight. *Rope* raises the frightening possibility that being fucked does *not* entail castration (so that "homosexuality would be characterized not by a problematics of castration, but on the contrary by an exemption from one"). More terrifying than the fear of castration is the "oddly compatible fear of the negation of castration." Miller, "Anal *Rope*," in *Inside/Out: Lesbian Theories, Gay Theories,* ed. Diana Fuss (New York: Routledge, 1991), pp. 135–38.

3. As Kenneth Lewes writes, "It is not accurate to speak of 'normal' or 'natural' development in the case of the Oedipus complex, since these terms suggest an orderly efflorescence of possibilities inherent in the individual before he enters the oedipal stage. The mechanisms of the Oedipus complex are really a series of psychic traumas, and all results of it are neurotic compromise formations. Since even optimal development is the result of trauma, the fact that a certain development results from a 'stunting' or 'blocking' or 'inhibition' of another possibility does not distinguish it from other developments. So all results of the Oedipus complex are traumatic, and, for similar reasons, all are 'normal.'" Lewes, *The Psychoanalytic Theory of Male Homosexuality* (New York: New American Library, 1988), p. 82. See also

the essay by John Fletcher, "Freud and His Uses: Psychoanalysis and Gay Theory," in *Coming On Strong: Gay Politics and Culture,* ed. Simon Shepherd and Mick Wallis (London: Unwin Hyman, 1989).

4. Judith Butler, *Gender Trouble: Feminism and the Subversion of Identity* (New York: Routledge, 1990), pp. 60–61.

5. Jonathan Dollimore makes an argument for the perverse "not as a unitary, pre-social libido, or an original plenitude, but as a transgressive agency inseparable from a dynamic intrinsic to social process." This dynamic "generates instabilities within repressive norms." Dollimore, *Sexual Dissidence: Augustine to Wilde, Freud to Foucault* (Oxford: Clarendon Press, 1991), p. 33.

6. Michael Warner, "Homo-Narcissism; or, Heterosexuality," in *Engendering Men: The Question of Male Feminist Criticism,* ed. Joseph A. Boone and Michael Cadden (New York: Routledge, 1990), p. 200.

7. Bonnie B. Spanier, "'Lessons' From 'Nature': Gender Ideology and Sexual Ambiguity in Biology," in *Body Guards: The Cultural Politics of Gender Ambiguity,* ed. Julia Epstein and Kristina Straub (New York: Routledge, 1991), pp. 334, 336.

8. Monique Wittig, *The Straight Mind and Other Essays* (Boston: Beacon Press, 1992), pp. 42–43.

9. Ibid., p. 29.

10. Lewes, *Psychoanalytic Theory of Male Homosexuality,* p. 80.

11. Wittig, *Straight Mind,* pp. 5, 13, 32.

12. Butler, *Gender Trouble,* pp. 120–121.

13. "Gender is an ontological impossibility because it tries to accomplish the division of Being. But Being as being is not divided." Wittig, *Straight Mind,* p. 81.

14. Butler, *Gender Trouble,* p. 114.

15. Ibid., pp. 5, 109–110, 132.

16. Ibid., pp. 121–22, 137, 124.

17. Ibid., p. 122.

18. Butler, *Bodies That Matter: On the Discursive Limits of "Sex"* (New York: Routledge, 1993), p. 94.

19. Butler, "Critically Queer," *GLQ: A Journal of Lesbian and Gay Studies,* 1.1 (1993), 21.

20. Butler, *Bodies That Matter,* p. 125. In a provocative review of *Paris Is Burning,* bell hooks has criticized the "imperial overseeing position" adopted by the filmmaker Livingston. See "Is Paris Burning," Z, Sisters of the Yam column (June 1991).

21. Butler, *Bodies That Matter,* p. 137.

Homosexuality and the Black Male

Robert Staples

Male friendships were regarded once by Aristotle as the most perfect of friendships. Indeed, masculine friendships were the only ones that he considered, with the exception of a brief allusion to the possibility of friendship between husband and wife. The average woman, in ancient Greece, was regarded as too ignorant, intellectually, to be capable of deep friendship with anyone.[1] The present state of male friendships is far from what Aristotle celebrated. According to other research studies and my own, single males have fewer meaningful friendships than most women, with either sex. A couple of reasons for the differences are clear. Women are more likely to be socialized into a nurturant role that complements the friendship role than are men who maintain a certain emotional distance from other men due to the fear of being labeled homosexual or weak.[2]

Homosexuality is the most difficult behavior of blacks to trace historically. Wherever social contact between persons of the same sex has existed, there has probably been some homosexual behavior. In pre-colonial Africa there was traditionally a division of labor, separate initiation training for males and females, in addition to economic and socio-political associations organized along gender lines. The practice, for instance, of some African tribes of sending young male children off to separate compounds may have produced some homosexual behavior. Such practices are rarely noted in the literature on African society. Instead, a noted Africanist asserts: "Although no proper studies of the problem have been made in traditional African societies, homosexual practices seem to be rare, or only confined to boys and girls before marriage. Part of the reason for this is that the psychological atmosphere from childhood to adolescence prepares one towards the goal of marriage, and a person, therefore, directs his sexual development towards relationship with the opposite sex."[3]

One of the effects of the sexual revolution is the increase in "visible" homosexuality. It is one area in the changing of sexual values that has significant black participation. However, the increase in people assuming overtly gay lifestyles is largely confined to black males. It is not known how many people in the United States are exclusively homosexual, but estimates range from 5 to 20 percent of the total population. The nation's prisons are the main places where homosexual preferences are evident. Some black men who acquired their homosexual behavior as prison inmates because of the unavailability of women continue it after their release. Their reasons for turning to homosexual lifestyles vary, ranging from a desire to escape family responsibilities to acquiring money through prostitution. An interesting side aspect of the sexual revolution is the development in San Francisco of "gay liberation" groups that are so politically powerful that few politicians dare run for office without seeking their support.

Despite a shortage of black males, relatively few black women have joined the community as overt lesbians. But since female homosexuals are not as visible as male homosexuals, the number of black lesbians is difficult to determine. As with the black male homosexual,

229

many black lesbians are deeply involved in the white homosexual community.

It is not known whether homosexuality is more or less prevalent in the black population than in the white because there is little data available on the subject for blacks. Some writers have claimed that blacks have a greater incidence of male homosexuality than whites. The reason for their belief is that female-headed households in the black community have resulted in a lack of male role models for male black children.[4] However there is no evidence to support this supposition.

After placing obstacles to self realization in the way of the black male, America then has its bearers of ideology, the social scientists, falsely indict him for his lack of manhood. There are various sociological and psychological studies which purport to show how black males are demasculinized, and suggest in fact, that they may be latent homosexuals. The reason cited is that black males reared in female-centered households are more likely to acquire feminine characteristics because there is no consistent adult male model or image to shape their personalities.[5] One sociologist stated that since black males are unable to enact the masculine role, they tend to cultivate their personalities. In this respect they resemble women who use their personalities to compensate for their inferior status in relation to men.[6]

If the above reasoning seems weak and unsubstantiated, the other studies of black emasculation are equally feeble. Many of the hypotheses about the effeminate character of black men are based on their scores on the Minnesota Multiphasic Inventory Test (MMPI), a psychological instrument that asks the subject to determine how over five hundred simple statements apply to him. Black males score higher than white males on the section which measures femininity. As an indicator of their femininity, the researchers cite the fact that black men more often agreed with such feminine choices as "I would like to be a singer" and "I think I feel more intensely than most people do."[7]

This is the kind of evidence that the dominant society has marshalled to prove the femi-

nization of the black male. The only thing this demonstrates is that white standards cannot always be used in evaluating black behavior. Black people live in another environment, with different ways of thinking, acting and believing from the white, middle class world. Singers such as James Brown and others represent successful role models in the black community. Black male youths aspire to be singers because this appears to be an observable means for obtaining success in this country—not because they are more feminine than white males. In addition, music is an integral part of black culture.

As part of their studies of sexual deviants, the Kinsey group investigated black homosexuality. They found that black men were more comfortable around homosexuals and did not perceive them as any kind of threat to their manhood. Consequently, black homosexuals (male and female) were not as isolated from the black heterosexual population. They were not relegated to their own bars or social cliques. Also, blacks were more likely to be bi-sexual than exclusively homosexual.[8]

The Sexual Solution

Finding a sexual partner is not a crucial or pervasive problem for many black singles, especially women. Achieving regular sexual gratification within the context of an emotionally satisfying relationship is. One alternative lifestyle that purports to resolve this problem is that of homosexuality. I realize the difficulty of positing this behavioral modality as an alternative to conventional marriage, still it is an option that is being discussed and, in some cases, adopted. Whether the increased visibility of homosexuality is due to the shortage of black men or to the conflict in male/female relationships, we do not know; however about 20 of the men we interviewed are homosexual or bisexual. These findings are part of a larger study of 500 black, college educated singles, of whom approximately 110 are males. These findings also could be due to the fact that all our interviews, and a large proportion of the questionnaires, come from the San Francisco Bay Area. In San Francisco itself gays constitute an estimated 25 percent of the adult population. We interviewed no known lesbians and our attempts to include them in the study were unsuccessful. Each quote, unless identified or footnoted comes from my black singles data.

Homosexuality is difficult to discuss as an option for black singles because it remains a subject fraught with controversy. Even understanding the nature of homosexuality is problematic because the research is permeated by bias. On the one hand, there are those who consider homosexuality to be a genetic disorder and everyone affected by it to be a pervert. More recently, there are those who declare homosexuals to be similar to heterosexuals in order to enhance the civil rights of gays. Some would claim that homosexuality cannot be a viable alternative for black singles because that tendency is formed in early childhood. However, we are in agreement with psychiatrist Richard Green who suggests that "at the present time the most one can say about the genesis of homosexuality is that it remains unknown."[9] In interpreting the importance of sexual orientation we might keep in mind the words of Erich Fromm: "the very first thing we notice about anybody is whether that person is male or female. And it's the one thing we never forget. Name, telephone number, profession, politics, all of these details may slip from our memory, but never the individual's sex."[10] Therefore our sexual preference, linked together, is an important source of a person's identity.

Not only have we failed to understand the causes of homosexuality, but we still know little about its nature. It is estimated that 10 percent of the male population is homosexual. Although no reliable figures are available, blacks are assumed to be proportionally representative in that gay population. The majority of gays are assumed to be male, but lesbians maintain a low profile and are less likely to reveal themselves. It appears that the majority of black homosexuals, both men and women, have less than a college education, although they are well represented, or perhaps more visible, in certain middle class occupations. Many live in urban locales where the possibility of discovery is less likely, although they can be found in all environments. Certainly those involved in an openly gay lifestyle live in large cities with sizeable gay populations. Today the most hospitable cities for them in the United States are New York, Los Angeles and San Francisco.

Black Male Homosexuals

A recent study entitled *Homosexualities* by Bell and Weinberg has attempted to refute some of the stereotypes about gays. Their book provides the source for most of our information about black homosexuals. In general they found that black male homosexuals tend to be younger than their white counterparts, with an average age of 27 in contrast to 37 for white males. They had less education and were employed at a lower occupational level than white gays. Members of the black group more often expressed the belief that their homosexuality and homosexual contacts had helped more than hurt their careers. Over two-thirds of black male gays reported they spent less than half of their leisure time by themselves in comparison to half of their white brethren. Both the black and white homosexual men claimed to have more good, close friends than the heterosexual men did. A similar difference existed in attitudes about job satisfaction. Black and white homosexuals expressed greater satisfaction with their jobs than did heterosexual men. About half of the black and white male homosexuals stated they had no regret whatsoever about being homosexual.[11]

It is worth noting that only one fourth of the black gay males said that all their friends were men.[12] The other gays probably constitute a large proportion of the platonic male friends many single women have. They make very good friends for many of these women because they share some of the same interests and they do not view women as sexual objects. A 26 year old gay male artist said:

I enjoy women a lot. I enjoy their companionship without emotional entanglements. I prefer having a platonic relationship with a woman rather than a man. Most of my male friends are gay and our interests overlap too much and we become competitive. I go out to dinners, movies, museums, plays and talk on the telephone with my female friends. They help me keep things in perspective and provide me with a balance to my life. However, they tend to lament the fact that I'm a man lost to them.

Another interesting characteristic of the black gay lifestyle is the extent of their involvement with whites. Over two thirds of the black male homosexuals said that half of their sexual partners had been white.[13] One of our respondents believed race was less important in the gay community. However, he acknowledged that whatever their sexual orientation, whites still have a certain insensitivity to blacks and cultural differences present problems. One black male gay declared that the majority of whites who are homosexually interested in blacks are misfits, that they desire a black mate only because they sense an identity between their own feelings of inferiority and the myth of black inferiority.[14] Whatever the reason, there is certainly some element of racism among white homosexuals. As a black male homosexual reported:

I've learned that in San Francisco's gay bars there's real racism—even overt racism—in terms of just being able to get in gay bars. They ask black gays for three pieces of I.D. with their pictures on them, but they don't ask whites for that. Or, they have a certain quota and after they've filled it, they won't let any Third World people in. And there are still the sexual myths about black people. The myth of the black man as a stud, for example.

Some non-white homosexuals began to confront the racism in gay bars in San Francisco. Since bars are the center of social life for gays, the exclusion of non-whites was of more than passing significance. In November, 1980, more than 20 non-white gays demonstrated in front of a San Francisco gay bar, charging racial discrimination against minority gays. According to a spokesman for the Gay Democratic Club, "Gay bar owners think it's bad for business to encourage minority gay patrons."[15] In the same city a rift is growing between the straight black community and white gays over the increasing displacement of black tenants by gays who are purchasing and renovating homes in the black ghettos. While the practice, known as "gentrification," is a commonplace practice in other cities, the large number of gays buying up homes in black neighborhoods has intensified black hostility to them and created speculation that most low-income blacks will be moved out of the city in a few years.

If black homosexuals stay in the black community they do not necessarily find a high degree of acceptance. Blacks may tolerate but will not openly approve of homosexual behavior. Ministers in the black church have preached that it is unnatural for men to burn for men, and women to burn for women. The A.M.E. church is on record as being strongly opposed to homosexuality.[16] Black physicians have tried to "cure" homosexuality in black patients. A Howard University newspaper called gays "freaks" and condemned the practice as capitalist depravity.[17] However, black male homosexuals were less likely to hide the fact of their homosexuality from their family and friends than their white counterparts.[18] As one black gay reported, "In a lot of ways the black community won't accept homosexuals, but, in a lot of ways I feel blacks will accept gays before the white community does—on a gut level—simply because blacks know what it's like to be oppressed."

Lack of approval by the black community, moreover, is not the only problem faced by male homosexuals. Sexual contacts are often fleeting ones, with one third of the men reported having had at least 500 different sexual partners during the course of their homosexual careers.[19] Despite those large numbers, two thirds of them complained of having trouble finding a suitable sexual partner.[20] Just as in the heterosexual world, youth and attractiveness are highly valued. Most younger gay men tended to rate their sex appeal higher than the older men did.[21] As one young gay male commented, "I hope I don't live much past 50. After that, nobody wants to look at you, and you always have to pay for sex." There was an interesting racial difference between the psychological adjustment of black and white male homosexuals, with the black males more likely to feel less happy at the present time than they did five years ago, to feel more tension and to feel lonely more frequently.[22]

With all these problems, homosexuality seems to be no trouble-free alternative, at least not for black males. Coupled with the stigma is the fact that many problems heterosexuals face are present in the homosexual world. Among them are the problems of finding a compatible partner. A number of gay males complained they were unable to find a compatible male with whom to establish a meaningful relationship. One male, a 35 year-old social worker told us:

Yes, I've lived with a lover in a homosexual relationship. The first four years were wonderful but the last six months were hell. I'm basically a relationship person. But the society reinforces butterfly relationships, where you light one second for sex. He wanted to continue living together but I wasn't willing. He was conventionally middle class while I'm more bohemian. He cares what people think and I don't.

Black Lesbians

Lesbians share the social stigma of their gay male counterparts but there are significant differences between the two groups. One of the reasons that lesbians are less visible could be attributed to the possibility that they are less socially acceptable in the black community. So thinks Audre Lorde, who declares: "If the recent hysterical rejection of lesbians in the black community is based solely upon an aversion to the idea of sexual contact between members of the same sex—why then is the idea of sexual

contact between black men so much more easily accepted, or unremarked."[23] Another black lesbian speaks thus about her oppression:

As a black lesbian I am in a weird situation. I am oppressed not only by society as a whole, but the black community too. The black community looks upon the lesbian as blacks do upon whites. This is particularly true of black males who consider lesbians a threat. Black males think that a lesbian is fair game sexually for anybody, because she can't get a man or is turned off by men.[24]

Those black women who chose lesbianism fared better than their male counterparts. They had fewer transient sexual contacts, for example, most of them had fewer than ten female sexual partners during the course of their homosexual careers and two-thirds of them reported that the majority of their sexual partners had been persons whom they cared about and for whom they had some affection.[25] In the lesbian culture, youthfulness did not carry the importance it had among male homosexuals or heterosexuals. Because members of the same sex are more sensitive to each other's sexual needs, many lesbians reported satisfactory sexual experiences. This was most evident in the fact that lesbians displayed greater skill in performing oral sex than did men engaged in performing oral sex with women.[26] Fewer than two-thirds of the black lesbians reported that they spent less than half of their leisure time alone.[27] Few of the lesbians encountered sexual problems or contracted a venereal disease.[28] However, black lesbians were more likely to report poorer health and more psychosomatic symptoms, to feel lonely more often, and to display more tension and paranoia.[29]

We know no more about the causes of lesbianism than we do about male homosexuality. A theory that covers both groups is that their homosexual orientation emerges in response to past difficulties in heterosexual relationships. It is true that a half of the black lesbians had been married at least once (compared to fewer than 20 percent of black male homosexuals).[30] And some black female singles in our study reported that they had considered a lesbian relationship if their relationship with men did not improve.

According to a 37 year-old teacher: "I'm not ready for homosexuality yet. If men keep playing games with me, I might consider switching in later life. Right now, I still know a few cool dudes." Probably a more typical response to lesbianism is that of a 39 year-old college administrator:

> Don't worry about me and the Daughters of Bilitis. Somehow I don't think deliberately complicating my life like that would net me anything I'm particularly in need of. For that kind of risk I'd have to be *assured* of something really great. Knowing what I know about human beings of both sexes and many races I have little hope that anybody can assure me of anything. So, I'll take my chances with my present lifestyle.

Indications are that most black women live primarily heterosexual lives. Some have recently turned to occasional bisexual experiences. Most of them do this in a clandestine manner, frequently between their serious relationships with men. Some have claimed that there is no such thing as bisexuality, only people who are basically homosexual with the ability to perform heterosexually. But our interviews with psychologists, leaders of women's groups and gay black males confirm a great deal of alternation between partners of different sexual orientations. A number of women reported having sexual experiences with men who were regarded as exclusively homosexual. Some of the women in our sample were formerly married to men who eventually came out of the closet. During the marriage they claimed to have experienced a normal frequency of sex relations. One of our male subjects, a 37 year-old professor said:

> I have considered an alternative lifestyle involving a male partner as well as legal marriage to a woman. I feel that I could do either and be happy. I prefer to do it with a woman for awhile because I would like children—perhaps

later with a man. I'm too conservative to do the both together.

Such an attitude has led some observers of the homosexual scene to speculate that homosexuality is nothing more than a trendy fad. They believe that some black males become homosexuals in order to take advantage of the gay network to gain access to better jobs and other perquisites of homosexuality. Considering the continued liabilities of being gay, such an explanation lacks much credibility. Another reason is given by feminist Michelle Wallace, who observes that, "I don't think that all of these people that are homosexual out here were born that way. I think that men and women are having a lot of problems now with each other and sometimes they think the easiest way to get around that is to go with the same sex: but of course, the same problems appear, because they're having problems with themselves and with people in general."[31]

Summary

Whenever men come into contact, homosexual behavior is a possible outcome. Sometimes it may be temporary activity, such as during the gender exclusive adolescence years, in prisons and among military men. In such cases, homosexual activity is time-contained, a function of the absence of women. American society inadvertently encourages homosexuality by the organization of gender-linked associations. Sports activity, for example, may lead to homosexuality because it brings men together in a common event from which women are largely excluded. According to one anthropologist, the aspects of male bonding in the game make "football a form of ritualized homosexuality. All the physical expression taboos in American society are converted in football into acceptable behavior—fanny patting—and symbolically the very structure of the game."[32]

As for the morality of homosexual behavior, that is not a judgment for this writer or the society to make. There is no reason to judge more harshly the behavior of men in private places than to judge any other deviation from the norm. Certainly it is behavior that has survived the years and constraints on its expression. And, many of our most admired and creative leaders have engaged in it. Recognizing the rights of homosexuals to lead their lives in peace, however, does not preclude the speculation that men indulge in it for a variety of motives, not all of them positive, and that problems exist in the internal structure of the homosexual community.

Notes

1. Works of Aristotle, *Friendship*, Encyclopedia Britannica, Volume 2, 1959, p. 459.

2. Louis M. Verborugge, "Multiplexity in Adult Friendships," paper presented at the American Sociological Association Meeting, New York, August 1976.

3. John S. Mbiti, *Love and Marriage in Africa*, (London: Longman, 1973) p. 35.

4. Robert Staples, "The Myth of the Impotent Black Male," *The Black Scholar* (June 1971):2–9.

5. Thomas Pettigrew, *A Profile of the Negro American*, (Princeton, New Jersey: D. Van Nostrand, 1964) pp. 17–22.

6. E. Franklin Frazier, *Black Bourgeoisie*, (New York, Crowell-Collier, 1962) p. 182.

7. Pettigrew, loc. cit.

8. Personal communication from Wardell Pomeroy, former Associate Director of the Institute for Sex Research, November, 1971.

9. Quoted in the *San Francisco Chronicle*, October 27, 1976, p. 16.

10. Quoted in the *San Francisco Chronicle*, May 19, 1979, p. 33.

11. Alan Bell and Martin Weinberg, *Homosexualities*, (New York: Simon and Schuster, 1978) pp. 34–215.

12. Ibid. p. 173.

13. Ibid. p. 85.

14. Levi Benton, "Case History: I'm a Black Homosexual," *Sexology*, March 1972, pp. 15–18.

15. "Minorities Charging Gay Bars with Bias," The *San Francisco Chronicle*, November 23, 1980, p. 9.

16. "Religious Leaders Say Black Church Untouched by Gay Rights Crusade," *Jet Magazine*, June 13, 1978, p. 8.

17. Jocelyn Johnson, "Faggots, Freaks and Macho Men," *The Hilltop*, February 9, 1979, p. 5.

18. Bell and Weinberg, op. cit. pp. 63–4.

19. Ibid. p. 85.

20. Ibid. p. 117.

21. Ibid. p. 104.

22. Ibid. p. 207.

23. Audre Lorde, "Scratching the Surface: Some Notes on Barriers to Women and Loving," *The Black Scholar*, (April 1978) p. 34.

24. Ann Allen Schockley and Veronica Tucker, "Black Women Discuss Today's Problems: Men, Families, Society," *Southern Voices*, 1 (August-September 1974) p. 18.

25. Bell and Weinberg, op. cit., p. 93.

26. Ibid. p. 105.

27. Sex Team Finds Few Surprises in New Study, *The San Francisco Examiner*, April 17, 1979, p. 6.

28. Bell and Weinberg, ibid. pp. 183–184.

29. Ibid. p. 215.

30. Ibid. p. 167.

31. Quoted in *The Sun Reporter*, August 30, 1979, p. 16.

32. Quoted in the *San Francisco Sunday Examiner and Chronicle*, January 20, 1980, p. c-7.

Powers of Observation: AIDS and the Writing of History

Simon Watney

*In a permanently transitional age we must expect unevenness,
contradictory outcomes, disjunctures, delays, contingencies, uncompleted
projects, overlapping emergent ones.*

> —Stuart Hall, Marxism Today, October 1988

Detachment is itself a moral position.

> —Isaiah Berlin, Four Essays on Liberty

For those actively involved in HIV/AIDS work, the time has not yet arrived for the writing of history. We have other priorities. Our writing tends to be strategic, and often directly instrumental; it provides information; it counters lies; it adapts its voice to its audience; it is as up-to-date as we can make it; it aims to provide the reassurance of reliability; it affirms values and experience that are elsewhere denigrated or denied. It strives to convince and it is almost entirely contingent, on a day-by-day, week-by-week basis. Because we are not observers, but closely engaged participants, we are also aware that our writings constitute their own form of historiography: we cannot however be expected to provide cool appraisal of the constantly changing and unpredictable circumstances in which we find ourselves. We are not dispassionate, and we are not seduced by fantasies about neutrality. As Isaiah Berlin has pointed out:

> The very use of normal language cannot avoid conveying what the author regards as commonplace or monstrous, decisive or trivial, exhilarating or depressing . . . I can say that so many million men were brutally done to death;

or alternatively, that they perished; laid down their lives; were massacred; or simply, that the population of Europe was reduced, or that its average age was lowered; or that many men lost their lives. None of these descriptions . . . is wholly neutral: all carry moral implications. What the historian says will, however careful he may be to use purely descriptive language, sooner or later convey his attitude. Detachment is itself a moral position. The use of neutral language ('Himmler caused many persons to be asphyxiated') conveys its own ethical tone.[1]

Moreover, AIDS has already been narrated many times, in many different genres. We possess an extensive testimonial literature in the form of books written by people living with HIV and AIDS; books written by and about their doctors and leading biomedical researchers; collections of poetry; AIDS fiction; collections of essays; historical accounts, and so on. There is also a vast periodical literature, which may be subdivided in different ways. For example, it is helpful and indeed necessary to contrast the national daily and weekly heterosexual press to the gay press. It is also helpful and necessary to note how, from early on in the history of the epidemic, community-based publications have played a vital role in translating the specialist scientific literature into more accessible and practically useful newsletters. These publications do not however stand on an equal social or economic footing with the *Lancet* or the *New England Journal of Medicine*. In no health crisis in history has the written word played such a central, extensive and heavily contested role. Hence the significance in this context of Isaiah Berlin's insistence that:

> History is not an ancillary activity; it seeks to provide as complete an account as it can of what men do and suffer; to call them men is to ascribe to them values that we must be able to recognise as such, otherwise they are not men for us. Historians cannot therefore (whether they moralise or not) escape from having some position about what matters and how much (even if they do not ask why it matters). This alone is enough to render the notion of a 'value-free' history, as the transcriber *rebus ipsis dictantibus*, an illusion.[2]

Indeed, it is precisely because so many people affected most directly by HIV are not widely regarded as fellow human beings that the question of the historiography of AIDS acquires such significance. AIDS is an especially contested subject because it focuses attention simultaneously on many of the most controversial topics of our times: abortion, reproductive sexual technology, homosexuality, bisexuality, 'the family', 'the nation', race, and so on. The wider public discursive formation surrounding AIDS is thus always heavily over-determined by this attendant litany of contingent issues.

The history and management of the British AIDS epidemic has, unsurprisingly, been largely determined by and in response to the wider disposition of power that we now know as Thatcherism. Considering the cultural roots and terrain of Thatcherism, Stuart Hall has noted how:

> Areas of contestation which may appear, to a more orthodox or conventional reading, to be 'marginal' to the main question, acquire in the perspective of an analysis of 'hegemony', an absolute centrality: questions about moral conduct, about gender and sexuality, about race and ethnicity, about ecological and environmental issues, about cultural and national identity. Thatcherism's search for 'the enemies within'; its construction of the respectable, patriarchal, entrepreneurial subject with 'his' orthodox tastes, inclinations, preferences, opinions and prejudice . . . its rooting of itself inside a particularly narrow, ethnocentric and exclusivist conception of 'national identity'; and its constant attempts to expel symbolically one sector of society after another from the imaginary community of the nation—these are as central to Thatcherism's hegemonic project as the privatisation programme or the assault on local democracy.[3]

Yet rather than relating AIDS to its specific, conjunctural national circumstances, the dominant historiographic tendency on the contrary locates it within a discrete 'history of epidemics' which is itself one tributary of an equally abstracted 'history of medicine'. Thus, for example, Professor Robert M. Swenson concludes a lengthy article on 'Plagues, history and AIDS' with the observation that:

> Although our advanced biotechnology has allowed us to apply sophisticated solutions to the biological problems of AIDS, our human responses have changed little from previous epidemics and hinder us from dealing effectively with many of the social problems that are part of the AIDS epidemic.[4]

In much the same vein, Elizabeth Fee and Professor Daniel M. Fox prefaced their influential anthology *AIDS: The Burdens Of History* with a quotation from Dr Frederick C. Tilney, on the polio epidemic: 'We have learned very little that is new about the disease, but much that is old about ourselves.'[5] The discursive and institutional pressure to articulate AIDS from within a continuous history of epidemics, understood to reflect a uniformly flawed human nature manifested in prejudice and discrimination, thus tends to displace any concrete consideration of the irreducible specificities of HIV and its multiple collisions with the late twentieth century.

In fact, Tilney's quote could hardly be less appropriate to our understanding of this epidemic. For we demonstrably now know far more about the microchemistry and natural history of HIV, than we do about the infinitely complex, unpredictable political, social, and psychological consequences of the epidemic, both in the lives of individuals and entire societies. Rather than inviting us to locate our understanding of the epidemic in the context of the political present and its recent history, Tilney's quotation is used to anchor the epidemic to the type of narrative which contrasts scientific progress to universal and invariant human frailties. Such an approach reveals the stance of the supposedly neutral observer, standing outside the epidemic, surveying its natural history.

Yet the international HIV pandemic is at least as much a socio-political phenomenon as it is biological or medical. AIDS has no 'natural history', at least in the sense of an inevitable, irreversible, biologically driven necessity. On the contrary, it is demonstrably amenable to prevention strategies.[6] Many of these problems seem to point back towards the constitutive metaphor of AIDS as a plague in the early years of the epidemic, a metaphor which many medical historians seem to have followed far too literally. David Black's early popular account of the epidemic, 'The Plague Years', first published in two parts in *Rolling Stone* early in 1985, opens with two quotations. The first, from Proust, depicts homosexual love derived 'not from an ideal of beauty . . . but from an incurable disease'.[7] The second cites Charles Creighton's *History of Epidemics in Britain*:

> The period from 1348 to 1352 [the time of the Black Death in England] is an absolute blank. . . . Most of the monastic chronicles are interrupted at the same point; if there is an entry at all under the year 1349 it is for the most part merely the words *magna mortalitas*.[8]

Thus, on the one hand AIDS is interpreted in the context of a pathological model of homosexuality, and on the other in relation to visions of premodern medical catastrophe. Such framing repeats and reinforces the initial mass-media presentation of the epidemic in the early 1980s as a 'gay plague', together with the implication that it is some kind of judgement, like the Biblical plagues of Egypt. Yet plague metaphors are singularly misleading and inappropriate in relation to AIDS for the simple reason that unlike the Black Death or cholera, HIV is *not* contagious. On the contrary, there is copious evidence concerning how infection may be prevented, by the introduction of needle-exchanges, and an energetic commitment to safer sex education, especially for risk groups—education that recognises and respects people's differing sexual needs and pleasures. Moreover, plague metaphors ignore the plain fact that, with few exceptions, the response to AIDS has not consisted of draconian quarantine measures, mandatory HIV testing, and so on, in spite of the fact that such practices have been widely implemented this century in relation both to contagious diseases such as tuberculosis, and sexually transmitted diseases such as syphilis.

This in itself fuels the suspicion that plague metaphors represent a form of cultural displacement away from other more appropriate interpretive models. In other words, it may be easier, and more convenient, to continue to think of AIDS in relation to the concept of plague, than to institutionalised homophobia and racism for example. The widespread acceptance of plague metaphors of AIDS as the central model for historical analysis only serves to encourage spurious analogies with the history of contagious disease. In this manner historians run the risk of introjecting a profoundly prejudiced model of the epidemic into the very heart of their work. Plague metaphors are not accidental. They embody a particular kind of ideological operation. To take just one example, in 1985 the *Sun* was already able to refute opposition to 'gay plague' interpretations of AIDS, on the grounds that people living with AIDS:

> have only themselves to blame for their terrible plight. But now gay campaigners are trying to turn the argument the other way round and

make the whole community bear some of the guilt. This is nonsense. The term Gay Plague upsets some people, but that effectively is exactly what it is. . . . Homosexual intercourse spreads a killer disease. Lay off it before it's too late.[9]

We may initially respond to such crude assertions in many different ways. We may refute their claims rationally, pointing out that HIV does not target gay men specifically; or any other social constituency. We may point to the great social diversity of the epidemic as it affects different nations and continents. We may argue that most people with AIDS were infected by HIV before anyone knew the virus even existed. We may insist that gay sex does not 'cause' AIDS, and that HIV can only be sexually transmitted by *unprotected* sex, whether anal or vaginal. Yet such rational responses do not begin to come to grips with the *unconscious* of such pronouncements: the wish to blame; the articulation of guilt; the more or less hysterically defensive tone; the imputation of conspiracy to gay men; the drawing of rigid boundaries between licit and illicit sex; the absence of any trace or vestige of concern, or sorrow, or sympathy, or urgency, or any sense whatsoever of AIDS as a vast and terrible human tragedy. The unconscious logic is clear: if AIDS is 'caused' by gay sex, only gay men are at risk, and if gay sex 'causes' AIDS, there is no reason for anyone else to be at all concerned. In this manner HIV is dismissed as a deadly by-product of homosexuality *per se,* and the 'solution' to the epidemic lies in the extinction of gay men. In this context it is also vital to note that homosexuality is imagined as a voluntary desire, a 'deadly choice' which amounts to suicide. It is the fact of sexual diversity which is the real target of such pronouncements, not HIV. From the perspective of homophobic fantasy, gay men must cease to exist. The only tolerable option is heterosexuality or death. When AIDS is depicted in this manner, as an essentially retributive spectacle, questions of government policy, the direction of medical research, or the provision of safer sex education, can all be equally *dismissed as irrelevant.*[10]

Such attitudes are by no means confined to the easily criticised tabloid press. After Elizabeth Taylor recommended the use of condoms at the memorial concert for the singer Freddie Mercury, the *Daily Telegraph* dismissed her advice as 'shamelessly immoral', whilst the *Independent* saw Mercury's death as 'a powerful and distressing cautionary tale'.[11] But a tale cautionary of what? The neglect of gay men's health education in Britain in the 1980s? The homophobia of the British press? It is sometimes assumed that press coverage of the epidemic has 'improved'. Any such opinion ignores the continued widespread confusion surrounding almost every aspect of HIV education, treatment, and degrees of relative risk. If the cultural response to AIDS is interpreted only from the point of view of a larger, general history of epidemics, such issues can be easily neglected, with renewed recourse to the familiar sorrowful note of disapproval concerning the supposed continuities of human 'folly'. Such an approach merely sustains the discursive construction of AIDS as plague by other means. In this manner the distancing, brutal prejudice of the UK press may be directly translated into articulate, scholarly, homophobic evasions on the part of the historian.

The history of medicine has much to teach us in this epidemic, but it has nothing to say about what is most specific to it, namely, the homophobic neglect of gay men's needs as those at greatest risk of infection. This is hardly surprising since the history of medicine has hitherto only acknowledged gay men as individual 'deviants', rather than as a social constituency. This is wholly in keeping with the wider discursive obliteration of gay men throughout the sociology of medicine, and in most modern epidemiology. Policies have thus been determined within a field of overlapping specialist disciplines that are homophobic. If gay men's needs have been consistently neglected throughout the epidemic, this needs to be interpreted in relation to the fact that we are not generally regarded as part of the general 'humanity' which is the subject of the social sciences, and medicine. It is this massive indifference to our lives that historians should attempt to explain, rather than emulate.

For it is precisely the discourse of 'History' that is so frequently employed in order to legitimate homophobic evasions in accounts of the epidemic written outside the domain of academic studies. Thus, writing in *Newsweek* in 1988, Matt Clark published an article in the Society and Medicine section, entitled 'Plagues, Man and History', with the sub-heading 'Lessons about AIDS from the Black Death', where we are quickly reassured that: 'the epidemics of the past hold medical lessons that can keep the AIDS threat in perspective'.[12]

According to Clark:

> To historians there's really nothing new about AIDS. Epidemics have changed the course of human events just as readily as wars, religious movements, royal houses and the imperatives of trade between nations.[13]

We are then treated to lengthy descriptions of the 1918–19 influenza epidemic, and the 'upsurge' of syphilis in the sixteenth century, which end with the pious conclusion that:

> If history remains a reliable guide, this epidemic too will run its vicious course, spreading acute misery. Then it will take its place in the background of the ecosystem, alongside the organisms that cause influenza, syphilis, measles and a host of other infections.[14]

In this manner, misleading and, at most, picturesque historical analogies are used to displace away any sense of social or political forces in conflict, or indeed any political dimension whatever. Instead, the epidemic is casually naturalised, made to seem *inevitable,* and all sense of human agency, or injustice, or ethical responsibilities, neatly and conveniently disappears.

Hence the inadequacy of accounts of the epidemic which do not address the central and indispensable role of the gay press in defining debate and information for gay men, and which choose to ignore the basic level of gay community experience, values, and institutions. The metaphor of plague naturalises homophobia, and makes it appear inevitable. It also naturalises the *impact* of HIV amongst gay men, and displaces attention away from the direct conse-

quences of homophobic denial of safer sex education to those in greatest need—a denial which may be accurately tallied in our mounting mortality statistics. All too often the whole complexity and richness of gay culture can be ignored, with perhaps at most a largely misleading footnote reference to the work of Randy Shilts.[15] Indeed, the tendency to refer to *And The Band Played On* as if it were an oracular text, explaining all gay men's responses to AIDS, is itself a typical example. Historical accounts of AIDS that overlook the achievements of the non-government AIDS service organisations, or treatment activism, or the role of gay men in the statutory sector, amount to nothing more than strategic disinformation.

Similar problems also afflict the other principal canonical text of AIDS criticism, Susan Sontag's *AIDS And Its Metaphors*.[16] For Sontag, what is 'new' about AIDS are metaphors of mutability and contemporaneity, as in the discourse of 'computer viruses'.[17] So homophobic is her text that, though writing in Manhattan in the late 1980s she does not even *mention* the word 'gay'. Furthermore, her complete embargo on war metaphors makes it difficult to convey the enormity of the consequences of government policies and government neglect in most countries. As the American AIDS activist group, Gran Fury, asked in a poster concerning HIV education for gay men: 'When a government turns its back on its people, is it civil war?' Plague metaphors for AIDS did not simply appear spontaneously in popular consciousness, carried over at some level of innate cultural memory from the distant past. On the contrary, they were mobilised by homophobic institutions in order to articulate their specific ideological and political vision of the epidemic. To accept historical analogies between people with AIDS and medieval plague victims, is to miss the point that whilst the plagues of history struck with arbitrary venom, demonstrably effective safer sex campaigns for those most at risk (gay men) have been almost everywhere either neglected, or subjected to many different forms of direct censorship and harassment. *This epidemic is unique in so far as its prevention has been prevented, rather than transmission.* Resources and education campaigns have been targeted at those at least risk of contracting HIV, as if the priority of preventing an epidemic amongst heterosexuals had been established at the expense of halting the epidemics that are actually raging throughout the developed world. One need only consider the paradoxical British response, which has successfully slowed down transmission amongst injecting drug users through the sharing of needles by introducing needle-exchanges. Yet almost nothing has been done for gay men, who are at much greater risk; in France, both groups are left to what is evidently thought of as their 'fate'.

If gay men have been regarded as expendable, and fundamental policies have been determined by homophobia, the historian can hardly sustain a neutral pose. For what she is 'observing' is, in effect, an ongoing massacre, quietly overseen and tacitly approved by the entire cultural and political system of the first world. Nobody may have set out with the intention that huge numbers of gay men should contract HIV, but that has been the inevitable consequence of government action, and inaction, all around the world, with only a handful of exceptions—Denmark, Australia and the Netherlands. In such circumstances, neutrality amounts to collusion. If we seek a historical model in the twentieth century it is not to the history of epidemics that we should initially turn, but to the history of medical atrocities, especially when these have been committed with state supervision and support.

What has happened is unprecedented, for the simple reason that the diaspora of gay identity is of very recent origin. Since we have not been widely accepted as a legitimate social constituency, our deaths are as unreal to most heterosexuals as our lives. Our situation is the more intolerable since we are not yet admitted into most notions of the common 'humanity' against which crimes may be said to be committed in such extraordinary and terrible circumstances. However, the history of medical atrocities directs us immediately to situations when specific groups of people have been treated inhumanely, in the wider name of 'care', or the advancement of science, because they themselves were not officially regarded as fully or properly 'human' in the first place.[18] When HIV is regarded as an agent of 'natural' extermination, it may be ignored in specific population groups where its effects will be taken for granted. This is not extermination by conscious policy, but by default, and the long-term consequences are not dissimilar.

We need to consider what happens in countries such as Britain, France and the US, where national identities are increasingly played out and defined in relation to demonised others—whose 'otherness' could hardly be made more apparent than in the spectacle of their suffering an epidemic, their dying like flies, like the non-humans they are thought to be. That gay men deserve to die from AIDS has never been challenged by heterosexuals, but has retained widespread legitimacy, as homophobic fanatics have successfully influenced governments of the left and the right alike. As an activist, I write from a position which has seen bad policies translated into inadequate actions. I have become extremely intolerant of those who have made no attempt whatsoever to educate themselves about HIV or AIDS. Their indifference to the epidemic is evidence of their wider indifference to whether gay men live or die. All around the world gay men have struggled to secure services for everyone affected by HIV, especially for those who are also marginalised as the result of their race, or gender, or class, or whatever. By so doing, however, we have frequently neglected 'our own'. Whilst vast sums of money have been squandered on generally dreadful AIDS education aimed at the 'general public', horribly little has been done on behalf of gay men, for whom nobody else will speak up. Hence the responsibility of historians to properly analyse this epidemic in its correct narrative contexts, which are overwhelmingly political. We cannot afford the luxurious delusion of some ultimate recognition of the scale of injustice perpetrated at all levels of the management of the epidemic, because we don't have time. Too many lives are still at stake. It is the historian's responsibility to narrate, and not to further legitimate the vast, ongoing atrocity that is AIDS.

Conclusion: The Horses of Achilles— An Allegory

In Book Seventeen of *The Iliad,* we read of the immortal horses sent by Zeus to Achilles, which weep for the untimely death of their brave young charioteer, Achilles's beloved, Patroclus. They weep at the news of his treacherous murder by Hector, Prince of Troy:

> Firm as a gravestone planted on the barrow of a dead man or woman, they stood motionless in front of their beautiful chariot with their heads bowed down to the earth. Hot tears ran from their eyes to the ground as they mourned for their lost driver, and their luxuriant manes were soiled.[19]

The immortal horses weep because they have been touched by mortal, human tragedy. Homer is very clear about this. They mourn an avoidable loss.

Eventually Zeus intervenes, and the horses recover their equilibrium. They gallop off to save Patroclus's squire, Automedon, who is in danger. After all, there was still everything to play for. The death of Patroclus had no direct effect on the course of the siege, save to harden Achaean resolve.

Notes

1. Isaiah Berlin, 'Introduction', *Four Essays on Liberty,* Oxford, 1982, p. XXIX.

2. *Ibid.,* p. XXX.

3. Stuart Hall, 'Introduction', *The Hard Road to Renewal,* Verso, London, 1988, p. 8.

4. Robert M. Swenson, 'Plagues, History, and AIDS', *The American Scholar,* vol. 57, no. 2, Spring, 1988, p. 200. Much the same universalist conclusion is also reached by Charles E. Rosenberg, in 'What is an epidemic? AIDS in historical perspective', *Daedalus* vol. 18, no. 2, Spring 1989, Cambridge MA, pp. 1–17.

5. Elizabeth Fee and Daniel M. Fox, *AIDS: The Burdens of History,* University of California Press, Berkeley and London, 1988, n.p.

6. See Simon Watney, 'Safer Sex as Community Practice' (in [Watney, *Practices of Freedom: Selected Writings on HIV/AIDS,* Duke University Press, Durham, 1994)].

7. David Black, 'The Plague Years', Parts One & Two', *Rolling Stone,* 28 March 1985, pp. 48–125; and *Rolling Stone,* 25 April 1985, pp. 35–62. Published in book form by Picador, London, 1986.

8. *Ibid.*

9. *Sun,* 11 April 1986.

10. *Ibid.*

11. 'The life and death of a star', *Independent,* 22 April 1992, p. 16.

12. Matt Clark, 'Plagues, Man and History: Lessons about AIDS from the Black Death', *Newsweek,* 9 May 1988, p. 65.

13. *Ibid.*

14. *Ibid.,* p. 67.

15. See Simon Watney, 'Politics, People and the AIDS Epidemic' (in [*Practices of Freedom*)]. See also Douglas Crimp, 'How to Have Promiscuity in an Epidemic', in D. Crimp (ed.), *AIDS: Cultural Analysis, Cultural Activism,* MIT, Cambridge MA, 1988, pp. 237–70.

16. Susan Sontag, *AIDS and Its Metaphors,* Allen Lane/The Penguin Press, London, 1988. See also Simon Watney, 'Guru of AIDS', *Guardian,* 10 March 1989; and David Miller, 'Sontag's Urbanity', *October,* no. 49, MIT, Cambridge MA, Summer 1989, pp. 91–102.

17. *Ibid.,* pp. 70–1.

18. See Hannah Arendt, *Eichmann In Jerusalem: A Report On The Banality Of Evil,* Penguin Books, Harmondsworth, 1977; also Robert Jay Lifton, *The Nazi Doctors: Medical Killing and the Psychology of Genocide,* Basic Books, New York, 1986; also Robert N. Proctor, *Racial Hygiene: Medicine Under The Nazis,* Harvard University Press, Cambridge MA, 1988; also Zygmunt Bauman, *Modernity and the Holocaust,* Polity Press, Oxford, 1989.

19. Homer, *The Iliad,* trans. E.V. Rieu, Penguin Books, Harmondsworth, 1976, pp. 327–8.

Present Tense:
Biphobia as a Crisis of Meaning[1]

Amanda Udis-Kessler

The lesbian and gay reaction to bisexuals has tended to veer between "You don't exist" and "Go form your own community; you're not welcome in ours," while the heterosexual reaction has tended to veer between "You don't exist" and "I hate all you queers." God knows we've heard enough of these sentiments, and I don't enjoy repeating them, but this particular set holds value for us if we consider the fear behind the anger. The denial of bisexuality by both straights and gays is common, as is our rejection from lesbian and gay communities and our designation as "homos" by heterosexuals. I believe that this biphobia has arisen as a result of American sexual discourse, the ways in which Americans understand sex and sexuality.

Specifically, I think it can be argued that a good deal of biphobia is the expression of a crisis of meaning posed by bisexuals which affects heterosexuals and homosexuals differently and which needs to be dealt with differently in the two cases. In each case, a collective myth is threatened, raising questions about the lesbian and gay past and the heterosexual future.[2] To appreciate the strength (and fragility) of these collective myths, we need to consider the uses they have in our society.

Sexuality is, of course, a biological aspect of our humanity, but it is also very much culturally constructed. Specific sexual practices, symbols, meanings, values, and power connections are located in concrete historical societies and vary over time and from culture to culture. For ex-

ample, sexual object choice is managed differently in different societies; a Native American, Pacific Islander, or African may engage in same-sex behavior without in any way having a lesbian or gay identity. The collective myth behind American sexual discourse includes two facets that lead directly to biphobia. First, we consider sexuality to be an essence, an unchanging core identity, and the way that lesbian and gay communities have adopted this view (which can be called essentialism) has led to a great deal of lesbian and gay biphobia. Second, we are still suffering the effects of a sex-negative cultural history which contributes greatly to homophobia and heterosexual biphobia.[3]

The extent to which sexuality is biologically or culturally determined is the subject of a debate between essentialists and constructionists. I indicated above that essentialism is the view that one's sexual orientation is an unchanging essence, which involves a transhistorical and transcultural identity. I also indicated that essentialism is not a universally accepted understanding of sexuality. An opposing view, constructionism, posits that categories of sexual identity are constructed and that human sexuality is wider in scope than the categories we assign it. This is to say that categories create, rather than reveal, social types. The essentialist versus constructionist debate has arisen as a result of changes in Western sexual discourse.

Before 1869, everyone was heterosexual and no one was heterosexual. By this I mean that all people were believed to be biologically oriented toward people of the opposite sex, there was no need for a word or category "heterosexual" since there was no opposite or conflicting category "homosexual." Certainly there were homosexual *acts,* homosexual *behavior,* but no homosexual people and no word "homosexuality." The fact that there could be behavior contrary to what was understood as natural did not cause anyone to rethink their concepts of the natural; rather, they simply labelled same-sex acts unnatural. Biblical injunctions against homosexual behavior must be seen in this light.

In 1869, the word "homosexuality" was coined and the concept—and category—of "the homosexual" came into existence, requiring the "discovery" of the heterosexual as well. I don't mean to suggest that heterosexuality was thought of as anything other than normative, or that homosexuality was taken seriously as a biological entity at that point. Physical and psychological understandings of homosexuality competed, but the constant which is of interest to us here is the depth of the homosexual identity which was brought to light. Sexuality was not simply a matter of acts. It involved an essence which did not change easily if at all. At the end of the nineteenth century, there were two identities to match sexual acts where none had been before, two categories of person: heterosexual and homosexual.

If we jump ahead a century to Stonewall, we notice a dramatic change in the *meaning* of the homosexual identity. The early gay liberation movement, revolting from decades of assimilation à la Mattachine Society and Daughters of Bilitis, took on an ethnic model of oppression and counterculture. In doing so, it maintained pre-Stonewall essentialism while adding a separatist politics. In this model, lesbians and gay men, drawing on the civil rights movement, defined themselves as an ethnic minority with sexuality rather than skin color the determining factor and with homophobia rather than racism the oppression.

Lesbian and gay activists had long taken the insight of experiencing sexuality as beyond choice and considering this proof that it was a natural part of their sex drive.[4] Interestingly enough, while this approach would seem to require a straightforward correlation between sexual behavior and core identity, such a correlation was not made. Many lesbians and gay men came out after being heterosexually active, and some of these people had enjoyed their heterosexuality; they simply enjoyed homosexuality more. Lesbian and gay essentialists simply switched the heterosexual assumption of prior ages and claimed that these people were essentially gay, regardless of their sexual behavior. Thus, a woman who came out at forty had really been a lesbian all along but had not been in touch with her true sexuality.

The acceptance of essentialism was not universal, however. Some psychologists and sexologists raised troubling questions about this conception which could invalidate forty years of a woman's life. They asked whether the experience of sexuality as beyond chosenness necessarily meant that it was biologically grounded. They asked why sexual identity appeared in such different forms in different cultures, and whether essentialism didn't carry with it a certain cultural imperialism. These constructionists posited that the categories of homosexuality and heterosexuality were *constructed* rather than *discovered* a hundred years ago, created because changing social circumstances dictated a need for such categories. Without denying the place of nature in our lives, they pointed out that socialization affects us tremendously, including the extent to which we think nature shapes us. They argued that sexuality is not simply the unfolding of one's natural essence. Rather, sexuality is learned, relational, contingent, and unpredictable; sexuality *is* as sexuality *does.* There are sexual scripts within every society and there are variations on those scripts in every society.

As we may imagine, the constructionist view of sexuality, with its fluidity and its connotation of choice, threatened lesbians and gay men as soon as it was proposed. Constructionism challenged the "oppressed ethnic minority" approach by arguing that sexuality could not be compared to skin color as a natural phenomenon. The response of lesbian and gay communities was understandably fierce; as Steven Epstein notes, "people who base their claims to social rights on the basis of a group identity will not appreciate being told that that identity is just a social construct."[5] Constructionism could not offer a sound political replacement for essentialism. "[O]nce we have deconstructed identity," so the fear went, "we will have nothing . . . which is stable and secure upon which to base a politics."[6] The upshot of this thinking was that sexual theorists continued the essentialist versus constructionist debate in academic journals and other settings, but it had little impact upon community members and their separatist culture and politics. This has remained true since the early days of gay liberation, with Steven Epstein noting in 1987 that "while constructionist theorists have been preaching the gospel that the hetero-homosexual distinction is a social fiction, gays and lesbians, in everyday life and in political action, have been busy hardening the categories."[7]

What does this have to do with bisexuality? Consider a lesbian who has gone through a traumatic coming-out process with loss of family and friends, but who is finally secure with a lesbian identity in a supportive community. Or consider a gay man who has spent his life being harassed and hurt for being gay, who knows personally that oppression means having one's choices removed but who has been able to rebuild his sense of having choices and his sense of humor within an urban gay male culture. Sexual essentialists are secure in their assertion that these two people may have had to suffer but that now they are home and able to build and love and fight back. But what if this man or this woman falls in love with someone of the opposite sex? What, then, was their pain and suffering about? Do the experiences which shaped them mean nothing? Was there an easier way? And should they have taken it? What is the connection of their pasts to a new and surprising present? Both of these people have come through tremendous soul-searching to reach their lesbian and gay identities, which provide them with a myth by which to structure their

lives, offering social and political meaning to their personal histories. Is the myth that fragile? Is their sexuality that fragile? How are they to be true to themselves and what does being true to themselves mean in this situation?

The larger lesbian and gay community carries a great deal of shared pain; indeed it is built on it. Stonewall would not have happened without a bunch of drag queens and some diesel dykes being sick and tired of being sick and tired. When lesbians and gay men who are deeply connected to their communities ask the questions above, the whole community feels the effect. If enough people ask them, the collective myth—and the community—are in danger. For both can only remain intact if the pain which built the community was in some way the inevitable product of being oneself in a heterosexist society. This brings us back to the essentialist verses constructionist debate, but with a clearer sense of the urgency behind the response to constructionism. Just as bisexuality would threaten the gay man and lesbian described above, the fluidity and connotation of choice within constructionism would seem to challenge both the history and the future of lesbian and gay communities.

Now we are in a position to see the leap of logic which has accounted for so much lesbian and gay biphobia: it is a leap which connects bisexuality and bisexuals to sexual constructionism and both to a crisis of meaning which may be both personal and communal. Lesbians and gay men, protective of the essentialist view of sexuality, equate the fluidity and apparent choice-making of bisexuality with that of constructionism and feel a tremor in the structure underlying their lives and identities.[8] No matter if, unlike the examples above, they do not experience bisexual feelings themselves, constructionism claims that the potential is always there, and that is enough of a threat.

When bisexuality equals constructionism, bisexuals become walking reminders of the potential crisis of meaning for lesbians and gay men, posing a threat to identity and community far greater than the one posed by heterosexuals. Lesbians and gay men have been able to define themselves as other than heterosexual; bisexuals challenge that definition regardless of our intention to do so. Behind the painful lesbian and gay biphobia which we have experienced is a poignant cry for a self; "you don't exist" means "I do exist." And, too, the rejection as a group ("go form your own communities; you're not welcome in ours") is a way for lesbians and gay men to claim a group identity, to say *we* exist, not just as individuals but as a community." This fragility may be hidden beneath flippancy, sarcasm, culture, and camp, but any bisexuality education which does not keep it in mind will not open barriers where it counts: in the heart.

What, then, about heterosexual biphobia? Is there, strictly speaking, such a thing? And if so, from whence does it come? Taking these questions seriously requires looking at some of the sexually problematic messages heterosexuals have internalized *without having to challenge them as lesbians and gay men do*. These messages basically revolve around the interface of sex negativity and dualistic thinking that permeates our culture.

Sex negativity comes down to us from Hellenistic idealism, gnosticism, and Christianity. For the equation of sex with sin we may thank Saint Paul and the mystery cults of his day, the early Church fathers, and the Puritans. This is a powerful history, and we feel its effects in our body hatred and our experience of sex as sick, shameful, and dirty, something done secretly and furtively. Sex negativity is visible in traditional Christian views on sexuality, in sodomy laws, in sexual dysfunction, and in the nonexistent or inadequate sex education in much of America.[9] The latter would be amusing if it did not lead directly to sexually transmitted diseases, unwanted pregnancies, and AIDS deaths, as well as indirectly fostering sex roles which contribute to rape.[10]

Sex negativity has always been closely related to hierarchical dualistic thinking. Philosophers from Plato to Descartes have held that the mind or spirit is superior to the body, that culture is superior to nature, and that men are superior to women. These various hierarchies are interconnected; the primary shapers of our culture have symbolically desexualized men, associating them with culture and the spirit, while women have been appointed representatives of sex, nature, and the body. This is not just an excuse for keeping women in their place, as we might imagine, but part of a collective myth used to manage men's fears of chaos and death (since neither culture nor the spirit die). With the discovery or creation of "the homosexual," lesbians and gay men were assigned the lowest place in the linkage of women, sexuality, and nature. They came to stand for sex as sin and to serve as the repository of America's deepest fears about sex and the body, representing lust out of control, promiscuity, dirtiness, and death. The fact that same-sex sex cannot produce a child only aggravated this symbolism, while the recent presence of AIDS brought these fears to a conscious level.

Bisexuals play an interesting role in this dynamic. We have been much less visible to mainstream America than lesbians and gay men, due primarily to our lack of a formal movement with significant numbers to capture the attention of the press. The onetime phrase of the sexual revolution, "everyone's really bisexual," has failed to have either accuracy or impact. Yet we do have a symbolic meaning for mainstream Americans who encounter us: We bring them closer to homosexuality and therefore to their deepest fears about being embodied creatures. As with lesbians and gay men, we bring about a personal and potentially collective crisis of meaning, though one oriented toward the future rather than the past.

Bisexuality can provoke this crisis of meaning for a heterosexual by casting her or his sexual future into doubt. Consider a woman who has always known herself to be heterosexual, who recognizes genuine attractions to men. She is quite clear that she is not a lesbian, but what happens on the day when she finds herself attracted to a woman? What does this mean about her sexual future? As with the lesbian and gay examples above, what might being true to herself mean in this situation? In a dualistic culture where nonheterosexuality is demonized and heterosexuality is made to represent all that is good and right and pure, this woman may have to face gremlins which society has tried very hard to keep hidden.

The essentialist-versus-constructionist debate about sexuality has not reached the American mainstream enough to be very troubling, but the challenge to categories posed by both constructionism and bisexuality would be a problem for any culture which uses categories as ours does to scapegoat some people in return for offering the rest peace of mind.

For if lesbians and gay men find the otherness of heterosexuals useful in defining themselves, consider how useful the otherness of homosexuals is in maintaining the American collective myth. There is a group upon which to project all of one's fears about being embodied, sexual, mortal, about having physical urges which sometimes seem out of control. Moreover, gay men and lesbians can represent godlessness, evil, and the decline of culture, which is the only way some parts of mainstream America can understand the social and sexual changes of the last twenty-five years. In order for this collective myth to work, however, the use of sexual categories must be thoroughly ingrained; they must not be seen as a useful if incomplete way of describing reality but rather as the truth, the whole truth, and nothing but the truth.

Bisexuality threatens this unconscious acceptance of good and evil, us and them dualism by throwing some grey in with the black and white, by representing a continuum. Once it is possible for a person to be both heterosexual and homosexual, then perhaps it is possible for a person to be both good and evil, mind and body, culture and nature. If this possibility creeps into the all-or-nothing dualism still used today to manage the fear of death and chaos, the collective myth is in danger. Bisexuality has not had the impact on the heterosexual culture that it has had on lesbian and gay communities, but it has the potential to challenge the meaning of heterosexuality as an experience and an institution. Here, too, the comment "you don't exist" really means something else, namely "I'm not gay," while "I hate all you queers" means

"gays are other," roughly translated as "I'm not gay." From this perspective, both the lesbian and gay and the heterosexual reactions to bisexuals center not around bisexuality as such, but around homosexuality. The heterosexual reaction to the bisexual is "I'm not gay." The lesbian and gay reaction to the bisexual is "I *am* gay."

The title of this paper, "Present Tense," has a double meaning. It refers to the challenge to the lesbian and gay past and the heterosexual future posed unintentionally by bisexuals, and it refers to the way that challenge takes place.[11] If bisexuality is a passing phase, a transitional period only, the lesbian and gay past and the heterosexual future retain their meaning and the present need not be tense for them. Yet if bisexuality is its own legitimate sexual identity as we know it to be, if we are not just confused or fence-sitting or in closets with revolving doors, if we live our bisexuality *in the present tense,* we will inevitably pose crises of meaning in American culture. We raise that dangerous question raised also by constructionism: to whom are we really similar and from whom are we really different? Who is our real enemy? Do we have one?[12]

How can this way of thinking about biphobia affect the educational work we do? First, I think it is extremely important when educating heterosexuals to work from their homophobia and do some education that may seem tedious or not in our best interest. If their crisis of meaning is based around a fear of homosexuality which has been driven into them since they were born, they need some of the same information and encouragement that lesbians, gay men, and bisexuals need; their biphobia may simply be homophobia in drag. From this perspective, once homosexuality is less threatening to them, bisexuality will be merely confusing rather than troublesome; we know very well how to educate in response to confusion.

It will be more difficult to educate in response to the lesbian and gay crisis of meaning without seeming to diminish its importance, but I suspect that there are two steps. First, we must be actively involved in lesbian and gay liberation, both because it is our liberation and because lesbians and gay men need to know that we are really with them. We need to grapple with the reality of heterosexual privilege and its links to sex and class stratification. Until we do this, we will never convince lesbians and gay men that we won't simply abandon them in hard times. Second, we must raise the essentialist versus constructionist question again with the aim of considering the strengths and weaknesses of both positions and moving beyond a one-or-the-other dichotomy.[13] We will want to raise questions about the common role of lesbians, gay men, and bisexuals in the future of sexual justice (not just sexual freedom) in America and elsewhere.

Just as lesbians and gay men do not personally choose to represent the worst aspects of embodiment, bisexuals do not personally choose to threaten the meaning systems by which lesbians, gay men, and heterosexuals live. But if we have this effect, we have all the more reason to work against the homophobia which injures and limits people of all sexualities and all the more reason to make the connections between homophobia and other supremacist systems which keep us alienated, disempowered, and afraid. We are not fence-sitters. Let us strive to be bridge-builders.

Notes

1. This paper draws extensively on an earlier paper, "Bisexuality in an Essentialist World," which appears in Tom Geller, ed., *Bisexuality: A Reader and Sourcebook,* Times Change Press, 1990.

2. There are, of course, more tangible issues present as well: Lesbian biphobia includes painful experiences around heterosexual privilege, while both lesbians and gay men have fears based in experience of abandonment by bisexuals, both as sexual partners and as partners in the struggle for liberation.

3. Clearly, sexual messages are transmitted and received differently depending on race and class, and different language is used to consider these problems. I can only speak out of my own experience as a white, middle-class, able-bodied, and college-educated woman. I offer this perspective with the confidence that people of many other backgrounds are asking these questions in ways most appropriate to them.

4. Ironically, the period around Stonewall is also the point at which some radical feminists began to choose political lesbianism and to publicize that choice; the question of choice in essentialist versus constructionist debates (and between bisexual and homosexual people) is double-edged, depending on one's politics.

5. Steven Epstein, "Gay Politics, Ethnic Identity: The Limits of Social Constructionism," *Socialist Review* 93, no. 4 (May–August 1987): 22.

6. Diana Fuss, *Essentially Speaking: Feminism, Nature, and Differences,* Routledge, 1989, p. 104.

7. Epstein, "Gay Politics, Ethnic Identity," p. 12.

8. There are certain links between constructionism and bisexuality, but they are not as substantial as they have been made to seem. It is as possible to be a bisexual essentialist, for example, as it is to be a lesbian Republican.

9. For excellent and thorough examinations of American body hatred, see James Nelson's *Embodiment: An Approach to Sexuality and Christian Theology,* Augsburg Publishing House, 1978; and Ernest Becker's *The Denial of Death,* Free Press, 1973. Some sections of Mary Douglas's *Purity and Danger,* Frederick Praeger, 1966, are also relevant.

10. There is another major discourse which has arisen in response to sex negativity and sex as sin, which can be called sex compulsivity and sex as salvation. *Embodiment* (ibid.) discusses some of its attributes, while Edwin Schur's *The Americanization of Sex,* Temple University Press, 1988, is primarily an extended discussion of the subject.

11. Incidentally, bisexuality also challenges lesbian and gay "eschatologies" (e.g., "someday the whole world will come out" or "someday we will have a society just of women") as well as an individual's exclusively heterosexual past by raising the question of moments of same-sex desire denied, distorted, or projected safely away.

12. For a discussion of the limits of the ethnic minority and separatist community approach, see Geller, pp. 61–62. Jana Sawicki offers a provocative thought along lines similar to my own: "Only if feminists democratize their struggles by giving equal respect to the claims of other oppressed minorities will they avoid . . . destructive Gemeinschaft [which] refers to the . . . sense of community in which conflict is experienced as an all or nothing contest . . . for the right to have one's feelings. Individuals involved in such conflicts sometimes become preoccupied more with bolstering their own identities than with their political goals. [This is] self-defeating insofar as it often leads

to internal struggles over who really belongs to the community" (in Irene Diamond and Quinby Lee, eds., *Feminism and Foucault: Reflections on Resistance,* Northeastern University Press, 1988, p. 187). Once lesbian and gay struggles are linked to international struggles of race, class, and gender, what is the logic of excluding bisexuals?

13. See Geller, pp. 60–61; Fuss, especially chapter 6, and Epstein are extremely useful as well.

It's Not Natural

Peter Ray

Old chestnuts don't come much older than the question 'what causes homosexuality?' In recent months, while the Western right has launched a 'cultural war' against lesbians and gay men, this issue has been receiving renewed attention as a result of the efforts of California-based neuro-biologist and gay campaigner Simon LeVay.

LeVay claims that research carried about by himself and other scientists demonstrates that the cause of homosexuality is biological. The media like what they hear. In America LeVay's results were greeted by *Newsweek* magazine with a front cover picture of a baby and the question 'Is this child gay?', while LeVay himself has been interviewed by everybody from *Oprah* to *Donahue*.

In Britain too LeVay's results have received an enthusiastic press reception, and in October he presented a Channel 4 documentary about his ideas. More recent research done by LeVay's colleagues, Laura Allen and Richard Gorski of the University of California Medical School, was reported by the *Guardian* as seeming 'to confirm what the gay community has maintained for decades: that homosexuals are born not made' (3 August 1992).

All in INAH3?

The truth is that none of the work LeVay has drawn attention to tells us very much about homosexuality. However, the enthusiastic reception he has received provides striking confirmation of the conservative and defensive approach to the right's attacks on homosexuals which is now being adopted by liberal opinion.

In an attempt to test for differences between heterosexuals and homosexuals, LeVay measured the size of certain cell nuclei known as INAH3 found in the hypothalamus area of the brain. The hypothalamus is closely linked to the pituitary gland which is one of the regulators of hormones involved in the human reproductive system. The results were described by *Newsweek* as showing 'that [this] tiny area believed to control sexual activity was less than half the size in gay men than in the heterosexuals' (24 February 1992).

In fact, LeVay's results are not so clear cut; are based on a dubious sample; and cannot demonstrate that homosexuals are 'born different'.

The cells which LeVay measured varied massively in size even among the male homosexuals. Although the cells of a third of the gay men clustered around the lower end of the range, some of them had large nuclei when compared with the straights. If some homosexuals also have large nuclei then, as leading science journal *Nature* commented, this means that 'nuclear size . . . is neither a unique nor an unambiguous determinant of homosexual behaviour' (J Maddox, 'Is homosexuality hard-wired?', 5 September 1991).

Sample Size

The sample that LeVay tested was very small. The cells of just 19 homosexual men were compared to those of only 16 heterosexual men and six heterosexual women. And the validity of the tests depended on the presumption that the individuals who reported themselves as straight were in fact exclusively heterosexual; a less than reliable source of information.

To the very limited extent that LeVay's results demonstrate a correlation between the size of the INAH3 nucleus and sexual orientation, that is all they demonstrate, as LeVay himself has cautioned. A correlation is not a cause; it could be that rather than the size of the nucleus determining sexual orientation, sexuality is the determinant of the size of the nucleus, or that both are a consequence of a third factor.

It should not be surprising that LeVay and his fellow researchers are having difficulties coming up with convincing results. As science, their whole approach is misconceived.

In the first place, since Alfred Kinsey researched the sexual experience of American men in the 1940s, it has been known that human sexual behaviour is more varied and complex than suggested by the simple concepts of hetero and homosexuality. How would LeVay's cells account for bisexuality? Do the nuclei change in size according to mood? Can they change suddenly and once and for all when a middle-aged married man 'comes out' as gay? Or do bisexuals fall in the middle of the size range?

And what about people who've got a thing for sheep, or men who like to have cream cakes thrown at them by prostitutes wearing Nazi uniforms? What will their INAH3 look like? You don't have to go to the wilder shores of desire, either. Apparently there are heterosexuals who get off on pretending to be football players during copulation, and why not? But exactly which gene is it that accounts for that?

Sex and Society

These questions cannot be answered because the things that turn us on are not the product of unchanging, natural processes. Everything to do with sex is continually shaped and reshaped by social pressures and developments. Even the question of which physical characteristics are regarded as sexy is more influenced by society

than it is by biology. Consider for a moment such standard contemporary fantasy objects as the Chippendales or page three girls, and ask yourself where the boys got those muscles or how anatomically well-suited the girls are for child-bearing. Nature has nothing to do with why people find them attractive.

What people consider to be desirable changes with society, both over time and between countries. A European woman who epitomised beauty a couple of centuries ago would today be regarded as almost obese. Where just a century ago, a glimpse of a woman's ankle was regarded as sexually provocative, today Madonna's posturing borders on the conventional. Things that might drive the English into a sexual frenzy would mean nothing to a native Amazonian.

It is difficult to see how nature could provide genes, cells and hormones able to distinguish, let alone determine preferences, between qualities that are the product of human history and social development. Indeed LeVay and his colleagues have hardly tried to come up with an explanation. As he admits, 'we do not . . . understand what makes people straight or gay' (Guardian, 9 October).

So why the disproportionate reaction of the press to the meagre and inconclusive results and the non-explanations that this research has produced? This is a particularly interesting question in the light of what is known about sexuality.

The Guardian's history is a little selective when it states that the 'gay community' has always maintained a natural view of homosexuality. The modern gay scene emerged in the wake of the militant self-assertion of the gay liberation movement in the early 1970s. Many gay liberationists explicitly rejected the idea that sexuality and even gender itself were natural. They believed that sexual liberation demanded the transcending of these categories.

Since the seventies, historical research has demonstrated that the entire project of trying to find biological factors that determine whether an individual will be homosexual or heterosexual is illogical because such categories of people were unknown before the nineteenth century.

Of course, from the ancient Greeks to Shakespeare's Elizabethans, there were always some people enjoying sex with others of the same sex. But the modern idea of homosexuality, as characteristic of a particular type of person (rather than just a sinful act that anybody might engage in) did not exist. This was because the possibility of living a modern homosexual lifestyle did not exist for any significant section of the population before the emergence of industrial capitalism.

In the backward, rural-dominated societies which predated capitalism, the traditional family was the institution through which economic production and survival were organised. While the odd sexual act was possible outside of the family's confines, there was no other way of life available for most people.

The industrial revolution of the eighteenth and nineteenth centuries broke down the traditional bonds and constraints of a society which had been tied to the land by economic necessity. Millions began to work in the cities for money wages, and for some at least the possibility arose of living outside the traditional family arrangements. Heterosexuality and homosexuality were concepts developed by the medical, moral and legal authorities at that time, in order to police the new society by demarcating acceptable and unacceptable behaviour. Male homosexuality was not specifically outlawed in Britain until 1885.

If the modern characteristics of hetero and homosexuality did not exist a couple of centuries ago, what sense can it make to project them backwards and try to discover their origins in humanity's biological make-up? In the 1990s, the attempt to do so marks a step backwards in our understanding. The fact that it is widely accepted as plausible is symptomatic of the profound conservatism that predominates in discussions of sex and sexuality today.

Faced with the right-wing attacks on lesbians and gay men, many liberals are welcoming the new 'scientific' proof that homosexuality is natural, since it appears to offer a way of getting around the right without having to fight its arguments. Liberal opinion hopes that by endow-

ing the sexual patterns of today with the unchanging, eternal validity of a natural scientific discovery, the fears of the fundamentalists can be assuaged. They can be told that, since homosexuality is inborn, persecution is doomed to fail and is also unnecessary if nobody can 'adopt' or be 'converted' to the homosexual lifestyle.

Naive and Dangerous

LeVay himself has a clear political agenda, believing that 'a better understanding of the innate differences between gay and straight people' may produce 'a rejection of homophobia based on religious or moral arguments' (*Guardian*, 9 October 1992). American gay activists like Randy Shilts welcomed the research because 'it would reduce being gay to something like being left-handed, which is in fact all it is' (*Guardian*, 3 August 1992). They hope that a demonstration of the 'immutability' of homosexuality will afford lesbians and gays constitutional protection against discrimination as a sort of ethnic minority.

The naivety of this idea is astonishing. In the first place, how have anti-discrimination laws prevented the continuing oppression of America's blacks? More dangerously, to argue that straight and gay are 'innately different' in a society where prejudice remains powerful can only reinforce the idea that one is innately superior and the other inferior.

Of course, LeVay or Shilts will argue that they are using the new research to ask for mutual toleration and respect between those who are 'different but equal'. But the hard fact is that difference will always mean inequality in a social order as fundamentally oppressive and exploitative as capitalism.

In case there is any doubt about this, the experience of the very first representatives of the *Guardian's* 'gay community' should be borne in mind. The world's first homosexual law reform campaign was started in Germany in 1897 by a doctor called Magnus Hirschfeld, who went on to found the prestigious Institute for Sexual Science in Berlin. Hirschfeld and his colleagues firmly believed that the route to justice was natural science. The demonstration of the naturalness of homosexuality, they thought, would destroy any rational argument for oppression.

'It's Nobody's Fault'

In the event, it was Hirschfeld's campaign and institute, not to mention many thousands of German homosexuals, which were destroyed by those most fervent believers in natural differences between people, the Nazis. History may not repeat itself, but it is certainly the case that turning social distinctions into natural ones can only ever reinforce existing divisions and antagonisms.

LeVay and Shilts accept the conservative agenda that the cause of homosexuality is the problem to be dealt with. The *Newsweek* article caught the defensive character of the discussion among liberals. One sympathetic researcher observed that:

'There is a tendency for people when told that homosexuality is biological, to heave a sigh of relief. It relieves the families and homosexuals of guilt. It also means that society doesn't have to worry about things like gay teachers.' (24 February 1992)

In other words, the important thing is to reassure bigots that while there is, naturally, something wrong with a fag, it's nobody's fault and it's not contagious.

This is some way down a slippery slope. To turn things around will require the recognition that the real problems to be identified and dealt with are not the origins of homosexuality, but the causes of bigotry and oppression. Those problems cannot be avoided with talk about natural difference. They have to be challenged through the struggle for a society in which lesbians and gay men have the right to live on exactly the same terms as everybody else.

Sexual Relations and the Class Struggle

Alexandra Kollontai

Among the many problems that demand the consideration and attention of contemporary mankind, sexual problems are undoubtedly some of the most crucial. There isn't a country or a nation, apart from the legendary "islands", where the question of sexual relationships isn't becoming an urgent and burning issue. Mankind today is living through an acute sexual crisis which is far more unhealthy and harmful for being long and drawn-out. Throughout the long journey of human history, you probably won't find a time when the problems of sex have occupied such a central place in the life of society; when the question of relationships between the sexes has been like a conjuror, attracting the attention of millions of troubled people; when sexual dramas have served as such a never-ending source of inspiration for every sort of art.

As the crisis continues and grows more serious, people are getting themselves into an increasingly hopeless situation, and are trying desperately by every available means to settle the "insoluble question". But with every new attempt to solve the problem, the confused knot of personal relationships gets more tangled. It's as if we couldn't see the one and only thread that could finally lead us to success in controlling the stubborn tangle. The sexual problem is like a vicious circle, and however frightened people are and however much they run this way and that, they are unable to break out.

The conservatively inclined part of mankind argue that we should return to the happy times of the past, we should re-establish the old foundations of the family and strengthen the well-tried norms of sexual morality. The champions of bourgeois individualism say that we ought to destroy all the hypocritical restrictions of the obsolete code of sexual behaviour. These unnecessary and repressive "rags" ought to be relegated to the archives—only the individual conscience, the individual will of each person can decide such intimate questions. Socialists, on the other hand, assure us that sexual problems will only be settled when the basic reorganisation of the social and economic structure of society has been tackled. Doesn't this "putting off the problem until tomorrow" suggest that we still haven't found that one and only "magic thread"? Shouldn't we find or at least locate this "magic thread" that promises to unravel the tangle? Shouldn't we find it now, at this very moment?

The history of human society, the history of the continual battle between various social groups and classes of opposing aims and interests, gives us the clue to finding this "thread". It isn't the first time that mankind has gone through a sexual crisis. This isn't the first time that the pressure of a rushing tide of new values and ideals has blurred the clear and definite meaning of moral commandments about sexual relationships. The "sexual crisis" was particularly acute at the time of the Renaissance and the Reformation, when a great social advance pushed the proud and patriarchal feudal nobility who were used to absolute command into the background, and cleared the way for the development and establishment of a new social force—the bourgeoisie. The sexual morality of the feudal world had developed out of the depths of the "tribal way of life"—the collective economy and the tribal authoritarian leadership that stifles the individual will of the individual member. This clashed with the new and strange moral code of the rising bourgeoisie. The sexual morality of the bourgeoisie is founded on principles that are in sharp contradiction to the basic morality of feudalism. Strict individualism and the exclusiveness and isolation of the "nuclear family" replace the emphasis on "collective work" that was characteristic of both the local and regional economic structure of patrimonial life. Under capitalism the ethic of competition, the triumphant principles of individualism and exclusive private property, grew and destroyed whatever remained of the idea of the community, which was to some extent common to all types of tribal life. For a whole century, while the complex laboratory of life was turning the old norms into a new formula and achieving the outward harmony of moral ideas, men wandered confusedly between two very different sexual codes and attempted to accommodate themselves to both.

But in those bright and colourful days of change, the sexual crisis, although profound, did not have the threatening character that it has assumed in our time. The main reason for this is that in "the great days" of the Renaissance, in the "new age" when the bright light of a new spiritual culture flooded the dying world with its clear colours, flooded the bare monotonous life of the Middle Ages, the sexual crisis affected only a relatively small part of the population. By far the largest section of the population, the peasantry, was affected only in the most indirect way and only as, slowly, over the course of centuries, a change in the economic base, in the economic relations of the countryside, took place. At the top of the social ladder a bitter battle between two opposing

social worlds was fought out. This involved also a struggle between their different ideals and values and ways of looking at things. It was these people who experienced and were threatened by the sexual crisis that developed. The peasants, wary of new things, continued to cling firmly to the well-tried tribal tradition handed down from their forefathers, and only under the pressure of extreme necessity modified and adapted this tradition to the changing conditions of their economic environment. Even at the height of the struggle between the bourgeois and the feudal world the sexual crisis bypassed the "class of tax-payers". As the upper strata of society went about breaking up the old ways, the peasants in fact seemed to be more intent on clinging firmly to their traditions. In spite of the continuous whirlwinds that threatened overhead and shook the very soil under their feet, the peasants, especially our Russian peasantry, managed to preserve the basis of their sexual code untouched and unshaken for many centuries.

The story today is very different. The "sexual crisis" does not spare even the peasantry. Like an infectious disease it "knows neither rank nor status". It spreads from the palaces and mansions to the crowded quarters of the working class, looks in on the peaceful dwelling places of the petty bourgeoisie, and makes its way into the heart of the countryside. It claims victims in the villas of the European bourgeoisie, in the fusty basement of the worker's family, and in the smoky hut of the peasant. There is "no defence, no bolt" against sexual conflict. To imagine that only the members of the well-off sections of society are floundering and are in the throes of these problems would be to make a grave mistake. The waves of the sexual crisis are sweeping over the threshold of workers' homes, and creating situations of conflict that are as acute and heartfelt as the psychological sufferings of the "refined bourgeois world". The sexual crisis no longer interests only the "propertied". The problems of sex concern the largest section of society—they concern the working class in its daily life. It is therefore hard to understand why this vital and urgent subject is treated with such indifference. This indifference is unforgivable. One of the tasks that confront the working class in its attack on the "beleaguered fortress of the future" is undoubtedly the task of establishing more healthy and more joyful relationships between the sexes.

What are the roots of this unforgivable indifference to one of the essential tasks of the working class? How can we explain to ourselves the hypocritical way in which "sexual problems" are relegated to the realm of "private matters" that are not worth the effort and attention of the collective? Why has the fact been ignored that throughout history one of the constant features of social struggle has been the attempt to change relationships between the sexes, and the type of moral codes that determine these relationships; and that the way personal relationships are organised in a certain social group has had a vital influence on the outcome of the struggle between hostile social classes?

The tragedy of our society is not just that the usual forms of behaviour and the principles regulating this behaviour are breaking down, but that a spontaneous wave of new attempts at living is developing from within the social fabric, giving man hopes and ideals that cannot yet be realised. We are people living in the world of property relationships, a world of sharp class contradictions and of an individualistic morality. We still live and think under the heavy hand of an unavoidable loneliness of spirit. Man experiences this "loneliness" even in towns full of shouting, noise and people, even in a crowd of close friends and work-mates. Because of their loneliness men are apt to cling in a predatory and unhealthy way to illusions about finding a "soul mate" from among the members of the opposite sex. They see sly Eros as the only means of charming away, if only for a time, the gloom of inescapable loneliness.

People have perhaps never in any age felt spiritual loneliness as deeply and persistently as at the present time. People have probably never become so depressed and fallen so fully under the numbing influence of this loneliness. It could hardly be otherwise. The darkness never

seems so black as when there's a light shining just ahead.

The "individualists", who are only loosely organised into a collective with other individuals, now have the chance to change their sexual relationships so that they are based on the creative principle of friendship and togetherness rather than on something blindly physiological. The individualistic property morality of the present day is beginning to seem very obviously paralysing and oppressive. In criticising the quality of sexual relationships modern man is doing far more than rejecting the outdated forms of behaviour of the current moral code. His lonely soul is seeking the regeneration of the very essence of these relationships. He moans and pines for "great love", for a situation of warmth and creativity which alone has the power to disperse the cold spirit of loneliness from which present day "individualists" suffer.

If the sexual crisis is three quarters the result of external socioeconomic relationships, the other quarter hinges on our "refined individualistic psyche", fostered by the ruling bourgeois ideology. The "potential for loving" of people today is, as the German writer Meisel-Hess puts it, at a low ebb. Men and women seek each other in the hope of finding for themselves, through another person, a means to a larger share of spiritual and physical pleasure. It makes no difference whether they are married to the partner or not, they give little thought to what's going on in the other person, to what's happening to their emotions and psychological processes.

The "crude individualism" that adorns our era is perhaps nowhere as blatant as in the organisation of sexual relationships. A person wants to escape from his loneliness and naively imagines that being "in love" gives him the right to the soul of the other person—the right to warm himself in the rays of that rare blessing of emotional closeness and understanding. We individualists have had our emotions spoiled in the persistent cult of the "ego". We imagine that we can reach the happiness of being in a state of "great love" with those near to us, without having to "give" up anything of ourselves.

The claims we make on our "contracted partner" are absolute and undivided. We are unable to follow the simplest rule of love—that another person should be treated with great consideration. New concepts of the relationships between the sexes are already being outlined. They will teach us to achieve relationships based on the unfamiliar ideas of complete freedom, equality and genuine friendship. But in the meantime mankind has to sit in the cold with its spiritual loneliness and can only dream about the "better age" when all relationships between people will be warmed by the rays of "the sun god", will experience a sense of togetherness, and will be educated in the new conditions of living. The sexual crisis cannot be solved unless there is a radical reform of the human psyche, and unless man's potential for loving is increased. And a basic transformation of the socio-economic relationships along communist lines is essential if the psyche is to be reformed. This is an "old truth" but there is no other way out. The sexual crisis will in no way be reduced, whatever kind of marriage or personal relationships people care to try.

History has never seen such a variety of personal relationships—indissoluble marriage with its "stable family", "free unions", secret adultery; a girl living quite openly with her lover in so-called "wild marriage"; pair marriage, marriage in threes and even the complicated marriage of four people—not to talk of the various forms of commercial prostitution. You get the same two moral codes existing side by side in the peasantry as well—a mixture of the old tribal way of life and the developing bourgeois family. Thus you get the permissiveness of the girls' house* side by side with the attitude that fornication, or men sleeping with

*In the traditional Russian villages, the young girls would often get together to rent an old hut or a room in someone's house. They would gather there in the evenings to tell stories, do needlework and sing. The young men would come to join in the merrymaking. Sometimes it seems that the merrymaking would become an orgy, though there are conflicting ideas about this.

their daughters-in-law, is a disgrace. It's surprising that, in the face of the contradictory and tangled forms of present-day personal relationships, people are able to preserve a faith in moral authority, and are able to make sense of these contradictions and thread their way through these mutually destructive and incompatible moral codes. Even the usual justification—"I live by the new morality"—doesn't help anyone, since the new morality is still only in the process of being formed. Our task is to draw out from the chaos of present-day contradictory sexual norms the shape, and make clear the principles, of a morality that answers the spirit of the progressive and revolutionary class.

Besides the already mentioned inadequacies of the contemporary psyche—extreme individuality, egoism that has become a cult—the "sexual crisis" is made worse by two characteristics of the psychology of modern man:

1. The idea of "possessing" the married partner;
2. The belief that the two sexes are unequal, that they are of unequal worth in every way, in every sphere, including the sexual sphere.

Bourgeois morality, with its introverted individualistic family based entirely on private property, has carefully cultivated the idea that one partner should completely "possess" the other. It has been very successful. The idea of "possession" is more pervasive now than under the patrimonial system of marriage relationships. During the long historical period that developed under the aegis of the "tribe", the idea of a man possessing his wife (there has never been any thought of a wife having undisputed possession of her husband) did not go further than a purely physical possession. The wife was obliged to be faithful physically—her soul was her own. Even the knights recognised the right of their wives to have *chichesbi* (platonic friends and admirers) and to receive the "devotion" of other knights and minnesingers. It is the bourgeoisie who have carefully tended and fostered the ideal of absolute possession of the "contracted partner's" emotional as well as physical "I", thus extending the concept of property rights to include the right to the other person's whole spiritual and emotional world. Thus the family structure was strengthened and stability guaranteed in the period when the bourgeoisie were struggling for domination. This is the ideal that we have accepted as our heritage and have been prepared to see as an unchangeable moral absolute! The idea of "property" goes far beyond the boundaries of "lawful marriage". It makes itself felt as an inevitable ingredient of the most "free" union of love. Contemporary lovers with all their respect for freedom are not satisfied by the knowledge of the physical faithfulness alone of the person they love. To be rid of the eternally present threat of loneliness, we "launch an attack" on the emotions of the person we love with a cruelty and lack of delicacy that will not be understood by future generations. We demand the right to know every secret of this person's being. The modern lover would forgive physical unfaithfulness sooner than "spiritual" unfaithfulness. He sees any emotion experienced outside the boundaries of the "free" relationship as the loss of his own personal treasure.

People "in love" are unbelievably insensitive in their relations to a third person. We have all no doubt observed this strange situation—two people who love each other are in a hurry, before they have got to know each other properly, to exercise their rights over all the relationships that the other person has formed up till that time, to look into the innermost corners of their partner's life. Two people who yesterday were unknown to each other, and who come together in a single moment of mutual erotic feeling, rush to get at the heart of the other person's being. They want to feel that this strange and incomprehensible psyche, with its past experience that can never be suppressed, is an extension of their own self. The idea that the married pair are each other's property is so accepted that when a young couple who were yesterday each living their own separate lives are today opening each other's correspondence without a blush, and making common property of the words of a third person who is a friend of only one of them, this hardly strikes us as something unnatural. But this kind of "intimacy" is only really possible when people have been working out their lives together for a long period of time. Usually a dishonest kind of closeness is substituted for this genuine feeling, the deception being fostered by the mistaken idea that a physical relationship between two people is a sufficient basis for extending the rights of possession to each other's emotional being.

The "inequality" of the sexes—the inequality of their rights, the unequal value of their physical and emotional experience—is the other significant circumstance that distorts the psyche of contemporary man and is a reason for the deepening of the "sexual crisis". The "double morality" inherent in both patrimonial and bourgeois society has, over the course of centuries, poisoned the psyche of men and women. These attitudes are so much a part of us that they are more difficult to get rid of than the ideas about possessing people that we have inherited only from bourgeois ideology. The idea that the sexes are unequal, even in the sphere of physical and emotional experience, means that the same action will be regarded differently according to whether it was the action of a man or a woman. Even the most "progressive" member of the bourgeoisie, who has long ago rejected the whole code of current morality, easily catches himself out at this point since he too in judging a man and a woman for the same behaviour will pass different sentences. One simple example is enough. Imagine that a member of the middle-class intelligentsia who is learned, involved in politics and social affairs—who is in short a "personality", even a "public figure"—starts sleeping with his cook (a not uncommon thing to happen) and even becomes legally married to her. Does bourgeois society change its attitude to this man, does the event throw even the tiniest shadow of doubt as to his moral worth? Of course not.

Now imagine another situation. A respected woman of bourgeois society—a social figure, a research student, a doctor, or a writer, it's all the same—becomes friendly with her footman, and to complete the scandal marries him. How does bourgeois society react to the behaviour of the hitherto "respected" woman? They cover her with "scorn", of course! And remember, it's so much the worse for her if her husband, the footman, is good-looking or possesses other "physical qualities". "It's obvious what she's fallen for", will be the sneer of the hypocritical bourgeoisie.

If a woman's choice has anything of an "individual character" about it she won't be forgiven by bourgeois society. This attitude is a kind of throwback to the traditions of tribal times. Society still wants a woman to take into account, when she is making her choice, rank and status and the instructions and interests of her family. Bourgeois society cannot see a woman as an independent person separate from her family unit and outside the isolated circle of domestic obligations and virtues. Contemporary society goes even further than the ancient tribal society in acting as woman's trustee, instructing her not only to marry but to fall in love only with those people who are "worthy" of her.

We are continually meeting men of considerable spiritual and intellectual qualities who have chosen as their friend-for-life a worthless and empty woman, who in no way matches the spiritual worth of the husband. We accept this as something normal and we don't think twice about it. At the most friends might pity Ivan Ivanovich for having landed himself with such an unbearable wife. But if it happens the other way round, we flap our hands and exclaim with concern, "How could such an outstanding woman as Maria Petrovna fall for such a nonentity? I begin to doubt the worth of Maria Petrovna." Where do we get this double criterion from? What is the reason for it? The reason is undoubtedly that the idea of the sexes being of "different value" has become, over the centuries, a part of man's psychological make-up. We are used to evaluating a woman not as a personality with individual qualities and failings irrespective of her physical and emotional experience, but only as an appendage of a man. This man, the husband or the lover, throws the light of his personality over the woman, and it

is this reflection and not the woman herself that we consider to be the true definition of her emotional and moral make-up. In the eyes of society the personality of a man can be more easily separated from his actions in the sexual sphere. The personality of a woman is judged almost exclusively in terms of her sexual life. This type of attitude stems from the role that women have played in society over the centuries, and it is only now that a re-evaluation of these attitudes is slowly being achieved, at least in outline. Only a change in the economic role of woman, and her independent involvement in production, can and will bring about the weakening of these mistaken and hypocritical ideas.

The three basic circumstances distorting the modern psyche—extreme egoism, the idea that married partners possess each other, and the acceptance of the inequality of the sexes in terms of physical and emotional experience— must be faced if the sexual problem is to be settled. People will find the "magic key" with which they can break out of their situation only when their psyche has a sufficient store of "feelings of consideration", when their ability to love is greater, when the idea of freedom in personal relationships becomes fact, and when the principle of "comradeship" triumphs over the traditional idea of "inequality" and submission. The sexual problems cannot be solved without this radical re-education of our psyche.

But isn't this asking too much? Isn't the suggestion utopian, without foundation, the naive notion of a dreaming idealist? How are you honestly going to raise mankind's "potential for loving"? Haven't wise men of all nations since time immemorial, beginning with Buddha and Confucius and ending with Christ, been busying themselves over this? And who can say if the "potential for loving" has been raised? Isn't this kind of well-meaning daydream about the solution of the sexual crisis simply a confession of weakness and a refusal to go on with the search for the "magic key"?

Is that the case? Is the radical re-education of our psyche and our approach to sexual relationships something so unlikely, so removed from reality? Couldn't one say that, on the contrary, while great social and economic changes are in progress, the conditions are being created that demand and give rise to a new basis for psychological experience that is in line with what we have been talking about? Another class, a new social group, is coming forward to replace the bourgeoisie, with its bourgeois ideology, and its individualistic code of sexual morality. The progressive class, as it develops in strength, cannot fail to reveal new ideas about relationships between the sexes that form in close connection with the problems of its social class.

The complicated evolution of socio-economic relations taking place before our eyes, which changes all our ideas about the role of women in social life and undermines the sexual morality of the bourgeoisie, has two contradictory results. On the one hand we see mankind's tireless efforts to adapt to the new, changing socio-economic conditions. This is manifest either in an attempt to preserve the "old forms" while providing them with a new content (the observance of the external form of the indissoluble, strictly monogamous marriage with an acceptance, in practice, of the freedom of the partners) or in the acceptance of new forms which contain however all the elements of the moral code of bourgeois marriage (the "free" union where the compulsive possessiveness of the partners is greater than within legal marriage). On the other hand we see the slow but steady appearance of new forms of relationships between the sexes that differ from the old norms in outward form and in spirit.

Mankind is not groping its way toward these new ideas with much confidence, but we need to look at its attempt, however vague it is at the moment, since it is an attempt closely linked with the tasks of the proletariat as the class which is to capture the "beleaguered fortress" of the future. If, amongst the complicated labyrinth of contradictory and tangled sexual norms, you want to find the beginnings of more healthy relationships between the sexes—relationships that promise to lead humanity out of the sexual crisis—you have to leave the "cultured quarters" of the bourgeoisie with their refined individualistic psyche, and take a look at the huddled dwelling-

places of the working class. There, amidst the horror and squalor of capitalism, amidst tears and curses, the springs of life are welling up.

You can see the double process which we have just mentioned working itself out in the lives of the proletariat, who have to exist under the pressure of harsh economic conditions, cruelly exploited by capitalism. You can see both the process of "passive adjustment" and that of active opposition to the existing reality. The destructive influence of capitalism destroys the basis of the worker's family and forces him unconsciously to "adapt" to the existing conditions. This gives rise to a whole series of situations with regard to relationships between the sexes which are similar to those in other social classes. Under the pressure of low wages the worker inevitably tends to get married at a later age. If twenty years ago a worker usually got married between the ages of twenty and twenty-five, he now shoulders the cares of a family only towards his thirtieth year. The higher the cultural demands of the worker—the more he values the opportunity of being in contact with cultural life, of visiting theatres and lectures, of reading papers and magazines, of giving his spare time to struggle and politics or to some favourite pursuit such as art or reading etc.—the later he tends to get married. But physical needs won't take a financial situation into consideration: they insist on making themselves felt. The working-class bachelor, in the same way as the middle-class bachelor, looks to prostitution for an outlet. This is an example of the passive adjustment of the working class to the unfavourable conditions of their existence. Take another example. When the worker marries, the low level of pay forces the worker's family to "regulate" childbirth just as the bourgeois family does. The frequent cases of infanticide, the growth of prostitution—these are all expressions of the same process. These are all examples of adjustment by the working class to the surrounding reality. But this is not a process characteristic of the proletariat alone. All the other classes and sections of the population caught up in the world process of capitalist development react in this way.

We see a difference only when we begin to talk about the active, creative forces at work that oppose rather than adapt to the repressive reality, and about the new ideals and attempts at new relationships between the sexes. It is only within the working class that this active opposition is taking shape. This doesn't mean that the other classes and sections of the population (particularly the middle-class intelligentsia who, by the circumstances of their social existence, stand closest to the working class) don't adopt the "new" forms that are being worked out by the progressive working class. The bourgeoisie, motivated by an instinctive desire to breathe new life into their dead and feeble forms of marriage, seize upon the "new" ideas of the working class. But the ideals and code of sexual morality that the working class develops do not answer the class needs of the bourgeoisie. They reflect the demands of the working class and therefore serve as a new weapon in its social struggle. They help shatter the foundations of the social domination of the bourgeoisie. Let us make this point clear by an example.

The attempt by the middle-class intelligentsia to replace indissoluble marriage by the freer, more easily broken ties of civil marriage destroys the essential basis of the social stability of the bourgeoisie. It destroys the monogamous, property-orientated family. On the other hand, a greater fluidity in relationships between the sexes coincides with and is even the indirect result of one of the basic tasks of the working class. The rejection of the element of "submission" in marriage is going to destroy the last artificial ties of the bourgeois family. This act of "submission" on the part of one member of the working class to another, in the same way as the sense of possessiveness in relationships, has a harmful effect on the proletarian psyche. It is not in the interests of that revolutionary class to elect only certain members as its independent representatives, whose duty it is to serve the class interests before the interests of the individual, isolated family. Conflicts between the interests of the family and the interests of the class which occur at the time of a strike or during an active struggle, and the moral yardstick with which the proletariat views such events, are sufficiently clear evidence of the basis of the new proletarian ideology.

Suppose family affairs require a businessman to take his capital out of a firm at a time when the enterprise is in financial difficulties. Bourgeois morality is clear-cut in its estimate of his action: "The interests of the family come first". We can compare with this the attitude of workers to a strikebreaker who defies his comrades and goes to work during a strike to save his family from being hungry. "The interests of the class come first". Here's another example. The love and loyalty of the middle-class husband to his family are sufficient to divert his wife from all interests outside the home and end up by tying her to the nursery and the kitchen. "The ideal husband can support the ideal family" is the way the bourgeoisie looks at it. But how do workers look upon a "conscious" member of their class who shuts the eyes of his wife or girlfriend to the social struggle? For the sake of individual happiness, for the sake of the family, the morality of the working class will demand that women take part in the life that is unfolding beyond the doorsteps. The "captivity" of women in the home, the way family interests are placed before all else, the widespread exercise of absolute property rights by the husband over the wife—all these things are being broken down by the basic principle of the working-class ideology of "comradely solidarity". The idea that some members are unequal and must submit to other members of one and the same class is in contradiction with the basic proletarian principle of comradeship. This principle of comradeship is basic to the ideology of the working class. It colours and determines the whole developing proletarian morality, a morality which helps to re-educate the personality of man, allowing him to be capable of positive feeling, capable of freedom instead of being bound by a sense of property, capable of comradeship rather than inequality and submission.

It is an old truth that every new class that develops as a result of an advance in economic growth and material culture offers mankind an appropriately new ideology. The code of sexual behaviour is a part of this ideology. However it is worth saying something about "proletarian ethics" or "proletarian sexual morality", in order to criticise the well-worn idea that proletarian sexual morality is no more than "superstructure", and that there is no place for any change in this sphere until the economic base of society has been changed. As if the ideology of a certain class is formed only when the breakdown in the socio-economic relationships, guaranteeing the dominance of that class, has been completed! All the experience of history teaches us that a social group works out its ideology, and consequently its sexual morality, in the process of its struggle with hostile social forces.

Only with the help of new spiritual values, created within and answering the needs of the class, will that class manage to strengthen its social position. It can only successfully win power from those groups in society that are hostile to it by holding to these new norms and ideals. To search for the basic criteria for a morality that can reflect the specific interests of the working class, and to see that the developing sexual norms are in accordance with these criteria— this is the task that must be tackled by the ideologists of the working class. We have to understand that it is only by becoming aware of the creative process that is going on within society, and of the new demands, new ideals and new norms that are being formed, only by becoming clear about the basis of the sexual morality of the progressive class, that we can possibly make sense of the chaos and contradictions of sexual relationships and find the thread that will make it possible to undo the tightly rolled up tangle of sexual problems.

We must remember that only a code of sexual morality that is in harmony with the problems of the working class can serve as an important weapon in strengthening the working class's fighting position. The experience of history teaches us that much. What can stop us using this weapon in the interests of the working class, who are fighting for a communist system and for new relationships between the sexes that are deeper and more joyful?

Capitalism and Gay Identity

John D'Emilio

This essay is a revised version of a talk I gave before several gay audiences during 1979 and 1980. I was searching for a large historical framework in which to set the history of the pre-Stonewall movement. Why, I wanted to know, did a movement begin only in 1950, when many of the elements of gay and lesbian oppression stretched much farther back in time? Michel Foucault in *The History of Sexuality* and Jeffrey Weeks in *Coming Out* had each argued that "the homosexual" was a creation of the nineteenth century, but without convincingly specifying why or how this came to be. I wanted to be able to ground social construction theory, which posited that gay identity was historically specific rather than universal, in concrete social processes. Using Marxist analyses of capitalism, I argued that two aspects of capitalism—wage labor and commodity production—created the social conditions that made possible the emergence of a distinctive gay and lesbian identity. I was not trying to claim that capitalism causes homosexuality nor that it determines the form that homosexual desire takes.

The essay had political motivation as well. Early gay liberationists had argued that sexuality was malleable and fluid ("polymorphously perverse") and that homosexuality and heterosexuality were both oppressive social categories designed to contain the erotic potential of human beings. By the late 1970s this belief was fading. In its place, gay activists laid claim to the concept of "sexual orientation," a fixed condition established early in life, if not at birth. This perspective was immediately useful in a political environment that sought "rights" for "minorities," but it also fudged some troubling issues, which the conclusion to this essay addresses.

*   *   *

For gay men and lesbians, the 1970s were years of significant achievement. Gay liberation and women's liberation changed the sexual landscape of the nation. Hundreds of thousands of gay women and men came out and openly affirmed same-sex eroticism. We won repeal of sodomy laws in half the states, a partial lifting of the exclusion of lesbians and gay men from federal employment, civil rights protection in a few dozen cities, the inclusion of gay rights in the platform of the Democratic Party, and the elimination of homosexuality from the psychiatric profession's list of mental illnesses. The gay male subculture expanded and became increasingly visible in large cities, and lesbian feminists pioneered in building alternative institutions and an alternative culture that attempted to embody a liberating vision of the future.

In the 1980s, however, with the resurgence of an active right wing, gay men and lesbians face the future warily. Our victories appear tenuous and fragile; the relative freedom of the past few years seems too recent to be permanent. In some parts of the lesbian and gay male community, a feeling of doom is growing: analogies with McCarthy's America, when "sexual perverts" were a special target of the right, and with Nazi Germany, where gays were shipped to concentration camps, surface with increasing frequency.

Everywhere there is a sense that new strategies are in order if we want to preserve our gains and move ahead.

I believe that a new, more accurate theory of gay history must be part of this political enterprise. When the gay liberation movement began at the end of the 1960s, gay men and lesbians had no history that we could use to fashion our goals and strategy. In the ensuing years, in building a movement without a knowledge of our history, we instead invented a mythology. This mythical history drew on personal experience, which we read backward in time. For instance, most lesbians and gay men in the 1960s first discovered their homosexual desires in isolation, unaware of others, and without resources for naming and understanding what they felt. From this experience, we constructed a myth of silence, invisibility, and isolation as the essential characteristics of gay life in the past as well as the present. Moreover, because we faced so many oppressive laws, public policies, and cultural beliefs, we projected this into an image of the abysmal past: until gay liberation, lesbians and gay men were always the victims of systematic, undifferentiated, terrible oppression.

These myths have limited our political perspective. They have contributed, for instance, to an overreliance on a strategy of coming out—if every gay man and lesbian in America came out, gay oppression would end—and have allowed us to ignore the institutionalized ways in which homophobia and heterosexism are reproduced. They have encouraged, at times, an incapacitating despair, especially at moments like the present: how can we unravel a gay oppression so pervasive and unchanging?

There is another historical myth that enjoys nearly universal acceptance in the gay movement, the myth of the "eternal homosexual." The argument runs something like this: Gay men and lesbians always were and always will be. We are everywhere; not just now, but throughout history, in all societies and all periods. This myth served a positive political function in the first years of gay liberation. In the early 1970s, when we battled an ideology that

either denied our existence or defined us as psychopathic individuals or freaks of nature, it was empowering to assert that "we are everywhere." But in recent years it has confined us as surely as the most homophobic medical theories, and locked our movement in place.

Here I wish to challenge this myth. I want to argue that gay men and lesbians have not always existed. Instead, they are a product of history, and have come into existence in a specific historical era. Their emergence is associated with the relations of capitalism; it has been the historical development of capitalism—more specifically, its free-labor system—that has allowed large numbers of men and women in the late twentieth century to call themselves gay, to see themselves as part of a community of similar men and women, and to organize politically on the basis of that identity.[1] Finally, I want to suggest some political lessons we can draw from this view of history.

*   *   *

What, then, are the relationships between the free-labor system of capitalism and homosexuality? First, let me review some features of capitalism. Under capitalism workers are "free" laborers in two ways. We have the freedom to look for a job. We own our ability to work and have the freedom to sell our labor power for wages to anyone willing to buy it. We are also freed from the ownership of anything except our labor power. Most of us do not own the land or the tools that produce what we need, but rather have to work for a living in order to survive. So, if we are free to sell our labor power in the positive sense, we are also freed, in the negative sense, from any other alternative. This dialectic—the constant interplay between exploitation and some measure of autonomy—informs all of the history of those who have lived under capitalism.

As capital—money used to make more money—expands so does this system of free labor. Capital expands in several ways. Usually it expands in the same place, transforming small firms into larger ones, but it also expands by taking over new areas of production: the weaving of cloth, for instance, or the baking of bread. Finally, capital expands geographically. In the United States, capitalism initially took root in the Northeast, at a time when slavery was the dominant system in the South and when noncapitalist Native American societies occupied the western half of the continent. During the nineteenth century, capital spread from the Atlantic to the Pacific, and in the twentieth, U.S. capital has penetrated almost every part of the world.

The expansion of capital and the spread of wage labor have affected a profound transformation in the structure and functions of the nuclear family, the ideology of family life, and the meaning of heterosexual relations. It is these changes in the family that are most directly linked to the appearance of a collective gay life.

The white colonists in seventeenth-century New England established villages structured around a household economy, composed of family units that were basically self-sufficient, independent, and patriarchal. Men, women, and children farmed land owned by the male head of the household. Although there was a division of labor between men and women, the family was truly an interdependent unit of production: the survival of each member depended on the cooperation of all. The home was a workplace where women processed raw farm products into food for daily consumption, where they made clothing, soap, and candles, and where husbands, wives, and children worked together to produce the goods they consumed.

By the nineteenth century, this system of household production was in decline. In the Northeast, as merchant capitalists invested the money accumulated through trade in the production of goods, wage labor became more common. Men and women were drawn out of the largely self-sufficient household economy of the colonial era into a capitalist system of free labor. For women in the nineteenth century, working for wages rarely lasted beyond marriage; for men, it became a permanent condition.

The family was thus no longer an independent unit of production. But although no longer independent, the family was still interdependent. Because capitalism had not expanded very far, because it had not yet taken over—or socialized—the production of consumer goods, women still performed necessary productive labor in the home. Many families no longer produced grain, but wives still baked into bread the flour they bought with their husbands' wages; or, when they purchased yarn or cloth, they still made clothing for their families. By the mid-nineteenth century, capitalism had destroyed the economic self-sufficiency of many families, but not the mutual dependence of the members.

This transition away from the household family-based economy to a fully developed capitalist free-labor economy occurred very slowly, over almost two centuries. As late as 1920, fifty percent of the U.S. population lived in communities of fewer than 2,500 people. The vast majority of blacks in the early twentieth century lived outside the free-labor economy, in a system of sharecropping and tenancy that rested on the family. Not only did independent farming as a way of life still exist for millions of Americans, but even in towns and small cities women continued to grow and process food, make clothing, and engage in other kinds of domestic production.

But for those people who felt the brunt of these changes, the family took on new significance as an affective unit, an institution that provided not goods but emotional satisfaction and happiness. By the 1920s among the white middle class, the ideology surrounding the family described it as the means through which men and women formed satisfying, mutually enhancing relationships and created an environment that nurtured children. The family became the setting for a "personal life," sharply distinguished and disconnected from the public world of work and production.[2]

The meaning of heterosexual relations also changed. In colonial New England the birth rate averaged over seven children per woman of childbearing age. Men and women needed the labor of children. Producing offspring was as necessary for survival as producing grain. Sex was harnessed to procreation. The Puritans did not celebrate heterosexuality but rather marriage; they condemned all sexual expression outside the marriage bond and did not differentiate sharply between sodomy and heterosexual fornication.

By the 1970s, however, the birth rate had dropped to under two. With the exception of the post–World War II baby boom, the decline has been continuous for two centuries, paralleling the spread of capitalist relations of production. It occurred even when access to contraceptive devices and abortion was systematically curtailed. The decline has included every segment of the population—urban and rural families, blacks and whites, ethnics and WASPs, the middle class and the working class.

As wage labor spread and production became socialized, then, it became possible to release sexuality from the "imperative" to procreate. Ideologically, heterosexual expression came to be a means of establishing intimacy, promoting happiness, and experiencing pleasure. In divesting the household of its economic independence and fostering the separation of sexuality from procreation, capitalism has created conditions that allow some men and women to organize a personal life around their erotic/emotional attraction to their own sex. It has made possible the formation of urban communities of lesbians and gay men and, more recently, of a politics based on sexual identity.

Evidence from colonial New England court records and church sermons indicates that male and female homosexual behavior existed in the seventeenth century. Homosexual behavior, however, is different from homosexual identity. There was, quite simply, no "social space" in the colonial system of production that allowed men and women to be gay. Survival was structured around participation in a nuclear family. There were certain homosexual acts—sodomy among men, "lewdness" among women—in which individuals engaged, but family was so pervasive that colonial society lacked even the category of homosexual or lesbian to describe a person. It is

quite possible that some men and women experienced a stronger attraction to their own sex than to the opposite sex—in fact, some colonial court cases refer to men who persisted in their "unnatural" attractions—but one could not fashion out of that preference a way of life. Colonial Massachusetts even had laws prohibiting unmarried adults from living outside family units.[3]

By the second half of the nineteenth century, this situation was noticeably changing as the capitalist system of free labor took hold. Only when individuals began to make their living through wage labor, instead of as parts of an interdependent family unit, was it possible for homosexual desire to coalesce into a personal identity—an identity based on the ability to remain outside the heterosexual family and to construct a personal life based on attraction to one's own sex. By the end of the century, a class of men and women existed who recognized their erotic interest in their own sex, saw it as a trait that set them apart from the majority, and sought others like themselves. These early gay lives came from a wide social spectrum: civil servants and business executives, department store clerks and college professors, factory operatives, ministers, lawyers, cooks, domestics, hoboes, and the idle rich; men and women, black and white, immigrant and native-born.

In this period, gay men and lesbians began to invent ways of meeting each other and sustaining a group life. Already, in the early twentieth century, large cities contained male homosexual bars. Gay men stalked out cruising areas, such as Riverside Drive in New York City and Lafayette Park in Washington. In St. Louis and the nation's capital, annual drag balls brought together large numbers of black gay men. Public bathhouses and YMCAs became gathering spots for male homosexuals. Lesbians formed literary societies and private social clubs. Some working-class women "passed" as men to obtain better-paying jobs and lived with other women—forming lesbian couples who appeared to the world as husband and wife. Among the faculties of women's colleges, in the settlement houses, and in the professional associations and clubs that women formed, one could find lifelong intimate relationships supported by a web of lesbian friends. By the 1920s and 1930s, large cities such as New York and Chicago contained lesbian bars. These patterns of living could evolve because capitalism allowed individuals to survive beyond the confines of the family.[4]

Simultaneously, ideological definitions of homosexual behavior changed. Doctors developed theories about homosexuality, describing it as a condition, something that was inherent in a person, a part of his or her "nature." These theories did not represent scientific breakthroughs, elucidations of previously undiscovered areas of knowledge; rather, they were an ideological response to a new way of organizing one's personal life. The popularization of the medical model, in turn, affected the consciousness of the women and men who experienced homosexual desire, so that they came to define themselves through their erotic life.[5]

These new forms of gay identity and patterns of group life also reflected the differentiation of people according to gender, race, and class that is so pervasive in capitalist societies. Among whites, for instance, gay men have traditionally been more visible than lesbians. This partly stems from the division between the public male sphere and the private female sphere. Streets, parks, and bars, especially at night, were "male space." Yet the greater visibility of white men also reflected their larger numbers. The Kinsey studies of the 1940s and 1950s found significantly more men than women with predominantly homosexual histories, a situation caused, I would argue, by the fact that capitalism had drawn far more men than women into the labor force, and at higher wages. Men could more easily construct a personal life independent of attachments to the opposite sex, whereas women were more likely to remain economically dependent on men. Kinsey also found a strong positive correlation between years of schooling and lesbian activity. College-educated white women, far more able than their working-class sisters to support themselves, could survive more easily without intimate relationships with men.[6]

Among working-class immigrants in the early twentieth century, closely knit kin networks and an ethic of family solidarity placed constraints on individual autonomy that made gayness a difficult option to pursue. In contrast, for reasons not altogether clear, urban black communities appeared relatively tolerant of homosexuality. The popularity in the 1920s and 1930s of songs with lesbian and gay male themes—"B. D. Woman," "Prove It on Me," "Sissy Man," "Fairey Blues"—suggests an openness about homosexual expression at odds with the mores of whites. Among men in the rural West in the 1940s, Kinsey found extensive incidence of homosexual behavior, but, in contrast with the men in large cities, little consciousness of gay identity. Thus even as capitalism exerted a homogenizing influence by gradually transforming more individuals into wage laborers and separating them from traditional communities, different groups of people were affected in different ways.[7]

The decisions of particular men and women to act on their erotic/emotional preference for the same sex, along with the new consciousness that this preference made them different, led to the formation of an urban subculture of gay men and lesbians. Yet at least through the 1930s this subculture remained rudimentary, unstable, and difficult to find. How, then, did the complex, well-developed gay community emerge that existed by the time the gay liberation movement exploded? The answer is to be found in the dislocations of World War II, a time when the cumulative changes of several decades coalesced into a qualitatively new shape.

The war severely disrupted traditional patterns of gender relations and sexuality, and temporarily created a new erotic situation conducive to homosexual expression. It plucked millions of young men and women, whose sexual identities were just forming, out of their homes, out of towns and small cities, out of the heterosexual environment of the family, and dropped them into sex-segregated situations—as GIs, as WACS and WAVES, in same-sex rooming houses for women workers who relocated to seek employment. The war freed millions of men and women from the settings where heterosexuality was normally imposed. For men and women already gay, it provided an opportunity to meet people like themselves. Others could become gay because of the temporary freedom to explore sexuality that the war provided.[8]

The gay men and women of the 1940s were pioneers. Their decisions to act on their desires formed the underpinnings of an urban subculture of gay men and lesbians. Throughout the 1950s and 1960s the gay subculture grew and stabilized, so that people coming out then could more easily find other gay women and men than in the past. Newspapers and magazines published articles describing gay male life. Literally hundreds of novels with lesbian themes were published.[9] Psychoanalysts complained about the new ease with which their gay male patients found sexual partners. And the gay subculture was not to be found just in the largest cities. Lesbian and gay male bars existed in places like Worcester, Massachusetts, and Buffalo, New York; in Columbia, South Carolina, and Des Moines, Iowa. Gay life in the 1950s and 1960s became a nationwide phenomenon. By the time of the Stonewall Riot in New York City in 1969—the event that ignited the gay liberation movement—our situation was hardly one of silence, invisibility, and isolation. A massive, grass-roots liberation movement could form almost overnight precisely because communities of lesbians and gay men existed.

Although gay community was a precondition for a mass movement, the oppression of lesbians and gay men was the force that propelled the movement into existence. As the subculture expanded and grew more visible in the post–World War II era, oppression by the state intensified, becoming more systematic and inclusive. The Right scapegoated "sexual perverts" during the McCarthy era. Eisenhower imposed a total ban on the employment of gay women and men by the federal government and government contractors. Purges of lesbians and homosexuals from the military rose sharply. The FBI instituted widespread surveillance of gay meeting places and of lesbian and gay organizations, such as the Daughters of Bilitis and the Mattachine Society. The Post Office placed tracers on the correspondence of gay men and passed evidence of homosexual activity on to employers. Urban vice squads invaded private homes, made sweeps of lesbian and gay male bars, entrapped gay men in public places, and fomented local witch-hunts. The danger involved in being gay rose even as the possibilities of being gay were enhanced. Gay liberation was a response to this contradiction.

*   *   *

Although lesbians and gay men won significant victories in the 1970s and opened up some safe social space in which to exist, we can hardly claim to have dealt a fatal blow to heterosexism and homophobia. One could even argue that the enforcement of gay oppression has merely changed locales, shifting somewhat from the state to the arena of extralegal violence in the form of increasingly open physical attacks on lesbians and gay men. And, as our movements have grown, they have generated a backlash that threatens to wipe out our gains. Significantly, this New Right opposition has taken shape as a "pro-family" movement. How is it that capitalism, whose structure made possible the emergence of a gay identity and the creation of urban gay communities, appears unable to accept gay men and lesbians in its midst? Why do heterosexism and homophobia appear so resistant to assault?

The answers, I think, can be found in the contradictory relationship of capitalism to the family. On the one hand, as I argued earlier, capitalism has gradually undermined the material basis of the nuclear family by taking away the economic functions that cemented the ties between family members. As more adults have been drawn into the free-labor system, and as capital has expanded its sphere until it produces as commodities most goods and services we need for our survival, the forces that propelled men and women into families and kept them there have weakened. On the other hand, the ideology of capitalist society has enshrined the family as the source of love, affection, and emotional security, the place where our need for stable, intimate human relationships is satisfied.

This elevation of the nuclear family to preeminence in the sphere of personal life is not accidental. Every society needs structures for reproduction and childrearing, but the possibilities are not limited to the nuclear family. Yet the privatized family fits well with capitalist relations of production. Capitalism has socialized production while maintaining that the products of socialized labor belong to the owners of private property. In many ways, childrearing has also been progressively socialized over the last two centuries, with schools, the media, peer groups, and employers taking over functions that once belonged to parents. Nevertheless, capitalist society maintains that reproduction and childrearing are private tasks, that children "belong" to parents, who exercise the rights of ownership. Ideologically, capitalism drives people into heterosexual families: each generation comes of age having internalized a heterosexist model of intimacy and personal relationships. Materially, capitalism weakens the bonds that once kept families together so that their members experience a growing instability in the place they have come to expect happiness and emotional security. Thus, while capitalism has knocked the material foundation away from family life, lesbians, gay men, and heterosexual feminists have become the scapegoats for the social instability of the system.

This analysis, if persuasive, has implications for us today. It can affect our perception of our identity, our formulation of political goals, and our decisions about strategy.

I have argued that lesbian and gay identity and communities are historically created, the result of a process of capitalist development that has spanned many generations. A corollary of this argument is that we are not a fixed social minority composed for all time of a certain percentage of the population. There are more of us than one hundred years ago, more of us than forty years ago. And there may very well be

more gay men and lesbians in the future. Claims made by gays and nongays that sexual orientation is fixed at an early age, that large numbers of visible gay men and lesbians in society, the media, and the schools will have no influence on the sexual identities of the young, are wrong. Capitalism has created the material conditions for homosexual desire to express itself as a central component of some individuals' lives; now, our political movements are changing consciousness, creating the ideological conditions that make it easier for people to make that choice.

To be sure, this argument confirms the worst fears and most rabid rhetoric of our political opponents. But our response must be to challenge the underlying belief that homosexual relations are bad, a poor second choice. We must not slip into the opportunistic defense that society need not worry about tolerating us, since only homosexuals become homosexuals. At best, a minority group analysis and a civil rights strategy pertain to those of us who already are gay. It leaves today's youth—tomorrow's lesbians and gay men—to internalize heterosexist models that it can take a lifetime to expunge.

I have also argued that capitalism has led to the separation of sexuality from procreation. Human sexual desire need no longer be harnessed to reproductive imperatives, to procreation; its expression has increasingly entered the realm of choice. Lesbians and homosexuals most clearly embody the potential of this spirit, since our gay relationships stand entirely outside a procreative framework. The acceptance of our erotic choices ultimately depends on the degree to which society is willing to affirm sexual expression as a form of play, positive and life-enhancing. Our movement may have begun as the struggle of a "minority," but what we should now be trying to "liberate" is an aspect of the personal lives of all people—sexual expression.[10]

Finally, I have suggested that the relationship between capitalism and the family is fundamentally contradictory. On the one hand, capitalism continually weakens the material foundation of family life, making it possible for individuals to live outside the family, and for a lesbian and gay male identity to develop. On the other, it needs to push men and women into families, at least long enough to reproduce the next generation of workers. The elevation of the family to ideological preeminence guarantees that a capitalist society will reproduce not just children, but heterosexism and homophobia. In the most profound sense, capitalism is the problem.[11]

How do we avoid remaining the scapegoats, the political victims of the social instability that capitalism generates? How can we take this contradictory relationship and use it to move toward liberation?

Gay men and lesbians exist on social terrain beyond the boundaries of the heterosexual nuclear family. Our communities have formed in that social space. Our survival and liberation depend on our ability to defend and expand that terrain, not just for ourselves but for everyone. That means, in part, support for issues that broaden the opportunities for living outside traditional heterosexual family units: issues like the availability of abortion and the ratification of the Equal Rights Amendment, affirmative action for people of color and for women, publicly funded daycare and other essential social services, decent welfare payments, full employment, the rights of young people—in other words, programs and issues that provide a material basis for personal autonomy.

The rights of young people are especially critical. The acceptance of children as dependents, as belonging to parents, is so deeply ingrained that we can scarcely imagine what it would mean to treat them as autonomous human beings, particularly in the realm of sexual expression and choice. Yet until that happens, gay liberation will remain out of our reach.

But personal autonomy is only half the story. The instability of families and the sense of impermanence and insecurity that people are now experiencing in their personal relationships are real social problems that need to be addressed. We need political solutions for these difficulties of personal life. These solutions should not come in the form of a radical version of the pro-family position, of some left-wing proposals to strengthen the family. Socialists do not generally respond to the exploitation and economic inequality of industrial capitalism by calling for a return to the family farm and handicraft production. We recognize that the vastly increased productivity that capitalism has made possible by socializing production is one of its progressive features. Similarly, we should not be trying to turn back the clock to some mythic age of the happy family.

We do need, however, structures and programs that will help to dissolve the boundaries that isolate the family, particularly those that privatize childrearing. We need community- or worker-controlled day care, housing where privacy and community coexist, neighborhood institutions—from medical clinics to performance centers—that enlarge the social unit where each of us has a secure place. As we create structures beyond the nuclear family that provide a sense of belonging, the family will wane in significance. Less and less will it seem to make or break our emotional security.

In this respect gay men and lesbians are well situated to play a special role. Already excluded from families as most of us are, we have had to create, for our survival, networks of support that do not depend on the bonds of blood or the license of the state, but that are freely chosen and nurtured. The building of an "affectional community" must be as much a part of our political movement as are campaigns for civil rights. In this way we may prefigure the shape of personal relationships in a society grounded in equality and justice rather than exploitation and oppression, a society where autonomy and security do not preclude each other but coexist.

Notes

1. I do not mean to suggest that no one has ever proposed that gay identity is a product of historical change. See, for instance, Mary McIntosh, "The Homosexual Role," *Social Problems* 16 (1968): 182–92; Jeffrey Weeks, *Coming Out: Homosexual Politics in Britain* (New York: Quartet Books, 1977). It is also

implied in Michel Foucault, *The History of Sexuality, vol. 1: An Introduction,* trans. Robert Hurley (New York: Pantheon, 1978). However, this does represent a minority viewpoint and the works cited above have not specified how it is that capitalism as a system of production has allowed for the emergence of a gay male and lesbian identity. As an example of the "eternal homosexual" thesis, see John Boswell, *Christianity, Social Tolerance, and Homosexuality* (Chicago: University of Chicago Press, 1980), where "gay people" remains an unchanged social category through fifteen centuries of Mediterranean and Western Europe history.

2. See Eli Zaretsky, *Capitalism, the Family, and Personal Life* (New York: Harper & Row, 1976); and Paula Fass, *The Damned and the Beautiful: American Youth in the 1920s* (New York: Oxford University Press, 1977).

3. Robert F. Oaks, "'Things Fearful to Name': Sodomy and Buggery in Seventeenth-Century New England," *Journal of Social History* 12 (1978): 268–81; J. R. Roberts, "The Case of Sarah Norman and Mary Hammond," *Sinister Wisdom* 24 (1980): 57–62; and Jonathan Katz, *Gay American History* (New York: Crowell, 1976), 16–24, 568–71.

4. For the period from 1870 to 1940 see the documents in Katz, *Gay American History,* and idem *Gay/Lesbian Almanac* (New York: Crowell, 1983). Other sources include Allan Bérubé, "Lesbians and Gay Men in Early San Francisco: Notes Toward a Social History of Lesbians and Gay Men in America," unpublished paper, 1979; Vern Bullough and Bonnie Bullough, "Lesbianism in the 1920s and 1930s: A Newfound Study," *Signs* 2 (Summer 1977): 895–904.

5. On the medical model see Weeks, *Coming Out,* 23–32. The impact of the medical model on the consciousness of men and women can be seen in Louis Hyde, ed., *Rat and the Devil: The Journal Letters of F. O. Matthiessen and Russell Cheney* (Hamden, Conn.: Archon, 1978), 47, and in the story of Lucille Hart in Katz, *Gay American History,* 258–79. Radclyffe Hall's classic novel about lesbianism, *The Well of Loneliness,* published in 1928, was perhaps one of the most important vehicles for the popularization of the medical model.

6. See Alfred Kinsey et al., *Sexual Behavior in the Human Male* (Philadelphia: W. B. Saunders, 1948)

and *Sexual Behavior in the Human Female* (Philadelphia: W. B. Saunders, 1953).

7. On black music, see "AC/DC Blues: Gay Jazz Reissues," Stash Records, ST-106 (1977) and Chris Albertson, *Bessie* (New York: Stein and Day, 1974); on the persistence of kin networks in white ethnic communities see Judith Smith, "Our Own Kind: Family and Community Networks in Providence," in *A Heritage of Her Own,* eds. Nancy F. Cott and Elizabeth H. Pleck (New York: Simon & Schuster, 1979), 393–411; on differences between rural and urban male homoeroticism see Kinsey et al., *Sexual Behavior in the Human Male,* 455–57, 630–31.

8. The argument and the information in this and the following paragraphs come from my book *Sexual Politics, Sexual Communities: The Making of a Homosexual Minority in the United States, 1940–1970* (Chicago: University of Chicago Press, 1983). I have also developed it with reference to San Francisco in "Gay Politics, Gay Community: San Francisco's Experience," *Socialist Review* 55 (January–February 1981): 77–104.

9. On lesbian novels see the *Ladder,* March 1958, 18; February 1960, 14–15; April 1961, 12–13; February 1962, 6–11; January 1963, 6–13; February 1964, 12–19; February 1965, 19–23; March 1966, 22–26; and April 1967, 8–13. The *Ladder* was the magazine published by the Daughters of Bilitis.

10. This especially needs to be emphasized today. The 1980 annual conference of the National Organization for Women, for instance, passed a lesbian rights resolution that defined the issue as one of "discrimination based on affectional/sexual preference/orientation," and explicitly disassociated the issue from other questions of sexuality such as pornography, sadomasochism, public sex, and pederasty.

11. I do not mean to suggest that homophobia is "caused" by capitalism, or is to be found only in capitalist societies. Severe sanctions against homoeroticism can be found in European feudal society and in contemporary socialist countries. But my focus in this essay has been the emergence of a gay identity under capitalism, and the mechanisms specific to capitalism that made this possible and that reproduce homophobia as well.

Dossier 4: Queer Desire

Dossier 4 provides texts that begin to account for the appearance of the new discourses of the "queer" (articulated here in the writings of Cherry Smith, Michael Warner, Dennis Cooper, Cherrie Moraga, Lauren Berlant and Elizabeth Freeman, Daniel Tsang, and David Halperin), which are markers of today's post-gay liberationist and ludic (post) modern sexual politics. Today's "queer" discourses are not an instance of history repeating itself: The term "queer" as used now develops out of new historical circumstances and its significance today is different from its significance in earlier moments. In fact today's "queer" theory has gone beyond its own recent origins: It both developed out of and has gone beyond the textual/sexual cultural understandings provided by ludic (post)modernism. Ludic (post)modernism proposes culture itself as basically a semiotically "playful" site of "autonomous desire," as a space of shifting, reversible, and undecidable representations; of hyperreality and simulation; of texts with no "outsides"; of decentering, *différance,* and the "free play of the signifier"; of *jouissance* and the pleasure of the text; of performativity and of em-body-ment; of libidinal rather than conceptual economy; of consumption rather than production; of undecidability and merely aleatory change and not determinate social change; of "reading justly" rather than justice. It is out of and along with these "unsettlings" of modernist and humanist discourses that the new queer discourses have developed, as the general introduction to this volume extensively argues.

The aim of Dossier 4 is not simply to make some of the new queer discourses available but more importantly to stage the differences between today's privileged mode of accounting for homosexuality, ludic queer theory, and an "other" account of "queerity" (derived from a critique of the existing dominant), which is a Marxist theory of sexualities. From the dominant "ludic" perspective, the goal of today's sexual politics is to "make everything perfectly queer," so that everyone (straight, lesbian, gay, bisexual) will end up living—as Michael Warner suggests in his text reprinted in this volume—on "a queer planet." The problem with such a proposal is that it ultimately defines the queer subject as primarily a *queer reader* trying to achieve a *queer state of mind:* In other words, the dominant understanding of "queerness" is basically hermeneutic, a form of textual/sexual politics (tending finally in the direction of an "erotics") that aims at changing modes of consciousness and defines the "material" not in historical terms, but—following Saussure—as the "material" part of the sign (the signifier).

On this view, queerity is that utterly "flexible" mentality that, for example (as we see in the text of Silverman in Dossier 2), allows the subject historically constituted as "female" to "become"—*as a reader*—a gay male subject. Silverman is able to "experience" "mentally" the reversibility of her subjectivity: She remarks that while writing a book on "deviant" masculinities, "I often felt myself to be 'outside' my corporeal 'envelope' and 'inside' the subjectivities I was exploring." Whereas within the dominant frame of textual/sexual politics, such a "queer" moment is understood as "liberating," from the perspective of a historical materialist politics, it is merely an instance of an ideologically mystified subject imagining herself to have escaped—via the "encounter" in reading with the "deviant" signifier—her own historical construction. It is, in other words, an instance of idealist, not materialist "explanation." What has happened here is not a structural change in society (the overthrow of capitalism and the inauguration of a socialist economy) that erases the exploitative practice of the capitalist extraction of surplus value from the labor of workers. Silverman's text provides just another instance of bourgeois "self-invention," a change of state of mind like that of Warner, which I critique in the introduction to the opening section of this volume ("Queer Consensus/Socialist Conflict"), brought about by a change of reading practices. (For more sustained discussions of the bourgeois idea of "invention"/"self-invention" in relation to sexualities, see The "Invention" of the Queer). Such moments of "liberation" like the one just described are typical of the Euramerican sexual common sense today. Such moments of new "desire" are actually encouraged in contemporary Western societies (which are, at the same time, busy recruiting the low-cost labor of peoples of the South and East to sustain their more comfortable lives and take care of their needs) for the very reason that they have little to do with overcoming social injustice: The basis of exploitation along the axes of class, race, gender, sexual orientation, and so on, lies not in the attitudes, opinions, mental states, or "states of desire" (to quote Edmund White) that people experience, but in the prevailing inequitable global system of resource distribution that has to be explained conceptually, that is, theoretically. Materialism argues that transformative social change cannot begin with the "liberation" of consciousness (however "real" such experiences may feel to the experiencer) since, in the words of Marx, "It is not the consciousness of men that determines their existence, but their social existence that determines their consciousness" (Marx 1970, 21).

Although the return of the queer is in fact the historical product of ludic (post)modernism, in its most "advanced" emergent form it is going beyond those parameters. In emergent queer theory, the textual/sexual queer reading is being replaced by a radical erotics. Although ludic (post)modernism makes discourses of the body a major focus of its inquiries, classic ludic reading strategies nevertheless insist on preserving the distinction between the "textual/sexual" as mode of signification, on the one hand, and the sensuous (sensations and impressions), on the other. In other words, textual/sexual reading follows Saussure in emphasizing the notion that the "signifier" is not "a purely physical thing" but a "sound image" (or "sight image") (Saussure 1966, 66) and also follows Derrida in speaking not of the sensory proper but of "something like the sensory" (Derrida 1982, 250). From this it follows that textual/sexual reading strategies place the emphasis on shifts, changes, and reversals in understanding brought about through the slippage of the signifier in the production of representations. In the textual/sexual ludic model, change is brought about by the disruption of the signified by the signifier, of denotation by connotations, of conceptuality by textuality, of literality by figurality. However, in today's emerging "queer" theory—which moves beyond the literal/figural distinction itself—what "unsettles" meaning is not signifiers but sensations: Change is brought about not by the slippage of the signifier (not by tropes, "turns" in representation) but by the body's "tropisms" (its "turns" in search of sensations and impressions). (For a more sustained discussion of these issues, see Morton 1993 and for examples of the new queer erotics, see Grosz and Probyn 1995 and Kiss and Tell 1994.)

From the materialist perspective, culture did not become ludic "in itself" or "on its own accord" or "by accident." The ludic cultural turn is a historical development produced by changes in the mode of production and the division of labor that required new subjectivities to help late capitalism sustain itself by providing ever newer terrains for the extraction of surplus value. What is of special significance in the present context is that the "becoming ludic" of Western culture has coincided historically not just with the increasing prominence or visibility of homosexual activity but also with the appearance of the homosexual—and now the new queer—subjectivities. This new prominence cannot be simply celebrated, but must also be carefully investigated. The materialist argument is not that homosexual activities are a creation of capitalism itself: In all cultures and in all historical moments, homosexual activity has always been a possibility and—whether socially approved or not—no doubt an actuality. The materialist view is instead that the particular form of (homo)sexual practices shifts as a consequence of changes in the prevailing mode and relations of production. Hence the prominence achieved by queer subjects in liberal capitalist democracies today (like that of female, African-American, and other marginal subjects) is far from unproblematic. The acceptability of the dominant form of the queer subject depends precisely on the degree to which it can be shaped as a "flexible" subject, a "good" "reader" with fluid—rather than fixed (in the sense of resistant)—affective modalities. Thus the increasing visibility of queer subjects today in liberal capitalist democracies is not so much the simple result of their self-liberating efforts (those "spontaneous reversals" of power articulated by Foucault) as it is the result of the reformative modifications undertaken by the system of late capitalism. In its earlier stages of development, capitalism—centered around the heterosexual extended family and then the heterosexual nuclear family as the productive and reproductive unit—did not have much use for queer subjects. In those earlier stages, the interests of capital and the interests of patriarchy tended to coincide, although to varying degrees in different historical moments.

Today, however, when the patriarchal family (in the 1950s version of which the husband "earned" and the wife "spent") has come under increasing pressure from, and indeed largely broken down under, the diverging needs of late capitalism in the (post)modern moment, the queer body—which may be sexually quite patriarchal (in the celebration, for instance, of the signifiers of a dominating masculinity) but non-patriarchal perhaps in exceeding to

some extent the domestic division of labor—is celebrated because it is a hyperefficient wage-earning *and* commodity-consuming body. One of President Clinton's early arguments in favor of gays in the military (before he moved, as in other issues, toward self-compromise) was that we "need everybody." This means that (post)-modern late capitalist society needs "queer" bodies as well. It may be argued that the Clinton presidency—which is situated in new historical contradictions that make it necessary to combine traditional "Republican" goals with traditional "Democratic" goals and thus aims at keeping U.S. capitalism healthy while including such marginalized groups as women, African-Americans, lesbians, and gays—is the (post)-modern presidency needed to produce and legitimize the new forms of subjectivity of labor and consumption that are required by late multinational capitalism. (For a sustained articulation of the changes in subjectivities in relation to the labor requirements of late capitalism, see Chapter 6 of Zavarzadeh and Morton 1994. Regarding the changes in sexualities and desire in relation to changes in exchange values under capitalism, see Morton 1995.)

The discourses of the Right on homosexuality are represented here in the text by David Horowitz, whose criticism aims basically at containing and policing, if not erasing altogether, "other" sexualities. What is needed instead—as I have argued throughout this anthology—is a historical, theoretical, and collective understanding of other sexualities, that is, a denaturalizing and historicizing of them that can only be provided by historical materialist critique of the existing dominant understandings. To conclude this volume, I have provided texts that inaugurate such an understanding. "What Can *Materialism* Mean to Poststructuralists?" by Kathryn Bond Stockton points up the idealist character of the (post)-structuralist notion of *the material,* without developing a historical materialist understanding of the term. The remaining texts share the historical materialist perspective. The texts by Sharon Smith and Nicola Field critique homosexual identity politics and reveal the idealist presuppositions of that kind of politics. The text by the Los Angeles Research Group (of lesbian Marxists) not only offers a theorization of homosexual oppression in relation to class and the social division of labor but also—in its critique of the analysis of homosexuality by another leftist group, the Revolutionary Union—points up the necessity of internal critiques over sexuality *within* the Left. Teresa L. Ebert's essay, "The Matter of Materialism," critiques the ludic understanding of the material that dominates the Euramerican academy and culture industry today and theorizes the resistant and oppositional understanding of the material that constitutes the basis for the new Red Theory that is emerging in the mid-1990s. (For developments in Red Theory, see for example Ebert 1995.) Robert Andrew Nowlan's "Critique as Radical Praxis" theorizes historical materialist critique as a political praxis. Finally, "Capitalism and Homophobia" by the 1917 Collective offers a broad Marxist-Leninist historical overview of homophobia.

References

Derrida, Jacques. (1982) *Margins of Philosophy*. Trans. Alan Bass. Chicago: University of Chicago Press.

Ebert, Teresa L. (1995) "(Untimely) Critiques for a Red Feminism." *Transformation 1. Post-ality: Marxism and Postmodernism.* (Spring):113–149.

Grosz, Elizabeth, and Elspeth Probyn, eds. (1995) *Sexy Bodies: The Strange Carnalities of Feminism.* London and New York: Routledge.

Kiss and Tell. (1994) *Her Tongue on My Theory: Images, Essays and Fantasies.* Vancouver, B.C.: Press Gang Publishers.

Marx, Karl. (1970) *A Contribution to the Critique of Political Economy.* New York: International Publishers.

Morton, Donald. (1993) "The Politics of Queer Theory in the (Post)Modern Moment." *Genders* 17 (Fall):121–150.

———. (1995) "Queerity and Ludic Sado-Masochism: Compulsory Consumption and the Emerging Post-al Queer." *Transformation: Marxist Boundary Work in Theory, Economics, Politics and Culture* 1:189–215.

Saussure, Ferdinand de. (1966) *Course in General Linguistics.* Trans. Wade Baskin. New York: McGraw-Hill.

Zavarzadeh, Mas'ud, and Donald Morton. (1994) *Theory as Resistance: Politics and Culture After (Post)structuralism.* New York and London: Guilford Press.

Zavarzadeh, Mas'ud, Teresa L. Ebert, and Donald Morton, eds. (1996) *The "Invention" of the Queer: Marxism, Lesbian and Gay Theory, Capitalism. Transformation 2: Marxist Boundary Work in Theory, Economics, Politics and Culture.* Washington, D.C.: Maisonneuve Press (forthcoming Spring).

What Is This Thing Called Queer?

Cherry Smith

Queer:

1. *Strange, odd, eccentric; of questionable character, shady, suspect; out of sorts, giddy, faint (feel queer); drunk; homosexual (esp. of man); in Q- street, in difficulty, debt, disrepute*

2. *Homosexual*

3. *Spoil, put out of order*

—**Concise Oxford English Dictionary**

1. *Drunk—Properly, not in your normal state of health, and still rarely used of a drunkard, with a suggestion that condition caused by something else.*

   "Queered in the drinking of a penny pot of malmsey." (Walter Scott: 1822 The Fortune of Nigel*)*

2. *Of unsound mind—'queer in the head'—a bit queer.*

3. *Homosexual: Almost always of males and equally common as an adjective: "I'm not, um, queer. Well, you know, I don't like boys . . ." (Theroux: 1975* The Great Railway Bazaar*)*

Queerdom is a tendency towards homosexuality.

—**The Faber Dictionary of Euphemisms, Faber 1989**

Queer means to fuck with gender. There are straight queers, bi-queers, tranny queers, lez queers, fag queers, SM queers, fisting queers in every single street in this apathetic country of ours.

—**Anonymous leaflet: 'Queer Power Now,' London 1991**

Queer is a symptom, not a movement, a symptom of a desire for radical change.

—**Keith Alcorn, 'Pink Paper,' Issue 208**

In April 1990 a group met in New York to discuss the frequent bashings of gays and lesbians in the East Village. Queer Nation was born with the slogan, 'Queers Bash Back' and stencils were drawn on the pavements: 'My beloved was queerbashed here. Queers fight back.' In classic postmodern fashion, Queer Nation borrowed styles and tactics from popular culture, black liberation struggles, hippies, AIDS activists, feminists and the peace movement to build its confrontational identity.

Queer Nationals are torn between affirming a new identity—'I am queer'—and rejecting restrictive identities—'I reject your categories'; between rejecting assimilation—'I don't need your approval, just get out of my face'—and wanting to be recognised by mainstream society—'we queers are gonna get in your face'. 'Outlook', No 11, Winter 1991

In London, OutRage was formed a few weeks later, with a similar 'in your face' agenda. *It was time.*

OutRage defines itself as:

A broad-based group of lesbians and gay men committed to radical non-violent direct action and civil disobedience to:

* assert the dignity, pride and human rights of lesbians and gay men
* fight homophobia, discrimination and violence against lesbians and gay men
* affirm the rights of lesbians and gay men to sexual freedom, choice and self-determination.

OutRage's first year produced a mass KISS-IN in Piccadilly Circus and a Queer Wedding in Trafalgar Square and provided plenty of sexy copy for a British press that had increasingly ignored or trivialised gay and lesbian politics.

Meanwhile, the legal system was introducing plenty of new challenges around which to rally disaffected queers. In December 1990, fifteen gay men were convicted on a series of charges for having consensual SM sex—a case that became known as Operation Spanner after the police code-name. In February 1992 their appeals were quashed. And in early 1991 the government introduced Clause 25 (now Section 27) of the Criminal Justice Act, which imposes stiffer sentences for certain sexual offences, including gay male procuring, solicitation and indecency, as well as child abuse, incest, rape, murder and sexual assault. The Clause was seen as the most serious move in over a century to increase the sentences for consenting homosexual behaviour and OutRage demonstrated outside Bow Street police station (chosen because it was where Oscar Wilde was charged almost

100 years ago), where activists 'turned themselves in' for crimes of importuning, indecency (kissing in the street) and procuring.

Legislation aimed at preventing lesbians from reproducing and lesbians and gay men from parenting also came to light. Paragraph 16 of the guidance notes to the 1989 Children Act contained an invidious little statement: '"Equal rights" and "gay rights" have no place in fostering', which was later amended, largely thanks to pressure from lesbian and gay campaigners. This followed closely on the Embryology Bill, which attempted to prevent lesbians using public A.I.D. services. The implication that only white, het, middle-class couples were fit parents had wide-reaching consequences for lesbian, gay, black and disabled parents, childcare workers, teachers and social services employees.

In March 1991, during the hysterical 'virgin births' furore about whether a woman who had not had penetrative sex with a man should be allowed artificial insemination, even the *Independent* newspaper supported the idea of dysfunctional lesbians:

How far is it reasonable to assume, on the basis of what we know of human psychology, that a woman who's been unable to establish a relationship with a man, will relate any better to a child?

For many women, lesbian or not, it has often amounted to the same thing.

OutRage rallied against all three threats and over 10,000 marched to Hyde Park in protest. In covering the event, an allegedly liberal, quality newspaper wrote:

Not unexpectedly, the rally was addressed by a lesbian woman [sic] from Australia with a daughter produced by artificial insemination. The mother now faces deportation as an illegal immigrant. People do go to the ends of the earth in order to land up in the most extraordinary fixes. 'Observer', 10 March 1991

This sort of reporting reinforces the insidious moral code in Britain which suggests that:

- lesbians choose to fall in love with the wrong object choice in the wrong country (and that we certainly don't want to encourage any more of them pouring in from foreign places and getting away with it)
- the only healthy way to reproduce is by good old-fashioned 'planned' hetero-fucking and only then if both people are the same colour, race, class and age—note the frenzy when older women mate younger men
- people get arrested on peaceful demos because they choose to get in the policeman's way
- people die of AIDS because they have chosen to contract the disease

You just have to look at the way the press has been condoning the attacks on the transsexual hookers in the Bois de Boulogne. It is being talked about as if transsexuals from the Third World come to Paris out of sheer bloody-mindedness, and that somehow they are, of their nature, 'infected', and the punters are 'innocent victims' of these terrible people. Roz Kaveney

By mid-1991, OutRage had sprouted several affinity groups including the Whores of Babylon (Queers Fighting Religious Intolerance); SISSY (Schools Information Services on Sexuality); and PUSSY (Perverts Undermining State Scrutiny). Their often extravagant actions signalled the emergence of a highly ironic, camp, theatrical politics of direct action which bullied its way to the heart of the complacent media and put fun back into a wearied lesbian and gay movement. 'We've lobbied our tits off,' said Anna-Marie Smith, a founder member of PUSSY, 'and it didn't get us anywhere.'

Action vs Assimilation

Tired of the gentlemanly approach, queer activists saw OutRage as distinctly anti-assimilationist compared to the parliamentary reform group, Stonewall, which had been established as a response to Clause 28 in 1989. The Stonewall agenda is described as:

> To work for equality under the law and full social acceptance for lesbians and gay men. Our approach is an innovatory one for lesbian and gay rights—professional, strategic, tightly managed, able and willing to communicate with decision-makers in a constructive and informed way. 'Interim Report', The Stonewall Group, 1990

This much-criticised, self-elected group of twenty lesbians and gay men has never professed to be representative:

> There really is no gay community. Most of us devise ways of keeping ourselves invisible. One feels one is on one's own. Sir Ian McKellen, 'Independent on Sunday', 10 November 1991

But Stonewall has been perceived as the legitimate voice of the 'lesbian and gay community' by government ministers, though it did not succeed in using the fame or prestige of Sir Ian McKellen and many 'poofs with privilege' to resist Clause 28, or as yet to obtain an equal age of consent.

Assimilationist strategies have nonetheless worked in other European countries. In the Netherlands and Scandinavia, for example, the lesbian and gay community has achieved greater access to the state and has been able to push though an impressive range of legal and social rights. Legalised gay and lesbian weddings (as in Denmark) are far from my own reading of what constitutes equality, whether queer or not, but the acknowledgement of gay and lesbian sexuality in sex education signals the possibility of building a society with a greater tolerance of diversity. Will the fact that legal reforms are being achieved mean that there will not be the same need for queer politics in these countries?

OutRage activists are not interested in seeking acceptance within an unchanged social system, but are setting out to 'fuck up the mainstream' as visibly as possible. It can also be argued that the extremism of OutRage actually facilitates the gains of Stonewall, who are seen as 'rational' and 'civilised' in comparison.

> In reality today, the main conflict is not simply between older 'gay' assimilationists . . . and 'queers' asserting their 'queerness'. Rather it is between those who think of the politics of sexuality as a matter of securing minority rights and those who are contesting the overall validity and authenticity of the epistemology of sexuality itself. Simon Watney

What's in a Name?

Each time the word 'queer' is used it defines a strategy, an attitude, a reference to other identities and a new self-understanding. (And queer can be qualified as 'more queer', 'queerer' or 'queerest' as the naming develops into a more complex process of identification.) For many, the term marks a growing lack of faith in the institutions of the state, in political procedures, in the press, the education system, policing and the law. Both in culture and politics, queer articulates a radical questioning of social and cultural norms, notions of gender, reproductive sexuality and the family. We are beginning to realise how much of our history and ideologies operate on a homo-hetero opposition, constantly privileging the hetero perspective as normative, positing the homo perspective as bad and annihilating the spectrum of sexualities that exists.

> I love queer. Queer is a homosexual of either sex. It's more convenient than saying 'gays' which has to be qualified, or 'lesbians and gay men'. It's an extremely useful polemic term because it is who we say we are, which is, 'Fuck You'. Spike Pittsberg

> I use queer to describe my particular brand of lesbian feminism, which has not much to do with the radical feminism I was involved with in the early 80s. I also use it externally to describe a political inclusivity—a new move towards a celebration of difference across sexualities, across

genders, across sexual preference and across object choice. The two link. Linda Semple

> I define myself as gay mostly. I will not use queer because it is not part of my vernacular—but I have nothing against its use. The same debates around naming occur in the 'black community'. Naming is powerful. Black people and gay people constantly renaming ourselves is a way to shift power from whites and hets respectively. Inge Blackman

> What's in queer, for X, Y, Z, is mostly what people decide to make it. I like dyke and TS. Roz Kaveney

> I don't use that term. I associate it with gay men and I'm dubious about reclaiming derogatory terms. The 'queer agenda', as you call it, isn't my struggle. I put my feminism before my lesbianism. Harriet Wistrich

> I've got a badge that says QUEER BISEXUAL. Alison Thomas

> I say 'I'm KHUSH', and that's from talking to Indian gay men and lesbians and finding that we want to find another word for ourselves that comes from our own culture. But I have used queer in the context of other queers. Pratibha Parmar

> I'm more inclined to use the words 'black lesbian', because when I hear the word queer I think of white, gay men. Isling Mack-Nataf

> Queer gives me politics for things I've always been interested in—like how I feel as a woman who's mistaken for a man, who's intrigued by men and gay male sexuality and as a lesbian and a feminist, connecting to my affinities with men's struggles around sexuality. Tori Smith

> I do have problems with it, but I use queer in the sense that I'M FUCKED OFF, like 'faggots with attitude'. My anger has come from the work I've done around policing. I had no idea how outrageous it was. Paul Burston

> I describe myself as a queer dyke. I never identified with the word lesbian because it seemed

quite medical, it was the word I used to come out to my mother and it seemed to have negative connotations. Queer was one of the ways of identifying with a mixed movement and challenging both separatism and misogyny at the same time. Tessa Boffin

While there is resistance to the word queer, it is useful to remember that there were also battles over 'gay', which was not a term without contradictions. In the early 70s, gay too was characterised as radical and oppositional. By the 80s, lesbians felt the term had rendered them invisible and the addition of 'lesbians and' became a necessary part of naming. For some people who have come out since the beginning of the AIDS epidemic, there is a tendency to associate 'gay' with AIDS and to fail to identify with its happy subtext. However, criticism of the term is hardly new.

> I never liked the word 'gay' (although I never said so), because it exuded a false optimism. It wasn't my word. I was in the party of miserabilists. Derek Jarman

While some older gay liberationists claim that gay is the only way to be, their earnest defence of the term fails to acknowledge either the evolution of self-naming, or the experiences of a younger generation. One of the most vehement members of the anti-queer lobby is Chris White, whose 'Inrage' mounts a one-man picket, complete with a placard claiming 'Homosexuals Are Not Queer', outside the London Lesbian and Gay Centre to discourage people from attending OutRage meetings.

> I shall continue to fight for as long as OutRage and their ilk believe it is part of their role to oppress us, split us and do our enemies' work for us. Chris White, 'Capital Gay', 24 January 1991

The debate has certainly produced lively political exchanges in the letters' pages of the gay press. Yet although for some of the older generation, the term 'queer' painfully recalls the homophobic abuse of a former era, for others it is merely a return to a word they used in a positive, self-parodying sense many years ago.

Back in the 60s when I was trying to figure out whether I was 'gay' or transsexual or what, the people I got to know in the TS/drag queen network in the north would use 'queer' in a 'what of it?' way. They'd sometimes use it in a self-deprecating manner and the two uses would shade into each other. 'Gay' was useful, but it changed nothing. The average homophobe uses it as derogatively as 'poofter' or 'homo'. It's just another word, it doesn't have intrinsic power for good. Roz Kaveney

Lesbians Fight Back

Queer politics is renowned for its sex-positive reclamation of words that have been used negatively against women and lesbians and gays, as well as for its outlandish acronyms. The OutRage affinity group, PUSSY (Perverts Undermining State Scrutiny) is a mixed gay and lesbian group set up to fight censorship, sexism and 'promote queer sex'. PUSSY's aim is to work actively to gain acknowledgement of lesbian sexual practices, both within and beyond the lesbian and gay community, rather than simply to campaign against prohibitive measures.

However, many of PUSSY's campaigns to date have been reactions to censorship from within the community—as in its organisation of protests when London gay and feminist bookshops Gay's the Word, Silver Moon and Sisterwrite refused to carry Della Grace's book *Love Bites* (although West & Wilde, the gay and lesbian bookshop in Edinburgh, and major bookshop chains stocked the title). PUSSY also worked to support the distribution of *Quim* (Britain's first lesbian sex mag), which encountered similar restrictions.

Other campaigns include defending the Terrence Higgins Trust's safer sex material and drawing attention to the Jenny White case. In 1991, White, a fifty-seven-year-old member of the London Older Lesbian Network, had ordered several porn tapes made by lesbians (Blush Productions and Fatale Videos) and sold through a lesbian sex shop in San Francisco. The tapes were seized by Customs and Excise and declared obscene, under the nineteenth-century law that prohibits the importation of 'obscene material'. With the support of FAC (Feminists Against Censorship) and PUSSY, White took the case to court, on point of principle, knowing that she would lose, but keen to highlight the inequality in the law. In court she explained that the videos were for private use and the depictions of safer sex and sexuality were less violent and 'obscene' than much of what is available through heterosexual outlets. The judge proceeded to view the most 'depraved, lewd and filthy' extracts and in a bizarre venture in voyeurism, lesbians in the gallery watched men watching lesbians. White's defence argued that it was absurd that these materials could be imported through the EC, but not from the US. It also seemed strange that this material was being banned, since many women had viewed at least two of the videos in screenings at the Rio cinema and National Film Theatre. Although the tapes were ordered to be destroyed, White did not have to pay costs and felt that this was a minor victory and could be claimed as a queer intervention into the anomalies of the law.

> Your sexuality is yours. It's not the state's, the Customs Officer's, or your husband's. It's yours and its exploration with another person is the only way to claim your birthright. Jenny White

In November of the same year a legal precedent was established concerning lesbian sexual practices which could be seen as a measure of the virulent hostility the threat of queer sex invokes. Jennifer Saunders, an eighteen-year-old, was sentenced to six years' imprisonment for dressing as a man and seducing two seventeen-year-old women. The age of consent laws could not be used against her—again revealing the anomaly whereby lesbians remain invisible—and so she was charged with indecent assault. In court, the two women said they would not have consented to sex if they had been aware of Saunders' true gender; in her defence, Saunders insisted that she had dressed as a boy at the women's request, to conceal the fact that they were having a lesbian relationship. Passing sentence in Doncaster, Judge Crabtree summed up:

> I suppose that both girls would rather have been raped by some young man ... I assume you must have some sort of bisexual feelings and I suspect that you have contested the case in the hope of getting some ghastly fame from it. I feel you may be a menace to young girls.

Saunders allegedly had sex with one of the women several times a week, using a strap-on dildo, in the course of a five-month affair. A new OutRage affinity group, LABIA (Lesbians Answer Back in Anger) took up the case and picketed the office of the Lord Chancellor to demand the dismissal of Judge Crabtree from the bench. In a letter to LABIA from prison, Saunders reiterated that the affairs were entirely consensual:

> She told her family I was a man to make herself clear, if you know what I mean ... I couldn't believe it when I was arrested. I went along with all the stupid things she was saying as I loved her more than anything in the world. I couldn't hurt her. So I promised to say nothing.

Without LABIA, the press would have ignored the fact that the case had anything to do with lesbians. And indeed there was a distinct failure of other lesbian feminist groups to rally to Saunders' defence—was this due to moral disapproval of the dildo or of the ultra-butch (ie perceived as het male) persona Saunders chose? In the same month as the case came to trial, there was a huge International Women's Day to End Violence Against Women march which focused on legal injustices to women. It highlighted the cases of Sara Thornton, Kiranjit Ahwalia and Amelia Rossiter, all of whom were given life sentences for killing their husbands. There was no mention of the Saunders' case in the publicity.

On the press front, the *Sun* not unexpectedly ran a headline: '6 Years for blonde who posed as boy to bed girls' (21 September 1991), while the *Guardian* ran a coy little piece on cross-dressing entitled 'Girls will be boys', in which Julie Wheelwright, author of *Amazons and Military Maids: Women Who Dressed as Men in Pursuit of Life, Liberty and Happiness,* opined that cross-

dressing was a 'forgotten historical phenomenon', and concluded:

> In the end, cross-dressing proves to be an un-
> satisfying alternative since it forces women to
> caricature male virility and fear their feminine
> self. 'Guardian', 24 September 1991

With moralising reactionary analysis like that,
all butch women should forget it. The article
omitted the 'L word' and made no attempt to
discuss why teenagers had been forced to use
such subterfuge in England in the late twentieth
century: *homophobia*. Saunders' six-year sentence was longer than most rape sentences and
it was clear that she was being punished for
being a woman who dared to step out of line. At
the time of writing Saunders is in Styal prison,
awaiting appeal.

To Out or Not to Out . . .

One of the most widely discussed queer strategies for the promotion of lesbian and gay visibility has been outing, which brought queer
politics into the headlines and strongly divided
opinion and support among lesbians and gay
men. The FROCS (Faggots Rooting Out Closeted Sexuality) outing campaign of August 1991,
which promised to out several MPs, gained more
column inches for lesbian and gay politics in one
week than in the whole of the previous year. The
campaign was allegedly an elaborate hoax designed to highlight the hypocrisy of the tabloid
press, who had been content to expose publicly
whomsoever they could, yet now began to bleat
about notions of 'privacy'.

For lesbians and gays, outing represented the
nub of the queer debate. For many, like Derek
Jarman, who argued that 'outing is a sign that
the gay [sic] movement has come of age', it was
a positive affirmation of the right to be open
about sexuality by a new generation of lesbian
and gay men who, content with their 'sexual
orientation', were refusing to toe the line sub-
missively, or accept discrimination and harassment. For others, the campaign raised moral,

ethical and political questions. Could someone
who'd been reluctantly dragged out of their
closet represent a positive role model? Wasn't
declaring Jason Donovan or Jodie Foster 'absolutely queer' fetishing the glamour of those in
public positions and their power to influence
opinion? The notion of 'claiming our own'
makes the assumption that all queers are progressive, have an essential awareness of oppression and therefore sympathise with the queer
cause; like 'gay lifestyle', it reinforces a spurious
idea of lesbian and gay homogeneity. And while
many yearn to reveal politicians' hypocrisy,
whipping up homophobia to discredit them
can only be destructive and ultimately counterproductive. Using outing as punishment raises
the question of who was choosing to out
whom?

The campaign denied the levels of coming
out we all have to consider—the closet door
often revolves—and ignored the different contexts for women and black people, for whom
being lesbian or gay intersects with the oppressions of sexism and racism. Are you more queer
the more outspoken you can risk being? The
more visible? The more vulnerable?

> Many of the younger Asian men and women in
> their early twenties I speak to are saying 'we're
> not interested in coming out that way, because
> if we do we won't have anywhere to live, we'll
> be chucked out from home'. It's not about
> their lack of confidence about their sexuality,
> it's about what choices are available. That's
> something that's always been seen by white les-
> bians and gay men as 'behind'. It creates a cer-
> tain kind of hierarchy from a white perspective
> and a white agenda. Pratibha Parmar

The separatism of the outing campaign made
no room for heterosexual or bisexual anti-
homophobes and in many ways went against
queer ethics in its reinforcement of the normative categories of the homo-hetero divide. We
constantly negotiate the territory in which it is
safe and appropriate to come out, so it follows
that there are times when queers may choose to
call themselves heterosexual, bisexual, lesbian

or gay, or none of the above. If queer develops into an anti-straight polemic, it will have betrayed its potential for radical pluralism. Nor can you simply substitute 'queer' for 'gay' and masquerade reactionary politics under a radical new guise.

The 'Bad' Girls

The attraction of queer for some lesbians is flavoured by a rebellion against a prescriptive feminism that had led them to feel disenfranchised by the lesbian feminist movement. There was a feeling that the importance of identifying politically as a lesbian had obscured lesbianism as a sexual identity. 'Acceptable' ideas of lesbian sexuality and desire were constructed around notions of sameness and a desexed androgyny, and anyone who disagreed with the 'right on' line, regardless of her sexual practice, would be dismissed at best as an SM dyke and at worst as a fascist. While the ground gained by identity politics in promoting equal representation and access to resources were important achievements of feminism, the rigid hierarchies of oppression rhetoric that privileged certain oppressions above others were considered divisive and futile.

> As a black lesbian, feminism let me down a lot, especially when debates stuck to gender and didn't include race or 'other' sexual practices. I want a context to look at more diversity. Isling Mack-Nataf

> Feminism as it has evolved can no longer accept difference and can only accept an orthodoxy that enforces 'if you don't fit that orthodoxy, you're not only wrong, you're dangerous'. Linda Semple

> The feminist movement was divided into the good, the bad and the ugly. The bad were women who fucked around but had serial monogamy and a sense of sex that had to do with love. The ugly were the women who were seen as male and had a sense of sex that had to do with consent. Queer was a way of retrieving

> that, of risking, of knowing there's no such thing as safe sex. There's safer sex. Sue Golding

> AIDS activism is far more effective than feminism ever was because it allows a broad diversity of opinion, while in feminism there was a tendency to block a range of analysis. Sarah Schulman

Discussions around HIV and safer sex soon highlighted the lack of information available on lesbian sexual practice. *The Joy of Lesbian Sex* was no longer in print and few booksellers would risk stocking the sex mag *On Our Backs*. The success of anti-porn campaigns had ensured that access to books like *Coming To Power* (SAMOIS) or *Sapphistry* (Pat Califia) was severely limited. (One bookseller told how she would find such volumes turned spine inwards or hidden behind more politically correct (PC) literature.) Perhaps there was something to be learned from a new generation of gay men who were rejecting the apologetic reactions and confused recommendations of abstention that had characterised the beginning of the AIDS epidemic and asserting a new confidence. If they had to fuck safely, they certainly weren't going to apologise for their desire.

> Dykes had to take the models of gay male sexual practice, apply them to lesbian sexual practice and say, 'what if?' There was an intellectual and theoretical need to ally with gay men around the politics of representation and sexuality which had been hijacked by radical lesbian feminists. Linda Semple

> For gay men the situation is 'we'll tolerate you being homos as long as you aren't sexual'. I'm going to be 'homo' and 'sexual'. Paul Burston

For other lesbians, queer has little to do with gay men; its roots are firmly embedded in the dyke camp, with its history of cross-dressing, role-playing, gender-fucking and subversion of patriarchy. The writings of women like Joan Nestle, Carole Vance, Gayle Rubin and Ann Snitow are considered some of the queerer elements to emerge from feminism.

Queer is a function of the debates around sexuality which were started by lesbians. We pushed back the borders and talked about SM, fantasies, taboos, butch-femme, violence in relationships, non-monogamy, penetration, ass-fucking etc. Many of us were doing it before HIV forced us to. Spike Pittsberg

We Lesbians from the fifties made a mistake in the early seventies: we allowed our lives to be trivialised and reinterpreted by feminists who did not share our culture. The slogan 'Lesbianism is the practice and feminism is the theory' was a good rallying cry, but it cheated our history . . . For many years now, I have been trying to figure out how to explain the special nature of butch-femme relationships to Lesbian-feminists who consider butch-femme a reproduction of heterosexual models. Joan Nestle, 'A Restricted Country'

One thing I hope as a historian is that the fact that feminists pioneered a lot of queer ideas doesn't get lost, so it becomes seen as something that only grew out of ACT UP or men's ideas. Tori Smith

Queer seems as chameleon as camp, which is also a useful vehicle for self-understanding and reading the signs of the moment, also labelled as self-oppressive. At times, the two interlink; certainly both can be viewed as subjective reinterpretations of the times, whether in art, politics or as a means of self-understanding.

For me, the taking back of negative words has been a survival strategy. I came out in the early 80s, when all the words available to me to articulate my desire were constructed negatively: lesbian, lessie, dyke ('gay' was never an option for self-naming as it was seen as definitively male in my radical feminist milieu), cunt, pussy, fuck . . . Or the words were non-existent: I didn't know I possessed a clitoris until I was eighteen. I was supposed to play with 'my bits', stroke someone else's and separate from all emotional and physical contact with men. I did. It has been a long haul back to reclaiming the right to call my cunt, my cunt, to celebrating the pleasure in objectifying another body, to fucking women and to admitting that I also love men and need their support. That is what queer is.

From *Fear of a Queer Planet*

Michael Warner

Heteronormativity in Social Theory

The essays in this volume [Editor's Note: That is, Warner's *Fear of a Queer Planet*] go beyond calling for tolerance of lesbians and gays. They assert the necessarily and desirably queer nature of the world. This extra step has become necessary, if only because so much privilege lies in heterosexual culture's exclusive ability to interpret itself as society. Het culture thinks of itself as the elemental form of human association, as the very model of intergender relations, as the indivisible basis of all community, and as the means of reproduction without which society wouldn't exist. Materialist thinking about society has in many cases reinforced these tendencies, inherent in heterosexual ideology, toward a totalized view of the social. I think this is what Monique Wittig has in mind when she writes that the social contract is heterosexuality: "[T]o live in society is to live in heterosexuality. . . . Heterosexuality is always already there within all mental categories. It has sneaked into dialectical thought (or thought of differences) as its main category."[1] Wittig notes that Aristotle grounds *The Politics* in the necessity of male-female union (42), and it is certainly true that Western political thought has taken the heterosexual couple to represent the principle of social union itself. In social thought this principle is typically mediated through such concepts as dependence and reproduction, and is thus naturalized in otherwise sophisticated work.

The core idea remains the same as the (literally) cartoon image of human society devised by Carl Sagan (and drawn, appropriately enough, by his wife, Linda) for use on NASA's *Pioneer 10* spacecraft (see figure). NASA's official explanation of this design reads: "The Pioneer 10 spacecraft, the first man-made object to escape from the solar system, carries this pictorial plaque. It is designed to show scientifically educated inhabitants of some other star system—who might intercept it millions of years from now—when Pioneer was launched, from where, and by what kind of beings. . . . The man's hand is raised in a gesture of good will."[2]

Although Sagan claims great care was taken to make a "panracial" image, the cartoon betrays several kinds of foolishness typical of bureaucrats, technicians, and Americans. (The designers, I would like to be able to say, weren't exactly rocket scientists.) It assumes that its space-alien, junk-dealer audience will be visually oriented, conceptually equipped with the conventions of outline drawing, and disposed to interpret the outlines not as individual objects but as generic persons, images for something like "humanity." There are other, more damaging assumptions here as well, for the NASA plates do not carry just any images of persons in their attempt to genericize humankind. They depict—if you share the imaging conventions of postwar U.S. culture—a man and a woman. They are not just sexually different; they are sexual difference itself. They are nude but have no body hair; the woman has no genitals; their heads are neatly coiffed according to the gender norms of middle-class young adults. The man stands square, while the woman leans

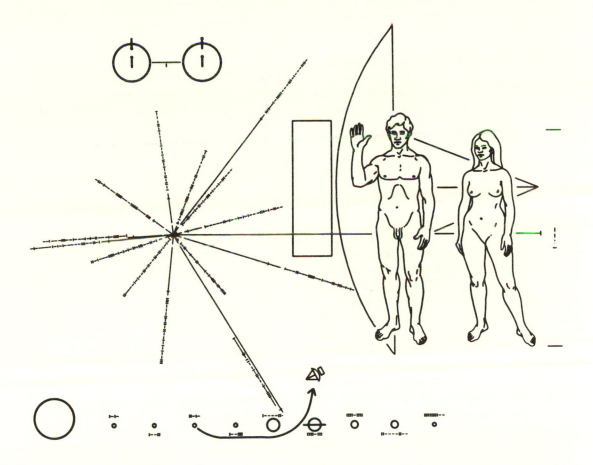

one hip slightly forward. To a native of the culture that produced it, this bizarre fantasy-image is immediately recognizable not just as two gendered individuals, but as a heterosexual couple (monogamous, one supposes, given the absence of competition), a technological but benign Adam and Eve. It testifies to the depth of the culture's assurance (read: insistence) that humanity and heterosexuality are synonymous. This reminder speeds to the ends of the universe, announcing to passing stars that earth is not, regardless of what anyone says, a queer planet.

Heteronormative thinking about society is seldom so cartoonish. Like androcentrism, it clothes itself in goodwill and intelligence. Much of the work of feminist social theory has con-

sisted of showing that basic conceptualizations—ways of opposing home and economy, the political and personal, or system and lifeworld—presuppose and reinforce a paradigmatically male position.[3] Queer theory is beginning to be in a position to make similar criticisms, sometimes with reference to the same oppositions (political and personal, intimate and public, market and lifeworld), but also with others—ways of distinguishing group members from nonmembers and the sexual from the nonsexual, ways of opposing the given and the chosen, and ways of identifying the intimate with the familial. Even the concept of oppression has to be reevaluated here, because in queer politics the oppression of a class of persons is only sometimes distinguishable from the repression of sexuality, and that in turn is a concept that has become difficult to contain since Foucault.

It is too early to say how many conceptualizations of this sort may have to be challenged, but many of them have been central to left social theory. I have already suggested that conceptions of culture as shared identity should be criticized in this way. Class may be another example. Andrew Parker suggests that at a fundamental level Marx's thought is especially bound up with a reproductivist conception of the social, falsely ontologized. Parker suggests that the language of theatricality in *The Eighteenth Brumaire* marks a crisis in the relation between production and interests, on one side, and politics and representation, on the other. Metropolitan sexuality appears unruly if not untheorizable given Marx's general productivist and economist commitments. Theatricality and metropolitan sexuality, in Parker's reading, are therefore related and indicative problems in Marx's thought because the othering of each helps to constitute the Marxian paradigm of production and reproduction.

This othering and the need to install it are not merely theoretical lapses but historical pressures that have conditioned Marxist thought from the moment the two writing bodies of Marx and Engels began to collaborate. By calling our attention to the homosocial dynamics of that collaboration, Parker suggests that Marxist thought is embedded in a history of sexuality, reproductivism, and homosociality in a way that prevents it from grasping these problems as conditioning its own project. Similar objections could be made against other traditions of social thought, of course, and Marxism has important countercurrents. But core elements of the Marxist paradigm may have to be seen as properly ideological moments in the history of reproductivist heterosexuality.[4]

Feminists and others have long objected to the general subordination of status conflict to class conflict in Marxist thought. It is instructive to consider, however, that at present there is no comparable category of social analysis to describe the kind of group or nongroup that queer people constitute. "Class" is conspicuously useless: feminism could at least have a debate whether women constituted a specific economic class; in queer theory the question is unintelligible. "Status," the classical alternative in social theory, is somewhat better but does not account for the way the ascribed trait of a sexually defined group is itself a mode of sociability; nor does it describe the terror and atomization by which its members become "members" before their presence in any codefined group; nor does it express the definitive pressure exerted by the assumption that this group, far from constituting one status among many, does not or should not exist. A lesbian and gay population, moreover, is defined by multiple boundaries that make the question who is and is not "one of them" not merely ambiguous but rather a perpetually and necessarily contested issue. Identity as lesbian or gay is ambiguously given and chosen, in some ways ascribed and in other ways the product of the performative act of coming out—itself a political strategy without precedent or parallel. In these ways sexuality defines—for most modern societies—a political interest-constituency unlike even those of gender or race. Queer people are a kind of social group fundamentally unlike others, a status group only insofar as they are not a class.

Queer Politics

The problem of finding an adequate description is a far from idle question, since the way a group is defined has consequences for how it will be mobilized, represented, legislated for, and addressed. Attempts have been made to use "nation," "community," even "ethnicity," just as "sexual orientation" has often been used as though it were parallel to "race" or "sex." But in each case the results have been partly unhappy, for the same reasons.[5] Among these alternatives the dominant concept has been that of a "gay and lesbian community," a notion generated in the tactics of Anglo-American identity politics and its liberal-national environment, where the buried model is racial and ethnic politics.

Although it has had importance in organizational efforts (where in circular fashion it receives concretization), the notion of a community has remained problematic if only because nearly every lesbian or gay remembers being such before entering a collectively identified space, because much of lesbian and gay history has to do with noncommunity, and because dispersal rather than localization continues to be definitive of queer self-understanding ("We Are Everywhere"). Community also falsely suggests an ideological and nostalgic contrast with the atomization of modern capitalist society.[6] And in the liberal-pluralist frame it predisposes that political demands will be treated as demands for the toleration and representation of a minority constituency.

It is partly to avoid this reduction of the issues that so many people in the last two or three years—including many of the authors in this volume—have shifted their self-identification from "gay" to "queer."[7] The preference for "queer" represents, among other things, an aggressive impulse of generalization; it rejects a minoritizing logic of toleration or simple political interest-representation in favor of a more thorough resistance to regimes of the normal. For academics, being interested in queer theory is a way to mess up the desexualized spaces of the academy, exude some rut, reimagine the publics from and for which academic intellectuals write, dress, and perform. Nervous over the prospect of a well-sanctioned and compartmentalized academic version of "lesbian and gay studies," people want to make theory queer, not just to have a theory about queers. For both academics and activists, "queer" gets a critical edge by defining itself against the normal rather than the heterosexual, and normal includes normal business in the academy. The universalizing utopianism of queer theory does not entirely replace more minority-based versions of lesbian and gay theory—nor could it, since normal sexuality and the machinery of enforcing it do not bear down equally on everyone, as we are constantly reminded by pervasive forms of terror, coercion, violence, and devastation. The insistence on "queer"—a term initially generated in the context of terror—has the effect of pointing out a wide field of normalization, rather than simple intolerance, as the site of violence. Its brilliance as a naming strategy lies in combining resistance on that broad social terrain with more specific resistance on the terrains of phobia and queer-bashing, on one hand, or of pleasure, on the other. "Queer" therefore also suggests the difficulty in defining the population whose interests are at stake in queer politics.

"Queer" is also a way of cutting against mandatory gender divisions, though gender continues to be a dividing line. Men in queer theory, as well as women who write about gay men or AIDS, tend to be strongly influenced by Foucault and constructionist theory in general. They infuse queerness into their work through a mixture of tempered rage and carnivalesque display. Women who write about women, by contrast, typically refer to French feminisms (Monique Wittig, Luce Irigaray, Julia Kristeva) and Anglo-American psychoanalytic feminism, especially in film theory (Teresa de Lauretis, Judith Mayne, Sue-Ellen Case, Judith Roof, but also Judith Butler and Diana Fuss). As Diana Fuss points out in her influential book *Essentially Speaking,* this tradition of lesbian feminism has made lesbian theorists more preoccupied with the theme of *identity*—the attempt to define (or, more recently, ironize) the common core of lesbian or female subjects. "A certain pressure is applied to the lesbian subject," Fuss points out, "either to 'claim' or to 'discover' her true identity before she can elaborate a 'personal politics.'"[8] For lesbian theorists, queer theory offers a way of basing politics in the personal *without* acceding to this pressure to clean up personal identity.[9]

Organizing a movement around queerness also allows it to draw on dissatisfaction with the regime of the normal in general. Following Hannah Arendt, we might even say that queer politics opposes society itself. Arendt describes the social as a specifically modern phenomenon: "[T]he emergence of the social realm, which is neither private nor public, strictly speaking, is a relatively new phenomenon

whose origin coincided with the emergence of
the modern age and which found its political
form in the nation-state."[10] She identifies society in this sense with "conformism, the assumption that men behave and do not act with
respect to each other"—an assumption embedded in economics and other knowledges of the
social that "could achieve a scientific character
only when men had become social beings and
unanimously followed certain patterns of
behavior, so that those who did not keep the
rules could be considered to be asocial or abnormal."[11] The social realm, in short, is a cultural form, interwoven with the political form
of the administrative state and with the normalizing methodologies of modern social
knowledge. Can we not hear in the resonances
of queer protest an objection to the normalization of behavior in this broad sense, and thus to
the cultural phenomenon of societalization? If
queers, incessantly told to alter their "behavior,"
can be understood as protesting not just the
normal behavior of the social but the *idea* of
normal behavior, they will bring skepticism to
the methodologies founded on that idea. The
essays in this volume, all at some level informed
by a skepticism about knowledges of the social,
may be regarded in that respect as reflecting the
modern conditions of queerness.

It would be a daredevil act of understatement
to say that not all gays and lesbians share this
view of the new queer politics. It will continue
to be debated for some time. I have made my
own sympathies clear because the shape of any
engagement between queer theory and other
social-theoretical traditions will be determined
largely by the political practice in which it
comes about. In fact, however, no term—even
"queer"—works equally well in all the contexts
that have to be considered by what I am nevertheless calling queer theory. Queer activists are
also lesbians and gays in other contexts—as for
example where leverage can be gained through
bourgeois propriety, or through minority-rights
discourse, or through more gender-marked language (it probably won't replace lesbian feminism). Queer politics has not just replaced older
modes of lesbian and gay identity; it has come

to exist alongside those older modes, opening
up new possibilities and problems whose relation to more familiar problems is not always
clear. Queer theory, in short, has much work to
do just in keeping up with queer political culture. If it contributes to the self-clarification of
the struggles and wishes of the age, it may make
the world queerer than ever.

Notes

1. Monique Wittig, *The Straight Mind* (Boston: Beacon Press, 1992), 40, 43.

2. I want to thank Max Cavitch for alerting me to this public release from NASA's Ames Research Center. Carl Sagan has commented on the controversy surrounding the design in his *The Cosmic Connection* (New York: Anchor, 1973), as has his collaborator F. D. Drake, in Drake and Sagan, *Murmurs of Earth* (New York: Ballantine, 1978).

3. I have in mind here especially Nancy Fraser, "What's Critical about Critical Theory? The Case of Habermas and Gender," *New German Critique* 35 (Spring/Summer 1985): 97–131; reprinted in her *Unruly Practices* (Minneapolis: University of Minnesota Press, 1989), 113–43.

4. Another blockage against sexual politics in the Marxist tradition, noticeable in the Melucci passage I quoted earlier, is the close connection between consumer culture and the most visible spaces of gay culture: bars, discos, advertising, fashion, brand-name identification, mass-cultural camp, "promiscuity." Gay culture in this most visible mode is anything but external to advanced capitalism and to precisely those features of advanced capitalism that many on the left are most eager to disavow. Post-Stonewall urban gay men reek of the commodity. We give off the smell of capitalism in rut, and therefore demand of theory a more dialectical view of capitalism than many people have imagination for.

5. For an explicit elaboration of this model, see Steven Epstein, "Gay Politics, Ethnic Identity: The Limits of Social Constructionism," *Socialist Review* 93, no. 94 (1987):9–54.

6. On this problem see Iris Marion Young, *Justice and the Politics of Difference* (Princeton, N.J.: Princeton University Press, 1990), 226–56.

7. On the logic of the term, see Lisa Duggan, "Making It Perfectly Queer"; Arlene Stein, "Sisters and Queers: The Decentering of Lesbian Feminism," *Socialist Review* 22, no. 1 (1992): 33–55; Jeffrey Es-

coffier and Allan Bérubé, "Queer Nation," *Out/Look* 11 (Winter 1991): 14–16; and the essays ... by Seidman, Berlant and Freeman, and Griggers.

8. Diana Fuss, *Essentially Speaking: Feminism, Nature, and Difference* (New York: Routledge, Chapman, and Hall, 1989), 99–101.

9. I have said more on the subject in a review essay on queer theory by lesbians in *VLS* (June 1992), from which the preceding paragraph is derived.

10. Hannah Arendt, *The Human Condition* (Chicago: University of Chicago Press, 1958), 28.

11. Ibid., 41–42.

Queercore

Dennis Cooper

I've been asked about Queercore, a term that refers to the punky, anti-assimilationist, transgressive movement on the fringe of lesbian and gay culture. But as a giddy and awestruck participant in this anything but settled scene, I'm torn as to how to describe it. A demystification would miss the point, since to those of us involved, the charisma of the thing is easily as much a draw as its politics. I *can* say that Queercore is a still vague, cross-generational phenomenon involving upwards of several thousand people in the U.S. and Canada who have long felt disenfranchised from official gay culture.

Up until a few years ago we were quirky outcasts—punk rockers, film buffs, artists, bookworms, etc. Now there's an intense if scattered community (ugh!) interconnected by zines like *J.D.'s, Homocore, Holy Tit-clamps, My Comrade,* and *Fertile LaToyah Jackson Magazine*—obsessive, personal little xeroxed rags some of us make and circulate as a way of formalizing our offbeat tastes and seeing if other like-minded people are out there. Zines are a kind of popular press that shapes, publicizes, and critiques the goings-on around them. Over the past year or so, their number has increased manyfold and become magnets for other lonely subcultural types: queer bands like Tribe 8 and Drance; filmmakers like Gregg Araki and Sadie Benning; countless performance artists; writers, club kids, and activists.

There's even an annual Queercore convention, Spew, at which one sees—in addition to the obvious growing pains—evidence of a relatively cohesive bunch of youngish folks who've figured out how to function in small units precisely because they don't expect anything close

to a consensus, and so are able to fight among themselves with a degree of affection. While this embrace of instability may put Queercore in danger of spinning its wheels as a political movement, the sentiment I most often hear expressed by participants is: Better an honest little spin out than a long, slow fudge.

You are entering a gay and lesbian-free zone. . . . Effective immediately, BIMBOX is at war against lesbians and gays. A war in which modern queer boys and queer girls are united against the prehistoric thinking and demented self-serving politics of the above-mentioned scum. BIMBOX hereby renounces its past use of the term lesbian and/or gay in a positive manner. This is a civil war against the ultimate evil, and consequently we must identify us and them in no uncertain terms. . . . So, dear lesbian womon or gay man to whom perhaps BIMBOX has been inappropriately posted . . . prepare to pay dearly for the way you and your kind have fucked things up.

—Johnny Noxzema and Rex Boy, *BIMBOX,* 1991

If you want to talk to a misogynist, talk to Andrew 'Dice' Clay, not to me. If you really want to confront racism, yell at David Duke or the Aryan Brotherhood, not at the nearest white male gay activist. Your voice will only be lost in the chorus of reactionary bullies who are already browbeating him, and what will you have gained?

—Arnie Kantrowitz, *QW,* 1992

I wasn't sure a hardcore queer movement existed until I read longtime activist Arnie Kantrowitz's attempt to paint queers as gay male culture's more hyper offspring. His recent piece in *NYQ* reminded me of how '60s radicals initially read punk as a mutiny within late hippiedom. In fact both punk and Queercore spring from an idealism that radicals have abandoned for the pleasures of a compromised but stable Left. In that tradition, Kantrowitz dismisses Queercore's most original ideas as reactionary when they're simply bewildering to him.

Specifically Kantrowitz singles out Toronto's queer provocateurs Johnny Noxzema and Rex Boy, editors of the zines *BIMBOX* and *S.C.A.B.*, for mock-gloating over the death of his friend Vito Russo, a man they'd never heard of but whose pious obituaries struck them as endemic of older gays' tendency to become self-righteous under the guise of pride. What Kantrowitz took personally, they meant as abstract. What they meant as creative he took as treacherous, labeling them self-hating and cowardly for their adoption of pseudonyms—as if this punk-related strategy of rejecting a given identity hasn't been used by militants since at least Malcolm X.

Far from being cowards, Noxzema and Rex Boy use their notorious zines to push unforeseen buttons. In proclamations like "ALL victims of gay bashing DESERVE what they get," and "*You* are the enemy, not Jesse Helms," they articulate an intense dissatisfaction with a knee-jerk gay "community" that can so easily disguise the complexity of homosexual desire in order to appease its conservative elements. "There is no dialogue here," Kantrowitz wrote of *BIMBOX*, "only an airing of the same old self-righteous indignation, which I have encountered for 22 years from various malcontents who find it easier to attack their allies than their enemies." But if he had actually read *BIMBOX*, he would know that heterosexual men receive easily as much abuse as do gay men. When Kantrowitz sees red, details don't matter. And this is exactly the kind of thing *BIMBOX* is critiquing.

Noxzema and Rex Boy incite an argument within queer culture that cannot be won. They pose questions about identity that are as lushly poetic as they are superficially irresponsible.

Like the Surrealists who tortured early 20th century political ideas into wittily gorgeous ambiguities, their points are both dauntingly sophisticated and antibourgeois. To become engaged in their illogic is to sense the idiocy that goes hand in hand with delusions of a united front.

Lately the Bimboxers' main target has been William Burroughs, whom they see as the accepted symbol of gay male disenfranchisement. In one of their recent one-shot zines, a little comic book called *Double Bill,* Burroughs is hunted down and killed by hack TV actor William Conrad (*Cannon, Jake and the Fatman*) for the crimes of senility and misogyny. Cheering queer bystanders hail Conrad as their new hero. By putting Burroughs in the same frame as a fake TV detective, Noxzema and Rex Boy are trying to debunk the sanctioned gay-outlaw mystique and emphasize where they think the power to disrupt actually resides—in the brain of any pissed-off queer with access to a xerox machine.

Still, even as they flirt with anthemic catcalls, Noxzema and Rex Boy speak for no one—not for an emerging generation and not even for themselves. If anything, they position themselves as savage cheerleaders feeding off and fueling their contemporaries' violent mood swings.

What are Johnny Noxzema and Rex Boy trying to say exactly? It's complicated. Certainly they're not advocating fascist behavior; they're trying to provoke a response from the lesbians and gays whom they know would never agree with their more absurd pronouncements. They pointedly adopt the most contentious stance possible because they want to keep an oppressed group from becoming too set and smug in its opinions. They attack gay sacred cows because they see the inflation of these people into untouchable symbols as a hierarchical device and, in classic anarchist style, they deeply distrust the institutionalizing of anyone or thing. They're aesthetic terrorists, and the fuss they're causing is beautiful to behold, assuming one accepts the world as essentially chaotic, as the new queers generally do.

*   *   *

How do you define Queercore?

Johnny Noxzema: Well, we're pissed off at the older gay set who set themselves up as leaders. People are just sick of the way dykes and fags behave toward each other.

Is that the only commonality?

Queers are embarrassed by traditional gay culture. The thing that really bugs me is that the only people who benefited from liberation were white gay men. It's like, queers aren't ashamed of being gay but we *are* ashamed of gays in general. This pride thing is disgusting. I mean, Jeffrey Dahmer picked up one of his victims at the gay pride parade!

Do you see Queercore as a reassertion of the homo libido post-AIDS?

For my friends and myself, sex is the last thing on our minds.

Does the scene have a central politic?

I don't concern myself with politics that much. But it's different up here in Canada. You can AIDS as a career. The government practically pays you to have it.

What do you think Queercore portends?

Hopefully it'll stop younger people from going down that same horrible path. So much party-line crap goes on in gay culture. Either you're an activist, or you're a prude. The whole *Village Voice/Advocate* establishment is corrupted by power. You can't take them seriously. It's a sick hierarchy.

*   *   *

Queercore's beginning to fight a certain gentrification within its own ranks. A current burning question goes: When exactly has one crossed the assimilationist line? It's thought that Bruce La Bruce, one of the earliest proponents of a punk/queer aesthetic via the seminal zine *J.D.'s,* might've sold out last year when his film *No Skin Off My Ass* met with a moderate underground success. Ever since, he's been careering with a Jayne Mansfieldian blatancy that many in the scene find cringeworthy. Then there are the growing number of zines that look

more like undercover agents from the gay porn world than bona fide rebel products.

Spew 2, held last winter at an alternative arts space in L.A., drew thousands of attendees—the largest gathering yet of the Queercore scene. In addition to the usual denizens, it attracted a number of activists, although not the sort one would find at a conference sponsored by the National Gay and Lesbian Task Force. At Spew 2, the highest level of participation came from a Queer Nation satellite group called Infected Faggot. These are outrageous HIV-positive women and men who straddle activism and radical aesthetics, functioning as a creative thorn in each. It would be wrong to think the new queers apolitical; they just see the world as too complicated to accommodate even conventional radical politics. Their ambivalence masks an offbeat, slippery philosophical temperament that makes them question just about everything.

In this way they break entirely from Queer Nation and ACT UP, direct-action groups with an in-your-face mentality that maintain subtle hierarchical structures within their one-for-all, all-for-one image. Queercore is a mess that can't be scaled. It may have stars, but it's never had anyone close to a Larry Kramer. (And if it ever does, please shoot it.) Perhaps most significantly of all, Queercore is both anti-assimilationist and anti-separatist. In fact the name *Queercore* is something of a misnomer since the scene involves a tenable mixture of queer, bisexual, and straight iconoclasts.

*   *   *

Pam Gregg is the director of the films *power boy* and *M.A.S.K.* She's also coeditor of the zine *Screambox.*

Is all this about the libido?

It's more about creativity, I think. If I want to be outrageously sexual, I feel like I can do it in my zine. I'm not sure I could do it in a sex club. The women I know who do zines are very sexual, but they're just as interested in exploring issues of power. A lot of them are even voyeuristically studying and enjoying gay men's porn.

Maybe Queercore allows for a new kind of role reversal where we can sexualize men back.

What were you doing before Queercore?

I was angry when I graduated from college. I was involved with a group of radical, militant feminists. It was so rigid, especially around issues of sex and gender. I went from my parents' white middle-class values to militant feminism's equally strict agenda. So it's definitely been a progression to where I am now.

*   *   *

As someone who's spent far more of my life happily locating homosexual signifiers in closetty artworks than standing around in bars eyeing svelte strangers, I'm hugely relieved by the emergence of a politically incorrect movement like Queercore. Not that it wasn't amusing and instructive to grow up estranged from my assigned subculture, to be one of the only fags frequenting hardcore punk clubs; because my secretiveness taught me to watch people carefully, and watching probably helped me avoid the platitudes that pass for political rhetoric in the gay mainstream. At its best, Queercore retains the mood of lovely ambivalence that my friends and I felt among disenfranchised, like-minded heterosexuals who happened to admire the same things we did.

Maybe the chief reason I've felt so alienated from gay culture is its insistence on exclusivity, its counterproductive if understandable need to establish havens where heterosexuals feel as unnerved as lesbians and gay men sometimes feel in the larger world. Like many queers, I grew up doing the same drugs, loving pretty much the same rock bands, books, movies, and TV shows as every hipster my age, whatever their sexuality. Currently my closest friends are a 19-year-old heterosexual boy and a heterosexual woman in her mid-thirties. I have as much or more in common with them as I do with my queer friends. For better or worse, I'd rather sit around in their company evaluating the new Sonic Youth LP than stay up all night in clubs badmouthing politically correct clones.

What I sense in Queercore—in its careless morality, its slippery rhetoric, its do-it-yourself aesthetic, etc.—is a new brand of queer defiance that claims part ownership of American culture's cutting edge but without demanding that everyone with talent turn out to be queer, too. I sense a little culture where *Taxi Driver*'s as cool as *My Own Private Idaho*, My Bloody Valentine's as cool as Morrissey, Mike Kelley's as cool as Nayland Blake, and Lynne Tillman's as cool as Jeanette Winterson. A place where "queer" defines not a specific sexuality, but the freedom to personalize anything you see or hear then shoot it back into the stupid world more distorted and amazing than it was before.

*   *   *

Dave Ehrlich is coeditor of the zine *Su Madre*. His novel-in-progress is called *Dreamy*.

Would the NEA Four fit comfortably into a so-called Queercore setting?

Yeah, except for Tim Miller.

Why not him?

Because all his work does is talk about why he's like everyone else. He wants everyone to think he's harmless, that he's the queer next door. I think that's totally assimilationist.

What's the difference between Queercore and Queer Nation?

Queer Nation's like sheep who trot together. Queercore's against predictable patterns. We're not all doing the same thing.

*   *   *

So where does Queercore begin and end? Wherever it fucking feels like it, is the answer it would like to give. Because anyone is welcome to participate; you don't have to meet some hard-to-define criteria to feel at home. The more flamboyant and loud-mouthed participants give the impression that Queercore revolves around pierced and tattooed anti-fashion plates. But the majority of people on the scene are physically uncategorizable. They range from 50-year-old nerds who've felt ostracized by gay culture since before Stonewall, to teenagers pissed off because they're too young to get into bars. There's a pretty good balance of women and men, of races and classes. Anarchism is the belief system of choice, which I guess explains people's cranky tolerance of activities like pedophilia and "sex magic," the Jungian reinterpretation of s&m. I have yet to meet anyone who doesn't write, paint, perform, take photographs, do graphic design, or make videos.

While the scene is fueled by sexual energy, I see horniness as less of a factor than it's been in traditional gay male culture, where women are considered turnoffs and straight men made into sex objects. Certainly Queercore assumes a world much raunchier than was possible even a few years ago, but it's not the focus of their identity. Spokescritics like Douglas Crimp, who stumps noisily for social-realist gay/lesbian art, have faded into grandparently positions as interest explodes in the kinds of transgressive activities that defined preliberation homosexuality.

In a way, the relatively privileged positions that lesbians and gay men now hold make secrecy the forbidden fruit. Radical queers reclaim outsider status, not out of a regressive chic, but rather archaeologically, as if to say, "Hey, those old closet cases were kind of cool in a strange way." This doesn't mean faggot heroes of the distant past like Judy Garland, Busby Berkeley, and Montgomery Clift are back in vogue. (Heroes in general are unacceptable except as fetish objects.) It *does* mean that drug experimentation, glory holes, s&m, drag, even a little quasi-spirituality are once again under consideration as potential tools of a cultural revolution.

Out of the closet doesn't begin to describe this stance. Radical queers operate from a point of such self-confidence about their sexuality that they find overt expressions of gay pride redundant. To generalize, they see homosexuality as a given, something they were born with. The world in which they make art and play does not find that particularly interesting or distasteful in and of itself. So they feel a freedom to invent

looks and ideas that both distort and take their sexual identity into account. It's as if they're saying, I refuse to manifest my homosexuality in a programmatic way—for instance by the wearing of activist T-shirts, pink triangles, and other clone accoutrements—just so you can pigeonhole me as a comrade. If you can't tell I'm queer, they're saying, that's your problem.

*   *   *

Danielle "Hell" Willis is a performer, sex worker, and the author of *Dogs in Lingerie*.

Define Queercore.

It's really diverse. There are goth kids, straights, punks, bisexuals, rockers, fags, dykes. Look at me, I'm a female who dresses like a rocker boy so I can go out with transvestites.

Where is Queercore heading?

Hopefully to a teenaged queer movement with kids running around in malls in drag. But I'm afraid the scene's becoming too homogenized. I guess that was inevitable, though, because most people are conformists. I'd say there's maybe another two to five years of vitality in Queercore, then we'll see what's next. It's already starting to produce clones. Ugh.

*   *   *

What do these new queers want gays to be? Based on everything I've read, heard, interpreted, and felt, they are disappointed that so many lesbians and gays have accepted the heterosexual model of normalcy, reiterating all of society's mistakes in Disneyesque ghettos like West Hollywood, the Castro, the Village. The new queers accept that assimilation's irreversible for much of lesbian/gay culture at this point. So they're trying to construct an alternate culture in and around it. They don't pretend for a moment that they can alter the dominant culture—gay or straight. They don't want to. All they really want is to be taken seriously. And left alone.

Queer Aztlán: The Re-formation of Chicano Tribe

Cherríe Moraga

How will our lands be free if our bodies aren't?

—Ricardo Bracho

At the height of the Chicano Movement in 1968, I was a closeted, light-skinned, mixed-blood Mexican-American, disguised in my father's English last name. Since I seldom opened my mouth, few people questioned my Anglo credentials. But my eyes were open and thirsty and drank in images of students my age, of vatos and viejitas, who could have primos, or tíos, or abuelitas raising their collective fists into a smoggy East Los Angeles skyline. Although I could not express how at the time, I knew I had a place in that Movement that was spilling out of barrio high schools and onto police-barricaded streets just ten minutes from my tree-lined working-class neighborhood in San Gabriel. What I didn't know then was that it would take me another ten years to fully traverse that ten-minute drive and to bring all the parts of me—Chicana, lesbiana, half-breed, and poeta—to the revolution, wherever it was.[1]

My real politicization began, not through the Chicano Movement, but through the bold recognition of my lesbianism. Coming to terms with that fact meant the radical re-structuring of everything I thought I held sacred. It meant acting on my woman-centered desire and against anything that stood in its way, including my Church, my family, and my "country." It meant acting in spite of the fact that I had learned from my Mexican culture and the dom-

inant culture that my womanhood was, if not despised, certainly deficient and hardly worth the loving of another woman in bed. But act I did, because not acting would have meant my death by despair.

That was twenty years ago. In those twenty years I traversed territory that extends well beyond the ten-minute trip between East Los Angeles and San Gabriel. In those twenty years, I experienced the racism of the Women's Movement, the elitism of the Gay and Lesbian Movement, the homophobia and sexism of the Chicano Movement, and the benign cultural imperialism of the Latin American Solidarity Movement. I also witnessed the emergence of a national Chicana feminist consciousness and a literature, art, and activism to support it. I've seen the growth of a lesbian-of-color movement, the founding of an independent national Latino/a lesbian and gay men's organization, and the flourishing of Indigenous people's international campaigns for human and land rights.

A quarter of a century after those school walk-outs in 1968, I can write, without reservation, that I have found a sense of place among la Chicanada. It is not always a safe place, but it is unequivocally the original familial place from which I am compelled to write, which I reach toward in my audiences, and which serves as my source of inspiration, voice, and lucha. How we Chicanos define that struggle has always been the subject of debate and is ultimately the subject of this essay.

*   *   *

"Queer Aztlán" had been forming in my mind for over three years and began to take concrete shape a year ago in a conversation with poet Ricardo Bracho. We discussed the limitations of "Queer Nation," whose leather-jacketed, shaved-headed white radicals and accompanying anglo-centricity were an "alien-nation" to most lesbians and gay men of color. We also spoke of Chicano Nationalism, which never accepted openly gay men and lesbians among its ranks. Ricardo half-jokingly concluded, "What we need, Cherríe, is a 'Queer Aztlán.'" Of course. A Chicano homeland that could embrace *all* its people, including its jotería.[2]

...

A Divided Nation: A Chicana Lésbica Critique

We are free and sovereign to determine those tasks which are justly called for by our house, our land, the sweat of our brows, and by our hearts.

Aztlán belongs to those who plant the seeds, water the fields, and gather the crops and not to the foreign Europeans. We do not recognize capricious frontiers on the bronze continent.

—From "El Plan Espiritual de Aztlán"

When "El Plan Espiritual de Aztlán" was conceived a generation ago, lesbians and gay men were not envisioned as members of the "house"; we were not recognized as the sister planting the seeds, the brother gathering the crops. We were not counted as members of the "bronze continent."

In the last decade, through the efforts of Chicana feministas, Chicanismo has undergone a serious critique. Feminist critics are committed to the preservation of Chicano culture, but we know that our culture will not survive marital rape, battering, incest, drug and alcohol abuse, AIDS, and the marginalization of lesbian daughters and gay sons. Some of the most outspoken criticism of the Chicano Movement's sexism and some of the most impassioned activism in the area of *Chicana* liberation (including work on sexual abuse, domestic violence, immigrant rights, Indigenous women's issues, health care, etc.) have been advanced by lesbians.

Since lesbians and gay men have often been forced out of our blood families, and since our love and sexual desire are not housed within the traditional family, we are in a critical position to address those areas within our cultural family that need to change. Further, in order to understand and defend our lovers and our same-sex loving, lesbians and gay men must come to terms with how homophobia, gender roles, and sexuality are learned and expressed in Chicano culture. As Ricardo Bracho writes: "To speak of my desire, to find voice in my brown flesh, I needed to confront my male mirror." As a lesbian, I don't pretend to understand the intricacies or intimacies of Chicano gay desire, but we do share the fact that our "homosexuality"—our feelings about sex, sexual power and domination, femininity and masculinity, family, loyalty, and morality—has been shaped by heterosexist culture and society. As such, we have plenty to tell heterosexuals about themselves.

When we are moved sexually toward someone, there is a profound opportunity to observe the microcosm of all human relations, to understand power dynamics both obvious and subtle, and to meditate on the core creative impulse of all desire. Desire is never politically correct. In sex, gender roles, race relations, and our collective histories of oppression and human connection are enacted. Since the early 1980s, Chicana lesbian feminists have explored these traditionally "dangerous" topics in both critical and creative writings. Chicana lesbian-identified writers such as Ana Castillo, Gloria Anzaldúa, and Naomi Littlebear Moreno were among the first to articulate a Chicana feminism, which included a radical woman-centered critique of sexism *and sexuality* from which both lesbian and heterosexual women benefited.

In the last few years, Chicano gay men have also begun to openly examine Chicano sexuality. I suspect heterosexual Chicanos will have the world to learn from their gay brothers about their shared masculinity, but they will have the most to learn from the "queens," the "maricones." Because they are deemed "inferior" for not fulfilling the traditional role of men, they are more marginalized from mainstream heterosexual society than other gay men and are especially vulnerable to male violence. Over the years, I have been shocked to discover how many femme gay men have grown up regularly experiencing rape and sexual abuse. The rapist is always heterosexual and usually Chicano like themselves. What has the Gay Movement done for these brothers? What has the Chicano Movement done? What do these young and once-young men have to tell us about misogyny and male violence? Like women, they see the macho's desire to dominate the feminine, but even more intimately because they both desire men and share manhood with their oppressor. They may be jotos, but they are still men, and are bound by their racial and sexual identification to men (Bracho's "male mirror").

Until recently, Chicano gay men have been silent over the Chicano Movement's male heterosexual hegemony. As much as I see a potential alliance with gay men in our shared experience of homophobia, the majority of gay men still cling to what privileges they can. I have often been severely disappointed and hurt by the misogyny of gay Chicanos. Separation from one's brothers is a painful thing. Being gay does not preclude gay men from harboring the same sexism evident in heterosexual men. It's like white people and racism, sexism goes with the (male) territory.

On some level, our brothers—gay and straight—have got to give up being "men." I don't mean give up their genitals, their unique expression of desire, or the rich and intimate manner in which men can bond together. Men have to give up their subscription to male superiority. I remember during the Civil Rights Movement seeing newsreel footage of young Black men carrying protest signs reading "I AM A MAN." It was a powerful statement, publicly declaring their humanness in a society that daily told them otherwise. But they didn't write "I AM HUMAN," they wrote "MAN." Conceiving of their liberation in male terms, they were unwittingly demanding the right to share the whiteman's position of male dominance. This demand would become consciously articulated with the emergence of the male-dominated Black Nationalist Movement. The liberation of Black women per se was not part of the program, except to the extent that better conditions for the race in general might benefit Black women as well. How differently Sojourner Truth's "Ain't I a Woman" speech resonates for me. Unable to choose between suffrage and abolition, between her womanhood and her Blackness, Truth's 19th-century call for a free Black womanhood in a Black- and woman-hating society required the freedom of all enslaved and disenfranchised peoples. As the Black feminist Combahee River Collective stated in 1977, "If Black women were free, it would mean that everyone else would have to be free since our freedom would necessitate the destruction of all the systems of oppression." No progressive movement can succeed while any member of the population remains in submission.

Chicano gay men have been reluctant to recognize and acknowledge that their freedom is intricately connected to the freedom of women. As long as they insist on remaining "men" in the socially and culturally constructed sense of the word, they will never achieve the full liberation they desire. There will always be jotos getting raped and beaten. Within people of color communities, violence against women, gay bashing, sterilization abuse, AIDS and AIDS discrimination, gay substance abuse, and gay teen suicide emerge from the same source—a racist and misogynist social and economic system that dominates, punishes, and abuses all things colored, female, or perceived as female-like. By openly confronting Chicano sexuality and sexism, gay men can do their own part to unravel how both men *and* women have been formed and deformed by racist Amerika and our misogynist/catholic/colonized mechicanidad; and we can come that much closer to healing those fissures that have divided us as a people.

The AIDS epidemic has seriously shaken the foundation of the Chicano gay community, and gay men seem more willing than ever to explore those areas of political change that will ensure their survival. In their fight against AIDS, they have been rejected and neglected by both the white gay male establishment and the Latino heterosexual health-care community. They also have witnessed direct support by Latina lesbians.[3] Unlike the "queens" who have always been open about their sexuality, "passing" gay men have learned in a visceral way that being in "the closet" and preserving their "manly" image will not protect them, it will only make their dying more secret. I remember my friend Arturo Islas, the novelist. I think of how his writing begged to boldly announce his gayness. Instead, we learned it through vague references about "sinners" and tortured alcoholic characters who wanted nothing more than to "die dancing" beneath a lightning-charged sky just before a thunderstorm. Islas died of AIDS-related illness in 1990, having barely begun to examine the complexity of Chicano sexuality in his writing. I also think of essayist Richard Rodríguez, who, with so much death surrounding him, has recently begun to publicly address the subject of homosexuality; and yet, even ten years ago we all knew "Mr. Secrets" was gay from his assimilationist *Hunger of Memory*.[4] Had he "come out" in 1982, the white establishment would have been far less willing to promote him as the "Hispanic" anti-affirmative action spokesperson. He would have lost a lot of validity . . . and opportunity. But how many lives are lost each time we cling to privileges that make other people's lives more vulnerable to violence?

At this point in history, lesbians and gay men can make a significant contribution to the creation of a new Chicano movement, one passionately committed to saving lives. As we are forced to struggle for our right to love free of disease and discrimination, "Aztlán" as our imagined homeland begins to take on renewed importance. Without the dream of a free world, a free world will never be realized. Chicana lesbians and gay men do not merely seek inclusion in the Chicano nation; we seek a nation strong enough to embrace a full range of racial diversities, human sexualities, and expressions of gender. We seek a culture that can allow for the natural expression of our femaleness and maleness and our love without prejudice or punishment. In a "queer" Aztlán, there would be no freaks, no "others" to point one's finger at. My Native American friends tell me that in some Native American tribes, gay men and lesbians were traditionally regarded as "two-spirited" people. Displaying both masculine and feminine aspects, they were highly respected members of their community, and were thought to possess a higher spiritual development.[5] Hearing of such traditions gives historical validation for what Chicana lesbians and gay men have always recognized—that lesbians and gay men play a significant spiritual, cultural, and political role within the Chicano community. Somos activistas, académicos y artistas, parteras y políticos, curanderas y campesinos. With or without heterosexual acknowledgement, lesbians and gay men have continued to actively redefine familia, cultura, and comunidad. We have formed circles of support and survival, often drawing from the more egalitarian models of Indigenous communities.

. . .

Madre Tierra/Madre Mujer: The Struggle for Land[6]

Journal Entry

I sit in a hotel room. A fancy hotel room with two walls of pure glass and pure Vancouver night skyline filling them. I sit on top of the bed and eat Japanese take-out. The Canadian t.v. news takes us east to the province of Quebec, to some desolate area with no plumbing or sewage, no running water, where a group of Inuit people have been displaced. To some desolate area where Inuit children stick their faces into bags and sniff gas fumes for the high, the rush, the trip, for the escape out of this hell-hole that is their life. One young boy gives the finger to the t.v. camera. "They're angry," an Inuit leader states. "I'm angry, too." At thirty, he is already an old man. And I hate this Canada as much as I hate these dis-United States.

But I go on eating my Japanese meal that has somehow turned rotten on my tongue and my bloody culpability mixes with the texture of dead fish flesh and no wonder I stand on the very edge of the balcony on the 26th floor of this hotel looking down on restaurant-row Vancouver and imagine how easy and impossible it would be to leap in protest for the gas-guzzling Inuit children.

*   *   *

The primary struggle for Native peoples across the globe is the struggle for land. In 1992, 500 years after the arrival of Columbus, on the heels of the Gulf War and the dissolution of the Soviet Union, the entire world is reconstructing itself. No longer frozen into the Soviet/Yanqui paradigm of a "Cold" and invented "War," Indigenous peoples are responding en masse to the threat of a global capitalist "mono-culture" defended by the "hired guns" of the U.S. military. Five hundred years after Columbus' arrival, they are spearheading an international movement with the goal of sovereignty for all Indigenous nations.

Increasingly, the struggles on this planet are not for "nation-states," but for nations of people, bound together by spirit, land, language, history, and blood.[7] This is evident from the intifada of the Palestinians residing within Israel's stolen borders and the resistance of the Cree and Inuit Indians in northern Quebec. The Kurds of the Persian Gulf region understand this, as do the Ukrainians of what was once the Soviet Union. Chicanos are also a nation of people, internally colonized within the borders of the U.S. nation-state.

Few Chicanos really believe we can wrest Aztlán away from Anglo-America. And yet, residing in those Southwestern territories, espe-cially those areas not completely appropriated by gringolandia, we instinctively remember it as Mexican Indian land and can still imagine it as a distinct nation. In our most private moments, we ask ourselves, *If the Soviet Union could dissolve, why can't the United States?*

Dreams of the disintegration of the United States as we know it are not so private among North American Indians. The dissolution of the Soviet Union has given renewed impetus to secessionist thinking by Indians here in the United States. One plan, the "North American Union of Indigenous Nations," described in Ward Churchill's book, calls for the reunification of Indian peoples and territories to comprise a full third of continental United States, including much of Aztlán. Not surprisingly, Chicano Nation is not mentioned as part of this new confederacy, which speaks to the still tenuous alliance between Chicano and Native American peoples. Nevertheless, the spirit of the plan is very much in accord with Chicano nationalists' most revolutionary dreams of reclaiming a homeland, side by side with other Indian Nations.

*   *   *

If the material basis of every nationalist movement is land, then the reacquisition, defense, and protection of Native land and its natural resources are the basis for rebuilding Chicano nation. Without the sovereignty of Native peoples, including Chicanos, and support for our land-based struggles, the world will be lost to North American greed, and our culturas lost with it. The "last frontier" for Northern capitalists lies buried in coal- and uranium-rich reservation lands and in the remaining rainforests of the Amazon. The inhabitants of these territories— the Diné, the North Cheyenne, the Kayapó, etc.—are the very people who in 1992 offer the world community "living models" of ways to live in balance with nature and safeguard the earth as we know it. The great historical irony is that 500 years after the Conquest, the conqueror must now turn to the conquered for salvation.

We are speaking of bottom-line considerations. I can't understand when in 1992 with 100 acres of rainforest disappearing every minute, with global warming, with babies being born without brains in South Tejas, with street kids in Río sniffing glue to stifle their hunger, with Mohawk women's breast milk being contaminated by the poisoned waters of the Great Lakes Basin, how we as people of color, as people of Indian blood, as people with the same last names as our Latin American counterparts, are not alarmed by the destruction of Indigenous and mestizo peoples. How is it Chicanos cannot see ourselves as victims of the same destruction, already in its advanced stages? Why do we not collectively experience the urgency for alternatives based not on what our oppressors advise, but on the advice of elders and ancestors who may now speak to us only in dreams?

What they are telling us is very clear. The road to the future is the road from our past. Traditional Indigenous communities (our Indian "past" that too many Chicanos have rejected) provide practical answers for our survival. At the Earth Summit in Río de Janeiro in June 1992, representatives from "developing countries," and grassroots, Indigenous, and people-of-color organizations joined together to demand the economic programs necessary to create their own sustainable ecologically-sound communities. In a world where eighty-five percent of all the income, largely generated from the natural resources of Indigenous lands and "Third World" countries, goes to twenty-three percent of the people, Fidel Castro said it best: "Let the ecological debt be paid, not the foreign debt."

And here all the connecting concerns begin to coalesce. Here the Marxist meets the ecologist. We need look no further than the North American Free Trade Agreement (NAFTA) to understand the connection between global ecological devastation and the United States' relentless drive to expand its markets. NAFTA is no more than a 21st-century plot to continue the North's exploitation of the cheap labor, lax environmental policies, and the natural resources of the South. The United States has no intention of responding to the environmental crisis. George Bush's decision to "stand alone on principle" and refuse to sign the Bio-Diversity Treaty said it all. Profit over people. Profit over protection. No sustainable development is possible in the Americas if the United States continues to demand hamburgers, Chrysler automobiles, and refrigerators from hungry, barefoot, and energy-starved nations. There is simply not enough to go around, no new burial ground for toxic waste that isn't sacred, no untapped energy source that doesn't suck the earth dry. Except for the sun . . . except for the wind, which are infinite in their generosity and virtually ignored.

*   *   *

The earth is female. Whether myth, metaphor, or memory, she is called "Mother" by all peoples of all times. *Madre Tierra.* Like woman, Madre Tierra has been raped, exploited for her resources, rendered inert, passive, and speechless. Her cries manifested in earthquakes, tidal waves, hurricanes, volcanic eruptions are not heeded. But the Indians take note and so do the women, the women with the capacity to remember.

Native religions have traditionally honored the female alongside the male. Religions that grow exclusively from the patriarchal capitalist imagination, instead of the requirements of nature, enslave the female body. The only religion we need is one based on the good sense of living in harmony with nature. Religion should serve as a justification against greed, not for it. Bring back the rain gods, corn gods, father sun, and mother moon and keep those gods happy. Whether we recognize it or not, those gods are today, this day, punishing us for our excess. What humankind has destroyed will wreak havoc on the destroyer. Fried skin from holes in the ozone is only one example.

The earth is female. It is no accident then that the main grassroots activists defending the earth, along with Native peoples, are women of all races and cultures. Regardless of the so-called "advances" of Western "civilization," women remain the chief caretakers, nurturers, and providers for our children and our elders. These are the mothers of East Los Angeles, McFarland, and Kettleman City, fighting toxic dumps, local incinerators and pesticide poisoning, women who experience the earth's contamination in the deformation and death occurring within their very wombs. We do not have to be mothers to know this. Most women know what it is to be seen as the Earth is seen—a receptacle for male violence and greed. Over half the agricultural workers in the world are women who receive less training and less protection than their male counterparts. We do not control how we produce and reproduce, how we labor and love. And *how will our lands be free if our bodies aren't?*

Land remains the common ground for all radical action. But land is more than the rocks and trees, the animal and plant life that make up the territory of Aztlán or Navajo Nation or Maya Mesoamerica. For immigrant and native alike, land is also the factories where we work, the water our children drink, and the housing project where we live. For women, lesbians, and gay men, land is that physical mass called our bodies. Throughout las Américas, all these "lands" remain under occupation by an Anglocentric, patriarchal, imperialist United States.

La Causa Chicana: Entering the Next Millennium

As a Chicana lesbian, I know that the struggle I share with all Chicanos and Indigenous peoples is truly one of sovereignty, the sovereign right to wholly inhabit oneself (*cuerpo y alma*) and one's territory (*pan y tierra*). I don't know if we can ever take back Aztlán from Anglo-America, but in the name of a new Chicano nationalism we can work to defend remaining Indian territories. We can work to teach one another that our freedom as a people is mutually dependent and cannot be parceled out—class before race before sex before sexuality. A new Chicano nationalism calls for the integration of both the traditional and the revolutionary, the ancient

and the contemporary. It requires a serious reckoning with the weaknesses in our mestizo culture, and a reaffirmation of what has preserved and sustained us as a people. I am clear about one thing: fear has not sustained us. Fear of action, fear of speaking, fear of women, fear of queers.

As these 500 years come to a close, I look forward to a new América, where the only "discovery" to be made is the rediscovery of ourselves as members of the global community. Nature will be our teacher, for she alone knows no prejudice. Possibly as we ask men to give up being "men," we must ask humans to give up being "human," or at least to give up the human capacity for greed. Simply, we must give back to the earth what we take from it. We must submit to a higher "natural" authority, as we invent new ways of making culture, making tribe, to survive and flourish as members of the world community in the next millennium.

Notes

1. An earlier version of this essay was first presented at the First National LLEGO (Latino/a Lesbian and Gay Organization) Conference in Houston, Texas, on May 22, 1992. A later version was presented at a Quincentenary Conference at the University of Texas in Austin on October 31, 1992.

2. Chicano term for "queer" folk.

3. In contrast to the overwhelming response by lesbians to the AIDS crisis, breast cancer, which has disproportionately affected the lesbian community, has received little attention from the gay men's community in particular, and the public at large. And yet, the statistics are devastating. One out of every nine women in the United States will get breast cancer: 44,500 U.S. women will die of breast cancer this year (*Boston Globe,* November 5, 1991).

4. See Rodríguez' essay "Late Victorians" in his most recent collection, *Days of Obligation: An Argument with My Mexican Father.*

5. This was not the case among all tribes nor is homosexuality generally condoned in contemporary Indian societies. See "Must We Deracinate Indians to Find Gay Roots?" by Ramón A. Gutiérrez in *Outlook: National Lesbian and Gay Quarterly,* Winter 1989.

6. I wish to thank Marsha Gómez, the Indigenous Women's Network, and the Alma de Mujer Center for Social Change in Austin, Texas, for providing me with statistical and other current information about Indigenous peoples' struggles for environmental safety and sovereignty, as well as published materials on the '92 Earth Summit in Brazil.

7. The dissolution of what was heretofore the nation-state of Yugoslavia, composed of Serbs, Slovenes, Croats, Albanians, and Macedonians, including the Muslim and Orthodox religions, represents the rise of bitter nationalist sentiment gone awry. It is a horror story of ethnic and cultural nationalism turned into nazism and serves as a painful warning against fascist extremism in nationalist campaigns.

From "Queer Nationality"

Lauren Berlant and Elizabeth Freeman

The key to the paradoxes of Queer Nation is the way it *exploits* internal difference. That is, QN understands the propriety of queerness to be a function of the diverse spaces in which it aims to become explicit. It names multiple local and national publics; it does not look for a theoretical coherence to regulate in advance all of its tactics: all politics in the Queer Nation are imagined on the *street*. Finally, it always refuses closeting strategies of assimilation and goes for the broadest and most explicit assertion of presence. This loudness involves two main kinds of public address: internal, for the production of safe collective Queer spaces, and external, in a cultural pedagogy emblematized by the post–Black Power slogan "We're Here. We're Queer. Get Used to It." If "I'm Black and I'm Proud" sutures the first-person performative to racial visibility, transforming the speaker from racial object to ascendant subject, Queer Nation's slogan stages the shift from silent absence into present speech, from nothingness to collectivity, from a politics of embodiment to one of space, whose power erupts from the ambiguity of "here." Where?

Inside: I Hate Straights, and Other "Queeritual" Prayers

Nancy Fraser's recent essay on postmodernity and identity politics argues that countercultural groups engage in a dialectic with mainstream public culture, shifting between internal self-consolidation and reinvestment of the relatively essentialist "internal" identity into the normal-izing discussions of the mass public sphere.[1] In this dialectic, the subaltern indeed becomes a speaking player in her own public identity, for the public is an intelligibly "dominant" space characterized by collective norms. Fraser's model does not work for Queer Nation, which neither recognizes a single internal or privatized interest nor certifies one mainstream whose disposition constitutes the terrain for counterpolitics. This distinguishing mark of Queer Nation—its capacity to include cultural resistance, opposition, and subcultural consolidation in a mix of tactics from identity politics and postmodern metropolitan information flows—will thus govern our inside narrative. We will shuttle between a dispersed variety of Queer National events, falsely bringing into narrative logic and collective intentionality what has been a deliberately unsystematized politics.

If there is one manifesto of this polyvocal movement, defining the lamination of a gay liberation politics and new gay power tactics, it is, famously, the "I Hate Straights" polemic distributed as a broadside at the Gay Pride parades in New York and Chicago in the summer of 1990. "I Hate Straights," printed (at least in Chicago) over the image of a raised clenched masculine fist, is a monologue, a slave narrative without decorum, a manifesto of rage and its politics. Gone, the assimilationist patience of some gay liberation identity politics; gone, the assertive rationality of the "homosexual" subject who seeks legitimacy by signifying, through "straight" protocols, that "civilization" has been sighted on the cultural margin.[2]

"I Hate Straights," instead, "proceeds in terms of the unavoidable usefulness of something that is very dangerous."[3] What is dangerous is rage, and the way it is deployed both to an "internal" audience of gay subjects and an "external" straight world. The broadside begins with personal statements: "I have friends. Some of them are straight. Year after year, I see my straight friends. I want to see them, to see how they are doing . . . [and] [y]ear after year I continue to realize that the facts of my life are irrelevant to them and that I am only half listened to." The speaker remains unheard, because straights refuse to believe that gay subjects are in exile from privilege, from ownership of a point of view that American social institutions and popular cultural practices secure: "Insiders claim that [gays] already are" included in the privileges of the straight world. But gay subjects are excluded from the privileges of procreation, of family, of the public fantasy that circulates through these institutions: Indeed, it seems that only the public discipline of gayness keeps civilization from "melt[ing] back into the primeval ooze."

In the face of an exile caused by this arrogant heterosexual presumption of domestic space and privilege, the speaker lights into a list of proclamations headed by "I hate straights": "I" hates straights on behalf of the gay people who have to emotionally "take care" of the straights who feel guilty for their privilege; "I" hates straights for requiring the sublimation of gay rage as the price of their beneficent tolerance. "'You'll catch more flies with honey,'" the speaker hears; "Now look who's generalizing," they say, as if the minoritized group itself had invented the "crude taxonomy" under which it labored.[4] In response, the flyer argues, "BASH BACK . . . LET YOURSELF BE ANGRY . . . THAT THERE IS NO PLACE IN THIS COUNTRY WHERE WE ARE SAFE."

The speaker's designation of "country" as the space of danger complexly marks the indices of social identity through which this invective circulates. "I" mentions two kinds of "we": gay and American subjects, all of whom have to "thank President Bush for planting a fucking tree" in public, while thousands of PWAs die for lack of political visibility. Here, the nation of the Bush and the tree becomes a figure of nature that includes the malignant neglect of AIDS populations, including, and especially (here), gay men. Straights ask the gay community to self-censor, because anger is not "productive": Meanwhile, the administrators of straight America commit omissions of policy to assert that healthy heterosexual identity (the straight and undiseased body) is a prerequisite to citizenship of the United States. The treatise goes on to suggest that the national failure to secure justice for all citizens is experienced locally, in public spaces where physical gay bashing takes place, and in even more intimate sites like the body: "Go tell [straights to] go away until they have spent a month walking hand in hand in public with someone of the same sex. After they survive that, then you'll hear what they have to say about queer anger. Otherwise, tell them to shut up and listen."

The distribution of this document to a predominantly gay population at Gay Pride parades underscores a fundamental Queer Nation policy. *Visibility* is critical if a safe public existence is to be forged for American gays for whom the contemporary nation has no positive political value. The cities where Queer Nation lives already contain local gay communities, locales that secure spaces of safe embodiment for capital and sexual expenditures. For Queer Nation, they also constitute sites within which political bases can be founded. This emphasis on safe spaces, secured for bodies by capital and everyday life practices also, finally, constitutes a refusal of the terms national discourse uses to frame the issue of sexuality: "Being queer is not about a right to privacy: it is about the freedom to be public . . . [i]t's not about the mainstream, profit-margins, patriotism, patriarchy or being assimilated. . . . Being queer is 'grass roots' because we know that everyone of us, every body, every cunt, every heart and ass and dick is a world of pleasure waiting to be explored. Everyone of us is a world of infinite possibility." Localness, here transposed into the language of worldness, is dedicated to producing a new politics from the energy of a senti-mentally and erotically excessive sexuality. The ambiguities of this sexual geography are funda-mental to producing the new referent, a gay community whose erotics and politics are tran-substantial. Meanwhile, in the hybrid Queer/American nation, orthodox forms of political agency linger, in modified form: For example, Queer Nation proclaims, "An army of lovers cannot lose!" But this military fantasy refers in its irony to a set of things: counterviolences in local places, sixties movements to make love, not war, and also the invigorated persecution of queer subjects in the United States military during the Reagan/Bush years.

Thus, too, the self-proclaimed "Queeritual" element in some Queer Nation productions ex-ceeds secular American proprieties, as in broad-sides that replace "I pledge allegiance to the flag" with "I praise life with my vulva" and "I praise God with my erection."[5] Although we might say that this queerituality is reactionary, reflecting a suprapolitical move to spiritual identity, we might also say that this is literally conservative, an attempt to save space for hope, prayer, and simple human relations—a Queer Nation "Now I lay me down to sleep." These pieties assert the luck the praying subjects feel to be sleeping with someone of their own sex, thus promoting homosexuality in the way Queer Nation wants to do, as a mode of ordi-nary identification and pleasure. But these prayers also parody the narrative convention of normative prayer to find a safe space for eluding official and conventional censorship of public sexuality: *Thing* magazine reports, indeed, that the broadside has come under criticism for seeming to promote promiscuity.[6] In our view, the prayers counter the erotophobia of gay and straight publics who want to speak of "life-styles" and not of sex. Finally, just as the genre of the circulating broadside reveals how gay and straight populations topographically overlap, so does this use of prayer itself avow the futility of drawing comprehensive affective boundaries between gay and straight subjects. Queer Nation's emphasis on public language and media, its exploitation of the tension between

local embodiment and mass abstraction, for-feits the possibility of such taxonomic clarity.

Outside: Politics in Your Face

On February 23, 1967, in a congressional hear-ing concerning the security clearance of gay men for service in the Defense Department, a psychiatrist named Dr. Charles Socarides testi-fied that the homosexual "does not know the boundary of his own body. He does not know where his body ends and space begins."[7] Pre-cisely, the spiritual and other moments of inter-nal consolidation that we have described allow the individual bodies of Queer Nationals to act as visibly queer flash cards, in an ongoing project of cultural pedagogy aimed at exposing the range and variety of bounded spaces upon which heterosexual supremacy depends. Moving out from the psychological and physi-cal safe spaces it creates, Queer Nation broad-casts the straightness of public space, and hence its explicit or implicit danger to gays. The queer body—as an agent of publicity, as a unit of self-defense, and finally as a spectacle of ecstasy—becomes the locus where mainstream culture's discipline of gay citizens is written and where the pain caused by this discipline is trans-formed into rage and pleasure. Using alternat-ing strategies of menace and merriment, agents of Queer Nation have come to see and conquer places that present the danger of *violence* to gays and lesbians, to reterritorialize them.

Twenty-three years after Dr. Socarides' mer-cifully brief moment of fame, New Yorkers began to display on their chests a graphic inter-pretation of his fear for the national defense. The tee shirt they wore portrays a silhouette of the United States, with the red tint of the East Coast and the blue tint of the West Coast fading and blending in the middle. Suddenly, the heartland of the country is a shocking new shade of Queer: Red, white, and blue make lavender. This, Queer Nation's first tee shirt, ex-tends the project of an earlier graphic produced by Adam Rolston, which shows a placard that reads "I Am Out, Therefore I Am." But Queer

Nation's shirt locates the public space in which the individual Cartesian subject must be out, transforming that space in order to survive. Queer Nation's design maps a psychic and bodily territory—lavender territory—that cannot be colonized and expands it to include, potentially, the entire nation. This lamination of the country to the body conjoins individual and national liberation: Just as Dr. Socarides dreaded, the boundaries between what constitutes individual and what constitutes national space are explicitly blurred. "National Defense" and "Heterosexual Defense" become interdependent projects of boundary maintenance that Queer Nation graphically undermines, showing that these colors *will* run.

While the Queer Nation shirt exploits heterosexist fears of the "spread of a lifestyle" through dirty laundry by publicizing its wearer as both a gay native and a missionary serving the spread of homosexuality, not all of their tactics are this benign. The optimistic assertion that an army of lovers cannot lose masks the seriousness with which Queer Nation has responded to the need for a pseudo-militia on the order of the Guardian Angels. The Pink Panthers, initially conceived of at a Queer Nation meeting (they are now a separate organization), provided a searing response to the increased violence that has accompanied the general increase of gay visibility in America. The Panthers, a foot patrol that straddles the "safe spaces" described in the first section and the "unsafe spaces" of public life in America, not only defend other queer bodies but aim to be a continual reminder of them. Dressed in black tee shirts with pink triangles enclosing a black paw print, they move unarmed in groups, linked by walkie-talkies and whistles. In choosing a uniform that explicitly marks them as targets, as successors of the Black Power movement, and as seriocomic detectives, the Panthers bring together the abstract threat implicit in the map graphic described above, the embodied threat implicit in individual queers crossing their subcultural boundaries, and the absurdity that founds this condition of sexual violence.

The Panthers' slogan is "Bash Back." It announces that the locus of gay oppression has shifted from the legal to the extralegal arena, and from national-juridical to ordinary everyday forms.[8] The menace of "Bash Back" reciprocates the menace of physical violence that keeps gays and lesbians invisible and/or physically restricted to their mythically safe neighborhoods. But rather than targeting specific gay bashers or lashing out at random heterosexuals, the Panthers train in self-defense techniques and travel unarmed: "Bash Back" simply intends to mobilize the threat gay bashers use so effectively—strength not in numbers but in the presence of a few bodies who represent the potential for widespread violence—against the bashers themselves. In this way, the slogan turns the bodies of the Pink Panthers into a psychic counterthreat, expanding their protective shield beyond the confines of their physical "beat." Perhaps the most assertive bashing that the uniformed bodies of the Pink Panthers deliver is mnemonic. Their spectacular presence counters heterosexual culture's will not to recognize its own intense need to reign in a sexually pure environment.

While the rage of "Bash Back" responds to embodied and overt violence, Queer Nation's "Queer Nights Out" redress the more diffuse and implicit violence of sexual conventionality by mimicking the hackneyed forms of straight social life. Queer Nights Out are moments of radical desegregation with roots in the civil rights era lunch counter sit-ins; whereas the sixties' sit-ins addressed legal segregation, these queer sorties confront customary segregation. Invading straight bars, for example, they stage a production of sentimentality and pleasure that broadcasts the ordinariness of the queer body. The banality of twenty-five same-sex couples making out in a bar, the silliness of a group of fags playing spin the bottle, efface the distance crucial to the ordinary pleasures straight society takes in the gay world. Neither informational nor particularly spectacular, Queer Nights Out demonstrate two ominous truths to heterosexual culture: (1) gay sexual identity is no longer a reliable foil for straightness; and (2) what looked like bounded gay subcultural activity has itself become restless and improvisatory, taking its pleasures in a theater near you.

Queer Nights Out have also appropriated the model of the surprise attack, which the police have traditionally used to show gays and lesbians that even the existence of their subcultural spaces is contingent upon the goodwill of straights. Demonstrating that the boundedness of heterosexual spaces is also contingent upon the (enforced) willingness of gays to remain invisible, queers are thus using exhibitionism to make public space psychically unsafe for unexamined heterosexuality. In one report from the field, two lesbians were sighted sending a straight woman an oyster, adding a Sapphic Appetizer to the menu of happy hour delights. The straight woman was not amused.[9] Embarrassment was generated—the particular embarrassment liberals suffer when the sphere allotted to the tolerated exceeds the boundaries "we all agree upon." Maneuvers such as this reveal that straight mating techniques, supposed to be "Absolutely Het," are sexual lures available to any brand of pleasure: "Sorry, you looked like a dyke to me."[10] This political transgression of "personal space" can even be used to deflect the violence it provokes. Confronted by a defensive and hostile drunk, a QN gayboy addresses the room: "Yeah, I had him last night, and he was terrible."

In this place of erotic exchange, the army of lovers takes as its war strategies "some going down and butt-fucking and other theatricals."[11] The genitals become not just organs of erotic thanksgiving but weapons of pleasure against their own oppression. These kinds of militant-erotic interventions take their most public form in the Queer Nation kiss-in, in which an official space, such as a city plaza, is transfused with the juices of unofficial enjoyment: Embarrassment,

pleasure, spectacle, longing, and accusation interarticulate to produce a public scandal that is . . . Queer Nation's specialty.

Notes

1. Nancy Fraser, "Rethinking the Public Sphere: A Contribution to the Critique of Actually Existing Democracy," *Social Text* 25/26 (1990): 56–80.

2. Identity is linked to territorialization, both geographical and ideological. We mean to offer an account of a subcultural *topology,* a description of how modern space requires negotiating a complex relation between situated identities and mobilized *identifications.* The shifting terrain in the meaning of the phrase *gay community* symptomatized in Queer Nation's practices has been splendidly explicated by Richard Herrell's "Symbolic Strategies of Chicago's Gay and Lesbian Pride Day Parade," in Gilbert Herdt, ed., *The Culture of Gay Men* (forthcoming).

3. Gayatri Chakravorty Spivak, "In a Word. Interview," *Differences* 1 (Summer 1989): 129.

4. See Sedgwick, *Epistemology of the Closet,* 1–63.

5. We cite the texts in their entirety. "I Praise Life": "I praise life with my vulva. I thank the gods for all the women who have kissed my lips. I praise life." "I Praise God": "I praise God with my erection. I thank God for all the men I've slept with. I praise God." They were created in 1990 by Joe Lindsay of Queer Nation Denver.

6. Robert Ford, "Sacred Sex: Art Erects Controversy," *Thing* 4 (Spring 1991): 4.

7. John D'Emilio, *Sexual Politics, Sexual Communities* (Chicago: University of Chicago Press, 1983), 216.

8. John D'Emilio, "Capitalism and Gay Identity," in *The Powers of Desire,* ed. Ann Snitow, Christine Stansell, and Sharon Thompson (New York: Monthly Review Press, 1983), 108.

9. Treybay, "In Your Face," 36.

10. The "Absolutely Het" series, parodies of the ads for Absolut vodka, were produced by the anonymous group OUTPOST.

11. Trebay, "In Your Face," 39.

Notes on Queer 'n Asian Virtual Sex

Daniel C. Tsang

The relationship between technology and sexuality is a symbiotic one. As humankind creates new inventions, people find ways of eroticizing new technology. Today, sex shops sell sex toys for all sorts of sex acts, but in fact, virtually anything can be a turn-on to someone. Once, lacking a real dildo, my partner and I dug out a frozen carrot from the refrigerator, thawed it under running water, and tried, rather unsuccessfully to use it as an organic replacement. The role sex plays in human endeavor is an area always worth exploring, and despite the contemporary focus on matters sexual, one could argue that society has paid attention to sex throughout recorded history. Tierney even argues that the

> erotic technological impulse dates back at least to some of the earliest works of art, the so-called Venus figurines of women with exaggerated breasts and buttocks, which were made by firing clay 27,000 years ago—15 millenniums before ceramics technology was used for anything utilitarian like pots.[1]

So it is not surprising that with the advent of the information super-highway, more and more folks are discovering the sexual underground within the virtual community in cyberspace.

Like the stereotypical computer nerd, I have sat in front of my computer, pressed some keys, and connected to a remote computer, perhaps twice daily, if not more often. But unlike the desexualized computer nerd, I have used the computer to connect to a Bulletin Board System (BBS) with a significant number of gay Asian members and used it to meet others for affection, romance, love and sex for several years. In fact, as I write, I have logged on to this board over 1,680 times, out of over 600,000 calls made by everyone to the board since its creation in September 1991. How many sexual partners I have met will remain a state secret. Of the 1,088 BBSers registered, some eighty-eight (8 percent) identify as Asian gay or bisexual males.

Initially this just seemed like the computerized, electronic version of placing or responding to a personal ad, as I had several times before. But as time went on, it dawned on me that this was something entirely different, with the potential for creativity (and mischief) largely untapped by myself and most of the others (I presumed) on the BBS.

One need not belabor the differences between pen and paper and the computer to recognize that with instantaneous communication now available, dating—and fulfilling our sexual desires—are much more immediately realizable.

Friends may bemoan months of BBSing without meeting anyone in the flesh, but they, alas, miss the point. The online experiences are ones that I cherish, not just the real live ones.

On the board, fantasy substitutes for hard reality. For a couple of years I had been chatting electronically with this college student; recently I called his college (he had given me his name and address) and found he did not exist, nor did his dormitory. Yet this was someone with whom I had even chatted "voice," i.e., on the phone. Could he have been a figment of my imagination? Or did he give me false identification? Or worse still, was an undercover government agent infiltrating the board to investigate my sex life? After all, the CIA has admitted collecting information about me and giving it away to a foreign government.[2]

It does pay to have a sense of "healthy paranoia" online. For despite the illusion of privacy, nothing one types is really truly private. The sysop [system operator] can "tap" your electronic conversations; who knows if the recipient is not "downloading" your love notes? Sometimes, in "open chat," the forum is deliberately not private, and several people can chat at once or almost at once. All participants get to read the messages flying back and forth. Without even the National Security Agency having its Clipper chip access, BBSing is arguably more open than chatting in public. Berlet (1985), for example, argues that today's BBS sysops "are merely the modern incarnation of the pesky and audacious colonial period pamphleteers like John Peter Zenger and Thomas Paine" and that today, "Zenger might well be a political dissident running a controversial BBS while listening to audio tapes of the 'Police' singing about surveillance," and should thus be protected by privacy laws from government intrusion.[3]

But despite the best efforts of these civil libertarians to protect the privacy of BBSers, those who chat online need a wake-up call: the notion of privacy is, in the end, an illusion. Like the HIV status of your electronic mate, don't be deluded. Play safe: treat every message as public, and every sexual partner as HIV positive. The BBS challenges traditional notions of privacy and obscures the lines between private and public.

One reason BBSing is so fascinating is that the online environment truly allows one to continually reinvent one's identity, including the sexual. For once, you are in total control of your sexual identity, or identities, or at least what you decide to show the outside world.

Indeed, it is our sexualities that are on display. In real life, but more so in virtual reality,

our sexualities are not fixed, but constantly in flux. In the Foucauldian sense, we re-invent our sexualities. Over time we can have more than one. And there are more than just gay or straight. And despite the protestations of the latest adherents to gay ideology that they were born gay, the online environment reminds us that our sexualities are ephemeral, to be changed with a stroke of a key. These are social constructs, not biological essentialisms.

In virtual reality, we can take on other identities than our current one, often with no one else the wiser. In time, these online identities may become more real than the physical one.

One student I know even signs on under a friend's I.D. so that he can maximize his time on the board; and he is on the board for hours daily even during exam week. Personally, I can't tell you how long it has been since I have been to a gay bar, except to pick up gay magazines; like numerous others, electronic cruising has replaced bar hopping.

The BBS I am most often on allows its members (those who pay or like me, were grandfathered in) to post not only a written biography of ourselves, answers to numerous questionnaires, but also digital portraits of ourselves. In turn, members can peruse (or "browse") these bios and questionnaire responses, as well as retrieve and download your digital image, and see you in the flesh, even nude.

Thus, with a keystroke, one can change one's biographical particulars, e.g., ethnicity, age, domestic partnership status, class, or even sexual orientation. This means, of course, that all the posted information should be taken with a grain of salt.

Age is one good example. This board, like many others, restricts membership to adults (eighteen and over). Hence, any minor who seeks access must lie about his age. In fact two had been kicked off the board because they were minors, according to the sysop. (The board is predominantly male, with only a handful of female, out of almost 1,100 members.) On the other end of the age scale, because of the disdain against them, some older men do not give their true age. When I went on I put my age as thirty-six; after several years, it has been changed only by one year, to thirty-seven.

Ethnicity or race is another characteristic that can be changed, almost at will. If being Vietnamese today is not what you want to be, you could pick some other category. One BBSer from Taiwan even picked "Caucasian," and found out lots more people wanted to chat with him than when he was "Chinese," a recognition that the electronic environment does not screen out racist sentiments.

Caucasians inhabit most of this virtual space, although there is significant Asian presence (on this board, as reported above, some 8 percent). Although Caucasians will describe themselves as being of various European backgrounds, depending on the person, the distinctions may not be revealing. If Caucasians see us as the "other," we admittedly often see the white race as just monolithic. Once, when I wrote about the "rice queen" phenomenon in a gay magazine, *Frontiers,* several white readers wrote in to argue that I was racist, because I lumped all whites together. It seems to be an empirical question as to whether or not white Americans really do identify as "Italian" or "German." The dominant role race plays in American society tends to obscure the diversities that exist in all cultures.

When I was growing up in Hong Kong, I definitely could tell the British colonials apart from the other *gwailos.* Ethnically Chinese, my Hong Kong I.D. card was stamped "American," because my mom was born in the U.S., but I never felt American, until years after I had lived in the States. As Dana Takagi argues elsewhere . . . the study of gay Asians also awakens us to the dangers of essentializing the Asian American. In fact, like sexualities, Asian American identities are not static, but in constant flux. The contemporary influx of Southeast Asians and other Asian subgroups to this country makes us realize that one can no longer limit our discourse to Chinese or Japanese subcultures.

The diversity of Asian identities in the U.S. is reflected in the Asian gay or bisexual male membership of the BBS. The figures for female

Asians or straight Asians on the board are too few for meaningful analysis. Although anyone can access this board by modem, given this particular BBS's location in Orange County, California, which has seen a 271 percent increase in its Vietnamese population in the decade since the 1980 census, it is surprising that only a few (thirteen) of the Asian gays or bisexuals on the board identify themselves as Vietnamese. That figure is identical to the number identifying as Japanese. In fact, the majority of the gay or bisexual Asians say they are Chinese (thirty-three in all). The 1990 census shows an increase of 191 percent in the Chinese population in the county. Pilipino gay or bisexuals are also a significant number on this board, adding up to seventeen. The 1990 census shows that Pilipinos have also increased in size in the county since the last census, by 178 percent. There are nine Amerasian or Eurasian gay or bisexuals and four Pacific Islander gays or bisexuals. There is only one Thai, and two East Indians. Although I have chatted with at least one Korean American on the board, he and any other apparently did not publicly identify their ethnicity.

Because this board was set up to serve gay males (in fact the sysop is a gay Vietnamese immigrant), there are few females on the board. Since some on the board specify they would only chat with other males, a female BBSer is at a disadvantage. She can continue to stay on the board as a female, or she can change her gender on her electronic biography. Whether anyone has done that remains an open question. Despite the preference of many to chat only with other males, the few hardy souls who are female have stuck it out, although one friend I know dropped out soon after, but also because she had relocated north.

One could argue that by signing up for the board, one is, in fact, taking the first step toward "coming out." Even though one can remain largely anonymous on the board with "handles" that are pseudonyms and not real names, the fact that a BBSer needs to identify his sexual orientation on the board makes it an important act of coming out. Many of the BBSers, for example, note in their biographies that they are just "coming out." Surprisingly, there are very few BBSers who identify as straight on the board. One might have thought that it would be easier, and less threatening to initially label oneself as straight. Undoubtedly a few do that, since they stay on the board quite a while and do engage in deep chats with those identifying as gay or bisexual. They are often asked why they are on a gay board. Yet the query is posed not to exclude but out of curiosity, I suspect, and out of a hope, perhaps, that the straight identity is indeed in flux, and moving toward a gay identity.

More of the Asians (like the non-Asians) identify themselves on the board as gay rather than bisexual. One might have thought that it would be less threatening to come out as bisexual. (If queried, many of the bisexuals would insist, however, that they are true bisexuals, and not just going through a phase). There are, however, differences within the various Asian groups as to the prevalence of bisexuals.

With the caveat that this is by no means a random sample, Japanese and Pilipinos appear to be the two groups of Asian gays with the highest percentage identifying as bisexual, if we discount the one case of a bisexual Thai man, or the two cases of East Indian men, one of whom calls himself bisexual. Thirty percent (or four out of thirteen) of the Japanese males call themselves bisexual, the rest label themselves as gay. Twenty-nine percent or five of all seventeen Pilipino males on the board identify as bisexual, with the rest calling themselves gay. One out of the four Pacific Islander males on the board identifies as bisexual. The rest identify as gay. Among Vietnamese males, only two out of thirteen (15 percent) identify as bisexual; the rest call themselves gay. Similar low percentages exist for Chinese males (almost 10 percent or three out of thirty-three). The others say they are gay. Only 11 percent or one out of the nine Amerasians or Eurasian males identifies as bisexual. The others identify as gay.

Age-wise, the Asian gay or bisexual males range from eighteen to fifty-five. Chinese gay males are generally younger (average age 24.8);

with Chinese bisexual males a bit older (25.6). Among Pilipinos, gay men average almost twenty-seven years old; bisexual men average over thirty-one years old. Japanese gay males are older (average thirty-two years old), although bisexual Japanese males are younger (twenty-seven years old). Vietnamese bisexual men show the reverse trend; they are older on average (thirty-two years old) than the gay Vietnamese men (twenty-eight). The one bisexual Amerasian is aged thirty-four; the average for the eight gay Amerasians is almost twenty-nine years old. Among Pacific Islanders, the age is 25.6 on average for gay men, and nineteen for the one bisexual man. Of the two East Indians, one is a bisexual eighteen-year old man, another a twenty-four year old gay man.

It should be noted, however, that identifying as gay or bisexual on a BBS is not the same as coming out to someone directly. Because of the presumed anonymity of the board, such a disclosure is made much more easily. Often, I have had prolonged chats with someone who pours out his love life online, something he would probably only do because I am a stranger. Hotline volunteers are familiar with this phenomenon.

As I write, Gay Asians have become more visible, the 1994 Lunar New Year celebrations marking the first time a gay and lesbian Asian contingent has marched in San Francisco's Chinatown. No one has done such a comparative study, yet, but one could postulate that it is harder for Asians (than Caucasians) to come out, given cultural and family traditions, and that the rate at which Asians come out varies by national origin.

Anthropologist Joseph Carrier and his colleagues have in fact studied the sexual habits of Vietnamese immigrants in Orange County, California. They have found that assimilated Vietnamese Americans are more ready to identify as "gay," whereas those who are more recent immigrants or less assimilated do not, even if they engage in homosexual behavior.[4] This supports Tomas Almaguer's observation that some Chicanos "come out" genitally but not cerebrally. In other words, they engage in gay sex, but without the self identification as gay or bi-sexual. Loc Minh Truong, who was almost bashed to death by two Caucasian youths later convicted of gay bashing, insists he is not gay, even though he was once convicted of lewd conduct on the same beach where the hate crime later occurred.[5]

In light of the above, it is surprising that so few on the BBS actually refuse to identify as gay or bisexual. Only a handful on the board who are Asian say they are straight.

I have also argued elsewhere that just as many homosexuals attempt to pass as straight, some Asians in North America attempt to pass as white.[6] I mentioned above the case of a college student from Taiwan who, in an apparent experiment, changed his ethnic identity from Chinese to Caucasian on the BBS, and almost immediately, received many more queries and invitations to "chat."

That there are others who are in fact uncomfortable with their ethnic identity is suggested by the several dozen, presumably of varying ethnicities, who identify as "others" in the category for ethnicity. To be sure, many may have found the categories listed inappropriate (especially those with a multiethnic heritage). But I suspect a certain percentage decline to state their ethnicity in the hopes that their chances on the board will be improved. Ethnic identity and age are the two identifying characteristics that flash on the screen whenever a BBSer tries to contact another BBSer to chat.

Online, it is of course possible to reconstruct not only one's sexual orientation, but also one's racial and ethnic identity. And indeed one's entire biography. In a racist society, it is perhaps surprising that not more do that. Fung has argued:

Gay society in North America, organized and commercial, is framed around the young middle-class white male. He is its customer and its product. Blacks, Asians and Latin Americans are the oysters in this meat market. At best we're a quaint specialty for exotic tastes. Native people aren't even on the shelves.[7]

Exoticized and eroticized, Gay Asian males are nonetheless considered a "quaint specialty."

This became quite clear with a recent mail message from a self-described "rice queen" on the board who wrote me:

Hi, they say opposites attract, so I am looking for an unabashed snow queen with nice patties! To rest upon my snowey [sic] slopes. . . . I have written to over fifteen Asians on this BBS but none of them has replied. Can you give me some helpful hints? Don't worry, I can take critisisms [sic].

Why are Asian males the subject of desire of so-called rice queens? A Japanese American I met on the board wrote in his short-lived print newsletter, *Daisuki-Men,* that there are three reasons: China Doll syndrome (i.e., Asian males are seen as feminine); perception that Asians are submissive; and the rice queens' obsession with things Asian (as indicated by decorating their residences with Asian knick knacks).[8]

One could go on, but the point is made. "[O]ur (presumed) racial characteristics are fetishized by the non-API gay communities as a frozen form of desirability—one that is derived from an Orientalist perspective. In this economy of desire, the trade is almost always unidirectional, where APIs are encouraged to use our 'exotic appeal,' our 'Oriental sensuousness,' to maximize our attractiveness . . ." according to Hom and Ma (1993).[9]

As Asians, we resent being treated as objects, or as the "Other," but given the mainstream definition of beauty in this society, Asians, gay or straight, are constantly reminded that we cannot hope to meet such standards. Fung writes that in commercial gay male representation, it is the image of white men that is set up as the ideal: "Although other people's rejection (or fetishization) of us according to the established racial hierarchies may be experienced as oppressive, we are not necessarily moved to scrutinize our own desire and its relationship to the hegemonic image of the white man."[10] With such lack of self-scrutiny, is it any wonder that some gravitate to the Great White Hope as their savior?[11]

For it is not just Caucasians who see Asians as a specialized taste. Asians are so specialized that for some Asians, fellow Asians are not even on the shelf.

A twenty-five-year old Japanese American sparked a recent debate on this very issue when he posted the following on a public bulletin board: "Like the stereotypical Asian, I prefer to date Caucasian men."

Now, as some subsequent BBSers pointed out, a stereotype has some basis in fact. To be sure there are Asians who feel attracted only to Caucasians. Hom and Ma have observed that since "many of us 'came out' in the Euro/American gay context, our ideals of male beauty are necessarily influenced by the dominant cultural standards of beauty and desirability."[12]

But it is probably safe to say that most Asians do not have exclusive attractions to one race. Even on this board, very few indicated publicly their attraction to their own race or strictly to another race. One suspects such a stereotype (that Asians prefer Caucasians) is based not only on self-hate and dominant beauty standards, but also because interracial couples stand out and thus are much more visible. In contrast, groups like Gay Asian Pacific Alliance (in the San Francisco Bay area) and Gay Asian Pacific Support Network (in Southern California), which provide safe spaces for Asian gays to meet each other, are largely invisible to the gay mainstream, in part because Caucasians are not in control and are in fact absent.[13] One could argue that the gay press will report the news of white gays much more than it will of nonwhite gays. It largely ignores the activities of people of color, except as they relate to HIV.

Furthermore, the online debate suffered from an implicit acceptance of a way of viewing sexuality and racial identity in dualistic terms: gay or straight, white or Asian (complementing mainstream media's black/white dichotomy). Not all Asians feel the same way, of course, nor do all Caucasians. Lumping each group together tends to obscure more than it unveils. Furthermore, there's more diversity (even on the BBS) than this white/Asian dichotomy allows. How about all the Latino Americans on the board? Or the African Americans? One can postulate, as I have argued, that our identifica-

tion with the struggles of the U.S. civil rights movement draws some of us in solidarity with other people of color, so that this focus on white/Asian relationships is misleading.[14]

As I explore BBSing further, I see more transgressing of these traditional dichotomies, Asians cohabiting with Blacks or Latinos. But not just racial barriers are transgressed. Monogamy is another. On the board, romance, marriage, love and lust are redefined. One bisexual Southeast Asian (who has a steady girlfriend he plans to marry) is an occasional fuckbuddy, visiting every so often in person, or more often, engaging in cybersex or phone sex.

The sexual practices that Asians on board find desirable run the gamut, from oral to anal sex, sadomasochism, and frottage. Some BBSers specifically ask other Asians to check out their electronic bios; others ask non-Asians to browse their sexual histories. Some readily admit their penis size, others say they are too shy. They report sizes ranging from five to eight inches. Many admit they have been tested for HIV, although some say it's too personal a question to answer. Some admit to smoking pot. Detailed analysis awaits further coding of the data.

BBSers provide more evidence that campaigns against sex in the schools have failed and that the Reagan/Bush years of sexual repression are over. The proliferation of sex boards suggests that a vibrant sexual underground has spawned right under the unsuspecting eyes of parents.

Given the prevalence of Asians in computer-related careers, one would not be surprised to find BBSers to be the places where gay or bisexual Asians gain entree into the sexual communities that now span the globe. Given restrictive drinking ages that bar anyone under twenty-one from gay bars, BBSers have become an easy way for young gays of whatever ethnicities to enter the sexual underground. And this is not just a U.S. phenomenon. France is in many ways ahead of us; authorities there banished the telephone book (thereby saving many trees). Instead, every household received a computer terminal, thus in one stroke, bringing the French into the electronic age. Inevitably, the sex boards on the Minitel became the hottest venues for a newly electronically enfranchised constituency.[15] A comparative study of Vietnamese in Orange County and in Paris cruising on their respective sex boards would be an exciting contribution to the study of Asian sexualities.

The prevailing, if contradictory images of the Asian male as Kung Fu expert or computer nerd is one that also renders him desexualized. In other words, the penis is missing in the dominant representation of the Asian male. In his "lifelong" quest for his lost penis, Fung found it in a Vietnamese American, going by various names including Sum Yung Mahn, who acted in gay porn videos.[16] In fact a BBSer claimed to be the same actor, but has since left the board so it has been impossible to confirm his identity.

BBSers, then challenge prevailing notions of Asian males as asexual. They provide Asians and Pacific Islanders an anonymous forum for sexually explicit dialog and for exploring their sexualities. On these boards, APIs are truly "breaking the silence" about taboo sexualities. In the process, APIs are empowered to voice our own forbidden desires and to re-construct our own sexual identities.

Notes

1. John Tierney, "Porn, the Low-Slung Engine of Progress," *The New York Times* (January 9, 1994), Section II:9.

2. For an early account of the case, Tsang v. CIA, see G.M. Bush, "Librarian Takes on CIA: UCI Employee Wants to Know About His File," *Los Angeles Daily Journal* (February 6, 1992), section II, 1, 18. The admission about releasing information about me to a foreign government appears in court documents. The student later explained online that because he lived in a homophobic dorm, he had given me fake identification information.

3. Chip Berlet, "Privacy and the PC: Mutually Exclusive Realities?" Paper prepared for the 1985

National Conference on Issues in Technology and Privacy," Center for Information Technology and Privacy Law, John Marshall Law School, Chicago, Illinois, June 21–23, 1985. Electronic version stored in publiceye database on PeaceNet.

4. Joseph Carrier, Bang Nguyen and Sammy Su, "Vietnamese American Sexual Behaviors and HIV Infection," *The Journal of Sex Research* 29:4 (November 1992):547–560.

5. Daniel C. Tsang, "The Attack on Loc Minh Truong: The Intersection of Sexual Orientation, Race and Violence," *RicePaper* 2:7 (Winter 1993):10–11.

6. Daniel Tsang Chun-Tuen, "Gay Awareness," *Bridge* 3:4 (February 1975):44–45.

7. Cited in Daniel Tsang, "Struggling against Racism," in Tsang, *The Age Taboo* (Boston: Alyson, 1981):163.

8. Sumo, "From the Editor . . ." *Daisuki-Men* 1 (1992):4.

9. Alice Y. Hom and Ming-Yuen S. Ma, "Premature Gestures: A Speculative Dialogue on Asian Pacific Islander Lesbian and Gay Writing," *Journal of Homosexuality* 26:2/3 (1993):38.

10. Richard Fung, "Looking for My Penis: The Eroticized Asian in Gay Video Porn." In Bad-Object Choices, editor, *How Do I Look? Queer Film and Video* (Seattle: Bay Press, 1991):149.

11. See Daniel C. Tsang, "M. Butterfly Meets the Great White Hope," *Informasian* 6:3 (March 1992): 3–4.

12. Hom and Ma, "Premature Gestures," 37–38.

13. A rare exception to usual mainstream non-coverage is when a major newspaper published my essay, "Laguna Beach Beating Opens Closed Asian Door," *Los Angeles Times* (January 18, 1993):B5, which focused on gay Vietnamese in Southern California. Cf. Daniel C. Tsang, "Asian-Americans Come Out Actively in Orange County," *Orange County Blade* (February 1993):39.

14. Daniel Tsang, "Lesbian and Gay Asian Americans: Breaking the Silence," *A/PLG Newsletter* (October 1990):14–17.

15. See chapter 8, "Télématique and Messageries Roses" in Howard Rheingold's *The Virtual Community* (Reading, Massachusetts: Addison-Wesley, 1993): 220–240.

16. Fung, "Looking for My Penis," 149–150.

The Queer Politics of Michel Foucault

David Halperin

What, specifically, might constitute a queer way of life? What might some of the new relationships of which Foucault spoke look like? Foucault gave a few hints about what he had in mind in some of his interviews with the gay press. The first challenge he saw was "to make ourselves infinitely more susceptible to pleasures" and, accordingly, to devise relationships that might offer strategies for enhancing pleasure and might enable us to escape the ready-made formulas already available to us—formulas which offer no alternative to purely sexual encounters, on the one hand, and the merging of identities in love, on the other.[1] Foucault protested against the paucity of choices.

> We live in a relational world that institutions have considerably impoverished. Society and the institutions which frame it have limited the possibility of relationships because a rich relational world would be very complex to manage. . . . In effect, we live in a legal, social, and institutional world where the only relations possible are extremely few, extremely simplified, and extremely poor. There is, of course, the fundamental relation of marriage, and the relations of family, but how many other relations should exist . . . !

Hence Foucault's interest in classical antiquity and its social methods for institutionalizing friendships between men, methods which in their time gave rise to "a system of supple and relatively codified relations" with its own panoply of "obligations, tasks, reciprocal duties, [and] hierarchy."[2] Foucault made it clear that he did not recommend reviving that classical form of social relations; he invoked it merely to dramatize the possibility of multiplying the forms of association beyond the small number that presently exist.

One possibility that intrigued Foucault—one which he put forward as an example of how we might pluralize the currently available kinds of legally institutionalized personal relationships while nonetheless accommodating, to some degree, the established institutions of law and modern society—was the possibility of expanding the practice of legal adoption. "We should secure recognition for relations of provisional coexistence, adoption . . . of one adult by another," he urged. "Why shouldn't I adopt a friend who's ten years younger than I am? And even if he's ten years older? Rather than arguing that rights are fundamental and natural to the individual, we should try to imagine and create a new relational right which permits all possible types of relations to exist and not be prevented, blocked, or annulled by impoverished relational institutions."[3] Adoption might also provide a mechanism for formalizing differences of wealth or age or education between lovers, acknowledging informal inequality while providing a framework of mutual support in which such inequality, accompanied by clearly marked rights and duties, might not devolve into exploitation or domination.

Such a project may be profitably compared to the queer practices of self-fashioning pursued by the members of an Italian feminist collective, the Milan Women's Bookstore group, and documented in a 1987 volume which has recently been the subject of a fascinating and illuminating essay by Teresa de Lauretis. Like Foucault, the anonymous authors of this volume are very much concerned with the problem of collective ethical and political self-fashioning: self-invention is for them, just as it is for queer culture, a practical necessity, insofar as it means inventing a freedom and a form of unmediated relationship that women have never enjoyed. "This book is about the necessity to give meaning, exalt, and represent in words and images the relationship of one woman to another," the introduction states. "[W]e are dealing, in part, with things that had no name. . . . What we have seen taking shape [in our group over the course of decades] is a genealogy of women, that is, a coming into being of women legitimated by the reference to their female origin."[4] It is less a question of attempting to realize a preexisting female nature than of calling a new social and individual identity into being. Commenting on the book's title, *Non credere di avere dei diritti: La generazione della libertà femminile nell' idea e nelle vicende di un gruppo di donne* ("Don't Think You Have Any Rights: The Engendering of Female Freedom in the Thought and Vicissitudes of a Women's Group"), de Lauretis observes,

> The bold injunction of the title, "don't think you have any rights" (a phrase of Simone Weil's, cited in the epigraph), with its direct address to women and its unequivocal stance of negativity, sharply contrasts with the subtitle's affirmation of a freedom for women that is not made possible by adherence to the liberal concept of rights—civil, human, or individual rights—which women do not have *as women*, but is generated, and indeed engendered, by taking up a position in a symbolic community, a "genealogy of women," that is at once discovered, invented, and constructed through feminist practices of reference and address.[5]

Rather than put pressure on a homogeneous identity-concept, such as "woman," in the way that lesbians and gay men in the United States have tended to do, relying on the use of pseudo-ethnic identity categories to secure civil rights according to a politically regulative ideal of liberal pluralism, the Milan collective explored, as it evolved, various practical devices for coping with differences among its members, especially with disparities of power and wealth, so as to be able to continue to build relationships among women who were and who would no doubt remain to some extent differently positioned with respect to one another in terms of economic and social power. One device invented in order to meet the challenge posed to the group by the social disparities among its members was the practice of "entrustment" (*affidamento*), which de Lauretis explicates as follows:

> Briefly, the relationship of entrustment is one in which one woman gives her trust or entrusts herself symbolically to another woman, who thus becomes her guide, mentor, or point of reference—in short, the figure of symbolic mediation between her and the world. Both women engage in the relationship—and here is the novelty, and the most controversial aspect of this feminist theory of practice—not in spite, but rather because and in full recognition of the disparity that may exist between them in class or social position, age, level of education, professional status, income, etc. That is to say, the function of female symbolic mediation that one woman performs for the other is achieved, not in spite but rather because of the power differential between them, contrary to the egalitarian feminist belief that women's mutual trust is incompatible with unequal power.[6]

The theoretical basis for this practice apparently lies in the distinction drawn by the earlier Italian feminist Carla Lonzi (the author of *Sputiamo su Hegel*) between "equality" and "difference." According to Lonzi, who is quoted by the volume's collective authorship to this effect, "[E]quality is a juridical principle . . . what is offered as legal rights to colonized people. And what is imposed on them as culture. . . . Difference is an existential principle which concerns the modes of being human, the peculiarity of one's experiences, goals, possibilities, and one's sense of existence in a given situation and in the situations one may envision."[7] This definition of "difference," though in its original application it refers to sexual difference—that is, to the difference between men and women—would seem to apply equally well to the various social differences among women. And it helps to explain why the immediate goal of the Milan collective was not simply to eliminate difference or to impose equality but rather to invent ways of dealing with difference so as to guard against whatever effects it might produce that would pose obstacles to "the engendering of female freedom." Rather than insist on fabricating a purely formal or procedural equality that would leave intact existing social disparities among its members, the Milan collective experimented with ways of negotiating those existing differences not only to prevent them from producing damaging side effects but also to transform them into vehicles of mutual assistance and of communal as well as individual strength. In order to achieve that goal, however, the collective first needed to invent new styles of life, new arts of existence. The project seems recognizably Foucauldian. As Foucault put it, "I don't see where evil is in the practice of someone who, in a given game of truth, knowing more than another, tells him what he must do, teaches him, transmits knowledge to him, communicates skill to him. The problem is rather to know how you are to avoid in these practices . . . the effects of domination. . . ."[8]

*   *   *

Of course, the classic case of the strategic use of power differentials to produce effects of pleasure instead of effects of domination is sadomasochistic eroticism. And so it is not surprising, perhaps, that some of Foucault's clearest indications of what might count as *queer praxis* occur in the context of his discussions of S/M. It is also in those discussions that Foucault's belief in the transformative potential of queer sex

emerges most eloquently, if still somewhat sketchily.

First of all, Foucault emphasizes that what goes by the name of "domination" in S/M is a strategy for creating pleasure, not a form of personal or political subjugation.

> What strikes me with regard to S/M is how it differs from social power. What characterizes power is the fact that it is a strategic relation that has been stabilized through institutions. So the mobility in power relations is limited, and there are strongholds that are very, very difficult to suppress because they have been institutionalized and are now very pervasive in courts, codes and so on. All that means that the strategic relations of people are made rigid.
>
> On this point, the S/M game is very interesting because it is a strategic relation, but it is always fluid. Of course, there are roles, but everyone knows very well that those roles can be reversed. . . . Or, even when the roles are stabilized, you know very well that it is always a game. Either the rules are transgressed, or there is an agreement, either explicit or tacit, that makes [the participants] aware of certain boundaries. This strategic game as a source of bodily pleasure is very interesting. But I wouldn't say that it is a reproduction, inside the erotic relationship, of the structure of power. It is an acting out of power structures by a strategic game that is able to give sexual pleasure or bodily pleasure.
>
> The practice of S/M is the creation of pleasure, and there is an identity with [i.e., a personal identity attached to] that creation. And that's why S/M is really a subculture. It's a process of invention. S/M is *the use* of a strategic relationship as a source of pleasure (physical pleasure). . . . What is interesting, is that in . . . heterosexual life those strategic relations [e.g., pursuit and flight] come before sex. It's a strategic relation in order to obtain sex. And in S/M those strategic relations are inside sex, as a convention of pleasure within a particular situation.[9]

So S/M is a game in which power differentials are subordinated to the overall strategic purpose of producing human pleasure; it is not a form of domination in which human beings are subordinated to the functioning of rigidly structured power differentials.

Next, Foucault saw S/M, especially as it was cultivated and elaborated in gay male urban enclaves in the United States as part of a wider practice of subcultural community formation, not as the expression of a deep psychological impulse which a permissive society had finally enabled people to indulge but rather as something new that modern subjects could *do* with the sexuality to which their identities had become so closely attached. S/M represented to Foucault "a process of invention," insofar as it detaches sexual pleasure from sexuality (in an S/M scene, the precise gender and sexual orientation of one's sexual partner may lose some of their importance as prerequisites of sexual excitement) and insofar as it frees bodily pleasure from organ specificity, from exclusive localization in the genitals. S/M thereby makes possible a new relation between the body and pleasure, and one effect of continued S/M practice is to alter one's relation to one's own body.

I don't think that this movement of sexual practices has anything to do with the disclosure or the uncovering of S/M tendencies deep within our unconscious, and so on. I think that S/M is much more than that; it's the real creation of new possibilities of pleasure, which people had no idea about previously. The idea that S/M is related to a deep violence, that S/M practice is a way of liberating this violence, this aggression, is stupid. We know very well what all those people are doing is not aggressive; they are inventing new possibilities of pleasure with strange parts of their body—through the eroticization of the body. I think it's a kind of creation, a creative enterprise, which has as one of its main features what I call the desexualization [i.e., the "degenitalization"] of pleasure. The idea that bodily pleasure should always come from sexual pleasure, and the idea that sexual pleasure is the root of *all* our possible pleasure—I think *that's* something quite wrong. These practices are insisting that we can produce pleasure with very odd things, very strange parts of our bodies, in very unusual situations, and so on.[10]

The notion of "desexualization" is a key one for Foucault, and it has been much misunderstood. When he speaks of "desexualization," Foucault is drawing on the meaning of the French word *sexe* in the sense of sexual organ. What he means by S/M's "desexualization of pleasure" is not that S/M detaches pleasure from all acts of a conceivably sexual nature (even if it does destroy the absolute dependence of sexual pleasure on sexual intercourse narrowly defined) but that S/M detaches sexual pleasure from genital specificity, from localization in or dependence on the genitals. S/M, along with various related (though often quite distinct) practices of bondage, shaving, tit torture, cock and ball torture, piercing, humiliation, flagellation, and fist-fucking, produces intense pleasures while bypassing, to a greater or lesser extent, the genitals themselves; it involves the eroticization of nongenital regions of the body, such as the nipples, the anus, the skin, and the entire surface of the body. And it finds other erotic uses for the genitals than that of stimulation to the point of orgasm. S/M therefore represents a remapping of the body's erotic sites, a redistribution of its so-called erogenous zones, a breakup of the erotic monopoly traditionally held by the genitals, and even a re-eroticization of the male genitals as sites of vulnerability instead of as objects of veneration. In all of those respects, S/M represents an encounter between the modern subject of sexuality and the otherness of his or her body. Insofar as that encounter produces changes in the relations among subjectivity, sexuality, pleasure, and the body, S/M qualifies as a potentially self-transformative practice (which does not mean, of course, that S/M is the *only* sexual activity practiced by [some] lesbians and gay men that has the potential to be transformative).

By invoking his term "desexualization," Foucault seems to be referring back to a 1978 interview with Jean Le Bitoux which did not appear in French until ten years later (in what seems to have been an imperfect transcript), has never been reprinted, and has never been published in English.[11] A prominent theme in that interview is Foucault's insistence on a distinction between gay and straight machismo, between even the hypermasculine "clone" style of gay male comportment, as it was elaborated in New York and San Francisco in the late 1970s, and the larger "phallocratic culture" (Foucault's term) in which we live. Foucault welcomes the possibility of a strategic alliance between gay men and feminism, "which has enabled homosexuals to demonstrate that their taste for men is not another form of phallocracy." Clone culture is not an expression of male supremicism or separatism, according to Foucault: "[O]ne has to look closer in order to grasp that this entire theatrical display of masculinity does not at all coincide with a revalorization of the male *as* male."

> On the contrary: in daily life, the relations between these men are filled with tenderness, with communitarian practices of life and of sexuality. Beneath the sign and under the shelter of these masculine theatrical displays, the sexual relations that take place reveal themselves to be, rather, valorizations of a masochist sort. Physical practices of the fist-fucking sort are practices that one can call devirilized, that is desexed [i.e., degenitalized]. They are in effect extraordinary counterfeit pleasures which one achieves by means of various devices, signs, symbols, or drugs such as poppers or MDA.
>
> What these signs and symbols of masculinity are for is not to go back to something that would be on the order of phallocratism, of machismo, but rather to invent oneself, to make one's body into the site of production of extraordinarily polymorphous pleasures, pleasures that at the same time are detached from the valorization of the genitals and especially of the male genitals. After all, the point is to detach oneself from this virile form of obligatory pleasure—namely orgasm, orgasm in the ejaculatory sense, in the masculine sense of the term.[12]

The hypermasculine look of gay clones is deceiving. What the new styles of gay virility represent, paradoxically, is a strategy for valorizing various practices of devirilization under the sign of masculinity, thereby forging a new asso-

ciation between masculinity and sexual receptivity or penetrability, while detaching male homosexuality from its phobic association with "femininity" (conceived in phallocratic terms as "passivity" or as an absence of phallic aggressivity). By desexing (that is, degenitalizing) bodily pleasure, gay male S/M practices make possible the creation of a masculine sexual identity that need no longer be centered in the penis (or that finds new uses for the penis which mortify rather than celebrate it). Masculinity can now be reconstituted in a devirilized form: that is, it can be constituted not phallocentrically but symbolically, or *performatively*. (If there is an argument to be made about the possible political congeniality of gay male hypermasculinity and feminism, it will have to be made on the basis of some such analysis of gender performativity, not—as Richard Mohr makes it—on the basis of a sentimental valorization of gay male active/passive role-switching, to which are imputed the standard liberal values of equality, fraternity, reciprocity, and democratic egalitarianism.)[13] Foucault similarly interprets lesbian S/M as the expression of a parallel struggle on the part of women to escape from constraining stereotypes of femininity.[14]

The creative and transformative potential of queer sex is especially clear in the case of fist-fucking,[15] the practice that Foucault singles out for mention and that he seems to have in mind when he speaks of "produc[ing] pleasure with very odd things, very strange parts of our bodies." Fist-fucking, after all, is a sexual practice that nonetheless differs in several important respects from "sexual intercourse" as the latter is conventionally defined. It is less an end-driven, teleological action aimed at achieving release of sexual tension through orgasm (as in the Freudian model of "full heterosexual genitality")[16] than a gradual, lengthy process—"an art," as Gayle Rubin describes it, "that involves seducing one of the jumpiest and tightest muscles in the body."[17] Intensity and duration of feeling, not climax, are the key values: the process can sometimes go on for hours, and it is possible that neither partner may come—or (in the case of men) even maintain an erection for long. It is also possible for the receptive male partner to come without being in a state of erection at the time. Hence, fist-fucking has been spoken of by its practitioners not as sex but as a kind of "anal yoga." As such, it would seem to represent a practical refutation of what Foucault considered, as we have seen, the mistaken "idea that bodily pleasure should always come from sexual pleasure, and the idea that sexual pleasure is the root of *all* our possible pleasure." The emergence of fist-fucking as both a sexual and a subcultural phenomenon therefore has the potential to contribute to redefining both the meaning and the practice of sex along the lines sketched out by Foucault in 1977 when, in an interview entitled "Down with the Dictatorship of Sex!" he announced, "I am for the decentralization, the regionalization of all pleasures."[18]

Notes

1. Bitoux et al., "De l'amitié comme mode de vie," 39; cf. Lévy, "Foucault: Non au sexe roi," 100.

2. Barbedette, "The Social Triumph of the Sexual Will," 38.

3. Ibid. Macey (*The Lives of Michel Foucault*, 367) reports a story told by Claude Mauriac in his memoirs to the effect that Foucault consulted a lawyer, shortly before his death, in order to inquire about the possibility—evidently abandoned—of adopting his lover of twenty years, Daniel Defert.

4. Qtd. in de Lauretis, "The Essence of the Triangle," 14.

5. Ibid., 14–15.

6. Ibid., 22.

7. Ibid., 18.

8. Fornet-Betancourt et al., "The Ethic of Care for the Self as a Practice of Freedom," 129. I wish to thank Jana Sawicki for calling my attention to this passage. I should emphasize, in this context, that Foucault did not easily or lightly make distinctions between power inequalities and domination; nor did he look on pedagogy as a politically neutral or harmless activity. It was not, for him, so much a matter of conceptually separating supposedly benign exercises of power (such as teaching) from nonconsensual impositions of force (such as imprisoning) as it was a matter of scrutinizing relations of power in order to discern the precise effects (of domination or other-

wise) produced by them. For an example of his skepticism about the supposed benignity of certain power asymmetries, see Foucault, "Politics and Ethics: An Interview," in *The Foucault Reader*, 373–80, esp. 378–79.

9. Gallagher and Wilson, "Michel Foucault," 29–30 (emphasis in original).

10. Ibid., 27–28 (emphasis in original).

11. The interview, conducted on July 10, 1978, was published in Dutch as "Vijftien vragen van homosexuele zijde san Michel Foucault," *Interviews met Michel Foucault*, ed. M. Duyves and T. Massen (Utrecht: De Woelrat, 1982), 13–23, and finally printed in two installments under the title "Le Gai savoir" in *Mec Magazine* during the summer of 1988. There is a transcription of the original interview in the Centre Michel Foucault in Paris; the text has unfortunately been omitted—it is one of several important omissions—from the new, four-volume collection of Foucault's papers, *Dits et écrits 1954–1988*, ed. Daniel Defert and François Ewald (Paris: Gallimard, 1994). (I wish to thank Diana Fuss for originally calling to my attention the existence of this interview, and to Michael West for supplying me with a copy of the text and sharing his unpublished translation with me.)

12. Foucault, "Le Gai savoir" (1), 34: Il faut néanmoins y regarder de plus près, pour saisir que toute cette mise en blason de la masculinité ne coïncide aucunement avec une revalorisation du mâle en tant que mâle. Au contraire, dans la vie quotidienne, les rapports entre ces hommes sont empreints de tendresse, avec des pratiques communautaires de vie et de sexualité. Sous les signes et à l'abri de ces blasons masculins, les rapports sexuels qui se déroulent se révèlent être plutôt des valorisations de type masochiste. Les pratiques physiques de type fist-fucking sont des pratiques que l'on peut nommer comme dévirilisées, voire désexuées. Ce sont en fait d'extraordinaires falsifications de plaisir que l'on atteint en s'aidant d'un certain nombre d'instruments, de signes, de symboles ou de drogues telles que le poppers ou le MDA. Si ces signes de masculinité sont là, ce n'est pas pour revenir à quelque chose qui serait de l'ordre d'un phallocratisme, d'un machisme, mais plutôt pour s'inventer, pour faire de son corps un lieu de production de plaisirs extraordinairement polymorphes, et en même temps détachés des valorisations du sexe et particulièrement du sexe mâle. Car il s'agit de se détacher de cette forme virile de plaisir commandé qu'est la jouissance, jouissance prise au sens éjaculatoire, au sens masculin du terme.

13. Richard D. Mohr, *Gay Ideas: Outing and Other Controversies* (Boston: Beacon Press, 1992), 135–203.

14. Gallagher and Wilson, "Michel Foucault," 29.

15. For the sake of clarity I'll quote Gayle Rubin's definition of fist-fucking (which, she notes, "is also known as fisting or handballing"): "It is a sexual technique in which the hand and arm, rather than a penis or dildo, are used to penetrate a bodily orifice. Fisting usually refers to anal penetration, although the terms are also used for the insertion of a hand into a vagina." See Rubin, "The Catacombs: A Temple of the Butthole," in *Leatherfolk: Radical Sex, People, Politics, and Practice,* ed. Mark Thompson (Boston: Alyson, 1991), 119–41 (quotation on p. 121 n). Macey, *The Lives of Michel Foucault,* 370, defines fist-fucking as "the gradual penetration of the rectum by a lubricated *and clenched* fist" (my emphasis); the last detail in this definition is an error (as well as a physical impossibility).

16. See Morrison, "End Pleasure."

17. Rubin, "The Catacombs," 126.

18. Madeleine Chapsal, "Michel Foucault: A bas la dictature du sexe," *L'Express,* January 24, 1977, 56–57: qtd. in Macey, *The Lives of Michel Foucault,* 364.

What Can *Materialism* Mean to Poststructuralists?

Kathryn Bond Stockton

In contemporary feminist theory, no issue is more vexed than that of determining the relations between the feminine body as a figure in discourse and as material presence or biological entity. The debates surrounding this question in recent years have been the most highly charged, but also perhaps the most fruitful.

—Mary Jacobus, Evelyn Fox Keller, Sally Shuttleworth,
in their introduction to *Body/Politics: Women and the Discourses of Science*

What if matter had always, already, had a part but was yet invisible, beyond the senses, moving in ways alien to any fixed reflection.

—Luce Irigaray, *Speculum of the Other Woman*

Poststructuralists and Victorians

Poststructuralist feminists are the new Victorians. What 'God' was to Victorian thinkers, 'the body' is to poststructuralist feminists: an object of doubt and speculation but also a necessary fiction and an object of faith.[1] Cultivating belief in 'real bodies' as 'material presence', poststructuralist feminists now want to compensate for deconstructive excesses and extreme forms of social constructionism, both of which so heavily stress how language constructs human beings and their world.[2] That is to say, poststructuralist feminists are becoming believers as they return to the fold of materialism.[3]

What can *materialism* mean to poststructuralists? Materialism is now difficult to think; it is the opaque impasse poststructuralists have reached. I don't mean materialism in the sense of ideologies by which we live out our relations to the real (ideology as "a material practice,"

Althusser would say).[4] Few would deny that materialism in this sense is laced with constructions. I mean materialism in its strongest sense: the material onto which we map our constructions, 'matter on its own terms' that might resist or pressure our constructions, or prove independent of them altogether. This materialism is the nondiscursive something poststructuralist feminists now want to embrace, the extradiscursive something they confess necessarily eludes them. This materialism stands as a God that might be approached through fictions and faith but never glimpsed naked. Real bodies are what never appear.

I want to speculate on this strange eclipse, as if to keep vigil with this newly emerging feminist tendency to spiritualize bodies, to endow bodies with sacred enigmas and mystical escapes—all in order to gesture toward bodies that stand apart from the constructions that render them. Poststructuralist feminists like

Jane Gallop, for example, admit that bodies elaborately present themselves as objects for construction. Yet, Gallop argues, bodies resist domination by the mind. The body is "a bodily enigma," "an inscrutable given," and "points to an outside—beyond/before language."[5] "The body is enigmatic," moreover, "because it is not a creation of the mind" and "will never be totally dominated by man-made meaning" (*TTB*, 18, 19).

Gallop exemplifies the poststructuralist feminist who, *in the act* of making problematic what (we think) Victorians often took for granted— the body's presence—ends up sounding like a Victorian believer. Stranger yet, poststructuralist feminists write versions of a *spiritual* materialism that remarkably echo Victorian discussions of bodies and God.[6] For instance, we find the Victorian Thomas Carlyle bent around conundrums that do not die out in the nineteenth century but that surface, resurgent, to plague poststructuralists. This bend is particularly true of Carlyle's discussion of bodies as "mystic unfathomable Visibilities." I seek to illuminate this unexpected join between poststructuralist feminists and Victorian intellectuals, such as Carlyle. By doing so, I believe, we can better locate the conceptual dilemmas these feminists face in their returns to materialism and can better understand why spiritualizing gestures suggest themselves to feminists as ways to produce escapes *back* to bodies.

Three exemplars of this feminist curve have emerged in Donna Haraway, Jane Gallop, and Luce Irigaray. Admittedly, Haraway and Gallop, along with Irigaray, are among those feminists I seek when I look to be shaken into feminist disturbance. Gallop and Haraway present, moreover, an intriguing pair, since they would not be, to my mind, likely candidates for spiritual gestures. Yet, both of these feminists, entirely sympathetic to, familiar with, and shaped by poststructuralist theory and its largely constructionist slant, now worry about where the body might stand apart from, or at times against, the representations that encode it at every turn. Unfolding their worry, we will find that Haraway and Gallop evince a more oblique

form of spiritual materialism. They, unlike Irigaray, do not overtly use Christian discourse in order to leverage their returns upon the body. In this way, we could distinguish between greater and lesser spiritual materialisms, or, as I prefer to regard them, materialisms which are oblique or overt in their spiritualizing character. Nonetheless, however we may cut between Gallop and Haraway on the one hand, and Irigaray (and Carlyle) on the other, I want to suggest that the antitranscendental bent of poststructuralist feminists only masks their deep dependence upon the kinds of gestures commonly deemed spiritual in Victorian writings. Most likely, it is precisely because of their differences that I have been struck by these feminists' surprising convergence on the plane of spiritual materialism.

Haraway, a biologist and philosopher of science, is clearly seeking new ways to conceptualize 'objectivity' and 'biology'; she thinks we lose too much if we see "the body itself" as only "a blank page for social inscriptions" without seeing how our bodies, by being agents themselves, resist linguistic capture.[7] Gallop, a psychoanalytic theorist and literary critic of French and American texts (quite removed from Haraway, in this respect), continues to explore the linguistic and materialist issues she has pondered for over a decade: the frictions between bodies and language and between political and psychoanalytic categories.[8] Hence her attempt in *Thinking Through the Body* to make *bedfellows* (her term) of Adrienne Rich and Roland Barthes, and to explore "the impossibility in our cultural tradition of separating an earnest attempt to listen to the material from an agenda for better control" (*TTB*, 4). For both Haraway and Gallop, political responsibility to real bodies and political rage against "agenda[s] for better control" (Gallop) spur their different "attempt[s] to listen to the material."[9] This responsibility and rage is shared by Irigaray, the widely read deconstructive feminist philosopher and psychoanalyst, steeped in French intellectual traditions. Irigaray is almost always read as an essentialist, sometimes dismissed but only superficially understood as a mystic, rarely seriously deemed a

materialist, and never read as a spiritual materialist, as I primarily wish to read her. It is curious
to me that her materialism always gets reduced
to essentialism, since her early works clearly
evince Gallop and Haraway's same strong concerns for (female) bodies that resist constructions and agendas for control.

It is time to scrutinize materialism in poststructuralist feminist thought and the undeniable ways in which spiritualizing means have
come to justify materialist ends. As a poststructuralist feminist schooled in theologies and
spiritual traditions, I confess my fascination
with these feminist returns. I confess again:
Though I am not necessarily arguing for their
claims, I continue to find these feminists inspiring. The problems and limits that stem from
these versions of spiritual materialism reveal, I
suggest, some of the most telling concerns we
encounter in feminist studies.

Notes

1. When I refer to *poststructuralist* feminists or
poststructuralists in this essay, I will be referring to
those theorists both who live in the postmodern age
(post–World War II) and who consciously borrow
heavily from deconstruction. Although I considered
using the term *postmodern* in this way—as signaling
both a period designation and a theoretical orientation—I decided to choose (what might be regarded
as) a narrower term. I wish, in this way, to mark my
awareness that some theorists (mostly European)
still distinguish between the terms *postmodern* and
poststructuralist as a way to distinguish philosophically oriented forms of deconstruction (which they
call *poststructuralist*) from the postmodern playfulness of Lyotard and Baudrillard.

2. Let me, from the outset, call attention to a ty-
pographical dilemma that relates to my essay's argument. In accordance with the *Chicago Manual of
Style,* I am required to enclose philosophical terms in
single quotation marks ('being', 'nonbeing', and 'the
divine' are examples this style book furnishes).
Words used as words are italicized (such as all the
words in this paragraph I have marked instead with
single quotation marks); words used ironically are
enclosed in double quotation marks, along with material quoted from texts. My dilemma is this: I wish
to mark several terms in this essay as terms post-

structuralists now consistently interrogate—terms
such as 'God', but also terms such as 'body', 'reality',
'man', 'woman', 'objectivity', and 'biology', which
have not traditionally been deemed philosophical
but which have been deemed so over the course of
poststructuralist discussions. Even so, the reader will
notice that in the case of 'body', 'real', and 'reality' I
will at times let quotation marks drop. By this move
I wish to emphasize that the body outside quotation
marks (real bodies that exist apart from cultural
markings) forms the object of poststructuralist feminist belief.

3. I use the word *return* to describe these feminists' reconsideration of what may look like posi-
tivist materialist claims, even though they return as
poststructuralists. I use this term because *going back*
and reexamining prior theories and assumptions is
how these feminists seem to view what they are
doing.

4. Althusser explains: "Where only a single subject (such and such an individual) is concerned, the
existence of the ideas of his [ideological] belief is
material in that his ideas are his material actions inserted into material practices governed by material
rituals which are themselves defined by the material
ideological apparatus from which derive the ideas
of that subject" (see Louis Althusser, *Lenin and Philosophy and Other Essays,* trans. Ben Brewster [New
York: Monthly Review Press, 1971], 169). Alex Callinicos provides this gloss: "Despite the repetition of
the word 'material' like an incantation, we can see
that the materiality of a set of ideological beliefs derives from the fact that they are, firstly, embodied in
particular social practices, and, secondly, the products of what Althusser calls an Ideological State
Apparatus (ISA)" (see Alex Callinicos, *Althusser's
Marxism* [London: Pluto Press Ltd., 1976], 63–64).

5. Jane Gallop, *Thinking Through the Body* (New
York: Columbia University Press, 1988), 13, 16. All
further references to this text will be abbreviated
TTB.

6. Thinking I had coined the phrase *spiritual materialism,* I was intrigued to discover that the phrase has
also been used by Chogyam Trungpa in his book *Cutting Through Spiritual Materialism* (Berkeley: Sham-
bhala, 1973).

7. Haraway captured feminists' attention with
her now-legendary essay "A Manifesto for Cyborgs:
Science, Technology, and Socialist Feminism in the
1980s," *Socialist Review* 80, no. 2 (March–April
1985):65–107. The publication of her masterpiece
on primatology, *Primate Visions: Gender, Race, and*

Nature in the World of Modern Science (New York: Routledge, 1989), has only strengthened her position as a leading theoretical voice.

8. Gallop's career began with her book on Sade (*Intersections: A Reading of Sade with Bataille, Blanchot, and Klossowski* [Lincoln: University of Nebraska Press, 1981]). Her next two books focused squarely on psychoanalytic theory: *The Daughter's Seduction: Feminism and Psychoanalysis* (Ithaca: Cornell University Press, 1982) and *Reading Lacan* (Ithaca: Cornell University Press, 1985). *Thinking Through the Body* follows as an extended meditation on and chal-

lenge to the mind-body split, containing a collection of Gallop's feminist essays written over a ten-year span.

9. On the issue of control, Haraway confesses her "nervousness about the sex/gender distinction in the recent history of feminist theory," by means of which "sex is 'resourced' for its representation as gender, which 'we' can control." See Donna Haraway, "Situated Knowledges: The Science Question in Feminism and the Privilege of Partial Perspective," *Feminist Studies* 14 (Fall 1988): 592. All further references to this text will be abbreviated SK.

Queer Revolution: The Last Stage of Radicalism

David Horowitz

Everyone who preached free love in the Sixties is responsible for AIDS. . . .
This idea that it was somehow an accident, a microbe that sort of fell from
heaven—absurd. We must face what we did.

—Camille Paglia

A specter is haunting the American academy, the last refuge of the political left. It is the specter of queer theory. Amidst the din and clatter of utopias crashing messily to earth, the true believers once again are burnishing the agendas of social revolution. In ivied trenches from Berkeley to Cambridge, lesbian and gay activists busily work to unveil the latest weapon in the intellectual armory of the tenured left. "Queer politics is no longer content to carve out a buffer zone for a minoritized and protected subculture," an academic manifesto proclaims. Its goal is "to challenge the pervasive and often invisible heteronormativity of modern societies." This is explained in less obfuscatory prose by a writer in the *Village Voice:* "It isn't enough to become parallel to straights. We want to obliterate such dichotomies altogether."

The "dichotomies" are already being obliterated in liberated zones of the popular culture. A San Francisco *Chronicle* reviewer describing Michael Jackson's video *Black and White,* which was seen by half a billion youngsters across the globe, waxes messianic: "The refrain in the *Black and White* video is 'It doesn't matter if you're black or white.' Most riveting is a computer-enhanced segment where a person changes ethnicity and sex in rapid succession. . . . In a world

threatened by racial tensions and overpopulation, the survival instinct could summon a new human, one who has no single race and who, by being . . . androgynous, is less subject to the procreative urge." Commenting on this, novelist Saul Bellow observed: "The idea is to clobber everything that used to be accepted as given, fixed, irremediable." The task (in the words of the previously cited manifesto) is "to confront . . . modern culture with its worst nightmare, a queer planet."

For the new radical theorists, the enemy is no longer a ruling class, a hegemonic race or even a dominant gender. Instead it is the sexual order of nature itself. Oppression lies in the very idea of the "normal," the order that divides humanity into two sexes. Instead of a classless society as the redemptive future, queer theorists envisage a gender free world.

Queer revolution is thus the ultimate subversive project: It proclaims not only the death of Society's God, but of Nature's Law—the very idea of a reality beyond human will. For these revolutionaries, not even biology grounds possibility or can limit human hope. Theirs is the consummate Nietzschean fantasy: a world in which humanity *is* God. On this brave new horizon, humanity will realize its potential as a self-creating species able to defy its own sexual gravity. The future will give birth to a new revolutionary people, no longer male and female, but queer.

*　　*　　*

The century behind us is littered with the corpses of millions who died on the cross of such new worlds. Before the collapse of the Communist empire, the quest for a "new man" and "new woman" consumed the lives of entire nations. But the effort to produce a super race created instead an unprecedented monstrosity, whose horror in the end was all too predictable. Indeed it *was* predicted by contemporary critics of Lenin and Marx, who saw how the revolutionary ideal bore within itself the seeds of its own undoing.

For behind the revolutionary pursuit of an impossible ideal lurks a deep hatred for the human norm and an unquenchable desire for its annihilation. The *in*humanity of the Communist ambition was what made its epoch so consummately evil. Self-hatred is the root of the communist ideal, a lesson too easily ignored. The totalitarian state was not an aberration of the progressive spirit, but its consummation. Totalitarian terror is the necessary means if the agenda is to erase the human past in order to remake the human soul.

The radical project is a war against nature. This is why the effort to reconstruct humanity according to socialist designs achieved Orwellian results. The promise of freedom produced a terrorist state; the promise of wealth a minimalist existence. In the end, the Adams and Eves of the liberated future proved to be only grotesque masks of their former selves, their all too human desires exiting the closet, the moment the socialist terror was removed.

Why should anyone have expected anything different? What else could have resulted from so calculated a rupture with the human past? What positive outcome could be achieved by so radical a rejection of tradition and law, by the wholesale destruction of tested institutions and the overthrow of existing states? What could an experiment like this produce, other than a social Frankenstein?

And yet, now that the monster is finally dead, the very premises of its birth are being resurrected on American campuses as the intellectual project of the tenured left. It is the totalitarian past that "radical feminism," "structuralism,"—and "queer theory" intend to resurrect in the name (once again) of a progressive future.

*　　*　　*

The paradox of progressive intentions and reactionary consequences is as old as the left itself. It springs from Rousseau's fantasy that social institutions are the root of all evil, which is the fountainhead of radical theory. It is the idea that human reality is "socially constructed" and thus the ills that flesh is heir to can be cured by social engineering or, in the discourse of the contemporary academy, by manipulating their social *context*. This is the idea that underpins both the Leninist project and the perverse doctrines of today's academic radicals, providing the intellectual paradigm of their latest incarnation as the "post-modern" left.

It is this very paradigm that constructs the utopian vision and also leads inexorably to its totalitarian conclusion. For if human nature is socially created, it can be socially molded to virtuous ends by a vigilant (and armed) political elite. Although they affect an intellectual superiority to their Communist forbears, the new campus puritans seek an identical result: the redemption of humanity through political power.

For Marxists, the key to this power was the proletariat, a majority class. Oppressed by its lack of property, the proletariat's liberation could be accomplished only by the abolition of property. This revolutionary act would not only re-constitute the proletariat as a liberated class, but all social classes, now freed from the chains that property had forged.

No one believes any longer in the revolutionary myth of the proletarian international, but Marx's discredited paradigm has been resurrected by his epigones in the American academy. The fulcrum of this revival has been the development of post-Marxist theories that substitute other "oppressed" groups—blacks, women and homosexuals—for the missing revolutionary term.

Behind each of these theories lies a version of the constructivist idea. The social construction of a race, class or gender creates the premise that it is socially "oppressed." Thus women have been historically excluded from certain roles not as a result of biological realities—for example, the hazards of childbirth before the development of modern medical techniques—but because "patriarchal society" has *defined* their roles in order that men can oppress them.

It should be obvious that radical theory is, in fact, a radical depreciation of the humanity and dignity of ordinary people. Only the successful are historical subjects; the rest are mere objects of others' "oppression." In the radical view, society reflects neither nature nor history and individual human beings have no complicity in their historical fates. They are only social creations.

The same constructivist fallacy creates the revolutionary potential of all those categories valorized and simultaneously depreciated by radical theory, i.e., stripped of their free will and reduced to the status of historical objects. It is their destiny to be reshaped and redefined by the radical vanguard. But because they were mere objects in the historical past, they are also objects in the radical future. This, in capsule, is the totalitarian paradigm, and the animating theme of all radical theory.

All theoretical relativisms, beginning with Nietzsche and culminating in the deconstructive postures of Derrida and his disciples have this absolute in common: there is no objective value, no natural standard, no insurmountable obstacle to human desire. This is the intellectual ground of a leftism that—to paraphrase Lenin—is an infantile disorder. "In this age of deconstruction," as one queer writer recently summarized, "the notion that sexual identities are 'essential'—that is, constituted by nature—is under attack [by revolutionary theorists]. Identity—in terms of race, ethnicity, gender or sexuality—is no longer seen as stable or even coherent; but as variable, provisional, and most of all

constructed." David Halperin, a leading queer theorist, puts this forcefully in describing the contribution of the father of structuralism (and the dominant sociological influence on the academic left): "Foucault did for 'sexuality' what feminist critics had done for 'gender.'. . . He divorced 'sexuality' from 'nature' and interpreted it, instead, as a cultural production." (*One Hundred Years of Homosexuality.*)

If sexuality is a "cultural production" and can be shaped to fit a conscious design, what area of human endeavor or desire cannot? Like their Communist predecessors, the Doctor Frankensteins of the newest left are intoxicated with the prospect of brave new worlds. Their agenda is to make a racist, sexist, homophobic humanity into a liberated entity in their own image. This is a secular idolatry identical to that of the Communist apocalypse, the displaced messianism that has so blighted the human prospect in our time.

*   *   *

For a century and a half after the French Revolution, America remained relatively immune to the destructive passions of this salvationist left. The offshoots of continental socialism that were planted on American shores, were an immigrant phenomenon, generally isolated from the cultural mainstream. This parochialism began to dissolve, however, during the Great Depression, when a second generation entered adulthood. It was further eroded during the Popular Front, when American Marxists expanded their influence and became part of a national political coalition. After 1941, when the Soviet Union joined the Allied Powers, American radicals also joined the American mainstream. But in the cold war that followed the Axis defeat, the allegiance of American Communists to the Soviet Union returned the Marxist faith to its intellectual ghetto. Marginalized by its Soviet commitments and disloyal agendas, American radicalism after World War II became again a parochial current, self-limiting and circumscribed.

By the mid-Fifties, the revolutionary left was a dead letter in American culture, although "progressives" refused to acknowledge the corpse. The conditions of its death were general and irreversible: The proletariat had failed to act as a revolutionary vanguard; Marx's analyses had not predicted the directions of modern industrial states; the utopias Marxists had created were without exception grotesque caricatures of the redemptive futures their prophets had promised.

Ironically, it was the death of Stalin that gave radicalism new life by giving new life to radicals' self-delusion. Leftists could now free themselves from the taint of their achievements. Stalinism was dead; long live socialism.

In the 1960s, radical born agains were readily received into the American mainstream. The battle cry of their new left—*you can't trust anyone over 30*—appeared to Americans as a claim to innocence. In practice it proved to be little more than the arrogant Rousseauist's contempt for experience.

The most important experience from which the new left refused to learn, of course, was its own. New left activists brazenly "answered" the questions that the epic crimes of socialism posed by refusing to confront them. The same refusal preserved the radical paradigm responsible for the catastrophe. Categories encumbered by the past, like "capitalism," were discarded. The "System"—a vague but untainted term—became the new left's code for that demonized complex of institutions and traditions that had made America one of the most decent and envied societies on the face of the earth. The new agenda of the radicals, however, was the same as the old—to first destroy and bury this society, and then to create a utopia in its ruins.

When it first appeared on the political horizon, the point of entry for the revived radical impulse was, ironically, a traditionalist movement for social reform. The civil rights movement, under the leadership of Martin Luther King, was guided by a conservative agenda. Its goal was to include black Americans in the existing social contract, especially in the segregated South, where the Constitutional covenant had been restricted to whites. King's dream was the American dream: inclusion and opportunity for all. *E pluribus unum.*

King's victories were achieved under the banner of "integration" into the very system that radicals despised. It was the worst nightmare of the rejuvenated left. As soon as the civil rights movement achieved its goal of ending legal discrimination, the radicals acted to push King aside. Led by racist demagogues like Stokely Carmichael, the new left rejected King's leadership (deriding him as "Uncle Martin") and embraced the violent racism of Malcolm X. The banner of integration was replaced by the call for separatism and "black power." The new political goal—"black liberation"—was defined as liberation *from* the American dream.

Underpinning the new vision was a bastard version of the old paradigm, as the discredited Marxist categories were re-cast in racial terms. In the new version, class war was replaced by race war and the liberators were no longer proletarians but a "third world" of non-white races, which presented no comparably universal claim. The Vietnam War provided a model for completing the conceptual framework. Radicals defined blacks as an internal colony in imperial America, the vanguard of third world peoples whom white Americans had conquered. A "war of national liberation"—waged at home and abroad—was necessary to set them free.

The problem with this new paradigm was that it lacked the basic coherence of its Marxist predecessor and, except as a rationale for destructive agendas, made little political sense. The international proletariat of the Marxist vision had been composed of all nationalities and races. The idea that it might represent the liberation of all humanity made a kind of sense. But the revolutionary force of the new paradigm was a minority within its own society. How could the triumph of *its* interest lead to the liberation of all?

Radical theorists attempted to overcome this problem by positing a revolutionary "coalition," and a hierarchy of liberators in which the "most oppressed" functioned as the political vanguard.

Blacks were the first to assume this privileged position in the revolutionary ranks. At the tactical level, there was a parallel hierarchy, with the most violent invariably being accorded pride of place. After his death, Malcolm X became the radicals' patron saint and "by any means necessary" its political slogan. A criminal street gang, the Black Panthers, was anointed as its political vanguard. The moderate politics of Martin Luther King—integration, compromise, and non-violence—were rejected in favor of racial confrontation and revolutionary conflict. This strategy was a dead-end vision, blocking those who followed its path from taking advantage of the opportunities of America's open system, with destructive consequences into the next generation.

When the idea of a universal class was discarded, however, there was no logical cutoff for new pretenders to the revolutionary throne. Women, Latinos, homosexuals, and Native Americans vied for possession of the victim's mantle. No reflexive embarrassment seemed to restrain them as they rushed forward to compare their own discomforts with the historic sufferings of American blacks. Even college students— among the most privileged of America's social ranks—experienced no difficulty in nursing their grievances into a revolutionary apotheosis, captured in the title of a Sixties tract called *Student As Nigger.*

But the most determined and successful claimants were radical women. Led by activists whose outlook had been shaped in Marxist polemics, radical feminists quickly appropriated the moral aura of the civil rights epic. Developing what came to be called a "politics of identity" (in contrast to the old politics of class), the feminists turned to the Marxist patriarchs as an intellectual source. From the poisoned well of the Communist past, they drew not only the specific terms but the general forms of their social analyses, creating a parodistic version of what had long been a bankrupt creed.

In a typical "contribution" to the new feminist theory Catharine MacKinnon crudely substituted sexual categories for Marx's economic terms, ignoring the absurdities that this intellectual sleight-of-hand inevitably produced. "As work is to marxism, sexuality [is] to feminism," she wrote in her pretentious opus, *Towards A Feminist Theory of the State.* To provide a theoretical underpinning, she simply abandoned the dialectic of history that had provided Marxism with a complex if erroneous view of human praxis, favoring a vulgar Lamarckism in which environment not only determined but actually created gender: "the molding, direction, and expression of sexuality organizes society into two sexes: women and men." This absurdity is now the prevailing "explanation" of sexual identity in elite universities across the United States.

No sooner had radical feminists grasped the revolutionary laurel, however, than the hierarchy of the oppressed asserted itself *within* the revolutionary ranks. Bisexual activists claimed a more revolutionary status than comrades who were straight; Lesbians rebelled. "Heterosexual sex," complained a lesbian theorist (and former Trotskyite) "is a site for male dominance that Marx ignored." (No doubt a shrewder one of his judgments.)

To establish their primacy in the revolutionary pecking order, radicals came up with a catchy slogan: *Feminism is the theory, lesbianism is the practice.* Catharine MacKinnon turned this into contemporary academese: "if feminism is the epistemology . . . lesbianism is the ontology."

The collision of feminist factions was replicated throughout the radical ranks. Lesbians clashed with gays. To provide an exit from the impasse of this political fragmentation, the idea of the "queer" was proposed as a unifying concept. "Queer" posited a universal sex to replace the absent universal class.

*   *   *

To the constructivist, all identities, gay *and* straight, are the product of a socially imposed ideal—heteronormativity—which also structures the system of oppression. This is the gender-patriarchy system through which heterosexual males oppress women and gays. In MacKinnon's formulation: "Women and men are divided by gender, made into the sexes as we know them, by the social requirements of its dominant form, heterosexuality, which institutionalizes male sexual dominance and female sexual submission." It is the task of the sexual revolutionary to overthrow the norm which structures this oppression.

In its queer formulation, the radical project appears to reach its outer limit, realizing what the young Marx might have called its species essence. For the concept of queer is really the modern revolutionary idea distilled into crystalline form as the cry of the Unhappy Consciousness: *That which is normal oppresses me.*

To the rest of humanity, the institutional forms of capitalist democracies appear as liberating structures in whose environment individuals can achieve, breathe free, and realize their desires, without engaging anarchy and chaos. It is the Hobbesian dilemma resolved. Liberty ordered by the rule of law and market constraints. To the alienated radical, however, democracy is a diabolical form of social oppression *because* of the freedoms it permits; because it *appears* to be free while failing to live up to radical expectations.

To the post-modern left, the institutional forms of capitalist democracies are not at all triumphs of an evolutionary process, nor reflections of the reality of who we are. To radicals, democratic government is not "a reflection on human nature" (as the authors of the *Federalist* maintained), but an instrument of class/gender/race oppression that social liberators like themselves are obliged to destroy.

But in this malevolent confrontation with democratic societies, radicals are confronted with a serious dilemma. Because democracies, like America's, are founded in conservative views of human nature, they embrace their opponents. Democratic societies institutionalize change and accommodate the unexpected. The reform of institutions is written into law as a necessary part of the democratic process, just as tolerance for difference is its central value. Not only do democracies not suppress their opposition, but they provide a haven even for those who hate the System. The democratic founders were conservatives who understood the inevitability of second thoughts.

It is this very principle of tolerance that queer revolutionaries and radicals most reject. For it is this rejection that defines them as radicals. For them, tolerance itself is repressive because it denies their most cherished illusion: that *they* are the authentic voice of humanity, and theirs the universal political solution.

Radicals, in short, do not want integration into a democratic system or equal status in a democratic state. Nothing could be more self-defeating than to be counted one among many. For radicals, accepting the idea of a democratic norm—or any norm at all—is merely to collude in one's own oppression; to embrace a "false consciousness" in place of a revolutionary vision. "Formally, the state is male, in that objectivity is its norm," explains the author of "Fear of A Queer Planet." In this radical conception of human freedom, the revolutionary goal is a queer state where norms no longer exist. At the recent 10th anniversary conference of the National Council for Research on Women, its feminist president cited the term "unwed mother" as an example of "androcentric" bias because "it presupposes that the norm is to be a *wed* mother." Hetero-normative, androcentric, Euro-centric: for the radical, the very idea of the normal community—the non-queer—is the mark of its oppression.

It is in this sense that the idea of the queer or—what is the same thing—the de-construction of the normal—can be seen as the core inspiration for all those experiments that produced this century's political nightmares. To those revolutionaries, all that existed deserved to perish.

Mercifully, the empires of the Communist future are no more. In their last refuge on American campuses, the academic Lenins appear pathetic in their inability to establish a base outside their radical studies programs and the departments of English Literature, or to muster instruments of repression more intimidating than speech codes and sensitivity seminars.

Yet the ideas of the left extend far beyond campus limits with ramifications for the culture at large. In the last decade, the de-construction of the normal has proceeded so rapidly in the mainstream of American life that even the nature of the family has been put into question. What is a family? A mother, father and child? An adult of either sex and a child? Two adults of the same sex and no child?

Are their consequences for not knowing or caring about the answers to such questions? For not having a sense of what is normal?

*   *   *

Normality is a term that can be either descriptive or prescriptive, or both. A "normal procedure" in medicine or in public health is a procedure that is *usually* prescribed. It is usually prescribed *because* it has been previously tried and proven successful. It is by trial that we arrive at methods, procedures, institutions, laws, that bring our efforts into conformity or coherence with the orders of our nature.

When homosexuals object to the term "abnormal," they are objecting to its prescriptive use—for example in the claim that homosexuality is unnatural or immoral or should be illegal. As a matter of description, homosexuality appears to be both a fact of nature and abnormal. According to the best statistics available, between two and five percent of a population will be homosexual in any given society, whether that society is tolerant or intolerant of homosexual behavior. Studies of identical twins indicate that upbringing has little bearing on homosexual development. The conservative conclusion will be that homosexuality is normal in that it is rooted in nature, but that socially it is abnormal in that the vast majority of people are not and will never be homosexually inclined.

But description in this sense does not necessarily lead to prescriptive conclusions. The claim that homosexuality is socially abnormal does not lead to any conclusion as to whether it is immoral or not. Such conclusions must be a matter of individual principles and communal preferences. Many communities and religions do view homosexuality as immoral. These attitudes may be "oppressive" to homosexuals, but no more so than are Christian attitudes towards Jews as souls condemned to eternal damnation. Jews can live with this attitude in a society that protects their rights and invokes tolerance of difference as its central virtue: *e pluribus unum.*

The demand that homosexuality should be made illegal, on the other hand, is not a matter of mere communal prejudice or individual preference. It is a demand that violates the social contract and its pluralist imperative, and runs counter to the very idea of America's unity as a nation. The ideal of American pluralism—the political norm that governs the behavior of its citizen democrats—is the necessary embrace of diverse communities: even communities in fundamental conflict. The pluralistic norm of American democracy *requires* that the deviant community and the abnormal citizen (black, homosexual, immigrant, Jew) be equal before the law and enjoy the same inalienable rights as everyone else. To violate this norm, to break the law of America's social contract, is to invite terrible consequences, as the bloodiest and most shameful pages of America's history attest.

But it is the normal "civil rights" solution to the problem of minority status, integration into America's civic foundation, that homosexual radicals—following the lead of all radicals who are at war with America and its social contract—reject. In rejecting America's normative institutions, while radically inventing the social future, however, they invite just those retributions that have historically attended the systematic violation of natural order. In so doing, they have created their own social Frankenstein, even without achieving state power, in the contemporary epidemic of AIDS.

*   *   *

Who would not have known in 1969, the year of "Gay Liberation," for example, that promiscuous anal sex was unsanitary for individuals and a potential danger to public health? Yet, gay liberation was defined by its theorists as just that:

promiscuous anal sex, a challenge to the repressive "sex-negative" culture of what queer theorists now call "heteronormativity," i.e., the heterosexual and monogamous norm. In the radical view, existing sexual norms reflected nothing about humanity's historic experience, but were merely a social construction to preserve the privileges of a dominant group.

Like black radicals before them, gay activists rejected the idea of integration into a normally functioning civil order. Gay liberation was identified with a sexual agenda that did not seek civic tolerance, respect, and integration of homosexuals into the public order of bourgeois life. It was defined instead as a defiant promiscuity, the overthrow of bourgeois morals and sexual restraints. And, consequently, of bourgeois standards of public hygiene. No natural or moral barriers were recognized to the realization of the radical project.

The effect of this radical agenda was immediate and unmistakable. In the years 1967–1969 —the flowering of the sexual revolution—the incidence of amoebiasis, a parasitic sexually transmitted disease increased *fifty* times in San Francisco because of promiscuous oral-anal sex among gays. Despite the consequences, a Toronto leftist paper defended the practice in an article titled "Rimming As A Revolutionary Act." During the next decade, the tolerant American civil order made room for the sexual revolutionaries. Public officials licensed sexual gymnasia called "bathhouses" and turned a blind eye towards homosexual activity in bookstore backrooms, bars and "glory hole" establishments, until a $100 million industry flourished by decade's end. At the same time, natural forces asserted themselves with ever more devastating results.

As opportunistic but still treatable infections flourished in the petrie dish of the liberated culture, gay radicals increased their defiance. Overloaded VD clinics became trysting places in the liberated culture. In his authoritative history of the AIDS epidemic, Randy Shilts describes the atmosphere on the eve of its outbreak: "Gay men were being washed by tide after tide of increasingly serious infections. First it was syphilis and gonorrhea. Gay men made up about 80% of the 70,000 annual patient visits to [San Francisco's] VD clinics. Easy treatment had imbued them with such a cavalier attitude toward venereal diseases that many gay men saved their waiting-line numbers, like little tokens of desirability, and the clinic was considered an easy place to pick up both a shot and a date."

Far from causing radical activists to rethink their agenda, the burgeoning epidemics prompted them to escalate their assault. When Dr. Dan William, a gay specialist warned of the danger of continued promiscuity, he was publicly denounced as a "monogamist" in the gay press. When playwright Larry Kramer issued a similar warning, he was accused in the *New York Native* of "gay homophobia and anti-eroticism." At a public meeting in the year preceding the first AIDS cases, Edmund White, co-author of *The Joy of Gay Sex* proposed that "gay men should wear their sexually transmitted diseases like red badges of courage in a war against a sex-negative society." Michael Callen, a gay youth present at the meeting, had already had 3,000 sexual partners and was shortly to come down with AIDS. When he heard White's triumphant defiance of nature's law, he remembers thinking: "Every time I get the clap I'm striking a blow for the sexual revolution." (Michael Callen, *Surviving Aids.*)

Callen's attitude was emblematic. The first clusters of AIDS victims were formed not by monogamous civil reformers who had come out of the closet to demand tolerance and respect, but by sexual revolutionaries who pushed their bodies' immune envelopes to advance the new order. Callen, who later founded People With AIDS, reflected on this revolutionary path: "Unfortunately, as a function of a microbiological . . . certainty, this level of sexual activity resulted in concurrent epidemics of syphilis, gonorrhea, hepatitis, amoebiasis, venereal warts and, we discovered too late, other pathogens. Unwittingly, and with the best of revolutionary intentions, a small subset of gay men managed to create disease settings equivalent to those of poor third-world nations in one of the richest nations on earth."

The diseases were being transformed as well. As Shilts explains, the enteric diseases—amoebiasis, Gay Bowel Syndrome, giardiasis and shigellosis—were followed by an epidemic of hepatitis B, "a disease that had transformed itself, via the popularity of anal intercourse, from a blood-borne scourge into a venereal disease." (Shilts, *And the Band Played On.*)

Where were public health officials, as these epidemics took their toll? Why didn't they intervene, sound the alarm, close the bathhouses, undertake vigorous education campaigns among gays to warn potential victims of the danger in their path? The reason was the revolution itself: So successful was the campaign of the radical activists, that it made traditional public health practices politically impossible, particularly when officials attempted to close sexual bathhouses regarded as "symbols of gay liberation." As Don Francis, the Center for Disease Control official in charge of fighting the hepatitis B epidemic told a reporter: "We didn't intervene because we felt that it would be interfering with an alternative lifestyle."

In the early Eighties, the AIDS epidemic was still confined to three cities with large homosexual communities. Aggressive public health methods might have prevented the epidemic's outward spread. But every effort to take normal precautionary measures was thwarted in turn by the political juggernaut the gay liberation movement had managed to create. Under intense pressure from gay activists, for example, the director of public health of the City of San Francisco refused to close bathhouses, maintaining that they were valuable centers of "education" about AIDS, even though their only purpose was to facilitate promiscuous sex.

Not only were measures to prevent the geographical spread of AIDS thwarted by radical politics, but measures to prevent its spread into other communities were obstructed as well. Thus when officials tried to institute screening

procedures for the nation's blood banks and asked the gay community not to make donations while the epidemic persisted, gay political leaders opposed the procedures as infringing the "right" of homosexuals to give blood. The San Francisco Coordinating Committee of Gay and Lesbian Services, chaired by Pat Norman, a city official, issued a policy paper asserting that donor screening was "reminiscent of miscegenation blood laws that divided black blood from white" and "similar in concept to the World War II rounding up of Japanese-Americans in the western half of the country to minimize the possibility of espionage."

The result of these revolutionary attitudes was to spread AIDS among hemophiliacs and some heterosexuals. Similar campaigns against testing and contact tracing—standard procedures in campaigns against other sexually transmitted diseases—insured the metasticism of AIDS, specifically into the black and Hispanic communities, which now account for more than 50% of the known cases.

*   *   *

The war against civilization and nature, which is at the heart of the radical enterprise, inevitably produces monsters like AIDS. The epidemic has killed 200,000 Americans, with a million more infected. The implementation of real public health methods is nowhere in sight. Even as the ashes of the Communist empire grow cold, the lessons of the disaster have not been learned. The nihilism that rejects nature and the idea of the normal, as it sets out to create a radical new world, is as blindly destructive as are its consequences predictable. Once in power—as the entire history of our bloody century attests—the radical impulse embraces radical evil in the futile attempt to enforce its rule and to realize its impossible ideal.

From "Mistaken Identity— Or Can Identity Politics Liberate the Oppressed?"

Sharon Smith

The Gay Movement of the 1970s

Like the women's movement, the gay movement developed first in the US and then exported its ideas elsewhere, mainly to Europe. The gay movement erupted with the Stonewall Rebellion in New York in 1969, when police tried to raid a gay bar and touched off a riot among gays which lasted for three days. Shortly afterwards, the Gay Liberation Front (GLF) was formed in cities all over the US, its name an identification with the Viet Cong's national liberation struggle against US imperialism. The early gay liberation activists saw themselves as part of a wider revolutionary movement, and took inspiration from those involved in the women's liberation and black power movements. They debated the Black Panthers and convinced them to formally endorse gay rights. In 1970 Black Panther leader Huey Newton announced his solidarity with the gay movement, stating that 'homosexuals are not given freedom and liberty by anyone in this society. Maybe they might be the most oppressed people in the society.'[1]

So the early gay liberation movement was genuinely radical in its outlook and practice, and identified with a larger social movement. But while the atmosphere was anti-capitalist, there was only a small socialist presence—and

virtually no socialist influence. Here again the politics of Stalinism bore much of the responsibility. Instead of welcoming the emergence of a new layer of gay revolutionaries, Stalinists condemned gay sexuality as a 'bourgeois deviation'; some Maoist groups called it 'petty bourgeois decadence'. And both agreed it would disappear after the revolution. Although some independent socialists and Trotskyists eventually participated in the gay liberation movement, there was an overriding mistrust of socialists, and a tendency to dismiss Marxism as a way to understand and fight against forms of sexual oppression. In an essay from the British Gay Left Collective's *Homosexuality: Power and Politics*, Simon Watney argued of the GLF in retrospect:

> For if gays had been left out of traditional Marxist analysis—together with most aspects of sexuality, which were seen as merely superstructural and reactive in an unproblematic way to the economic 'base' of society—then class analysis itself was likely to be left at the back of the political cupboard in the general excitement which characterised the development of sexual politics in the late sixties, and the gradual rethinking of the base/superstructure model of society.[2]

The gay liberation movement, particularly in the US, did not place the same emphasis on the development of theory as the radical feminists. But both movements shared a rejection of class politics, which led to an early emphasis on lifestyle politics. Thus Watney concluded in the same essay, 'The major division in early GLF was between the organised leninist [sic] party supporters, and the diffused forces of the alternative society. This division between what might be termed "actionists" and "life-stylers" is clearly evident in the history and theory of the GLF, and in its Manifesto [in 1971].'[3]

It wasn't long, however, before the politics of separatism also grew in influence inside the gay movement, and led to its fracture. Lesbians began splitting from the gay movement, using much the same rationale used by radical feminists who split off from the New Left. As Shane Phelan argues in *Identity Politics: Lesbian Feminism and the Limits of Community,* 'Lesbians in the gay rights and gay liberation movements found themselves in the position of women in the civil rights, anti-war, and New Left movements: conceptual appendages, and organisational housekeepers/secretaries/sexual partners.' Lesbians argued that when they tried to raise specifically lesbian demands within the gay movement, male leaders denied that lesbians faced any special problems because they were women. One male leader reportedly responded by saying that, 'the lesbian IS, after all, a homosexual, first and foremost—subject to *all*—yes all—of the problems of the male homosexual and with *no* special problems as a lesbian.'[4]

So undoubtedly sexist attitudes existed within the gay movement. But, as the experience between the GLF and the Black Panthers showed, it is possible to convince others within a movement to break with backward ideas in the context of solidarity and struggle. Nevertheless, groups of lesbians broke off without sticking around long enough to find out whether it was possible to successfully challenge sexist ideas within the movement. Instead the conclusion drawn by this Canadian lesbian was typical of the time: 'Gay liberation, when we get right down to it, is the struggle for gay men to achieve approval for the only thing that sepa-

rates them from the "Man"—their sexual preference.'[5] But many lesbian feminists were equally disappointed with the atmosphere in radical feminist groups, coining the term 'heterosexism' to describe an atmosphere which many felt was exclusive, placed too much emphasis on the problems between men and women, or avoided taking the issue of lesbian liberation seriously by arguing that sexual orientation shouldn't matter. The differences erupted early on. In 1970 the lesbian feminist Martha Shelley put out a pamphlet which stated:

> I am personally sick of liberals who say they don't care who sleeps with whom, it's what you do outside of bed that counts. This is what homosexuals have been trying to get straights to understand for years. Well, it's too late for liberalism. Because what I do outside of my bed may have nothing to do with what I do inside—but my consciousness is branded, is permeated with homosexuality. For years I have been branded with your label for me.[6]

A section of lesbians within the radical feminist movement began to develop the argument that women must reject heterosexuality if they are to become full human beings. This idea was first put forward at the Congress to Unite Women in 1970, by a group of lesbians calling themselves Radicalesbians, in a position paper called, 'The Woman-Identified Woman'. This idea was carried to its logical conclusion over the next few years, as the notion that lesbians were the only true resisters of patriarchy began to take hold. The lesbian author Rita Mae Brown asked in an essay printed in 1975, 'If you can't find it in yourself to love another woman, and that includes physical love, then how can you truly say you care about women's liberation?' Later in the essay she concluded, 'Straight women are confused by men, don't put women first, they betray lesbians and in its deepest form, they betray their own selves. You can't build a strong movement if your sisters are out there fucking the oppressor.'[7]

Lesbian separatism represented the politics of radical feminism carried to their furthest extreme, and this led to a series of lesbian splits from the women's liberation movement between 1972 and 1974 in the US. Therefore, separatism was much more clearly articulated among lesbians than within the gay men's organisations. Nevertheless, the politics of movementism were echoed there. Among more political gay male activists the tendency was to accept the need for separate movements and the need for 'autonomy' generally. Thus, for example, the Gay Left Collective in Britain was founded in 1974 as an all male collective, because it accepted the 'division of interests and activities' between gay men and lesbians which had led to the split of lesbians from the GLF.[8] The call for 'autonomy' led gay men to the same kind of conclusions that radical feminists had drawn, as this explanation of autonomy from a member of the Gay Left Collective demonstrates:

> The theory of autonomy asserted our right to have control of our movement and formulate our own activities, independent of existing organisations which had for so long been oppressive in their attitudes towards homosexuality and unconcerned with sexual relationships in general . . . There was a rejection of authority, hierarchy and formal structure both in small groups and large meetings . . . The process involved in consciousness-raising groups and the participation in movement activities were important steps in building self-confidence and mutual support.[9]

Autonomy is more than an acknowledgement that separation is unavoidable. It is a positive affirmation of dissimilarity. In the same way that some lesbian feminists concluded that their sexual orientation to women made them more authentic feminists, the British GLF manifesto printed in 1971 stated that since gays existed 'already outside the family', they were 'already more advanced than straight people'. That same year it produced a handout which read:

> We are fighting an entire culture . . . Conversion on a personal level is fundamental to our existence . . . We must be 'rotten queers' to the straight world and for them we must use camp,

drag, etc in the most 'offensive' manner possible. And we must be 'freaks' to the gay ghetto world. Our very existence must provoke a questioning of society.[10]

The Decline of the Women's and Gay Movements of the 1970s

As the gay and lesbian movements went into decline, the emphasis on the personal and on the notion of autonomy led to still further divisions between different groups of lesbians and gay men. Among gay men splits developed between drag queens and 'machos', while among lesbians rifts occurred between political and non-political lesbians, who were accused of being 'male-identified' because they remained in the bar scene. These sorts of divisions had plagued the movement from early on, but became more common as time went on.

The emphasis on autonomy also led to an increasing focus on personal, or individual, liberation. The act of coming out was an important feature of the gay liberation movement, and remains a precondition for developing a sense of gay pride in a homophobic society. However, as activism declined, coming out became an end in itself, rather than a way to build a broad, fighting movement. Moreover, it's important to understand that, so long as capitalism exists, coming out will be impossible for very many lesbians and gays. Most gays are forced to stay in the closet to keep their jobs or are married or otherwise unable to break from their families or communities. Seen as an end in itself, coming out will probably only be possible for a minority of lesbians and gays, most of them middle class.

Even the notion of 'power', once it has been divorced from the realm of class society and placed in the category of personal relations, becomes virtually meaningless. One can feel 'powerful' without including anyone else at all. Hence the term of personal 'empowerment' became the mantra of movementism in the 1980s. As one lesbian feminist argued, 'The subject of revolution is ourselves.'[11] Having divorced the source of oppression from class society, and raised the notion of autonomy to a principle, it was only a short step from the politics of movementism to the politics of identity.

The women's and gay movements declined in size and shifted rightward politically along with the rest of the left during the 1970s and throughout the 1980s. As the movements declined, discussions of left wing ideas became divorced from any role in the struggle. In this context postmodernism flourished, particularly in the US, as former Marxists discovered they could build their academic careers by discovering new ways to prove class politics wrong. Volume after volume of theory was churned out at an ever higher level of abstraction. It was in these circumstances that the ideas of postmodernism, with their emphasis on language and ideology, found a wider audience—first among veterans of the 1960s social movements. For example in 1972 gay socialist Jeffrey Weeks, author of *Coming Out,* had argued, 'it is within the specific context of the capitalist family that modern concepts of homosexuality have developed . . .'.[12] By 1980, citing the influence of Foucault, Weeks had changed his viewpoint on this central issue:

> we must begin to think much more in terms of the various forms of social definition of sexuality and their social conditions of existence rather than try to speak in terms of 'capitalism' oppressing 'sexuality' as if there could be a simple relationship between the two . . . The rejection of an 'essentialist' view of sexuality in turn challenges the orthodox model of the nuclear family as the sole locus of the oppression of sexuality in general and homosexuality in particular.[13]

The Politics of Difference

In a 1985 article 'queer' theorist Jeffrey Escoffier summarised identity politics as follows: 'the politics of identity must also be a politics of difference . . . The politics of difference affirms limited, partial being.'[14] For Escoffier, arriving at this conclusion involved a conscious repudia-

tion of working class agency, and an accompanying sense of demoralisation at the 'flawed vision' of socialism:

> We are now in a period of decline and discouragement. We have no objective guarantee that the working class recognises capitalism as the cause of the injustice and inequalities of American life. The recent history of the American working class clearly shows that it lacks the organisational and political capacity to struggle effectively for the fundamental transformation of society.[15]

The essence of 'queer nationalism' is the belief that gays *should* live in a separate culture from the rest of society. This approach necessarily engenders an atmosphere of extreme moralism and an emphasis on lifestyle. Writer/director Todd Haynes summed up these politics when he argued recently in the liberal magazine *The Nation,* 'I'd prefer that subjectivity as a queer *not* be ceremoniously confirmed by Hollywood. For the most that we can expect is that we will be depicted as "ordinary" ie, *just like every heterosexual*' [his emphasis].[16]

Perhaps the experiences of the organisation Queer Nation in the US best exemplify the problems inherent in identity politics. At their best, Queer Nation activists have been able to tap into the very real anger felt by millions of lesbians and gays in US society today. For example, in September 1991, after California governor Pete Wilson bowed to business pressure and vetoed a bill which would have outlawed job discrimination against gays, Queer Nation activists played an agitational role in the riots by outraged lesbians and gays in downtown San Francisco. In 1991 Queer Nation activists also took part in organising sit-ins and pickets against the Southern based Cracker Barrel restaurant chain after it began firing its lesbian and gay employees for violating 'American family values'. These sort of activities, which at times have attracted hundreds of gay activists, have shown the potential which exists for building a broad, militant movement among lesbians and gays in the US.

In addition, Queer Nation activists have been consistently involved in the abortion rights movement, and have organised marches against gay-bashing in major cities around the US over the last few years. And Queer Nation doesn't usually endorse political candidates from either the Democratic or Republican parties, reinforcing the appearance of radicalism. These factors convinced many on the left that Queer Nation represented the future for gay liberation. This remark by *Nation* contributor Andrew Kopkind is a common view on the left:

> What has changed the climate in America is the long experience of gay struggle, the necessary means having been first, coming out, and second, making a scene. Sometimes it is personal witness, other times political action, and overall it is the creation of a cultural community based on sexual identity.[17]

But the dominance of identity politics is a guarantee against building a lasting movement. The tendency among groups organised around identity politics has been to grow—sometimes substantially—for a short period of time, and then fairly rapidly to shrink to a much smaller 'core' membership. For example, the New York chapter of the Women's Action Coalition (WAC), a women only organisation, claimed a membership of 1,500 within a few months of its founding in early 1992. Within a year it was reduced to a small fraction of that size. Queer Nation's short history has followed a similar pattern. All of the problems which led to the fragmentation of the women's and gay liberation movements in the 1970s are magnified in Queer Nation: an emphasis on autonomy, rather than unity with other struggles; an atmosphere of self righteous moralism; and an overwhelming emphasis on personal, lifestyle issues. Instead of growing in size, Queer Nation chapters tend to grow smaller and disappear with the passage of time.

Queer Nation was formed in March 1990 by a group of New York lesbian and gay anti-AIDS activists interested in applying 'direct action' tactics to the gay rights movement. They vowed that Queer Nation chapters would be organised in a 'non-hierarchical and non-patriarchal' structure, to ensure democracy and prevent any person or persons from dominating or intimidating the rest of the group. In an interview later that year two founding members of Queer Nation were asked why they chose to call themselves 'queer', a term of anti-gay abuse. One replied, 'It's the idea of reappropriating the words of our oppressors and actually recontextualising the term "queer" and using it in a positive way to empower ourselves . . . Now we can really rally around the word, and that confuses our oppressors. It makes us feel stronger.' The other added, 'We have disempowered them by using this term.'[18]

This reflects the belief that using certain 'politically correct' language can affect the actual conditions facing the mass of gays and lesbians in society. It does not. Whether or not Queer Nation activists feel personally 'empowered' by using the term 'queer', the vast majority of people will continue to regard it as a term of abuse. Indeed, many people will undoubtedly—and with some validity—regard their use of the term 'queer' as an acceptance of oppression, rather than an attempt to challenge it in any purposeful way. Whatever Queer Nation activists claim, words cannot be meaningfully 'reappropriated' without massive struggle. In the 1960s black power activists demanded—and won—the widespread usage of the term 'black', replacing the term 'coloured'. Women's rights activists demanded that the term 'women' replace the term 'girls' to describe adult females. And the slogan of the Gay Liberation Front was 'gay pride', expressing the optimism of a movement which hoped to achieve dignity and respect for gays within society as a whole. In each of these social movements activists fought for social equality—and this was reflected in their demands.

If anything, today's usage of the derogatory term 'queer' shows just how much political distance stands between today's gay activists and those who formed the Gay Liberation Front after the Stonewall rebellion. The equivalent would be using the term 'bitch' among women's rights activists, or the word 'nigger' by blacks. Few would argue that this would represent a step forward, even among those who have adopted the term 'queer'. Formulations such as those of Queer Nation's founders, noted above, represent defeat and demoralisation, and an expectation that the gay movement will remain a small group of the 'enlightened few', marginal to the rest of society. But 'queer identity' quickly proved itself to be about more than simply redefining the language of oppression. The Queer Nation founding manifesto was headlined, 'I Hate Straights'. It said, 'Go tell [straights] to go away until they have spent a month walking hand in hand in public with someone the same sex. After they survive that, then you'll hear what they have to say about queer anger. Otherwise, tell them to shut up and listen.' So from the very beginning Queer Nation ruled out the possibility of building the kind of movement which could act in solidarity with heterosexuals who supported gay rights. Black lesbian feminist Barbara Smith, a veteran of the 1970s movement, argued why such an approach is a recipe for disaster:

> Queer activists focus on 'queer' issues, and racism, sexual oppression and economic exploitation do not qualify, despite the fact that the majority of 'queers' are people of colour, female, or working class ... Building unified, ongoing coalitions that challenge the system and ultimately prepare a way for revolutionary change simply isn't what 'queer' activists have in mind ... In 1990 I read Queer Nation's Manifesto, 'I Hate Straights,' in Outweek and wrote a letter to the editor suggesting that if queers of colour followed its political lead we would soon be issuing a statement titled, 'I Hate Whitey', including white queers of European origin.[19]

Furthermore, the call for 'direct action' has not usually meant building large, angry demonstrations. Most Queer Nation activity has been limited to fairly small groups of activists staging events often designed to do nothing more than startle passers by or create publicity. For example, one early activity called the 'Queer Shopping Network' brought groups of activists to area shopping malls, where men wearing tutus and women dressed in macho leather jackets staged kiss-ins. The GLF's 1971 demand that gay activists behave like 'rotten queers' in the most 'offensive' manner possible has been carried out by Queer Nation in the 1990s.

The controversial tactic of 'outing' perhaps best reflects the emphasis on moral witness which grew hand in hand with the development of identity politics. It first began in 1989, when the New York based magazine Outweek began exposing the homosexuality of gay celebrities on the grounds that they were remaining silent while thousands of gay men were dying of AIDS. In February 1990 the National Gay and Lesbian Task Force media spokesman Robert Bray threatened to expose the identities of all the gays serving in Congress:

> We have a list of many of the over 50 gays in the US Congress. Many are very gay and vote pro-gay. Two of them are out of the closet. The others ... hurt us yet they benefit from progress made for gays, like going to our bars and buying gay literature, and they benefit from the protection we have for protecting our privacy. We know who they are ...[20]

There is a serious problem with this reasoning. Lesbians and gays should never be forced to come out of the closet, no matter who they are or what job they hold. The idea that those who remain in the closet 'benefit' from the actions of those who come out is dangerous, particularly when applied to ordinary working class gays. Moreover, instead of understanding that the nature of the system makes it impossible for vast numbers of gays to be open about their sexuality, this approach assumes the opposite: that coming out is the way to change the prevailing ideas in society.

The underlying assumption of identity politics is that only those who actually experience a form of oppression may define it or voice an opinion about how to fight against it. Rather than leading to collaboration, this assumption has often led to bitter divisions among lesbians and gays, frequently within the same organisations. For example, some lesbians and gays have argued that bisexuals are not really oppressed, because they enjoy 'heterosexual privilege'. Meanwhile, some bisexuals have argued that they are oppressed by 'both gay and straight communities'. This sort of atmosphere damaged the internal life of Queer Nation chapters from early on. The commitment to 'non-hierarchical' structures meant that groups generally operated by 'consensus'. This meant that a single dissenting opinion could embroil the group in hours of argument. Not infrequently meetings degenerated into shouting matches, and eventually into organisational splits.

The short history of San Francisco's embattled Queer Nation chapter is not atypical. Attendance at weekly meetings peaked at 350 when Queer Nation first formed in the summer of 1990. The group set up autonomous 'focus' groups for lesbians and bisexuals, as well as those who were racially oppressed. At every meeting two members acted as 'vibes watchers' to make sure that no one felt intimidated. At first the atmosphere was very positive and co-operative. Members dressed in drag and converged on suburban malls. They staged kiss-ins in the middle of Fisherman's Wharf, San Francisco's biggest tourist spot. When *Basic Instinct*—which depicts a bisexual character as a murderer—began filming, they disrupted production. But by December 1991 Queer Nation San Francisco had shattered—after a fierce argument over the wording for guidelines prohibiting racist, sexist, anti-Semitic and homophobic comments within the group. After the meeting, which one member described as an 'incredible free for all', the handful of remaining members of Queer Nation San Francisco decided to disband. After the split one member concluded, 'Twelve people can reach a decision more easily than 500 can. If these 12 need help, they work with another group of 12. I don't know if we'll ever have a cohesive national gay organisation.'[21]

The April 1993 gay rights march in Washington, DC, attracted a million demonstrators. Again this showed the tremendous potential which exists for building a broad movement among lesbians and gays. After the demonstration, however, an anonymous group calling itself 'QUASH (Queers United Against Straight-Acting Homosexuals)' issued a newsletter called, 'Why I hated the march on Washington.' The newsletter argued against the 'assimilation' of gays into the rest of society. It stated that 'the racism, sexism, classism and internalised homophobia within our own communities devastates us more than the vicious attacks from the likes of [right wingers such as] Anita Bryant, Jesse Helms, George Bush and Sam Nunn.' Thus it concluded, 'Were there a million people? Maybe. But who gives a shit!' This sort of raving is not left wing. As Barbara Smith put it, 'When the word "radical" is used at all, it means confrontational, "in your face" tactics, not strategic organising aimed at the roots of oppression.'[22] Rather, these sorts of politics can be summed up as 'middle class radicalism'—which, as Smith points out, isn't particularly radical at all.

Notes

1. Quoted in B D Adam, *The Rise of a Gay and Lesbian Movement* (Boston, 1987), p80.

2. Gay Left Collective, ed, *Homosexuality: Power and Politics* (London, 1980), p66.

3. Ibid, p67.

4. S Phelan, *Identity Politics: Lesbian Feminism and the Limits of Community* (Philadelphia, 1989), p37.

5. M Robertson, 'We Need Our Own banner,' in *Flaunting It!* (Vancouver, 1982), p177.

6. 'Gay Flames pamphlet', quoted in S Phelan, op cit, p44.

7. R M Brown, 'The Shape of Things to Come', in N Myron and C Bunch, eds, *Lesbianism and the Women's Movement* (Baltimore, 1975), pp70 and 74.

8. Gay Left Collective, op cit, pp8–9.

9. Ibid, pp87–88.

10. Ibid, pp68 and 72.

11. S Phelan, op cit, p105. The source quoted is K Barry, *Female Sexual Slavery* (NJ, 1979).

12. J Weeks, *Coming Out* (London, 1972), p5.

13. Gay Left Collective, op cit, pp13–14.

14. J Escoffier, 'Sexual Revolution and the Politics of Gay Identity,' in *Socialist Review* (US), 1985, p149.

15. Jeffrey Escoffier, 'Socialism as Ethics' (1986), in Socialist Review Collectives, eds, *Unfinished Business: 20 Years of Socialist Review* (London, 1991), p319.

16. Contribution in 'A Queer Nation,' in *The Nation*, 5 July, 1993.

17. A Kopkind, 'The Gay Moment,' in *The Nation*, 3 May 1993.

18. Interview in *Outlines*, October 1990.

19. Ibid.

20. Quoted in *Outlines*, February 1990.

21. M Cunningham, 'If you're queer and you're not angry in 1992, you're not paying attention', in *Mother Jones*, May/June 1992; *San Francisco Examiner*, 26 December, 1991.

22. Contribution in 'A Queer Nation', op cit.

From *Over the Rainbow:*
Money, Class and Homophobia

Nicola Field

The Romantic Origins of Lesbian and Gay Identity

Is there such a thing as a gay community? 'Yes. Our starting point is a shared sexuality and a shared oppression.'

At the very heart of all thought and activity in the modern lesbian and gay movement is the concept of *identity*. This idea of shared identity across classes is no more real than the nationalistic concept of shared national interest across classes. Nevertheless, the entire edifice of gay political culture is based upon unity through sexuality and a common experience of oppression. Gay identity specifically consists in being sidelined, ignored, criminalised, made invisible in mainstream society. It is seen as being shared by a specific group of people who have a mutual and *exclusive* interest in getting rid of gay oppression. The developing gay commercial scene offers apparent havens (venues, events, publications) for gay self-expression. What is contained in these havens amounts to the components of gay identity, *sold as the essence of what it is to be lesbian or gay in modern society.* In that these clubs, magazines, events are targeted at a gay market, they provide the focus for lesbians and gay men to lead apparently separate lives from heterosexual people. We come to believe that gay and straight people are essentially different from one another, with separate social and sexual experiences and aspirations. This 'specialness' contains the ideas that gay people are particularly sensitive (as a result of suffering persecution) and sexually explorative (as a result of not being formally sexually 'educated'). This section aims to show where these ideas have come from and the elements of romanticisation contained in the concepts of lesbian and gay identity.

Capitalist history shrink-wraps events and social relationships, packaging them into superficial and repetitive stories about ruling class personages (kings and queens, prime ministers, declarations of war and key speeches). This romanticisation is extended, rather than countered, by the history of gay sensibility. To look for evidence of a common thread of experience, based on sexual preference, through the past, present and future, is akin to chauvinistic rhetoric about 'being British' (stiff upper lip, sense of fair play, sympathy for the underdog) or 'being an American' (land of the free, true grit, pioneering spirit). Both of these patriotic delusions, in the true tradition of romance, blur and distort a gruesome track record of imperialism, murder, repression, slavery and vicious class oppression. This is because they are ideology: part of the awesome weaponry of social control.

The idea that sexuality can be explained in terms of orientation comes from social and scientific developments in the latter half of the nineteenth century. These originate in the work of two German reformists: Karl Heinrich

Ulrichs and Magnus Hirschfeld. Their writings and research led them to call for the repeal of Paragraph 175, the Prussian law which criminalised male homosexuality. Through them, homosexuality ceased to be regarded as a type of unnatural behaviour and came to be seen as the characteristic of a group or sub-species within society.

Ulrichs began in 1864 to publish a series of pamphlets about 'uranian' love—or love between men, showing the extent of discrimination against uranians and arguing forcefully for an end to oppression and prejudice. As his ideas developed he asserted that uranians were men and women belonging to a 'third sex', biologically different from the majority of society. They could be detected through their behaviour and their tastes in activities, uranian girls preferring boys games, uranian boys preferring traditionally feminine activities like knitting. He argued that uranians had existed throughout history and in all societies, born that way and ultimately unchanging. Same-gender sexual acts were not, as was the dominant view of the time, activities any person might choose to participate in if they were sufficiently depraved, but the particular characteristics of an oppressed minority. Since they were born that way they should not be said to have committed a crime by acting on their nature. Ulrichs's writings were banned on the grounds that they undermined marriage and the family.

Ulrichs's ideas, though, were not the brainchild of a maverick thinker out of touch with the norms of his own society. Times were changing and his writings were a reflection of changing concerns within emergent industrial capitalism. Germany was establishing itself as a highly industrialised nation. The development of the modern family and the social and moral codes surrounding sex and reproduction, together with the appalling living and working conditions of most of the labour force, meant that people were beginning to organise around issues of common interest. Workers' organisations, political parties, and a feminist movement began to coordinate a culture of resistance. There was also a flowering of all kinds of

'New Age' interests such as vegetarianism, natural healing, mysticism and nudism. It was in this context in 1897 that Dr Magnus Hirschfeld, a pioneer in the new science of sexology, founded his Berlin centre for sexual research: the Scientific Humanitarian Committee (SHC). Established with the aim of bringing about enlightenment on matters of sexuality and the legalisation of gay sex, the SHC continued its research and campaigning work until it was forcibly closed down after the Nazi party came to power.

Hirschfeld developed the theory of the Third Sex through interviewing and observing thousands of people who did not conform to the conventional stereotypes of masculinity, femininity and heterosexuality. He believed strongly that homosexuals (as they had now begun to be called) were physiologically and psychologically different from heterosexuals, to varying degrees. Hence people who had sex with both women and men could be seen as a variant of the Third Sex. Again, the argument that people were born like that and that they could not be changed by legal restraint or punishment was at the centre of Hirschfeld sexological theory. The theory of the Third Sex was the inspiration behind the first organised homosexual rights movement which gained considerable ground at the beginning of the twentieth century. He was an idealist, in the sense that he believed you could change society by the introduction of enlightened ideas. He mistook a symptom of oppression in society for its cause and believed that a rational, convincing case would surely put an end to backward ideas, superstitions and prejudices. Hirschfeld failed to recognise the connection between gay oppression and the material and economic organisation of the society he lived in. Although Paragraph 175 was repealed in 1929, the Nazis came to power in 1933 and homosexuals were recriminalised, many of them rounded up during raids on private clubs and homes. Thousands perished alongside Jews, Gypsies, socialists and others.

Hirschfeld's romanticism leaves a cultural legacy which has remained influential to this day. His idea that homosexuals were a particular group of people with their own characteristic way of life has stayed at the centre of political campaigning around issues of sexual liberation and lesbian and gay equality. Being lesbian or gay is now more or less a prerequisite for inclusion in the perceived lesbian and gay rights movement. Hirschfeld's reforming agenda has defined a set of criteria for defining lesbian and gay sex and identity and created a space for the development of gay sensibility, a gay way of looking at the world, a gay consciousness. The notion of an essential 'difference' between gay and straight holds an important position in contemporary gay culture, feeding into the romantic construction of *a race apart,* or a *queer breed.* It is this idea which lies behind the politics of queer and the establishment or recognition of a Queer Nation, a parallel dimension which pretends to operate outside the margins of society. In effect, the Queer Nation is a virtual reality kingdom.

Hirschfeld was not the last proponent of scientific 'evidence' for theories of essential difference. In 1991 gay neuroscientist Simon LeVay developed his own theory that a part of the brain called the hypothalamus was smaller in gay men than in heterosexual men. His research was based on dissecting the brains of men 'presumed gay' who had died of AIDS, but his findings were dubiously received mainly because the size of the hypothalamus can change as a result of sexual behaviour and illness. LeVay's claims were followed in 1993 by the publication of US cancer researcher Dean Hamer's research into the possibility of there being a 'gay gene', detectable before birth. Mark Brown, commenting on the sensation surrounding press reports of these research projects, points to the material motivation of apparently neutral media and scientific interest in sexual identity:

> It became increasingly clear that the work of the likes of Hamer and LeVay is given a high media profile not as a result of any outstanding scientific merit but due to the relations their claims have to the enduring argument about the 'cause' of homosexuality. That is to say without homophobia such 'findings' would be irrelevant, and, in fact, such research would never have been undertaken.

Both LeVay's and Hamer's findings reached interested ears amongst gay 'community leaders'. Peter Tatchell of the reformist campaigning group Outrage! argued that while there was a danger that suspected 'gay foetuses' might be aborted, science might well offer parents a chance to choose gay offspring. Richard Kirker of the Lesbian and Gay Christian Movement echoed Hirschfeld's view that science had proved that discrimination was unjustified because gay sexuality is 'natural', inborn or God-given. None of the findings addressed the question of lesbians or the challenge of bisexuality to the 'fixed sexuality' tradition—and few gay commentators saw fit to point out these discrepancies.

. . .

The Future of the Nation

Some lesbians and gays, especially those involved in the media, see the politics of queer as a way of uniting people of all sexualities who want to fight for sexual liberation. Others see the term 'queer' simply as a shorter and more pugilistic way to say 'lesbian and gay'. In relation to romantic ideas about 'community' and common interests, few queer devotees can agree on a common political agenda for sexual liberation across class. Extraordinary confusions arise around working out who is 'us' and who is 'them'. For instance, film-maker Inge Blackman sees solutions in language: 'Naming is powerful. Black people and gay people constantly renaming ourselves is a way to shift power from whites and hets respectively.'

Harriet Wistrich, a member of Justice for Women, can't bring herself to align even with gay men: 'I don't use that term (queer). I associate it with gay men and I'm dubious about reclaiming derogatory terms. The "queer agenda", as you call it, isn't my struggle. I put my feminism before my lesbianism.'

'Queer dyke cultural activist' Tessa Boffin seizes on queer as a way of resolving the inadequacies of sexual labelling and as a way of showing anger and defiance in the face of oppression: 'I never identified with the word lesbian because it seemed quite medical . . . Queer was one of the ways of identifying with a mixed movement and challenging both separatism and misogyny at the same time.'

Unfortunately queer is largely an alternative form of sexual labelling and its politics far from clear cut about whom it includes and excludes. It does nothing to relocate sexual liberation within the politics of class. This is the quandary of gay romanticism and the contradiction of seeking social change without changing the class system. You are special; you are the same. You are just as good; you are better. You alone can understand your oppression; the rest of the world should understand. You need to form a self-reliant community; you want to be incorporated into the mainstream. You need to separate, you need to integrate. You want to protect; you want to take a risk. You want massive social change but you don't want to tamper with the class system. You want gay liberation but you don't want to look at the causes of gay oppression.

The gay business class (highly developed in the US and on the rise in the UK) uses an open rhetoric of liberation and self-expression through commercial strength and consumer power. It offers a version of gay freedom which is based on the visibility and power of gay markets. Whilst most gay people have no illusions about the aim of any commercial enterprise—gay or straight or just making money—the frustration, anger and sense of political vacuum means that sometimes business appears to be the only way to develop, the only way of attaining bargaining power. The positive, thrusting confidence of the gay marketeers appears to make a refreshing change from the familiar reiteration of suffering, persecution and passive victimhood:

> The higher-than-average disposable income of gays and lesbians makes them an attractive target for marketers. Yet advertisers invariably shy away from targeting them because they do not wish to be identified with them. Can the advertising industry continue to ignore a group that forms an estimated 10% of the buying public?

Capitalist ideology continually aims to make workers see their role in society as *consumers* of products rather than *producers* of wealth and commodities, necessities and pleasures. The politics of gay power through consumer power are no different. Most lesbians and gays are obviously not high earners and yet the corporate identity being pushed is one of well-heeled individuals with taste and money. The implication is that the gays who will make it into the millennium with impunity will be those who can afford to buy into the trappings of corporate gay sensibility. The substitution of one set of romantic ideas for another, under the guise of radical or liberal intervention, does not constitute social change. We need to bring about an environment where all consensual sex can be freely enjoyed without fear of censure, persecution or intrusion. Romance is a barrier, not a channel.

Material Oppression

Los Angeles Research Group

Once again, the Revolutionary Union fails to stop and think, or even investigate what it is saying, when it writes:

> "Imperialism profits directly from the oppression and exploitation of women. This is not true for gay people. They are not materially oppressed as a group, and the denial of their democratic rights does not secure great profits for the ruling class."

But in real life it is rarely such a simplistic matter as the direct immediacy implied in the formula "oppression equals great profits." Rather, in advanced capitalist society there are many superstructural and ideological forms that do not *directly* "secure great profits" but which are indirectly "useful" in that they help maintain conditions (disunity, apathy, cynicism, backwardness) that allow the continued expropriation of "great profits."

To say that there is no profit to the capitalist in the oppression of gays is to ignore the basic theorems of the science of Marxism. Does the RU believe that it is simply an accident, or "natural," that gays are oppressed? The fact is that gay people are materially oppressed and the material basis for that oppression indeed lies in the maintenance of profit and power for the capitalist.

Our investigation leads us to believe that the material basis for the oppression of gays can be found in the role of the bourgeois nuclear family under class society in the maintenance and perpetuation of the division of labor. The bourgeois nuclear family is the economic institutionalization of personal relationships under capitalism. It is a socially isolated unit consisting of a husband, a wife, and their children. The husband works outside the home. The wife, whether or not she also works outside the home, works within it at invisible labor which maintains and reproduces the labor force. The purpose of the bourgeois family is to: first of all, socialize children into understanding and accepting class relationships as they exist in this country today; secondly, reproduce the class structure in microcosm; and thirdly, privatize the maintenance and reproduction of the working class. Class society establishes, maintains, and perpetuates divisions of labor, including sexual divisions. Sexual division of labor is of incalculable use to the bourgeoisie, dividing workers into two great camps, those in social labor and those in private labor; those in private labor can and have been called forward as a reserve army of labor according to the needs of the bourgeoisie.

Historical Perspectives: Historically, as collective economies broke down and economic relations based on patriarchy and rising capitalism emerged, man's labor was increasingly that of commodity production and his role included the provision of the material necessities for the maintenance and propagation of the family. (The sexual division of labor had existed prior to this historical development, but it was not accompanied by the superstructural characteristic of sex-roles—standards of personal character and behavior according to gender.)

349

Woman's labor was increasingly individualized and restricted to items of use value, i.e., for private and indirect consumption. Her role included the maintenance of current labor power (husband), the rearing and education of future labor power (children), and the care of expended or discarded labor power (sick, injured, and elderly).

The sexual division of labor, reified as "natural," is of material benefit to the bourgeoisie in a capitalist society where collective replacement of daily needs is not provided for. The working woman in the home does not directly sell her labor power as such. Under capitalism, the value of her "invisible" labor power is appropriated by and benefits the bourgeoisie through her role in the family, which requires her to shop for food, clothing, etc.; cook, maintain the home, and look after the family, including the wide range of emotional and psychological needs, such as defusing her husband's anger from the exploitation of his job.

With the industrial revolution and the full development of capitalism, some women were incorporated into the public sector of the working class. Nevertheless, the working woman's role at home has not changed materially. Because her nurturing and service role has not been recognized as having economic value necessary to the maintenance of capitalism, but only as a "natural" and biologically determined sex characteristic, it is likewise considered "natural" that the working woman continue to bear the primary burden of creating a healthy home life for the family.

To maintain the division of labor so crucial to the maintenance of its rule, the bourgeoisie has developed a powerful and pervasive ideology. It includes the radically opposing sex models which permeate education and culture: women learn to be supportive and passive, men are to be physically strong, courageous and combative. Starting with childhood, both boys (cars, mechanical sets, guns) and girls (dolls, sewing kits, play stoves) receive the toys which will train them for their eventual roles in the economy. Bourgeois ideology and institutions make sure this indoctrination continues throughout a person's life.

Sexuality, Reproduction, and Sex-Roles: Similarly, anti-gayness is a necessary part of bourgeois ideology. Implicit in the fact of two men or two women relating to each other is a rejection of the necessity of basing a relationship of the socially defined "inferiority" or "superiority" (according to physical characteristics) of its participants. When men and women see themselves as equal the bourgeoisie loses one of its basic "divide and conquer" weapons. Working men can recognize that the sexual privileges and short range benefits they derive from the bourgeois oppression of women are minimal and not in their class interest. Likewise, women in rejecting definitions of inferiority can see themselves as workers and become militant fighters for socialist revolution. The bourgeoisie, terrified by the communist spectre of the equality of women and men, labels sexual equality as unnatural. Gayness is also labeled "unnatural," and therefore a threat to bourgeois dominance, precisely because it rejects the "natural" bourgeois society as reflected in the "natural" bourgeois/proletarian relationship of the nuclear family; it also implies that sexual relationships need not be tied to reproduction.

The ruling class should be encouraged by the fact that they are not alone in this perception. They have what we consider to be some very unlikely allies. The October League strongly condemns gay relationships on the grounds that they cannot produce children and thus are anti-social and attack the family. There are two basic errors in this position. One is the confusion of sexuality with reproduction. The other is the failure to understand that when societies undergo a qualitative change, so do all the basic institutions that uphold them—including personal relationships and childrearing, and the dominant and subordinate nature of sexuality and reproduction within them.

Sexuality and reproduction are not synonymous. The history of civilization has been in part the ruling class's attempts to enforce the connection between sexuality and reproduction in order to preserve private property through the institution of inheritance. Repressive laws against adultery, pre-marital sex, illegitimacy and homosexuality (which often carries the heaviest penalties), are examples of the repressive measures taken by the ruling class to punish those who rebel against its false unity of sexuality and reproduction. Of course this does not mean that as communists we advocate that people place primary emphasis on the gratification of their sexual urges. At this time, love relationships between two people are probably the best way of meeting people's emotional and sexual needs. Also for most people these relationships are now the most practical way of carrying out reproduction. But if two women, for example, should choose to build such a relationship, this does not mean that they either will not or have not had children. Indeed, many gay people do have children; some of us were involved in heterosexual relationships before we came out, and we have fought long and hard for the right to keep our children from being taken away by the judicial arm of the bourgeoisie. As scientific socialists, we cannot deny the possibilities of the role that the continuing development of science and technology may come to play in reproduction. Just as it is possible to avoid reproduction through scientific methods of birth control, it is also possible to aid reproduction through artificial insemination.

Reproduction, as the primary basis for personal relationships, is already decreasing in importance under capitalism. This process would be accelerated under socialism. In a society run by workers, the needs of one are the needs of all. The care and upbringing of children is a social obligation in which every citizen takes part. For example, the People's Republic of China has long recognized the foolishness of keeping most of the female workforce at home with their children. Continuous child care centers are set up, staffed by members of the community, thus freeing parents from direct responsibility. There is no reason why gay people could not participate fully in such programs.

*   *   *

In summary, the bourgeoisie does not oppress people because it thinks such oppression is funny; and the oppression of gay people is anything but funny, nor is it so slight that it can be dismissed as negligible. It runs the gamut from denial of democratic rights, such as housing, employment and education, to police repression and brutality, to the imprisonment, castration and lobotomizing of gays, to the use of adversive conditioning (chemical and electrical shock) to "cure" gays in state prison hospitals such as Vacaville. Economically, it is our experience that many open gays are forced to work in the lowest paying, non-unionized small manufacturing shops where the boss is not much concerned with whom a person sleeps with, but who uses a worker's status as added leverage for increased exploitation. Denial of child custody, over-priced "gay ghettos," Mafia-controlled bars—all provide evidence of the material oppression of gay people. It is no less heinous because its victims are determined by sexuality instead of by color or class. Rather, it is the conscious oppression of gay people by a class conscious bourgeoisie acting only out of its own material interests.

The Matter of Materialism

Teresa L. Ebert

The issue of feminism and "materialism" in the 1990s involves two conflicting but related problems. The first is the crisis of *materialist feminism* itself. The term *materialist feminism* can best be defined as those efforts since the 1970s (especially in Britain) to bring feminism together with *both* Marxism and postmodern theories. But this project has been troubled not only by some of the contradictions between feminism and Marxism but also by poststructuralism's "deconstruction" and discrediting of Marxism itself. This conflict has led many materialist feminists to abandon Marxism altogether in favor of poststructuralism. However, for others, including myself, it has led to a renewed insistence on the necessity of Marxism for a *revolutionary* feminism in late capitalism. At stake here is the question: How effective is a *materialist* feminism without Marxism?

The second problem takes up the other side of the issue and concerns the (non-Marxist) rethinking of materialism in postmodern theories. The problem here, especially for poststructuralist feminists, is the question of the limits of language: specifically, is there an "outside" to language? Postmodern feminists do not simply address language in its everyday sense of a *means* of communication, rather they focus on they way it *shapes* what we communicate and mediates between us and the world. Whether they treat language as "discourse" (following Foucault) or as "textuality" (following Derrida), it signifies the entire meaning-making *practices* in society. Language, in other words, is seen as a form of "matter" or "materiality" in and of itself. Many postmodern feminist theorists commonly

argue as Derrida says, "There is nothing outside of the text."[1] However, some of these feminists are now trying to find an "outside" to discourse and return to a reality that is shaped not just by language. Their efforts most often involve a return to the "matter" of the body and raise the issue what is materialism for feminism and what kind of politics does it enable?

I consider two books to be exemplary of several of the issues around materialism and to demonstrate some of the historical, political, and theoretical problems the issues pose for feminist and queer politics. *Materialist Feminisms* by Donna Landry and Gerald MacLean is especially representative of the poststructuralist erasure of Marxism, and Judith Butler's *Bodies that Matter* is a major contribution to the rethinking of materialism in postmodern theories of discourse. Both books participate—with varying degrees of critical awareness—in the familiar debate in Western philosophy over whether reality produces discourse and consciousness (materialism) or whether discourse—consciousness—constructs reality (idealism). How feminist theory understands materialism—that is, how it understands reality—sets the terms for the way we understand, explain, and intervene in everyday life and sexual politics.

Materialist Feminisms begins by drawing on the legacy of Marxist-socialist feminism. In fact, it opens by saying "this is a book about feminism and Marxism written when many people are proclaiming the end of socialism and the end of feminism . . . We find these claims to be both premature and misleading" (vii). At the same time, the authors are deeply invested in poststructuralism, especially deconstruction, as the ground of their knowledge. This leads them to turn Marxism into a *textuality* that they try to deconstruct. In fact, they expend considerable energy throughout the book trying to erase Marxism altogether from materialist feminism. The book does not so much critically examine the crisis in materialist feminism as replay it in a way that privileges poststructuralism. Thus, although the book begins by treating Marxist, socialist, and materialist feminism as nearly synonymous, it concludes by saying "Need materialism be only an alias for Marxism? We hope that by now the distinction between Marxist feminism and materialist feminism is clear" (229). But in writing a materialist feminism without Marxism, the book ends up offering little more than a general, poststructuralist identity politics.

For many, *Materialist Feminisms* will seem, at first, to be a very promising book because of the claims it makes "to present a history of the debates between Marxist and feminist social and cultural theorists in the 1960's, 1970's and early 1980's, primarily in Britain and the United States, and to analyze what has happened to transform those debates in recent years" (ix). *Materialist Feminisms*, however, is in many ways a disappointing book because of the eclectic and philosophically inadequate way in which it develops its argument and, more important, for dehistoricizing the issues. As deconstructionists, the authors are quite ambivalent about the very project of writing a history and end up with what they themselves describe as a "schematic and inconsistent chronological narrative." Their argument relies heavily on summaries of key texts (mostly essays rather than more sustained works) by such feminists as Michele Barrett, Rosalind Coward, Gayle Rubin, Toril Moi, Gayatri Spivak, Barbara Christian, Hortense Spiller, Judith Butler, and Donna Haraway. They give special attention to telling the "stories" of such poststructuralists as Derrida, Lacan, Foucault, Said, and the ecologist, Murray Bookchin, in order to map the importance of postmodern theories, particularly Derridean deconstruction, in "shift[ing]

the terrain" of feminism. Poststructuralism is, for them, the means to overcome the "impasse" of efforts to bring Marxism and feminism together. But they do not so much provide a way out of this impasse as offer a series of disjointed summaries that confuse opposing positions and simplify complex issues to the point of misrepresentation.

The notion of materialism Landry and MacLean put forth is based on Raymond Williams's concepts of "cultural materialism" and "green socialism" (a combination of ecologism and socialism), which they graft onto deconstruction. Although they continue to call their position "historical materialism" (following Williams), they in fact subscribe to what is, in effect, a *discursive materialism*. There is a fundamental difference between historical materialism and a cultural or discursive materialism. It is the difference over whether the priority should be given to the economic (the *base*) or to the cultural and ideological (the *superstructure*) in trying to understand and change society. Of course, such a difference is itself largely suppressed in poststructuralist discourses that have tried to discredit the base/superstructure model and displace the economic.

Historical materialists argue that the way women and men produce and reproduce the material conditions of their lives—how they are able to provide for their basic human needs, their subsistence—provides the basis (the *base*) for producing social and cultural life, including our ideas and consciousness (the *superstructure*). As Marx says, it is not "the consciousness of men that determines their existence, but their social existence that determines their consciousness."[2] Materialism is not simply "human activity," as Landry and MacLean claim, rather it is based on human activity understood as the transforming practice of labor.[3] For historical materialists "the degree of economic development . . . form(s) the foundation upon which the state institutions, . . . the art and even the religious ideas . . . have been evolved, and in the light of which these things must therefore be explained instead of *vice versa*."[4]

Cultural materialists, on the other hand, question the primacy of the economic and argue instead that cultural processes are largely autonomous. For them, the main site of social struggle has become discourse and ideology. As Landry and MacLean summarize this position,

> the production of signs, of signifying systems, of ideology, representations, and discourses is itself a material activity with material effects. Instead of arguing that the material or economic base produces certain effects, like culture and ideology, as part of its superstructure, a cultural materialist would argue that ideology and the discourses generated by social institutions are themselves located in material practices which have material effects that affect even the economic structures of the base. (61)

This notion of cultural materialism seems to many to be a more complex way to approach the problem because it emphasizes the way the cultural affects the base. As a result, it is quite widely used in place of historical materialism. For Landry and MacLean, in particular, it seems to overcome the "economic reductionism" they find in the historical materialist emphasis on the base. But in practice cultural materialists, especially those embracing poststructuralism, so overemphasize culture and discourse, they almost entirely exclude the economic issues of production and labor. They are unable to explain the dialectical relation of the cultural to the economic or to develop an effective politics to end economic exploitation. The culturalist dismissal of the economic as "reductive" is itself a "reductive" understanding of the dialectics of historical materialism, which is concisely described by Engels:

> According to the materialist conception of history, the *ultimately* determining element in history is the production and reproduction of real life. More than this neither Marx nor I have ever asserted. Hence if somebody twists this into saying that the economic element is the *only* determining one, he transforms that proposition into a meaningless, abstract, senseless phrase. The economic situation is the basis, but the var-

> ious elements of the superstructure . . . also exercise their influence upon the course of the historical struggles . . .

> We make our history ourselves, but, in the first place, under very definite assumptions and conditions. Among these the economic ones are ultimately decisive.[5]

In place of an economic "determinism," Landry and MacLean, like other poststructuralists, substitute a defacto "discursive determinism" (a discursive "reductionism") under the cloak of deconstructive undecidability. Following the post-Marxists, Ernesto Laclau and Chantal Mouffe, they argue that both "history and the real *are* discursive" (140). In short, they reduce the social to a form of textuality, to simply problems of representation and rhetorical or semiotic differences.

Landry and MacLean thus claim that the "more adequately materialist feminist reading" is one that reads both Marx and the world "*as* texts" (65). An important part of their argument against the primacy of the economic in Marxism is their "reading" of the central concept of "surplus value" as a linguistic "pun"—or rather their summary of Gayatri Spivak's reading of surplus value "as a catachresis or pun" (64). Such an emphasis, they claim, "not only shifts the grounds of debate from a tendency towards economic reductionism but opens up potentially productive contradictions in Marx's *texts*" (emphasis added, 64). They engage in a rhetorical deconstruction of "surplus value" as a "signifier for which there is no adequate literal referent," as a trope or "pun," in which there is a "perpetual sliding of the signified (the concept being referred to)" (64). However, for Marx, "surplus value" is a historically necessary concept (what Maria Mies would call a "struggle concept"[6]): Surplus value explains how profit is gained in capitalism by having workers produce more than they are paid for. Surplus value, in short, is the result of the exploitation of people's surplus (unpaid) labor. This has been a fundamental issue for historical materialist feminists, who have expanded the Marxist understanding of labor to include the work of women, as in the domestic labor debates, and more effectively, by The "German School" of (historical) materialist feminists, notably Maria Mies. Mies understands labor to mean not only wage labor but, more importantly, the "subsistence" (nonwage) labor needed to reproduce and sustain life and that is performed primarily by women, peasants, and colonized people.[7] Landry and MacLean entirely neglect the work of German materialist feminists (even though they address French feminists when necessary). As their privileging of poststructuralism would suggest, they deal with the issue of labor only briefly and mostly in passing. Their cultural materialism is concerned not so much with the social realities Marx and historical materialists are trying to explain in order to change as it is with "*reading* . . . a patient and careful teasing out of the way texts may work against themselves . . . their text-uality, sometimes going against the grain of their ostensible arguments" (64). In short, they privilege the materiality of language and discourse and largely suppress the material conditions of production and economic exploitation.

Poststructuralists like Landry and MacLean pose the question, what is the cost of abandoning the economic and focusing almost exclusively on discourse? Materialist feminism for these critics becomes a pluralist "politics of difference" sensitive to the "leaky distinctions" among "questions of race, sexuality, ethnicity, nationality, postcoloniality, religion, and cultural identity, as well as class and gender" (90). Materialist feminism is reduced, in short, to what Landry and MacLean call a poststructuralist "identity politics of undone identities" (Landry and MacLean, p. 145). Identity politics has become so widely accepted that such a move may seem a virtue to many. But identity politics—even of deconstructed, "undone identities"—is seriously limited. As A. Sivanandan (the editor of *Race and Class*) points out: "How do you extend a 'politics of food' to the hungry, a 'politics of the body' to the homeless, a 'politics of the family' for those without an income? . . . The touchstone of any issue-based or identity-based politics has to be the lowest common denominators in our society. A women's movement that does not derive its politics from the needs, freedoms, rights of the most disadvantaged among them is by that very token reformist and elitist."[8] Identity politics is most commonly based not on a commitment to ending the exploitation of the most oppressed but rather to liberating the *desires* of those whose basic material *needs* are already met. It produces a fragmented and divisive cultural politics that marginalizes the struggle for social and economic emancipation against the "'interlocking' systems of oppression—racial, sexual, heterosexual, and class oppression" (Landry and MacLean, p. 145) called for by earlier materialist feminists, such as those of the Combahee River Collective.

The move from the economic to discourse is duplicated in the very structure of *Materialist Feminism*, which begins with the "inconsistent" chronological narrative of the "origins" of materialist and Marxist feminism but, after two chapters, devotes the rest of the book to a deconstructive cultural critique and identity politics. Thus the first chapter stresses the work of such (historical) materialist feminists as Michele Barrett, who in her earlier work, insists on "not letting go of economic relations" and warns against a "discursive imperialism." However, the rest of the book treats these as "past" knowledges, superseded by deconstruction and has no hesitation in now embracing "discursive imperialism." In so doing, Landry and MacLean are following the same trajectory taken by a number of socialist and materialist feminists, who like Michele Barrett, have largely abandoned Marx for Foucault; materialism for discourse, and are, as Barrett says of herself: "nailing my colours to the mast of a more general post-Marxism."[9] There is very little theoretical self-reflexivity in *Materialist Feminism*, and consequently no critical explanation of the relation between the historical materialism of the earlier feminists and the discursive materialism of more recent feminism. Rather *Materialist Feminism* follows the common sense (in commodity capitalism) that whatever is "newest" is best. In fact, the last half of the book drops the concept of materialism almost entirely, and its descriptions of the debates around an anti-essentialist identity politics of sexuality, race, postcolonialism, and "green cultural criticism" become little more than an eclectic left-liberal postmodern politics of difference that could easily appear in any survey of postmodern cultural studies.

Only in the final chapter do Landry and MacLean, again unself-reflexively, remember the economics they started with but had eclectically erased under the sign of deconstruction. Here they briefly address the problem of the international division of labor and the "exploitative proletarianization" of women in global capitalism. Significantly, it is only "from a radical ecological point of view"—put forth in this final chapter—that they argue that "social and economic iniquities must be overthrown" (216) and are sympathetic to "a total reorganization of economic, political, and social life on a global scale" (211) without dismissing these as totalizing—as they do with Marxism. But even here their "Green solutions," following Williams, rewrite the economic in terms of a cultural materialism, especially the cultural practice of consumption. They stress that the basic issue is a problem of "unequal consumption of the earth's resources" rather than one of unequal relations of production and appropriation of people's labor. They give just as much, if not more, attention here to the problem of "hunting," "the critique of anthropocentrism" and "exploitation of non-human" as they do to the increasing "exploitation and immiseration [of humans] within the New World Order."

Landry and MacLean acclaim Judith Butler's work, and we can better see the consequences of rethinking materialism in terms of discourse by turning to her *Bodies that Matter: On the Discursive Limits of "Sex,"* which explores the problem of the "materiality of the body" in terms of a feminist poststructuralism that is heavily indebted to Derrida and Foucault. Many will find this book to be an important contribution to postmodern feminism and "queer theory" as well as a significant extension of Butler's critical inquiries into the ways in which bodies are "sexed": a task she began in her previous book, *Gender Trouble. Bodies that Matter* demonstrates a theoretical complexity and philosophical erudition that has become all too rare in feminism. Yet, on a more careful reading, Butler's text turns out to be an eclectic combination of contradictory and untenable positions.

Bodies that Matter consists of a series of lectures and essays (some like the "Lesbian Phallus" and "Critically Queer" already quite well known) that engage a wide range of philosophical, psychoanalytical, and literary texts: from Plato, Irigaray, Foucault, Freud, and Lacan to Willa Cather, Nella Larson, and the "psycho-postmarxism" of Slavoj Zizek as well as the film *Paris is Burning* and the discourses of "queerness." One of the major tasks of the book is to write the lesbian in(to) these diverse texts, or rather to articulate the "exclusion" of the lesbian and the way this exclusion in turn constitutes the heterosexual norm. Another concern of the book is Butler's attempt to address some of the problems raised by her theory of the "performativity" of gender—by which she means the way the body acquires its sexual identity through acts of "speaking" and "performing" the norms of heterosexual discourse. She also extends her thinking on these issues to the problem of the "social regulation of race." One of the main questions her work invites asks "what about the materiality of the body, *Judy?*" In response, her book develops a series of theoretical speculations on "the materiality of sex" and "the sex of materiality."

However, Butler does not answer the question in a conventional way. She breaks with the common sense and deconstructs the dominant philosophical and psychoanalytical understandings of such concepts as the body, materiality, gender, sexuality, and lesbian, offering instead, a complex poststructuralist rethinking of these terms. Any discussion of Butler's work for the general reader is, thus, caught in a contradiction: To make her work more accessible requires translating it into the very "common sense" language that she is writing against. Nor is it possible to "fix" the meaning of Butler's own terms because, following the deconstructive logic, she places them in a sliding chain of signifiers with no fixed or stable meanings. For example, her main concept of "performativity" is a form of performance, but Butler warns against reducing its meaning to performance—especially theatrical notions of performance as role playing. The meaning of performativity slides into a kind of "speech act" that enacts, repeats, or "cites" the *norms* of sex. The "construction" of sexual identity for Butler is an act of "performativity," but this is not a conventional process of social or even psychoanalytic identification. Rather the body for Butler "assumes" or "materializes" its sex through a process of "citationality"—a form of *speaking* in and through bodies—in which the symbolic laws, norms, and discourses of heterosexuality are "cited" in the same way, according to Butler, that a judge cites a law. In fact, "performativity" is rethought in Butler's book as "citationality."

It is through the process of "citationality" that Butler tries to explain how heterosexuality operates as a compulsory symbolic law, or what she calls, following Foucault, a "regulatory regime" of discourse (that is, a system of discourse that compels and regulates our identities, practices, and ways of understanding the world). "Citationality," for Butler, is part of a circular operation of power: The "regulatory regime" of heterosexuality compels us to repeat (cite) its sexual norms and at the same time our very act of repeating the law, invokes it and helps establish the chain of binding conventions that in turn compels us.

Butler tries to link the question of the materiality of the body to the performativity of gender, but in so doing, she puts forward a very different understanding of *materiality, matter, materialization*. Again her poststructuralist rethinking of these concepts makes it difficult to "translate" them into the common sense where these terms refer to a reality or referent *outside* language. For Butler, matter, materialization, materiality are all aspects and effects of the citational practice of the power of discourse, which produces the effects that it names. For Butler,

sex is not "a bodily given . . . but . . . a cultural norm which governs the materialization of bodies" (3). Butler construes "matter," itself, "not as a site or surface, but as *a process of materialization that . . . produces the effect of boundary, fixity and surface we call matter*" (9). In short, "matter" (the body) is given its boundaries, shape, fixity, and surface—it is "materialized"—through the "citationality" of discourse. The materiality of sexuality, then, is not outside language but is the *effect* of discourse.

Butler, however, argues that "there is an 'outside' to what is constructed by discourse," but she understands this to be "a constitutive 'outside,' it is that which can only be thought—when it can—in relation to that discourse" (8). Butler's "outside" to discourse, in other words, is *what discourse itself constructs* through "exclusion, erasure, violent foreclosure, abjection." But this "outside" is also a "disruptive return" that constitutes what excludes it. For example, the primacy of masculinity in Western metaphysics is, Butler argues, "founded . . . through a prohibition which outlaws the spectre of a lesbian resemblance" (the lesbian phallus); masculinity, then, is an "effect of that very prohibition . . . dependent on that which it must exclude" (52). The "outside" (the excluded lesbian), in other words, is the necessary ground "constituting" the "inside" of masculinity and heterosexuality. Butler is following here the classic poststructuralist erasure of the boundaries between inside and outside (what is called "supplementarity"). As she says in discussing the "materiality of the signifier (a 'materiality' that comprises both signs and their significatory efficacy) . . . it is not that one cannot get outside of language in order to grasp materiality in and of itself; rather, every effort to refer to materiality takes place through a signifying process which . . . is always already material" (68).

Butler attempts to move beyond this limitation by writing materiality as the "effect of power." As she says, "What constitutes the fixity of the body, its contours, its movements, will be fully material, but materiality will be rethought as the effect of power, as power's most productive effect" (2). In so doing, she is following Foucault's lead in "basing" her theory of social and cultural processes in his notion of a diffuse, autonomous power. For poststructuralists like Butler, power becomes the *constitutive* "base" of society, substituting for the Marxist concept of a *determining* economic base. Butler denies, however, that she makes "'materiality' into the effect of a 'discourse' which is its cause." Instead she claims there are no cause-effect relations because causal connections are displaced by a Foucauldian notion of power "where effects are the dissimulated workings of power." Butler thus rewrites materiality as "the dissimulated effect of power"— but one that "appears only when its status as contingently constituted through discourse is erased, concealed, covered over" (251). This is an extraordinarily circular logic: Materiality, for Butler, is constituted in and through discourse—but such processes are covered over, concealed, and can only be effects of power, which by definition is a displaced and dissimulating (non)cause. Materiality in Butler's poststructuralist argument is thus entirely confined to the level of the "superstructure," to discourse. Such a logic understands power as a closed, self-legitimating operation. This logic completely suppresses the economic: the real material conditions of our working day—the production of profit (surplus value) through the exploitation of our unpaid and subsistence labor.

Butler is, of course, among the most sophisticated of a generation of feminist theorists who are basing their social analytics on a Foucauldian notion of the regime of power-discourse. In fact, the Foucauldian theory of power has become so hegemonic in feminism, so taken for granted as *the way things are,* that only a few materialist feminists, such as Nancy Hartsock, risk critiquing it. The Foucauldian theory of power (which traces its genealogy back to Nietzsche) posits power as diffuse and dispersed without a cause or originary source. Or as Butler says, power is "a reiterated acting . . . in its persistence and instability": It is established through a chain of "citations," repetitions, and mimings, in short, "performatives"

(225). The politics of such a Foucauldian theory is that it blurs the lines between the powerful and powerless, the oppressor and oppressed, and produces a social analytic that turns the historical binaries of social class into reversible matters of discourse in which exploiter and exploited become shifting positions in the (Lacanian) Symbolic, open to rearticulation, or what Butler calls "resignification."

Butler argues that the materialization of "sexed positions" in the discourse-power regime of heterosexuality "is a question of *repeating* that [heterosexual] norm, citing or miming that norm" (225). But such a theory of power and "citational practice" raises the problem of how to account for change or resistance. Butler resolves this by arguing that the practice of repeating and citing—this "reiterative acting" of power in the "juridical domain" of heterosexuality—is an unstable process that includes its own subversion. Since any citation or repetition of a norm will involve a *difference* from every other citation, it opens up a space for changing—what Butler calls, "resignifying"—the norm and its symbolic regime. In other words, each citing provides an opportunity to alter the meaning of the norm and the way it organizes signification. According to Butler, the symbolic "law provides *the discursive occasion* for a resistance, a resignification, and potential self-subversion of that law" (109). The prime example of this resignification is, of course, the way the derogatory term *queer* has been "resignified" in a positive way as a site of affirmation and resistance. However, Butler's politics of resignification, like any Foucauldian theory of power, is a series of individual resistances in and through discourse. It substitutes a superstructural, that is, a discursive project of resistance for the collective project of socioeconomic emancipation and revolutionary change.

In contrast, a historical materialist concept of power argues that power is not simply an autonomous, compulsory process, rather it is fundamentally related to the historical conditions of production. Power is the effect of the relations of production and the social divisions of labor; it is constructed in the production process to enforce the appropriation of surplus labor. The "superexploitation" of subsistence labor, in particular, depends on violence and coercion. In capitalism—which organizes the social division of labor around differences of gender, race, (hetero)sexuality, nationality— this means especially the expropriation of the surplus labor of women, lesbians, gays, people of color, and the colonized. The current anti- lesbian and gay backlash clearly demonstrates this. However, Butler's theory of citationality is unable to *explain* this material reality, and it is quite significant that Butler momentarily moves toward a class analysis of resisting sexu- alities in order to ask, "For whom is outness a historically available and affordable option? Is there an unmarked class character to the de- mand for universal 'outness'?" For historical materialist feminists and lesbian/gay critics, "outness," and the possibility of exploring alter- native sexualities, is not simply a function of desire, as most queer theory insists. It is, in- stead, determined by the heterosexual division of labor and one's own position in it.[10]

Labor and the relations of production are the suppressed, "covered over," "exclusionary," and "constitutive outside" of Butler's theory. They especially haunt her opening essay, "Bodies that Matter," in which she attempts to "discern the history of sexual difference encoded in the history of matter" (54) through a "rude and provocative" rereading of Plato (36). She begins by positing matter within the metaphysical bi- nary of matter and form, and confines her ar- gument to this metaphysical circuit. But at two points in her text, when she attempts to explain *why* Plato has constituted the category of the "excluded" in the way he has, she is forced to move beyond the domain of discourse to the *re- lations of production and the division of labor*. As Butler explains, "this xenophobic exclusion op- erates through the production of racialized Others, and those whose 'natures' are consid- ered less rational by virtue of their appointed task in the process of laboring to reproduce the conditions of private life" (48). And again, she says, "there is no singular outside, for the Forms require a number of exclusions; they are and

replicate themselves through what they ex- clude, through not being animal, not being the woman, not being the slave, whose propriety is purchased through property, national and racial boundary, masculinism, and compulsory heterosexuality" (52). All these exclusions are part of the same "singular outside": the material relations of production that construct all of the social divisions and differences around labor and the appropriation of social resources. In other words, for all Butler's discursive displace- ments, the concealed, sutured over *base* of her theory—as it is of any theory or knowledge practice—is still the (occluded) *economic base*.

Power for historical materialists is always linked to relations of production and labor. In any society divided by the unequal division and appropriation of labor, power is a binary rela- tion between exploiter and exploited and pow- erful and powerless, and cannot be translated into a plurality of differences as if all sites of power are equally powerful. The resolution of these binaries does not come about through a linguistic resignification but through revolu- tionary praxis to transform the system of ex- ploitation and emancipate those it exploits. It is telling that Butler (in her review of Drucilla Cornell) adopts the post-Marxist position that proclaims "the unrealizability of 'emancipation' is the condition of the possibility for a political field."[11] Emancipation, for Butler, has a "contra- dictory and untenable" foundation and thus becomes part of a sliding chain of significa- tions. But for historical materialists, emancipa- tion is a necessary "struggle concept" for ending the exploitation of people's surplus labor and the unequal distribution of social resources.

We can see the consequences of these differ- ent theories of materialism by briefly examin- ing the construction or "materialization" of female gender—what Butler calls "girling." To describe this process, Butler adapts Louis Althusser's concept of interpellation, which means the ideological process of "calling" a person to take up (identify with) the posi- tion "named" (e.g., girl). According to Butler, "medical interpellation . . . (the sonogram notwithstanding) . . . shifts an infant from an 'it' to a 'she' or a 'he,' and in that naming, the girl is 'girled,' brought into the domain of language and kinship through the interpellation of gender. . . . The naming is at once the setting of a boundary, and also the repeated inculcation of a norm" (7–8). Butler understands this naming ("girling") as placing the infant in a "regulatory regime" of discourse (language and kinship). But for historical materialists, ideological interpellation does not simply place the infant in discourse but, more important, it also places the child in the relations of production, in the social division of labor (according to gender, heterosexuality, race, nationality). Butler's theory of performativity completely eclipses this dialectical relation between ideology and the economic. Butler is concerned with changing how "bodies matter," how they are valued. But without relating ideological "interpellation" to the relations of production, no amount of resignification in the symbolic can change "what counts as a valued body"—for what makes a body valuable in the world is its *economic value*.

This *truth* is painfully clear if we move beyond the privileged boundaries of the upper-middle class in the industrialized West (for whom basic needs are readily fulfilled) and see what is happening to "girling" in the international division of labor—especially among the impoverished classes in India. Here the "medical interpellation" (naming) of infants/fetuses, particularly through the use of the sonogram, immediately places "girled" fetuses not only in discourse but also in the gender division of labor and unequal access to social resources. About 60 percent of the "girled" fetuses are being immediately aborted or murdered upon birth (female infanticide) because the families cannot afford to keep them. The citational acts, rituals, and "performatives" by which individuals are repeatedly "girled"—such as expensive ear-piercing ceremonies and exorbitant bridal dowries—are not simply acts of discourse but economic practices. In India, under postcolonial capitalism, the appropriation of women's surplus labor is increasing to such an extent that these rituals and "performatives" of "girling" are becoming highly popular and widely exploited

sources of capital and direct extraction of surplus labor. So much so, the unmarried woman's *family* is itself being "girled" in order for its combined labor to collectively produce the surplus value taken from the "girled body" (e.g., bridal dowries). Revolutionary praxis and not simply "resignification" is necessary to end the exploitation and murdering of hundreds of thousands of economically devalued ("girled") bodies.

Both *Materialist Feminisms* and *Bodies that Matter* are likely to gain a wide readership and will contribute to the prominence of poststructuralist understandings of materialism. But we are left to ask whether the cultural and discursive materialism they offer is not yet another antimaterialism and whether feminism's embrace of poststructuralism and postmodernism betrayed the possibility of a radical, historical materialist politics. Feminism and progressive cultural studies are at a crisis point in late capitalism. The eclipse of Marxism and historical materialism—as demonstrated in both of the books discussed—is a considerable loss for feminism and greatly impairs our ability to develop a revolutionary materialist feminism capable of challenging capitalism and working to end the very real exploitation of women's lives and labor.[12] "Resignification" and a "politics of undone identities" may help with some aspects of the ideological struggles, but they do little to explain and transform the economic deprivation and injustices—to meet the needs—of the most oppressed women. What is postmodern materialist feminism becoming? If it is no longer engaging the economic; if it is no longer a struggle to emancipate *all* people from *need* but instead has become a politics of (undone) identities, concerned with liberating the desires of those whose basic needs are already met—does it just become another middle-class feminism for the already privileged?

Notes

1. Jacques Derrida, *Of Grammatology,* trans. Gayatri Spivak (Baltimore: The Johns Hopkins University Press, 1974), p. 158.

2. Karl Marx, *A Contribution to the Critique of Political Economy,* ed. M. Dobb (New York: International Publishers, 1970), p. 21.

3. Karl Marx, *Capital,* 1 (New York: Vintage, 1977), p. 283.

4. Frederick Engels, "The Funeral of Karl Marx" in *When Karl Marx Died: Comments in 1883,* ed. Philip Foner (New York: International Publishers, 1973), p. 39.

5. Frederick Engels, Letter to Joseph Bloch, 21–22 September 1890 in *The Marx-Engels Reader,* 2nd ed, ed. R. Tucker (New York: Norton, 1978), pp. 760–761.

6. Maria Mies, *Patriarchy and Accumulation on a World Scale: Women in the International Division of Labour* (London and Atlantic Highlands, NJ: Zed Books, 1986), p. 36.

7. Mies, see especially chapter 2.

8. A. Sivanandan, "All that Melts into Air is Solid: The Hokum of New Times," *Race and Class,* 31.3 (1989):18.

9. Michele Barrett, *The Politics of Truth: From Marx to Foucault* (Stanford: University of Stanford Press, 1991), p. vii.

10. See for example, Donald Morton, "Practice, *Not* Performance: For a Materialist Queer Theory," Session on "Queer Theory Inside and Outside the Academy," Modern Language Association Convention, Toronto, December 29, 1993.

11. Judith Butler, "Poststructuralism and Postmarxism," *diacritics* (Winter 1993):8.

12. I attempt to develop a historical materialist postmodern feminism in my book, *Ludic Feminism and After* (Ann Arbor: University of Michigan Press, 1996) as well as in my text, "Ludic Feminism, the Body, Performance, and Labor: Bringing *Materialism* Back into Feminist Cultural Studies," *Cultural Critique* 23 (Winter 1992–1993):5–50.

References

Butler, Judith. (1993). *Bodies That Matter: On the Discursive Limits of 'Sex.'* New York: Routledge.

———. (1990) *Gender Trouble: Feminism and the Subversion of Identity.* New York: Routledge.

Landry, Donna, and Gerald MacLean. (1993) *Materialist Feminisms.* London: Blackwell Publishers.

Critique as Radical Praxis

Robert Andrew Nowlan

It is well-known that "being critical" is something of crucial and indeed even central importance to what "radicals," and especially marxists, are all about. After all, one of the most well-known quotations from Karl Marx is his call for "a ruthless criticism of all that exists." Yet more often than not what this means and how it is (to be) done is greatly misunderstood.

There are several reasons for this misunderstanding. First, it is not just radicals, and certainly not just marxists, who prize "critical thinking": in fact, all intellectual disciplines and all kinds of mental labor require learning some form of "critical thinking," and, because of this, workers in different fields of intellectual work will tend to understand "radical criticism" in relation to the notion of what criticism means that prevails in their field. Second, "being critical" is just as frequent a part of the "common sense" of everyday life, and in fact, common sense teaches us as much and as often about what are "critical" versus "non-critical" ways of thinking, acting, and interacting as does any form of "technical sense"; therefore, "radical criticism" may also be understood in relation to commonsensical notions of what criticism is and does. Third, and this is of key importance, it is often assumed, from the vantage point of either common or "technical" senses, and also by many radicals themselves, that the only difference in the way that radicals are critical from the way in which everyone else is critical is that radicals simply are more critical—and also, more often, and of more things—than non-radicals.

"Radical" criticism which is understood, and, more importantly than understood, *practiced* as simply *more* of the same kind of criticism as that which prevails among those working "critically" from the vantage point of non-radical common or technical senses is neither genuinely radical, nor effectively crucial—or central—to radical praxis. Radical criticism is *qualitatively* different from non-radical criticism. This does not mean that radical criticism bears no resemblance to non-radical criticism; on the contrary, radical criticism is a kind of criticism which develops out of a critique of the limitations of non-radical criticism, and this means that radical criticism is an attempt to supersede the limitations of non-radical criticism—in particular, the limitations of non-radical criticism that make it difficult if not impossible for this non-radical criticism either to imagine or to enable radical social change.

Radical criticism is criticism which aims to enable radical social change: change which strikes at the "root," at the "source," at the "structural foundations" of the social "system," pushing change forward towards transformation of the social totality rather than mere reformation or even conservation of this existing system. The ultimate aim of radical criticism is to enable the emergence and development of a new social system—governed by a new essential logic—to replace the existing system. To be radical in today's world, therefore, means, minimally, to work towards the transformation and replacement of capitalism with a social system that will enable the most radically progressive resolution of the principal contradictions and thereby the most radically progressive solution of the most egregious problems and the most radically progressive supersession of the most egregious limitations of capitalism; and this means the replacement of capitalism with socialism. Radical criticism must be criticism which is both first and last directed towards and genuinely capable of making a significant and substantial contribution towards this end.

Radical criticism, therefore, does not simply come to (prospective) radicals "naturally"; it must be studied and learned. A merely cognitive study of radical criticism, however, is insufficient to insure mastery: radical criticism must be learned by focusing, developing, sharpening, and refining cognitive understanding in practice. In fact, only when critique becomes a principal mode of radical praxis—and in all areas of radical activity—will the radical activist have made effective use of the real potential of *critique as radical praxis.*

What I propose to do in this essay is briefly to provide an introduction to critique as such a principal mode of radical praxis. My aim is to outline how to begin to go about this process. Providing such an outline involves a serious risk: the risk that this "general guide" will be used as a kind of mechanical apparatus, when my purpose is merely to enable a rudimentary understanding and to provide a provisional framework from which to begin to engage in critique. If this guide is applied as a mechanical apparatus, the "critiques" that this guide enables will tend towards an idealist (and perhaps more precisely, a rationalist) abstractness rather than a materialist concreteness.

I think it is worth taking this risk, however, because the risks of not developing a more precise and rigorous understanding of what is critique and of how to do it are worse. Too often, supposedly "radical" criticism is ineffective because it is unsystematic, undisciplined, and deficient in precision and rigor. When this is the case, "radical criticism" tends towards a largely uncritical—and also, as I shall explain, an often *anticritical*—mode of evaluation that is principally dependent upon moral rather than political categories. Use of these kinds of categories tends to support criticism which (idealistically) reifies its object: criticism which conceives of its

object as an isolated and disconnected, fixed and frozen thing rather than a complex of relations and processes that is interdeterminately interconnected with many other complexes of relations and processes within the context of a concrete real totality. For example, Dan Quayle is mocked as simply a "stupid" and—"bigoted"—man, rather than critiqued as a man who exercises significant power (despite, or perhaps even because of his apparent stupidity) as a representative of the interests of the capitalist class. Likewise, Quayle's attack on *Murphy Brown* is criticized as an example of his "stupid" inability to distinguish "fact" from "fiction" rather than contested for its reactionary political implications—delegitimation of women's struggle for liberation from enslavement within the patriarchal family.

My point, however, is that critical praxis which refuses methodological precision and rigor tends towards eclecticism, empiricism, relativism, pragmatism, mysticism, dogmatism, and irrationalism. Radical criticism that exhibits strong tendencies in any one or more of these directions will not be able to make an effective contribution to radical social change. Nonetheless, it should be emphasized very clearly and forcefully, right at the beginning, that A CRITIQUE IS NOT A MECHANICAL EXERCISE, but rather an *investigation* which requires *imagination* and *creativity* as well as rigor and precision.

Criticism is, of course, something we all do—and at many different times and in many different places. Criticism also can take many different forms: we think, feel, read, write, speak, listen, act, and interact critically. Criticism is, in fact, one of the most important ways in which we engage in the world in which we live to make and re-make this world. What is criticism? Very generally, to "criticize" is to evaluate—to judge—something according to certain standards. Commonsensically, critical judgment is often understood to be simply and entirely negative as "to criticize" is most often understood as simply involving finding fault with, or putting down someone or something, and "criticism" is often understood as merely that which points out what is "bad" or "wrong" about something. Commonsensically, to criticize capitalism, for example, would involve simply expressing the opinion that "capitalism sucks." A critique is a more useful mode of criticism. A critique does not simply point out that "capitalism sucks." A critique explains first, what is means by "capitalism" and by "sucks"; second, *how* and *why* capitalism sucks; and third, what can be done to transform capitalism so that the "suckiness" of capitalism is overcome.

I prefer to call "commonsensical criticism"—critical judgment which offers no explanation for its judgment—non-critical *criticism*. Non-critical criticism merely evinces an *opinion*—usually negative—rather than producing an *argument* for and from a *position*. Simply to declare that "capitalism sucks" is merely to express an opinion. An argument differs from an opinion in several ways. First, an argument *explains* its *claim,* and this involves the use of various means—for example, deductive and inductive reasoning and factual and counterfactual evidence—to *support* and *substantiate* the claim. An argument in support of the claim that "capitalism sucks" would involve explanation of the logic of capitalist development supported by reference to actual history and to real historical possibilities which demonstrate this logic at work. Second, an argument *accounts* for the *terms and definitions* it uses (it explains why it uses the particular terms and definitions it does). An argument in support of the claim that "capitalism sucks" would explain what it means by "capitalism" and, if it still wants to make a case for the claim that capitalism "sucks," (and a rigorously *theoretical* argument would, of course, tend to make use of much different—much more rigorously theoretical and far less colloquial and moralistically reductive—categories than "sucks"), then also for what it means by "sucks." Third, an argument accounts for the *philosophical-ideological assumptions and presuppositions* which underlie its claim, the *philosophical-ideological vantage point or perspective* from which these assumptions and presuppositions are derived, and the *social-political (pre)conditions* which make possible

and which further enable the articulation and defense of this claim, from this philosophical-ideological vantage point, at the particular historical time and place in which the argument is made. An argument that "capitalism sucks" would want to explain that marxism is the scientific study and the revolutionary ideology of (the possibility of) proletarian self-emancipation, how this is so, and, in particular, what this means at this concrete moment in the historically ongoing struggle to transform capitalism into socialism. Fourth, an argument accounts for *the philosophical-ideological* and *the social-political implications and consequences* of accepting and agreeing with the claim it makes: in other words, an argument accounts for the philosophical-ideological and social-political *ends* it advances and the philosophical-ideological and social-political *interests* it serves. An argument that "capitalism sucks" would want to suggest how revelation of what capitalism really is doing, to whom and for whom, can provide at least something of the impetus for organization and mobilization of radical resistance and opposition to the interests of capital, and ultimately to the interest of capital in maintaining and reproducing capitalism. Fifth, and finally, an argument accounts for the relations—and especially any and all *contradictions*—that *connect*—and disconnect—its assumptions and presuppositions, the claim it makes, the explanation it provides in support and defense of this claim, its selection and deployment of terms and definitions, and the implications and consequences that follow from accepting and agreeing with its claim. An argument in support of the claim that "capitalism sucks" would want to show how and why even the most progressive reform within capitalism is enabled by discerning the true nature of capitalist exploitation and alienation and developing a long-term strategic perspective on what is and is not possible at this concrete historical moment in the struggle to end and overcome these problems.

In addition to non-*critical criticism,* I think it is useful also to distinguish another mode of evaluative praxis from genuinely "critical criticism," and this is what I call *anti-critical criticism*. Anti-critical criticism does provide an explanation for the judgment it makes, and yet this is an explanation which is not only so abstract but also so partial and limited as to provide little real explanation at all: anti-critical criticism typically marshals sweepingly simplistic and reductive—and usually transhistorically essentialist—kinds of reasoning and evidence to support its claims. A common anti-critical argument against socialism is that socialism is impossible because it runs contrary to human nature: human beings are, supposedly, by nature hopelessly and inevitably, always (already and forever) essentially uncooperatively competitive, selfishly greedy, and cruelly and callously corrupt. This argument usually involves citing the entirety of hitherto recorded human history as proof without realizing that this history has not been so monolithically anti-socialistic, and, furthermore, that even if this were the case, what is and what has been is not necessarily what will or must be.

A critique attempts to judge its object on the basis of an accurate interpretation of what this object really is and does. This means that a critique aims to be scientific: it seeks to determine precisely what the object is and does, how so, and for what. Such a determination enables the critic not only to recognize the problems and the limitations inherent in the object for what and for how serious they really are, but also to recognize the *contradictions* inherent within the object that provide the source both of these problems and limitations and of a possible solution to these problems and an overcoming of these limitations by means of a development and transformation of possibilities inherent within the object of critique itself. A critique of capitalism, for example, will look to the principal contradictions of capitalism (especially the fundamental contradiction of capitalism, the contradiction between socialization of the forces of production and privatization of relations of production) to explain both the problems and limitations of capitalism (especially the determinate relation, within and across global capitalism, between a very few who enjoy sumptuous wealth and a great many who suffer miserable poverty) and the basis upon which these problems can be solved and these limitations overcome through a resolution of these contradictions, and thereby a transformation and supersession of capitalism (especially through the expropriation and redistribution of private wealth as the wealth of the collective whole).

A critique should be both objective *and* interested. It should be *objective* insofar as it seeks to determine what is true and what is not about its object. It should be *interested* insofar as its aim is not simply to explain what is and is not, but rather to point the way towards the most radically progressive possible resolution of the contradictions (and thereby the most radically progressive possible solution of the problems and overcoming of the limitations) inherent in this object. Critique is motivated by a concern to *intervene* in, effect, and (re)direct the course of change—change both in and of the object, and change in what the object effects as it changes. A critique, therefore, not only seeks the *truth* about its object, but also seeks to make use of this discernment of what is and is not true as a foundation upon which to advance a radical *political agenda* in relation to what should be done with or about its object so as to enable radical political *ends* and *interests,* and the ultimate end and interest of radical praxis is to enable transformation of the structural foundations of the existing social system so as to enable an exponential leap forward in the realization of human emancipation, collective equality, social justice, and ecological harmony.

The first stage of critique involves determination of the meaning of the object of critique. The meaning of an object refers to what that object *is* and *does*. The meaning of an object is a unity of its *content* (what it is about), its *form* (how it goes about this), and its *purpose* or *function* (why it goes about this, and why in this way). As an object can be and do many different things in many different ways for many different ends as part of many different relations and processes, it can mean many different things, and yet it is important to understand that meaning refers to what an object *truly* is and does—meaning refers to what is *objectively* real about an object. The different meanings that adhere to a single object always refer to what are different aspects or dimensions of its objectively *real* existence within different relations and as part of different processes. Meaning is, therefore, different from *signification:* from what an object is *understood* to mean, what the object "signifies." What people think and feel about an object, even about its relation to themselves, may or may not be true. Meaning refers to what is objectively real and signification to what is subjectively imagined to be real. For example, many workers for capitalist corporations do not think they are exploited and do not feel alienated and yet they are both. What working for capital signifies to these workers is therefore not what it actually means.

Interpretation of meaning is much more complex than merely discerning what is objectively real from what is subjectively imagined to be real. Meaning must be understood concretely. This means that it is necessary to study the meaning of an object *in context.* In other words, because an object "is" something, moreover, ultimately only in and through the various real relations and processes in which it really "does" something, an object is only meaningful, therefore, in context, and a critique should always seek to determine the meaning of an object by inquiring into what the object does in the context of its precise, reallocation(s) within an historically concrete society.

Recognition of the multiplicity of meaning should not, however, be misunderstood in a relativist fashion: it is necessary to recognize the meaning of an object refers not only to the *concrete forms of appearance* of the object, its *concrete manifestations* in particular *concrete situations,* but also to its *abstract essence* (which unites in common, and more precisely governs, the ways, and the range of ways, in which the object manifests itself concretely), and to the *mediations* (connections and transformations) which link the essence of the object with its various concrete forms of appearance. The meaning of capitalism, for example, involves refer-

ence not only to what capitalism looks like at very particular places and times, but also to what are the fundamental laws of motion of capitalism in general, and to the ways these laws of motion are mediated through the uneven development of these laws of motion within and between various nations and regions, branches and sectors, and industries and firms.

It is, in fact, useful to inquire into the meaning of an object as it exists on—and across—multiple, different levels of natural and social reality. I suggest investigating the meaning of an object as it exists on seven general levels of meaning, inquiring into what are its specific locations, and what are its specific functions and significances, within and as a part of what specific relations and processes on each of these levels of meaning. Allow me to illustrate with the example of "capitalism" once more:

Level of Meaning 1:   What does capitalism mean—what are its specific forms and effects—at the level of what is uniquely particular about the present conjuncture, the immediately here and now, i.e. in late capitalist america today?

Level of Meaning 2:   What does capitalism mean—what are its specific forms and effects—at the level of what is uniquely particular to the present stage in its historical development and transformation, i.e. in late capitalism?

Level of Meaning 3:   What does capitalism mean at the level of what is uniquely particular to capitalism in general as a dominant mode of social organization, as a dominant mode of articulation of the forces and relations of social production?

Level of Meaning 4:   What does capitalism mean at the level of its place within the history of class society in general?

Level of Meaning 5:   What does capitalism mean at the level of its place within the history of human society in general?

Level of Meaning 6: What does capitalism mean at the level of its place within the (history of the) animal world in general?

Level of Meaning 7: What does capitalism mean at the level of its place within (the history of) nature in general?

Of course, both within and between each of these levels of meaning, many other "sublevels" are possible as well. What is important is that the critic indicate clearly at what level(s) of generality and particularity (and of abstractness and concreteness) she is working in explaining what an object means. Moreover, it is also important that she indicate what particular aspects or dimensions of reality she is concerned with at these levels and sublevels and from what particular vantage point(s) or perspective(s) she is focusing upon what her object of critique means in relation to these aspects and dimensions of reality at these levels and sublevels of meaning. The importance of working at (or across) different levels and sublevels of meaning, focusing upon different aspects and dimensions of reality at these different levels and sublevels, and working from (and moving between) different vantage points will vary both from one kind of object of critique to another kind of object of critique, and according to what *objective* the critic seeks to accomplish in and through her critique. A critique of how and why "capitalism sucks," for instance, will probably want to explain how and why capitalism is dependent upon the perpetuation of exploitation and alienation of working class productive and reproductive activity. This kind of critique will probably want to work not only at level one, but also level two and level three; it will probably want to focus not only upon economic relations but also upon forms of consciousness and the relations—and mediations—between the two; and it will probably want to examine capitalist alienation and exploitation from the vantage points of both "subject" (under capitalism) and "structure" (of capitalism), of both capitalist and proletarian,

of both capitalist ideology and anti-capitalist ideology, and of both capitalist subjectivity and anti-capitalist subjectivity.

In all cases, it is always important to realize that what an object is and does within and as a part of any particular relation or process—and therefore also what it means on any level and sublevel, in relation to any aspect or dimension of reality, and from any vantage point or perspective—is always, in actuality, not only *multiple* but also *contradictory*. It is particularly important, for instance, in critiquing capitalism to be able to assess what contribution capitalism has made to the "universal" development of humanity—to progress in the development of human culture and civilization—versus what is "independent" of this universal development and, as such, functions to maintain and reproduce capitalism rather than to push forward through and beyond capitalism: here, of course, the tendency of capitalism to support socialization of the process of (social) production is "universal" while the tendency of capitalism to maintain and even greatly expand the privatization of ownership in the means and ends of (social) production is "independent."

The actual evaluation—the judgment—of the object of critique develops immediately out of the interpretation of what the object means: critical evaluation involves assessing the object's problems and limitations in relation to the contradictions inherent within the object which both give rise to these and to the possibility of their supersession. Interpretation should have already prepared the way for the first step in this second stage of critique: determination of what are the principal—and the most serious—problems and limitations in what the object of critique is and in what it does. What is necessary here is for the critic to account for what she seizes upon as (the most serious) problems and limitations by explaining from what *vantage point*, according to what *standards for evaluation* (of importance and seriousness), and in relation to the *advancement of what ends* and the *service of what interests* these problems are (such important and serious) problems and these limitations are (such important and serious) limitations. In the case of capitalism, of course, she would explain her commitment towards finding the way past the exploitation and alienation of labor—and the resulting destruction and dehumanization of life—which she has already shown is intrinsically indispensable to the normal workings of capitalism itself.

Because critical evaluation is not interested in merely stopping with determination of what is "bad" about or "wrong" with its object, it is necessary to move from this point to investigate the real possibilities—in the real struggle of real forces and tendencies—for resolution of the principal contradictions inherent within the object that provide the *source of its problems and limitations.* This requires a very precisely concrete analysis of what are and are not possible and useful sites of prospective intervention in this struggle so as to push these contradictions towards crisis and to strengthen the forces and tendencies representative of the most radically progressive resolution of these contradictions at—and beyond—their development to the point of crisis (the point in which a fundamental change in the balance or configuration of opposing forces *must* occur because the possibility of a continuation of the status quo has been exhausted). Upon the basis of such a concrete analysis, then, it is the final aim of the critique to intervene exactly as possible and as useful where possible and where useful both to push forward the contradictions in its object further towards crisis and to push forward the most radically progressive tendencies for resolution of these contradictions at and beyond this point of crisis. The critic pushes the most radically progressive tendencies more strongly to the fore(front), and pushes these over and against competing counter-tendencies which she at the same time attempts to push back, disrupt, and subvert.

Capitalism and Homophobia: Marxism and the Struggle for Gay/Lesbian Rights

The 1917 Collective

Revolutionists must seek to understand the gay and lesbian question for both scientific and programmatic reasons. Marxists have always sought to understand society as a whole, and to develop a historical materialist analysis of all social phenomena—from the relations of production to religion, the family, and so on. As Lenin noted in *What Is To Be Done?*, it is not sufficient to give attention only to questions immediately affecting the proletariat:

> "The consciousness of the working masses cannot be genuine class-consciousness, unless the workers learn, from concrete, and above all from topical, political facts and events to observe *every* other social class in *all* the manifestations of its intellectual, ethical, and political life; unless they learn to apply in practice the materialist analysis and the materialist estimate of *all* aspects of the life and activity of *all* classes, strata, and groups of the population."

We uphold the Leninist conception of a party of the proletariat as the "tribune of the people," which seeks to lead the working class in the fight against all forms of oppression under capitalism, and to link the struggles of the oppressed to the struggle for working-class rule. Marxists oppose all capitalist oppression, and in that spirit clearly oppose the persecution of both male and female homosexuals and others who are oppressed on the basis of sexually related behaviour, such as transvestites and transsexuals, sado-masochists, etc. As long as there is informed consent between participants, we adamantly oppose state intervention.

Capitalism does not concentrate the pain it causes in a single identifiable class easily mobilized as a united force. If that were the case our task would be simple. Capitalism distributes its pain in seemingly chaotic patterns, leaving its victims to fight for their interests in isolation, each separated from the others—disabled groups, immigrants, religious minorities, the elderly and the young. It is the task of the revolutionary party to champion the interests of all the oppressed, and to organize their struggles around the axis of proletarian revolution.

As Lenin explained, a Marxist must be a:

> . . . *tribune of the people*, who is able to react to every manifestation of tyranny and oppression, no matter where it appears, no matter what stratum or class of the people it affects; who is able to generalise all these manifestations and produce a single picture of police violence and capitalist exploitation; who is able to take advantage of every event, however small, in order to set forth *before all* his socialist convictions and his democratic demands, in order to clarify for *all* and everyone the world-historic significance of

the struggle for the emancipation of the proletariat.—*What is to be Done?*

This conception was not some temporary
tactical stance adopted by the immature Lenin;
the defense of democratic rights and the oppressed was integral to Bolshevism. Lenin explicitly disagreed with the notion that as a
Marxist, you should "concern yourself only with
your own class," and rejected the Mensheviks'
advice to "abandon 'Blanquist dreams' of leading all the revolutionary elements of the people. . . ." (*Collected Works,* v. 16).

The classical case in which the issue of the
Marxist vanguard as tribune of the people was
posed was the Dreyfus case. In 1894, Captain
Alfred Dreyfus, a Jewish officer of the French
general staff, was court-martialed for treason,
degraded, and sent to prison. When it subsequently became clear that he was innocent, the
right-wing, clericalist, anti-Semitic general staff
did their best to suppress the truth. Throughout
1898–99 there were frequent street clashes between the Dreyfusards (Intellectuals, socialists
and bourgeois radicals) and the French right.
While some leftists argued that the working class
had no interest in defending a bourgeois military officer who had no connection to the workers' movement, this conflict shook the Third
Republic almost to its foundations. The majority
of French socialists understood that it was important to uphold democratic rights and to connect this struggle to the movement against capitalist rule.

Historically homosexuality has been persecuted because of its "unnaturalness" and the
supposed threat it poses to the reproduction of
the species. These two rationalizations are in
fact closely related, as what is supposed "unnatural" about homosexual activity is that it is not
procreative. In fact there is no reason to think
that homosexuality has any more impact on reproductive statistics than recreational heterosexual intercourse, masturbation or celibacy.

It is simply not possible to know for sure how
biogenetic and social influences interact to determine sexual preference, although, while
there is no demonstrated biological function

for a unidirectional sexuality, it is clear that in
contemporary society there is very substantial
social pressure encouraging an exclusively heterosexual orientation. A more tolerant social atmosphere may lead to an increase in homosexual behavior, but that does not necessarily
imply an increase in the proportion of people
with a homosexual preference, or a decline in
reproductively significant heterosexual behavior. Certainly the need to reproduce the human
population is not threatened by homosexuality;
the quantity of heterosexual activity necessary
for reproductive purposes is a small fraction of
what goes on.

Homosexuality Before Capitalism

The intensity of social prejudice, and the legal
sanctions employed against male and female
homosexual behavior, has varied considerably
with time and place. On the whole, homosexuality (in particular patterns) was accepted in
classical antiquity. In 1980, a Yale University
professor, John Boswell, published *Christianity,
Social Tolerance, and Homosexuality,* which described how, from the mid-eleventh to the mid-
twelfth century in Catholic Europe, there was a
veritable flowering of explicitly gay activity and
writing, including erotic poetry, in the priesthood. This corresponded with the enforcement
of the ban on priestly marriage, which until
that time had been permitted (as it still is in
the Eastern Church). Homosexual priests were
among the strongest supporters of the ban on
heterosexual marriage, but the fundamental
basis for the shift was the need for the church to
adapt itself to the feudal mode of production.
In most feudal societies land was inherited by
the eldest son, and that principle could have
rapidly depleted church landholdings. Consequently it was necessary to prevent the clergy
from marrying and having sons.

The outlawing of heterosexual activity in the
priesthood required either accepting homosexuality as a norm, or, alternatively, banning homosexual activity as well. The matter was decided at the Third Lateran Council in 1179,

which imposed sanctions against homosexuality. The decision was not immediately reflected in local legal codes, but between 1250 and 1300 sodomy passed from being legal to being punishable by death in most countries in feudal Europe.

Although its origins lay in the requirements of the church, it is hardly surprising that the doctrine of sodomy as a particularly iniquitous sin applied universally, or that it soon became an ecclesiastical crime for the whole population, and later a crime before the king's courts. Nor is it surprising that there was an uneven tendency over time for the prohibition to lose its force.

Capitalism and the Nuclear Family

Persecution of homosexuals declined from the 14th to 19th centuries, and then increased sharply in the late 1800s. This outburst of homophobia was clearly linked to the promotion of the nuclear family as the social norm, and the associated prohibition on extra-marital sex.

In the *Communist Manifesto* of 1848, Marx and Engels described the proletarian family (as distinct from the bourgeois family) as a vestigial and decaying institution. However, within a couple of generations the nuclear family was firmly established as the characteristic form of proletarian domestic life under capitalism.

The capitalist mode of production does not require any particular form of domestic arrangement for the working class. As long as there is a sufficient supply of new workers ready to sell their labor power, the manner in which working-class reproduction takes place should not, at least in the abstract, be a matter of vital concern to the bourgeoisie. In the early days of the industrial revolution, proletarian domestic life was characterized by decaying pre-capitalist, multi-generational family forms. The transition from the field to the factory was a traumatic one, marked by massive social dislocation and domestic disorder (with associated drunkenness, child abuse, etc.). The employment of men, women and children for very long hours

at subsistence wages proved an impediment to the development of the nuclear family. This is what the *Manifesto* described as "the bourgeois clap-trap . . . about the hallowed co-relation of parent and child" when the development of large-scale industry meant that "all family ties among the proletarians are torn asunder, and their children transformed into simple articles of commerce and instruments of labour."

The absence of strongly patterned domestic arrangements in the early proletariat did not serve capitalism well. It did not prove easy to integrate childbearing, nursing and child-raising into the factories and other enterprises. Over time, bourgeois society accepted that these functions could best be carried on outside the factory. This is the material basis of the proletarian nuclear family. That is its origin, and even today that is its sustenance.

The historical development of the family was conditioned by the necessity for socializing young proletarians, looking after the aged, and providing healthcare and emotional support for the laboring population. It was shaped ideologically by the practices of the ruling class (developed earlier to meet its own needs).

The nuclear family also provided a measure of social cohesion and stability for the bourgeois order. A male wage earner, demeaned at work, could accept his lot more readily if he had his personal needs met at home where he was "boss." He thereby became an important participant in moulding the next generation of workers into acceptance of the hierarchical nature of class society. At the same time his domestic responsibilities reinforced the power of the employer—a worker had to consider his dependent wife and children before slugging the foreman or voting to go on strike.

For all its utility, however, the nuclear family proved difficult to entrench in the proletariat, and required considerable ideological as well as legal and material support. In England there were a battery of props—from the Factory Acts limiting hours of work for women and children, to the emphasis on plebeian chastity, temperance and self sacrifice by the various nonconformist Christian denominations. By the end of the 19th century, as the hegemony of the nuclear family was gradually established, childhood became prolonged, motherhood was promoted as the proper full-time occupation for women, prostitution become an outcast occupation, and homosexuals were despised and victimized.

Homophobia and the Proletarian Family

The bourgeois family discussed by Marx and Engels was based on the premise that an individual bourgeois male must have exclusive sexual access to his wife (in order to guarantee that his property be eventually inherited by his own blood relatives). This did not require prohibiting extra-marital sexual activity (whether heterosexual or homosexual) for the husband. Such activities did not threaten the line of property succession, so there was no obvious necessity for their prohibition. However, the establishment of the nuclear family as the primary domestic social institution for the proletariat and other plebeian strata required such taboos.

In part it was simply a matter of suppressing alternatives to the nuclear family, with their potential counter-exemplary effects. If you are trying to convince a population that bliss consists in a man working in a factory, with a woman looking after five children at home—not an inherently easy task—then it is not useful to permit more agreeable domestic configurations. Homosexual couples or bachelor groupings with access to prostitutes, or other more bohemian combinations, might be seen as more interesting, fulfilling, or more materially comfortable than membership in a proletarian family.

There is another, related strand to the genesis of modern homophobia. Under nineteenth-century capitalism the central conditioning fact of proletarian domestic life was that the entire cost of raising the next generation was a private rather than a social responsibility. Children could not sustain themselves financially, nor could their caregivers. The nuclear family required that mothers and children be supported by a male, who must be productive enough to command a wage sufficient for that purpose.

This required that childbearing be delayed, which, in the absence of modern technologies of family planning, required a high degree of teenage chastity. This was not easily achieved. It involved a certain level of frustration and social tension, and required the backing of authoritative religion as well as state intervention through age-of-consent laws and the like.

There are difficulties with banning teenage heterosexual intercourse while permitting homosexual activity, unless teenage homosexuality is carefully institutionalized, as in English public schools. Consequently, in the latter part of the 19th century, there was considerable fear that without powerful counter-pressures, libidinous male teenagers would channel their energies in a homosexual direction. The fear that heterosexuality would succumb before the homosexual onslaught was frequently cited as the justification for anti-homosexual measures in this period. The fear of the "corruption of youth," together with the importance of maintaining the power of the father in the family as against any homosexual competitor, were themes of the prosecuting lawyers, judges and newspapers during the trials of Oscar Wilde in the 1890s, which were crucial in the articulation and structuring of anti-homosexual moralism in Britain and elsewhere (see, for example, H. Montgomery Hyde, *Oscar Wilde*, 1976).

Women were seen as less socially significant, and as essentially asexual. Their sexual lives were therefore not subject to such active persecution. Young women were far more closely supervised than men and much more likely to be confined to the home. The greater success in suppressing teenage female sexuality meant that lesbianism was largely ignored, and in general the extremes of homophobic prejudice were reserved for men. Lesbian activity was generally described as women engaging in "male" behavior.

Early Socialists and Homophobia: The Schweitzer Case

There is a considerable history of opposition in the workers' movement to the oppression of homosexuals, particularly in Germany, home to the largest and most influential socialist movement in the period before World War I. In August 1862, two elderly ladies enjoying a quiet stroll through a public park in Mannheim came across a talented young lawyer named Jean Baptiste von Schweitzer and an unidentified youth in a highly compromising situation. As a result Schweitzer spent two weeks in jail and was disbarred. It was suggested that this incident made him unfit for membership in Ferdinand Lassalle's General German Workers Association (see James D. Steakley, *The Homosexual Emancipation Movement in Germany*, 1975). Lassalle defended Schweitzer as follows:

> "What Schweitzer did isn't pretty, but I hardly look upon it as a crime. At any rate, we can't let ourselves lose someone with such great ability, indeed a phenomenal person. In the long run, sexual activity is a matter of taste and ought to be left up to each person, so long as he doesn't encroach upon someone else's interests. Though I wouldn't give my daughter in marriage to such a man."—John Lauritsen and David Thorstad, *The Early Homosexual Rights Movement (1864–1935)*, New York, 1974

In 1864 Lassalle died as a result of a duel (over a woman) and Schweitzer became the leader of the Lassalleans for the next eight years. While the Eisenachers, the grouping supported by Marx and Engels, engaged in sharp political exchanges with the Lassalleans, the public polemics do not seem to have been polluted by homosexual baiting. In May 1875 the two groups fused to form the German Social-Democratic Party (SPD), which became the leading section of the Second (Socialist) International.

The SPD and the Homosexual Question

August Bebel (a leader of the Eisenachers and the preeminent leader of the SPD) spoke up on a number of occasions in the Reichstag in defence of homosexuals and against the penal provisions of the criminal code. He is quoted as saying on one occasion:

> "But gentlemen, you have no idea how many respectable, honorable and brave men, even in

high and the highest positions, are driven to suicide year after year, one from shame, another from fear of the blackmailer."—Lauritsen and Thorstad, *op cit.*

One case taken up by German Marxists was that of Oscar Wilde in England, prosecuted in 1895 under the 1885 Labouchere amendment which illegalized homosexual activities. Eduard Bernstein, leading theoretician of the SPD's right wing, wrote a substantial article defending Wilde in the April and May 1895 issues of *Die Neue Zeit*. Bernstein commented that:

> "Although the subject of sex life might seem of low priority for the economic and political struggle of the Social Democracy, this nevertheless does not mean it is not obligatory to find a standard also for judging this side of social life, a standard based on a scientific approach and knowledge rather than on more or less arbitrary moral concepts."—Lauritsen and Thorstad, *op cit.*

He rejected the notion that homosexual acts should be persecuted as "unnatural," and pointed out that very little done by human beings is "natural"—including carrying on a written discussion. He observed that judgments of what is natural or unnatural for human beings are reflections of the state of development of society rather than nature, and made the point that "moral attitudes are historical phenomena."

Bernstein noted that in most of the great civilizations of antiquity (the Egyptians, the Greeks and the Romans) homosexual love was freely practiced and remarked that: "same-sex intercourse is so old and so widespread that there is no stage of human culture we could say with certainty were free from this phenomenon." He denounced theories of homosexuality as illness, as a form of disguised moralism, a point taken up by another Social Democrat, Adolf Thiele, in the 1905 Reichstag debate on the subject. Karl Kautsky, representing the SPD's left wing, also came out against the oppression of homosexuals. Yet despite the public statements of many of its most prominent representatives, the party as a whole did not take a position on the subject.

The founders of the Marxist movement shared many of the prejudices of their times on the question of homosexuality. Marx apparently made only a single written reference to the subject, although in 1869 he had passed on to Engels a copy of a book on the subject by K. H. Ulrich, who was the first person to seriously work for a liberalization of the law on homosexuality. There is no indication that Marx actually read the book (almost certainly *Die Geschlechtsnatur des mannliebenden Urnings*) lent to him by Wilhelm Strohn, a German communist who lived in Bradford. In a letter to Engels dated 17 December 1869, Marx remarked: "Strohn will be returning from here to Bradford, and desires you to return him the *Urnings* or whatever the paederast's book is called."

Engels had commented on the book in a letter to Marx of 22 June 1869. He prefaced his remarks with a complaint that Wilhelm Liebknecht, their German co-thinker, was being too conciliatory with the Lassalleans, who were led by Schweitzer:

"The *Urning* you sent me is a very curious thing. These are extremely unnatural revelations. The paederasts are beginning to count themselves, and discover they are a power in the state. Only organisation was lacking, but according to this source it apparently already exists in secret. And since they have such important men in all the old parties and even in the new ones, from Rosing to Schweitzer, they cannot fail to triumph. '*Guerre aux cons, paix aus trous-de cul*' will now be the slogan [translated by the editors of the *Marx-Engels Collected Works* as "War on the cunts, peace to the arse-holes"]. It is a bit of luck that we, personally, are too old to have to fear that, when this party wins, we shall have to pay physical tribute to the victors. But the younger generation! Incidentally it is only in Germany that a fellow like this can possibly come forward, convert this smut into a theory, and offer the invitation *introite,* [enter] etc. . . . If Schweitzer could be made useful for anything, it would be to wheedle out of this peculiar honourable gentleman the particulars of the paederasts in high and top places, which would certainly not be difficult for him as a brother in spirit."

In his published work, Engels made only three unenlightened and moralistic remarks (all within a short section of the second chapter of his groundbreaking *Origin of the Family, Private Property and the State*).

Homosexuality in Czarist Russia

In Russia under the Czars, the climate was relatively liberal. Russia had not experienced the feudal wave of homophobia that swept Western Europe. The Romanov dynasty by the late 19th century was attempting to implant capitalist industry, but it was not seeking to promote the proletarian nuclear family. There were only two articles in the Tsarist criminal code related to homosexuality. Article 995 prohibited anal sex (but not other homosexual activities), and article 996 covered homosexual rape and the seduction of male minors or mentally retarded men (see: Simon Karlinsky, in *Hidden from History: Reclaiming the Gay and Lesbian Past,* London, 1989). One historian cited by Karlinsky claims that the only known prosecution under these articles in the 1890s concerned a male schoolteacher who seduced a thirteen-year-old pupil—within five years the teacher was back on the job.

In the 1890s there were a number of prominent gay sets in Russia. The flamboyant Grand Duke Sergei Alexandrovich frequently took his current lover to public functions. Those in Diaghilev's circle did not hide their homosexuality, and there was also a highly significant gay literary milieu including national celebrities like Kuzmin and Kliuev. "Their homosexuality was known to everyone and caused no problems in their social or professional lives" (Karlinsky, *op cit.*).

In this relatively liberal climate the Bolsheviks (like Marx and Engels before them) were not compelled to address the question of the oppression of homosexuals, and neither Lenin nor Trotsky are thought to have written anything on this issue either before or after the October Revolution. It is quite clear, however, that Trotsky had a relaxed and tolerant attitude to the question. In *Literature and Revolution,* published in 1924, he produced some literary criticism of some openly homosexual poetry without any homophobic bias. He also wrote a sympathetic—almost tender—obituary in the 19 January 1926 issue of *Pravda* for Sergei Esenin, an openly bisexual poet (see *Leon Trotsky on Literature and Art,* New York, 1972).

Homosexuality After the Russian Revolution

After the Russian Revolution, the revolutionary regime repudiated all Czarist laws deemed to "contradict revolutionary conscience and revolutionary legal awareness" (Decree on the Judicature issues by the Council of People's Commissars, 5 December [22 November], 1917). This implicitly decriminalized homosexuality, and when a new criminal code was promulgated after the Civil War in 1922, all mention of homosexuality was deleted.

The new regime's progressive attitude on the question of homosexuality was indicated by the appointment in early 1918 of Georgi Chicherin, a flamboyant and open gay, as People's Commissar of Foreign Affairs. No bourgeois state would have put such a figure in charge of foreign affairs.

(Chicherin's early relationship and continuing correspondence with the preeminent Russian gay poet, Mikhail Kuzmin, is documented in John E. Malmstead, "Mixail Kuzmin: A Chronicle of His Life and Times" [in English], in volume III of Kuzmin's collected poetry, *Sobranie stikhotvorenii* [in Russian], edited by Malmsted and Vladimir Markov, Munich, 1977. An account of his unconventional attire and style of work as Foreign Commissar can be found in Alexander Barmine's *One Who Survived: The Life Story of a Russian under the Soviets,* New York, 1945).

Scientific opinion in the early Soviet Union was not determined by the "general line," but many early Soviet sexologists seem to have had a progressive attitude on homosexuality. In 1923 Dr. Grigorii Batkis, the Director of the Moscow Institute of Social Hygiene, wrote the following approving description of the new legal code:

"Soviet legislation bases itself on the following principle: *It declares the absolute non-interference of the state and society into sexual matters, so long as no one's interests are encroached upon.* "Concerning homosexuality, sodomy, and various other forms of sexual gratification, which are set down in European legislation as offenses against public morality—Soviet legislation treats these exactly the same as so-called 'natural' intercourse. Only when there's use of force or duress, as in general when there's an injury or encroachment upon the rights of another person, is there a question of criminal prosecution."—*Die Sexualrevolution in Russland* (Berlin, 1925, apparently a reprint of a Russian original published in 1923, quoted in Lauritsen and Thorstad, *op cit.*)

At the same time, however, there remained professionals who regarded homosexuality as a serious illness. In *Sexual Life of Contemporary Youth,* published by the State Publishing House in 1923, Izrail Gel'man asserted:

"Science has now established, with precision that excludes all doubt, [that homosexuality] is not ill will or crime, but sickness.... The world of a female or male homosexual is perverted, it is alien to the normal sexual attraction that exists in a normal person."—quoted by Karlinsky, *op cit.*

Over time, as the Stalinist bureaucracy gradually took over the levers of power within the Soviet workers' state, this view of homosexuality grew in influence. One symptom of the deteriorating situation of gays was the rapid decline of Chicherin's influence after Lenin's death in early 1924. By the time the *Great Medical Encyclopedia* was published in 1929, homosexuality had been fully pathologized. Homosexuals were increasingly persecuted—the old German revolutionist Klara Zetkin intervened on behalf of some of the victims.

Finally, in 1933–34, homosexuality was formally recriminalized. The reintroduction of state-sponsored homophobia, like the accompanying attacks on women's rights (e.g., the re-criminalization of abortion) were aimed at reinforcing the nuclear family as the basic unit of a conservative social order.

Stonewall and After

In the past few decades the visibility and political clout of the homosexual population has grown considerably, particularly in Europe, North America and Australasia. An important factor in this development has been the militant political struggles waged for homosexual rights, signaled by the 1969 Stonewall riot in New York's Greenwich Village. The aggressive and self-confident gay liberation movement of the early 1970s developed in the context of a generalized shift to the left politically and a liberalization of attitudes towards sexuality in general. The explosive growth of the women's liberation movement in this period challenged the legitimacy of the "normal" patriarchal family. Elements of the women's movement embraced lesbianism ("women-identified women") as the most consistent expression of feminism.

The limited progress recorded by gays and lesbians is integrally connected to changes in the operation of the nuclear family. The growth of the white-collar sector with jobs that could be performed by either sex, the massive expansion of the female workforce, and the impossibility of maintaining living standards on a single (male) wage, undermined traditional stereotypes about men's and women's "rightful places" in the world. Another important change—connected to the increased efficacy of contraceptive techniques—was the surrender to the teenage sex drive. Widespread teenage heterosexual activity in turn reduces the "danger" that appetites which would otherwise develop in a heterosexual direction would be diverted towards homosexuality, and obviates the need for special measures to counter that "danger." Homosexual activity is still a potential counter-example to the nuclear family, but in societies where extra-marital sex is tolerated, that threat is merely one of many.

Yet the nuclear family remains a powerful institution in modern capitalist society. It is where the most important emotional needs of individuals (for love, intimacy and emotional security) are supposed to be met. Even for those whose experience of the family is one of misery and alienation, the myth continues to exert considerable influence. With the erosion of working-class living standards, the collapse of social services and growing levels of chronic unemployment within the metropolitan imperialist heartlands, the proletarian family has also become an increasingly important source of support for a substantial section of young adults who might otherwise be destitute. Moreover, at least within the layers of the working class and petty bourgeoisie affluent enough to own real estate or some other substantial material assets, parental control over a potential inheritance operates as a disciplinary mechanism in much the same way as within the bourgeoisie.

The gains recorded by gays and lesbians in the past several decades are substantial, but they are also fragile and reversible. Extra-marital sex, and particularly homosexuality, are still ferociously condemned by powerful forces, of both a clerical-fundamentalist and secular-conservative character. The furious opposition of the Pentagon (and most of Congress) to Bill Clinton's tentative gestures toward letting open gays and lesbians serve in the military provided a reminder of just how precarious the rights of homosexuals are. Last August the U.S. Senate voted overwhelmingly "to cut off Federal money to schools that teach acceptance of homosexuality as a way of life" (*New York Times*, 2 August 1994). One of the items cited as "disgusting, obscene material" purveyed to students was a book about a lesbian couple entitled "Heather Has Two Mommies."

As the logic of global economic competition compels the capitalists continually to increase pressure on working-class living standards, the bonds that once united people in the nuclear family are stretched to the breaking point or beyond. Homosexuals, "secular humanists," abortion-rights advocates and feminists are scapegoated for the collapse of family life, as "family values" becomes the rallying cry of social reaction.

The overlapping anti-abortion, anti-pornography and anti-gay campaigns provide a natural recruiting ground for the fascists, who are currently on the rise in Europe and North America. Gay-bashing is often used as an organizing tool by these fanatical defenders of capitalist irrationality and inequality.

The AIDS epidemic has given rise to a wave of moral panic used to foster anti-gay prejudice, to promote a general fear of sex, and to reinforce religion. Prevention, care and research on HIV/AIDS has been scandalously underfunded by the capitalist rulers of the "New World Order." Like every other social evil under capitalism, AIDS hits those at the bottom of the social ladder hardest.

In the imperialist heartland it is those who are most dependent on the decaying public health services—the poor and oppressed minorities—who suffer the most. The desperately poor neo-colonies have, of course, been hit far worse than the imperialist countries, with growing proportions of the population in the most productive age groups disabled and dying.

In recent years militant gays and lesbians have aggressively campaigned for more resources to fight AIDS, and have exposed some of the most glaring examples of negligence and abuse. We respect the considerable courage displayed by these activists in confronting the medical establishment and the state, and seek opportunities to engage in common work with them in the future. It is vitally important that deeper social layers become involved in these struggles, and particularly that the organizations of the working class take up these issues as a key part of the struggle for free universal quality health care.

Marxists recognize, however, that there is nothing inherently revolutionary about homosexuality, or about the struggle against AIDS. The gains won by lesbians and gays over the past

several decades have led to the development of an upwardly mobile layer of openly homosexual professionals (many associated with the AIDS industry) who desperately crave bourgeois respectability.

Tactics in the Gay Movement

The tactics of militant gay groups vary considerably in their effectiveness. One approach, involving the ostentatious display of gay affection in unexpected settings, is intended to shock heterosexuals into changing their consciousness. This is harmless, and we certainly support the right of homosexuals to be open about their sexual orientation. But as a political strategy it presupposes that the roots of homophobia lie in the consciousness of individuals rather than in the requirements of the capitalist social order.

Another approach involves encouraging gay men and lesbians to "come out" in less ostentatious ways—to be open about their sexuality in the course of their daily lives. Coming out is considered by most gay people not so much as a political strategy as a personal step toward self-esteem and adjustment, to be made by the individual concerned, depending on his/her circumstances. There are still many homosexuals who understandably fear exposure, who value their right to privacy, and who do not wish to come out.

Inevitably, various bourgeois functionaries are closeted homosexuals, and some of them may engage in the worst kind of homophobic politics. In recent years gay activists have engaged in "outings," i.e., publicly revealing the sexual identities of such prominent right-wing closeted homosexuals. This tactic is not new. It was known in the early German homosexual rights movement as "the path over the corpses," and was used in the early 1900s with disadvantageous results (see Steakley, *op cit*, and Oosterhuis and Kennedy, *Homosexuality and Male Bonding in Pre-Nazi Germany*, New York, 1991). Although Marxists share the gay liberationists' disgust with most targets of outing, as well as a sense of frustration with the lack of progress in gay rights, in general we oppose this tactic. It tends to add to the fears of exposure that burden the ordinary inoffensive closeted homosexual, and creates a climate for the worst kind of muckraking homophobic journalism and an anti-gay backlash.

It is the job of the Marxist party to inculcate scientific consciousness and to lead the proletariat in transcending moralism and mystification. This means opposing the Stalinist promotion of the "socialist family" and the attendant social backwardness toward women and homosexuals. Homophobia, like every other reactionary social prejudice in capitalist society, serves to divide, demoralize and discipline the proletariat, and undercut its capacity to understand its own historic interests. Common participation in class struggle and the fight for social and economic justice can undercut homophobia in the working class and other layers of the oppressed.

A revolutionary party must embody a scientific consciousness of society as a totality. It must seek to incorporate people who feel the oppression of capitalism in every form, and to connect their struggles to the necessity to overturn the social system from which oppression derives. Just as it is useful to have comrades of different generations, different political histories, and different cultural backgrounds, so the particular forms of alienation of gay men and lesbians gives them a variety of perspectives on bourgeois society which significantly enrich the collective Marxist consciousness of the proletarian vanguard.

Against Sectoralism, for Transitional Organizations

Marxists fight against all forms of special oppression (whether of women, blacks, youth, aboriginal peoples or homosexuals) without losing sight of the fact that it is *class society* which lies at the root. Revolutionaries support every reform which advances the situation of the oppressed, but know that, ultimately, social oppression can only be uprooted through the fight for a socialist society—one based on production for human need, not profit.

Unlike sectoralists, Marxists recognize that, because of its economically strategic position, the working class is the decisive factor in the struggle for fundamental social change. Attempts to organize gays as gays, women as women, or blacks as blacks, inevitably lead to cross-class formations, and to confining the struggle within the framework of capitalist rationality. Yet the oppression of gays and lesbians (in common with other forms of social oppression) can only be successfully challenged with a program that transcends the limits of the existing social order.

A revolutionary party needs transitional organizations to focus the struggles of the oppressed and to recruit the most politically advanced elements to the struggle for workers' power. Where there is the possibility of intervention in a significant gay or lesbian political arena, then a revolutionary party will seek to build a transitional organization for this work. The activities of such an organization, which would be part of a common revolutionary movement with a common discipline, would center on fighting the oppression of gays and lesbians while advancing a program that links these struggles to the necessity for working-class rule.

The fact that Marxists fight all forms of oppression under capitalism does not imply that all forms are equally important for revolutionary strategy. Gay and lesbian oppression is not entirely analogous to the oppression, for example, of blacks in the United States, or of women. Gays and lesbians are not concentrated in particular, crucial parts of the working class, they do not constitute a large or easily organized constituency, and besides, sexual orientation is not as immediately apparent as race or sex. Moreover, on the whole, there is not an important economic component to the oppression of homosexuals—indeed there are economic advantages to childlessness, which in the current social climate is often concomitant with being gay or lesbian.

Whatever progress has been made in recent decades, homophobia remains a "hot button" for the reactionary right, and a powerful tool for the defense of the status quo. The question of the oppression of homosexual men and women is a vital one for Marxists to take up, but it is not a strategic one for socialist revolution—unlike, for example, the woman question.

The oppression of homosexuals is rooted in the requirements of the capitalist system, and their liberation can be achieved only through the rational employment of humanity's immense productive capacity to eliminate poverty, ignorance and social inequality. In a classless society, the state, along with the nuclear family, will start to wither away and be replaced by freer, voluntary forms of human association in which the remarkable plasticity of human sexuality can be expressed without the fear, prejudice and anxiety with which patriarchal, capitalist society has traditionally treated sexual "deviants."

MATERIALIST QUEER THEORY: A WORKING BIBLIOGRAPHY

Compiled by Tamara Powell, Annie Adams, Angie Albright, Angela Athy, James R. Bennett, Heath Diehl, Kristi Johansen, Joe Sanders, Jeff Schwartz

Introduction

Material and *materialist* are terms familiar to traditional sociocritique or sociocriticism (expressed by the term *social*) and to contemporary cultural critique. However, these notions have found new articulations in postmodern critical theory (for discussion of some differences in the concepts, see Zavarzadeh, "Post-ality"). The concept "material" in postmodern theory (the very conceptuality of which is often questioned) refers not to the property of the object but to the resistance to paraphrasable "meaning." The "body," for example, is understood to be "material" not because it is three-dimensional and has volume and weight but because its "meanings" are not exhaustible by discourse. It is, in other words, more than its meanings; it is a material "excess." This sense of the "material" underlies one of the best-known discussions of materiality/materialism in postmodern criticism: J. Hillis Miller's Modern Language Association "Presidential Address 1986." Initially, Miller shows some sympathy with the notion of the material, but he then subjects the idea to a sustained textual critique. In the postmodern mode, Miller "deconstructs" the notion of the material in order to show that the material is not the reliable base of culture but is displaced in language and therefore resistant to it (see Zavarzadeh, "J. Hillis Miller, Materialism, and the Joy of Reading"). In short, the "material" in postmodern theory is understood not as the objective reality of historical processes but as the excess of meanings that functions as resistance to the established representations of

culture. This is why such writers as Judith Butler oppose the material to "discourse" (*Bodies That Matter*, 27–55), and writers like Deleuze and Guattari (*Anti-Oedipus*) identify the material with desire and critique Freud for his idealization of "pleasure" (as opposed to the supposed materiality of the "real"), as in "the pleasure principle" (Freud, *Beyond the Pleasure Principle*).

In sharp contrast to the material as appropriated by postmodernists stands the concept of "materialism" articulated and argued by Marx and Engels. For them, *materialism* is not simply a matter of resistance to social representations but is rooted in the praxis of labor and is closely tied to the objective properties of the historical world. Not only do they refuse to reduce *materialism* to postmodern *materiality* but they are also very careful not to allow it to become identical with the *matterism* that informs the writings of such critics as Raymond Williams and other cultural materialists. In fact, in their critique of Feuerbach, Marx and Engels make it clear that matterism/materiality are simply idealist understandings of objective reality. As Zavarzadeh suggests, V. L. Lenin calls these various (postmodern) materialities "objective idealism" in his *Materialism and Empirio-Criticism* (13–30). Several quotations from Marx and Engels bear on these questions. For example, Marx declares that "Our wants and pleasures have their own origin in society; we therefore measure them in relation to society; we do not measure them in relation to the objects which serve for their gratification" (*Wage-Labour*, 33). Or: "The production of ideas, of conceptions of consciousness, is at first directly interwoven with the material activity and the material intercourse of men, the language of real life" (*German Ideology*, 47). Marxist theory connects objective reality (modes of production, class conflict) with meanings that arise from social reality and with resistance to meaning (*Wechselwirkung*, interaction of base and superstructure, oppositional writers). All meanings have a material base—from advertising to national symbols (flag, eagle) to meanings embodied in written or printed texts; that is, they are embedded in history, culture, society, politics, institutions, class and gender conditions, social contexts, and conditions of production, technology, distribution, and consumption.

Materialism is not merely a new jargon term for the "social," but a theory of objective historical processes and the objective structure of conflicts and class antagonisms. That is, the Marxist notion of the material embodies the objective reality of labor: "Labour is . . . a process between man and nature, a process by which man, through his own actions, mediates, regulates, and controls the metabolism between himself and nature. . . . Through this movement he acts upon external nature and changes it, and in this way he simultaneously changes his own nature" (*Capital*, Vol. 1, 283).

Like the idea of the "material," the term *queer* used here also has a complicated history, from marking "deviation" in the moralistic sense of the old order to its postmodern implication of "at oddness," which points to the queer as an exemplary site of resistance to the old order and its social representations (see T. de Lauretis, *Queer Theory*). In its postmodern sense, it is more inclusive than "gaylesbian," encompassing also bisexual, transgendered, and transsexual persons. It covers everything but normative heterosexuality. A political strategy is also involved, that of an oppressed group itself reclaiming a pejorative term from its persecutorial uses.

"Queer theory," however, as Donald Morton explains, is a manifestation of "ludic postmodernism" and embodies at least two politically unproductive characteristics. Ludic postmodernist queer theory embraces a commitment to pleasure in place of Enlightenment and civil rights/feminist/gay-lesbian aspirations for progressive liberation, equity, democracy, and social justice ("Birth of the Cyberqueer," 371); and it functions as an agency of predatory capitalist commodification of all things ("Queerity," 189–190).

Thus "queer materialism" (in opposition to the dominant "queer theory") is the examination of the complex social conditions (division of labor, production, distribution, consumption, class) through which sexual preference/orientation, hierarchy, domination, and protest develop dialectically at a particular time and place. Morton emphasizes the challenge to idealist notions of homosexuality posed by the "material queer" insistence that sexuality and desire are not autonomous in people but are produced through economics.

Nor is the term *theory* denotatively simple in our usage here. Miller explains it as the displacements and elaborations of social representations in language and refers to "materialist" reading as shifting "from a focus on the meaning of texts to a focus on the way meaning is conveyed" (283). He continues: "Put another way, theory is the use of language to talk about language. Put yet another way, theory is a focus on referentiality as a problem rather than as something that reliably and unambiguously relates a reader to the 'real world' of history, of society, and of people acting within society on the stage of history" (283). Of course, the Marxist view of theory is radically different: Theory is an accounting of the objective processes of labor as producer of history, which provides a reliable guideline for praxis. Theory does not simply explain the world but helps to change it.

This bibliography emphasizes Marxist materialist works (such as those by Engels, Luxemburg, Zetkin, Kollontai, Fernbach, Reed, German, D'Emilio, and others, which argue that sexual relations are produced by economics, class, etc.), but a wide range of other kinds of materialist treatments of sexuality are included: the neo-Marxists of the Frankfurt School (Marcuse, Reich, and others), post-Marxists like Zizek, poststructuralists such as Deleuze and Guattari, various kinds of "materialist" feminists (Moi and Radway, Butler, Haraway), among other kinds. Not all of the entries in the bibliography are strictly or mainly about homosexuality, but all express at least some implications for its material understanding.

James R. Bennett

Works Cited

Butler, Judith. (1993) *Bodies that Matter: On the Discursive Limits of "Sex."* New York: Routledge.

de Lauretis, Teresa, ed. (1991) *Queer Theory*. Spec. issue of *Differences* 3.2:i–xviii, 1–159.

Deleuze, Gilles, and Felix Guattari. (1977) *Anti-Oedipus: Capitalism and Schizophrenia*. Trans. Robert Hurley, Mark Seem, and Helen R. Lane. New York: Viking.

Freud, Sigmund. (1975 [c. 1961]) *Beyond the Pleasure Principle*. Trans. James Strachey. New York: Norton.

Lenin, V. L. (1972) *Materialism and Empirio-Criticism: Critical Comments on a Reactionary Philosophy*. New York: International Publishers.

Marx, Karl. (1977) *Capital*, vol. 1. New York: Vintage.

———. (1988) *Wage-Labour and Capital*. New York: International Publishers.

Marx, Karl, and Frederick Engels. (1970). *The German Ideology*. New York: International Publishers.

Miller, J. Hillis. (1987) "Presidential Address 1986. The Triumph of Theory, the Resistance to Reading, and the Question of the Material Base." *PMLA* 102.3:281–291.

Morton, Donald. (1995) "Birth of the Cyberqueer." *PMLA* 110.3: 369–381.

———. (1995) "Queerity and Ludic Sado-Masochism: Compulsory Consumption and the Emerging Post-al Queer." *Transformation* 1 (Spring):189–215.

Zavarzadeh, Mas'ud. (1994) "J. Hillis Miller, Materialism, and the Joy of Reading." *Minnesota Review*, 41–42: 188–194.

———. (1995) "Post-ality: The (Dis)Simulations of Cybercapitalism. Book One." *Transformation* 1 (Spring):1–75.

———. (1996) "Post-ality: The (Dis)Simulations of Cybercapitalism. Book Two." *Transformation* 2: Marxist Boundary Work in Theory, Economics, Politics and Culture (Spring, forthcoming).

Selected Bibliography

Abelove, Henry, Michèle Aina Barale, and David M. Halperin, eds. (1993) *The Lesbian and Gay Studies Reader*. New York: Routledge.

Adam, Barry D. (1995) *The Rise of a Gay and Lesbian Movement*. Rev. ed. Boston: Twayne Publishers.

al-Hibri, Azizah Y., and Margaret A. Simons, eds. (1990). *Hypatia Reborn: Essays in Feminist Philosophy*. Bloomington: Indiana University Press.

Allen, Jeffner, ed. (1990) *Lesbian Philosophies and Cultures*. Albany: State University of New York Press.

Allison, Dorothy. (1993) "A Question of Class." In Arlene Stein, ed., *Sisters, Sexperts, Queers: Beyond the Lesbian Nation*. New York: Plume, 133–135.

Altman, Dennis. (1993) *Homosexual Oppression and Liberation*. New York: New York University Press.

———. (1982) *The Homosexualization of America: The Americanization of the Homosexual*. New York: St. Martin's Press.

Anzaldúa, Gloria. (1987) *Borderlands/La Frontera: The New Mestiza*. San Francisco: Aunt Lute.

Bad Object Choices, ed. (1991) *How Do I Look?: Queer Film and Video*. Seattle: Bay Press.

Barbin, Herculine. (1980) *Herculine Barbin: Being the Recently Discovered Memoirs of a Nineteenth-Century French Hermaphrodite*. Brighton, England: Harvester Press.

Barrett, Michelle. (1995) "Capitalism and Homophobia: Marxism and the Struggle for Gay/Lesbian Rights." *1917*. 15:32, 26–31.

———. (1980) *Women's Oppression Today: Problems in Marxist Feminist Analysis*. London: Verso.

Barthes, Roland. (1985) *The Grain of the Voice: Interviews 1962–1980*. Berkeley: University of California Press.

———. (1992) *Incidents*. Berkeley: University of California Press.

———. (1977) *Roland Barthes by Roland Barthes*. New York: Hill and Wang.

———. (1974) *S/Z: An Essay*. New York: Hill and Wang.

Baudrillard, Jean. (1981) *For a Critique of the Political Economy of the Sign*. Trans. Charles Levin. St. Louis: Telos.

———. (1975) *The Mirror of Production*. Trans. Mark Poster. St. Louis: Telos.

———. (1990) *Seduction*. Trans. B. Singer. New York: St. Martin's Press.

———. (1993) *Simulations*. Trans. Paul Foss and Paul Patton. New York: Semiotext(e).

Beckwith, Sarah. (1994) "Passionate Regulation: Enclosure, Ascesis, and the Feminist Imaginary." *South Atlantic Quarterly* 93:803–824.

Bell, Robert R., and Michael Gordon, eds. (1972) *The Social Dimension of Human Sexuality*. Boston: Little, Brown.

Bergmann, Emilie L., and Paul Julian Smith, eds.(1995) *Entiendes?: Queer Readings, Hispanic Writings*. Durham, N.C.: Duke University Press.

Berlant, Lauren, and Elizabeth Freeman. (1992) "Queer Nationality." *Boundary 2* 19.1:149–180.

Bersani, Leo. (1995) *Homos*. Cambridge, Mass.: Harvard University Press.

Blasius, Mark. (1994) *Gay and Lesbian Politics: Sexuality and the Emergence of a New Ethic*. Philadelphia: Temple University Press.

Boone, Joseph, and Michael Cadden, eds. (1990) *Engendering Men: The Question of Male Feminist Criticism*. New York: Routledge.

Braun, Lily. (1987) *Selected Writings on Feminism and Socialism.* Trans. Alfred G. Meyer. Bloomington: Indiana University Press.

Bredbeck, Gregory W. (1993) "The Postmodernist and the Homosexual." In Bill Readings and Bennet Schaber, eds., *Postmodernism Across the Ages: Essays for a Postmodernity that Wasn't Born Yesterday.* Syracuse, N.Y.: Syracuse University Press, 254–259.

Brett, Philip, Elizabeth Wood, and Gary C. Thomas, eds. (1994) *Queering the Pitch: The New Gay and Lesbian Musicology.* New York: Routledge.

Brown, Norman O. (1996) *Love's Body.* New York: Random House.

Browning, Frank. (1993) *The Culture of Desire: Paradox and Perversity in Gay Lives Today.* New York: Crown.

Bullough, Vern L. (1979) *Homosexuality: A History From Ancient Greece to Gay Liberation.* New York: New American Library, 1979.

Burston, Paul, and Colin Richardson, eds. (1995) *A Queer Romance: Lesbians, Gay Men, and Popular Culture.* New York: Routledge.

Butler, Judith. (1993) *Bodies that Matter: On the Discursive Limits of "Sex."* New York: Routledge, 1993.

Butler, Judith, and Biddy Martin, eds. (1994) "Critical Crossings." Special issue of *diacritics* 24.2–3 (Summer-Fall).

———. (1990) *Gender Trouble: Feminism and the Subversion of Identity.* New York: Routledge.

Callari, Antonio, Steven Cullenberg, and Carole Biewener, eds. (1995) *Marxism in the Postmodern Age: Confronting the New World Order.* New York: Guilford Press.

Cant, Bob, and Susan Hemmings, eds. (1988) *Radical Records: Thirty Years of Lesbian and Gay History, 1957–1987.* New York: Routledge.

Cardea, Caryatis. (1990) "Lesbian Revolution and the 50 Minute Hour: A Working-Class Look at Therapy and the Movement." In Jeffner Allen, ed. *Lesbian Philosophies and Cultures.* Albany: State University of New York Press, 193–217.

Case, Sue-Ellen. (1995) "Performing Lesbian in the Space of Technology: Part I." *Theatre Journal* 47:1–18.

———. (1988–1989) "Towards a Butch-Femme Aesthetic." *Discourse* 11.1:55–73.

———. (1991) "Tracking the Vampire." *Differences* 3.2:1–20.

Case, Sue-Ellen, and Janelle Reinelt, eds. (1991) *The Performance of Power: Theatrical Discourse and Politics.* Iowa City: University of Iowa Press.

Castle, Terry. (1993) *The Apparitional Lesbian: Female Homosexuality and Modern Culture.* New York: Columbia University Press.

Champagne, John. (1995) *The Ethics of the Margins: A New Approach to Gay Studies.* Minneapolis: University of Minnesota Press.

———. (1992) "Seven Speculations on Queens and Class." *Meditations* 17.1 (December):5–20.

Clark, Danae. (1991) "Commodity Lesbianism." *Camera Obscura* 25–26:181–201.

Clum, John M. (1992) *Acting Gay: Male Homosexuality in Modern Drama.* New York: Columbia University Press, 1992.

Cohen, Ed. (1992) *Talk on the Wilde Side: Towards a Genealogy of a Discourse on Male Sexualities.* New York: Routledge.

Cornell, Drucilla. (1991) *Beyond Accommodation: Ethical Feminism, Deconstruction, and the Law.* Thinking Gender Series. Ed., Linda J. Nicholson. New York: Routledge.

———. (1992) *The Philosophy of the Limit.* New York: Routledge.

Cornwell, Anita. (1993) *Black Lesbian in White America.* Tallahassee, Fla.: Naiad Press, 1983.

Crimp, Douglas, ed. (1988) *AIDS: Cultural Analysis, Cultural Activism.* Cambridge, Mass · MIT Press.

"Critical Studies of Lesbian, Gay, and Bisexual Issues." Special issue of *Critical Sociology* 20.3 (1994).

Cruikshank, Margaret. (1992) *The Gay and Lesbian Liberation Movement.* New York: Routledge.

Cruikshank, Margaret, ed. (1992) *Lesbian Studies: Present and Future.* Old Westbury, N.Y.: Feminist Press.

Daumer, Elizabeth. (1992) "Queer Ethics, or the Challenge of Bisexuality to Lesbian Ethics." *Hypatia* 7.4:91–105.

Dawes, James. (1995) "Narrating Disease: AIDS, Consent, and the Ethics of Representation." *Social Text* 43:26–44.

De Cecco, John P., and John P. Elia, eds. (1993) *If You Seduce a Straight Person, Can You Make Them Gay?: Issues in Biological Essentialism Versus Social Constructionism in Gay and Lesbian Identities.* New York: Haworth Press.

De Jongh, Nicholas. *Not in Front of the Audience: Homosexuality on Stage.* New York: Routledge, 1992.

D'Emilio, John. (1983) "Capitalism and Gay Identity." In Ann Snitow, Christine Stansell, and Sharon Thompson, eds., *Powers of Desire: The*

Politics of Sexuality. New York: Monthly Review Press, 100–113.

———. (1992) *Making Trouble: Essays on Gay History, Politics, and the University.* New York: Routledge.

———. (1983) *Sexual Politics, Sexual Communities: The Making of a Homosexual Minority in the United States, 1940–1970.* Chicago: University of Chicago Press.

de Lauretis, Teresa. (1994) *The Practice of Love: Lesbian Sexuality and Perverse Desire.* Bloomington: Indiana University Press.

de Lauretis, Teresa, ed. (1991) *Queer Theory.* Spec. issue of *Differences* 3.2:i–xviii, 1–159.

Deleuze, Gilles. (1989) *Masochism.* Trans. Jean McNeil. New York: Zone Books.

Deleuze, Gilles, and Felix Guattari. (1977) *Anti-Oedipus: Capitalism and Schizophrenia,* vol. 1. Trans. Robert Hurley, Mark Seem, and Helen R. Lane. New York: Viking Press.

———. (1987) *A Thousand Plateaus: Capitalism and Schizophrenia,* vol. 2. Trans. Brian Massumi. Minneapolis: University of Minnesota Press.

Deutelbaum, Wendy, and Cynthia Huff. (1985) "Class, Gender, and Family System: The Case of George Sand." In Shirley Garner, Claire Kahane, and Madelon Sprengnether, eds., *The (M)other Tongue: Essays in Feminist Psychoanalytic Interpretation.* Ithaca: Cornell University Press, 261–279.

Dews, Peter. (1987) *Logics of Disintegration: Post-Structuralist Thought and the Claims of Critical Theory.* New York: Verso.

Dickinson, James, and Bob Russell. (1986) "Introduction: The Structure of Reproduction in Capitalist Society." In Dickinson and Russell, *Family, Economy, and State.* New York: St. Martin's Press, 1–22.

Dickinson, James, and Bob Russell, eds. (1986) *Family, Economy, and State.* New York: St. Martin's Press, 1986.

Doan, Laura. (1994) *The Lesbian Postmodern.* New York: Columbia University Press.

Dollimore, Jonathan. (1991) *Sexual Dissidence: Augustine to Wilde, Freud to Foucault.* Oxford: Clarendon Press.

———. (1994) "Shakespeare Understudies: The Sodomite, the Prostitute, the Transvestite, and Their Critics." In Jonathan Dollimore and Alan Sinfield, eds., *Political Shakespeare: Essays in Cultural Materialism.* Ithaca: Cornell University Press, 129–152.

Dorenkamp, Monica, and Richard Henke, eds. (1995) *Negotiating Lesbian and Gay Subjects.* New York: Routledge.

Doty, Alexander. (1993) *Making Things Perfectly Queer: Interpreting Mass Culture.* Minneapolis: University of Minnesota Press.

Doty, Alexander, and Corey K. Creekmur. (1994) *Out in Culture: Gay, Lesbian, and Queer Essays on Popular Culture.* Durham, N.C.: Duke University Press.

Douglas, Carol Anne. (1990) *Love and Politics: Radical Feminist and Lesbian Theories.* San Francisco: Ism Press.

Duberman, Martin. (1993) *Stonewall.* New York: Plume.

Duberman, Martin, Martha Vicinus, and George Chauncey, Jr., eds. (1989) *Hidden from History: Reclaiming the Gay and Lesbian Past.* New York: Meridian.

Dyer, Richard. (1981) "Getting Over the Rainbow: Identity and Pleasure in Gay Cultural Politics." In G. Bridges and R. Brunt, eds., *Silver Linings: Some Strategies for the Eighties. Contributions to the Communist University of London.* London: Lawrence and Wishart, 53–67.

———. (1990) *Now You See It: Studies on Lesbian and Gay Film.* New York: Routledge.

Ebert, Teresa L. (1995) "The Crisis of Ludic Socialist Feminism." *Genders* 21:339–369.

———. (1996) *Ludic Feminism and After: Postmodernism, Desire, and Labor in Late Capitalism.* Ann Arbor: University of Michigan Press.

———. (1992–1993) "Ludic Feminism, the Body, Performance, and Labor: Bringing *Materialism* Back into Feminist Cultural Studies. *Cultural Critique* 23:5–50.

———. (1995) "(Untimely) Critiques for a Red Feminism." *Transformation* 1:113–149.

Edelman, Lee. (1994) *Homographesis: Essays in Gay Literary and Cultural Theory.* New York: Routledge.

Edwards, Tim. (1990) "Beyond Sex and Gender: Masculinity, Homosexuality and Social Theory." In Jeff Hearn and David Morgan, eds., *Men, Masculinities and Social Theory.* London: Unwin Hyman, 110–223.

———. (1994) *Erotic Politics: Gay Male Sexuality, Masculinity, and Feminism.* New York: Routledge.

Engels, Friedrich. (1986) *The Origin of the Family, Private Property and the State.* New York: Penguin.

Evans, David T. (1993) *Sexual Citizenship: The Material Construction of Sexualities.* London: Routledge.

Faderman, Lillian. (1991) *Odd Girls and Twilight Lovers: A History of Lesbian Life in Twentieth Century America.* New York: Columbia University Press.

———. (1981) *Surpassing the Love of Men: Romantic Friendship and Love Between Women from the Renaissance to the Present.* New York: William Morrow.

Farnsworth, Beatrice. (1980) *Aleksandra Kollontai: Socialism, Feminism, and the Bolshevik Revolution.* Stanford: Stanford University Press.

Ferguson, Ann. (1990) "Is There a Lesbian Culture?" In Jeffner Allen, ed., *Lesbian Philosophies and Cultures.* Albany: State University of New York Press, pp. 63–88.

Fernbach, David. (1981) *The Spiral Path: A Gay Contribution to Human Survival.* Boston: Alyson Publications.

———. (1980) "Towards a Marxist Theory of Gay Liberation." In Pam Mitchell, ed., *Pink Triangles: Radical Perspectives on Gay Liberation.* Boston: Alyson, 148–163.

Field, Nicola. (1995) *Over the Rainbow: Money, Class, and Homophobia.* London: Pluto.

Findlay, Heather. (1994) "Queer Dora: Hysteria, Sexual Politics, and Lacan's 'Intervention on Transference.'" *GLQ: A Journal of Lesbian and Gay Studies* 1.3:323–347.

Foreman, Ann. (1977) *Femininity as Alienation: A Marxist View.* London: Pluto.

Foster, David Williams. (1994) *Gay and Lesbian Themes in Latin American Writing.* Austin: University of Texas Press.

Foucault, Michel. (1986) *The Care of the Self: The History of Sexuality Volume 3.* New York: Vintage.

———. (1989) *Foucault Live: Interviews 1966–1980.* New York: Semiotext(e).

———. (1978) *The History of Sexuality: Volume 1: An Introduction.* New York: Vintage.

———. (1984) "Michel Foucault, An Interview: Sex, Power, and the Politics of Identity." *The Advocate* (August 7), pp. 26–30, 58.

———. (1988) *Politics, Philosophy, Culture: Interviews and Other Writings 1977–1984.* Trans. Alan Sheridan et al. Ed. Lawrence D. Dritzman. New York: Routledge.

———. (1980) *Power/Knowledge: Selected Interviews and Other Writings, 1972–1977.* New York: Pantheon.

———. (1991) *Remarks on Marx: Conversations with Duccio Trombadori.* New York: Semiotext(e).

———. (1985) *The Use of Pleasure: The History of Sexuality Volume 2.* New York: Vintage.

Fout, John C. ed. (1992) *Forbidden History: The State, Society, and the Regulation of Sexuality in Modern Europe. Essays from the Journal of the History of Sexuality.* Chicago: University of Chicago Press.

Fromm, Erich. (1992) *The Revision of Psychoanalysis.* Ed. R. Funk. Boulder: Westview Press.

Fuss, Diana. (1989) *Essentially Speaking.* New York: Routledge.

———. (1991) *Inside/Out: Lesbian Theories, Gay Theories.* New York: Routledge.

Gallop, Jane. (1988) *Thinking Through the Body.* New York: Columbia University Press.

Garber, Marjorie. (1993) *Vested Interests: Cross-Dressing and Cultural Anxiety.* New York: Harper.

———. (1995) *Vice Versa: Bisexuality and the Eroticism of Everyday Life.* New York: Simon and Schuster.

Gay Left Collective. (1980) *Homosexuality: Power and Politics.* London and New York: Allison and Busby.

———. (1980) "Why Marxism?" In Pam Mitchell, ed., *Pink Triangles: Radical Perspectives on Gay Liberation.* Boston: Alyson, 98–106.

"The Gender of Homosexuality." Special issue of *Thamyris: Mythmaking from Past to Present.* 2.1 (1995).

German, Lindsay. (1989) *Sex, Class, and Socialism.* London: Bookmarks.

Gever, Martha, Pratibha Parmar, and John Greyson, eds. (1993) *Queer Looks: Perspectives on Lesbian and Gay Film and Video.* New York: Routledge.

Gevisser, Mark, and Edwin Cameron, eds. (1994) *Defiant Desire: Gay and Lesbian Lives in South Africa.* New York: Routledge.

Goldberg, Jonathan. (1994) "The History that Will Be." *GLQ: A Journal of Lesbian and Gay Studies* 1:385–403.

———. (1994) *Reclaiming Sodom.* New York: Routledge.

Goodman, Paul. (1977) "The Politics of Being Queer." In his *Nature Heals: The Psychological Essays of Paul Goodman.* Ed. Taylor Stoehr. New York: Free Life Editions, 216–255.

Greenberg, David F. (1988) *The Construction of Homosexuality.* Chicago: University of Chicago Press.

Greene, Beverly, and Gregory M. Herek, eds. (1994) *Lesbian and Gay Psychology: Theory, Research, and Clinical Applications.* Thousand Oaks, Calif.: Sage.

Greene, Gayle, and Coppelia Kahn, eds. (1993) *Changing Subjects: The Making of Feminist Literary Criticism*. New York: Routledge.

Grosz, Elizabeth. (1994) *Volatile Bodies: Toward a Corporeal Feminism*. Theories of Representation and Difference Series. Ed., Teresa de Lauretis. Bloomington: Indiana University Press.

Grosz, Elizabeth, and Elspeth Probyn, eds. (1995) *Sexy Bodies: The Strange Carnalities of Feminism*. London and New York: Routledge.

Gumbrecht, Hans Ulrich, and K. Ludwig Pfeiffer, eds. (1994) *Materialities of Communication*. Trans. William Whobrey. Stanford: Stanford University Press.

Haggearty, George E., and Bonnie Zimmerman, eds. (1995) *Professions of Desire: Lesbian and Gay Studies in Literature*. New York: Modern Language Association of America.

Halperin, David. (1990) *One Hundred Years Of Homosexuality and Other Essays on Greek Love*. New York: Routledge.

———. (1995) *Saint Foucault: Towards a Gay Hagiography*. New York: Oxford University Press.

Hamer, Diane, and Belinda Budge, eds. (1994) *The Good, the Bad and the Gorgeous: Popular Culture's Romance with Lesbianism*. London: Pandora.

Hamilton, Roberta. (1978) *The Liberation of Women: A Study of Patriarchy and Capitalism*. London: Allen and Unwin.

Haraway, Donna. (1991) *Simians, Cyborgs, and Women: The Reinvention of Nature*. New York: Routledge.

Hart, Lynda. (1994) *Fatal Women: Lesbian Sexuality and the Mark of Aggression*. Princeton: Princeton University Press.

Hart, Nett. (1990) "Lesbian Desire as Social Action." In Jeffner Allen, ed., *Lesbian Philosophies and Cultures*. Albany: State University of New York Press, 295–303.

Hartsock, Nancy C. M. (1983) *Money, Sex, and Power: Toward a Feminist Historical Materialism*. New York: Longman.

Harwood, Victoria, David Oswell, Kay Parkinson, and Anna Ward, eds. (1993) *Pleasure Principles: Politics, Sexuality and Ethics*. London: Lawrence & Wishart.

Hearn, Jeff. (1987) *The Gender of Oppression: Men, Masculinity, and the Critique of Marxism*. New York: St. Martin's Press.

Heger, Heinz. (1995) *The Men With the Pink Triangles*. Trans. David Fernbach. Boston: Alyson.

Hekma, Gert, Harry Oosterhuis, James Steakley, eds. (1995) *Gay Men and the Sexual History of the Political Left*. New York and London: Harringon Park Press.

Hendriks, Art, Rob Tielman, and Evert van der Veen, eds. (1993) *The Third Pink Book: A Global View of Lesbian and Gay Liberation and Oppression*. Buffalo, N.Y.: Prometheus Books.

Hennessy, Rosemary. (1993) *Materialist Feminism and the Politics of Discourse*. Thinking Gender Series. Ed., Linda J. Nicolson. New York: Routledge.

———. (1994) "Queer Theory, Left Politics." *Rethinking Marxism* 7.3:85–111.

———. (1994–1995) "Queer Visibility in Commodity Culture." *Cultural Critique* 29:31–76.

Herdt, Gilbert, ed. (1994) *Third Sex, Third Gender: Beyond Sexual Dimorphism in Culture and History*. New York: Zone.

Hoagland, Sarah Lucia. (1992) "Lesbian Ethics and Female Agency." In Eve Browning Cole and Susan Coultrap-McQuin, eds., *Explorations in Feminist Ethics*. Bloomington: Indiana University Press, 156–162.

Hocquenghem, Guy. (1978) *Homosexual Desire*. Trans. Danielle Dangoor. London: Allison and Busby.

Hodges, Andrew, and David Hutter. (1979) *With Downcast Gays: Aspects of Homosexual Self-Oppression*. 2d ed. Toronto: Pink Triangle Press.

Howells, Kevin, ed. (1984) *The Psychology of Sexual Diversity*. New York: Basil Blackwell.

Humm, Maggie. (1986) *Feminist Criticism: Women as Contemporary Critics*. New York: St. Martin's Press.

Humphreys, Laud. (1975) *Tearoom Trade: Impersonal Sex in Public Places*. Enlarged Edition. Observations Series. Chicago: Aldine Publishing Company.

Hyam, Ronald. (1994) *Empire and Sexuality*. Manchester and New York: Manchester University Press.

In the Spirit of Stonewall. Atlanta: World View Publishers, 1979.

"The Invention of the Queer: Marxism, Lesbian and Gay Theory, Capitalism." *Transformation 2: Marxist Boundary Work in Theory, Economics, Politics and Culture*. (Spring 1996).

Irigaray, Luce. (1985) *Speculum of the Other Woman*. Trans. Gillian C. Gill. Ithaca: Cornell University Press.

———. (1985) *This Sex Which is Not One*. Trans. Catherine Porter with Carolyn Burke. Ithaca: Cornell University Press.

Jay, Karla, ed. (1995) *Lesbian Erotics*. New York: New York University Press.

Johnson, Barbara. (1987) *A World of Difference*. Baltimore: Johns Hopkins University Press.

Johnston, Gordon. (1979) *Which Way Out of the Men's Room?: Options for the Male Homosexual*. South Brunswick, N.J.: A. S. Barnes.

Katz, Jonathan Ned. (1992) *Gay American History: Lesbians and Gay Men in the U. S. A.* Rev. ed. New York: Meridian.

———. (1995) Jonathan. *The Invention of Heterosexuality*. New York: Dutton.

Kipnis, Laura. (1993) *Ecstasy Unlimited: On Sex, Capital, Gender, and Aesthetics*. Minneapolis: University of Minnesota Press.

Knight, Julia. (1995) "The Meaning of Treut?" In Tamsin Wilton, ed., *Immortal, Invisible: Lesbians and the Moving Image*. New York: Routledge, 34–51.

Koestenbaum, Wayne. (1993) *The Queen's Throat: Opera, Homosexuality, and the Mystery of Desire*. New York: Vintage.

Kollontai, Alexandra. (1981) *A Great Love*. Trans. Cathy Porter. New York and London: W. W. Norton.

———. (1977) *Selected Writings*. Trans. Alix Holt. Westport, Conn.: Lawrence Hill.

Kovel, Joel. (1982) *The Age of Desire: Reflections of a Radical Psychoanalyst*. New York: Pantheon Books.

Laing, R. D. (1967) *The Politics of Experience*. New York: Ballantine.

Lash, Scott. (1985) "Postmodernity and Desire." *Theory and Society* 14.1 (January):1–33.

Lauritsen, John, and David Thorstad. (1974) *The Early Homosexual Rights Movement (1864–1935)*. New York: Times Change.

Lenin, V. I. (1965) *On the Emancipation of Women*. Moscow: Progress Publisher.

Lochrie, Karma. (1995) "Don't Ask, Don't Tell: Murderous Plots and Medieval Secrets." *GLQ: A Journal of Lesbian and Gay Studies* 1.4:405–417.

Los Angeles Research Group. (1980) "Toward a Scientific Analysis of the Gay Question." In Pam Mitchell, ed., *Pink Triangles: Radical Perspectives on Gay Liberation*. Boston: Alyson, 117–135.

Luxemburg, Rosa. (1985) *Reform or Revolution*. New York: Pathfinder Press.

———. (1991) *Rosa Luxemburg Speaks*. Ed. Mary-Alice Waters. New York: Pathfinder Press.

———. (1971) *Selected Political Writings of Rosa Luxemburg*. Ed. Dick Howard. New York: Monthly Review Press.

Lyotard, Jean-François. (1993) *Libidinal Economy*. Trans. Iaian H. Grant. Bloomington: Indiana University Press.

Lyotard, Jean-François, and Jean-Loup Thébaud. (1985) *Just Gaming*. Trans. Wlad Godzich. Minneapolis: University of Minnesota Press.

Marcuse, Herbert. (1956) *Eros and Civilization: A Philosophical Inquiry into Freud*. Boston: Beacon Press.

———. (1969) *An Essay on Liberation*. Boston: Beacon.

———. (1970) *Five Lectures: Psychoanalysis, Politics, and Utopia*. Trans. Jeremy J. Shapiro and Shirley M. Weber. Boston: Beacon.

———. (1964) *One-Dimensional Man: Studies in the Ideology of Advanced Industrial Society*. Boston: Beacon Press.

Marks, Elaine, and Isabelle de Courtivron, eds. (1981) *New French Feminisms: An Anthology*. New York: Shocken.

Marx, Karl. (1977) *Capital*. Vol. 1. New York: Vintage.

———. (1988) *The Communist Manifesto*. Ed. Frederic L. Bender. New York: Norton.

———. (1981) *A Contribution to the Critique of Political Economy*. New York: International Publishers.

———. (1988) *Wage-Labour and Capital*. New York: International Publishers.

Marx, Karl, and Frederick Engels. (1970) *The German Ideology*. New York: International Publishers.

McCubbin, Bob. (1993) *The Roots of Lesbian and Gay Oppression: A Marxist View*. 3d ed. (Formerly titled: *The Gay Question: A Marxist Appraisal*. 1st ed. 1976.) New York: WW Publishers.

Meese, Elizabeth A. (1992) *(Sem)erotics: Theorizing Lesbian: Writing*. New York: New York University Press.

Mercer, Kobena. (1994) *Welcome to the Jungle: New Positions in Black Cultural Studies*. New York: Routledge.

Meyer, Moe, ed. (1994) *The Politics and Poetics of Camp*. London and New York: Routledge.

Michel, Frann. (1995) "Lesbian Panic and Mary Shelley's *Frankenstein*." *GLQ: A Journal of Lesbian and Gay Studies* 2.3:237–252.

Miller, D. A. (1992) *Bringing Out Roland Barthes*. Berkeley: University of California Press.

Miller, James. (1993) *The Passion of Michel Foucault*. New York: Simon.

Miller, Neil. (1995) *Out of the Past: Gay and Lesbian History from 1869 to the Present.* New York: Vintage.

Miller, Toby. (1995) "A Short History of the Penis." *Social Text* 43:1–26.

———. (1993) *The Well-Tempered Self: Citizenship, Culture, and the Postmodern Subject.* Baltimore: Johns Hopkins University Press.

Milligan, Don. (1993) *Sex-Life: A Critical Commentary on the History of Sexuality.* London: Pluto Press.

Mills, Patricia Jagentowicz. (1987) *Woman, Nature, and Psyche.* New Haven: Yale University Press.

Mitchell, Pam, ed. (1980) *Pink Triangles: Radical Perspectives on Gay Liberation.* Boston: Alyson.

Moi, Toril. (1994) "Conversation with Juliet Mitchell." In Toril Moi and Janice Radway, eds., *Materialist Feminism,* 925–949.

———. (1985) *Sexual/Textual Politics: Feminist Literary Theory.* London and New York: Methuen.

Moi, Toril, and Janice Radway, eds. (1994) *Materialist Feminism.* Special issue of *South Atlantic Quarterly* 93.

"More Gender Trouble: Feminism Meets Queer Theory." Special issue of *differences* 6.3–4 (Summer–Fall 1994).

Morrison, Paul. (1993). "End Pleasure." *GLQ: A Journal of Lesbian and Studies* 1.1:53–78.

Morton, Donald. (1995) "Birth of the Cyberqueer." *PMLA* 110.3:369–381.

———. (1996) "The Class Politics of Queer Theory." *College English* 58.4 (April):471–482.

———. (1996) *The Material Queer: A Lesbian and Gay Cultural Studies Reader.* Boulder: Westview Press.

———. (1993) "The Politics of Queer Theory in the (Post)Modern Moment." *Genders* 17:121–150.

———. (1995) "Queerity and Ludic Sado-Masochism: Compulsory Consumption and the Emerging Post-al Queer." *Transformation* 1:189–215.

Mullaney, Marie Marmo. (1983) *Revolutionary Women: Gender and the Socialist Revolutionary Role.* New York: Praeger.

Munt, Sally. (1993) *Critical Essays: Gay and Lesbian Writers of Color.* New York: Haworth Press.

Munt, Sally, ed. (1992) *New Lesbian Criticism: Literary and Cultural Readings.* New York: Columbia University Press.

Nahem, Joseph. (1981) *Psychology and Psychiatry Today: A Marxist View.* New York: International Press.

Nowlan, Bob. (1992) "Marxist Theory of Homosexuality: Past, Present and Future." *The Alternative Orange* 2.2:5–8, 10, 14.

———. (1993) "Marxist Theory of Homosexuality." *The Alternative Orange* 2.6:11, 14–16.

———. (1996) *Queer Theory, Cultural Studies, Marxism.* Urbana and Chicago: University of Illinois Press.

———. (1994) "We're Here, We're Queer, We're Fabulous, Get Used to It!: (Radical) Queer Politics and Culture in the 1990s." *The Alternative Orange* 3.3:45–53.

Nowlan, Bob, and Mark Wood. (1991) "Marxism, Socialism, and the Politics of Gay and Lesbian Liberation." *The Alternative Orange* 1.2:9–10.

Ollman, Bertell. (1979) *Social and Sexual Revolution: Essays on Marx and Reich.* Boston: South End Press.

Osborn, Reuben. (1965) *Marxism and Psychoanalysis.* New York: Dell.

Owens, Craig. (1992) *Beyond Recognition: Representation, Power and Culture.* Berkeley: University of California Press.

Patton, Cindy. (1995) "What is a Nice Lesbian Like You Doing in a Film Like This?" In Tamsin Wilton, ed., *Immortal, Invisible: Lesbians and the Moving Image.* New York: Routledge, 20–33.

Penelope, Julia. (1994) *Out of the Class Closet: Lesbians Speak.* Freedom, Calif.: Crossing.

Penelope, Julia, and Susan J. Wolfe, eds. (1993) *Lesbian Culture: An Anthology: The Lives, Work, Ideas, Art and Visions of Lesbians Past and Present.* Freedom, Calif.: Crossing Press.

Penley, Constance, and Sharon Willis, eds. (1993) *Male Trouble.* Minneapolis: University of Minnesota Press.

Peraldi, François, ed. (1981) *Polysexuality.* Special issue of *Semiotext(e)* 10.

Phelan, Shane. (1994) *Getting Specific: Postmodern Lesbian Politics.* Minneapolis: University of Minnesota Press.

Plant, Richard. (1986) *The Pink Triangle: The Nazi War Against Homosexuals.* New York: Henry Holt.

Plummer, Kenneth, ed. (1981) *The Making of the Modern Homosexual.* Totowa, N.J.: Barnes and Noble.

———. (1992) *Modern Homosexualities: Fragments of Lesbian and Gay Experiences.* New York: Routledge.

Ponse, Barbara. (1978) *Identities in the Lesbian World: The Social Construction of Self.* Westport, Conn.: Greenwood Press.

"The Queer Issue: New Visions of America's Lesbian and Gay Past." Special issue of *Radical History Review* 62 (Spring 1995).

"Queer Relations: The Lesbian/Gay Movement and the U.S. Left." Special issue of *CrossRoads: Contemporary Political Analysis and Left Dialogue* 15 (November 1991).

Rand, Erica. (1995) *Barbie's Queer Accessories.* Durham, N.C.: Duke University Press.

Ray, Peter. (1992) "It's Not Natural." *Living Marxism* (December):21–32.

Reed, Evelyn. (1969) *Problems of Women's Liberation.* New York: Pathfinder.

Reich, Wilhelm. (1960) *Selected Writings: An Introduction to Orgonomy.* New York: Farrar, Straus, and Cudahy.

———. (1974) *The Sexual Revolution: Toward a Self-Regulating Character Structure.* Trans. T. Pol. New York: Farrar, Straus, and Giroux.

Reiter, Rayna R., ed. (1975) *Toward an Anthropology of Women.* New York: Monthly Review Press.

Riggs, Marlon. (1992) "Unleash the Queen." In Michelle Wallace and Gina Dent, eds., *Black Popular Culture.* Seattle: Bay Press, 99–105.

Ringer, R. Jeffrey, ed. (1994) *Queer Words, Queer Images: Communication and the Construction of Homosexuality.* New York: New York University Press.

Roof, Judith. (1991) *The Lure of Knowledge: Lesbian Sexuality and Theory.* New York: Columbia University Press.

Roscoe, Will. (1995) "Was We'wha a Homosexual: Native American Survivance and the Two-Spirit Tradition." *GLQ: A Journal of Lesbian and Gay Studies* 2.3:193–235.

Rose, Jacqueline. (1983) "Femininity and its Discontents." *Feminist Review* 14:5–21.

Roszak, Theodore. (1969) *The Making of a Counterculture: Reflections on the Technocratic Society and Its Youthful Opposition.* Garden City, N.Y.: Anchor.

Rouse, A. L. (1977) *Homosexuals in History: A Study of Ambivalence in Society, Literature, and the Arts.* New York: Carroll and Graf.

Rowbotham, Sheila, and Jeffrey Weeks. (1977) *Socialism and the New Life: The Personal and Sexual Politics of Edward Carpenter and Havelock Ellis.* London: Pluto.

Rubin, Gayle. (1995) "The Traffic in Woman: Notes on the 'Political Economy' of Sex." In Rayna R.

Reiter, ed., *Toward an Anthropology of Women.* New York: Monthly Review Press, 157–210.

Russo, Vito. (1981) *The Celluloid Closet: Homosexuality in the Movies.* New York: Harper and Row.

Ryan, Michael. (1992–1993) "Foucault's Fallacy." *Strategies* 7:132–154.

Sachs, Karen. (1995) "Engels Revisited: Women, the Organization of Production, and Private Property." In Rayna R. Reiter, ed., *Toward an Anthropology of Women.* New York: Monthly Review Press, 211–234.

Sargent, Lydia, ed. (1981) *Women and Revolution: A Discussion of the Unhappy Marriage of Marxism and Feminism.* Boston: South End.

Scott, Darieck. (1994) "Jungle Fever? Black Gay Identity Politics, White Dick, and the Utopian Bedroom." *GLQ: A Journal of Lesbian and Gay Studies* 1.3:299–321.

Seccombe, Wally. "Marxism and Demography: Household Forms and Fertility Regimes in the Western European Transition." In Dickinson and Russell, eds., *Family, Economy and State,* 23–55.

Sedgwick, Eve Kosofsky. (1985) *Between Men: English Literature and Male Homosocial Desire.* New York: Columbia University Press.

———. (1990) *Epistemology of the Closet.* Berkeley: University of California Press.

———. (1993) *Tendencies.* Durham, N.C.: Duke University Press.

Seidman, Steven. (1992) *Embattled Eros: Sexual Politics and Ethics in Contemporary America.* Thinking Gender Series. New York: Routledge.

Shaviro, Stephen. (1993). *The Cinematic Body.* Minneapolis: University of Minnesota Press.

Signorile, Michelangelo. (1993) *Queer in America: Sex, the Media, and the Closets of Power.* New York: Random House.

Simpson, Mark. (1994) *Male Impersonators: Men Performing Masculinity.* New York: Routledge.

Sinfield, Alan. (1994) *Cultural Politics-Queer Reading.* Philadelphia: University of Pennsylvania Press.

———. (1994) *The Wilde Century: Effeminacy, Oscar Wilde and the Queer Moment.* New York: Columbia University Press.

Smith, John H. (1995) "Queering the Will." *Symploke* 3.1:7–28.

Snitow, Ann, Christine Stansell, and Sharon Thompson, eds. (1983) *Powers of Desire: The Politics of Sexuality.* New Feminist Library Series. New York: Monthly Review.

Solie, Ruth, ed. (1993) *Musicology and Difference: Gender and Sexuality in Music Scholarship.* Berkeley: University of California Press.

Sontag, Susan. (1989) *AIDS and Its Metaphors.* New York: Farrar, Straus, and Giroux.

Stein, Arlene, ed. (1993) *Sisters, Sexperts, and Queers: Beyond the Lesbian Nation.* New York: Plume.

Stein, Edward, ed. (1992) *Forms of Desire: Sexual Orientation and the Social Constructionist Controversy.* New York: Routledge.

Stryker, Susan. (1994) "My Words to Victor Frankenstein Above the Village of Chamounix: Performing Gender Rage." *GLQ: A Journal of Lesbian and Gay Studies* 1:237–254.

———. "On Not Being Lady Macbeth: Some (Troubled) Thoughts on Lesbian Spectatorship." In Tamsin Wilton, ed., *Immortal, Invisible: Lesbians and the Moving Image.* New York: Routledge, 143–162.

Sullivan, Andrew. (1995) *Virtually Normal: An Argument About Homosexuality.* New York: Knopf.

"Symposium: Queer Theory/Sociology: A Dialogue." *Sociological Theory* 12.2 (July 1994):166–248.

Thomas, Kendall. (1993) "Corpus Juris (Hetero)-Sexualis: Doctrine, Discourse, and Desire in *Bowers vs. Hardwick.*" *GLQ: A Journal of Lesbian and Gay Studies* 1.1:33–51.

Todd, Janet. (1988) *Feminist Literary History.* New York: Routledge.

Traub, Valerie. (1992) "The (In)significance of 'Lesbian' Desire in Early Modern England." In Susan Zimmerman, ed., *Erotic Politics: Desire on the Renaissance Stage.* New York: Routledge, 150–169.

Tripp, C. A. (1987) *The Homosexual Matrix.* 2nd ed. New York: New American Library.

Trotsky, Leon. (1970) *Women and the Family.* New York: Pathfinder Press.

Tucker, Scott. (1990) "Gender, Fucking, and Utopia: An Essay in Response to John Stoltenberg's 'Refusing to Be a Man.'" *Social Text 27*:3–34.

Ursel, Jane. (1986) "The State and the Maintenance of Patriarchy: A Case Study of Family, Labour and Welfare Legislation in Canada." In James Dickinson and Bob Russell, eds., *Family, Economy, and State.* New York: St. Martin's Press, 150–191.

Vaid, Urvashi. (1995) *Virtual Equality: The Mainstreaming of Gay and Lesbian Liberation.* New York: Anchor Doubleday.

Valverde, Mariana. (1985) *Sex, Power, and Pleasure.* Toronto: Women's Press.

Vogel, Lisa. (1983) *Marxism and the Oppression of Women: Toward a Unitary Theory.* New Brunswick, N.J.: Rutgers University Press.

Voloshinov, V. N. (1987) *Freudianism: A Critical Sketch.* Trans. I. R. Titunik. Bloomington: Indiana University Press.

Waldrep, Shelton. (1992) "Deleuzian Bodies: Not Thinking Straight in *Capitalism and Schizophrenia.*" *Pre/text* 13.3–4:137–156.

Warner, Michael, ed. (1993) *Fear of a Queer Planet: Queer Politics and Social Theory.* Minneapolis: University of Minnesota Press.

Watney, Simon. (1987) *Policing Desire: Pornography, AIDS, and the Media.* Minneapolis: University of Minnesota Press.

———. (1994) *Practices of Freedom: Selected Writings on HIV/AIDS.* Durham, N.C.: Duke University Press.

Weeks, Jeffrey. (1985) *Sexuality and Its Discontents: Meanings, Myths, and Modern Sexualities.* London: Routledge & Kegan Paul.

Weinberg, George H. (1972) *Society and the Healthy Homosexual.* Garden City, N.Y.: Anchor/Doubleday.

Weinstein, Jeff, Jim Fouratt, Vito Russo, Kate Millet, Arthur Bell, Edmund White, and Bertha Harris. (1990) "Extended Sensibilities." In Russell Ferguson, William Olander, Marcia Tucker, and Karen Fiss, eds., *Discourses: Conversations in Postmodern Art and Culture.* Cambridge, Mass.: MIT Press, 130–153.

Weiss, Andrea. (1992) *Vampires and Violets: Lesbians and Film.* New York: Penguin.

Weston, Kath. (1995) "Get Thee to a Big City: Sexual Imaginary and the Great Gay Migration." *GLQ: A Journal of Lesbian and Gay Studies* 2.3:253–277.

Whittle, Stephen, ed. (1994) *The Margins of the City: Gay Men's Urban Lives.* Brookfield, Vt.: Ashgate.

Wicke, Jennifer. (1994) "Celebrity Material: Materialist Feminism and the Culture of Celebrity." In Toril Moi and Janice Radway, eds., *Materialist Feminism,* 751–778.

Williams, Susan. (1980) "Lesbianism: A Socialist Feminist Perspective." In Pam Mitchell, ed., *Pink Triangles: Radical Perspective on Gay Liberation.* Boston: Alyson, 107–116.

Wilton, Tamsin, ed. (1995) *Immortal, Invisible: Lesbians and the Moving Image.* New York: Routledge.

Wittig, Monique. (1992) *The Straight Mind and Other Essays.* Boston: Beacon.

Yaeger, Patricia. (1988) *Honey-Mad Women: Emancipatory Strategies in Women's Writing.* New York: Columbia University Press.

Zaretsky, Eli. (1986) "Rethinking the Welfare State: Dependence, Economic Individualism and the Family." In James Dickinson and Bob Russell, eds., *Family, Economy, and State*. New York: St. Martin's Press, 85–109.

Zavarzadeh, Mas'ud. (1994) "Ideology, Poststructuralism, and Class Politics: Rethinking Ideology Critique for a Transformative Feminist Politics." In Ann Kibbey, Kayann Short, and Abouali Farmanfarmaian, eds., *Sexual Artifice: Persons, Images, Politics. Genders* 19. New York: New York University Press, 292–324.

Zetkin, Clara. (1984) *Selected Writings*. New York: International Publishers.

Zizek, Slavoj. (1989) *The Sublime Object of Ideology*. New York: Verso.

CREDITS

"A Note on Cultural Studies" is excerpted from Donald Morton, "The Politics of Queer Theory in the (Post)Modern Moment," *Genders* 17 (Fall 1993):121–150. Reprinted by permission of the University of Texas Press.

Queer Consensus/Socialist Conflict

Michael Warner,"Tongues Untied: Memoirs of a Pentecostal Boyhood," *Village Voice Literary Supplement*, February 1993. Reprinted by permission of the author and the *Village Voice*.

Lance Selfa, "What's Wrong with 'Identity Politics,'" *Socialist Worker* (June 1992). Reprinted by permission of the International Socialist Organization (*Socialist Worker*, P.O. Box 16085, Chicago, IL 60616, phone 312-665-8996, fax 312-665-9651.)

Chicago Gay Liberation, "Working Paper for the Revolutionary People's Constitutional Convention," in *Out of the Closets*, edited by Karla Jay and Allen Young (New York: New York University Press, 1977). Reprinted by permission.

Dossier 1: Outing the Concepts

Heraclitus, "Selections from the Fragments, with Commentaries of Hegel and Engels": excerpts from *The Art and Thought of Heraclitus* by Charles H. Kahn (Cambridge: Cambridge University Press, 1984 [1961]). Reprinted with the permission of Cambridge University Press. Excerpts from G.W.F. Hegel, *Lectures on the History of Philosophy*, (London: Routledge, 1974), pp. 278–279, 285–286, 293–294, 295, reprinted by permission. Excerpts from Friedrich Engels, *Socialism: Utopian and Scientific*, translated by Edward Aveling (New York: International Publishers, 1972), pp. 45–47, 48, 49, reprinted by permission.

Plato, selections from the *Symposium*, from *The Collected Dialogues of Plato*, edited by Edith Hamilton and Huntington Cairne (Princeton: Princeton University Press, 1961), pp. 534–535, 537–538, 542–545, 533–563. Copyright © 1961 by Princeton University Press. Reprinted by permission of Princeton University Press.

Jean d'Alembert and Denis Diderot, "A Conversation," reprinted with the permission of The Free Press, an imprint of Simon & Schuster, from *Eighteenth-Century Philosophy* by Lewis White Beck, pp. 172–180. Copyright © 1966 by Lewis White Beck.

Pages 1–28 from *Three Essays on the Theory of Sexuality* by Sigmund Freud. Copyright © 1962 by Sigmund Freud Copyrights, Ltd. Reprinted by permission of BasicBooks, a division of HarperCollins Publishers, Inc.

V. N. Vološinov, "The Content of Consciousness as Ideology," from *Freudianism: A Marxist Critique*, translated by I. R. Titunik and edited in collaboration with Neal H. Bruss (Orlando: Academic Press, 1976), pp. 85–91. Copyright © 1976 by Academic Press, Inc. Reprinted by permission.

"Surplus Repression," from Herbert Marcuse, *Eros and Civilization* (Boston: Beacon Press, 1974), pp. 34–35. Copyright © 1955, 1966 by Beacon Press. Reprinted by permission of Beacon Press and Routledge.

Ann Foreman, "Femininity as Alienation" (London: Pluto Press, 1977), pp. 42–63.

Excerpt from Dennis Altman, *Homosexual: Oppression and Liberation* (New York: New York University Press, 1993), reprinted by permission.

by Amanda Udis-Kessler (Boston: Alyson Publications, 1991). Reprinted by permission of the author.

Peter Ray, "It's Not Natural," *Living Marxism* (December 1992). Published by Junius Publications Ltd. Reprinted by permission.

Alexandra Kollontai, "Sexual Relations and the Class Struggle," from *Selected Writings of Alexandra Kollontai* (Chicago: Lawrence Hill Books, 1977). Reprinted by permission.

John D'Emilio, "Capitalism and Gay Identity," from Ann Snitow, Christine Stansell, and Sharon Thompson, eds., *Powers of Desire* (New York: Monthly Review Press, 1982), pp. 100–113. Copyright © 1983 by Snitow, Stansell, and Thompson. Reprinted by permission of Monthly Review Foundation.

Dossier 4: Queer Desire

"What Is This Thing Called Queer?" (pp. 17–27) and Smith's definition of queer (p. 4) from *Lesbians Talk Queer Notions*, by Cherry Smith (London: Scarlet Press, 1992). Reprinted by permission.

Michael Warner, "Introduction: Fear of a Queer Planet," *Social Text* 29. Copyright © Duke University Press, 1991. Reprinted with permission.

Dennis Cooper, "Queercore," *Village Voice*, June 30, 1992. Reprinted by permission.

"Queer Aztlán: The Re-formation of Chicano Tribe," excerpted from *The Last Generation*, by Cherríe Moraga (Boston: South End Press, 1993). Reprinted by permission.

Lauren Berlant and Elizabeth Freeman, "Queer Nationality," *boundary 2*, 19, 1 (Spring 1992): 149–174. Copyright Duke University Press, 1992. Reprinted with permission.

Daniel C. Tsang, "Notes on Queer 'N Asian Virtual Sex," from *Amerasia* 20, 1 (1994). Reprinted by

permission of University of California, Los Angeles, Asian American Studies Center.

"The Queer Politics of Michel Foucault," from *Saint Foucault: Towards a Gay Hagiography* by David M. Halperin (New York: Oxford University Press, 1995). Copyright © 1995 by David M. Halperin. Reprinted by permission of Oxford University Press, Inc.

Kathryn Bond Stockton, "What Can *Materialism* Mean to Poststructuralists?" from "Bodies and God: Poststructuralist Feminists Return to the Fold of Spiritual Materialism," *boundary 2* 19, 2 (Summer 1992):129–133. Copyright Duke University Press, 1992. Reprinted with permission.

"Queer Revolution: The Last Stage of Radicalism," originally published as David Horowitz, "The Queer Fellows," *The American Spectator* 26, 1 (January 1993). Reprinted by permission of the author.

Sharon Smith, excerpted from "Mistaken Identity— Or Can Identity Politics Liberate the Oppressed?" *International Socialism* (Spring 1994):12–21. Reprinted by permission.

From *Over the Rainbow: Money, Class and Homophobia*, by Nicola Field (London: Pluto Press, 1995). Reprinted by permission.

Los Angeles Research Group, "Material Oppression," in Pam Mitchell, ed., *Pink Triangles: Radical Perspectives on Gay Liberation* (Boston: Alyson Publications, 1980).

"The Matter of Materialism," by Teresa L. Ebert, is first published in this book.

Robert Nowlan, "Critique as Radical Praxis," *The Alternative Orange* (October 1992). Reprinted by permission.

The 1917 Collective, "Capitalism and Homophobia: Marxism and the Struggle for Gay/Lesbian Rights," from *1917 Journal of the International Bolshevik Tendency* 15 (1995):26–32 (BT, Box 332, Adelaide St. Stn., Toronto, Canada M5C 1J0). Reprinted by permission.